GILBERT OF SEMPRINGHAM
AND THE GILBERTINE ORDER

GILBERT OF SEMPRINGHAM AND THE GILBERTINE ORDER
c. 1130–*c.* 1300

Brian Golding

CLARENDON PRESS · OXFORD
1995

Oxford University Press, Walton Street, Oxford OX2 6DP
Oxford New York
Athens Auckland Bangkok Bombay
Calcutta Cape Town Dar es Salaam Delhi
Florence Hong Kong Istanbul Karachi
Kuala Lumpur Madras Madrid Melbourne
Mexico City Nairobi Paris Singapore
Taipei Tokyo Toronto
and associated companies in
Berlin Ibadan

Oxford is a trade mark of Oxford University Press

Published in the United States
by Oxford University Press Inc., New York

British Library Cataloguing in Publication Data
Data available

Library of Congress Cataloging in Publication Data
Golding, Brian.
Gilbert of Sempringhan and the Gilbertine Order / Brian Golding.
p. cm.
Includes bibliographical references (p.   ) and index.
1. Gilbert, of Sempringham, Saint, 1083?–1189. 2. Christian
saints—England—Biography. 3. Gilbertines—History. I. Title.
BX4700.G65G64 1995
271'.49—dc20 94–44891
ISBN 0–19–820060–9

1 3 5 7 9 10 8 6 4 2

Typeset by Graphicraft Typesetters Ltd., Hong Kong

Printed in Great Britain
on acid-free paper by
Bookcraft Ltd., Midsomer Norton,
Bath, Avon

For Flora
and in memory of my parents

Preface

This book has been long in the making, and over the years I have accumulated great debts. My first, especial debt is to my parents for their early support and encouragement. Many institutions have aided my research financially, and particular thanks are due to Wolfson College, Oxford, for electing me to a research fellowship during the early years of this work, and to the Wolfson Foundation, the British Academy, and the University of Southampton for their assistance over the years. Library staff have been without exception courteous and understanding: I am particularly grateful to the British Library, the Bodleian Library, the Public Record Office, the Institute of Historical Research, the National Library of Wales, and the library of the University of Southampton. There could have been no more careful and supportive supervisor than Miss Barbara Harvey, who oversaw my thesis on the Gilbertine priories of Alvingham and Bullington which first stimulated my interest in the Gilbertines, and has encouraged, advised, and chivvied for many years more. Drs Christopher Harper-Bill and Sally Thompson, as well as my colleagues Professor Colin Morris and Drs Bella Millett and Tessa Webber, have read substantial drafts of the book: their comments and criticisms have been invaluable. My thanks go especially to Dr Janet Burton, who has read the complete text and discussed it at great length over countless cappucini at Conti's. Many others, including Professors Constable and Holdsworth, Sister Benedicta Ward, and Miss Brenda Bolton, have been generous in their advice. Ms Dorothy McCarthy has been a most careful and helpful editor at the Press, and saved me from many embarrassments. My greatest debt is to my wife, Dr Flora Lewis, who has read and re-read innumerable drafts (sometimes under duress), for her advice and criticism, and above all for her love and support throughout the Gilbertine years.

BRIAN GOLDING
University of Southampton
1993

Contents

Abbreviations

AASRP	*Associated Architectural Societies Reports and Papers*
BAR	British Archaeological Reports
BIHR	*Bulletin of the Institute of Historical Research*
BL	British Library
Book of Fees	*The Book of Fees*, 3 vols., HMSO (London, 1920–31)
Book of St Gilbert	*The Book of St Gilbert*, ed. and trans. R. Foreville and G. Keir (Oxford, 1987)
Cal. Ch. R.	*Calendar of Charter Rolls preserved in the Public Record Office*, 6 vols., HMSO (London, 1903–27)
Cal. Cl. R.	*Calendar of Close Rolls preserved in the Public Record Office*, HMSO (London, 1902–)
Cal. Inq. Misc.	*Calendar of Inquisitions Miscellaneous preserved in the Public Record Office (Chancery)*, HMSO (London, 1916–)
Cal. Inq. p. m.	*Calendar of Inquisitions post Mortem and other analogous documents in the Public Record Office*, HMSO (London, 1904–)
Cal. Liberate R.	*Calendar of Liberate Rolls preserved in the Public Record Office*, HMSO (London, 1916–)
Cal. Papal Letters	*Calendar of Entries in the Papal Registers relating to Great Britain and Ireland*, ed. W. H. Bliss, C. Johnson, and J. A. Twemlow, HMSO (London, 1893–)
Cal. Pat. R.	*Calendar of Patent Rolls preserved in the Public Record Office*, HMSO (London, 1901–)

CRR	*Curia Regis Rolls*, HMSO (London, 1922–)
Danelaw Charters	*Documents illustrative of the Social and Economic History of the Danelaw from various Collections*, ed. F. M. Stenton, British Academy Records of the Social and Economic History of England and Wales, 5 (1920)
EETS	Early English Text Society
EHR	*English Historical Review*
Elkins, *Holy Women*	S. Elkins, *Holy Women of Twelfth-Century England* (Chapel Hill, NC, 1988)
EYC	*Early Yorkshire Charters*, ed. W. Farrer and C. T. Clay, 12 vols., Yorkshire Archaeological Society Record Series, Extra Series, 1–12 (1914–65)
GEC	G. E. Cokayne, *The Complete Peerage*, ed. V. Gibbs, H. A. Doubleday, *et al.*, 12 vols. (London, 1910–59)
Gilbertine Charters	*Transcripts of Charters relating to the Gilbertine Houses of Sixle, Ormsby, Catley, Bullington and Alvingham*, ed. and trans. F. M. Stenton, Lincoln Record Society, 18 (1922)
Golding, 'Gilbertine Priories'	B. J. Golding, 'The Gilbertine Priories of Alvingham and Bullington: Their Endowments and Benefactors', D.Phil. thesis (Oxford University, 1979)
Graham, *St Gilbert*	R. Graham, *St Gilbert of Sempringham and the Gilbertines* (London, 1901)
Heads of Religious Houses	M. D. Knowles, C. N. L. Brooke, and V. London, *The Heads of Religious Houses: England and Wales, 940–1216* (Cambridge, 1972)
JEH	*Journal of Ecclesiastical History*
Lincolnshire Domesday	*The Lincolnshire Domesday and the Lindsey Survey*, ed. C. W. Foster and T. Longley, Lincoln Record Society, 19 (1924)

LRS	Lincoln Record Society
Medieval Religious Houses	M. D. Knowles and R. Neville Hadcock, *Medieval Religious Houses: England and Wales* (2nd edn., London, 1971)
Monasticon	W. Dugdale, *Monasticon Anglicanum*, ed. J. Caley, H. Ellis, and B. Bandinel, 6 vols. (London, 1846)
PL	*Patrologiae cursus completus, series latina*, accurante J.-P. Migne, 221 vols. (Paris, 1844–64)
PRS	Pipe Roll Society
Registrum Antiquissimum	*The Registrum Antiquissimum of the Cathedral Church of Lincoln*, ed. C. W. Foster and K. Major, 10 vols., Lincoln Record Society, 27–9, 32, 34, 41, 46, 51, 62, 67 (1931–73)
Sempringham Charters	'Charters relating to the Priory of Sempringham', ed. E. M. Poynton, *The Genealogist*, NS 15 (1899), 158–61, 221–7; 16 (1900), 30–5, 76–83, 153–8, 223–8; 17 (1901), 29–35, 164–8, 232–9
Taxatio	*Taxatio Ecclesiastica Angliae et Walliae auctoritate P. Nicholai IV, circa AD 1291*, ed. T. Astle, S. Ayscough, and J. Caley, Record Commission (London, 1802)
Thompson, *Women Religious*	S. P. Thompson, *Women Religious: The Founding of English Nunneries after the Norman Conquest* (Oxford, 1991)
TRHS	*Transactions of the Royal Historical Society*
VCH	*Victoria History of the Counties of England*
VE	*Valor Ecclesiasticus temp. Henrici VIII, auctoritate Regis institutus*, ed. J. Caley and J. Hunter, 6 vols., Record Commission (London, 1810–34)

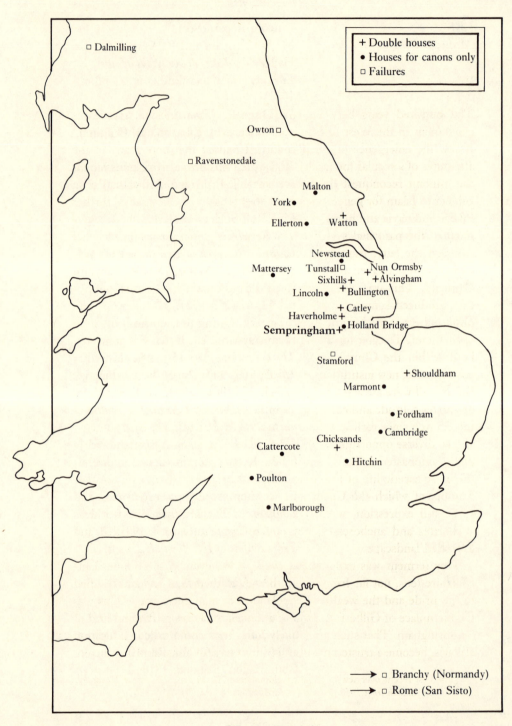

□ Dalmilling

Owton □

□ Ravenstonedale

Malton

York ●

Ellerton ●   + Watton

Newstead

Mattersey   Tunstall □   □ Nun Ormsby
Sixhills +   + Alvingham
Lincoln ●   + Bullington

+ Catley

Haverholme +

Sempringham +   ● Holland Bridge

□
Stamford

+ Shouldham

Marmont ●

● Fordham

● Cambridge

Chicksands

Clattercote ●   +

● Poulton   ● Hitchin

● Marlborough

+ Double houses
● Houses for canons only
□ Failures

⟶ □ Branchy (Normandy)
⟶ □ Rome (San Sisto)

Gilbertine Foundations

Introduction

The hundred years between *c.*1050 and *c.*1150 witnessed a religious excitement in the West unparalleled since the era of the Early Church.[1] It saw the emergence of a self-confident papacy that bore many of the attributes of a secular monarchy, and which was primarily responsible for the militant reconquest (however short-lived) of regions that had been subject to Islam for generations and the extension of Christianity further into Scandinavia and north-eastern Europe. At a local level, the development of the parochial system and a parochial clergy consolidated belief amongst the laity, though at the same time some were drawn towards heresy, now perceived as a real threat to the Church as it had not been for centuries. This was also a period of extraordinary intellectual enquiry that produced some of the most remarkable scholars, theologians, and philosophers of the Middle Ages: men such as Anselm, Abelard, or Hugh of St Victor. To cater for the new demand for learning that was generated both within the Church and from increasingly bureaucratized secular governments, new institutions, particularly the universities, were to emerge. But not all were attracted by public clerical careers; many looked to lives of greater solitude and contemplation. Monasticism had been a feature of the Church since earliest times, but never before had there been so many and so diverse opportunities in the religious life. Long-established Benedictine monasteries like Cluny or Winchester flourished; others sought the more ascetic life of the 'new' orders that sprang up all over western Europe, of which the Cistercians were only the most widespread and successful expression, while yet others lived apart from the world as anchorites and anchoresses, now a familiar feature of the settled and unsettled landscape.

This ferment was experienced everywhere, even in the remote Lincolnshire fens, not far from where the new cathedral of Lincoln testified to the pride and the wealth of the Anglo-Norman episcopacy. This was the birthplace of Gilbert, the son of a modest Norman settler and lord of Sempringham. That such a relatively lowly man could gain an education at Paris, become a trusted member of the episcopal household at Lincoln,

---

[1] The best recent overview of these developments is C. Morris, *The Papal Monarchy: The Western Church from 1050 to 1250* (Oxford, 1990).

and ultimately a close friend of king Henry II, testifies to the new opportunities within the twelfth-century Church. But it is as a monastic founder that Gilbert is most remembered, the founder of the only native English religious order, which in its structured provision for the care of both nuns and canons was, though not unique, at least a highly unusual experiment.

Though the Gilbertines have received little attention by comparison with other orders, two scholars, above all, have been responsible during this century for ensuring that the Gilbertine order has never been forgotten. In 1901 Rose Graham published her *St Gilbert of Sempringham and the Gilbertines*, which at the time was unusual as an analysis of a religious order which was not only concerned with its organization and foundations but also with its temporal development and economy. My debt to it is great. Even greater is that owed to Raymonde Foreville, whose study of Gilbert's canonization process, published in 1943 in wartime Paris, for long remained the only supplement to Graham's work.[2] Foreville never lost her interest in the Gilbertines; in 1984 she published on the revolt of the Gilbertine lay brothers, and in 1987 produced (with Gillian Keir) *The Book of St Gilbert*, an edition and translation of the canonization dossier which for the first time made available to a wider public the most important primary source for the order's early history.[3]

More recently, the Gilbertines have attracted attention as part of a growing interest, after a long period of marginalization, in women's experience of the religious life in medieval Europe. Perhaps at least subconsciously persuaded by the rhetoric of monastic reformers themselves, many commentators have considered religious women only as adjuncts to the dominant male dynamic of monasticism.[4] This neglect can be partly attributed to a scarcity of sources—which is itself a result of the relative poverty of most medieval nunneries when compared with male communities, but is also due to a value judgement that ascribed a lower role to women than men in the spiritual hierarchy. Happily, this imbalance is now being rectified. For many years the only general study of nunneries in medieval England was that of Eileen Power, which was solely concerned

---

[2] *Un procès de canonisation à l'aube du XIIIᵉ siècle (1201–1202), Le Livre de saint Gilbert de Sempringham* (Paris, 1943).

[3] 'La Crise de l'ordre de Sempringham au XIIᵉ siècle: nouvelle approche du dossier des frères lais', *Anglo-Norman Studies 6 (1983)*, ed. R. A. Brown (Woodbridge, 1984), 39–57; *The Book of St Gilbert*, ed. and trans. R. Foreville and G. Keir (Oxford, 1987).

[4] The doyen of English monastic historians, Dom David Knowles, devoted a mere 3 pages to nunneries and 3 to the Gilbertines in his *Monastic Order*, a work of more than 700 pages (M. D. Knowles, *The Monastic Order in England* (2nd edn., Cambridge, 1963), 205–7).

with late-medieval conditions, but, as a result of the pioneering work of Janet Burton, Sharon Elkins, and Sally Thompson in particular, the women religious of medieval England are at last emerging from obscurity.[5] These historians have laid down solid foundations for further research in the religious, social, and economic life of these women, and have drawn heavily on the Gilbertine experience to illumine general problems and developments. The Gilbertines are central to Elkins's thesis of growing restriction, if not repression, of autonomous female religious communities during the second half of the twelfth century, while Thompson has similarly argued that the sophisticated articulation of the Gilbertine Rule was a response to the ambivalences and ambiguities inherent in the attitudes of so many monastic reformers to the role of religious women.

However, Graham's account of the Gilbertines is now somewhat dated, while neither the studies of Thompson or Elkins paid much attention to the relationship of the Gilbertine communities with their benefactors, or to their economy. The success of a religious community depended neither merely on the charismatic leadership of its founder, nor on a well-structured Rule, but on a continuing appeal to lay supporters and a dynamic economy. What follows aims to provide an analysis of the Gilbertine order from its mid-twelfth-century origins up to the early fourteenth century. Such an aim is, of course, only possible for a small order, and has been attempted only once in England, in Colvin's pioneering account of the Premonstratensians (with whom the Gilbertines shared some characteristics), while Milis's magisterial analysis of the Arrouaisians provides a Continental model.[6]

The first section of this book examines both the life of the founder within the context of twelfth-century monastic reform and the gradual creation of the Gilbertine Rule. It then considers the Gilbertine foundations from the first eremitical community at Sempringham to the last, and very different, houses established at the beginning of the fourteenth century, before looking at general patterns of endowment and the extent to which these were determined both by economic constraints on

---

[5] E. Power, *Medieval English Nunneries c.1275–1535* (Cambridge, 1922); J. E. Burton, *The Yorkshire Nunneries in the Twelfth and Thirteenth Centuries*, Borthwick Papers, 56 (York, 1979); S. Elkins, *Holy Women of Twelfth-Century England* (Chapel Hill, NC, 1988); S. P. Thompson, *Women Religious: The Founding of English Nunneries after the Norman Conquest* (Oxford, 1991).

[6] H. M. Colvin, *The White Canons in England* (Oxford, 1951); L. M. Milis, *L'Ordre des chanoines réguliers d'Arrouaise. Son histoire et son organisation de la fondation de l'abbaye-mère (vers 1090) à la fin des chapîtres annuels (1471)*, 2 vols. (Bruges, 1969).

benefactors and by shifts in pious giving away from the monasteries towards other more 'individual' expressions of piety such as the chantries. This investigation leads into an analysis of the Gilbertine economy, its organization and the sources of revenue. Like other communities of canons, the Gilbertines derived a great part of their income from *spiritualia*, and from the beginning the order was concerned to attract and retain grants of parish churches with a view to their appropriation and the concomitant appointment of vicars. Their relative success in this policy, by contrast with other English nunneries, which held very few churches, is one factor in explanation of the Gilbertines' economic strength when compared with other female communities established in England after the Conquest. Another was the order's ability to attract benefactors, who found in the Gilbertines a well-regulated community that offered a greater range of spiritual benefits (such as confraternity rights) than was available from the early Cistercians, while at the same time providing a secure home for entrants, both male and female, recruited from local knightly families who would not normally be recruited into larger, more prestigious foundations.

This study ends at the beginning of the fourteenth century. There are several reasons for this. One is practical. An already lengthy book would become unmanageable if continued till the Dissolution. By 1300 the order had reached its maximum extent: thereafter benefactions fell off rapidly, and families which had long supported the order now turned to other expressions of pious giving, concentrating their activities on the support of chantries and parish churches. But the most fundamental justification is that by 1300 the Gilbertine experiment was largely dead. What had begun as an unusual, though not quite unique, creation of an organizational structure in which men and women could live in harmony and discipline ended as an order in which the men, the canons, were everywhere dominant while the nuns were sidelined and almost irrelevant.

PART I

'An Unheard-Of Order': Gilbert of Sempringham and the Shaping of his Communities

I

The Making of a Saint

From Sempringham to Cîteaux

The early years

The *Vita* of Gilbert of Sempringham, often styled the *Liber Sancti Gilberti*, is by far the most important surviving source both for the life of the founder and for the early history of the communities. It is also unquestionably one of the most illuminating documents for the history of monasticism in twelfth-century England: it ranks with the life of Christina of Markyate as a spiritual biography, while being at the same time a major source for the understanding of the dynamics of monastic reform.[1] The *Vita* was written shortly after the translation of the newly canonized Gilbert's relics on 13 October 1202. The author, who was almost certainly Ralph de Insula, sacrist of Sempringham and one of the envoys to Rome during Gilbert's canonization process, dedicated it to archbishop Hubert Walter of Canterbury.[2] It was prepared at the request of Roger, Gilbert's successor as Master of the order, and of Albinus, chaplain and close friend of the saint. An earlier, shorter version of the Life was taken to Rome to further the canonization campaign: the final expanded version was undertaken on the commission of the archbishop and corrected by William de Montibus, chancellor of Lincoln.[3]

In some respects the work's prologue resembles that of other hagiographies. It is undertaken to edify the faithful by proclaiming the virtues of the saint, and is itself a meritorious act: 'to reveal them [sc. Gilbert's acts] is to secure not only the praise of God and the honour of his saints but also the profit of mankind.' The good works of Gilbert *confessor* are to be proclaimed 'as a model of faith and pattern of justice'.[4] The author's assertion of his own unworthiness is also a commonplace of such

---

[1] The recent edition of this work and associated documents by Foreville examines the *Vita* in detail: *The Book of St Gilbert*, ed. and trans. R. Foreville and G. Keir, Oxford Medieval Texts (Oxford, 1987). Substantial extracts from the Life were published in *Monasticon*, vi, pt. ii. v–xxix from the British Library manuscript, Cotton Cleopatra B. I.

[2] *Book of St Gilbert*, pp. lxxi–lxxv.   [3] Ibid. 8.   [4] Ibid. 4–6.

literature.[5] At the same time, however, there is an intriguing difference between most contemporary hagiographies and Ralph's work, for it is aggressively defensive in tone. While most hagiographers took the sanctity of their subject as read, here the author presents a belligerent vindication of Gilbert, which is the more surprising since it was written *after* the saint's canonization when his status in heaven and earth might have been thought assured. Traditionally, hagiographies had been designed to interpret the saint's life and works to those who came to visit the shrine and venerate the relics, but the saint constructed here is a saint for the canons and nuns of the order, many of whom figure among the *miraculés*. Though the laity occur in the story, they are tangential and incidental.

Ralph first identifies Gilbert as an explicitly English saint and claims that God has so favoured the nation as to make 'men all but cut off from the world equal to the glory of the eastern world'. He then compares Gilbert the *confessor* with Thomas the *martir*, following this with a long excursus on why some confessors should be held in equal respect with those whose blood was shed for the Church Militant. Gilbert has done great things for the Church and is an example to many. Then Ralph makes a revealing comment: 'even if he had not performed the miracles that he did, he would have been a match for most who accomplished them', and cites Gregory the Great that deeds were a truer indicator of worth than signs.[6] Ralph seems very concerned that Gilbert would be compared unfavourably with England's most prestigious martyr, and that contemporaries might criticize the relative paucity of Gilbertine miracles. The Gilbertines were facing an uphill task if they thought Gilbert would replace Thomas as a national cult-figure, and Ralph's fears were justified in that Sempringham was never remotely to approach Canterbury in popularity.

Ralph returned to this theme even more explicitly in chapter 30 of the *Vita*: 'Miracles performed during his lifetime.'[7] 'This is not an age of miracles', he writes; Gilbert paid more attention to deeds than miracles. He goes on to relate the vision of Adam de Amundeville, himself a benefactor of Sempringham, who dreamed that Thomas of Canterbury, in whose household Adam had been, appeared to him. Adam greeted the archbishop: 'we reckon that there was never anyone in our land, and never will be, to give rise to such rejoicing.' Thomas contradicted him, with the name 'Gilbert'. Ralph boldly asserts that this is 'our' Gilbert,

---

[5] Compare Adam of Dryburgh's similar protestations in the prologue to his Life of Hugh of Lincoln (*Magna Vita Sancti Hugonis*, ed. and trans. D. L. Douie and D. H. Farmer, 2 vols. (Oxford, 1985), i. 1–2).   [6] *Book of St Gilbert*, 2–8.

[7] Ibid. 93–7.

'for we are certain that there has not yet been a man like him, and we conclude that there will not be one in the future either'. Thus the rival saint is himself brought in to authenticate Gilbert's claims.

But there is more to Ralph's protestations than his justifiable concern that Gilbert could not replace Thomas. For in the prologue he goes on to accuse contemporaries of failing to recognize Gilbert's virtues. Even though they knew the man, saw his deeds, and heard from witnesses, even though Rome had ruled in his favour, 'still they detract from what he did, contradict those who praise him, and oppose his veneration'. While foreigners laud his memory, his own people, through malice, neglect him.[8] These charges go far beyond hagiographic commonplace in expressing real hostility. Behind the formal approval of Rome and the lavish 'establishment' ceremonies at Gilbert's translation lie division and discontent.

We may find a clue to this scepticism in the very structure of the *Vita*. This contains much more than the usual recital of the life and miracles. The prologue describes the method and chronology of its composition, and then lists its contents. It commences with the saint's life and miracles performed during his lifetime, follows with the canonization and translation processes, letters sent in Gilbert's cause during his lifetime (i.e. those relating to the lay brothers' revolt) and after his death (i.e. those concerning the canonization), the *post-mortem* miracles, and finally *lectiones* extracted from this account for use on the saint's feast-day.[9] The most significant inclusion is the material relating to the lay brothers' revolt. This incident, and the preceding scandal of the nun of Watton which had partly precipitated it, had come close to wrecking the order. Worse, the canonization came at a time when the position of women within male communities was increasingly being questioned. This is the context for the *Vita*. It is both an account of the founder intended primarily for his order and a *pièce justificative* directed against hostile critics.

How reliable a source, then, is the *Vita*? History and hagiography overlap, but they operate by different conventions. There are no external sources by which we may check Ralph's account of the order's founder and its early history. Like all saints' lives, that of Gilbert is thoroughly permeated by biblical allusions and images. His virtues are the same as those found in hundreds of similar works—with perhaps a special emphasis placed, not surprisingly, on his chastity. Gilbert is a wonder-worker

---

[8] Ibid. 8.

[9] Responses and antiphons would be extracted from the Scriptures (*Book of St Gilbert*, 8–10). The text here is somewhat ambiguous: Foreville believes (p. lxv) that the author did not intend to include these responses and antiphons, but this is not readily apparent from the text.

before and after death; he can quell natural forces by his words or prayers, he is a prophet, he experiences visions. Certainly, the hagiography is, in Foreville's words, 'integrated into the historical narrative' and Gilbert's deeds are often firmly rooted in a historical context. But what we are reading is an official history generated within and for the order. This audience felt itself under threat, its very way of life was suspect: only the sanctity of its founder could provide its validation.

While the *Vita* borrowed heavily from Gilbert's now-lost autobiographical account of the establishment of the order, *De Constructione Monasteriorum*, it is unclear whether this text also contained details of its author's early life.[10] The *Vita*'s opening chapters include elements common in contemporary and earlier hagiographies, and care must therefore be taken in their interpretation. Thus, before the saint's birth his mother is said to have had a vision in which the moon came down from heaven and lay in her womb, symbolizing the light to the world her unborn son would be. Again, such stories of pre-natal prophecy are commonplace: Stephen of Obazine's mother dreamt that she gave birth to a lamb which when full-grown brought a large flock to her, while the vision of Bernard of Clairvaux's mother in which the saint was foreshadowed as a small white dog is well known.[11] Similarly, the author stresses the nobility of Gilbert's parents. Gilbert's Norman father, Jocelin, is described as an active knight (*miles strenuus*) and a wealthy man (*opulentus*) with many possessions in Lincolnshire, while his mother is said to have been of lesser social status and English by birth. The connection between nobility and sanctity was often made by twelfth-century commentators, and many of Gilbert's contemporary reformers were described in similar terms.[12] Yet we should beware of accepting the *Vita*'s assessment of Jocelin's wealth too readily. He was a Domesday tenant of Alfred of Lincoln with holdings, which amounted to some twelve carucates, concentrated in Lindsey.[13]

---

[10] These sources are discussed in more detail below, Appendix II.

[11] *Book of St Gilbert*, 10–2; *Vita Stephani Obazinensis*, ed. M. Aubrun, Institut d'études du massif central. fasc. VI (Clermont-Ferrand, 1970), 42–3; *S. Bernardi Vita Prima PL* 185, cols. 227–8.

[12] *Book of St Gilbert*, 10. See A. Murray, *Reason and Society in the Middle Ages* (Oxford, 1978), pt. 4, 316–415. The modestly noble parentage of Gilbert's contemporary, Stephen of Obazine, is similarly stressed by his hagiographer (*Vita Stephani Obazinensis*, 4). See also the case of Hugh of Lincoln (K. Leyser, 'The Angevin Kings and the Holy Man', in H. Mayr-Harting (ed.), *St Hugh of Lincoln* (Oxford, 1987), 57–8).

[13] *The Lincolnshire Domesday and the Lindsey Survey*, ed. C. W. Foster and T. Longley, with an introduction by F. M. Stenton, LRS, 19 (1924, repr. 1976), 126, 130. The family is discussed in *Early Yorkshire Charters*, ed. C. T. Clay, 12 vols., Yorkshire Archaeological Society Record Series, Extra Series, 1–12 (1914–65) vi. 252–4. Other Jocelins are recorded in Domesday but are probably different individuals.

It is clear, therefore, that he was only a member, albeit a relatively prosperous one, of the knightly class of post-Conquest Lincolnshire: he was not a tenant-in-chief and was merely of local status. The marriage between Jocelin and his anonymous English wife was typical of many such after 1066, and we may postulate that it was through her that Jocelin acquired his landed rights.[14] But in stressing Gilbert's dual nationality the *Vita* may also be indicating his potential as a mediator between the two races: such a task was frequently fulfilled by holy men in post-Conquest England.[15]

Gilbert's first years were clearly a disappointment to his parents. He was said to have had some physical deformity and was, perhaps primarily for this reason, despised within the household, so that he himself related how the household (*famuli*) refused to eat with him. This story is used by the author of the *Vita* to stress God's grace in raising up a saint from the dust. While this portrayal of the saint as outsider is again a hagiographical topos, Gilbert's disability may well have been the reason why, as the *Vita* asserts, he was sent to school, the implication being that he was not fit enough to follow his father, whose eldest son he probably was, in a military career.[16]

His first years as a student were equally inauspicious. As Southern has illuminatingly demonstrated, there were two educational routes in twelfth- and thirteenth-century England: the high road to Paris and Bologna that led on to fame and sometimes fortune, and the low road via the limited but widely established English schools that took the scholar to posts in 'middle management' either in the Church or in lay administration.[17] For the former, considerable resources, either through family wealth or the support of a patron, were almost essential for survival during the years of study and in order to gain satisfactory employment on graduation. It is difficult to imagine that Jocelin had the means to send Gilbert abroad, belonging as he did to that class which, in Southern's words, 'neither grovelled nor aimed high', who 'were satisfied with a competent prosperity'.[18] In Lincolnshire educational options were fairly limited. Foreville has suggested that he went either to Crowland, the only local monastic foundation of any size, or to a parish school.[19] The extent of the network

[14] C. Clark, 'Women's Names in Post-Conquest England: Observations and Speculations', *Speculum*, 53 (1978), esp. 224–9.

[15] See H. Mayr-Harting, 'Functions of a Twelfth-Century Recluse', *History*, 60 (1975), 344–5.   [16] *Book of St Gilbert*, 12.

[17] R. W. Southern, *Robert Grosseteste: The Growth of an English Mind in Medieval Europe* (Oxford, 1986), 49–62.   [18] Ibid. 55.

[19] *Book of St Gilbert*, p. xviii.

of local schools run by the parish priest (like the priest who taught Gilbert's slightly older contemporary, Orderic Vitalis, or, indeed, such as Gilbert himself a few years later) has probably been underestimated.[20] Another possibility is Lincoln. Certainly by the middle of the twelfth century the cathedral had a flourishing school and possessed a substantial library. Perhaps more importantly in the present context, a song school run by the precentor was already in existence by the middle of the century.[21] Gilbert's presence at Lincoln, though undistinguished, may have given him his first introduction to the episcopal household which he was to enter a few years later.

Wherever he was first educated, it was only when firmly taken to task for his slow progress and laziness that he is said to have fled, through shame or fear, to France. This flight may be exaggerated; it is hard to see how he could have supported himself without some assistance from his family, though he is said to have been aided by modest contributions to his studies from friends.[22] The *Vita* does not indicate where Gilbert studied. He may, of course, have moved from centre to centre. It has been suggested that he could have gone to Normandy, perhaps to the west of the duchy to Avranches or Caen, but it is just as likely that he went to Paris.[23] There is, however, an intriguing possibility that Gilbert was educated at Laon. In a tract addressed to Gilbert by Maurice, of the Augustinian priory of Kirkham in Yorkshire, and probably written in the 1160s, he refers to Gilbert and himself hearing *magister* Anselm teach on the heresy of the Salomites forty-five years earlier. This must be Anselm of Laon. Gilbert can only have been in Laon at the very end of Anselm's career, for the latter died in 1117 when Gilbert was in his early thirties.[24]

[20] F. Barlow, *The English Church, 1066–1154* (London, 1979), 228–9; M. Clanchy, *From Memory to Written Record: England 1066–1307* (2nd edn., Oxford, 1993), esp. 224–52.
[21] *The Registrum Antiquissimum of the Cathedral Church of Lincoln*, ed. C. W. Foster and K. Major, 10 vols., LRS, 27–9, 32, 34, 41, 46, 51, 62, 67 (1931–73), i. 262–3. Other schools of elementary education also existed in the city (N. Orme, *English Schools in the Middle Ages* (London, 1973), 60–8, 308; D. M. Owen, *Church and Society in Medieval Lincolnshire*, History of Lincolnshire, 5 (Lincoln, 1971), 38–9).
[22] Gilbert's experience is similar to that of Robert of Arbrissel (from perhaps a more lowly background), who went to Paris to study when he was approaching 30, after more rudimentary education (*PL* 162, col. 1047).   [23] *Book of St Gilbert*, p. xviii.
[24] The tract is found in Oxford, Bodl. Lib. MS Hatton 92, fos. 4–38, and in an abbreviated version in Oxford, Lincoln College, MS 27, fos. 3–5. These MSS were discussed by M. R. James in 'The Salomites', *Journal of Theological Studies*, 35 (1934), 287–97. Maurice writes: 'quam (sententiam) et vos olim sicut dixistis ab illo magno et insigni doctore vestro Anselmo habuistis, cuius apud nos in psalterio tractatus et glosule ab annis ferme xlta et vque habentur.' I owe this reference first to Beryl Smalley and later to Christopher Holdsworth, who notes that Maurice refers to Gilbert as 'reverendo ac vero sancto patri', which suggests a date by which Gilbert had established his reputation as a monastic leader.

Gilbert seems to have stayed in France for several years. He returned as a *magister*.

In the bishop's household

On his return it might have been expected that Gilbert would have taken up a post in a cathedral or urban school and/or have proceeded to major orders. He did neither. Instead he began to teach the children, both boys and girls, of his neighbourhood. The precise locality is not given, but since the author of the *Vita* explicitly regarded this school as the prototype of the later community at Sempringham, it is reasonable to suppose that it was sited there. The establishment was organized on quasi-monastic lines—indeed, the *Vita* explicitly states that the children followed monastic discipline ('statuta monasteriorum'). The boys had to keep silence except in places where speech was authorized and to sleep together as in a dormitory.[25] However, the *Vita* is at pains to point out that Gilbert still wore costly and elegant secular dress. The saint's position was clearly an ambivalent one within the lay world: provided with an income by his father, still not a priest, and yet following in many respects a monastic regime.[26] This ambivalence was heightened when Jocelin presented his son to his two demesne churches of Sempringham and West Torrington. The author of the *Vita*, writing perhaps some eighty years after these events, was clearly embarrassed by this episode in the life of his saint, and tries to excuse Gilbert's behaviour in accepting these churches. For not only was such provision suspect, the churches would, of course, be held in plurality, and Gilbert was not yet in major orders. When the grant was made (perhaps in the late 1110s) the lay patron might still expect to receive some profits from 'his' church, but by 1200 the *ius proprietatis* had clearly been superseded by the *ius patronatus*, so Gilbert is said only to have accepted his father's gift because otherwise the latter's rights in them would have been jeopardized—which was perhaps a poor defence in canon law.[27] The *Vita* stresses that Gilbert was lawfully and canonically admitted and instituted, and that it took many lawsuits before his father's advowson rights and his own rights to the rectories were confirmed. Details of these actions, which obviously pre-date the assize of darrein

[25] *Book of St Gilbert*, 14–16. Tessa Webber has suggested to me that, just as the school was seen as the foreshadower of the community, so too the reference to the education of girls may be a device to stress how the rule of women was an integral part of Gilbert's design from the beginning. However, there is some evidence that girls could receive elementary education in the 12th century. See Barlow, *The English Church, 1066–1154*, 219.

[26] *Book of St Gilbert*, 16. This ambiguity was also noted in the early life of Stephen of Obazine (*Vita Stephani Obazinensis*, 44). It is possible that Gilbert was a deacon at this time.

[27] M. Brett, *The English Church under Henry I* (Oxford, 1975), 140–6, 229–30.

presentment, cannot be recovered, but it is probable that they arose from a situation where the right to the advowson in a village divided amongst several lords could not be determined, and that the family's enemies took advantage of Gilbert's uncertain position to press their claim.[28]

Though thereafter Gilbert is said to have duly discharged his office, it was presumably because he himself was unable to administer the sacraments that he now employed a chaplain, Geoffrey, to assist him in his pastoral duties at Sempringham. The *Vita* tells how the two originally lodged with a family in the village—an interesting and unusual reference to the housing of twelfth-century parish clergy. However, following a dream in which Gilbert saw himself fondling the breasts of his host's daughter (a fantasy to which Geoffrey also admitted), the two left and built themselves a house in the churchyard.[29] Thereafter Gilbert proceeded to the reform of the parish. He turned the people from their drinking feasts and spectacles to what is described as a monastic life, so that they became locally famous for their devotion.[30] In particular he seems to have insisted on the payment of church dues and tithes, and a graphic account is given of how a recalcitrant parishioner who kept back his tithe was severely rebuked by being obliged to carefully measure out his corn, the tithe of which Gilbert then piled in the street and burnt.[31] The *Vita* explains that Gilbert's chief objective was to maintain justice and ecclesiastical law. This authoritarianism is an aspect of Gilbert's character we shall frequently encounter.

Some time before 1123 Gilbert left his parish in order to serve in the episcopal household of Robert Bloet, bishop of Lincoln.[32] The *Vita* suggests that he did this because he judged it better to serve under the rule of the bishop rather than be like those who without authority ('more acephalorum') ran hither and thither with dissolute liberty. Here it seems as if the *Vita* may be trying to exonerate the unpriested and theoretically

[28] In 1086 Jocelin held a quarter of the church at Sempringham, Gilbert de Gant another half, and the third portion was probably held, though it is not specified, by the third Domesday tenant, Robert de Todeni (*Lincolnshire Domesday*, 98, 114, 130). West Torrington was also a divided village.

[29] *Book of St Gilbert*, 16–18. Not surprisingly, the dream is given a spiritual interpretation by the *Vita*.

[30] Ibid. 18. Drinking in church had long exercised the authorities. See e.g. Aelfric's pastoral letter (993 × *c*.995) in *Councils and Synods. I. 871–1066*, ed. D. Whitelock, M. Brett and C. N. L. Brooke (Oxford, 1981), 217–18.

[31] *Book of St Gilbert*, 18–20. Opposition to tithe payment is frequently encountered in contemporary *exempla*: see G. Constable, 'Resistance to Tithes in the Middle Ages', *JEH*, 13 (1962), 172–85, esp. 180.

[32] *Book of St Gilbert*, 20. For the Lincoln household see *English Episcopal Acta. I. Lincoln 1067–1185*, ed. D. M. Smith (Oxford, 1980), pp. xxxix–xlvii and references there cited.

irregular Gilbert from charges of unlicensed preaching, a problem which troubled ecclesiastical authorities throughout the century.[33] The *Vita* certainly implied in its reference to Gilbert instructing his hearers that he did preach in his parish, but the level at which this was practised is unknown.[34] On Robert's death in 1123 Gilbert was retained in the employment of his successor, Alexander 'the Magnificent'. While he was with the bishop, Gilbert used his income from Sempringham church for his living expenses, but any surplus from rents, annual pensions, and other income was directed for the relief of the poor (a theme which is frequently found in the *Vita*), while all the income from West Torrington was employed for this purpose.[35] As an episcopal chaplain Gilbert's personal piety was noted, and the *Vita* draws particular attention to his habit of repeating the Psalter with prostrations whenever the name of God was mentioned, his frequent private prayer, fastings, and self-scourgings: all, of course, part of the expected activity of a contemporary holy man. It was at this point that the bishop prevailed on Gilbert (much against his will) to become a priest.[36] Alexander's intention seems to have been to make Gilbert a penitentiary for the diocese, if this is what is meant by the *Vita*'s statement that he wished to commit to his chaplain the keys of binding and of loosing, and to appoint him to discover and judge the sins of all his (i.e. the bishop's) people, though it may be that this merely refers to a licence to preach within the diocese.[37] Certainly his new post involved travel, for a cryptic passage in the *Vita* records how Gilbert took with him his travelling allowance as a pilgrim on his journey. This done, Gilbert is said to have redoubled his spiritual exercises, so that he would have been thought a regular canon rather than a secular clerk.[38] Of his clerical activities we are not informed. He witnesses very few episcopal charters, yet he clearly made sufficient of an impression to be a candidate

---

[33] *Book of St Gilbert*, 20. See Morris, *Papal Monarchy*, 289, 305–9, and H. Leyser, *Hermits and the New Monasticism* (London, 1984), 69–77.

[34] *Book of St Gilbert*, 26. This may indicate that he had been granted a *licentia docendi* by the bishop (see Barlow, *English Church*, 226).

[35] *Book of St Gilbert*, 20. The church of West Torrington was later granted to Sempringham priory before being ceded to the much nearer priory of Bullington in return for a quitrent.

[36] Ibid. 24–6. His unwillingness to take priestly office on the grounds of his unworthiness is a common hagiographic topos (see e.g. ibid. 26 n. 2).

[37] Ibid. 24. English bishops were beginning to appoint deputies as penitentiaries to reduce their own increasing commitments (Barlow, *English Church*, 140, 155). Barlow suggests that Gilbert was also the bishop's justiciar: 'it would seem that Gilbert was made presiding judge in the bishop's audience as well as his penitentiary.' In the vast diocese of Lincoln a justiciar was clearly essential, particularly as the volume of ecclesiastical judicial business increased. If Barlow is right, Gilbert would have been a most valued official. It should be noted (*pace* Barlow) that Gilbert became penitentiary before, not after, he was offered an archdeaconry.   [38] *Book of St Gilbert*, 24.

for one of the eight archdeaconries of the diocese.[39] Gilbert refused on the grounds that the temptation of avarice so often associated with the office might lead him to evil.[40] It was shortly after this that he resolved to return to Sempringham and to follow the path of poverty by selling his goods and distributing to the poor. It may be that his reluctance to accept office had caused offence to the bishop; certainly the offer seems to have been a catalyst to Gilbert's later career.[41]

The first communities

The *Vita*'s emphasis on Gilbert's devotion to voluntary poverty places him firmly in the mainstream of contemporary monastic reformers, particularly those who derived their inspiration from the eremitical tradition.[42] It explicitly criticizes those who believe earthly possessions convey honour when really they bring degradation: surely a reference to those monastic reformers who saw the increase of the material prosperity of a community as an indicator of its spiritual state.[43] The gospel text the author cites: 'If you wish to be perfect, go and sell all that you have, and give to the poor, and come follow me' (Matt. 19: 21), is frequently associated with the twelfth-century reformers. Gilbert's action is paralleled, to cite one example, by that of Norbert of Xanten, who, when he resigned his prebend, sold his property and gave it to the poor.[44] There is one

[39] For Gilbert's activities in the episcopal household see *English Episcopal Acta. I*, p. xli, nos. 61, 62, 77, 158, 161. This archdeaconry is described as the richest and most distinguished, and presumably therefore relates to that of Lincoln itself. Gilbert may have been the preferred candidate before William of Bayeux took this office some time before 1132 (*Book of St Gilbert*, 28–9 and n.; J. le Neve, *Fasti Ecclesiae Anglicanae 1066–1300. III. Lincoln*, compiled by D. E. Greenway (London, 1977), 24–5).

[40] For the office of archdeacon see Barlow, *English Church*, 48–50, 154–6, and C. N. L. Brooke, 'The Archdeacon and the Norman Conquest', in D. E. Greenway, C. Holdsworth and J. Sayers (eds.), *Tradition and Change: Essays in Honour of Marjorie Chibnall* (Cambridge, 1985), 1–20.

[41] *Book of St Gilbert*, 28–30. However, Gilbert *sacerdos* of Sempringham is still found witnessing (in the company of Aelred of Rievaulx, Gervase of Louth Park, Walter of Kirkstead, and other Cistercian dignitaries) a charter of the canons of Lincoln as late as 1147, shortly before he set out for Cîteaux. It has been suggested that these were all assembled for the foundation of Vaudey abbey on 23 May 1147 (*Registrum Antiquissimum*, iii. 263).

[42] See e.g. Leyser, *Hermits and the New Monasticism*, 52–6, 59–62; L. K. Little, *Religious Poverty and the Profit Economy in Medieval Europe* (London, 1978), esp. 78–96.

[43] *Book of St Gilbert*, 28–30. The connection between temporal and spiritual prosperity is discussed by J. van Engen in 'The "Crisis of Cenobitism" Reconsidered: Benedictine Monasticism in the Years 1050–1150', *Speculum*, 61 (1986), 269–304, esp. 288–91.

[44] Little, *Religious Poverty*, 88.

significant difference, however, between the almsgiving of Gilbert and that of many of his contemporaries. Their giving seems to have been non-discriminatory: they gave to whomsoever asked. By contrast Gilbert is said to have chosen those poor whose poverty was rendered honourable by their fear and love of God.[45]

All commentators are agreed that the first community at Sempringham was established in 1131, though the *Vita* merely records that it was during the reign of Henry I.[46] This account, which is not always easy to follow and whose chronology is sometimes obscure, states that seven girls of the village decided to leave the world for a heavenly bridegroom, that is, they wished to live as anchoresses, or (perhaps) nuns. Gilbert wished his goods to be used in the service of God and, we are told, originally intended these to be used for the support of a male community, but, since he could not find men willing to live so austere a life as he required, he made over his property for the support of the girls. This choice of women is stressed again shortly afterwards: 'he did not at first make friends for himself of men but . . . called together women as his friends.'[47] Gilbert's own account is a little different. He writes that he could not find men, and so 'I found girls, who had been frequently taught by us, and who wished, having put aside earthly cares, to devote themselves to divine service without hindrance.'[48] This has recently been interpreted to mean that Gilbert never intended to establish a community for women.[49] If this is so, then here is an interesting paradox. The man described by William of Newburgh as supreme amongst those who took on the care and governance of religious women did not apparently have this as his original intention.[50] But it is important to see Gilbert's first community in its context. Thompson has demonstrated how frequently nunneries developed from small communities of anchoresses. This often occurred over a long period of time, and depended on the level of support the women could obtain from local monasteries or lay patrons.[51] Thompson comments that at Markyate the first of Christina's followers were styled *puellae* rather than

---

[45] His discriminatory and 'correct way of giving' is again emphasized in the account of the first community (*Book of St Gilbert*, 30). For a recent and stimulating account of undiscriminating and discriminating charity see M. Rubin, *Charity and Community in Medieval Cambridge* (Cambridge, 1987), esp. 68–71. As we shall see, the relief of poverty continued to be a central feature of Gilbert's spirituality, though when this is mentioned again his almsgiving does not appear to discriminate.

[46] This date is found in the *Successio Magistrorum Ordinis* (PRO 31/9/16, fo. 2). The foundation is discussed below, Ch. 4: 'Sempringham'.   [47] *Book of St Gilbert*, 30.

[48] *Monasticon*, vi. 2. xix.   [49] Elkins, *Holy Women*, 79.

[50] *Chronicles of the Reigns of Stephen, Henry II and Richard I*, 4 vols., Rolls Series (London, 1884–9) i. 54–5.   [51] Thompson, *Women Religious*, 16–37.

sanctimoniales, living under the authority of a *domina* rather than a *priorissa*, and argues that 'the change from a community grouped around a holy recluse who exercised considerable authority, to a nunnery with its more formal organisation, was a slow and almost imperceptible process'.[52] *Mutatis mutandis*, these words could be applied to Gilbert at Sempringham. It is significant, then, that Gilbert's followers are called *puellae* or *ancillae Domini*, never, in these early years, nuns.

Many of the nunneries Thompson describes were supported by and dependent (in more than one sense) upon local communities of men. This is true, for example, of Sopwell (St Albans), Crabhouse (Castle Acre), and Kilburn (Westminster). Other nunneries would later have links with, and would probably be served by, local Augustinian canons.[53] Gilbert's problem was (at least in part) geographical. There were no nearby monasteries that could have ministered in this way to his female followers. Thus in a literal sense Gilbert was unable to find local men to minister to the women. He had, therefore, to go it alone. Early charters relating to the first communities of Sempringham and Haverholme (both of which pre-date Gilbert's abortive visit to Cîteaux discussed below) demonstrate that the care of religious women was central in his design. The very early charter of Roger fitzJocelin (Gilbert's brother) was to the 'handmaidens of Christ' in their poverty: the foundation charter of bishop Alexander in favour of Haverholme was similarly addressed to Christ's handmaidens, 'serving God under the care and teaching of Gilbert the priest'.[54] Two additional points can be made. The *Vita* clearly assumes that the parish girls were already prepared to dedicate themselves to religious life before Gilbert ceded his property to them, and indeed does not state that Gilbert did not intend to establish a community for women, but that he wished to use his *resources* for the support of a male community. One final important point. We must remember that Gilbert and the author of the *Vita* are often apologists: both wrote after crises and scandals had rocked the youthful order and at a time when the role of women in the monastic commonwealth as a whole was increasingly coming into question. To imply that he was not intending to found a female community but that

[52] Ibid. 21.

[53] S. P. Thompson, 'The Problem of the Cistercian Nuns in the Twelfth and Early Thirteenth Centuries', in D. Baker (ed.), *Medieval Women*, Studies in Church History, Subsidia 1 (Oxford, 1978), 248. One of these 'Cistercian' nunneries, Swine, was probably founded by a priest very like Gilbert who gathered a group of women round him, but here the priest was able to find a local community to take over the burden (ibid. 251 and n. 168).

[54] For the Sempringham charter see *Sempringham Charters*, xv. 158–9, and for Haverholme see *English Episcopal Acta. I*, 24–5.

his hand was forced by circumstances may be a way in which he and his biographer attempted to deflect criticism.

Gilbert's own account goes on to describe how houses and a cloister were built and how the seven girls were enclosed by bishop Alexander of Lincoln.[55] Thereafter they would never leave, and, Gilbert adds, he did not think at that time that more would be added to this small community. The *Vita* is, as we might expect, fuller. Gilbert provided for all the girls' necessities. Again the aid of Alexander is acknowledged, and the girls are said to have been enclosed to live a solitary life in buildings erected against the north wall of the parish church. The only way in which necessities could be passed through to them was by a single opening. These were made the responsibility of certain secular women, while Gilbert himself had the only key to the door, never unlocked except at his command and only for his entry to them, not for their exit. Indeed, the *Vita* states that the window itself would never have been opened if humans could have lived without human things.[56]

What, then, was the nature of this community? Elkins has drawn a contrast between the type of female monasticism of northern England (including Lincolnshire) and the south.[57] She rightly stresses that until the 1130s there were no monastic possibilities for women in the north; this is contrasted with the south, where there was a long tradition of activity which had evolved over many years and had given rise to a wide variety of organizational forms, ranging from the interest of old-established Benedictine houses to that of individual hermits who took an active part in the encouragement of religious women. In the north, she argues, there was greater homogeneity. There were few monasteries for men and few hermits to influence the spiritual life of women; moreover, in the north benefactors supported the new orders while in the south they looked to the Benedictines. As a result of these factors, twelfth-century northern nunneries were typically based on forms created by the new orders and included religious men within their walls. This hypothesis requires further investigation: what will be examined here is how far the first community at Sempringham reflected this allegedly specific northern mentality.

---

[55] *Monasticon*, vi. 2. xix. Dyson has suggested (with little evidence) that Alexander's support 'took the form of buildings' since Alexander had a considerable expertise in architecture, but it is hard to place the simple constructions next to Sempringham parish church in the context of the bishop's elaborate structures, such as Newark castle (A. G. Dyson, 'The Monastic Patronage of Bishop Alexander of Lincoln', *JEH*, 26 (1975), 16).

[56] *Book of St Gilbert*, 32–4.   [57] Elkins, *Holy Women*, esp. 76–7.

The antithesis between north and south may be overstated. In particular, the community established at Sempringham in the early 1130s was essentially eremitical rather than cenobitic, and hence had considerable affinities with developments elsewhere in England (and beyond). The language of both Gilbert himself and of the *Vita* employed to describe the seven is primarily that applicable to anchoresses. Gilbert refers to their inclusion by the bishop ('per dompnum Alexandrum . . . septem inclusimus'): the role of the bishop in the enclosure of anchorites was already established by this time and was to become the norm during the thirteenth century.[58] Later he refers to them as *inclusae Christi*, a term typically applied to anchoresses.[59] The *Vita*'s account of the girls' life, of the window and the door whose key was held by Gilbert alone, are all reminiscent of the organization of a community of anchoresses rather than nuns. So too are the similes and metaphors used in the description. The girls are segregated from the world, pledged to eternal virginity, and reserved for the heavenly bridegroom. They are said to be enclosed as *ancillae Christi*; they are exiles from their land, family, and father's house, 'imprisoned' from the world.[60] It is also worth noting the parallel between the Sempringham community with its cells against the walls of the parish church and the home of the women of the *Ancrene Wisse*, which lay under the eaves of the church.[61] These women can surely be classed amongst those described by the author of the *Libellus de Diversis Ordinibus* as taking up Christ's yoke 'with holy men or under their guidance'.[62] The same writer emphasized without disapproval the diversity of the hermits' life and organization.[63] This eclecticism is paralleled in Gilbert's arrangements for his female followers, and later in his establishment of a Rule.

Parallels can easily be found in twelfth-century England. A number of writers and clerics, of whom Anselm is only the most famous, had written

---

[58] *Monasticon*, v. 2. xix; A. K. Warren, *Anchorites and their Patrons in Medieval England* (Berkeley and Los Angeles, 1985), 53–91, esp. 56–7.

[59] It should be stated, however, that Gilbert later referred to the nuns 'quas Deo incluseram'.

[60] This vocabulary of enclosure is discussed by Warren, *Anchorites and their Patrons*, 93–7. The term *ancilla Christi* is used, for example, to describe Christina of Markyate (*The Life of Christina of Markyate*, ed. and trans. C. H. Talbot (corr. repr., Oxford, 1987), 52). For an illuminating recent discussion of marriage similes in anchoretic literature see T. Head, 'The Marriages of Christina of Markyate', *Viator*, 21 (1990), 75–101.

[61] *Ancrene Wisse, edited from MS Corpus Christi College Cambridge 402*, ed. J. R. R. Tolkien, EETS 249 (1962), 74.

[62] *Libellus de Diversis Ordinibus et Professionibus qui sunt in Aecclesia*, ed. G. Constable and B. Smith (Oxford, 1972), 4.   [63] Ibid. 14–16.

for the instruction of anchoresses or had been their patrons, companions, and teachers. Anselm's letter of advice was written at the request of a group of women living under the care of a priest, Robert, who probably followed much the same sort of life as Gilbert's seven followers.[64] As Warren has written: 'The twelfth-century Englishwoman who desired a religious life had three choices: she could become a nun, an anchoress, or a hermitess', that is, an unenclosed solitary.[65] As we have already seen, many of these women were later organized in nunneries, and indeed may have been pressurized into this.[66] There is no direct evidence that the community at Sempringham came under similar pressure, but its lack of organization and, seemingly, of significant income apart from Gilbert's own inheritance may well have limited its growth and been one of the stimuli for Gilbert's attempt to abandon his followers in 1147.

While Gilbert cannot be regarded as a hermit in the same way as many of the other contemporary founders of small orders, such as Gaucher of Aureil or Stephen of Obazine (both of whom welcomed women as followers), there are a number of similarities between Gilbert's career and theirs.[67] Gilbert showed some reluctance to lead his communities and thus decided to cede them to the Cistercians; his asceticism owed as much to the eremitical as to the monastic tradition; he refused to be clothed in the habit of a canon until persuaded, in old age and with reluctance, by his followers: all these features testify to his desire to withdraw from active involvement in the cenobitic life. Ultimately, Gilbert and his houses were integrated into fully organized monastic communities, but there had clearly been tensions in that slow transition. Like so many of his contemporaries, the very success of the holy man and the growing needs, temporal as much as spiritual, of his followers meant a choice had to be made between flight or organization.[68] Gilbert chose the

[64] *Sancti Anselmi Opera Omnia*, ed. F. S. Schmitt, 6 vols. (Edinburgh, 1946–61), iv. 134–5, v. 359–62. The women at Haverholme were described as being 'sub custodia et doctrina Gilberti sacerdotis'.

[65] A. K. Warren, 'The Nun as Anchoress: England 1100–1500', in J. A. Nichols and L. T. Shank (eds.), *Medieval Religious Women. I. Distant Echoes*, Cistercian Studies, 71 (Kalamazoo, Mich., 1984), 199.

[66] Warren, 'The Nun as Anchoress', 200; C. J. Holdsworth, 'Christina of Markyate', in Baker (ed.), *Medieval Women*, 189 and n. 18.

[67] For hermits and their attitude to women see the brief survey in Leyser, *Hermits and the New Monasticism*, 49–51. I have considered Stephen of Obazine's female followers in 'Hermits, Monks and Women in Twelfth-Century France and England: The Experience of Obazine and Sempringham', in J. Loades (ed.), *Monastic Studies: The Continuity of Tradition* (Bangor, 1990), 127–45.

[68] These pressures are discussed by L. Milis, 'Ermites et chanoines reguliers au XIIe siècle', *Cahiers de Civilisation Médiévale*, 22 (1979), 57–60.

first alternative when he went to Cîteaux: when that failed he had perforce to create an order and a Rule.

It is also clear that, just as in so many other communities both of the old and new orders, eremitical elements remained in Gilbert's twelfth-century communities.[69] When Thomas Becket was fleeing from Northampton *en route* for France, he is said to have come to a remote spot some forty miles from Lincoln and accessible only by water, called *hermitorium*, which belonged to the congregation of the nuns of Sempringham.[70] A little earlier, in 1160, Adam, the first abbot of the Cistercian abbey of Meaux, left his monastery to become a recluse at Watton priory, where he remained for seven years until a fire destroyed his home and he returned to the abbey.[71]

The community at Sempringham was for a short time looked after by lay women who passed all necessities to the *ancillae* through the window.[72] Again, this arrangement is more suggestive of an eremitical community than a small nunnery. There is a parallel here with the anchoresses of the *Ancrene Wisse*, who, it was understood, would have servants, who seem, like those at Sempringham, not to have been resident.[73] Yet the use of female servants brought problems of temptation to which Benedict of Aniane had long ago drawn attention, though in his case he was concerned for the well-being of canonesses. It was precisely this fear to which Aelred gave vivid expression in his guide for recluses, when he wrote of the anchoress being led astray by the chatterings of the gossip who sat before her window.[74]

The solution was the introduction of a lay sisterhood. According to Gilbert's own account, this was done on the advice of the first abbot of

[69] See G. Constable, 'Eremitical Forms of Monastic Life', in *Istituzione monastiche e Istituzione Canonicali in Occidente (1123–1215)*, Miscellanea del Centro di Studi Medioevali, 9, (Milan, 1980), 239–64, esp. 259–64.

[70] This has been plausibly identified by Foreville with the small dependent priory established at Wyberton *c*.1180 for two canons by Ralph de Wyperton, and dedicated to Becket. Though this grant post-dates Becket's flight, it may well have been established on the site of the earlier hermitage (*Book of St Gilbert*, p. xxxv and n.; see *Sempringham Charters*, xv. 76, and below, Ch. 4 n. 4). While the term *hermitorium* may merely mean a place of solitude, in this instance it almost certainly refers to a hermitage H. Dauphin, 'L'Erémitisme en Angleterre aux xiᵉ et xiiᵉ siècles' in *L'Eremitismo in Occidente nei Secoli XI e XII*, Miscellanea del Centro di Studi Medioevali 4 (Milan, 1965).

[71] *Chronica Monasterii de Melsa, a fundatione usque ad annum 1396, auctore Thoma de Burton, abbate*, ed. E. A. Bond, 3 vols., Rolls Series (London, 1866–8), i. 107.

[72] *Book of St Gilbert*, 34.

[73] Discussed in Warren, *Anchorites and their Patrons*, 31, 33.

[74] M. Parisse, *Les Nonnes au Moyen Âge* (Le Puy, 1983), 142; Aelred, *De Institutis Inclusarum*, ed. C. H. Talbot, in *Aelredi Rievallensis Opera Omnia I*, ed. A. Hoste and C. H. Talbot, Corpus Christianorum: Continuatio Medievalis 1 (Turnhout, 1971), 638. For further criticism of worldly speech see Warren, *Anchorites and their Patrons*, 108–10.

Rievaulx (i.e. William, abbot from 1132 to 1145). If this was so, then the model for these women was presumably the *conversi* of the Cistercians.[75] The first recruits were the original servants of the community who requested that they too be given a habit. Gilbert's response was to attempt to dissuade them by giving them a Rule of the utmost austerity in order to test their vocation, and he obliged them to wait for a year before acceptance. The lay sisters are the element of Gilbert's communities about which least is known: all we are told in the *Vita* is that they had experienced great poverty and had resorted to begging, and that this experience certainly helped persuade them to join the community.[76] The next development was the introduction of *conversi*. Gilbert wrote how since he only had 'seculares' to look after his goods, he acquired hired labourers ('mercenarii') to whom he offered identical conditions to the lay sisters, and to whom he gave the same habit as the Cisterciaan *fratres*.[77] The *Vita*'s account is similar, and tells how men were employed as *famuli* to carry out the more external and heavier tasks of the community. Like the lay sisters, they were said to have been recruited from the poorest elements of rural society: some were those raised by Gilbert himself from their youth at his own expense, others were escaped serfs who had been freed in the name of religion, and others were extremely poor and beggars. These men, just as their female counterparts, pleaded with Gilbert to allow them to join the community. This version of events is expanded in the first chapter of the lay brothers' Rule ('de institutione et ordinationi fratrum'), which tells how, shortly after the nuns were settled at Sempringham, Cistercian monks arrived, dressed and living in great simplicity, accompanied by *laici* who were poorly dressed and content with the food of the poor. The labourers at Sempringham were allegedly so impressed on hearing this that they expressed a wish to live 'with us [sc. Gilbert's community] in the same order'.[78]

During the 1130s the group at Sempringham must have been very similar to eremitical and semi-eremitical communities that could be found all across contemporary western Europe. It probably continued to rely for its sustenance upon the income from the two churches of which Gilbert was rector, combined with local alms, and perhaps additional sums from Gilbert's patrimony. There is no surviving charter or other evidence that any local lord had as yet made any landed endowment for the group's

[75] *Monasticon*, vi. 2. xix. The *Vita* (*Book of St Gilbert*, 34) merely states that he acted on the advice of prudent and religious men. The rule for the lay sisters is discussed below, Ch. 2: 'The Gilbertine Rule': 'The lay sisters'. [76] *Book of St Gilbert*, 34–6.
[77] *Monasticon*, vi. 2. xix. [78] *Book of St Gilbert*, 36–8.

maintenance. Grants, like those early ones to Sempringham and Haver-holme mentioned above, were addressed to an individual and his fol-lowers, not to an institution.[79] The community at Sempringham was not yet Sempringham priory. Just like eremitical communities elsewhere in western Europe, that change would take several years.[80]

Between c.1132 and 1147 Gilbert's followers marked time. Contrary to Gilbert's account (echoed by the *Vita*) of how the life of his nuns found approval with wealthy lords who gave him lands on which to build, there was in fact no major expansion and only one new foundation, and Gilbert's version of events is given within the context of his visit to Cîteaux in 1147 and is an attempt to explain why Gilbert wished to hand over his commu-nities to the Cistercians' control.[81] The author of the *Vita* writes in more expansive style of how wealthy and noble Englishmen brought land, estates, and many possessions, and how under Gilbert's guidance they began to build many monasteries in many regions. The roles of bishop Alexander, who began the work, and Henry II, who finished it, are singled out for individual mention.[82] Yet there is no evidence that any substantial grants were being made at this time, and no Gilbertine foun-dation other than Sempringham and Haverholme can be certainly dated before c.1150. Indeed, as will be discussed in more detail below, there is no evidence (*pace* previous accounts of the order) that Sempringham was endowed by 1139, or that Gilbert de Gant played a leading role in its establishment.[83] According to the *Vita*, Gilbert was reluctant to receive these grants, and indeed rejected many, only accepting some because he was reluctant to oppose God's will, hinder the devotion of benefactors, or neglect the support of God's servants.

The one new community to be founded during this period was Haverholme.[84] Bishop Alexander's foundation charter can be firmly dated to the last weeks of December 1139 and is worth detailed consideration. The grant was made for the relief of the necessities of the handmaidens of Christ, the nuns serving Christ under the care and teaching of Gilbert the priest ('sub custodia et doctrina Gileberti'). These women were said to follow a hard and holy life, the life of the Cistercian monks as far as the weakness of their sex allowed. We do not know if this community of nuns

[79] For an analogous case at Sopwell see Thompson, *Women Religious*, 23–4.

[80] Discussed by Milis, 'Ermites et chanoines reguliers', 39–80. See also J. Herbert, 'The Transformation of Hermitages into Augustinian Priories in Twelfth-Century England', in W. J. Sheils (ed.), *Monks, Hermits and the Ascetic Tradition*, Studies in Church History, 22 (1985), 131–45.   [81] *Monasticon*, vi. 2. xix.

[82] *Book of St Gilbert*, 38–40.   [83] See below, Ch. 4: 'Sempringham'.

[84] *English Episcopal Acta*. I, 24–5. See below, Ch. 4, 'Haverholme'.

was sent out from Sempringham because the original group there was becoming too large, or whether this was an entirely new group, nor can we tell how it was ministered to, though clearly Gilbert himself could not look after Sempringham and Haverholme at the same time, even though the two communities were not many miles apart. Most interesting is the reference to the women following the Cistercian way of life.[85] While the Rules followed by both the lay sisters and brethren were said to be based on Cistercian models, there is no other evidence that the *ancillae* followed a version of the Cistercian Rule at this time. The later Rule of the nuns as defined by Gilbert after his return from Cîteaux was Benedictine, and while this does not necessarily deny a Cistercian interpretation, it is likely that the *Vita* would have specified that the nuns followed the Cistercian way of life if they did so. It is, of course, possible, or even probable, that abbot William also advised Gilbert on the Rule of his community, as well as suggesting a way of life for the lay sisters, but since the Cistercians at this time had no houses for women any such Rule must have had to be substantially modified for Gilbert's use. Perhaps a more likely explanation for Alexander's description is that by this time the term 'Cistercian' may have become almost generic, synonymous with any reformed monastic grouping following the Benedictine Rule.

The founding of a second house forced Gilbert to face up to the difficult problem of how to order a community primarily established for women but which necessarily also included men. Though this question had always perplexed the Church, it acquired considerable urgency at the end of the eleventh and through the twelfth century, as women came in increasing numbers to follow the hermits and reformers of western Europe and to demand guidance for their own spiritual life. The response to the problem varied considerably. One solution frequently employed was for a community of women to be linked to a neighbouring house of monks, who would provide spiritual services and who often had a supervisory role over the women.[86] This arrangement was that adopted, for example, at Marcigny, the early double houses of Prémontré, and at Fontevrault. At Arrouaise the communities, though constitutionally linked, seem to have been physically some way apart.[87] Proximity was dangerous: sometimes communities were moved in order that they be further away from each other. Some reformers were not so prepared to compromise. Stephen of Muret allegedly moved away from Gaucher of Aureil to avoid

---

[85] Elkins has drawn attention to this feature (*Holy Women*, 81–2).

[86] English examples are discussed by Thompson, *Women Religious*, 54–82.

[87] See below, Ch. 2: 'Models and options'.

the temptation of Gaucher's female followers; Ailbert of Rolduc moved himself when the women who entered the community with Embricon themselves refused to move to new, more distant quarters.[88] By contrast, Gilbert was not troubled by the presence of his women followers: his flight to Cîteaux seems to have been rather a flight from responsibility. In this his response was similar to that of most of the 'eremitical' monastic reformers of the early twelfth century. Bruno of La Grande Chartreuse, Robert of Arbrissel, Robert of Molesme, Norbert of Xanten all at some time or other left their communities in the lurch. Whatever its reason, the journey to Cîteaux marked a turning point in the history of the Gilbertine communities.

Cîteaux and beyond

According to his own account, since the communities were expanding and he could not recruit clerks ('religiosi literati') necessary for the rule of the women and the lay brothers, Gilbert travelled to the 1147 council at Cîteaux in order that he might commit 'our house, the handmaidens of Christ, and our brethren to their rule'. However, he was totally frustrated in his purpose ('omnino repulsam sustinui'), and so, forced by necessity, he appointed Augustinian canons to undertake the care of the order.[89] His initial choice is explained by the *Vita*: he knew more about the Cistercians since they had often given him hospitality, and they were more perfect and stricter than others in their observance of the religious life.[90] Such an explanation is certainly plausible: abbot William had, as we have seen, already played an important part in helping Gilbert devise regulations for his followers, and there were now Cistercian abbeys in Lincolnshire such as Louth Park or Revesby of which Gilbert must have known.[91] It is possible that arrangements for the journey were finalized earlier in 1147 (perhaps in May), when Gilbert is known to have been with the abbots of Rievaulx, Louth Park, and Kirkstead.[92] Such an occasion would have given Aelred and his fellow white monks the opportunity of discussing Gilbert's plans: perhaps he even travelled to Cîteaux in their company. The Cistercians were a good choice for a local reformer who wanted to leave the direct care of his communities to others. Gilbert's reluctance is explicitly pointed out by the *Vita*: he was conscious of his own weakness

[88] Both examples cited in Leyser, *Hermits and the New Monasticism*, 50.
[89] *Monasticon*, vi. 2. xix.   [90] *Book of St Gilbert*, 40.
[91] Louth Park was founded in 1137 by Gilbert's early patron, bishop Alexander; Revesby, whose abbot in 1147 was Aelred, had been founded by William de Romara, earl of Lincoln, in 1143.   [92] *Registrum Antiquissimum*, iii. 263.

(which may have been physical as much as spiritual: he was already in his mid-sixties) and wished to commit the group to those stronger and more capable than himself.[93] Such a move made sense to Gilbert: it did not make equal sense to the Cistercians.

The chapter of 1147 was a busy one.[94] In addition to the internal agenda of the order, the Cistercians also assumed control of the orders of Savigny and that founded by Stephen of Obazine. This was not the first example of aggrandizement by the order—for example, Cadouin with its dependent communities had been affiliated to Cîteaux in 1119—but the takeovers of 1147 were on a grand scale. There were thirty-two Savigniac houses and seven communities associated around Obazine; the reception of these two groups marked a significant increase in the Cistercian empire.[95] Why, then, were these communities accepted while Gilbert's were rejected? Gilbert himself offered no explanation. In the following generation it was recorded that the pope and the Cistercian abbots said that their order was not allowed authority over the religious life of others, especially over that of women.[96] Yet both Savigny and Obazine had facilities for women, and though this may have occasioned the Cistercians' initial reluctance (revealed in the *Vita* of Stephen) to take on the Obazine communities, they overcame their scruples and absorbed both orders. Writing at the very beginning of the thirteenth century, when the Gilbertine order was at the peak of its popularity, it must have been difficult for the *Vita*'s author to explain Cistercian misgivings other than by reference to their distrust of women in their houses, and he may well have been unaware that Savigny and Obazine had been accepted in 1147.[97] Viewed from the Cistercians' perspective, however, the 'appeal' of Gilbert was limited. He was offering two not very well-endowed communities in distant Lincolnshire. Both Savigny and Obazine were more accessible to Cistercian centres and most of their houses were in France.[98] Again, Gilbert had no powerful patrons. Bishop Alexander, whose support is in any case hard to determine, had just died; William, abbot of Rievaulx,

---

[93] *Book of St Gilbert*, 40.

[94] *Statuta Capitulorum Generalium Ordinis Cisterciensis ab anno 1116 ad annum 1786*, ed. J. M. Canivez, 6 vols. (Louvain, 1933–41), i. 37–8.

[95] I have discussed aspects of the chapter in 'Hermits, Monks and Women', 127, 139–40.

[96] *Book of St Gilbert*, 42.

[97] 'Cistercian' nunneries are discussed below, Ch. 2: 'Models and options': 'Continuity and native tradition'.

[98] Distance from the mother house was, after all, the prime reason why the Gilbertines refused to take on the responsibility of care for San Sisto at Rome some 50 years later. See below, Ch. 4: 'Failures': 'Rome'.

had died two years earlier.[99] By contrast, Stephen had the active support both of the pope and of the abbot of Cîteaux, while Bernard seems to have supported Serlo of Savigny in his desire to bring his houses under Cistercian control.[100] What is more, Gilbert's 'Rule' was inchoate; his own commitment to his followers less than certain. For the Cistercians to take over Gilbert's houses was a gamble; the fact that they consisted *primarily* for women (unlike both Savigny and Obazine, where the care of religious women was not central to the communities' life) probably tipped the balance. It was a difficult enough task (as would shortly be seen) for two relatively flourishing and well-organized orders to be affiliated to the Cistercians; the Gilbertines posed much greater problems.[101]

Nevertheless, Gilbert is said to have made a good impression on the pope and Bernard of Clairvaux.[102] Eugenius ordered Gilbert to continue the rule of his communities. Gilbert protested his age and general unfitness for this burden, fearing too that he would be prevented from meditation by administrative duties, a fear that is a further indication of his eremitical leanings. The *Vita* (though not Gilbert's own account) implies, though does not state directly, that Gilbert moved from Cîteaux to Clairvaux, for discussions with Bernard and Malachy of Armagh. If this is so, then he must have been at Clairvaux in October 1148, for Malachy did not arrive there till then, and it is likely that he stayed in France for more than a year, from September 1147 (the general chapter) till *c.*November 1148, when Malachy died.[103] But did Gilbert engage in discussions with Bernard at Clairvaux at all? Elkins has recently argued that he did not.[104] This case needs careful examination, for it affects the interpretation of the Gilbertine Rule and its relation to Cistercian models. As already noted, Gilbert himself made no mention of a meeting with

---

[99] For Alexander's support see Dyson, 'Monastic Patronage', 16.

[100] Golding, 'Hermits, Monks and Women', 139–41.

[101] For the later history of the Obazine nuns see B. Barrière, *L'Abbaye cistercienne d'Obazine en Bas-Limouisin: les origines—le patrimoine* (Tulle, 1977), 91–108, and for the post-union problems of Savigny see B. D. Hill, *English Cistercian Monasteries and their Patrons in the Twelfth Century* (Chicago and London, 1968), 105–15.

[102] The pope is said to have regretted not having made Gilbert archbishop of York (*Book of St Gilbert*, 44).

[103] Foreville (*Book of St Gilbert*, p. xli n. v) has suggested that Gilbert may have returned to England after the council and then made a second visit.

[104] S. Elkins, 'All Ages, Every Condition, and Both Sexes: The Emergence of a Gilbertine Identity', in J. A. Nichols and L. T. Shank (eds.), *Medieval Religious Women. I. Distant Echoes*, Cistercian Studies, 71 (Kalamazoo, Mich., 1984), 177–80, and *Holy Women*, 132–3, 207–8 n. 22. This view is shared by Giles Constable (pers. comm.).

Bernard. The *Vita*'s account is also hardly explicit. The relevant passage on which the argument for Bernard's influence on the Gilbertine Rule has been based reads: 'Gilbert also became so intimate (*familiaris*) with St Malachy, archbishop of Ireland, and St Bernard, abbot of Clairvaux, on that journey that in the presence of those men alone he was present when it is recorded that through their prayers health was restored to a sick man. Moreover he received tokens of the love of both bishop and abbot, in the shape of a staff from each, the instruments of certain miracles; and the abbot gave him a stole and a maniple as keepsakes.'[105] The only other account of Gilbert's meeting with Bernard is found in William of Newburgh, who, in the *Historia Rerum Anglicarum* written *c*.1196, tells how Gilbert thought of going to St Bernard and 'instructed by his [i.e. Bernard's] respected counsel and strengthened in his purpose he did not cease to pursue the more fervently and confidently what had been devoutly begun'.[106] Elkins has argued that the *Vita*'s account is a later addition.[107] She stresses the fact that Gilbert did not refer to the stay at Cîteaux, that he would hardly have stayed over one year there, and that, while the *Vita* does not mention Cistercian influence on the lay brethren and sisters, it was responsible for the introduction of the canons. Central to Elkins's argument is a belief that Gilbert's and the *Vita*'s differing versions represent two ideologies or perceptions of the communities, and more particularly that the *Vita* writes up Cistercian and Bernardine influence to justify the continuation of the order after Gilbert's death.[108]

This thesis has much to commend it. Certainly Bernard is not known to have been at Clairvaux for any length of time during the period when Gilbert is said to have been devising the Rule with his advice. Neither can archbishop Malachy have had a great impact on Gilbert since he only arrived at Clairvaux for his last visit in October 1148, and by the

---

[105] *The Life of St Gilbert*, 44–5. This version of events is embroidered by Capgrave, in whose account Gilbert is accompanied home by Malachy and Bernard, the cure of the sick man is attributed to Gilbert not the other saints, and Malachy's gift of the maniple is said to have contained a relic (ibid. 358–9; *John Capgrave's Lives of St Augustine and St Gilbert of Sempringham*, ed. J. J. Munro, EETS, os 140 (1910), 91).

[106] William of Newburgh, *Historia Rerum Anglicarum*, in *Chronicles of the Reigns of Stephen, Henry II and Richard I*, ed. R. Howlett, 4 vols., Rolls Series (London, 1884–9), i. 54.

[107] Elkins, *Holy Women*, 133 and 207–8 nn. 22–3. She cites Foreville's statement in *Un Procès de canonisation*, pp. xvii–xviii that the chapters of the *Vita* headed *Quod commissum est ei a domino papa regimen ordinis sui* (the chapter under discussion here) and *de constantia eius* post-date the canonization, since they alone refer to Gilbert as *beatus* rather than the more usual *magister*, *dominus*, or *pater*. Foreville did not repeat this suggestion in her more recent edition. William of Newburgh's account is seen as representing a later tradition.

[108] Elkins, 'All Ages', 178–80.

beginning of November he was dead.[109] Certainly, too, by the time the *Vita* was produced new orders, particularly those which made provision for women, were everywhere under criticism. To stress the intimacy with Bernard may have been one way for the Gilbertines to protect themselves from attack. But it is important to note that the *Vita* itself does not explicitly refer to Bernard and Malachy's role in devising the Gilbertine Rule: instead it emphasizes Gilbert's friendship with the two saints. Two conclusions follow. The differences between the two sources, the *Vita* and the autobiography, are not of great significance, and both in particular stress that Gilbert was frustrated in his plans at Cîteaux: the most that can be suggested is that the author of the *Vita* was *implying* that Gilbert was directed by Bernard in the construction of the Rule. But it must now appear unlikely that Gilbert and Bernard met for any length of time. Does this necessarily mean that Bernard had no influence on the formulation of the Gilbertine Rule? His role in its creation is explicitly acknowledged in early papal confirmation charters:

The nuns also in church observe in all things that order of the Office that was instituted by saint Gilbert, first prior of the order of Sempringham, and which was first approved by blessed Bernard along with many other religious persons; that is, [the nuns conduct the Office] not by singing musically but by chanting or reading in a dignified, measured and distinct manner.

This account is ambiguous. Elkins has observed that it refers to a specific rule only, that the nuns should chant or read rather than sing the offices; yet should we necessarily thus infer that this was Bernard's only contribution?[110] Certainly, as we shall see, the Gilbertine Rule for *conversi* was closely modelled on the Cistercian equivalent, and Cistercian influences are noticeable elsewhere. What remains unclear is how far these were direct borrowings, or how far they were filtered through other channels, such as those of the reformed Augustinian congregations which had themselves borrowed so heavily from the white monks. To summarize: perhaps the most likely scenario is that Gilbert was already well aware of Cistercian

---

[109] *PL* 182, cols. 1114–18.

[110] 'Moniales quoque in omnibus illum modum officii sui in ecclesia servent qui a . . . Gileberto primo priore ordinis de Sempingham institutus et a beato Bernardo . . . nec non et aliis plerisque religiosis personis primo fuerat approbratus, scilicet non musice cantando sed honeste et moderate psallendo atque legendo.' Elkins, 'All Ages', 177–8. Her case is weakened in one respect, since, while she correctly dates the papal bull given in *Monasticon*, vi. 2. 960–1 to the pontificate of Innocent IV, 'a pontiff unlikely to have any special information about the Gilbertines', the same phrasing is found in a bull of Alexander III's dating from 1178 (C. R. Cheney, 'Papal Priveleges for Gilbertine Houses', in *Medieval Texts and Studies* (Oxford 1973), 59–60).

customs through his ties with Cistercian abbeys in Lincolnshire and his friendship with William of Rievaulx (and maybe already at this stage with Aelred). The journey to Cîteaux gave him the opportunity to observe Cistercian organization and practice at first hand and at the centre. Bernard may well have encouraged him, as pope Eugenius did. We do not need to accept that Bernard gave Gilbert detailed instructions in person but rather that contemporary Cistercian customs were an influence and were adopted subject to necessary modifications. Thereafter Bernard may have continued to give advice by letter or through the agency of Cistercians visiting Sempringham.

If it is difficult to determine the chronology and origins of the Rule's prototype, equally unclear is the date of the next development, which was to be crucial in establishing the ultimate shape of the order: the introduction of the canons. Gilbert wrote how he associated clerks in his work, who would have the rule and custody of the nuns and the lay brethren, would follow the Augustinian Rule 'in vigils and fasts', and who would have no access to the nuns except to administer the last rites, and then under close supervision. Masses were to be celebrated in the conventual churches, which would be divided by a wall preventing the nuns and the canons from seeing each other. The canons' own church and domestic buildings were to be separated at some distance from those of the nuns.[111] The *Vita* amplifies Gilbert's writing, emphasizing that the Gilbertine canons were priests and well educated, and it describes the elaborate mechanisms for the separation of the nuns and men—though it may be that this is a description of conditions that obtained when the author was writing rather than those operative in the 1150s and 1160s.[112] Indeed, the degree of separation may have been deliberately emphasized in order to reduce criticism of the order. Certainly these arrangements, if they existed, could be circumvented, as events at Watton would shortly demonstrate.

The choice of Augustinian canons as the male element in Gilbert's nunneries made a great deal of sense. Gilbert could obviously no longer look to local Cistercian abbeys for resources, and there were already several Augustinian communities in the region.[113] Care for religious women was the sort of practical responsibility for which the Augustinians were

---

[111] *Monasticon*, vi. 2. xix.   [112] *Book of St Gilbert*, 46.

[113] Such as Bourne and Thornton, though whether Gilbert actually recruited canons from these houses (as suggested by Elkins, *Holy Women*, 83) is far from certain. It is interesting that the brethren of a number of 'Cistercian' nunneries, such as Legbourne, Stixwould, and Swine, were described as canons (Thompson, *Women Religious*, 68–71).

well suited, and at least two Augustinian congregations, those of Arrouaise and Prémontré, had already experimented with nunneries. Though the latter had abandoned double houses a decade before Gilbert introduced canons, there remained close links between communities of Premonstratensian canons and neighbouring nunneries of various observances.[114] A more important influence may have been Fontevrault. Though recently this influence has been denied, and there were certainly considerable differences between the two, it is significant that the male religious at Fontevrault followed the Augustinian Rule.[115] Whatever the reason for Gilbert's choice of the Augustinian Rule, it was to change the entire direction of the order, and ultimately to make Gilbertine double houses indistinguishable from other nunneries that were totally controlled by male religious.[116]

Were the canons introduced immediately on Gilbert's return from France in 1148? Unfortunately, none of the early Gilbertine double foundations (save Haverholme) can be securely dated, though most have—on little evidence—been ascribed to the years 1148 to 1154.[117] There is some indication, however, that even after Gilbert's return to England communities were established without canons. The most compelling evidence comes from Watton. Eustace fitzJohn's foundation charter is addressed to the 'nuns who serve God at Watton': no mention is made either of the canons or the lay brethren. Between 1151 and 1153 archbishop Henry Murdac issued a detailed confirmation charter at the request of William Fossard, Eustace's lord.[118] In this William also remitted the service of two knights owed by Eustace 'specially for the maintenance of thirteen canons who are to serve and provide for (*servituri et provisuri sunt*) the said nuns for ever, both in spiritual and temporal matters, according to the *instituta* of the order of Sempringham'. These words are echoed by the archbishop's confirmation 'in order that the thirteen canons might rule over the said nuns, and religiously minister to them according to the order of Sempringham'. These are the first explicit references to the existence of a Rule and an Order of Sempringham. Similar evidence is found from Sixhills. Here, Thomas son of William, the son of the founder, gave to

---

[114] See below, Ch. 2: 'Models and options', and Thompson, *Women Religious*, 139–45.
[115] This is discussed in more detail below: for denial of a Fontevraudine model see Foreville, *Book of St Gilbert*, pp. xliii and n., liii–liv.
[116] I have discussed this development in more detail in 'The Distortion of a Dream: Transformations and Mutations of the Rule of St Gilbert', *Word and Spirit*, 11 (1989), 60–78.   [117] See below, Ch. 4.
[118] This charter can probably be dated to 1151 (*English Episcopal Acta. V. York 1070–1154*, ed. J. E. Burton (Oxford, 1988), 100–2, no. 129).

'our nuns' the churches of Saleby and East Rasen 'to support thirteen canons who will serve God and the said nuns for ever in the church of St Mary, Sixhills'.[119] Unfortunately, this charter cannot be precisely dated, but its similarity to the Watton document is clear and indicates the same pattern of development: a community of nuns to which was shortly added in a second stage the apostolic number of canons. Finally, a charter in favour of Sempringham issued by William de Rames, and dated to the 14th year of king Stephen (Dec. 1149–Dec. 1150), is addressed solely to the nuns of Sempringham, with no mention of *conversi* or canons. This might suggest that at Sempringham too the canons had still not arrived.[120] Yet if archbishop Murdac's charter can be dated to 1151, then by this date canons were already at Watton and the rudiments, at any rate, of Gilbert's order had been established. The canons were certainly in existence by 1153, as both Murdac's charter and Gilbert's own reference to pope Eugenius' approval of the Rule indicate. How far the Rule had 'solidified' is another question: the two interrelated crises that were shortly to beset the communities suggest an order in tension, one that was still feeling its way towards that resolution acclaimed as the 'chariot of Aminadab' by the *Vita*.[121]

The Years of Crisis

Following Gilbert's return from Cîteaux a number of new foundations were made, and by the end of the 1150s all but one of the double houses had been established.[122] All now included nuns, canons, lay brethren, and lay sisters, though, as we have seen, in some cases at least, the canons were introduced subsequent to the nunneries' foundation.[123] However, the crises that soon broke suggest that arrangements within the priories were still fairly informal and that the clearly defined Rule apparent in succeeding generations had not yet been fully codified.

The nun of Watton

The *Vita* takes constant pains to emphasize the propriety of the relations between men and women in Gilbertine houses and the lack of any scandal.

---

[119] *Gilbertine Charters*, 3–4.   [120] *Sempringham Charters*, xvi. 157.

[121] *Book of St Gilbert*, 50–4.

[122] These were Alvingham, Bullington, Catley, Chicksands, Nun Ormsby, Sixhills, Tunstall (which did not survive), and Watton. The precise dates of foundation are very difficult to determine.

[123] There were also two priories for canons only: Malton and St Katherine's, Lincoln.

We have only one account to set against this: Aelred's narrative of the nun of Watton, which itself survives only in a single manuscript.[124] It is hardly surprising that an episode that reflected so badly on the internal discipline of the Gilbertines was not reported in Gilbertine sources: it is perhaps more surprising that it was not picked up by contemporaries such as Walter Map or Gerald of Wales, both of whom made veiled, and perhaps sarcastic, reference to the double houses.[125] But the events narrated by Aelred have moved from being silenced and marginal to centre-stage, and enforce their own comment on the protestations of the Gilbertine advocates.

Aelred seems to have written his account shortly before the beginning of his last illness in December 1166; it is addressed to a distant friend, who has been variously but inconclusively identified.[126] According to Aelred, the events he wrote about had happened long before.[127] After a brief opening section in which Aelred describes the re-foundation of Watton by Gilbert and the reputation for sanctity and spirituality of its nuns, he tells how archbishop Murdac (d. 1153) had requested that the community receive a girl of about 4 years of age. As she grew up, it was clear that she had no vocation for the religious life. She met one of the brethren 'to whom the care of external affairs was entrusted', who had entered the nuns' quarters to work. This *frater* was almost certainly a lay brother; though he is said to have worn a habit, this was not confined to the choir monks.[128] The two fell in love, and illicit meetings resulted in

---

[124] See G. Constable, 'Aelred of Rievaulx and the Nun of Watton: An Episode in the Early History of the Gilbertine Order', in Baker (ed.), *Medieval Women*, 205–26, which provides a full bibliography and on which the following paragraphs heavily depend; but see also Elkins, *Holy Women*, 106–11. The text of Aelred's account can be found in *PL* 195, cols. 789–96.

[125] See below, Ch. 3: 'Disciplining the community': 'The view from outside'. Foreville and Constable suggest that the *Vita*'s reference to Gilbert's cure of a lustful nun with a sharp reproof may be a veiled allusion to the nun of Watton, but it is more likely that this refers to the episode recorded by Gerald of Wales in the *Gemma Ecclesiastica* where Gilbert allegedly showed his naked and emaciated body to a nun in order to cure her of her desires (*Book of St Gilbert*, p. liv, 60; *Giraldi Cambrensis Opera*, ed. J. S. Brewer, J. F. Dimock, and G. F. Warner, 8 vols., Rolls Series (London, 1861–91), ii. 247–8).

[126] Constable, 'Aelred of Rievaulx', 209 n. 11.

[127] However, the age of the girl makes it unlikely that the events happened before 1160; see Elkins *Holy Women*, 201 n. 2.

[128] Constable ('Aelred of Rievaulx', 218–19) suggests that he may have been a canon since Murdac's confirmation charter to Watton mentions the canons who serve the nuns in secular as well as divine affairs, but the implication of Aelred's account is that he had entered the nuns' area as a workman. Moreover, Gilbert's own account of the foundation of the order refers to the *conversi* as those 'qui laboribus exterioribus se dederant' (*Monasticon*, vi. 2. xix).

her pregnancy. Discovered by the other nuns, the girl was accused by 'matronae sapentiores' (whom Constable suggests may have been the three religious and discreet nuns to whom the Rule entrusted special responsibility).[129] On confession she was beaten up, narrowly avoided worse punishment, and was imprisoned on a meagre diet.[130] Indeed, the fury of the nuns at the discovery may suggest that this was an exceptional case, and there was in fact no general laxity of relations. The young man had already fled the house, but his hiding place was revealed by his lover and by a ruse he was recaptured by some brethren sent out by Gilbert himself. They held him in custody, but the nuns persuaded them to hand him over on the grounds that they wanted some information from him. Once he was in their hands they brought the two together and forced the girl to castrate her lover. 'Then one of the bystanders snatched the parts of which he had been relieved and thrust them into the mouth of the sinner just as they were, befouled with blood.' The young man was given back to the brethren, and no more is heard of him. The girl was returned to prison.

Then came the miracle, which for Aelred was the point of the narrative. The nuns, now calmer, daily with tears prayed to Christ for mercy against the danger and infamy which they recognized threatened their house. The girl herself cursed Henry Murdac for placing her in the community. Murdac then appeared to her in a vision, together with two women, who miraculously removed her baby and cleansed her of all signs of pregnancy. Accusations of infanticide could not be sustained and all but one of her fetters miraculously fell away. Gilbert was next informed of events and called on Aelred for advice. The latter visited the girl, verified the miracle, and decided that the chains should not be replaced but her fate should be left to God. After Aelred had returned home, Gilbert wrote to him that the final fetter had fallen.

These events still retain their power to shock, though our focus is now on the treatment of the girl and her lover rather than on their violation of the vows of chastity: a terrible deed which necessitated a terrible vengeance. It has been pointed out that the castration in itself was not necessarily exceptionally harsh in medieval terms, and it was the fact that it was carried out by the nuns and their use of the girl as an instrument

---

[129] Constable, 'Aelred of Rievaulx', 207 and n. 7.

[130] This became the standard punishment prescribed for nuns who committed adultery (ibid. 214 n. 29). See below, Ch. 3: 'Disciplining the community', for the Gilbertine Rule on immorality.

which clearly most disturbed Aelred.[131] Nevertheless, though it was indeed available as a judicial punishment, castration still seems to have been seen as an act of particular horror. It is often associated, most famously in the case of Abelard, with situations of strong emotion where the 'wronged' families—in this case the nuns—take the law into their own hands and exact vengeance, or with instances of despotic power.[132] It would clearly not normally have been invoked in this situation. The nuns' prayers and tears afterwards suggest that they recognized that their own part in the events would also be a matter of scandal. The miracle undoubtedly was welcomed for its reconciling power.[133] Not only was the girl freed and cleansed of her child, her virginity seemingly restored, but the community itself was cleansed. Only the mutilated young man has to vanish, into the silence that the Gilbertine sources would have preferred to cover the whole affair.

Why, then, did Aelred later break this silence, and write this account? The events had clearly made a deep impression on him, and he was writing at a time of crisis for the Gilbertines, when the relationship of the sexes within the order was a central issue. Both the recent commentators have pointed out the silent influence knowledge of the scandal must have had on the affair of the lay brethren, and it is surely the latters' accusations which were the stimulus for Aelred to set down his account. He writes, as he says, 'in order both to deprive the envious of an opportunity and yet not to keep hidden the glory of Christ', to 'my dearest friend who is far removed from these parts': perhaps in this way he could unburden himself, at a safe distance from the crisis unfolding around him.

Aelred clearly considered Gilbert to have been too insouciant in disciplinary matters. While it was Gilbert's decision to authorize the trick by which the brother was trapped, he is otherwise presented as ignorant about the whole affair. Though this may be in part a protective measure of Aelred's, the initiative throughout these happenings is nearly always taken by the nuns, over whom Gilbert cannot or does not exercise effective authority. Yet the scandal was obviously threatening to the

---

[131] Constable, 'Aelred of Rievaulx', 214–16. His chief example is the castration and blinding of the defeated but innocent party in a case of judicial combat, related in a miracle story of William of York (who restored the victim). Constable points out that this shows judicial castration was not unknown in the 12th century, but it also demonstrates that it could also be seen as cruel and excessive, even taking into account that the victim here is innocent. It is presented as an act of bestial savagery, horrible to see, which made the crowd wonder at the victor's rage and the judges abhor his cruelty.

[132] As in Constable's example of Geoffrey of Anjou ordering the castration of several clerics and that their parts be brought to him in a basket (ibid. 215 n. 31). For family vengeance see ibid. 217.   [133] Ibid. 214, 218.

stability of the whole house, perhaps the whole order. Gilbert's call on Aelred as adviser seems an admission of failure: certainly it was the Cistercian who took the dominant role in proceedings after the miracle of the removal of the fetters. Gilbert travelled to Rievaulx for advice, rather than Aelred going to Watton. As we have seen in other contexts, and as was to be apparent later, Gilbert on occasions showed himself very little concerned with the *minutiae* of management, with potentially disastrous consequences; Aelred provided the necessary support, just as Aelred's predecessor as abbot of Rievaulx, William, had advised on the early arrangements at Sempringham. Aelred was certainly a close friend and admirer of Gilbert and his nuns, whom he mentions with approval in one of his sermons.[134] A friendly critic was a useful asset as the new order struggled for survival. At the same time, it may well be that it was Aelred's own misgivings about Gilbert's communities and about the association of religious men and women in general (revealed, for example, in his *De Institutione Inclusarum*) which led to the introduction of stricter rules amongst the Gilbertines.[135] Finally, the story-book question, 'and what happened to them next', is worth asking here. However silenced, these events would still have been strong in the memory during the Gilbertines' worst institutional crisis, that precipitated by the lay brethren; and, indeed, at least some of the protagonists could still have been at Watton.

The story of the nun of Watton is the most important surviving source to illustrate conditions in Gilbertine double communities in the first generation after their foundation. One of the chief problems in assessing the development of the Gilbertine Rule is the fact that it survives in only one manuscript, which is clearly a composite document including both fragments of Gilbert's own *scripta* and later additions made up until 1238.[136] By that time the order was fully organized with elaborate institutional and architectural arrangements to ensure that nuns and men, whether laity, *conversi*, or choir monks, rarely met, and then only under the strictest supervision. But Aelred's account reveals a much less ordered arrangement. The carefully articulated structure of the mature Gilbertine Rule made no room for recruits like the nun of Watton, for it forbade the reception of novices until they had reached the age of 15. Following the practice general amongst the new orders, the Gilbertines refused oblates, yet the 4-year-old was certainly to be included amongst

---

[134] Ibid. 210–11.   [135] Ibid. 219–20, and Elkins, *Holy Women*, 106.
[136] See below, Appendix II.

their number.[137] In the early years, however, oblates were probably not
wholly rejected. There were young children at Obazine, where they accompanied their parents, and other hermits received whole families into
their communities.[138] Analogous to Murdac's support for the Watton
recruit is perhaps Marbod of Rennes' request of Vitalis of Savigny that he
take a young girl whose father had become a *conversus* and whose mother
could not afford a dowry for her to enter a nunnery.[139] Thus Professor
Foreville's interesting suggestion that the 'nun' of Watton may not have
been a nun at the time of the scandal since she was at most only about 15
may not be necessary. Certainly Aelred's reference to her as 'virgo Christi'
strongly suggests that he thought of her as a nun, though it is possible
that she was still a novice, and the fact that she was 'sponsored' by an
archbishop suggests that she was intended to be a nun rather than a lay
sister.[140] Reception of child recruits, easy association between the female
and male elements of the community, the apparent absence of an authority at Watton to curb the nuns' excesses: all indicated laxity. This was the
context for the scandal to become a catalyst to institutional development.
It brought about the effective end of that free association between Gilbert
and his nuns that had begun in 1131 and which had been under increasing restriction ever since.

Gilbert and Becket

At about the same time that Gilbert had to contend with the disorder at
Watton he was faced with another crisis, which in a different way threatened the survival of his communities, and indeed his own freedom. In
1164 Becket fled secretly from the Council of Northampton. The *Vita*
states merely that Becket found refuge in Gilbertine houses and that it
was in them that plans for his flight to France were drawn up, and that
Gilbert provided the archbishop with servants and companions amongst
his brethren (presumably the *conversi*). Further details (though they do
not always tally) are found in other Becket sources.[141] It would seem that
while at Northampton Becket planned his escape in collaboration with
two guides, Robert de Cave and Scaiman, who may have belonged to St
Katherine's priory, Lincoln. They were almost certainly lay brethren,

---

[137] The rule for novices is discussed below, Ch. 3: 'Entering the house': 'The Rule and
the novice'.   [138] Barrière, *L'Abbaye cistercienne*, 123–5.

[139] Examples cited in Leyser, *Hermits and the New Monasticism*, 49–51.

[140] *Book of St Gilbert*, p. liv n. 1. The girl cannot have been born after 1149, and Watton's
foundation can scarcely be before 1148. See Constable, 'Aelred of Rievaulx', 210 n. 14, 218.

[141] See *Materials for the History of Thomas Becket, Archbishop of Canterbury*, ed. J. C.
Robertson and J. B. Sheppard, 7 vols., Rolls Series (London, 1875–85), ii. 399–400, iii.
318–25, iv. 53–7, vi. 77.

rather than canons. It is noteworthy that they were already at Northampton, where they were perhaps staying with Becket in St Andrew's priory: Becket's flight was not a sudden decision. These two accompanied Becket via Grantham to Lincoln, where they stayed in hiding with a fuller, James *ad pontem*, who was known to one of them.[142] Moving on from the city, they progressed through the Lincolnshire fens, where they rested at Gilbertine communities, including a hermitage (which has been variously identified as a cell of Sempringham on Holland Marsh later dedicated to Thomas the Martyr, or as Catley priory) and Haverholme, as they made their way to Boston.[143] Then, with Becket disguised as a Gilbertine *conversus*, they moved westwards towards the Gilbertine priory of Chicksands, where the archbishop obtained the services of Gilbert, a chaplain-canon, who (with Scaiman) was to accompany Becket across the Channel. How long they remained with Becket is not known; Scaiman was certainly associated with the archbishop, perhaps acting as a messenger, until the end of 1166, when he was captured in England, though he soon succeeded in escaping to Christ Church, Canterbury; at about the same time Gilbert the chaplain is found in Thomas's entourage in France.[144]

Why should Gilbert of Sempringham have supported Becket? There are no obvious ties between the two men, Becket had no great friends among the leaders of the reformed orders, and there is no evidence of earlier connections between them.[145] The escape from Northampton was clearly well orchestrated between Becket and the Gilbertines; perhaps Gilbert himself was there. Northampton was in the diocese of Lincoln, but Gilbert's diocesan bishop, Robert de Chesney, was no particular supporter of his archbishop.[146] Whatever the reason for Gilbert's support, it did not end with the provision of escorts and guides, for he was also accused of providing the exile with large funds against the king's

[142] The author of the Anonymous *I Vita* writes that James was a brother of one of the two companions (*Materials for the History of Thomas Becket*, iv. 54). James's family was quite prominent in Lincoln, and members of it are found amongst the benefactors of Alvingham priory. See G. W. F. Hill, *Medieval Lincoln* (Cambridge, 1948), 394–5. It is possible that the chapel of St Thomas of Canterbury on the High Bridge (ibid. 149) was erected on the site of, or near, James's house.

[143] *Book of St Gilbert*, p. xxxv; F. Barlow, *Thomas Becket* (London, 1986), 115. In 1392 a chapel was said to have been founded at the Holland Marsh hermitage on account of the miracles performed there through St Thomas the Martyr (*Cal. Papal Letters*, iv. 431).

[144] Barlow, *Thomas Becket*, 161, 171.

[145] Though in his letters (written while in exile) to Gilbert at the commencement of the lay brothers' revolt, Becket does describe himself as a close friend and supporter (*Book of St Gilbert*, 346–8).

[146] Philip of Broi, the notorious canon of Bedford supported by Becket when accused of murder, was priest of the church of Hawnes, which belonged to Chicksands priory, but this seems a very tenuous association to explain Gilbertine involvement.

commands. Though the *Vita* alleges that this was a false accusation, such aid would accord with Gilbert's earlier support for Becket. As a result of this accusation he was cited, together with all the priors and proctors of the communities, to appear before the royal justices.[147] The allegation, even if false, was serious: support for the exile was often a dangerous and costly business and the fears of Gilbert's companions are very understandable. Henry had probably already ordered the arrest of all those who had aided Becket's flight from Northampton; any further assistance would be seen as compounding that crime.[148] In spite of an offer of release if Gilbert swore that the charges were untrue, he refused, saying that he would rather go into exile.[149] In a long excursus the *Vita* attempts (not wholly successfully) to explain Gilbert's refusal. Meanwhile the case dragged on and Gilbert's companions became increasingly concerned. Finally, as they were giving up hope, royal messengers arrived from France ordering their release until the king could investigate the charges in person.[150] Gilbert thereupon declared his innocence, and the case would appear to have been entirely dropped. While the author of the *Vita* may have been concerned to stress his subject's support for Becket (as Constable suggests), it seems certain that for a time Gilbert was indeed an ally of Becket.[151] Fortunately for the Gilbertines, in this instance Henry did not bear a grudge against the order and he was to continue as its patron. In the coming years his support was to be vital.

The lay brothers' revolt

The outbreak of discontent and the setting up of the papal inquiry

Scarcely, if at all, had the matter of his involvement with Thomas Becket been resolved when Gilbert was faced by the most serious crisis yet. Together with the episode of the nun of Watton, the rebellion of the Gilbertine *conversi* is the most notorious incident in the early history of the order.[152] It is one of the first (perhaps the first) recorded revolt of

---

[147] *Book of St Gilbert*, 72.   [148] Barlow, *Thomas Becket*, 125–7.

[149] *Book of St Gilbert*, 72.

[150] Henry II was in France from February till May 1165 and from March 1166 till October 1170 (R. W. Eyton, *Court, Household and Itinerary of Henry II* (London, 1878), 78–9, 92–135).   [151] Constable, 'Aelred of Rievaulx', 224 n. 67.

[152] The chronology of events and the issues raised by the revolt have been examined by Knowles and Foreville: see M. D. Knowles, 'The Revolt of the Lay Brothers of Sempringham', *EHR*, 50 (1935), 465–87; R. Foreville, 'La Crise de l'ordre de Sempringham au XIIe siècle: nouvelle approche du dossier des frères lais', *Anglo-Norman Studies 6 (1983)*, ed. R. A. Brown (Woodbridge, 1984), 39–57; and *Book of St Gilbert*, pp. lv–lxii, 76–85, 134–167.

conversi. The causes of these revolts were various—the first major rising at the Cistercian house of Schönau in 1168 arose over the question of the supply of boots to the lay brothers—but they normally share one feature in common: a belief, real or mistaken, that the powers of the *conversi* were being restricted.[153] This can be seen most clearly at Sempringham, but at Grandmont too, which experienced considerable unrest in the 1180s, the agreement made in 1187 shows that the central issue was the balance of power between the clerical and lay brothers.[154]

Details of the Gilbertine rebellion are found in a long chapter entitled in the *Vita* 'Vexatio falsorum fratrum'.[155] This incorporates two paragraphs from Gilbert's own account in *De Constructione Monasteriorum*. In addition the *Book of St Gilbert* includes the texts of six letters sent to the pope in Gilbert's defence, the reports of two inquiries set up by the pope, a letter of support and advice from William of Norwich to Gilbert himself, and three letters from the pope to Gilbert, the bishops, and the king. These letters constitute only a sample of the total correspondence relating to the revolt—and it must be remembered that they represent the Gilbertines' own selection—but their survival enables the account as presented in the *Vita* to be considerably augmented.[156] Conflating Gilbert's story and the letters, the events of the rising can be reconstructed, though the chronology remains ambiguous.[157]

The rising was led by two lay brothers to whom the Master had entrusted the care of all the houses. These were accompanied by two more, including Ogger, who emerges as the ultimate and most determined leader. Not surprisingly, the *Vita* and associated documents paint a very black picture of the lay brothers. Ogger's rebellion was felt all the more bitterly since in the early days of the order Gilbert had rescued Ogger and his family from beggary and taught the boy a trade. As the *Vita* says, 'the men who shared his peace and partook of his bread, whom he trusted and had loved most dearly, enlarged their crookedness against him, which caused him to grieve even more deeply'.[158] According to

---

[153] The fullest treatment of *conversi* rebellions remains J. S. Donnelly, *The Decline of the Cistercian Laybrotherhood*, Fordham University Studies, History Series, 3 (New York, 1949). For Schönau see ibid. 34–5.

[154] The precise causes of the revolt here are not spelled out. J. Becquet, 'La Première crise de l'ordre de Grandmont', *Bulletin de la Société Archéologique et Historique du Limousin*, 87 (1960), 283–324. [155] *Book of St Gilbert*, 76–84.

[156] Ibid. 134–62. The inclusion of the letters in the *Vita* is explicitly stated in its Prologue (ibid. 8).

[157] My interpretation of the chronology of events differs considerably from that presented by Foreville, for which see below, Appendix III.

[158] *Book of St Gilbert*, 76–8.

Gilbert's account, Ogger and Gerard had stolen possessions belonging to the order, and, defying all attempts to restrain them, had slandered the founder (i.e. himself) and the canons so that the latter became the object of slanderous gossip. They had turned away from their profession and religious life and 'chased hither and thither on their own mounts with very little respect for continence and honest living until they became objects of mockery and derision to clergy and people'.[159] The charge of theft was repeated by Henry II, who also maintained that the Master and some of his canons would have been expelled or even killed were the rebels not frightened of royal action. Indeed, they had attempted to bribe the crown with 300 marks (which is surely an exaggeration) to allow the canons to be removed and the rule amended as the *conversi* wished.[160] The fact that the rebels were 'villeins and lay brethren and those who before entering the religious life were tied to the soil' clearly made their revolt all the more deplorable.[161] As the *Vita* complains, 'servants presumed to attack their master, contemptible men to assail a person of distinction, and obscure men one of noble birth'.[162] The bishop of Winchester complained about the 'insolence' of the lay brothers, and the prior of Bridlington characterized them as 'men of lower nature, men who love only themselves, men dedicated only to flesh and blood'.[163]

No date is given for the beginning of the dispute, but the context in the *Vita* strongly suggests that events came to a head early in 1165, as the account follows immediately upon Gilbert's citation before the royal judges to explain his support of Becket. Indeed, it is possible that the lay brothers sought to take advantage of the difficulties Gilbert was encountering at the royal court. They appealed in person to pope Alexander III, then in exile at Sens. Here they complained of mistreatment and of scandalous behaviour in the Gilbertine houses. Alexander took their complaints seriously, wrote to Becket, and ordered the archbishop, himself a fellow exile, to examine the allegations and to reform the order if necessary.[164] As Knowles remarked, one of the most surprising features of the affair is how the *conversi*, presumably illiterate, were able to travel to France, gain audience with the pope, one of the finest canon lawyers of the age, and convince him of the justice of their cause. Yet, since the *conversi* had for long administered all the temporal affairs of the houses, it may well be that their leaders were rather more learned than has been thought.[165]

[159] Ibid. 78–80.   [160] Ibid. 142–4, letter 3.
[161] Ibid. 162, letter 12.   [162] Ibid. 78.
[163] Ibid. 146, letter 4; 156, letter 8.   [164] The letter does not survive.
[165] 'The Revolt of the Lay Brothers of Sempringham', 465.

Becket thereupon wrote to Gilbert and the order. Neither this letter, nor a later letter of Becket's, was included in the Gilbertine collection of relevant documents. Becket expressed his dismay at the news of the *maxima scandala*, and urged Gilbert to reform and put both the order and the houses into better state, in accordance with the papal letters which accompanied the archbishop's own letter. He also cited Gilbert to appear before him on 2 February 1166 and explain any failure to obey.[166] The messenger who brought these letters to Gilbert was Ogger, and the fate of the papal letters (which do not survive) was one of the objects of the subsequent inquiry. Ogger charged that Gilbert said the letter was forged and had excommunicated Ogger; whereas Gilbert claimed he had never received it, and had only spoken a general excommunication of 'those who overturned his order, together with thieves and robbers' (presumably these were descriptions of the lay brothers), from which he had excluded Ogger out of reverence for the letter (a denial which Ogger admitted).[167] It seems clear that Ogger's return with the papal letter had precipitated an angry confrontation and that either Ogger had been unwilling to deliver the letter or (quite probably) Gilbert had refused to accept it. A letter from William Turbe, bishop of Norwich, and one of Gilbert's closest supporters on the episcopal bench, to Gilbert survives. It is written in the warmest terms: William begins by assuring Gilbert of his love and pleading with him to recognize that he is writing purely out of this affection. He then comes to the point: 'Letters from the pope will be coming to you which I advise you to receive with godly respect, and do not provoke those who bear them with any roughness of speech or fierce looks.' This letter may anticipate Ogger's arrival with the letter and express William's premonitions of the likely result of Ogger's return—in which case William's pleas clearly had little effect—but it seems more likely that William had heard of the stormy arrival of the first letters from the pope and was trying to prevent a similar scene happening again. His whole letter is a plea for Gilbert to show patience and obedience to the pope and to take advice only from the wise who love peace; advice which William evidently felt Gilbert was much in need of.[168]

Since Gilbert had apparently failed to act on the letters, and had not appeared with an explanation at the archiepiscopal court, Becket wrote

---

[166] Printed in *Book of St Gilbert*, 346–7. Becket stresses his love and support for the order and his wish that nothing substantial should be done in the order without his advice.

[167] William of Norwich's report to the pope (ibid. 136, letter 1). The report from the archbishop of York and bishop of Durham also considered the accusation of forgery, and there also Gilbert denied receiving or seeing the letter (ibid. 152, letter 7).

[168] Ibid. 146–8, letter 5.

again later in the year (this time as papal legate) urging him in even stronger terms to reform. This letter refers to two specific grievances. Gilbert had forced his lay brothers to take an oath on profession such as Becket had never heard that any other religious community exacted. Secondly, he urges Gilbert to temper the severity of his zeal. This is the first, albeit oblique, reference to the harshness of the early Gilbertine discipline.[169]

However, Gilbert was also marshalling his supporters, and the establishment was closing ranks. There appears to have been an orchestrated campaign of letters to the pope on his behalf from the king and leading prelates. Those of the king, the archbishop of York, the bishops of Winchester and Norwich, and the prior of Bridlington are preserved in the *Book of St Gilbert*.[170] There is a strong possibility that this support of Gilbert was conceived as part of the anti-Becket policy of the crown. Gilbert was a friend of the Angevins, and the letters of the pope and archbishop of Canterbury ordering reforms in the order could easily be interpreted as unwarranted interference in English ecclesiastical affairs.[171] There are interesting parallels in the wording of several of these letters, which may indicate that they were not written independently. Virtually all refer to Gilbert's great age and the need for papal support for him; the letters from both the bishop of Norwich and Henry of Blois apply to the lay brothers the metaphor of the man who looks back having put his hand to the plough, and that of the archbishop of York echoes the king's warning that the communities' patrons had specifically given their property to the double houses and might withdraw their benefactions if judgement

---

[169] For Becket's second letter, see ibid. 347–8. Becket was appointed papal legate in April.

[170] The sending of the episcopal letters is referred to in the *Vita* account, ibid. 82. The letter of archbishop Roger of York (ibid., 148–50, letter 6) poses some problems. It only appears in MS Cotton Cleopatra B.I (and MS Harl. 468). I have followed Knowles, Constable, and Elkins in accepting the traditional attribution. Foreville has argued that this letter is wrongly attributed to the archbishop since he refers three times to double *houses* (my italics), and there was only one double house (Watton) in his diocese. She suggests therefore that this letter was written by Robert de Chesney and hence should be dated before his death at the end of 1166. However, this is a general letter of support, not necessarily confined to his own diocese, and the single direct reference to houses in his diocese merely states that they are ruled with complete integrity and the strictest regard for the religious life—which could refer to both single and double houses. Foreville would also associate the letters of the bishop of Norwich and prior of Bridlington with a second hearing at the Curia which she suggests occurred between 1169 and 1176. As I have argued below (Appendix III), I think there is little evidence that such a second inquiry was held.

[171] A suggestion first made by Constable, 'Aelred of Rievaulx', 223–5, though he fails to distinguish between the episcopal letters of support and the reports of the inquiries sent by William of Norwich, Roger of York, and Hugh of Durham.

went against Gilbert.[172] Henry asked the pope to consider the letters from Gilbert's ecclesiastical supporters, which suggests they were sent as a concerted appeal—they were certainly carried by the two royal messengers who took Henry's letter.

While Gilbert's ecclesiastical supporters concentrated on rebutting the charges against him, Henry II's own letter was a threat rather than an appeal.[173] He insisted that he would protect the order as established with its canons in control, and asked the pope to order the contumacious rebels to observe their vows, and, if they did not, to ensure that the diocesan bishops used their powers to ensure compliance. This was combined with threats that the king and his magnates would resume all lands granted to the Gilbertines if the pope did not support Gilbert. It is uncertain whether these letters were sent in advance of the subsequent inquiry, or as supporting material with the inquiries' reports. However, the former seems most likely. It seems doubtful that William of Norwich and Roger of York would have written both their reports and appeals on the same occasion, and Henry of Blois, who was appointed to the inquiry but unable to attend through sickness, would surely have alluded to his absence in his appeal.

Perhaps not surprisingly, given such forthright royal interference, this campaign evidently moved Alexander to reconsider, and he arranged two inquiries, one to examine the Lincolnshire priories, and the other to consider the situation at Watton, the only double priory in the York province. In the province of Canterbury William Turbe, bishop of Norwich, and Henry of Blois were appointed judges-delegate, though since the latter was too ill to attend William invited other unnamed religious to help in the investigation.[174] In the provinces of York, the judges were archbishop Roger and Hugh du Puiset, bishop of Durham. Thus all but the bishop of Durham had already shown themselves to be supporters of Gilbert.

Though Alexander's mandate setting up the inquiries of 1166–7 has not survived, its terms can be determined by reference to the reports of the judges' findings. Their task was to investigate the allegations made by Ogger and his companions to the Curia, and their treatment on return. Gilbert, some of the canons, and the rebel *conversi* were to attend. There

---

[172] *Book of St Gilbert*, 150, letter 6; 162, letter 12.

[173] Unlike Foreville, I follow the text of the letters of Henry II as found in Oxford, Bodl. Libr., MS Digby 36, as did Knowles; for a discussion of the textual problems with these letters see below, Appendix III.

[174] For William Turbe's activities as papal judge-delegate, see C. Harper-Bill, 'Bishop William Turbe and the Diocese of Norwich, 1146–1174', in *Anglo-Norman Studies 7 (1984)*, ed. R. A. Brown (Woodbridge, 1985), 147–9.

were two main areas of enquiry: the treatment of the lay brothers and the
question and validity of the new profession, and the allegations of sexual
impropriety between the canons and the nuns. The charge that Gilbert
had claimed that the pope's letter was a forgery and had excommunicated
Ogger, the bearer, was also examined.

The inquiry: the lay brothers

In his second letter Becket had written that the lay brothers had been
obliged to take an oath on profession which no other order had been
accustomed to exact.[175] William of Norwich seems to have been the most
well informed of Gilbert's supporters about the issues. He insisted in his
letter of support that the only obligation laid by Gilbert on the lay
brothers was to keep their profession, 'and this they have promised in my
presence faithfully to do'.[176] Both he and the archbishop of York also
referred to the extraction of the oath in their reports. The latter wrote
that Gilbert had not exacted any sort of oath contrary to the brothers'
first profession, while William Turbe's report is fuller, and more tantalizing. He states that the *conversi* had alleged that Gilbert had forced them
to make a new profession to the abbey of *Sabaneia* (which must, as
Knowles suggested, be Savigny) and to swear oaths 'secundum formam
ordinis Cistercie', contrary to the first profession they had made to
Sempringham. Those who refused to take this oath Gilbert had excommunicated.[177] According to William, Gilbert denied all these charges,
stating that they had never made a profession based on that of the
Cistercians, nor had they been compelled to make a profession at Savigny
contrary to their first profession, or, indeed, any profession at all. None
had been forced to take any oath. Some had taken a voluntary oath to
maintain the order, but this had already been dispensed 'long ago' in the
presence of the bishop of Lincoln. William called upon the lay brothers
to supply proof of their allegation, but they were unable to do so.[178]

The 'voluntary' oath and its dispensation seem to refer to earlier attempts by Gilbert to hold his order together, and by the bishop of
Lincoln to mediate in the dispute.[179] The question of the new profession
following the custom of the Cistercian order is evidently connected with
the adoption of Cistercian customs, which it is argued below probably
took place on Gilbert's introduction of the canons after his visit to Cîteaux

---

[175] *Book of St Gilbert*, 347.
[176] Ibid. 140, letter 2. This perhaps refers to a previous peace-making attempt of William.
[177] Ibid. 134–6, 150; Knowles, 'The Revolt of the Lay Brothers of Sempringham', 470
and n. 1.   [178] *Book of St Gilbert*, 134–6.
[179] The bishop should almost certainly be identified as Robert de Chesney, who was dead
by the end of 1166. The nature of this oath is uncertain.

in 1147, and which drastically reduced the authority of the lay brothers.[180] While the lay brothers maintained that they had had a new profession forced on them, the letters in Gilbert's support in turn accused them of choosing to abandon their profession. Prior Gregory of Bridlington also states specifically that Gilbert had brought in the canons to look after the temporal affairs and religious observance of the priories, and that they had authority over the *conversi*. It is indeed this power struggle which lies behind the lay brothers' complaints.[181]

It is William's references to Savigny which are the most puzzling. Unfortunately, the constitutions of Savigny while it was independent have not survived.[182] It has been suggested that the Savignacs did not have their own Rule, but merely followed that of the Benedictines. However, it is apparent that their economy was based on the grange system and that they had *conversi*. Orderic Vitalis refers to their new customs, and it is probable that like the early Gilbertines they modelled themselves on the Cistercian *ordo*. When the Savignacs were taken over by the Cistercian houses, the English Savignacs led by the abbot of Furness refused to accept the new regime and only agreed to make a profession to Savigny after several years and the application of papal pressure.[183] The adoption of the Cistercian *Usus Conversorum* by the Gilbertines must have seemed an uncomfortable parallel to the events at the English Savignac houses.[184] The reference to the enforced oath to Savigny is probably either a garbled rendering of fears expressed by the lay brothers of similar absorption or an actual misunderstanding on their part.

From William Turbe's report it is evident that the pope wished Gilbert to receive Ogger and his companions back into the order. This requirement would follow from their earlier expulsion from the order and subsequent persuasion of Alexander of the justice of their claim. However, William reported, many of the disaffected lay brothers had already left the order, having received dimissory letters and absolution (again this suggests a degree of compromise and, indeed, that the case had reached the pope after the dispute had continued for some time). Two of these, W. and Denis, were insistent that they would not return, but wished

---

[180] See below, Ch. 2: 'The Gilbertine Rule': 'The lay brotherhood'.

[181] *Book of St Gilbert*, 154–6, letter 8. Gregory also refers to the papal privileges granted to the order by Eugenius III and Adrian IV, which laid down that no changes should be introduced to the institutions.

[182] For the fullest account, though not always satisfactory, see Hill, *English Cistercian Monasteries*, 80–115, and also J. Buhot, 'L'Abbaye normande de Savigny, chef d'ordre et fille de Cîteaux', *Le Moyen Âge*, 46 (1936), 1–19.

[183] Hill, *English Cistercian Monasteries*, 105–9.

[184] For Gilbertine use of the *Usus Conversorum*, see below, Ch. 2, 'The lay brotherhood'.

instead to transfer to another order. The extremer elements, led by Ogger, were looking for a more radical solution and one which would have irrevocably reshaped the order, or, at any rate, restored it to its early condition. Ogger demanded that the four elements of the order should be ruled by one man (presumably the *magister*) and submit equally to him— a desire to reconfigure the order and return it more to its 'original' state, which again indicates discontent with the rule of the canons.

The northern inquiry appears to have run very smoothly. The judges reported that at Watton 'Master Gilbert has not demanded from its inhabitants either an oath or anything else contrary to their first profession; he has sent none of them to prison; he has excommunicated no one'. Here the lay brothers and Gilbert were reconciled, though the former continued to ask for some moderation of the Rule: this was probably associated with their demand for better conditions.[185] The lack of trouble in the north may be associated with the later foundation of these houses; it was only in the earliest foundations in Lincolnshire that the lay brothers would have experienced the contrast between their previous authority and their present demotion.

The inquiry: sexual scandal

The lay brothers had undoubtedly raised the question of scandal in their case to the pope, perhaps in the hope that it would gain papal sympathy for their own demands and criticisms of Gilbert and be further ammunition against the canons. It is certainly the charge that Alexander found most worrying, as is seen by his concentrating the inquiry on the double houses.[186] Gilbert's supporters also saw this as the central issue—or, at least, as Gilbert's most vulnerable point, given the recent scandal at Watton, though for Henry II what was at stake was a usurpation of power by the lay brothers.[187] In his letter of support William Turbe stresses the maligned chastity of the canons. He stated that none of them, even the priest who performed the offices, had access to the nuns, that at mass neither the giver nor the receiver of communion saw each other, and that in general the canons lived totally apart from the nuns.[188] Henry of Blois admitted that he had never seen a Gilbertine community but acknowledged the Gilbertines' reputation and the total segregation of the canons

---

[185] That was only settled with the final adjudication of bishop Hugh of Lincoln at the end of Gilbert's life.

[186] That the inquiry was not primarily concerned with the houses for canons only is borne out by the letter of the archbishop of York and bishop of Durham in which they state that their task was easy since there was only one double house (Watton) in the province.

[187] The letters from Robert of York and the prior of Bridlington (nos. 1 and 8) concentrate entirely on the charge of sexual scandal.   [188] *Book of St Gilbert*, 138, letter 1.

and nuns, who only met (and then under supervision) in direst necessity.[189] Archbishop Roger of York echoed the other bishops' remarks.
The men and women were kept apart, and if the men were moved a long
way from the nuns (presumably in the same sort of way as existed at the
double community at Obazine) then the communities would die, since
the lay patrons would revoke their grants.[190] In an impassioned letter
prior Gregory of Bridlington made few additional points, but did expand
some of those made by his fellow writers. The canons lived not in the
nuns' cloister but within the lay brothers' enclosure. This arrangement
may further indicate that the canons were newcomers in the double
communities, having been literally intruded into the lay brothers' place.[191]

The lay brothers had charged that the canons and nuns shared the
same church, a charge William rebutted again in his report to the pope.
He pointed out that in all the houses the canons had entirely separate
oratories and cloisters and only came to the conventual church once a day
for mass. However, the pope had clearly given instructions that in future
only two or three canons should come to mass while the majority stayed
in their own quarters. This was reluctantly accepted by Gilbert, though
he wanted papal confirmation of the measure, and considered that the
new regulation was harmful to the order. As for the *conversi*, they had
been used to coming to the nuns' church for the night office, but now
they were to attend the canons' church. Delinquent nuns and lay sisters
were not in future to be admitted to the offices.[192] When we turn to the
northern inquiry we find a similar account.[193] The bishops emphasized
(though in less detail) that in the double house of Watton the canons and
nuns lived apart. Nevertheless, Gilbert was still ordered to separate the
canons from the nuns.

The issues are resolved

When the case was again heard in the Curia, Gilbert was cleared of the
charges against him and Alexander issued two privileges in the order's
favour in the summer of 1169.[194]

---

[189] Ibid. 144–6, letter 4.   [190] Ibid. 148–50, letter 6.   [191] Ibid. 154, letter 8.

[192] Ibid. 140, letter 1. William told the pope that 'the Master showed himself patient and
agreeable to this measure, although it is harmful to the Order, until he receives your answer
on this matter'.   [193] Ibid. 150–2, letter 7.

[194] One, dated 30 July, was issued in favour of Malton priory, and it is possible that the
other priories received similar individual documents (*Papsturkunden in England*, ed. W.
Holtzmann, 3 vols. Abhandlungen der Gesellschaft der Wissenschaften zu Göttingen, Phil-
Hist. Klasse. neue Folge, xxv. 1–2: Dritte Folge, xiv–xv, xxxiii (Berlin and Göttingen,
1930–52), i. 377–9, no. 112). The other is a general privilege to the order and is dated 20
Sept. (*Book of St Gilbert*, 156–8).

But, after the dust had settled, had anything changed? The papal letters to the king, Gilbert, and the diocesan bishops make it clear that in the central issue of control of the order the *status quo* was strengthened. The claims of the *conversi* and their attempts to recover a leading role in the organization of the order had failed. In his letter to Henry II Alexander asked that the king should continue to protect the nuns and canons against the rebels, and that those who refused to submit to ecclesiastical penalties should be coerced by royal authority. A similar letter to the bishops and archdeacons urged them to support the canons and to censure the rebels if necessary. Anyone who physically attacked a canon should be excommunicated and should be required to come to Rome for penance. The letter to Gilbert of 20 September 1169 included the privilege that only he or his successors were empowered (in consultation with the priors) to make changes to the Rule. Any member of the order who disobeyed the statutes could be excommunicated by Gilbert, who would be supported by his diocesan bishops.[195] On the question of authority Gilbert had undoubtedly emerged the winner. On that of the conditions of the *conversi*, which Gilbert had promised to ameliorate, no action was taken until shortly before his death, when he agreed to make concessions regarding the lay brothers' clothing and food, evidently in an effort to settle any remaining causes of dispute before he died, though to the end he refused to budge on the issue of the first profession.[196] Although this suggests that the issue still rankled, it seems that the lay brothers in the main accepted the situation, however unwillingly, or joined another order, and it was only Ogger who continued in open revolt and 'almost to the day both of his own death and that of St Gilbert, he lost no opportunity to attack the saint'.[197]

The most important repercussions for the order were the changes in the internal organization of relations between the canons and nuns. The tightening of the rules concerning contact between the nuns and the men insisted on by the pope was perhaps inevitable, particularly in the light of the Watton affair that had occurred only a few years earlier. This 'reform' was accepted by Gilbert, though the tone of bishop William Turbe's comment that it was harmful to the order suggests that it may not have been unanimously welcomed, even by some of the bishops.[198]

The lay brothers' rebellion threatened the very existence of the new order. It actually achieved a strengthening of the canons' control over the

[195] A paraphrase of this letter is given in the *Vita* (*Book of St Gilbert*, 84).
[196] Ibid. 80, 116–18.   [197] Ibid. 80.
[198] Ibid. 138. See also Elkins, *Holy Women*, 114.

conversi that the latter had most resented. It also ensured that the double houses would lose much of the institutional freedom that they had enjoyed during Gilbert's time as *magister*. The nuns would increasingly forfeit whatever authority and independence they had once enjoyed, and when in the mid-1170s Gilbert finally handed over the government of his priories to Roger, prior of the canons-only house of Malton, a new period in Gilbertine history would begin.

Master and Saint

The personal rule

Until that date Gilbert continued to lead his order. Comparatively little is known of his life as *magister*. The *Vita*, hardly surprisingly for a work explicitly intended to present its subject as a confessor comparable with his contemporary, the martyred Thomas, concentrates on the trials he experienced, notably the lay brothers' revolt and the difficulties occasioned by his support for Becket. Nevertheless, something can be gleaned from a careful reading of the life and the miracles. One of the most striking features of Gilbert's rule to which the *Vita* testifies was its peripatetic nature. Given the supreme authority vested in the Master by the Gilbertine constitution, and the very personal nature of Gilbert's disciplinary control, this was perhaps to be expected. The *Vita* explains that all major issues and decisions, including individual disciplinary measures, were left to him. While visiting the houses he would preach, but would also undertake various manual tasks including manuscript copying and building work.[199] We see Gilbert prevented by a unfavourable wind from crossing the Humber estuary when 'he was anxious to visit the monasteries on the other side' and waiting at Hessleskew (a grange of Watton) for more favourable conditions, and then setting out on horseback with his companions, including his successor as *magister*, Roger.[200] On these journeys he was normally accompanied by one *conversus* and two canons, and further details of how these visitations were conducted can be gathered from some of the miracle stories. Several involve Albinus, Gilbert's chaplain. He was probably the saint's closest friend and companion and is described in the *Vita* as the most intimate ('familiarissimus') of Gilbert's chaplains; significantly, the author of the *Vita* undertook his work at the request both of prior Roger and of Albinus. Albinus often accompanied Gilbert on his visitations, once being delayed by fever at Sempringham

---

[199] *Book of St Gilbert*, 58–60. [200] Ibid. 110–12.

and 'unable to go on his usual circuit of the monasteries with father Gilbert'. Gilbert went on without him to 'Insula' (most probably Newstead on Ancholme), where he waited for the recovered chaplain to join him. Albinus was also with Gilbert on his visitation of Chicksands and his visit to Elstow nunnery.[201]

For Gilbert's travels were not confined to visiting his own communities: he was also a spiritual adviser to members of other orders and to the laity, and this is perhaps what is meant by the *Vita*'s reference to his preferral of virtuous outsiders ('extraneos') to some of his own kin whom he regarded as rebels and wicked.[202] No further details are given of what appears to have been a rift within Gilbert's family, but this certainly suggests that not all of his kin were committed supporters of his activities. It seems to have been while on a visit to Chicksands that the nuns of the neighbouring Benedictine nunnery of Elstow invited him to preach to them, while Agnes, prioress of the nunnery of Nun Appleton (Yorkshire), knew Gilbert well. The author of the *Vita* points out that she belonged not to the Gilbertines but to another order, but during her vision of the saint's reception into heaven she exclaimed: 'Do you think that I do not know master Gilbert? I know him extremely well . . . I know that he is my lord and a patron (*advocatus*) of this house and I have known him almost the whole of his life.'[203] Elkins has drawn attention to the close kinship ties between the founders of Nun Appleton, Gilbertine Bullington, and two Benedictine nunneries in Yorkshire.[204] Such ties may have led to the close association between Gilbert and this community; alternatively, they may have been a consequence of it. What does seem certain from the tone of the prioress's remarks is that Gilbert was sufficiently closely involved with Nun Appleton to be regarded as its patron. The instances of Elstow and Appleton remind us that Gilbert's influence

---

[201] Ibid. 62, 96–8, 108. Albinus witnessed charters to Nun Ormsby (*Gilbertine Charters*, 42, 62). Another miracle story tells how Gilbert cured a lay brother of Chicksands while he was visiting the priory (*Book of St Gilbert*, 100).

[202] *Book of St Gilbert*, 60. Some of his family were supporters of Gilbert's foundations, but we know little but their names.

[203] Ibid. 108, 124–6. Nun Appleton had been founded by Alice of St Quentin between *c*.1148 and 1154 and was thus an exact contemporary of the early Gilbertine double houses. It is usually regarded as a 'Cistercian' nunnery, but its status (at any rate during the 12th century), like that of other Yorkshire nunneries such as Sinningthwaite or Swine, was ambiguous. Indeed, the fact that the foundation charter was addressed to a prior as well as the nuns may suggest that it had a similar organization to that of the Gilbertine houses. (*EYC* i, no. 541; Burton, *Yorkshire Nunneries*, esp. 7, 12, 18–19. The vision is discussed in Elkins, *Holy Women*, 130–1.)   [204] Elkins, *Holy Women*, 94–6.

was wide-ranging across nuns from various monastic traditions. It is also of note that there is no mention in the sources of his similarly advising male religious.

Gilbert is also said to have attended (not always successfully) not only the royal but episcopal and baronial courts on both sides of the Channel on behalf of his order. In the Angevin world such journeys were inevitable, but they should persuade us that Gilbert's activities were not confined to the shires of Lincoln and York.[205] He also continued to appear at the episcopal court of Lincoln, where he witnessed several episcopal charters between 1147 and the 1160s.[206] Even allowing for hagiographic hyperbole, it is clear that Gilbert was held in high regard by the Angevin establishment, both ecclesiastical and secular; indeed, it was this support which largely contributed to Gilbert's success in dealing with the lay brothers' revolt. Henry II (together with his court) is recorded as having visited Gilbert in his lodgings, perhaps in London, where the order already held property during the founder's lifetime.[207] Both the king and queen are portrayed as enthusiastic supporters of the saint, who in his turn is seen as their advocate in heaven. In a well-known passage, the *Vita* tells how Henry II, then campaigning against his sons and nearing the end of his own life, broke out on hearing of Gilbert's death: 'Truly I now know that he has left this life for these troubles have come upon me because he no longer lives.'[208] The king was himself responsible for founding at least one Gilbertine priory, Newstead; he also made a small grant to Sixhills priory, but, apart from issuing confirmation charters in favour of that house and Catley as well as to the order in general, there is no evidence that this support amounted to much.[209] Professor Leyser recently placed Hugh of Lincoln in the context of twelfth-century holy men, stressing especially his relationship with the Angevin kings; it seems that Gilbert also fulfilled this role.[210] If Gilbert was seen, like Hugh and others, as an outsider and 'hinge man' possessing extraordinary, and

---

[205] *Book of St Gilbert*, 58.

[206] *English Episcopal Acta. I*, 52, 94, 96; *Registrum Antiquissimum*, i. 250, 265; iii. 268 (a charter of 1147 in which he witnesses as *sacerdos* of Sempringham); iv. 266 (when he is found as a witness with bishop Robert to a grant by Hugh of Bayeux to Thornton abbey).

[207] *Book of St Gilbert*, 92, 112. See below, Ch. 8, 'Urban property': 'London'.

[208] *Book of St Gilbert*, 92.

[209] Henry may also have founded St Margaret's, Marlborough. See below, 225–6. For the confirmation charters of Sixhills and Catley, see *Gilbertine Charters*, 35–8, 90, and for Henry II as patron of the order, below Ch. VII.

[210] Leyser, 'The Angevin Kings and the Holy Man', 49–74.

perhaps frightening, spiritual powers, this might explain how Gilbert was able to retain the close support of the crown both in the matter of the lay brothers' revolt and as patron, even though he had rendered very considerable assistance to Thomas Becket. One episode in the Becket affair seems to typify the holy man's attitude to worldly authority: Gilbert's insouciance in the face of apparent danger. While his followers were terrified that their leader's support of the exile would lead to their own expulsion from the realm, Gilbert remained calm and remote from what was happening around him, buying some spinning-tops from a boy in order to amuse and divert his companions. This studied unconcern can be compared with bishop Hugh's sparkling repartee when faced with Angevin anger at Woodstock.[211] Similarly, the reluctance and fear of the royal justices to convict Gilbert of support for Becket 'because his sanctity was known to all of them' echoes Henry's officials' grudging respect for Hugh. Henry's letters to the pope in support of Gilbert at the time of the lay brothers' rebellion are also couched in terms that suggest the king saw Gilbert not only as a founder of an order of which both the king and his magnates were benefactors, but also as a holy man of distinction, 'a venerable man of God' (Gilbert's great age would have contributed to his reputation for sanctity).[212]

Undoubtedly, too, Gilbert was held in high regard by many bishops, as was most clearly demonstrated at the time of the lay brothers' revolt, and again during the saint's canonization process. Bishops from overseas are reported to have begged items of clothing from Gilbert to expand their relic collections. Archbishop Hubert Walter is said to have known Gilbert well, and the *Vita* was dedicated to him.[213] William aux Blanchemains, who became archbishop of Rheims and who supported Gilbert's canonization at the Curia, is reported to have known Gilbert while he was a young man in England. William was a nephew of king Stephen and had an illustrious ecclesiastical career: he was perhaps typical of the high-ranking clerics with whom Gilbert was familiar.[214] There are also some indications in the miracle stories of the saint's aristocratic friends or patrons. They include the wife of Simon II de Beauchamp, to whom Gilbert gave a piece of bread he had blessed which remained incorrupt for fourteen years. Simon was the son of Payn de Beauchamp and his wife

[211] *Book of St Gilbert*, 74; Leyser, 'The Angevin Kings and the Holy Man', 58–60.

[212] *Book of St Gilbert*, 142–4, 160–2.

[213] Ibid. 168. It is clear that the archbishop was the leading force in procuring Gilbert's canonization. [214] Ibid. 176–8.

Rohaise, the founders of Chicksands priory, of which he too was a bene-factor.[215] Gilbert also sometimes witnessed charters issued by the laity, though he appears surprisingly rarely as a witness to any Gilbertine charter.[216] Very occasionally he also witnessed charters in which the order had no direct interest.[217]

The last years

By the time that Gilbert faced the succession of attacks on his communi-ties in the 1160s he was already an old man. As early as 1147 he had pleaded his age as an excuse for handing over control of his communities to Cîteaux, and he is described as 'senex noster' in the *Vita*'s account of the troubles over his support of Becket, where his defence of the Church is explicitly compared with the example given by aged Eleazar to younger believers. In telling of the lay brothers' revolt the *Vita* describes how Gilbert was not only troubled by old age but by bodily exhaustion.[218] Old age and infirmity did not result in any mitigation of the saint's austerity. His asceticism is stressed, in particular his fasting and sparse diet and clothing.[219] Towards the end of his life Gilbert went blind, which added to his physical weakness. He slept in a separate chamber from the breth-ren, but insisted on continuing to eat with them in the refectory, despite having problems with the stairs; and although he now had to be carried

---

[215] Ibid. 116. For the family, see C. G. Chambers and G. H. Fowler, 'The Beauchamps, Barons of Bedford', *Publications of the Bedfordshire Historical Record Society*, 1 (1913), 3–25, and for their patronage of Chicksands, below, Ch. 4: 'The mid-century expansion': 'Chick-sands'. For other lay witnesses to Gilbert's sanctity as revealed by visions and miracles during his lifetime, see *Book of St Gilbert*, 94–6, 98, 114, 126–8 (the vision of the wife of Ralph de Hauville, founder of the small Gilbertine priory of Marmont in Cambridgeshire).

[216] Gilbert appears amongst the witnesses at Lincoln when the grant of William Tisun of land at Thrussington was confirmed to the nuns of Sempringham. (*Sempringham Charters*, xvi. 83 (before 1160). See also *Gilbertine Charters*, 62.) He also witnessed two charters issued (probably at the same time) by Agnes and her husband Robert, constable of Flamborough, to Watton priory. These are dated between 1150 and 1157 (*EYC* ii. 406, 408).

[217] 'Master Gilbert, prior of the order of Sempringham' stands as first witness (accom-panied by the prior of Watton and a chaplain of Watton) to a grant of land in Brompton by Robert, son of Lemeri of Watton, to *magister* Henry of Willoughby. This charter is dated to the 1170s (*EYC* ii, no. 1233, p. 503). Philip of Kyme's grant of Sotby church to Bardney, in a charter dated between 1148 and 1155, is witnessed by the abbots of Kirkstead, Revesby, and Bourne, and by 'Gilbert of Sempringham and the convent of nuns in that place' (London, BL. MS Cotton Vespasian E XX, fo. 91ʳ), and between 1156 and 1166 he witnessed a charter by Rohaise, wife of Gilbert, earl of Lincoln, in favour of Kirkstead (London, BL, Harl. Chart. 50 F 32).   [218] *Book of St Gilbert*, 42, 72–4, 78.

[219] Ibid. 60–8.

round the priories on a litter, his only concession to his worsening health was to withdraw from secular business (that is, the rule of the temporal affairs of the priories).[220]

This delegation of responsibilities, forced on Gilbert particularly by the loss of his eyesight, made it necessary to choose a successor: Roger, prior of Malton. This can probably be dated to the end of the 1170s (by which time Gilbert was already in his nineties).[221] The significance of his choice will be stressed later, but it should be noted here that the acceptance of Roger as *magister* does not appear to have been unanimous.[222] It is made clear in the *Vita* that this was a transfer of responsibility, but not of ultimate authority: 'To Roger, prior of Malton, he entrusted the care of all the religious houses, in such a way that this man handled the more important business *following his advice*' (my italics). Inspectors (the *summi scrutatores*) were appointed beneath Roger, but they were always to refer the more serious matters to Gilbert: 'For as the head over them all, surpassing all in understanding and in holiness, he referred the cases of them all to himself and, as long as he lived, he received the written professions of all.'[223] In discussing this event in a previous section, the *Vita* takes pains to emphasize Roger's authority, and how 'thereafter as long as [Gilbert] lived he displayed such great reverence and such obvious humility towards Roger that (for although he commanded all, he was himself under Roger's command) he would take scarcely any decisions about what should be done for those in his care without Roger's advice and approval, and he would cancel nothing that Roger did'.[224] However, Roger's position was clearly awkward, and he certainly did not have a free hand. The necessity for the election of a successor after Gilbert's death

---

[220] Ibid. 88–90.

[221] The chronology of these events is hard to determine, since here as elsewhere the author of the *Vita* does not follow a logical progression. He discusses the transition to Roger in two places. In the first instance he goes on to argue that it was Gilbert's association of Roger as an almost coequal authority to put the order's foundations on a secure foundation that inspired the Devil to attempt to overthrow the order during the Becket crisis of 1164–5 (*Book of St Gilbert*, 70). He then returns to the subject after dealing with the lay brothers' revolt, discussing Gilbert's old age and blindness (ibid. 86). However, in 1169 Gilbert was still styled prior of Malton, and the letter of the papal legate of 1176 is addressed to Gilbert in terms that suggest that he was still effective head of the order. Roger is first cited as head in the privileges of 1178, evidently shortly after his appointment (C. R. Cheney, 'Papal Privileges for Gilbertine Houses', in *Medieval Texts and Studies* (Oxford, 1973), 51–2). The author of the *Vita* constantly stresses Roger as Gilbert's natural successor, and may here be trying to push the choice of Roger back, but the confusion may be simply the result of the amplification of the *Vita*.   [222] *Book of St Gilbert*, 68.

[223] Ibid. 86–8.   [224] Ibid. 68.

shows that it was far from being so smooth a transition as the author of the *Vita* seeks to maintain.

It seems to have been at this point, in the 1170s, that Gilbert finally joined his own order, though the chronology is not certain.[225] Both decisions are linked by a concern with the future of the order after his death, though in the event he lived far longer than would have been expected. Gilbert made his own profession to Roger not at Sempringham but at Bullington, perhaps during one of the periodic visitations of the community. One of the most interesting features of Gilbert's career is his resistance to the adoption of a monastic habit until towards the end of his life. Even then it was only reluctantly that he took the habit.[226] The *Vita* points out that, though he had dressed in a grey garment, he had not worn the canon's habit that he had given to his followers nor had he made any special vow to any rule.[227] With his outer garment of linen, and a woollen layer between that and his hair shirt, his clothing was typical of individual hermits and eremitical foundations of the twelfth century: white or grey wool or linen being preferred to the more traditional black for a variety of reasons, but especially to stress the difference between them and the Benedictines.[228] To the author of the *Vita*, Gilbert's reluctance to make his own profession was attributable to his humble belief that he would be accused of arrogance if he took vows to obey a Rule that he himself had written.[229] But this is also the last instance of Gilbert's unwillingness (that had been apparent since at least the time of his journey to Cîteaux in 1147) to commit himself to an *ordo*. Not surprisingly, the canons saw things differently. They feared that if Gilbert was not formally received into the order, then after their founder's death it was possible an outsider might be intruded to take control. Such fears were doubtless accentuated by the fact that new orders were being increasingly

[225] Gilbert's profession is associated in the *Vita* with the appointment of Roger, which seems to have taken place *c.*1177 (see above, n. 221). In any case the profession must be post-1169, as Roger, to whom Gilbert made his profession, only became prior of Malton (his position before he became head of the order) some time between 1169 and 1174.

[226] There is some evidence that Christina of Markyate was similarly reluctant to be professed and had to be persuaded by abbot Geoffrey of St Albans (Thompson, *Women Religious*, 21–2). [227] *Book of St Gilbert*, 66–8.

[228] Leyser, *Hermits and the New Monasticism*, 67–8. See in general A. d'Haenens, 'Quotidienneté et contexte: pour un modèle d'interprétation de la réalité monastique mediévale (XIᵉ–XIIᵉ siècles)', in *Istituzioni monastiche e istituzioni canonicali in occidente (1123–1215)*, Miscellanea del Centro di Studi Medioevali, 9 (Milan, 1980), 567–97.

[229] *Book of St Gilbert*, 66–8. 68.

viewed with suspicion by the Church, and it is probably for this reason that the *Vita* at this point stresses the fact that the order had received papal approbation. Which privileges this refers to is uncertain, as there are several references to unidentified privileges and confirmations. However, if Gilbert's profession to Roger was related to Roger's appointment as head of the order, in *c*.1177, as seems likely, it may refer to the papal privileges of 1178. It has been argued that these privileges testify to a final settlement of the lay brothers' revolt, but it seems far more likely that they mark the transition of the order from the rule of Gilbert to the rule of Roger.[230] It is clear from the *Vita* that the order—as was Gilbert himself—was extremely anxious about what would happen on Gilbert's death and new papal privileges in Roger's name would have been a desirable insurance policy.

Gilbert's concern over his order's future seems to have clouded his last years. His desire for peace within the order even led him finally to relent over the question of the lay brothers' conditions, and shortly before his death, with the chapter's consent, he came to an accord with the lay brethren in the presence of bishop Hugh of Lincoln. All parties reached agreement over the question of rations, clothing, and other customs, though Gilbert continued to argue that 'if anything was determined which contravened their first profession he would have nothing to do with it and he did not wish to be held up as its author'.[231]

Realizing he was close to death, he wrote to all his communities asking for their prayers and blessing, and again urged unity upon his followers.[232] One of these letters survives, addressed to the canons of Malton.[233] Apart from the fragments of Gilbert's *Instituta* preserved in the later Rule, and of his autobiography in the *Vita*, this is Gilbert's only writing to have survived. Its opening is striking: 'Gilbert of Sempringham, by the mercy of God whatever he is, or rather was.' These are humble words, but they also testify to Gilbert's ambivalent position, no longer head of his order, and yet inevitably still the ultimate authority. Gilbert writes of his visits to the priory and his teachings. Now he is too weak for such activity and awaits release from the life that has become bitter. He urges the canons to continue steadfast and to keep the rules of the order. Gilbert asks them for their prayers and concludes with a last attempt to exert his influence and ensure his order's future after his death: 'I also absolve all those who shall in future love our order and defend the unity

---

[230] For a full discussion of these see below, Appendix III.
[231] *Book of St Gilbert*, 116–18.   [232] Ibid. 118–20.
[233] Ibid. 164–6, letter 13. This letter is dated by Foreville to 1176–8 or 1186–7, but it is clearly one of those described in the *Vita*.

of our congregation, from all the offences which, through ignorance, weakness, negligence or contempt, they committed against the rules of our order. But those who scheme to bring about dissension and discord in our community must know that my absolution can be of no use to them, for, unless they are penitent and arrive at a suitable penance, it is clear that they remain guilty in the sight of God.'[234] The fear of dissension that had been triggered by the lay brothers' revolt remained potent to the end.

Gilbert spent Christmas 1188 at Newstead priory, where he received the last sacraments. Since he did not die immediately, his household resolved to move him to Sempringham and carried him secretly and quickly to the mother house, fearing that if he died away from Sempringham he might be captured by lords over whose property they passed in order that they might bury him in their own churches or monasteries. This concern to protect the body of a local holy man or monastic founder is of course a common hagiographic topos; relics brought prestige and, sometimes, prosperity.[235] At Sempringham he was visited by all the heads of the Gilbertine priories, to whom he again stressed the need for unity within the order: 'they were most carefully advised and instructed how to preserve the order's peace, unity and strict discipline after his days were over.' After all the other heads of houses had left Gilbert's deathbed, Roger only remained, to hear his last words, 'Upon you the responsibility rests, from now on.' Since the *Vita* was written at Roger's request, he is presented throughout as the natural candidate for the succession. If there were any other candidates, they have been airbrushed out.

Gilbert died early on Saturday morning, 4 February 1189. Immediately after his death the priors and prioresses of the communities assembled for the funeral. This was attended by a large crowd of mourners including the religious of other orders and the laity. The body was washed (the water effecting a number of cures) and vested, and then buried in the middle of the conventual church in the wall dividing the nuns' half from the canons' so that the tomb could be venerated from both sides. Immediately following the burial the communities proceeded to the formal election of Gilbert's successor, and Roger's unanimous election is presented

[234] Ibid. 164.
[235] Ibid. 118–24. A similar concern to save the body was shown by the followers of Stephen of Obazine on his death. For the acrimonious struggles that could accompany the burial of a holy man, see the *Vita* of Wulfric of Haselbury (*Wulfric of Haselbury by John, Abbot of Ford*, ed. M. Bell, Somerset Record Society, 47 (1933), 126–9).

as the first post-mortem miracle of the saint, since 'it was thought almost certain by some, and by nearly all those belonging to the province (*ab omnibus comprovincialibus*) that immediately so vigorous a head was lost then a secession of his limbs from the [mother] house of Sempringham would follow'.[236] This is taken by Foreville to be a reminiscence of the lay brothers' revolt, but it seems to indicate a deeper fear of dissension within the order following the death of a charismatic leader—a fear Gilbert had clearly shared—and to suggest that the acceptance of the prior of Malton as *magister* was by no means certain.[237] However, Roger's position was at last unambiguous, and a new period in the order's history opened: the founder could now be raised to the company of the saints.

Miracles and canonization

According to the *Vita*, in his old age Gilbert had already performed a number of miracles of various types.[238] After his death these miracles, recorded in the canonization dossier, increased considerably. The first recorded occurred a few months later, when on 24 June 1189 a nun of Haverholme was cured of a fishbone stuck in her throat by application of some of the water in which Gilbert's body had been washed, and at about the same time a boy of Haverholme who later became a canon there was cured of a paralysis of his right leg.[239] However, though locally Gilbert was clearly regarded as a saint, there was no formal move for his canonization until 1200. According to the official Gilbertine version, this was because the brethren of Sempringham did not wish to make these miracles public knowledge since it was vainglorious, and it was only in 1200 that some of them decided that it was dishonourable to God and the Church to suppress them in this way. Such statements suggest that the Gilbertines felt some explanation of the delay was necessary. In part this may be attributable to the growing centralization of canonization procedure at the Roman Curia: indeed, Gilbert's canonization has attracted considerable attention as the first to be carried through according to the new rules established by Innocent III. In essence there was a shift from local, episcopal proclamation of canonization to papal control of the process, backed by full legal inquiries with written testimonies into the candidate's sanctity, which was itself a result of the extension of the *plenitudo*

---

[236] *Book of St Gilbert*, 128–32.   [237] Ibid. 130 and n. 4.

[238] The canonization process has been fully examined by Foreville in *Un Procès de canonisation à l'aube du XIIIᵉ siècle (1201–1202), Le Livre de saint Gilbert de Sempringham* (Paris, 1943), and more recently in *Book of St Gilbert*, pp. lxii–lxiii, xc–cviii.

[239] *Book of St Gilbert*, 168, 284, 264–6.

potestatis during this period.[240] This does not fully explain, however, why the Gilbertines themselves did not press for canonization until 1200. It is possible that Hugh, bishop of Lincoln, was not favourable to the cause. Hugh died in November 1200, only a few months after Gilbert's canonization was initiated. Certainly the *Vita* is silent concerning any friendship between Gilbert and his diocesan bishop, a silence which should perhaps be compared with Gilbert's well-attested good relations with two of Hugh's predecessors, Alexander and Robert de Chesney. Only once are Gilbert and Hugh recorded as coming into contact, when Gilbert finally agreed to moderate his stance on the conditions of the lay brothers. It may also be that Hugh perceived Gilbert as too close to the Angevin establishment to merit his support. This suggests a more likely explanation for the delay until 1200. As we have seen, Gilbert was a close friend of Henry II and his family, from whom he gained much support, particularly at the time of the lay brothers' revolt. Henry died very shortly after Gilbert. The absence of his successor, Richard, from England for long periods was hardly propitious for Gilbert's canonization if royal backing was needed. It may not be coincidental that moves for canonization began very shortly after the accession of John. John certainly wrote to the pope in support of the canonization, as did his chief justiciar, Geoffrey fitzPeter, earl of Essex, who was himself the founder of a Gilbertine house, Shouldham.[241] John was also present at the first canonization inquiry at Sempringham early in 1201. Just as the letters sent to Alexander III in support of Gilbert against the *conversi* read as an orchestrated campaign of the senior ecclesiastical hierarchy and the king, so too the letters sent to Innocent III in favour of the canonization suggest a carefully planned operation by the establishment. Gilbert was a less 'dangerous' saint than Becket for the Angevins: his career did not set off resonances which could disrupt the government. Gilbert (though a supporter of Becket) was essentially a king's man.[242]

The account of the canonization and the letters concerning it which are transcribed in the *Book of St Gilbert* enable the enterprise to be reconstructed in considerable detail. Official proceedings began with a letter of Philip, the papal notary, to all the prelates of England, in which he urged

---

[240] See ibid., esp. pp. xc–xcvi; R. Foreville, 'Canterbury et la canonisation des saints', in D. Greenway, C. Holdsworth, and J. Sayers (eds.), *Tradition and Change: Essays in Honour of Marjorie Chibnall* (Cambridge, 1985), 63–76, esp. 71–5; E. W. Kemp, *Canonization and Authority in the Western Church* (Oxford, 1948). [241] *Book of St Gilbert*, 214, 232–4.

[242] It may be significant that Hubert Walter is said to have particularly supported Gilbert because he was a native of the country. For this reason he could be seen as a figure to inspire political unity (ibid. 168).

them to support the canonization, investigate the case promptly, and report to Rome the results of their enquiry. The letter makes clear that unofficial proceedings were already in hand: members of the order had asked some of the prelates to investigate the miracles themselves.[243] The account of the canonization stresses that the chief supporter of the Gilbertines was the archbishop of Canterbury. Archbishop Hubert Walter oversaw the canonization of two English saints: Gilbert and Wulfstan of Worcester. It has been suggested that one of the reasons the archbishop sponsored Gilbert was because he was native-born. This can be taken further. Both Gilbert and Wulfstan spanned the Anglo-Norman divide, both were 'acceptable' priests who while protecting ecclesiastical liberties had rocked but never overturned the boat.[244] Philip was establishing the papal claim to control canonization, but at the same time was prepared to support the Gilbertine initiative. The archbishop responded by asking three heads of houses in the Lincoln diocese to hold an inquiry into the alleged miracles at Sempringham and to report back to himself and the pope. This inquiry was duly held by the delegates on 9 January 1201 in the presence of four more heads, including the priors of the Gilbertine houses of Chicksands and Catley. More importantly for the success of the venture, it occurred in the presence of many other leading clergy and on the very day that king John and his court visited the priory. Such timing cannot be coincidental: John was lending royal support to the venture in the clearest possible way.[245] The delegates reported on the miracles they had examined and swore to their authenticity, while *magister* Roger himself testified to two miracles he had experienced. In their covering letter to the archbishop they added their support for Gilbert's canonization both on account of the miracles and also because of Gilbert's success as a monastic founder. All seven abbots and priors wrote in similar vein to Innocent III. The delegates' letter formed part of the first dossier for the canonization that was assembled by the archbishop, who was clearly continuing to co-ordinate the campaign in England. This role is demonstrated in a letter he addressed to bishops William of London, Eustace of Ely, and Geoffrey of Coventry, and abbots John of St Albans, Walter of

[243] This letter was written after Philip's return from England, where he had been during the spring and early summer of 1200 in order to arrange collection of the papal fortieth for the Crusade. For Philip's visit, see C. R. Cheney, 'Master Philip the Notary and the Fortieth of 1199', *EHR*, 63 (1948), 342–50. See also *Book of St Gilbert*, p. xcvii n. 1.

[244] Ibid. 168. For Wulfstan's canonization, see *The Vita Wulfstani of William of Malmesbury*, ed. R. R. Darlington, Camden Society, 3rd ser. 40 (1928), pp. xlvi–xlvii, 148–50, 184; and E. Mason, *St Wulfstan of Worcester, c.1008–1095* (Oxford, 1990), 278–91; Foreville, 'Canterbury et la canonisation des saints', 74. [245] *Book of St Gilbert*, 168–70.

Waltham, and Martin of Chertsey, urging them to write in their own words supporting the cause. He included a copy of his own letter in order that they might see what he had written.[246] The dossier also contained a letter written by *magister* Roger proclaiming his predecessor's miracles and his fame in the foundation both of monasteries and of houses for the poor and infirm.[247] In return for papal assent to the canonization the Gilbertines pledged to place Innocent's name in their martyrology and include him as a *confrater* of the order. Not surprisingly, in the light of the archiepiscopal suggestion, the letters of the bishops and priors are all couched in similar language. To these were added letters from bishops John of Norwich, Gilbert of Rochester, and Robert of Bangor as well as from a large group of abbots and priors from a wide range of orders. Though there are no letters from the bishops of the archdiocese of York, a number of Yorkshire heads of houses wrote, including the abbot of Kirkstall and prior of Bridlington. Indeed, virtually all the monastic letters were from houses in either the diocese of Lincoln or York. Since the bishopric of Lincoln was vacant, a letter was also forwarded from the dean and chapter.[248]

When these letters were assembled they were sent off to Rome, along with letters from king John and members of the lay aristocracy, of which that of Geoffrey fitzPeter has survived. By this time a short life of the saint had been compiled, which was later to be the basis of the *Vita*, and this too was sent as supporting evidence to the Curia.[249] Two canons, Gamel and W., acted as messengers, and in the face of considerable hardships reached Rome in the summer of 1201. Their testimonials make it clear that these two were responsible and perhaps high-ranking members of the order.[250] They were not, however, immediately successful, and were sent back to England with the instructions that four judges-delegate including the archbishop of Canterbury should reassemble at Sempringham and after a three-day fast of the community reopen the inquiry, this time

---

[246] Ibid. 214–16. It is not clear whether Hubert expected all the bishops in his province to write. The letter was only addressed to three of them, but, as noted below, a number of other episcopal letters were included in the collection.   [247] Ibid. 206–10.

[248] These are printed ibid. 216–32.

[249] This is mentioned in the prologue to the surviving *Vita* (ibid. 8).

[250] W. cannot be identified, though Foreville stated that he 'must be the canon William' who witnessed two miracles (ibid., p. lxxii n. and 266, 290). Gamel is a fairly unusual name. He is likely to be that Gamel who, with Albinus (probably Gilbert's chaplain), witnessed a cure of a blind man, and may be the same Gamel who was prior of Alvingham in 1202 and of Bullington in 1209 (ibid. 316; M. D. Knowles, C. N. L. Brooke, and V. C. M. London (eds.), *Heads of Religious Houses: England and Wales, 940–1216* (Cambridge, 1972), 200–1).

relying on sworn witnesses to the miracles as well as statements of evidence. This material was to be taken directly to the Curia, where the messengers would confirm this evidence on oath. On 26 September the inquiry opened under the archbishop, the bishops of Ely, Bath, and Bangor, and the abbots of Peterborough and Bourne, and for four days evidence was heard and written down. The cause was aided by a miracle which occurred at the tomb during the time of the inquiry; its recipient was one of those sent to Rome to testify. The new team of messengers comprised five Gilbertine canons (including Gamel, and probably W.) and six laymen, who had either received or witnessed miracles. The account of the canonization hints at difficulties during their preparation. The nuns, 'who are often more fervent in devotion', and especially a nun of Haverholme who had a vision in which the Christ-child himself accompanied the mission, lent their prayers. The venture was unquestionably risky and uncertain: no wonder visions were required to strengthen the canons' resolve. One of them, Ralph de Insula, whom Foreville has convincingly suggested to be the author of the *Vita*, dreamed he saw Gilbert himself assuring them of their success, while at the same time the saint initially reproved Gamel for being the cause of the delay in returning to Rome the second time.[251] On 2 January 1202 they reached Anagni, where the pope was staying, and after ten days achieved their aim, aided by a vision experienced by Innocent which was interpreted to him by his confessor and adviser, the Cistercian abbot Reiner of Ponza.[252]

The bull of canonization was issued on 30 January 1202 and sent to the two English archbishops and to the Gilbertine order. Hubert Walter was further instructed to make arrangements for the translation of the new saint's body, and the bull included collects for Gilbert's commemoration.[253] The good news was also formally conveyed to the order by the archbishop, who at the same time notified his diocesans of the decision and exhorted them to keep Gilbert's feast. In turn they then passed on this instruction to their archdeacons.[254] A similar procedure was followed when the translation was organized. On 13 September *magister* Roger and

[251] *Book of St Gilbert*, 182.

[252] For Reiner, see B. Bolton, 'For the See of Simon Peter: The Cistercians at Innocent III's Nearest Frontier', in J. Loades (ed.), *Monastic Studies: The Continuity of Tradition* (Bangor, 1990), 150. Another vision of Gilbert was experienced by one of Innocent's kinsmen (*Book of St Gilbert*, 184).

[253] Ibid. 252. According to the account of the canonization, Innocent is supposed to have composed a special prayer immediately on waking from his vision of the saint, and to have later written the secret and the post-communion (ibid. 174).   [254] Ibid. 252–8.

the senior members of the order met Hubert Walter and other bishops and leading members of the lay aristocracy at Sempringham to ask that the translation be arranged for 13 October. The archbishop then issued letters to his diocesans urging their attendance at the ceremony. The account is not specific as to who did attend, apart from the archbishop himself, the bishops of Norwich, Hereford, and Llandaff, and numerous other churchmen. It is likely that had king John been there his presence would have been noted—as it is, we are merely told that princes and leading men of England attended and helped to carry the new reliquary. The occasion was marked by the usual manifestations of bright lights, sweet odours, and incorrupt clothing. Additionally, the archbishop himself was privileged with a cure from an illness which threatened to prevent him continuing with the lengthy ceremonies. Following his recovery, Walter preached a sermon in the new saint's honour, and presented a silk cloth in which the relics were to be wrapped. The proceedings concluded with the placing of a short document describing Gilbert's life, death, and canonization, together with a lead strip carrying a brief epitaph, in the chest, which was then sealed and returned to its old site in the middle of the church, placed in the longitudinal wall dividing the men's from the women's choir, probably near the east end.[255] The archbishop then issued an indulgence of forty days and an additional one of 160 days from bishops assisting at the translation, to all those visiting the shrine, or making grants to the priory.

The canonization of Gilbert had taken something over two years from the first moves by his community and the archbishop of Canterbury to its triumphant conclusion on 13 October 1202. The shrine was to survive until the Dissolution, though no further miracles at it are recorded. Its shape is unknown, though it probably resembled those of comparatively unfrequented saints, such as that of Osmund at Salisbury or Bertolin at Eyam, where openings in the side enabled the sick to approach as close as practically possible to the holy one's bones. Some would stretch themselves upon the tomb, others would lie down beside it, sometimes wearing items of the saint's clothing, such as his scapular or shoe. Visitors

---

[255] Ibid. 190–2. The shrine's position is discussed in R. Graham and H. Braun, 'Excavations on the Site of Sempringham Priory', *Journal of the British Archaeological Association*, NS 5 (1940), 91–2. See also *Book of St Gilbert*, pp. xxvi and n. 1, lxxxiii and n. 2. Two of those cured are said to have been in the 'inner chancel' of the church, in contrast to the outer chancel, where some of those who accompanied the sick watched and waited (ibid. 294, 298).

might sleep before the tomb, spending several days and nights in expectation of a cure.[256] We know nothing of later pilgrims to the shrine, or anything of offerings made there, but it is likely that it was fairly soon overshadowed by other cult centres, such as those of Hugh of Lincoln or 'Little' St Hugh, or by Walsingham, not so far away in north Norfolk.[257] Gilbert's cult remained a minor one and his life seems to have attracted little attention outside his own communities.

A constructed saint?

Without the *Vita* we would know virtually nothing of the life of Gilbert of Sempringham. Two or three mentions in late twelfth-century chronicles, a scattering of references in contemporary pipe rolls and charters: that is all. Any consideration of Gilbert, therefore, is founded within a hagiographic context and, like all hagiographies, the *Vita* looks both back, to earlier models of sanctity, and forwards, to the needs of its audience— in this case the Gilbertine community that desired the formal canonization of its founder. Hagiography is grounded in selective memory; a saint is made through the recollections of others, and the saint's specific *virtus* must be capable of assimilation into the collective mentality and values of those seeking his or her honour.[258] Elements of the saint's life which could not thus be incorporated had either to be omitted or reconfigured to these norms. Much hagiography was concerned primarily with promoting and publicizing a cult by drawing attention both to the saint's virtues and, above all, to the miracles achieved through the saint's relics. It had also another, linked function: a didactic intention to edify its readers or hearers. It is this aim that underlies Gilbert's *Vita*.

We have already seen that Gilbert's cult was not widely disseminated,

---

[256] Permission to remain at the shrine was normally granted by the prior (*Book of St Gilbert*, 264–79, 288–303, 320–3).

[257] The later fate of the relics is uncertain. Those exhibited in a modern reliquary in the ambulatory of St Sernin, Toulouse, adjacent to relics of St Edmund, seem to be misidentified, according to David Farmer (pers. comm.) In 1290 the body of Gilbert was said to lie in the priory church at Sempringham (*Cal. Papal Registers*, i. 516). A post-Dissolution transcript of the relics of Waltham abbey (CUL, Addit. MS 3041, fo. 48), lists *os de sancti Gilberto de Semplingham* among relics given by Nicholas, prior of St Gregory's, Canterbury (presumably Nicholas de Shotindon, elected 1241). I am indebted to Nicholas Rogers for this information.

[258] Discussions of hagiography are legion. Fundamental are the studies of H. Delahaye, and R. Aigrain, *L'Hagiographie: ses sources, ses methodes, son histoire* (Paris, 1953). I have found the sociological overview of P. Delooz, 'Towards a Sociological Study of Canonised Sainthood in the Catholic Church', in S. Wilson (ed.), *Saints and their Cults* (Cambridge, 1983), 189–216, challenging, though not wholly convincing.

nor were his relics highly prized. Though the Gilbertines did not go so far as the Cistercian abbot who is said to have ordered Bernard of Clairvaux not to perform any posthumous miracles since the excitement they caused disturbed the cloister's tranquillity, many of Gilbert's miracles were for the benefit of members of his communities, and those laity whose cures were recorded were mostly very local to the shrine.[259] Likewise the *Vita* did not circulate outside the order, and the only contact the laity would normally have had with Gilbert's life would be through the *lectiones*, themselves of course in Latin, that were derived, sometimes verbatim, from the *Vita* and which would be read on the saint's feast-days.[260] In other words, the cult of Gilbert was primarily intended for the enclosed, private world of the cloister; the characteristic virtues stressed in the *Vita* are for the edification of Gilbert's spiritual *familia*.

Delooz drew a distinction between the 'saint réel' and the 'saint construit'. It has been argued that this opposition is too rigid, particularly in the case of saints whose lives were written long after their death so that they were 'in many ways no more than bundles of *topoi*' and what was described in the lives was the only 'reality' their audience knew.[261] The same, it might be argued, could be applied to Gilbert, of whom virtually everything we know is a construction of the *Vita*. At the same time, however, Gilbert's *Vita* was composed within a few years of his death. Though inevitably retrospective, Gilbert's memory was fresh, and the *Vita* is informed by the testimony of eyewitnesses and disciples; there was no necessity to resort in their absence to presenting him in terms of long-established hagiographic topoi and traditions, though these could of course be borrowed if desired. Gilbert should be seen in the context of those described by J.-C. Schmitt as 'saints contemporains ayant une individualité bien reconnue'.[262] These 'contemporary' saints were a new phenomenon of the twelfth century. They might be venerated as holy even before their death, though they could only be formally canonized after death, when their merits and miracles were evident. The new emphasis on the saint's individuality and character is in part at least another result of the 'discovery of the individual'. Its function is partisan: its context Gilbert's canonization process.

---

[259] Discussed in B. Ward, *Miracles and the Medieval Mind* (London, 1982), 180.

[260] Oxford, Bodl. Libr., MS Digby 36, fos. 110ᵛ–116ᵛ. Printed in *The Gilbertine Rite*, ed. R. W. Woolley, 2 vols., Henry Bradshaw Society, 59, 60 (1921, 1922), i. 113–26.

[261] T. Head, *Hagiography and the Cult of Saints: The Diocese of Orleans, 800–1200* (Cambridge, 1990), 117–18.

[262] J.-C. Schmitt, 'La Fabrique des saints', *Annales: Economies, Sociétés, Civilisations*, 39 (1984), 293.

In the light of these constraints, can those of us outside the cloister and separated by some eight hundred years from his life recover anything of Gilbert's personality, or are we left only with a saint constructed from conventional description and hagiographic topoi? All saints' lives were standardized to a greater or lesser extent; they followed models both of literary convention and construction and of certain norms of virtue which varied over time and which were related to specific types of saint: the warrior, the martyr, the hermit, and so on. They consciously borrowed from the Bible and earlier saints' lives, to which were added more specific individual details.[263] It is in these details, if anywhere, that we will find the 'real' Gilbert.

When John Odonis, a kinsman of pope Innocent III, had a vision of Gilbert during the canonization process he described the saint's appearance to the canons. He was, he said, an old man with a broad face, bald but for a few white hairs, and his head was bowed down to his chest.[264] This is perhaps a commonplace description of old age, and it is also a hagiographic convention, but it is none the less likely to be an accurate, if not very informative, portrait of Gilbert the centenarian, blind, sick, and infirm.[265] But for the biographer more noteworthy was the fact that Gilbert's mental abilities and spiritual awareness remained unimpaired until the day he died.

The author of the *Vita*, for all he is concerned to demonstrate Gilbert's austerity as a man of God, emphasizes the saint's cheerfulness and eloquence. He is a pleasant companion, well spoken and generous, though abstemious himself. When a child is born to a couple at whose house Gilbert has stayed and is named after the saint, Gilbert, 'a happy and generous man', sends the boy a cow as a present. His coolness in the face of royal persecution during the Becket crisis is demonstrated by his buying some spinning-tops from a boy and playing with them to amuse his disconsolate companions. Doubtless we are expected to infer Gilbert's steadfastness in adversity through this episode, but we also glimpse the saint's pleasure in the toys themselves.[266] He worked hard at practical things, copying manuscripts, helping to make household utensils, and working on buildings. In the description of his death there is real emotion at the passing of 'a father and pastor, a brother and a friend', the sole

---

[263] Biblical citations in the *Vita* are discussed by Foreville, *Book of St Gilbert*, pp. lxxvi–lxxvii.

[264] Ibid. 184. The wife of Ralph de Hauville also had a vision of Gilbert as a bald man 'though he had the face of a boy' (ibid. 127).   [265] Ibid. 84–6, 118.

[266] Ibid. 60, 62, 112, 74.

father and protector of his spiritual children, a charismatic leader to the last. All this, of course, is connected with the communities' fear of the future.[267]

But the affable saint is comparatively rarely seen. Much more often it is the harsh disciplinarian, the cantankerous holy man, the authoritarian leader. These characteristics are perhaps inevitably stressed given his career, and we encounter them continually, from his forbidding the school-boys under his care from jesting and wandering about at will, to his rejection of the peasant's tithes, to his striking of a recalcitrant canon and his cursing of obdurate nuns.[268] Gilbert is presented throughout as a demanding taskmaster who requires unquestioning submission to his authority, while at the same time he himself finds it hard to relinquish authority and obey another. It seems no coincidence that the first form his community takes is that of the master in charge of children.

Gilbert's autocracy must also be seen in the context of contemporary eremitical behaviour. In communities that were, almost by definition, less structured than those of traditional monasticism, disorder, even anarchy, were ever-present threats. Discipline and obedience were cardinal virtues in the eremitical life, and if authority was not self-imposed and regulated there was a danger that it might be imposed from without.[269] And herein lay the tension and the ambivalence that is a constant, if unstated, theme of Gilbert's *Vita*. Nowhere is this more clearly seen than in Gilbert's unwillingness to take the habit in old age, which surely reflects a reluctance to submit himself to authority, even though he had created it, while at the same time he kept the responsibility for overseeing the order and adjudicating on the more serious matters, even while Roger was nominally *magister*.[270]

The saint whom the *Vita* constructs is an uncomfortable one. He is autocratic, almost despotic, at times. He does not readily inspire love but respect. The *Vita* hints at conflict within his own family; there were clearly critics of Gilbert after his death, though these may have rather more to do with misgivings about his double houses, and the author's prologue makes it clear that some refused to acknowledge Gilbert's sanctity: 'they detract from his deeds, contradict those who praise him, and

---

[267] 'He was not such a father as others under monastic authority possess and lose' (ibid. 122–3).

[268] Ibid. 14, 18–20, 102–4. A holy man's curses were to be feared, as the *Vita* of Wulfric of Haselbury makes clear (Mayr-Harting, 'Functions of a Twelfth-Century Recluse', 339).

[269] Leyser, *Hermits and the New Monasticism*, 43–5, has some stimulating comments.

[270] *Book of St Gilbert*, 58, 66, 86–8.

oppose his veneration.'[271] Gilbert was a controversial figure, and his order from the first was regarded with some suspicion. This is the context for the tension apparent in the hagiographer's account of Gilbert's last days. He stresses Gilbert's desire for peace and concord. Gilbert makes a final agreement with the lay brothers and modifies their Rule, but then, immediately backtracking, insists that he will have nothing to do with any changes that are contrary to the brothers' first profession. Similarly, he blesses all those who love his order, but denies forgiveness to all those who plot discord.[272] The *Vita* ends with praise of Gilbert as a man of peace—but it is peace on his own terms.[273]

---

[271] Ibid. 6–8, 56, 60.   [272] Ibid. 116–18.   [273] Ibid. 130–2.

2

The Making of the Rule

The Twelfth-Century Context

One of the most striking features of the twelfth-century Church was the growing desire and demand of women for a place in the new spiritual commonwealth.[1] Typically they were described by an anonymous contemporary writer as those 'who sweetly take up Christ's yoke with holy men or under their guidance'.[2] Until *c*.1100 there were few nunneries, and many of these were considered by contemporary reformers to be suspect and lax. The lack of cenobitic opportunities for women was especially apparent in England, where in 1066 there were only ten nunneries. All were royal or aristocratic foundations which offered no opportunity for the spiritual desires of the majority of women. In the next century the number increased tenfold.

The spiritual aspirations of women during this period, however, were expressed in a wide range of possible options. Some found a place as anchoresses and recluses, and it was for these individuals, rather than communities, that letters of spiritual advice tended to be written (such as Aelred's *De Institutione Inclusarum* or Goscelin's *Liber Confortatorius*).[3] Likewise, it was with an anchoress that a religious was most likely to develop a close relationship, as was the case between Geoffrey, abbot of St Albans, and Christina of Markyate.[4] But the life of the anchoress could of its nature only be open to a comparatively small number of religious

[1] From amongst a copious and ever-increasing literature, the most useful in the context of this study are Thompson, *Women Religious*, and Elkins, *Holy Women*, while J. E. Burton, *The Yorkshire Nunneries in the Twelfth and Thirteenth Centuries*, Borthwick Papers, 56 (York, 1979), provides a brief but excellent regional study.

[2] *Libellus de Diversis Ordinibus et Professionibus qui sunt in Aecclesia*, ed. G. Constable and B. Smith (Oxford, 1972), 4–5.

[3] For a discussion of these works, see Elkins, *Holy Women*, 21–7, 152–6, and references there cited.

[4] *The Life of Christina of Markyate*, ed. and trans. C. H. Talbot (Oxford, 1959), esp. 138–40, 150.

women; there was a large and increasing number of women who looked for some communal role within the Church.

The Lives of virtually all the monastic reformers of the period draw attention to their female followers. Though the appeal of these preachers to women is most forcefully exemplified in the experience of men such as Gilbert of Sempringham or Robert of Arbrissel, it is also seen at a very local level, for example, in the activities of Salomon, a little-known follower of Robert of Arbrissel, who founded several communities for women and a double house at Nyoiseau.[5] The reasons for this development have been the subject of considerable and growing discussion, but undoubtedly one of the contributory factors was the scarcity of female religious foundations in western Europe. Another lay in the new orders' refusal to accept oblates; instead, they appealed to mature entrants who might frequently be married with families. In many cases this meant that their wives and daughters needed security which could most easily be found in religious houses. The women either accompanied the new recruit *en famille*, or entered another house. Some communities were indeed established primarily to receive such entrants, as appears to have been the case at Marcigny, the first Cluniac nunnery, or Jully, which was closely associated with the early Cistercians.[6] It can also be suggested that there was a demographic imbalance, with women outnumbering men; many nunneries fulfilled a crucial social role, often providing the only refuge for widows, or a convenient home for surplus daughters who could not be given dowries, or for women who had little chance of inheriting their parents' lands. Thus social and religious pressures combined to increase the demand for places for women in communities, and all contemporary reformers had in some way to react, even if only negatively.

The spectrum of their response was a wide one, ranging from those who feared and fled from women, like Stephen of Muret or Guigo of La Chartreuse, who declared that rather than touch a woman he would prefer to walk on burning coals, through those whose attitude was ambivalent and distrustful, such as the early Cistercians, to men like Robert of Arbrissel, who practised syneisactism and who wished to place all members of his foundation at Fontevrault under the authority of the prioress. The rule of Grandmont, drawn up during the priorate of Stephen de Liciac (1139–63) but deriving much of its content from the wishes

---

[5] J. B. Bienvenu, 'Aux origines d'un ordre religieux: Robert d'Arbrissel et la fondation de Fontevraud (1101)', *Cahiers d'Histoire*, 20 (1975), 235 n.

[6] See Thompson, *Women Religious*, 84–8.

of the order's founder, Stephen of Muret, was particularly outspoken in its opposition to women. They were to be totally excluded, since by a woman man was expelled from the earthly paradise, while 'mildest David, wisest Solomon, and strongest Samson' were unable to resist their blandishments.[7] Certainly the appeal of the new foundations to women recruits was deeply disturbing to all shades of opinion within the Western Church. Even those who did not (like St Bernard) wholly fear the temptations of women could see difficulties. Clearly the female followers of Robert of Arbrissel or Vitalis of Savigny could not imitate their leaders as itinerant evangelists. They required a community, a Rule, and, above all, enclosure.

Nunneries did not only need considerable supervision, they also demanded substantial endowments, and these were seldom forthcoming. The greatest problem nunneries had to face throughout the medieval centuries was simply one of survival. Benefactions tended to be smaller than those made to houses for men; partly this was a consequence of chronology—the later a foundation, the less substantial tended to be its endowments. A rapid influx of recruits, with no accompanying benefactions, could seriously jeopardize a nunnery's existence. Even more importantly, at a time when grants were explicitly regarded as a *quid pro quo* for prayers for the donor's salvation, the intercessions of monks (who were during this period increasingly priests as well) were generally regarded as more efficacious than those of women religious.[8] As a consequence, more, and larger, endowments were directed to male than to female communities.

The denial of clerical status to women denied ultimate autonomy to all communities of religious women, however much they might seem to be independent institutions under the authority of a freely elected abbess. The requirement for a priest or group of priests to administer the sacraments meant that all founders of religious houses for women had to make some arrangements for their spiritual supervision, and hence had also to face the problems of the relationship between the female and male elements of the community and of their segregation. One possible solution

---

[7] *Scriptores Ordinis Grandimontensis*, ed. J. Becquet, Corpus Christianorum, Continuatio Mediaevalis, 8 (Turnhout, 1968) 86–7. Stephen's hostility to women is also recorded in an apocryphal story which tells how he was a disciple of Gaucher of Aureil, whose followers included many women, and asked Gaucher if he could move further away from the community at Aureil in order to avoid them (Leyser, *Hermits and the New Monasticism*, 50).

[8] C. H. Lawrence, *Medieval Monasticism* (London, 1984), 178.

to these problems was the establishment of a 'double monastery'. This
phenomenon demands both definition and explanation.[9] In its broadest
sense the term can be, and often is, applied to all communities where
women and men lived alongside each other in a religious community,
either within the same precinct though in different buildings, as typically
in the Gilbertine double houses, or at a short distance from each other,
as was found, for example, in the early days of Obazine. It is therefore
possible to style any nunnery where the sacraments were administered by
resident males a double house, and it is not surprising to find a significant
proportion of all new foundations for women in the twelfth century to be
of this sort. Other solutions, such as using the services of non-resident
but local monks, were possible, but these were often neither as convenient nor as easy to control.[10]

According to Bateson, the chief dynamic for the earlier double houses
of the Anglo-Saxon age came as a reaction to religious enthusiasm which,
if unregulated, would have threatened the chastity and good order of the
nascent communities. The introduction of the double monastery marked
a growing institutionalization and regulation of reform and is in that
sense an invention of those who would restrict the religious radicals. So
she argued that later (that is, in the twelfth century, a period with which
her own study was not concerned) 'the double monastery reappears with
the religious revivals which gave birth to new orders: it is notably absent
from the revivals which were directed rather to systemisation than to new
spiritual conceptions'.[11] Other commentators, such as Schmitz and de
Fontette, have stressed that a double monastery consists of two communities that are subject to one authority and which form a juridical unity.[12]
In her recent study of religious foundations for women in twelfth-century
England, Elkins has forsworn the use of the terms 'double' and 'quasi-
double' on the grounds that this is to distinguish unnaturally between

---

[9] The fullest general studies are M. Bateson, 'Origin and Early History of Double
Monasteries', *TRHS*, ns 13 (1899), 137–98, which is an overview of their development in
western Europe till *c*.1050; U. Berlière, 'Les Monastères doubles aux XIIe et XIIIe siècles',
Mémoires de l'Académie Royale des Sciences etc. de Belgique, 2nd ser. 18 (Brussels, 1923), 1–
32; A. H. Thompson, 'Double Monasteries and the Male Element in Nunneries', in *The
Ministry of Women: A Report by a Committee Appointed by His Grace the Lord Archbishop of
Canterbury* (London, 1919), app. viii, 145–64. There is also much of value in P. Schmitz's
study of Benedictine double houses in *Histoire de l'Ordre de Saint-Benoit*, 7 vols. (Gembloux,
1942–56), vii. 45–53, 229–31.   [10] Elkins, *Holy Women*, p. xvii.
[11] Bateson, 'Origin and Early History', 197–8. *Pace* her observation, double houses were
found in the 'systematic' Benedictine reform as well as elsewhere.
[12] Schmitz, *Histoire de l'Ordre de Saint-Benoit*, vii. 45–6; M. de Fontette, *Les Religieuses
à l'âge classique du droit canon* (Paris, 1967), 17.

them and other arrangements 'in which celibate men and women affiliated with each other'. As she indicates, the term is an anachronistic one and was not used by contemporary commentators; she is right also to emphasize that the double house was an element in a wide continuum of institutional arrangements.[13] However, it will be argued here that the term is a useful one and should be retained, so long as it is remembered that it can be applied to a number of organizations which often differ radically in their origins and intentions from each other. This is a point well made by Schmitz, who distinguished between those communities ruled by an abbot and those by an abbess, contending that in the first type (originally found in fourth-century Egypt) groups of nuns attached themselves to pre-existing monastic communities for spiritual benefits and temporal protection, while in the second instance (occurring from the sixth century in the West) the reverse was the case and men joined a community of women. This institution was particularly found in, though it was not exclusive to, the Celtic Churches. Here the monks were generally subject to the abbess. Thus the role of the women in these communities was necessarily determined by the nature of their organization: in some, such as Fontevrault, the women were dominant and the men served them in a self-conscious spirit of humility, while in others the women's chief function seems to have been, as at Obazine and Prémontré, to wash and make clothes and to cook. There are also indications that at some houses the women were nurses in hospitals attached to the monastery.[14] Every double foundation must be considered as an individual entity with its own distinctive regulations which were often very different from other such houses. From house to house the proportion of women to men might vary substantially, and the topography of the convent might also show markedly differing characteristics. Thus, for example, though we normally find the church of a double house divided into two, one part for the canons or monks and the other for the nuns, at some houses like Sempringham the building was divided longitudinally, at others like Obazine the monks worshipped in the choir, the nuns in the nave.

Suspicion of women in the religious life focused on two aspects: the fact that many communities of women were initially reluctant to accept a Rule, and (more importantly) the problems created by the inevitably close proximity of women to men in religious communities and the necessity of

---

[13] Elkins, *Holy Women*, pp. xvii–xviii.
[14] As they also were in the Gilbertine priory of St Katherine's, Lincoln.

segregation. There is much evidence that double houses were regarded as at best a necessary evil. From at least the sixth century there were criticisms, found most clearly in archbishop Theodore's statement: 'It is not permissible for men to be with monastic women, nor women with men; nevertheless we shall not overthrow that which is the custom in this region.'[15] Similar distrust is expressed later in the *Regularis Concordia*, and certainly in England there was a gradual transformation of the double house in the late tenth and the eleventh centuries.[16] During the second quarter of the twelfth century, as communities of religious women increasingly sought official or unofficial ties with male houses, ecclesiastical legislation indicates growing unease. In 1139 the second Lateran Council condemned those women who styled themselves nuns without submitting to a Rule; nuns who, though living the common life, built dwellings for their individual use to receive guests; and nuns who joined themselves to the choir of monks or canons.[17] This was the most trenchant of many statements reflecting contemporary disquiet over the role of women in the Church, and in particular their function as religious. Above all it indicates a suspicion of women who were not securely organized in a Rule, preferably under the control of a male monastery. It reveals a tension within the Church, faced as it was with a large influx of women recruits, particularly into the new orders.

Gratian, that yardstick of establishment opinion, provides evidence of the hardening of opinion against double houses.[18] Though he generally cites much earlier legislation in support of the *causae*: 'it is not lawful for nuns to live with monks'; 'monks and nuns should not live together in the same place', and 'a community of women should be established far from a monastery of monks', these rulings are clearly directed against contemporary phenomena. One in particular (derived from Gregory VII) provides a general context for the action of the Premonstratensians, who were then engaged in the dismantling of their double houses: 'if there are many such [sc. double houses] they should be divided into communities for monks and for nuns, and the property which they have in common should be divided amongst them according to due law.' Gratian also laid

---

[15] Cited in B. Yorke, '"Sisters Under the Skin"? Anglo-Saxon Nuns and Nunneries in Southern England', *Reading Medieval Studies* 15 (1989), 107.

[16] *Regularis Concordia*, ed. and trans. T. Symons (London, 1953), 2, 4–5. See below, 'Continuity and native tradition'.

[17] H. Hefele, *Histoire des Conciles*, ed. and trans. H. Leclercq, 8 vols. in 16 (Paris, 1902–21), v. i. 732–3. Cited in Gratian, *Decretum*, C. 18, q. 2, c. 25.

[18] *Decretum*, C. 18, q. 2, cc. 21–4.

down rudimentary regulations for the controlling of relations between the sexes in nunneries, and between communities of men and women. Necessities of life brought by men to the community were to be received outside the gate by the abbess accompanied by an aged nun, and if a monk wished to see a kinswoman who was in a nunnery then they were only to meet briefly in the presence of the abbess. These arrangements were to be replicated and expanded in the double communities of Sempringham. But Gratian went further. He also cited legislation under a *causa* entitled 'communities of women to be ruled by the governance and administration of monks' which laid down that men should be chosen both to protect and to teach nuns, but even then under the strictest supervision of the abbess or prioress and in the presence of two or three nuns. The ground rules of legislation were therefore well established by the time Gilbert came to draw up his own institutes. In fundamental respects these were to run contrary to Gratian's canon law and were a legal anomaly: it is for this reason that we find the author of Gilbert's *Vita* laying such stress on the separation of the male and female elements. It also accounts for his quotations from these very sections of the *Decretum* when he justifies the new order by demonstrating how canon laws were observed.[19]

To sum up, the early twelfth century saw an unparalleled demand amongst women for access that was in part at least generated by the perceived inadequacies of existing nunneries. Many women converts followed charismatic preachers and teachers of the period, who then found themselves in a quandary as to how to respond to their disciples' needs. This difficult situation, which centred on the crucial question as to how women and men could coexist in a community, provoked a number of experiments and solutions. It is in this framework of experimentation and radical reform, which paradoxically both appealed to women and sought to distance itself from them, so creating tensions that were extremely difficult to resolve, that the evolution of the Gilbertine Rule must be set. Gilbert needs to be seen within the mainstream of twelfth-century monastic reform and to be placed in the context not merely of the Lincolnshire fens but of similar foundations in western Europe, particularly in France.

---

[19] *The Book of St Gilbert*, 46–8. I am indebted to Mrs Maire Wilkinson for her helpful suggestions in this matter. Abelard similarly cited with approval the Council of Seville's firm regulations concerning the supervision of double communities in his long letter of direction to Heloise.

The Search for a Structure

Choosing a Rule

When Gilbert travelled to Cîteaux in 1147 he went, in the words of the *Vita*, 'to divest his shoulders of what was at once a burden and an honour, and to find one or more to whose power he might entrust it as more suited and stronger'.[20] This desire was typical of many contemporary reformers who realized that some regularization of their communities was essential for their survival. The creation of a Rule was indeed an inevitable consequence of success. A rapid increase in the number of followers and recruits made it very difficult for one man (often styled the *magister*) to exercise personal discipline over them. But though the evolution of a Rule was part of the continuous process of a community's growth, it also marked a faultline in the group's development which was most characterized by a shift from the personal authority of the founder to institutional control. The chronology and motivation for change varied from group to group; frequently, however, it was generated from within, and was the consequence of fear that the community would collapse, or even be suppressed, on the death of the founder.[21] Though a Rule was necessary if the community was to be more than ephemeral, and if it was to be free-standing, it is clear that in many cases its adoption both irrevocably changed the character of the original foundation and did not always correspond to the founder's desires. In particular, many reformers had begun their careers as charismatic *wanderprediger*, and the establishment of houses at Prémontré, Fontevrault, or Savigny marked literally, as well as symbolically, the 'stabilization' of their founders' careers and their transition to a less active, more contemplative life.

The choice of a Rule and customs was often the most difficult task a founder had to face, for though there were in the West only two Rules available, those of Benedict and Augustine, the diversity of forms of the religious life had never been greater, and the array of possibilities was startling, and even disturbing, to contemporaries.[22] The formal adoption of a Rule could be a long-drawn-out process, often achieved only after

---

[20] *Book of St Gilbert*, 40.

[21] This fear is clearly apparent in the canons' urging of Gilbert to accept the habit (*Book of St Gilbert*, 66–8).

[22] The most comprehensive and measured contemporary assessment is contained in the *Libellus de Diversis Ordinibus et Professionibus qui sunt in Aecclesia*. For an elegant recent analysis of this *embarras de richesses*, see C. N. L. Brooke, 'Monk and Canon: Some Patterns in the Religious Life of the Twelfth Century', in W. J. Shiels (ed.), *Monks, Hermits and the Ascetic Tradition*, Studies in Church History, 22 (Oxford, 1985), 109–29.

much discussion with local religious leaders, each of whom might suggest different solutions and possibilities.[23] Many groups relied initially on the basic framework provided by the Augustinian and Benedictine Rules (often mediated through Cistercian observances), and only gradually was a need felt for fully worked out legislation, while the adding of ingredients of observance that imparted their specific flavours to the community might take several generations.

Sometimes the practices of another community were taken over more or less in entirety; completely new customs might be created, or a Rule constructed incorporating elements from many others. This latter course was that followed by Gilbert. The *Vita* stresses the eclecticism of the Gilbertine *institutio* and shows how, after adopting the Benedictine Rule for his nuns and the Augustinian for his canons, Gilbert, finding that these Rules were not sufficient for his communities, carefully assembled a collection of regulations 'from the statutes and customs of many churches and monasteries' which he then wrote down as *scripta* and sent to pope Eugenius III for his approbation.[24]

The transition from unorganized community to a structured order could often be painful. It is not the place here to examine the patterns of evolution in general, but it is important to be aware of the pressures that underlay the proliferation of monastic orders. Present interpretations of these developments can conveniently (though inevitably at the risk of some simplification) be divided into those which argue that most reformers did not wish to be 'regularized' but were more or less coerced into this action by outside forces, especially diocesan bishops, and those who assert that the reformers were content and even enthusiastic to either organize themselves or to be organized into a more cenobitic and 'traditional' way of life.[25] There is certainly considerable evidence to suggest that there was

---

[23] There was about a 10-year space between the foundation of Prémontré and its first statutes (Colvin, *The White Canons*, 3–6; C. Dereine, 'Les Origines de Prémontré', *Revue d'Histoire Ecclésiastique*, 42 (1947), 352–78), and Obazine and Oigny also took several years to work out their *modus vivendi*.

[24] *Book of St Gilbert*, 48–50. The composite nature of the Rule is further eulogized in the famous comparison of the Rule to the chariot of Aminadab: 'St Augustine steers the clerks and St Benedict the monks' (ibid. 52).

[25] For the first interpretation, see especially L. Milis, 'L'Évolution de l'érémitisme au canonicat régulier dans la première moitié du douzième siècle: transition ou trahison', in *Istituzioni monastiche e istituzioni canonicali in occidente (1123–1215)*, Miscellanea del Centro di Studi Medioevali, 9 (Milan, 1980), 223–8, and 'Ermites et chanoines réguliers au xiie siècle', *Cahiers de Civilisation Médiévale*, 22 (1979), 39–80; for the second, Leyser, *Hermits and the New Monasticism*, esp. 87–96. For a convenient summary of the relationship between hermitages and monasteries see Morris, *Papal Monarchy*, 68–74, 237–40.

opposition in many communities, or sections of them, to incorporation into a pre-existing order, or to the creation of a regular institution. At the same time the reformer was frequently exhorted by local prelates to adopt a Rule, and Church councils were increasingly suspicious of amorphous 'fringe' groups which could so easily cross the boundary of accepted behaviour into heresy. The difficulties encountered were so much the worse when, as often happened, the nascent communities included a significant female element.

It may be possible to reconcile these two interpretations of development, which see the evolution of eremitic to cenobitic life as either a process of evolutionary transition or a betrayal of ideals. Most of the reformers began their careers either as itinerant preachers or as hermits. Often they combined both vocations. The success of their apostolic efforts lay at the heart of their predicament; the attraction of followers inevitably distorted their own preferred way of life. As the *Vita* of Stephen of Obazine puts it, he had not gone into the wilderness in order to attract crowds.[26] The pressure of followers obliged their leaders to provide for their needs by building houses and churches for them, and by the establishment of some rules of conduct. At the same time their way of life attracted benefactions which could not always be refused. An endowed hermitage was scarcely different from a monastery in its economic base. Often a reformer also feared (as did his supporters) that on his death his community might be threatened; ultimately written regulations were stronger and more acceptable than the *dicta* of the *magister*.[27] Permanence required a structured Rule. The primacy of written over mere spoken words was gaining momentum. Any hermit who found himself the victim of his own success was obliged to resolve the tensions by in some way compromising strict eremitical ideals. The pressure for regularization was internally generated and inevitable; it is perhaps less relevant to argue whether or not it was welcomed.

Moreover, as Constable has reminded us, there was no rigid dichotomy between the eremitic and cenobitic way of life; individuals easily moved between these states, and traditional cenobitic communities might well harbour an individual or even a group of anchorites, while eremitic communities might become cenobitic and groups of monks might leave to form communities of hermits.[28] So we find Adam, first abbot of Meaux, leaving that abbey in order to become an anchorite at Watton, before

---

[26] *Vita Stephani*, 58–60.   [27] Milis, 'L'Évolution de l'érémitisme', 61–4.
[28] As happened at St Mary's, York in 1132. See G. Constable, 'Eremitical Forms of Monastic Life', in *Istituzioni Monastiche e istituzioni canonicali in occidente (1123–1215)*, Miscellanea del Centro di Studi Medioevali, 4 (Milan, 1980), 239–64.

returning to resume his old office following a fire at the Gilbertine priory in 1167.[29] There was, therefore, two-way traffic between the two religious life-styles, or, to change the metaphor, we can figure much of the twelfth-century reform movement as three overlapping circles, comprising those who followed a reformed Benedictine way, those who adapted the imprecision of the Augustinian Rule, and hermits living alone or in groups.

Though Gilbert was scarcely typical of the hermit-preacher transmuted into monastic founder, there were some similarities. He came from the same social milieu as many contemporary reformers, and followed a similar educational path; like Norbert of Xanten, for example, he first found advancement in an episcopal household.[30] Nor was it unknown for a monastic reformer to have earlier followed a career as parish priest. Stephen of Obazine, having given up his life as a seigneur, took over a parish, which perhaps like Gilbert's Sempringham belonged to his patrimony, but here his and Gilbert's paths diverge.[31] Stephen had a local reputation as preacher, but then abandoned his post to 'live in exile' as a solitary: Gilbert, however, continued to serve his parishes, at least until the foundation of the community at Sempringham. The *Vita* makes it clear that the pressure for its creation came from the women who requested Gilbert's spiritual patronage in their anchoretic life; there is little evidence that till that date Gilbert had wished to be other than an ascetic and conscientious parish priest, though if we take the *Vita*'s account of his quasi-monastic school at Sempringham literally we might see there the germ of Gilbert's later foundation. He became a religious leader *malgré lui*. This could be said of most of his contemporaries: the difference is that most of them began as hermits; by contrast, Gilbert was not a hermit, though his later attitudes to acceptance of authority were certainly coloured by eremitical leanings.

The organization of the first communities

Very little is known of the earliest arrangements for the governance of the community at Sempringham. The surviving unique version of the Gilbertine Rule dates from between 1220 and 1223, and though it incorporates elements from earlier periods these are generally overlaid by later additions and amendments.[32] It is consequently impossible to recover

---

[29] *Chronica Monasterii de Melsa, a fundatione usque ad annum 1396, auctore Thoma de Burton, abbate*, ed. E. A. Bond, 3 vols., Rolls Series (London, 1866–8), i. 107.

[30] Colvin, *The White Canons*, 1–2.

[31] *Vita Stephani*, 44–6, 164. *Magister* Robert de Verli, the probable founder of Swine (Yorkshire) nunnery, may well have been priest at Swine church (Thompson, *Women Religious*, 69 n. 99).

[32] Discussed below, App. II: 'The Documentary Sources'.

arrangements in the first generation with any certainty. Gilbert's own account (which probably derives from his lost work, *De Constructione*) is clearly the most primitive version of events at Sempringham, and probably the most authoritative. It seems to date from the pontificate of Alexander III (1159–81), perhaps from the period immediately following the lay brothers' revolt, and is contained in the first two sections of the *institutiones*. The second of these is divided into two parts: *de exordio canonicorum et provisione quatuor procuratorum*, and *de nuncio misse domino papae*, which appears to be incomplete and breaks off after three sentences. The next chapter, written in the third person, *de electione magistri et eius auctoritate*, follows immediately, and seems to derive from a later stage in the Rule's evolution.[33] Gilbert's account can be supplemented by what can be gleaned from the *Vita* (which was itself prepared in a generation after Gilbert, and with the intent of procuring its subject's canonization); from incidental references in the dossier relating to the lay brothers' revolt; early papal privileges, and slight indications in early charters.

Gilbert's prologue to his Rule, with its account of the early years and foundation of Sempringham, is similar in content to that of other institutions. Thus, for example, the *consuetudines* of Oigny commence with a *propositum* in which the early eremitical years of the community and its transition to the cenobitic life are described.[34] There are obvious parallels between Gilbert's account and those of both the Cistercians and Oigny. Just as at Cîteaux, where the early monks were advised by 'many religious men including bishops', and at Oigny, where 'religious men' counselled the hermits to adopt a more ordered life, so at Sempringham Gilbert tells how he received the counsel of William, abbot of Rievaulx.[35] This account is echoed in the *Vita*, which is at pains to stress that Gilbert was ready to seek and take advice from other 'religious and prudent men'. While such references are frequently found in accounts of new foundations at this time—Stephen of Obazine took counsel from (amongst others) the monks

[33] *Monasticon*, vi. 2. xix–xx. There are also traces of Gilbert's original regulations elsewhere in the institutes. For example, a statement on the retention of property by entrants to the order reads 'redicere dico' (*Monasticon*, vi. 2. lvi).

[34] *Le Coutumier de l'abbaye d'Oigny en Bourgogne au XIIᵉ siècle*, ed. Pl. F. Lefevre and A. H. Thomas, Spicilegium Sacrum Lovaniense, Études et Documents, fasc. 39 (Louvain, 1976), pp. viii–ix, xxxv–xxxvi, 43–4. The model for this type of introduction may well have been the *Exordium Parvum* and/or the *Exordium Cistercii*, both of which commence with an account of the origins of the Cistercians before reciting the early statutes (see *Les Plus Anciens textes de Cîteaux*, ed. J. Bouton and J. van Damme, Cîteaux: Commentarii Cistercienses: Studia et Documenta, ii (1974), 56–86, 112–14).

[35] *Monasticon*, vi. 2. xix; *Les Plus Anciens Textes*, 64; *Le Coutumier de l'Abbaye d'Oigny*, 43. It is also worth noting that the rubric heading Gilbert's account of the canons reads 'de exordio canonicorum', which may be a conscious imitation of the Cistercian *Exordium*.

of Dalon, his diocesan bishop, and abbot Guigo of La Chartreuse—and this hagiographical commonplace may in part be a device to validate the new foundations' legitimacy and orthodoxy, it is likely that in many cases advice was indeed sought.[36]

William, abbot of Rievaulx, and Alexander, bishop of Lincoln, were amongst Gilbert's counsellors; Aelred should probably be added to them, and there were doubtless others. In his own account Gilbert tells how he was visited by abbot William, who advised him to institute lay sisters. It was probably on William's recommendation, too, that lay brothers were introduced.[37] The influence of Gilbert's old employer, Alexander, is more difficult to assess. He may well have hoped that reforming ideals would be disseminated by Gilbert through the diocese. Dereine showed with regard to the early years of Prémontré that Norbert was supported by Bartholomew, bishop of Laon, who provided him with sites for settlement and with lands, with the intention of harnessing the dynamism of the reformer to the advantage of his diocese.[38] Like Norbert, Gilbert was active in the household of his diocesan bishop; the cathedral of Lincoln was organized on similar lines to that of Laon; and Alexander certainly employed his chaplain as a diocesan confessor and perhaps as a preacher, and wished to promote him to an archdeaconry.[39] Dyson has argued strongly that the *Vita* underplayed the bishop's role in support of Gilbert during the early days.[40] He based this hypothesis on a passage in the fourteenth-century *Chronicon Angliae Petriburgense* which, though largely dependent upon sources such as the Peterborough Chronicle and Henry of Huntingdon for its earlier entries, also incorporates fragments of material from other, now lost, contemporary twelfth-century works. The entry for 1136 is presumably derived from one of these: 'Iste Alexander munificans valde potentissimus erat in Anglia et in Romana curia; unde cetera magnifica opera sua ordinem Sempringhamensem ardentissime promovit.' How reliable is this source? Since its date and provenance are uncertain, it is impossible to say: it may emanate from a writer close to the bishop and eager to promote Alexander's role as a monastic patron, though it is worth noting (as Dyson himself points out) that Henry, archdeacon of Huntingdon in Lincoln diocese, makes no mention of Alexander's support of Gilbert, which might suggest that the bishop's patronage was of

---

[36] *Book of St Gilbert*, 34; *Vita Stephani*, 96. [37] *Monasticon*, vi. 2. xix.
[38] Colvin, *The White Canons*, 2–3. Bartholomew is called the founder of the Premonstratensians in one source (ibid. 31).
[39] A. G. Dyson, 'The Career, Family and Influence of Alexander le Poer, Bishop of Lincoln' B.Litt. thesis (Oxford University, 1971), 149–68.
[40] Dyson, 'Monastic Patronage', 14–24.

less note. Alexander was certainly interested in the religious movement for women in his diocese: he supported Christina of Markyate and attended the consecration of Sopwell and Godstow nunneries, bestowing on the latter important benefactions and privileges. Yet this does not make him exceptional amongst his episcopal colleagues.[41] A part at any rate of Alexander's activities was standard diocesan practice; though he was not frustratingly obstructive, as his predecessor had been, to Christina of Markyate, she certainly owed far more to the patronage of abbot Geoffrey of St Albans than she did to Alexander, while many other prelates were generous to Godstow at its consecration, which was predictable, given the amount of royal support it also enjoyed.[42] Dyson also suggests that Gilbert owed as much to the order of Arrouaise with its double houses as to the Cistercians, and that since Alexander was a patron of the Arrouaisian communities he may have influenced the adoption of some of their regulations by Gilbert. However, though a number of such foundations were made in the diocese during Alexander's episcopate, all but one, Harrold, were for canons only, and Alexander is not known to have been a particular benefactor of Harrold.[43] Moreover, Gilbert did not introduce double houses until after his return from Cîteaux in 1148, and perhaps not for several years thereafter; Alexander died in 1148, so it is hard to see how he could have influenced Gilbert. Finally, it is argued that Alexander's two visits to pope Eugenius III, the second of which almost coincided with the fateful chapter at Cîteaux in September 1147, were in order to press the cause of his former chaplain with the pope. This hypothesis seems extremely unlikely. Alexander was in poor health to undertake an arduous journey; indeed, he was to contract the illness from which he died during the second visit. It is hardly credible that loyalty to Gilbert with his two small and insignificant communities would be sufficient to persuade the bishop of Lincoln to journey to Auxerre, and we must look elsewhere for explanations of this visit. That neither Henry of Huntingdon nor the *Vita* mention it is not a conspiracy of silence, but rather due to the fact that there was nothing to report. Alexander's role was limited to that of a conscientious diocesan rather than an enthusiastic patron of his chaplain's foundations. His one Gilbertine foundation was hardly generous. It is clear that Haverholme's endowment was too unproductive to support the new group, and only a year later a

---

[41] A number of the Anglo-Norman episcopate, including such distinguished figures as Anselm of Canterbury and Thurstan of York, were patrons of religious foundations for women. For episcopal patronage of women religious, see Elkins, *Holy Women*, 13–8; Thompson, *Women Religious*, 191–210.   [42] Elkins, *Holy Women*, 13–8, 62–4.

[43] Dyson, 'Monastic Patronage', 10–11, 19–20.

benefactor made special reference to the poverty of the Gilbertine nuns there. In fact Alexander's interest seems to have been half-hearted and limited to requesting potential lay benefactors to favour his foundation.[44]

Then there is Aelred. Undoubtedly the abbot of Rievaulx was a close friend of Gilbert during the 1160s; the problem is to determine when that friendship began. It may well date from 1143, when Aelred became first abbot of the Lincolnshire abbey of Revesby, only a few miles from Sempringham (and even nearer to Haverholme). However, he had entered Rievaulx in 1134 during the abbacy of William, and the latter's connection with Gilbert may have prompted the friendship. He writes warmly, though not uncritically, of Gilbert and the community in his account of the nun of Watton, and in his second sermon on Isaiah he highly praises the 'holy father Gilbert' and a nun in one of his communities (probably also Watton) who was the recipient of visions.[45] Certainly, too, Ailred had a close interest in the life of anchoresses, as demonstrated in his Rule written for a sister in the early 1160s.[46] Though Ailred's support for Gilbert in the 1130s and 1140s cannot be proven, it seems a likely hypothesis.

Gilbert's account reveals nothing of the life followed by his nuns: the *Vita* tells how Gilbert gave his infant community precepts concerning life and discipline, emphasizing chastity and humility, obedience and charity.[47] Until 1147 Gilbert was in sole charge of the community at Sempringham (and after 1139 at Haverholme too), and the implication of the *Vita* is that Gilbert was entirely responsible for their governance. The first anchoretic community had, then, no written Rule. Neither do the lay sisters appear to have been guided by any formal institutes other than the principles already cited. Additionally, Gilbert prescribed them a sparse diet of a pound loaf 'vilis et rusticanus', two dishes of pottage, and water to drink. Their clothing was of the poorest.[48] The *Vita*'s fuller account tells how Gilbert laid down their way of life. This is described as having all the rigour of monastic discipline and a stricter way of life than they

---

[44] He had earlier offered the site to the monks of Fountains, who, in spite of the fact that the bishop had already provided buildings ready for their use, rejected it on the grounds of its unsuitability, which is hardly surprising given its position in a near-marsh. He persuaded Ralph d'Aincurt to make a substantial gift to the nuns of land in Scopwick, Kirkby, and Blankney (London, BL, MS Lansdowne 207a, fo. 115ʳ).

[45] *PL* 195. cols. 370d–371d; Constable, 'Aelred of Rievaulx', 210–11.

[46] *De institutione inclusarum*, ed. C. H. Talbot, Corpus Christianorum, Continuatio Mediaevalis, 1 (Turnhout, 1971), 633–82.

[47] *Book of St Gilbert*, 32. This should be compared, for example, with the *Vita* of Stephen of Obazine, who is said to have taught his followers 'humility, obedience, poverty, discipline, and above all constant charity' (*Vita Stephani*, 70).

[48] *Monasticon*, vi. 2. xix.

had ever experienced or seen.[49] Such a regime is also found in other contemporary saints' lives, such as that of Stephen of Obazine, where the author is keen to demonstrate that the way of life followed by a community was no less strict than that of a monastic Rule: such reassurances are another way to deflect criticism of, and to validate, an unregulated group.[50] The lay brothers who were introduced soon afterwards received the same food as the sisters, but are said to have been given the same habit as that of the Cistercian *conversi*, which suggests that they were now organized along Cistercian lines, and were thus the first of the constituent parts which made up the Gilbertine community to be regularized.[51]

By 1147 it is likely that Sempringham and its daughter house at Haverholme were organized much as were other small communities of holy women, of which that at Markyate is the best known, with its church, cloister, and modest conventual buildings.[52] Gilbert, assisted perhaps by one or more chaplains (such as Geoffrey, his chaplain while parish priest of Sempringham, or Albinus, who plays a prominent role in the *Vita*), was responsible for celebrating mass and performing other spiritual services as occasion required. His *ancillae Christi* had made a profession to bishop Alexander, just as had Christina of Markyate and her companions, but this does not necessarily imply that they were now formally regarded as nuns, and indeed it may be anachronistic at this date to draw too rigid a distinction between the anchoress, the nun, or the more imprecise *soror*.[53] To categorize Sempringham at this stage as either a nunnery or a hermitage would, therefore, be misleading: it was a community grouped around its *magister*. Change, and that only gradual, would only come in the 1150s.

The chariot of Aminadab[54]

After returning from Cîteaux Gilbert was on his own. He had first to choose an order, then to formulate a Rule. Both decisions presented substantial difficulties. As we have already seen, the nature and scope of the assistance given to Gilbert at Cîteaux is hard to determine. It should,

---

[49] *Book of St Gilbert*, 36.   [50] *Vita Stephani*, 96.

[51] *Monasticon*, vi. 2. xix; *Book of St Gilbert*, 38.

[52] Holdsworth, 'Christina of Markyate', 187–8.

[53] Certainly the account of the novitiate and profession of Gilbertine nuns that is contained in the Rule reflects a much greater formalization typical of the 13th century. See Thompson, *Women Religious*, 22–3, for some illuminating remarks on this subject.

[54] For an elucidation of the obscure reference in which the order is compared to the chariot of Aminadab, driven by Gilbert, and guided by Augustine and Benedict (*Life of St Gilbert*, 50–2), see *Life of St Gilbert*, 336–7.

however, be stressed again that, though the *Vita* emphasizes the respect felt for Gilbert by pope Eugenius, Bernard, and Malachy of Armagh, and implies their role in drawing up the Gilbertine Rule, this is never explicitly stated.

Gilbert's women were already as strictly enclosed as any but the most ascetic of anchoresses, but the growth in their numbers demanded a more secure organizational structure. However, neither the Benedictine nor the Augustinian Rule was wholly adequate for women. The former could not be adopted by communities of women without considerable modification. Its shortcomings had been shrewdly recognized by Heloise in her letter to Abelard asking both for a history and justification of nuns, and for a suitable Rule for her and her nuns to observe at the Paraclete. Her letter contains a detailed critique of the Rule's deficiencies.[55] Its gist is that though Benedict designed his Rule for men it is followed by both men and women. Women's needs differ from those of men; the Rule contains much that is unsuitable or irrelevant for women. As Benedict had himself acknowledged, just as the Rule could be amended to take account of natural frailties amongst men, so it had to be changed to be acceptable for women in the religious life. Heloise went on to ask specific questions about daily life in the nunnery, including diet and clothing. Abelard's detailed and lengthy reply was a thoughtful attempt to refashion the Benedictine Rule for women's use, and provided a detailed set of regulations for the nunnery covering the day-to-day operation of the community and its organization, which he envisaged as a double house subject to the overall authority of the abbot.

The Rule of Augustine presented other problems. The early history of the works that together make up the Augustinian monastic dossier has been the subject of much debate. In particular, scholars have varied in arguing whether or not the Rule was originally addressed to women and then rewritten for a male community or vice versa.[56] There is no indication as to the intended recipients of his Rule, though many commentators (including Verheijen) have suggested that it was intended for the lay monastery of Hippo.[57] However, even if it was intended for a lay

---

[55] *PL* 178, cols. 213–26.

[56] There is a vast literature on this vexed topic, but G. Lawless, *Augustine of Hippo and his Monastic Rule* (Oxford, 1987), provides a recent succinct and persuasive overview. The Rule itself has been edited with a commentary by L. Verheijen, *La Règle de Saint Augustin*, 2 vols. (Paris, 1967).

[57] The *ordo monasterii* and the other monastic documents of Augustine were not originally addressed to monks who were also clerics, they make no mention of the sacramental office, and assume that there will be one presbyter who will undertake spiritual duties for

community of either sex, it could be, and soon was, adopted as the Rule *par excellence* for regular clergy. The female version of the Rule seems to have been little used for centuries after its compilation, though it was certainly consulted by Caesarius of Arles shortly after Augustine's death, and it was also employed by Spanish compilers of Rules for religious women at the end of the sixth century.[58] Significantly, very few manuscripts of Augustine's Rule in the version for nuns are known until the thirteenth century, and in general by the twelfth century the Rule was believed to have been written for men.[59] The Rule of Augustine was now understood to be intended neither for women or lay monks, but for the ordained clergy. Thus it was impossible for nuns to adopt it without making such alterations to the canonical *raison d'être* as to make it nugatory.

A possible explanation for the general failure of nuns to adopt the Augustinian Rule may lie in an ethos specific to the regular canons. In her exciting but controversial studies of the spirituality of the canons during this period, Bynum has argued that what made the canons distinct from monks was not differences in their communal way of life or varying degrees of austerity, or even a stronger attachment to preaching, but a concern to edify their fellow men. This did not necessarily mean that they served in parish churches or took their message to the laity, but they did have a commitment to educate—to teach, in a phrase that was as much a cliché in the twelfth century as it is today, by word and example.[60] The canons emphasized this aspect of their vocation because they were, as monks were not, clerics by definition. Even if regular canons did not preach or exercise the priestly function outside their cloisters, their clerical status was not in doubt. Monks were not always priests, nuns could never be.[61]

the community. Instead, they appear to be based on conditions that had obtained at Thurgaste, Augustine's 'lay' or even 'house' monastery, where he himself was not yet a priest. But they were written after Augustine had moved from Thurgaste to Hippo and had been ordained priest (with great reluctance). As bishop of Hippo Augustine again presided over a monastery, but this time his household was 'a monastery of clerics' while another monastery existed in the city for laymen (Lawless, *Augustine of Hippo*, 62, 148–5, 158–9).

[58] Ibid. 140.

[59] However, there was a rumour circulating during the Premonstratensians' early years accusing them of using the Rule, which Norbert himself allegedly claimed was written for women. See ibid. 137–41 for a discussion of this intriguing and complex issue. In his letter of direction to Heloise, Abelard, quoting from the *ordo monasterii* (interestingly in its female version) wrote that Augustine set up a monastery for clerks and wrote a rule for them.

[60] C. W. Bynum, *Docere Verbo et Exemplo: An Aspect of Twelfth-Century Spirituality*, Harvard Theological Studies, 31 (1979), and 'The Spirituality of Regular Canons in the Twelfth Century', in *Jesus as Mother: Studies in the Spirituality of the High Middle Ages* (Berkeley and Los Angeles, 1984), 22–58.

[61] Though nuns might preach, as did Hildegard of Bingen (Bynum, 'The Spirituality of Regular Canons', 31, 54–7).

The denial of clerical status to women was therefore of critical importance in determining which Rules were available to them. Where women were attached to reformers like Norbert of Xanten or Roger, the founder of Arrouaise, who adopted the Augustinian Rule as the framework for their own organizations, they were anomalous and difficult to legislate for. It was indeed the tension between the appeal of the reformers' message to their female followers and the adoption of an unsuitable Rule that underlay the problems both the Premonstratensians and Arrouaisians were to face within a generation of their foundation.[62] In the light of these factors, Gilbert's solution was seemingly inevitable: 'he imposed a double discipline of monastic life on his followers, giving the nuns the Rule of St Benedict to observe, but to the clerks the Rule of St Augustine.'[63] It remains to consider why he did not also adopt the Benedictine Rule, perhaps following Cistercian customs, for his clerks.

Various explanations have been offered. Foreville has stressed the dual role of Bernard of Clairvaux, representing the Cistercian tradition and influence, and Malachy of Armagh, who maintained close ties with reformed canons, especially the Arrouaisians.[64] Malachy's activities as a reformer are well attested, though, given the fact that he died shortly after Gilbert's arrival at Cîteaux in the autumn of 1147, the extent of his direct influence may have been limited.[65] Foreville has also suggested that Gilbert was already familiar with the canons' way of life, which was moreover more adaptable to varied spiritual and charitable functions than was that of the Cistercians.[66] This seems very likely. By this time there were a number of Augustinian (including Premonstratensian and Arrouaisian) priories in the neighbourhood of Sempringham. Alexander of Lincoln, like so many of his episcopal contemporaries, had been a patron of the canons.[67] If (as seems likely) the Gilbertine priory of St Katherine's, Lincoln (which was for men only), was founded shortly after 1148, and if it had indeed from the time of its foundation an eleemosynary role, then it made sense for it to adopt an Augustinian Rule. Moreover, it is possible that Gilbert, who may have been a student at Laon,

---

[62] See below, 'Models and options—Arrouaise' and 'The Premonstratensian solution'. For the fullest discussion of Augustinian involvement with women religious in England, see Thompson, *Women Religious*, 132–57. That there was considerable vagueness as to what Rule women followed is clear (ibid. 214, 216).

[63] *Book of St Gilbert*, p. 48. This too had been the solution adopted at Fontevrault.

[64] Ibid., pp. xliv–xlviii.

[65] J. Watt, *The Church and the Two Nations in Medieval Ireland* (Cambridge, 1970), 19–28.

[66] Though her suggestion that bishop Robert de Chesney, founder of the priory of St Katherine's, Lincoln, may have been instrumental in the adoption of the Augustinian way of life cannot be substantiated.   [67] Dyson, 'Monastic Patronage', 10–14.

had come into contact with the Premonstratensians in their north-eastern French heartland, and he may even have encountered Norbert himself, who was summoned to Laon in 1119.[68] Fontevrault, too, had already adopted the Augustinian Rule for its brethren: it too may have influenced Gilbert in his choice. Elkins has argued that though it might have been more appropriate and 'symmetrical' to incorporate monks, and that though in southern England monks were often priors of communities of women, in the north there were fewer such opportunities and most monastic recruits were joining the Cistercian order which had rejected Gilbert. By contrast, the Augustinians were increasing in numbers locally and could fulfil both a teaching and an active role within a nunnery.[69]

But the most compelling reason for Gilbert's choice of the Augustinians was that he had no option. He wanted a reformed Rule; the Cistercians had closed their doors to him. Old-style Benedictinism was not appropriate: nearly all of the new orders of the twelfth century were Augustinian rather than Benedictine in tone. Two that were essentially Benedictine, Grandmont and La Chartreuse, refused all contact with women, and in any case had made no settlements in England. The Augustinian Rule provided a framework round which Gilbert could build a way of life for his communities. His next task was to turn to that construction.

It must always be remembered that Gilbert belonged to the second generation of the 'new monasticism'. By the time he, along with his advisers or those who may have helped him draw up the Rule after the Cîteaux meeting of 1147, prepared his 'institutes' a number of potential solutions to these problems had already been tried, and many of them had failed. Prémontré had experimented with double houses only to abandon them c.1140; Fontevrault was now securely under the control of abbess Petronilla, and the original intentions of Robert of Arbrissel had been largely distorted; Abelard had produced a new reading of the Benedictine Rule for the Paraclete.[70] Those who drafted the Gilbertine institutions would have known of these experiments and could evaluate their success. These were possible models for Gilbert: before looking at his solution we need to consider the available options as they presented themselves in 1148.

---

[68] I owe this suggestion to Christopher Holdsworth.

[69] Elkins, *Holy Women*, 83. For criticism of some aspects of this interpretation, see above, Ch. 1: 'Cîteaux and beyond'.

[70] Though Dr Thompson has suggested (pers. comm.) that Robert may always have wished a woman to rule at Fontevrault as part of the penitential subservience of men to women.

Models and Options

Fontevrault

The order that most invites comparison with the Gilbertines is that of Fontevrault, founded a generation or more earlier. Gilbert would almost certainly have known of it when he came to draw up his Rule, and while in France in 1147–8 it is not unlikely that he came into contact with the new order, which had already attracted the patronage of the Angevins.[71] Some years ago I rashly suggested that the Gilbertine constitutions partly derived from its practices. This view has been justifiably criticized by Foreville. She has argued that though Fontevrault was founded by Robert d'Arbrissel as a double community it was soon 'changed into a mixed community merely', in which the male element was reduced to the status of clerical servants and the house became recognized solely as a nunnery. In contrast to the aristocratic women and their powerful supporters who came to dominate Fontevrault, Gilbert 'held to his first ideal', and he gained the support of powerful patrons who apparently did not seek or manage to impose themselves on the founder. Moreover, at Sempringham it was undeniably the canons who within a generation emerged as the dominant partners.[72] There are certainly striking differences between Fontevrault and Sempringham. Robert does not seem originally to have wanted to found an order of nuns, and his first foundation at La Röe was for canons only. It was only later, as a large number of female followers were attracted to his teaching, that he diverted his attention to their welfare and submitted himself and his male followers to their leadership in a self-conscious act of humility and self-denial.[73] There were also some real differences in the authority wielded over the two houses by Gilbert and Robert. Though Gilbert was the *magister* and Robert the

---

[71] Though no houses of the order were founded in England until after the Gilbertine double houses had been established, we must recall that Fontevrault was well enough known in England for a suggestion to be made to Christina of Markyate that she join that house. It is also worth remembering that Gilbert's most powerful patron, Henry II, was also a major patron of Fontevrault, where he and many of his family found burial. The fullest study of Fontevraudine houses in England is now Thompson, *Women Religious*, 113–32.

[72] B. J. Golding, 'St Bernard and St Gilbert', in B. Ward (ed.), *The Influence of St Bernard* (Oxford, 1976), 50; *Book of St Gilbert*, pp. xliii, 1 n., liii–liv. Elkins has pointed out that in England the male members of the Fontevraudine house of Grovebury seem to have been made responsible for all the business affairs of the order's houses in the country. Thus the men here were also emerging as the controlling force (*Holy Women*, 122–3). Thompson (*Women Religious*, 128–30) is more cautious.

[73] Thompson, *Women Religious*, 114–15. See also D. Iogna-Prat, 'La Femme dans la perspective pénitentielle des ermites du Bas-Maine (fin xiᵉ–début xiiᵉ siècle), *Revue d'Histoire de la Spiritualité*, 53 (1977), 54–64.

magister or *dominus*, and neither adopted the style 'abbot' or 'prior', Gilbert's magisterial control was quasi-despotic, while that of Robert was far less evident.[74]

It remains unclear, however, how far these differences were the result of later developments within both orders. As we have seen, there is much evidence to suggest that Gilbert's own vision for his foundation was distorted by outside pressures. Similarly, Robert's programme for Fontevrault was undoubtedly changed by the accession of Petronilla of Chemillé.[75] Moreover, there were similarities in the organization of the two communities. Like Gilbert, Robert gave his canons the Rule of Augustine, while the nuns followed that of Benedict. In both communities, though the male and female elements lived in separate houses, they shared the same church. This custom was followed elsewhere (for example, at Obazine), but, again, Gilbert may well have derived the idea from Robert. There is one other significant parallel. Both men were unwilling to accept any institutionalized authority over their foundations and ceded such power as they did claim to a successor before their deaths. Robert first elected Hersende as head of Fontevrault and then Petronilla of Chemillé as his successor, whereupon he seems to have withdrawn from active supervision of the community, while Gilbert chose Roger, prior of Malton, and similarly retired from direct government of his houses.[76]

The influence of Robert of Arbrissel on Gilbert must remain unproven. Fontevrault provided one model of how to deal with the problem of the *cura monialium*, but was a creation of an earlier age when double houses were not so suspect. Gilbert lived in a later generation. It must be considered extremely doubtful whether by the last third of the twelfth century any woman could have been appointed to the position of power wielded by Petronilla, and even in Fontevraudine houses there are hints of rising discontent among the brethren at their subservient role.[77] For Gilbert, compiling his Rule in the early 1150s, some of the features of Fontevrault could not be adopted at all, others not without considerable modification. The freedom enjoyed by the abbess of Fontevrault, and to a lesser extent by the prioresses of the order too, could not now be contemplated.

---

[74] J. Smith, 'Robert of Arbrissel: *Procurator Mulierum*', in D. Baker (ed.), *Medieval Women*, Studies in Church History, Subsidia 1 (Oxford, 1978), 183–4.   [75] Ibid.

[76] Thompson, *Women Religious*, 116–19; Smith, 'Robert of Arbrissel', 181–4.

[77] Thompson, *Women Religious*, 118. It is also worth noting that Petronilla and her successors were of high social status, in contrast to the prioresses of Gilbertine foundations.

Arrouaise

Women were also found at Arrouaisian communities, though they do not seem to have been an element in the earliest priories. Unfortunately, little is known of the organization of the women in these early Arrouaisian houses, though at Beaurepaire the prioress seems to have had overall control of the house, and there is evidence from several of the priories that they were arranged as double houses with the nuns living in buildings separate from, but adjacent to, those of the men.[78] There has been considerable debate whether there was a rigid distinction at this time between professed nuns and lay sisters at Arrouaise; certainly the terms *soror* and *conversa* seem to have been used very loosely, but this may merely reflect the fact that there was as yet no clear organization of female personnel within the communities. What is certain is that at Arrouaise, as at Prémontré, moves were made by the mid-twelfth century to establish separate communities for the women of the order away from the canons, and that by the end of the century strict measures were being taken to reduce the number of Arrouaisian sisters.[79]

The women's chief patron seems to have been the third abbot of Arrouaise, Gervase, who was responsible for founding the first Arrouaisian house for women in England at Harrold (Bedfordshire) *c*.1136–8.[80] Thus it was almost exactly contemporaneous with Sempringham, and its arrangements are worth considering in a little detail. The foundation was probably made primarily for a kinswoman (?sister) of Gervase. Gervase had been primarily responsible for the recovery of the nascent order, and for resolving the tensions between the factions who wished to follow a cenobitic way of life and those who wanted to continue as solitaries following an Augustinian Rule, and it has recently been suggested that he may have been particularly concerned to foster religious women within his communities.[81] Harrold's foundation chronicle tells how he admitted

---

[78] The fullest discussion of the Arrouaisian sisters is L. M. Milis, *L'Ordre des chanoines réguliers d'Arrouaise. Son histoire et son organisation de la fondation de l'abbaye-mère (vers 1090) à la fin des chapîtres annuels (1471)*, 2 vols. (Bruges, 1969), 502–17. See also Thompson, *Women Religious*, 145–56.

[79] J.-B. van Damme, 'La "Summa Cartae Caritatis": source de constitutions canoniales', *Cîteaux* 23 (1972), 6–9; Thompson, *Women Religious*, 149–50.

[80] Milis, *L'Ordre des chanoines*, 114–17; *Records of Harrold Priory*, ed. G. H. Fowler, Publications of the Bedfordshire Historical Record Society, 17 (1935), 16; *Cartulary of Missenden Abbey*, ed. J. G. Jenkins, 3 vols., Buckinghamshire Records Society, 2, 10, 12 (1938–62), iii. 182, no. 809. The foundation is discussed in Thompson, *Women Religious*, 150–5.　　　　　　　　　　　　　[81] Thompson, *Women Religious*, 145.

to *conversio* almost all those who came, both men and women, and goes on to state how he took advice from Bernard of Clairvaux and many other religious men in drawing up his Rule, which laid stress on manual work and continual silence.[82] To the women at Harrold were added a prior and canons, to whose care they were entrusted. Harrold was certainly originally intended as a double foundation, though the relative status of its nuns and canons is hard to assess. One charter was addressed to the nuns 'and the brethren protecting them', which seems to imply the dominance of the women, while a contemporary charter is directed to the prior, canons, and sisters, suggesting the reverse.[83] Priors were appointed from Arrouaise until the 1180s. In 1177 an abortive attempt was made to pass the governance of Harrold to the neighbouring Arrouaisian abbey of Missenden, but by *c.*1188 the sisters had gained their independence from the mother house, perhaps because of difficulties in maintaining authority at so considerable a distance. Thereafter Harrold was ruled by a prioress. Before its emancipation it, like all dependencies of the order, was subject to Arrouaise, which did not allow independent priories and had, in spite of Bernard's influence, no devolution of authority such as that enjoyed by the Cistercians; under such control the prior of Harrold may have been a cipher, and hence more dispensable when the nuns gained their freedom. How far did the Arrouaisian experiment influence Gilbert? Certainly bishop Alexander of Lincoln was their patron, and archbishop Malachy had close ties with them and was largely responsible for introducing the order into Ireland.[84] The house at Bourne was founded in 1138 and lay only a few miles from Sempringham; it may have been linked with an obscure foundation for women at Wothorpe near Stamford.[85] Gilbert could have looked to conditions at Harrold when he came to draw up his own institutes. Yet it is not possible to prove any direct links. Gilbert's order was in no way modelled upon the organization at Arrouaise, and by the time he came to draw up his own Rule the canons of Arrouaise were having second thoughts about the wisdom of having women in their communities.

The Premonstratensian solution

Though the early Lives of Norbert play down his ministry to women, preferring to stress his apostolic vocation and the canonical structure of

---

[82] Milis, *L'Ordre des chanoines*, i. 62–5. There are obvious parallels here with the development of the early Gilbertine rule.   [83] Thompson, *Women Religious*, 152.

[84] Dyson, 'Monastic Patronage', 20; Watt, *The Church and the Two Nations*, 25–7.

[85] Thompson, *Women Religious*, 155–6.

his order, Herman of Laon, a contemporary and authoritative source, leaves no doubt that Norbert's preaching inspired many female as well as male converts. These had to be provided for; at the time when Herman was writing there were allegedly more than a thousand women in the order serving God in an austerity and silence that could scarcely be found in the strictest communities of men.[86] Like most of the other new orders, the Premonstratensians adopted double houses to cater for these women. The organization and layout of these houses was very similar to those of the Gilbertines. Prémontré itself consisted of a double set of claustral and other buildings for the canons and nuns, both of which were contained within a single precinct, and with the church used by both communities. Contemporary and near-contemporary accounts make it clear that the women prepared the canons' clothes, cooked, and carried out most of the domestic duties of the abbey.[87] The earliest surviving collection of statutes dates from after their first redaction by Hugh de Fosse in 1131.[88] Eight of these concern the *sorores*. They emphasize the strict dependence and enclosure of the women and stress the silence in which they were to live. Enclosure was total, and whenever the prioress dealt with the outside world she had to be accompanied by two of the mature sisters who had care of the guests.[89] No sister might leave the cloister; men were not allowed in. The only exceptions were the *provisor*, who was responsible for the provisions; the priest who administered communion, made sick visits, and conducted funerals; and the abbot, who could enter to hear confessions or preach a sermon, when he had to be accompanied by two brethren. Normally men could only communicate with the sisters through a window (as at Sempringham or Obazine) and then never alone. The sisters were ruled by their prioress, who regulated their life in the dormitory and refectory, supervised them at church and at work, while they heard sermons and attended chapter, and was responsible for visiting the sick. She was also responsible for disciplinary matters amongst the *sorores*. However, in all important matters she was subject to the abbot, with whom she communicated not directly but through the *magister exteriorus*. The abbot also

[86] Quoted in Colvin, *The White Canons*, 335 n. The fullest study of the Premonstratensian nuns is A. Erens, 'Les Sœurs dans l'ordre de Prémontré', *Analecta Praemonstratensia*, 5 (1929), 5–26, and there is an excellent survey in M. de Fontette, *Les Religieuses à l'âge classique du droit canon* (Paris, 1967), 14–25.   [87] De Fontette, *Les Religieuses*, 16.

[88] See R. van Waefelghem, 'Les Premiers Statuts de Prémontré', *Analectes de l'Ordre de Prémontré*, 9 (1913), 63–6.

[89] Though this may be merely an echo of the Augustinian *ordo monasterii*, which stipulated that two monks should always go if anything was needed outside the monastery (Lawless, *Augustine of Hippo*, 76).

had authority to determine some of the minutiae of the nuns' daily living, their clothes to wear, and their books to read.

These communities did not survive for long. They attracted the criticism of the more austere, notably Bernard of Clairvaux, while Jacques de Vitry drew attention in the *Historia Occidentalis* to the growing laxity of these communities where the windows (i.e. for communication between the sisters and men) were changed into doors when the first fervour of the institutions abated.[90] However, in, or shortly before, 1141 the nuns were transferred from Prémontré to the neighbouring site of Fontenelle. Though this action was not followed universally and immediately through the order, the nuns were gradually established in communities which, though now separated from the canons' quarters, remained constitutionally linked and subordinate. They often continued to be sited very close to the male priories. However, charters in favour of both Orford (Lincolnshire) and Broadholme (Nottinghamshire) were addressed to both the nuns and the brethren, a phrase used frequently in the early Gilbertine charters, which seems to suggest a less segregated arrangement similar to that of the Gilbertine houses before the introduction of the canons.[91] This anomalous position probably contributed to their obscurity and poverty when compared with the Gilbertine double houses. The Premonstratensian solution to the *Frauenfrage* brought the worst of both worlds: the nuns were both dependent on the canons and distanced from them. It was not one that would obviously commend itself to Gilbert as he drew up his own institutes.

Continuity and native tradition

We have now examined some of the possible Continental models with which Gilbert would have been familiar, but of course there were communities nearer home which could equally have served as exemplars. Reference has already been made to double monasteries. In England they had enjoyed a long, and in many respects illustrious, history. Double monasteries such as Whitby or Wimborne were a familiar feature of the landscape of Anglo-Saxon monasticism.[92] Most, if not all, were intimately

---

[90] *PL* 182, col. 200; *The Historia Occidentalis of Jacques de Vitry*, ed. J. F. Hinnebusch (Fribourg, 1972), 134–5. These arrangements are very similar to those obtaining at Obazine before 1147.　　　　　　　　　　　　　　[91] Thompson, *Women Religious*, 143–4.

[92] There is now a substantial literature on this subject, but for pre-Conquest English communities see in particular, Bateson, 'Origin and Early History', 137–98; Thompson, 'Double Monasteries', app. viii, 145–64; J. Godfrey, 'The Double Monastery in Early English History', *Ampleforth Journal*, 79 (1974), 19–32; Yorke, ' "Sisters under the Skin"?', 95–118.

connected with a royal house: all were undeniably 'aristocratic'. Normally they were 'single-site' communities, though Dr Yorke has recently suggested that there were also 'dual-site' double communities at Beverley and Chertsey. All, however, appear to have been under an abbess, though since we do not know what Rule, if any, was followed at these houses it is impossible to have any clear idea of their organization. It does seem that the men and women were segregated and the women were expected to be enclosed.[93] The fullest description of the layout of a double house in England is found in Rudolf's *Vita* of Leoba, which describes conditions at Wimborne. Here there was apparently a wall separating men from women in the church and the abbess only spoke to her priests and other men about the affairs of the monastery through a window. If this was the arrangement then it was very similar to that which was to be adopted at Sempringham and Obazine centuries later. However, Dr Yorke reminds us that this description was written after Carolingian legislation had tightened up the rules relating to segregation and enclosure and draws attention to another (unidentified) seventh-century double house where though the men and women were in separate choirs they do not seem to have been invisible from one another and both male and female lectors read the lessons. What is clear is that during the heyday of the double communities before the Viking invasions each followed its own eclectic 'Rule' and there was no standardization of observance.[94]

During the tenth century the double monastery in England declined. While religious women frequently continued to live near male communities (which sometimes included their own relatives), some at any rate of these women were individual nuns and vowesses rather than forming a specific community. The tenth-century reform movement was both critical of double houses and the possibilities for scandal they afforded, while seeking at the same time to increase the segregation of nunneries. Many of these were now served by secular, non-residentiary chaplains financed through prebends, rather than by clerics of the same community. It seems increasingly likely that such arrangements survived the Conquest and that immediate post-Conquest establishments were organized in a similar way. There is clear evidence that many post-Conquest monasteries had associated with them groups of holy women, though it remains a matter of debate how far these were institutionally linked to the male

[93] Nevertheless, in a famous passage Bede describes the laxity of the community at Coldingham.

[94] Yorke, ' "Sisters Under the Skin"?', 107–9. See also D. M. Wilson (ed.), *The Archaeology of Anglo-Saxon England* (London, 1976), 205–7.

community. Dr Thompson has demonstrated that some Benedictine abbeys like St Albans and Peterborough were closely connected with nuns, but that by the middle of the twelfth century they were literally distancing themselves from these women by creating independent nunneries such as Sopwell or St Michael's, Stamford. She argues that the Gilbertines were not a unique phenomenon in the twelfth century, but that they should be seen in a pre-existing context of double organization. Growing suspicion of double communities in the latter part of the twelfth century 'would obscure the importance of links between men and women and the possibility that some communities of women developed from double monasteries'.[95] The earliest example of the separation of a double community appears to have occurred in the late 1150s. The Augustinian house of Marton in Yorkshire contained both canons and nuns until early in the reign of Henry II. By 1158 the nuns had received a separate endowment and were established nearby at Moxby. This division seems to have taken place gradually, but it was irreversible.[96] It has been suggested that the founder intended Marton as a double house on Arrouaisian lines or even modelled it on Gilbertine arrangements.[97] There is no evidence for the former hypothesis, and in any case the foundation of Marton may well precede those of the Gilbertines. Here, then, we have a double house that seems remarkably similar to those of the Gilbertines, but which was transformed at just the time when the Gilbertine double houses were undergoing their greatest expansion. Dr Thompson's argument is striking, but it does raise a more fundamental problem which is not really addressed in her analysis. If these ties did exist but were under growing threat from the mid-century, then why did Gilbert continue with this type of organization precisely at a time when it was beginning to disappear elsewhere?

Dr Thompson has unquestionably shown that there were a significant number of nunneries which included canons and *conversi* in twelfth-century England. These were almost certainly laid out on a very similar pattern to the Gilbertine double houses. A high percentage of the twelfth-century Lincolnshire nunneries seem to have contained a significant male element, and Dr Thompson draws attention to the fact that the geographical distribution of these double houses, primarily in Lincolnshire and Yorkshire, is just that of the Gilbertine double houses.[98] Gilbert was clearly not an isolated phenomenon. However, since few of these

[95] Thompson, *Women Religious*, 56–63.   [96] Ibid. 65–6.

[97] Burton, *Yorkshire Nunneries*, 7–8, 48 n. 29.

[98] Thompson, *Women Religious*, 77–8.

foundations can be precisely dated (though Stixwould appears to date from *c.*1135) it remains unclear how far he was the model for these non-Gilbertine foundations, or whether conversely they influenced his own institutions.[99] Certainly contemporaries found it very difficult to distinguish between them: Gervase of Canterbury's *Mappa Mundi* refers to Nun Cotham, Stixwould, Wykeham, and Hampole nunneries as containing *canonici albi et moniales*, the term Gervase usually uses to describe the Gilbertines, while Catesby nunnery is explicitly said to be a house of *moniales de Simplingham*. In the following century all five non-Gilbertine houses are described as Cistercian, though there is no evidence that they were regarded as Cistercian during the twelfth century.[100] The *Mappa Mundi* also lists seven communities of *moniales albae*. One of these (Amesbury) was a Fontevraudine house, three were later regarded as Cistercian, one (Brewood White Ladies) was probably for Augustinian canonesses though a Cistercian affiliation has been suggested, one ('Camesturne') cannot be identified, while the last, Shouldham, was a double Gilbertine community. Such classification suggests considerable uncertainty concerning status and reflects the lack of clear distinguishing features between the communities.[101]

The best-known of these nunneries that closely resembled the Gilbertines in organization is Swine (Yorkshire). This remained a double house until at least the second half of the thirteenth century, when in 1267/8 the visitation of archbishop Walter Giffard shows that it included both canons and *conversi* and that the men's quarters were divided from those of the nuns by walls with windows through which food was passed.[102] If (as seems likely) a similar organization obtained during the early years of Nun Appleton (Yorkshire), then the friendship between Gilbert and the community there might have included some reciprocal influences between that house and Sempringham.[103]

Swine and Nun Appleton were both founded *c.*1150; both were later described as Cistercian. In 1147 Gilbert had been told by the Cistercian

---

[99] Stixwould is discussed in C. V. Graves, 'The Organization of an English Cistercian Nunnery in Lincolnshire', *Cîteaux*, 33 (1982), 331–50.

[100] *The Historical Works of Gervase of Canterbury*, ed. W. Stubbs, 2 vols., Rolls Series (London, 1879–80), ii. 429, 431, 432, 439, 441; S. P. Thompson, 'The Problem of the Cistercian Nuns', 227–52, esp. 242–52.

[101] Thompson points out (ibid. 246–7) that most of these orders may have worn similar habits with white the predominant visible colour.

[102] *The Register of Walter Giffard, Lord Archbishop of York, 1266–79* ed. W. Brown; Surtees Society, 109 (1904), 147–8.

[103] Nun Appleton is discussed by Burton, *Yorkshire Nunneries*, 17.

general chapter that the white monks were not able to take over the rule of nuns. 'The problem of the Cistercian nuns' is indeed both complex and controversial. On the one hand there is clear evidence that the early Cistercians, and Bernard in particular, were determined to exclude women from their abbeys at all costs. On the other, by the middle of the following century there were many flourishing Cistercian nunneries throughout Europe, apparently fully integrated into the order.[104] Even the first Cistercian generation saw religious women seemingly residing in, or close by, Cistercian abbeys, while there were at least two female communities, Jully and Tart, under Cistercian aegis. The nature of their affiliation to the order is, however, a matter of dispute and it may be that their links were personal (perhaps stemming from ties of kinship), unofficial, and (as far the monks were concerned) unsolicited.[105]

By 1147 there were at least three nunneries (Heynings, Legbourne, and Stixwould) in Lincolnshire which later claimed to be Cistercian.[106] The organization of these houses requires some attention, for they were communities local to Sempringham whose *modus vivendi* Gilbert might be expected to know, and perhaps imitate. They included canons and *conversi* shortly after their foundation, and seem to have been structured in a manner very similar to the Gilbertine double houses.[107] The nuns followed a Benedictine Rule, based on Cistercian custom, while the canons seem to have observed the Augustinian Rule.[108] By the 1170s at least two other nunneries (Nun Cotham and Sinningthwaite) were recognized by Alexander III as observing Cistercian custom.[109] All these communities, therefore, seem to have perceived themselves as essentially Cistercian,

[104] S. Roisin, 'L'Efflorescence Cistercienne et le courant féminin de piété au treizième siècle', *Revue d'Histoire Ecclésiastique*, 39 (1943), 342–78.

[105] The clearest analysis of these early nunneries is found in Thompson, 'The Problem of the Cistercian Nuns', 227–52. Her conclusion that nunneries may have followed Cistercian customs at this period, but were not incorporated into Cistercian organizational structure, is not universally accepted, and for an interesting counter-argument see C. H. Berman, 'Men's Houses, Women's Houses: The Relationship between the Sexes in Twelfth-Century Monasticism', in A. Macleish (ed.), *Medieval Studies at Minnesota 2: The Medieval Monastery* (St Cloud, Minn., 1988), 43–52. See also de Fontette, *Les Religieuses*, 27–33.

[106] In 1270 six Lincolnshire nunneries; Stixwould (1139 × 1142); Greenfield (1148 × 1166); Nun Cotham (1148 × 1153); Legbourne (−1148 × 1166); Gokewell (1147 × 1175); and St Michael's, Stamford (?1135 × 1154), claimed Cistercian status.

[107] Arrangements were also paralleled at Catesby (Northamptonshire, *c*.1150 × 1176), and Swine (Yorkshire, *c*.1143 × 1153). Interestingly, Gervase of Canterbury explicitly styled Catesby a Gilbertine house in his *Mappa Mundi* (*Historical Works*, ii. 431). Gervase also mentioned canons at Nun Cotham, Wykeham, and Catesby (Thompson, 'The Problem of the Cistercian Nuns', 247–8).   [108] Ibid. 248.

[109] Ibid. 249; *Papsturkunden in England*, iii. 370–1 (Nun Cotham); *Monasticon*, v. 466 (Sinningthwaite).

even if they were not formally subject to Cîteaux. On occasion, and particularly in the thirteenth century, they did claim full Cistercian status, primarily in order to acquire fiscal advantage. Like Gilbert's Haverholme, they followed the Cistercian way of life as far as the strength of their sex allowed.[110]

In the 1150s, therefore, there was a significant group of communities for religious women, but including monks or canons and lay brethren under the authority of a *magister*, sometimes aided by a prioress. Most of these houses were situated in Lincolnshire and Yorkshire. They were organized as double houses, though at this date we cannot be certain that the full monastic plan had been established, and it may be that in some houses at least there was considerably more freedom of access between the women and men than would later be thought acceptable.[111] Their status and affiliation is unclear, but since they were denied a place in the Cistercian order they were probably more or less autonomous bodies, though perhaps nominally subject to the diocesan bishop. Nevertheless, their life-style reflected that of the white monks, and the communities were to make frequent and unsuccessful claims that they were formally Cistercian. Essentially they were on the Cistercian fringes, and as such were anomalous and potentially dangerous to the stability of an order which denied full membership to women. These small-scale, quasi-autonomous communities provide a context for the Gilbertine Rule. Sempringham and Stixwould, Haverholme and Heynings, Nun Ormsby and Nun Cotham emerged from the same social and spiritual milieu. The Gilbertine achievement was to provide an organizational framework for the nunneries that the 'Cistercian' houses lacked.

The Gilbertine Rule

Structures of command

The magister *and his deputies*

One of the most significant developments to the Gilbertine Rule was the shift away from the personal control of Gilbert to the more institutionalized

---

[110] There is an echo here of Herman of Laon's remarks about those women who followed the Cistercians in manual work and who imitated the monks of Clairvaux in every way they could (cited in Thompson, 'The Problem of the Cistercian Nuns', 232).

[111] This is particularly true of the Gilbertines. See Constable, 'Ailred of Rievaulx', 219, 222–3.

role of the *magister*.[112] Cheney demonstrated that Gilbert, though sometimes described as *magister ordinis*, was also styled by other descriptive titles such as *primus inventor ordinis*. It does not appear that there was a clear understanding of a specific institutionalized headship, and the issue is further confused by the fact that Gilbert was also an academic *magister*.[113] Gilbert's successor, Roger, was variously described as *magister* or *prior ordinis*, as was Gilbert II (1205–25). Only thereafter does *magister* become the usual designation. Cheney argued that this lack of precision can be related to Gilbert's reluctance to found an order, still less lead one, and followed Foreville in suggesting that the term *magister* could have been borrowed from Fontevrault. This change in the nature of government was perhaps inevitable; it is certainly observable, though to a less marked extent, in a number of other twelfth-century orders. It can be illustrated in a number of ways, but nowhere more clearly than in the changes in Gilbertine visitations. In Gilbert's own time visitations were conducted by the founder himself in conjunction with a *conversus* and two canons. When Roger took over as *summus prior* he was assisted in his visitations by the *summi scrutatores* (or *circatores*); by the early thirteenth century this system had been refined into an elaborate arrangement for the maintenance of good order and discipline.

Though masters were also found in other contemporary communities of women, their role was generally more limited than at Sempringham. At the 'Cistercian' nunneries of Nun Cotham and Stixwould they were elected by the nuns, though (as with the Gilbertines) their appointment was confirmed by the diocesan.[114] Their chief function was to supervise the pastoral care of the nuns; otherwise they functioned as the executive arm of the prioress, accounting to her for the community's income and expenditure, and representing her in financial and legal matters in the world. By contrast, the authority of the Gilbertine *magister* or *prior omnium* was virtually untrammelled. Supreme in the order, the fact that the Gilbertines were exempt from diocesan visitation, and episcopal interference was limited to the ordination of canons and the blessing of nuns, meant that the *magister* was independent of his local bishop too. He was elected by an elaborate process from which the nuns were excluded; his

---

[112] The fullest discussion of the status and origin of the Gilbertine *magister* is provided by Cheney, 'Papal Privileges', 45–52.

[113] The *Vita* states that Gilbert was known by the title *magister* in his lifetime (*Book of St Gilbert*, 312), but its connotations are not spelled out.

[114] Graves, 'Organization of an English Cistercian Nunnery', *Cîteaux*, 33 (1982), 336–8.

rule graphically indicated the control the canons had achieved in the order in the generations following Gilbert's death.[115] The *magister* had normally served as a prior, but on election he left his community and began what was in theory an endlessly peripatetic career visiting each house at least once a year, accompanied by two canons as assistants. These frequent visitations meant that almost all major decisions, and many minor ones, could be left to his discretion. Not only did he regulate the spiritual life of each community—for example, receiving all novices and later hearing their profession, as well as acting as confessor to the nuns when necessary—he also controlled the economic activity of every house, his assent being necessary for all but the most insignificant transactions, and his seal was required on all documents issued by the order. He (apart from his own companion, a trustworthy canon) was the only male member of the order allowed to enter the nuns' enclosures.[116]

The *magister* also presided at the annual chapter of the order, which was normally (though not exclusively) held at Sempringham. In attendance were the prior, cellarer, and two prioresses from each house, the general inspectors, including those who had served in that office during the previous year, and those elected for the following year. All others were excluded, except any that the *magister* might co-opt.[117] The women travelling to and from the chapter were carefully secluded and chaperoned, and the strictest penalties laid down for any who had unlicensed conversation with them.[118] The chapter functioned as the paramount disciplinary body in the order, proclaiming excommunications and maintaining harmony and unity within the communities, while at the same time amending and adding to the order's statutes when necessary.

Amongst contemporary monastic orders only the Master General of

---

[115] *Monasticon*, vi. 2. xx. For a full description of the election process in the 13th century, see *The Rolls and Register of Bishop Oliver Sutton, 1280–1299*, ed. R. M. T. Hill, 8 vols., LRS, 39, 43, 49, 52, 60, 64, 69, 76 (1948–86), i. 230–4.   [116] *Monasticon*, vi. 2. xx–xxi.

[117] Ibid. lvii. The Gilbertines followed the Cistercians in explicitly denying attendance to the grangers, i.e. the most senior of the lay brethren. All the community at Sempringham heard the *magister*'s opening address before leaving the chapter in closed session.

[118] The chapter placed considerable strain on the food resources of Sempringham, and in 1256 Philip of Kyme made arrangements for the nuns of Bullington to have men fish in Dogdyke 'for the two days in the year when the nuns of Bullington go to the great chapter at Sempringham' (*Gilbertine Charters*, 92). Alice de Gant gave land in Heckington in the third quarter of the 12th century for the nuns travelling to the chapter to have a hostel, presumably so that they need not stay at the priory itself (*Sempringham Charters*, xv. 161). For similar logistic problems, though on a larger scale, experienced by Cîteaux, see Lawrence, *Medieval Monasticism*, 159.

the Templars (in very different circumstances) enjoyed such power.[119] The origins of this power clearly lay in the authority exercised by Gilbert before his retirement in the 1170s. His replacement by Roger, prior of Malton, marked the beginning of the institutionalization of magisterial rule, but the context in which the *magister* now worked had changed considerably. Gilbertine priories were by this time widely established and potentially difficult to control. Not for nothing did the institutes constantly reiterate the need for harmony and uniformity. By his reluctance to establish a firm organizational framework and his reliance on personal charisma and power Gilbert ensured that his successors, if they were to retain his authoritarian autocracy, establish a rigid hierarchy. At the same time, however, it was clear that the *magister* needed deputies. Like the *magister* himself, these stood outside the ambit of any one priory, and, being chosen solely by the *magister*, constituted an executive arm unprecedented in other orders, and one which in many ways was divorced from, and certainly superior to, the authority wielded by priors and prioresses in individual communities.

The most important of the *magister*'s 'staff' were the *summi scrutatores*, two canons and a lay brother. According to the *Vita*, they were appointed after Gilbert had ceded control of the order to Roger.[120] They served when necessary as the *magister*'s deputies in carrying out the visitation of each house that occurred at least once a year. Their own authority was limited to this disciplinary function, though in the absence of a prior the senior inspector sat in his place. Each house was visited for at least a week, when irregularities were corrected and any matter too serious to be left to their discretion was referred to the general chapter. In double houses their office was paralleled by two nuns and a lay sister. These women, whose travel from house to house was as closely supervised as their journey to the general chapter, were expected to visit each nunnery once, and perhaps twice, a year. This institution is not exactly paralleled in any other order. However, both Prémontré and Oigny had *circatores*. These officers, whose function appears to have been based on Cluniac models, were responsible for informing on delinquent brethren, bringing accusations in the chapter, and in particular detecting unauthorized conversation. They also kept the keys of the cloister and were entrusted

---

[119] M. D. Knowles (*From Pachomius to Ignatius* (Oxford, 1966), 36) regarded the power of the Gilbertine *magister* as the most innovative, and perhaps significant, feature of the Rule: 'it had, what all the monastic and canonical orders had hitherto lacked, a single supreme head.'   [120] *Book of St Gilbert*, 86–8.

with all security matters.[121] These officials may well have been the model for the Gilbertines, but whereas they seem to have been accountable to the chapter, the Gilbertine inspectors were responsible to the *magister* alone.

The *magister*'s hold on disciplinary matters throughout the order was strengthened by his appointment of a general confessor. While the priors were licensed to hear confessions of the men in their priories, and the *summus scrutator* could hear confessions of the prior and all men in the order, the general confessor (or *sacerdos confessionis*) and the *magister* alone could provide sacramental confession for the women.[122] The confessor travelled round the priories: his needs were provided for by the *circatores*, while his activities were themselves monitored by two 'discreet' nuns.

The task of the general inspectors and confessor was further aided by the appointment within each double house of three lesser inspectors, chosen by the *magister*, and the *summae speculatrices*, chosen from amongst the nuns 'of proven piety and discretion'. These, too, were accountable only to the *magister* or his nominee, and two or three times a year were required to reveal any faults within the community. Though as members of the community they were nominally subject to the prioress, the latter was expected to defer and show obedience to them, while her own authority was effectively bypassed by their privilege of making their confession directly to the *magister*.[123]

By the beginning of the thirteenth century the Gilbertines had, therefore, devised an inquisitorial system unmatched in Western monasticism. Though in part it owed something to Cluniac and Premonstratensian models, as a whole it was unique. It represented a response to the challenge and the potential dangers inherent in a double community at a time when such organizations were on the defensive. Its essentially autocratic and authoritarian nature was perhaps the only way the Gilbertines could have survived at a time when everywhere women were being moved out from reformed congregations. In their almost paranoid obsession with harmony and good government the institutes and the *Vita* are at one.[124]

[121] van Waefelghem, *Institutiones Premonstratenses*, 19; *Le Coutumier de l'abbaye d'Oigny*, pp. lxiii, 48–9. See also H. Feiss, '*Circatores*: From Benedict of Nursia to Humbert of Romans', *American Benedictine Review*, 40 (1989), 346–79, for a wider survey.

[122] *Monasticon*, vi. 2. xxi, liii. Another priest, the *magister*'s chaplain, whose function is more shadowy, seems to have accompanied the confessor on his visitations (ibid., p. xxii).

[123] *Monasticon*, vi. 2. xxiii. The prioresses did have the authority to hear the confessions of the other nuns.

[124] See e.g. ibid. xxiv, and the lavish eulogy of the order in *Book of St Gilbert*, 50–6.

Both stress the pivotal role of the *magister* as supreme head of the organization; both look back to the charismatic leadership of Gilbert himself. But in both there is perhaps a tacit recognition that Gilbert's rule, though harsh, had not been wholly effective. This had brought about crises that had almost wrecked the community; only by formalizing the command structure could the future of the order be assured.

The prioresses and senior nuns

The most striking and significant difference between the organization of the Gilbertine double houses and that of other contemporary nunneries was the relative lack of power enjoyed by Gilbertine prioresses in their communities. The abbess of Fontevrault had supreme control, not only over the abbey itself but over its dependencies; her authority extended over the men as well as the women, and she and her deputy, the prioress, travelled widely, approved the appointment of prioresses, and directed the sending of confessors for the male element in the community.[125] The prioress of 'Cistercian' Stixwould was elected by the nuns, had absolute control over all members of the community, including its canons, and both she and the cellaress were allowed to leave the house on convent secular business.[126] By contrast, the powers of the Gilbertine prioresses were limited to the administration, care, and discipline of the women within their cloister. They did have the authority to hear confessions and impose penances and also oversaw the liturgy.[127] The most unusual feature of the nuns' organization was the arrangement whereby three prioresses were appointed, and exercised their power in turn, each ruling for a week. This seems to have been unique, and doubtless contributed to their relative lack of power.[128] Though the prioresses were elected by the nuns, if the nuns failed to do so within fifteen days of the death of the previous one, the choice reverted to the *magister*—a further restriction of their authority.

Below the prioresses, arrangements were closely parallel to those obtaining in male Benedictine communities. The sub-prioress's role was strictly subordinate to that of the prioresses. She could not normally be promoted to the senior position, and was not permitted to enter the novices' quarters unless called, nor to go to the window-room without a

---

[125] De Fontette, *Les Religieuses*, 68–72.

[126] J. A. Nichols, 'The Internal Organisation of English Cistercian Nunneries', *Cîteaux*, 30 (1979), 27.

[127] *Monasticon*, vi. 2. xlvi–xlvii, l, liii. Elkins (*Holy Women*, 208 n. 34) points out that, since Innocent III in 1210 forbade abbesses to hear confessions, this privilege is relatively early.   [128] *Monasticon*, vi. 2. xlvi.

mature colleague. The cellaress was responsible for the provisioning of the nuns' quarters, while the precentrix had varied roles: she sometimes served in the kitchen, when she kept the cupboard keys; she looked after the book cupboard and gave the nuns their books on the first Sunday in Lent. The sacrist, like her male equivalent in a Benedictine abbey, supervised the decoration of the church and its ornaments, and summoned the community to the hours and chapter.[129]

The organization of the male communities

In nearly all respects, the hierarchy of the Gilbertine canons, both within the double houses and in the priories for canons only, followed arrangements common throughout Western monasticism, with officials such as the cellarer and his deputy responsible for the provisioning of the house, the sacrist in charge of the conventual church, and so forth. Within each house there were eight senior office holders, some canons, others *conversi*, all of whom were appointed, and could be deposed, by the *magister*.[130] At their head was the prior. It is by no means clear when the first Gilbertine priors were elected, though it is possible that it was not until well into the 1150s.[131] Until that date Gilbert may have been the only institutional link between Sempringham and the other early priories, which would explain his frequent journeys of visitation. The prior's authority, though wholly subordinate to the *magister*'s, was, in the latter's absence, considerable within the male community. He presided at the chapter and preached the weekly sermon to the entire house in the conventual church.[132] Just as the *magister* was assisted by the inspectors, each prior had a small team, comprising the cellarer, the senior granger, and another lay brother. These four proctors made collective decisions on the administration, and particularly the economy, of the priory and negotiated with the senior nuns who kept the treasury about expenditure, though (as noted above) all major purchases required the sanction of the *magister*.[133] The cellarer,

[129] Ibid. xlvii–xiii, l.

[130] These comprised the prior, sub-prior, cellarer, proctor, *grangiarius abbatiae* or chief granger (an office clearly borrowed from the Cistercians), the chief shepherd, and the wardens of the works and of the nuns' sheep. At St Katherine's, Lincoln, these were joined by the sub-cellarer of the brethren and the warden of the infirmary. All other obedientiaries were appointed by the prior (*Monasticon*, vi. 2. xxi).

[131] The first to be recorded is probably Torphinus, who occurs as prior of Chicksands between 1154 and 1158 (*Heads of Religious Houses*, 202).

[132] *Monasticon*, vi. 2. xxiv–xxv.

[133] Ibid. xxiv–xxvi. It was hoped that their decisions would be unanimous; if not, a majority of 3 to 1 sufficed, while unresolved differences were referred to the *magister* or chief inspectors.

as well as overseeing the internal economy of the priory and being responsible for keeping the priory accounts, which were shown annually to the chief inspectors, also supervised all the priory's granges and servants.

The nuns

The surviving early thirteenth-century version of the Gilbertine institutes reveals very clearly the arrangement of the houses and the observances of the nuns as practised in the generation following Gilbert's death. How far they can be extrapolated back to the order's earlier years is open to question. The account of the nun of Watton suggests a much more informal, less closely segregated society, and pressure for a more rigid Rule may have only come (as Constable suggests) following the shock of that incident and the lay brothers' revolt.[134]

The Rule is divided under thirty-five rubricated headings; in addition there are ten sections that apply both to the nuns and to the lay sisters, and a separate group governing the operation of the infirmary. These sections are not arranged in any clear order, and may well represent the gradual accumulation of regulations by succeeding general chapters, the new ordinances being added to the collection as necessary.[135] They open with a statement, seemingly dating from the early years of the order, that the brethren's chief duty is to minister to the *ancillae Christi*, and that should any be negligent in this duty he is to be disciplined by relegation

[134] Constable, 'Ailred of Rievaulx', 219–20, 225–6.

[135] *Monasticon*, vi. 2. xliv–lii, lvi, liii–liv. The lack of formal arrangement is a common feature of the customaries relating to nunneries of this period, such as Marbach, briefly considered by Parisse, *Les Nonnes au moyen âge*, 76–80. The ten sections headed *Capitula institutionum communiter ad moniales et sorores pertinentium* (*Monaticon*, vi. 2. lvi) are presented even more haphazardly, and may well represent decisions taken at an early general chapter. They include a number of both weighty and trivial prohibitions: on the reception of anyone (including men, a puzzling reference which may date from the very early days when the nuns had more authority and there was a closer association of the sexes) into the nuns' community without the nuns' consent; on nuns making all but the plainest purses; on particular friendships amongst the women; on nuns and lay sisters going out to work in any way; on anyone wishing to leave one house for another of their own will. Transgressors would be degraded for fifteen days, beaten three times in chapter, and prevented from ever leaving the community. Other chapters relate to the cutting of the women's hair and bathing (which was discouraged); punishments for disobedient nuns and sisters; and a provision for the Rule to be read four times a year to the community, the nuns reading to the lay sisters 'far from any seculars'. Ch. ix stands out from the rest, and is the most interesting of this collection. It is a forthright appeal for harmony in the order which hints at some unrest, perhaps resentment amongst the nuns at the increasing powers of the canons: 'We beseech our nuns and sisters, in the name of our Lord Jesus Christ, that they bear themselves peacefully towards their brethren in Christ.'

to lay rank for a year.[136] The nuns followed the Rule of St Benedict, their community being largely organized along lines found in most twelfth-century nunneries. In general the nuns followed the same liturgical round as the canons, and like the latter the literate nuns were expected to read in the cloister. They copied manuscripts and other works as laid down by the *magister*, as well as performing such tasks as sewing and in particular aiding the lay sisters in the making of habits for the whole community.[137] The nuns themselves wore white tunics with black veils and caps. Though the cloth was cut out and made up within the community, it might be purchased from outside, and provision was made, subject to the *magister*'s approval and that of the canons and brethren, for the manufacture of vestments. The habits were washed by the nuns and lay sisters together, two canons passing the canons' clothes through the revolving window and receiving them again when ready.[138]

Where the Gilbertine Rule for nuns does show some originality is in the arrangements made both for the financial support of the nuns and for the internal security of the community. Most nunneries were under-endowed in comparison with male communities, and the lack of a firm economic base for communities of religious women was a frequent cause of their failure. The Gilbertine Rule stipulated that a tenth of all the order's sheep should be made over every year for the women's exclusive use.[139] A faithful *frater* was to have their care and to seek to increase the flocks' numbers. All income from the sale of wool was to be administered, not by the four proctors of the Gilbertine priories, but by the nuns themselves for the construction and maintenance of their buildings and for the purchase of small necessities. Any surpluses could be used for the purchase of bedding for the relief of the poor who came to the priory at night (which might indicate that the sisters were responsible for these charitable activities), and if there was still money left over it could be assigned for any necessary purchase. All financial transactions of the nuns were in the hands of a canon and *conversus*, who were to be appointed by the *magister* and to act in consultation with the priories' proctors and the

[136] *Monasticon*, xliv. With its reference to *fratres* rather than *canonici*, this section probably pre-dates the introduction of the canons in the early 1150s.   [137] Ibid. l.

[138] Careful prohibitions were made against excessive ornamentation of dress, or too frequent washing. Moreover, all the community's vestments, with one or two exceptions, were in the nuns' care, and draconian penalties were laid down for any canon or *conversus* who dared to usurp their prerogative in these matters (ibid. xlvii–xlviii).

[139] Ibid. xliv. A charter of Shouldham refers to the sheep possessed for the use of the nuns (G. W. Watson, 'Charters to Shouldham Priory', *The Genealogist*, NS 36 (1919–20), 76).

inspectors. The brother who actually had the care of the money was to pass it to the nuns through the window dividing their quarters from those of the men in the presence of the prior. The Rule makes it clear that everything, including gold and silver and all receipts from lands and sales of produce, was in the custody of the nuns and passed to them through the connecting window. Though a canon was in charge of all the written deeds and documents relating to financial transactions, all his receipts after report to the prior and proctors had to be transferred to the nuns. A special privilege allowed the proctors 30 or 40 shillings to purchase necessities in order to avoid frequent visits to the window.[140]

In a neat progression from the nuns' financial arrangements to their absolute segregation, with which the next few chapters of the Rule are concerned, it was provided that three marks per annum from the nuns' income should be spent on increasing the security of their enclosure. No expense was to be spared in preserving the nuns from the outside world. No one should enter their dwellings without serious cause and the permission of the prior; anyone who disobeyed this ruling was to be temporarily removed to another priory, where he was to fast and suffer beatings in the weekly chapter. If he refused this punishment he was to be expelled from the order. Anyone who was detected secretly sending messages or small gifts from any of the women, or receiving them, was also to be removed to another house and degraded for as long as the *magister* saw fit, 'ut alii timorem habeant et caveant'.[141] Again, if the accused refused to repent he was to be expelled as if sacrilegious. The same punishment was prescribed for any woman who transgressed in the same way, though in her case she was to be imprisoned or heavily punished rather than expelled, in order to avoid scandal. Such prohibitions were not confined to written messages: the fear of unlicensed communication extended to conversation as well. No clerk or lay member of the community was allowed to speak with even his mother or other female relative who might be in the same priory, while no man, except the *magister*, the *fenestrarius*, and the priest who heard confession, might speak to a female member of the community except in the presence of the *magister* or in the chapter, and then only on business of the house or when preaching in the

---

[140] *Monasticon*, vi. 2, xliv.

[141] Ibid. xlv. It is important to note that this provision seems to be closely modelled on that in the Augustinian *ordo monasterii*, which suggests that Gilbert was looking to Augustinian as well as Benedictine precedents when he drew up his rule for nuns (Lawless, *Augustine of Hippo*, 92).

segregated church. Again, severe penalties, including the transfer of an erring nun to another house, were laid down for those who disobeyed. Licensed communication was restricted to specific areas, and in particular to the window-house and the parlour.[142]

The Gilbertine institutes therefore refashioned traditional rules for enclosed religious women. They preserved the basic organizational framework while ensuring as far as possible that the nuns would be financially and physically secure. The presence of men, both clerical and lay, as integral members of the Gilbertine nunneries freed the nuns for contemplative and liturgical life, but at the same time it posed a potential threat to the women's physical and spiritual well-being.

The lay brotherhood

As in most of the new religious communities of the twelfth century, the Gilbertine economy and organization relied heavily upon the *conversi* or *laici fratres*.[143] These servants, typically recruited from the peasantry, though at least in the first generations they included some of noble birth, 'lived a life of consecrated labour'.[144] Their work was the *sine qua non* of the highly contemplative and liturgic life of the monks, while at the same time they made possible the economic and agricultural expansion that so typified the new orders: Mary could not exist without Martha. In addition to their presence in all-male houses, *conversi* were also found in double communities and nunneries, where they fulfilled an identical function, attending to everything outside the convent buildings. Lay brothers are recorded, for example, at the English 'Cistercian' nunneries of Nun Cotham and Stixwould, where it is clear that they were

---

[142] *Monasticon*, vi. 2. xlv–xvi. Nuns were even forbidden to visit their relatives or lay notables except for due cause. They were required to describe the route they would take and could only stay one night if illness or dire necessity intervened.

[143] The introduction of lay brethren into the monastic commonwealth has been much discussed. See, especially, K. Hallinger, 'Woher kommen die Laienbrüder?', *Analecta Sacri Ordinis Cisterciensis*, 12 (1956), 1–104; Donnelly, *The Decline of the Cistercian Laybrotherhood*; J. Dubois, 'L'Institution monastique des convers', in *I laici nella 'societas christiana' dei secoli XI e XII*, Miscellanea del Centro di Studi Medioevali, 5 (1968), 183–261; J. Leclercq, 'Comment vivaient les frères convers', ibid. 152–81. For Premonstratensian *conversi*, see Colvin, *The White Canons*, 360–2.

[144] C. J. Holdsworth, 'The Blessings of Work: The Cistercian View', in D. Baker, (ed.), *Sanctity and Secularity: The Church and the World*, Studies in Church History 10 (Oxford, 1973), 75. This essay (59–76) is a valuable interpretation of 12th-century monastic attitudes to manual labour.

responsible for the running of the nunneries' granges and for *ruralia officia*.[145]

The lay brothers occupied an integral place in the Gilbertine houses: they were, as the *Vita* put it, one of the four wheels of the chariot being steered to its heavenly reward by St Gilbert.[146] The *Vita*'s account of their introduction into the community at Sempringham makes no mention of their Rule as such, though Gilbert is said to have obliged them to take a vow to serve and to live in humility, obedience, and patience.[147] Elsewhere the *fratres laici* of the Gilbertines were said to observe the customs of the Cistercians, except where any new rules had been made to decrease the first rigour of the order.[148]

Now, while there can be no doubt (as will be shown in more detail below) that the Gilbertine Rule (at any rate as we have it in the first surviving version) did borrow heavily from the Cistercian Rule and customs, it is by no means clear when the Gilbertines took over this Rule. It is interesting that the account written by Gilbert himself, though acknowledging that the lay brethren wore the same habit as the Cistercians, does not explicitly state that he gave them the Rule, while the *Vita* likewise omits any mention of a Rule. But there is further evidence that the Cistercian Rule may well not have been adopted until comparatively late in Gilbert's career. The Cistercian *conversi* system could only function in a community which also possessed monks: there was a clear distinction between *conversi* and choir monks, their roles were carefully defined and demarcated, and it was impossible for a lay brother ever to become a choir monk. At the same time there was a symbiotic relationship between the two: the Cistercian constitution was a translation into monastic terms of the division between those who prayed and those who worked to the benefit of the community as a whole. As we have seen, Gilbert did not institute canons until after 1147 at the earliest. Until that time it is most likely that the Gilbertine *conversi* had a role much more similar to that of their Grandmontine than their Cistercian counterparts, and that they were (as the *Vita* and Gilbert's own account state) in charge of the temporal affairs of the community, a responsibility and status that went well beyond that of the Cistercian brethren. There is further evidence to

---

[145] *Monasticon*, v. 677; Graves, 'Organization of an English Cistercian Nunnery', 343–4; Nichols, 'Internal Organisation', 32–4; see also Elkins, *Holy Women*, 86–7 and references n. 31, 193–4. They are also found in Arrouaisian communities in England (such as Harrold) and elsewhere, as well as at small Benedictine nunneries (Elkins, *Holy Women*, 53–6).

[146] *Book of St Gilbert*, 50–2.   [147] Ibid. 36–8.

[148] *Monasticon*, vi. 2. xxxvi. For the Gilbertine Rule for the *conversi*, see below, 'The lay brotherhood'.

support this hypothesis. Early grants to the Gilbertines are usually made in favour both of the nuns and of their brethren, and no distinction is made between lay and clerical men.[149] Such an association of the lay brethren is, of course, unknown in the charters of Cistercian abbeys. The dossier of material relating to the revolt of the lay brethren at Sempringham reveals a little more.[150] Gilbert wrote that the leaders were two lay brothers to whom he had 'entrusted the care of all our houses'.[151] Such delegation of power was unthinkable in a Cistercian context: it would not have been unfamiliar to the Grandmontines. There is a further hint of the lay brethren's freedom of action in Gilbert's reference to their accumulating property for themselves.[152]

It has already been observed that the Gilbertine Rule for *conversi* owed much to its Cistercian model. But when were the Gilbertine regulations compiled? As shown above, though Gilbert wrote how he had given his *fratres* 'the habit of religion such as the Cistercian brothers have', there is no explicit mention of their adoption of the Cistercian Rule, neither is it mentioned in the *Vita*'s account. Later, in the 1160s, Gilbert would specifically deny the rebellious lay brothers' charge that he had forced them to take oaths of profession *secundum formam ordinis Cistercie*. Yet a comparison of the Gilbertine rule *de susceptione fratrum, et eorum capitulo, et professione* with the rite (known to have been established prior to 1183) for profession of *conversi* in Cistercian houses makes it very clear that the former was based very closely on the Cistercian observance and that, though the verbal borrowings are not as pronounced as they are in some sections of the Rule, there are strong parallels between the two. Though in places there are obvious and necessary amendments (the Cistercian *conversus* makes his promise of obedience *flexis genibus coram abbati*, the Gilbertine *coram magistro*), in general a reading of the Gilbertine Rule

---

[149] The foundation charter of Bullington was addressed to the 'sanctimonialibus ordinis de Sempingham et fratribus earum clericis et laicis ibidem deo servientibus', that of Ormsby is made to the 'sanctimonialibus et fratribus suis', while an early charter in favour of Alvingham is to the 'sanctimonialibus ibi deo servientibus et fratribus earum' (*Gilbertine Charters*, 91, 39, 102). Bishop Alexander of Lincoln's foundation charter to Haverholme is couched in similar terms, and it may be significant that, while Alexander refers to the nuns modelling their lives, as far as they were able, on the Cistercians, there is no mention that the lay brethren were doing the same (*English Episcopal Acta. I*, 24–5).

[150] The events of the revolt are considered above, Ch. 1: 'The years of crisis': 'The lay brothers' revolt'.   [151] *Book of St Gilbert*, 78.

[152] 'qui aggregaverunt sibi proprietates' (ibid. 78). Henry II also seems to allude to this in his letter to the pope supporting Gilbert. The rebels had secretly removed the possessions of the houses, but the king and the other founders would in no way allow those *laici* to take over the running of the communities (ibid. 142–4).

demonstrates that the Gilbertine profession was, indeed, *secundum formam ordinis Cistercie.*[153]

Like the Gilbertine Rule, the Cistercian *Usus Conversorum* was a long time in the making. The 1119 Constitutions contained only four *capitula* dealing with the *conversi*; two of these dealt with the economic role of the brethren, one with the probation of a *conversus*, and the fourth stipulated that a lay brother could never be made a choir monk. Thereafter the Rule gradually evolved until it reached its 'final' form in the *Usus Conversorum* contained in MS Dijon 114, and dated by Lefèvre between 1183 and 1188. It is not the place here to recite in detail the stages of this compilation as Lefèvre reconstructed it, except in so far as they affect the reception of the Cistercian Rule into Gilbertine houses.[154] The *Usus Conversorum* contains twenty-two chapters. Nearly all of them are reproduced in full or in part in the Gilbertine institutions, but two, the last, are conspicuously missing. These, *quod aliter alteri caput non lavet* and *quas pelles non operentur*, were added to the Cistercian use before 1183.[155] The fact that they do not appear in the Gilbertine Rule strongly suggests that its core was compiled from Cistercian models before that date. Is it possible to date them more precisely? Lefèvre has rightly observed that the 'custom of a living institution cannot remain fixed and one can say, without paradox, that the last code in date is already out of date on publication'.[156] For this reason, manuscripts of the *Usus* had continually to be modified. Either new fair copies were produced, as is most clearly seen in MS Dijon 114, or existing copies were amended, erasures made, marginal entries inserted, or supplementary statutes added as new rulings were made at the annual chapters. Lefèvre showed this procedure in action at the end of the 1150s and early 1160s, when statutes promulgated in 1157, 1159, and 1161 were added to the *Usus Conversorum*.[157] Only one of these five amendments (an addition to chapter viii of the *Usus* made in 1161) appears in the parallel Gilbertine text and it seems probable, therefore, that the Gilbertine Rule was established prior to 1157. The comparison between the two Rules can, however, be taken further. Lefèvre argued convincingly that the text of the 1151 version of the *Usus Conversorum* is contained in MS Paris, BN, n.a.l. 430 and consisted of seventeen

---

[153] *Monasticon*, vi. 2. xxxvii.

[154] J. Lefèvre, 'Les Traditions manuscrites des "Usus Conversorum" de Cîteaux', and 'L'Évolution des "Usus Conversorum" de Cîteaux', *Collectanea Ordinis Cisterciensium Reformatorum*, 17 (1955), 11–39 and 65–97.   [155] Lefèvre, 'L'Evolution', 78.
[156] Ibid. 76.   [157] Ibid. 77–8.

chapters.[158] Between 1152 and 1153 three further chapters were added, making a total of twenty. The last of these, *de campanis*, is the last to be found in the Gilbertine use. After 1153 and before 1157 a number of amendments were made to 'working' manuscripts of the *Usus*. None of these are to be found in the Gilbertine Rule. It is thus this version of the *Usus* that Gilbert relied upon when drawing up his own Rule, and the argument then is strong that the Gilbertine Rule (at any rate that for the lay brethren) was crystallized *c*.1153, some six years after Gilbert's visit to Cîteaux.

A study of the development of the *Usus Conversorum* is therefore essential to an understanding of the development of the Gilbertine use for the order's own *conversi*. But it is possible to take this argument further. The *Usus* was not the only Cistercian source for the Gilbertine Rule: the *Instituta* were another.[159] For the present purpose the chapter *de tabernis* is the most revealing. Most commentators on the early development of the Cistercian Rule (notably Lefèvre and van Damme) have indicated the importance of this text in dating the *Instituta*. It is generally accepted that MS Laibach 31 is the best text of the institutes codified in 1151 and that it incorporates capitular decisions of earlier years. The Laibach text contains only one correction—to the section *de tabernis*. The shorter text, preserved in Paris, Bibl. nat. lat. 4221 (a manuscript slightly anterior to MS Laibach 31), has been erased, and a longer, more prohibitive version written over the erasure in smaller characters. This correction can be dated to 1151, or at any rate before the general chapter of 1152. It is this later version that is used verbatim in the Gilbertine Rule for lay brethren, *de euntibus ad nundinas*. This, then, would further suggest that the Gilbertine Rule was not formalized until early in the 1150s.[160]

To sum up so far. The lay brethren attached to the Gilbertine houses may well have had considerable power and autonomy in the early years of the communities, analogous to that of the Grandmontines. Though Gilbert

---

[158] A comparison of Paris, Bibliothèque Nationale, MS n.a. 1. 430 with Trent, MS 1711 enabled Lefèvre to argue reasonably that the latter manuscript was anterior to the codification of 1151, while the Paris manuscript contained the new formulation of the *Usus* established in 1151, to which were added by 1153 the three new chapters (ibid. 16, 80).

[159] van Damme, 'La "Summa Cartae Caritatis" ', 33; Lefèvre, 'L'Évolution', 164–5.

[160] Other chapters also indicate, though less conclusively, the same interpretation. Ch. ix of the Rule for Gilbertine canons, *de canonicis ad nova loca mittendis*, is copied from the 1151 *Instituta* (ch. xii of Laibach, MS 31) and not from the earlier and textually very different version of 1119. Similarly, the prohibition on the building of houses outside the priories in ch. xv of the Rule for lay brethren is taken from ch. xxi of the Laibach manuscript, not from the shorter version in the 1119 constitutions.

was influenced by the example of the Cistercian *conversi*, he did not immediately adopt the Cistercian Rule. On his return from Cîteaux and consequent upon the introduction of canons, the role of the lay brethren was considerably reduced and they were given (perhaps in 1153) a Rule that was based upon that of the Cistercians as it existed in the early 1150s. The very adoption of the Cistercian *Usus* implied the downgrading of the lay brethren's authority. This was probably the root cause of the revolt of the following decade. The rebels realized that the Rule had been changed, and it was this realization that underlay their claim that they had made an oath of loyalty 'secundum formam ordinis Cistercie professionem'. Gilbert, for his part, testified that no such profession had been made, and his word was apparently accepted by the papal delegates. It seems most likely that the Gilbertines had indeed taken the Cistercian Rule for *conversi* but that those lay brothers who had joined prior to its adoption had not been obliged to swear an oath though they did have to abide by its regulations. Such a confused transitional state of affairs can only have contributed to the lay brothers' discontents.

The Gilbertine lay brotherhood was typical in that it provided a ready labour force for the communities it served while at the same time offering a place within monasticism for those who had previously been excluded. It was also typical in that it early saw a demotion of the brethren's status and their replacement by the choir canons in the priories' hierarchy. This denial of power led to outright rebellion and defeat; but the *conversi* were still necessary to the Gilbertine economy.

The Gilbertine Rule for *conversi* is divided into thirty-three chapters, whose titles are rubricated in the Douce manuscript.[161] However, it is immediately apparent that not all of this section (which is entitled *Scripta de fratribus*) relates solely to the lay brethren. Some of the chapters contain a variety of unconnected material. Chapter xxiv can illustrate both these points.[162] It begins with a general prohibition on members of the order undertaking lawsuits, moves to a prohibition of visits to kin or *notos seculares* without permission, then forbids unauthorized visits to houses of anchoresses or nuns of another order, and ends by forbidding individual members of the community to give their own or the priory's goods to their kin. Here, as throughout, the impression is given of a composite work, compiled at various times, and incorporating the *dicta* of Gilbertine general chapters.

---

[161] *Monasticon*, vi. 2. xxxvi–xliv. There are marginal entries in the Douce manuscript cross-referencing the chapters to other related sections (such as those of the lay sisters) elsewhere in the Rule.   [162] Ibid. xlii.

Though many of the chapters relating to the lay brothers can be traced to Cistercian antecedents, the Gilbertine version is normally considerably expanded. In general their clothing was to accord with that for their Cistercian equivalents.[163] Specialist workers were given some rewards: oxherds, carters, and shepherds had clothes of fuller material and smiths were allowed to have smocks or rochets. Clothes were either to be washed by the brethren themselves, if there were no fullers (which seems to suggest a reliance on hired labour), or given by the doorkeeper to be washed by the poor.

The chapters describing the life of the *conversus* within the community and his role in the spiritual polity are also heavily dependent upon Cistercian models. No one could become a lay brother until he was 24. On arrival he was received by the *magister* in the nuns' chapter, where the activities and responsibilities of his future life were outlined to him. He was then accepted by the community which he was to join and immediately given tasks, such as ploughing. For a year he was assigned to the novice-master. On Sundays and feast-days the *conversi* and novices went to the canons' chapter and heard the prior's sermon, after which the novices left. At this point a novice could be professed, but only in the presence of the *magister*, who would examine him, while another *conversus* would briefly explain the rigours of a lay brother's life, after which the novice would go to the nuns' chapter for profession. The other *conversi* would then proceed with their own chapter along the same lines as prescribed for the canons, and when this was ended the novice made his vows in the hands of the *magister* and again at the altar. He was now a *conversus* and could undertake the responsibilities previously denied him. He could carry out temporal affairs for the convent on his own, or become a *grangiarus*; he could never become a canon. He could have no books, and such prayers as he was allowed to learn were to be learnt by rote, not by reading.[164]

The daily spiritual life of the *conversi* was modelled on that of the canons, though they only communicated (normally at the morning mass) eight times per annum.[165] The offices were said, with slight variations, in both the granges and the priories. Between 15 September and Easter the

---

[163] Ibid. xxxvi. Each brother had three white tunics, a grey cloak reaching to mid-calf and lined with coarse skins, a grey cape reaching nearly to the feet, together with a cowl just covering the shoulders and chest. This could be of any colour as long as it was suitable for the religious life ('dummodo verae religione conveniat').   [164] Ibid. xxxvi–xxxvii.

[165] The text of the Rule here reads 'tam ad vigilias quam ad horas diei faciant orationes suas sicut mos est', but *mos est* is probably a misreading of *monachi*, which appears in the Cistercian Rule.

brethren were woken by a bell on working days and were not normally allowed to rise before this time. Matins, Lauds, and Prime, if time permitted, were said before going out to work, the other Hours were said wherever they happened to be working. During the summer months the brethren were allowed to sleep till Lauds to compensate for the fact that they had no midday break. Non-working feast-days largely followed the Cistercian prototype but there were rather more than amongst the white monks.[166] In addition, to avoid scandal any brother staying amongst the laity was to keep feast-days generally observed by them. On non-working days identical Hours were kept with the canons.

Every week a chapter was held for the brethren under the chairmanship of the prior or sub-prior, and in the presence of one or two canons.[167] Attendance was obligatory and absence punished; only at the busiest times of the agricultural year, hay-making and during August, did it not meet. The brothers' refectory was similar to that of the canons.[168] Meals were presided over by the granger or by the senior brother (*prior illorum*). Though their diet was generally sparse, they were allowed pittances on major feast-days, just as were the canons, as well as the mowers during hay-making.

Lay brothers were particularly useful as representatives of the community on secular business outside the cloister. These activities had necessarily to be closely monitored for disciplinary reasons. They were not allowed to stay in neighbouring towns except in the order's own guesthouses, though if a brother travelled on his own he might lodge at the hostel of another order provided it was occupied by a canon or brother. They were not to be absent from the convent for longer than allowed, and if they did so delay they were to be severely punished and treated as a fugitive.[169]

The lay brothers' *raison d'être* was to labour for the community. They were therefore valuable commodities, and for this reason the Rule stipulated that they should neither injure any of their draught animals, or

---

[166] Thus four, rather than three, days after Christmas were feast-days, and the feasts of the Purification, SS Matthew, Mary Magdalene, Peter *ad vincula*, the Decollation of St John, and the Invention and Exaltation of the Cross were added, together with some feasts of special importance in England or in the order, such as St Gilbert's day and the feast of his translation, the translation of St Thomas Becket, and the feast of St Hugh of Lincoln. This last feast dates from 1220, and is an important dating device for this version of the Rule.   [167] *Monasticon*, vi. 2. xxxviii.

[168] Ibid. xxxviii–xxxix.

[169] Ibid. xl, xlii–xliii. They were expressly forbidden from unlicensed attendance at the dedication feasts of churches belonging to the order, the over-indulgence that frequently accompanied such occasions being explicitly acknowledged ('nec ibi comedere vel inordinate bibere attemptet').

indeed themselves, through excessive loads. The loss of an animal was a serious offence, and the careless brother was regarded as a *dissipator domus suae*. As such he was to fast and be severely beaten.[170] Though the majority laboured on the priories' granges, they were also employed as specialist workers and craftsmen within the conventual precincts.[171]

The lay sisters

All communities of nuns, particularly if they were strictly enclosed, would normally require the services of female servants. Lay sisters were as necessary as the *conversi* in any community of the 'new monasticism' which included women. Indeed, it could be argued that they were more indispensable, since it was doubly essential to ensure that the nuns remained untainted by the world. The sisters could serve as one more line of defence between secularity and community; they occupied a key position at this boundary. Their role as frontier guards in the Gilbertine houses is symbolized by the fact that it was to them, and not to the nuns, that the male community made known its daily food requirements.[172] Additionally, and as importantly, the lay sisters gave the nuns greater freedom for contemplation and thus functioned as Marthas to the professed religious Marys.[173]

Lay sisters were frequently recruited from local women of humble means, and it was from the secular servants of the first anchoretic community at Sempringham that the earliest Gilbertine lay sisters came. These were given their first Rule by Gilbert shortly afterwards.[174] Their introduction preceded the recruitment of lay brethren. Though other nunneries had servants, their regularization by Gilbert was an initiative as radical as the Cistercian introduction of *conversi*.[175] At the same time, however, they occupied an ambivalent (and lowly) position in the Gilbertine hierarchy. The distinctions between the nuns and sisters seem to have been less clear than those between the canons and the *conversi*, who were legally and formally segregated by the fact that the canons were clerks. For the women the lines of demarcation were based on class and, later perhaps, also on educational attainments or potential. By the beginning of the thirteenth century the author of the *Vita* in his eulogy of the order

---

[170] Ibid. xlii. [171] These functions are discussed in more detail below, pp. 415–18.

[172] A similar arrangement was found at Obazine-Coyroux, where a corridor linked the nuns' cloister with the outside world. The passage of goods through this was supervised by a portress, who was almost certainly a lay sister (Golding, 'Hermits. Monks and Women', 132). [173] See above, n. 144.

[174] *Book of St Gilbert*, 34–6.

[175] It has been seen by one scholar as 'the most original' part of the Gilbertine Rule (B. Bolton, *The Medieval Reformation* (London, 1983), 85).

could write of the two sorts of women: those who were lettered and those who were illiterate.[176] This distinction was reinforced by the Rule's insistence that the lay sisters, like the *conversi*, speak only in English, which was also the language in which they made their profession.[177] Yet the literacy of the nuns was itself fairly rudimentary. They were expected to know the Psalter and other essential liturgical texts by heart, and the nuns who could read were required to study their one book a year.[178] But this begs a question. How many nuns could not read? The Rule certainly acknowledges that there were nuns incapable of reading, specifically referring to nuns *literata vel illiterata*, and it was normal to waive even the requirement to learn the Psalter for a nun who entered as a mature woman.[179] The evidence of literacy as a test to divide the nuns from the lay sisters is at best open to question.

A more realistic distinction was social. Virtually nothing is known of the recruitment of the *conversae*, though a single Watton charter is of interest. Early in the thirteenth century Agnes Engayne, daughter of Walter Engayne the younger, gave a carucate in Kilnwick with herself, two daughters, and Edusa her *ancilla*. It is likely that Agnes was entering the nunnery in retirement, with her maid being received as a lay sister. How far this situation was typical is impossible to determine, but it probably represents a frequent scenario. Accounts of twelfth-century monastic recruitment often tell of whole families and households entering religion; in such circumstances it is surely most likely that the servants exchanged one master (or mistress) for another, arrangements within the community replicating social divisions outside.[180] According to the *Vita*, the early recruits were willing to undertake the hardships imposed upon them by Gilbert's Rule since they were compelled by poverty and reduced

---

[176] 'et duas feminarum, litteratarum et litteras nescientium' (*Book of St Gilbert*, 52). In Abelard's arrangements for the Paraclete it was stipulated that the nun obedientiaries (with the exception of the chantress) be recruited from those 'quae litteris non intendunt', so that those who were literate might be free for study (*PL* 178, col. 281).

[177] Oxford, Bodl. Lib., MS Douce 136, fos. 88ᵛ, 100.

[178] This is discussed further in Ch. 3 below. The question of the literacy/illiteracy of nuns at this period requires further examination, but see E. N. Millett, 'Women in No Man's Land: English Recluses and the Development of Vernacular Literature in the Twelfth and Thirteenth Centuries', in C. Meale (ed.), *Women and Literature in Britain, c.1150–1500* (Cambridge, 1993), 86–103. Dr Millett suggests that there was a 'spectrum' of literacy amongst nuns and recluses, and points out (pers. comm.) that knowing texts by heart is not necessarily evidence for literacy.   [179] *Monasticon*, vi. 2. xlvii.

[180] *Yorkshire Deeds VI*, ed. C. T. Clay, Yorkshire Archaeological Society Record Series, 76 (1930), 96, no. 309. A particularly interesting example is recorded in the *Vita* of Stephen of Obazine where a lord left his castle for the monastery 'on carts with his children, wife, all the people of his house both men and women, each with their baggage and their animals' (*Vita Stephani*, 86–8. See also Barrière, *L'Abbaye cistercienne*, 123–5).

to beggary, so long 'as they were assured of payment for the rest of their lives'.[181] Indeed, the author even admits that their motives for joining the community may at best have been mixed, when he explicitly states that a virtue was made of necessity, and that in the case of some of them 'the object of their original resolution was perhaps less than ideal'.

In the 1160s the bishop of Norwich wrote of *sanctimoniales* and *sorores*, and by the time the *Vita* was written a clearer view of the distinguishing characteristics of the nun and lay sister had emerged.[182] But was it ever thus? Here we should compare the experience of other orders which provided for women in the twelfth century. Not all gave prominence in their rule to the lay sisterhood. The (admittedly exiguous) regulations for Fontevrault refer only once to *conversae*, who were responsible for looking after the nuns' dormitory.[183] In Abelard's letter of direction on the conventual life he distinguishes between the lay sisters (*conversae*) and the nuns (*moniales*). The former are said to have renounced the world and to have dedicated themselves to serving the nuns. They wear a religious, though not, it is emphasized, a monastic, habit, and like the infantry in the army are of lower rank than the nuns. Later, however, the sisters (*sorores*) are said to be responsible for all indoor women's work, such as making and washing clothes for all the community, bread-making, the dairy, and feeding hens and geese. No distinction is made between lay sisters and nuns; all seem expected to partake of this work.[184]

It has recently been suggested that in many nunneries the differences between nuns and *conversae* were for a long time blurred, and that the term *soror* is capable of varying interpretations. It was only as an increasing emphasis was placed on the contemplative duties of the women, which itself may have been the result of their growing isolation from men, that a gap opened between the contemplative nun and the lay sister who performed menial tasks.[185] At Prémontré in the early days the women

---

[181] 'dummodo de perpetuo vite stipendio fierent secure' (*Book of St Gilbert*, 36).

[182] Ibid. 34, 138. Yet sometimes the term *sorores* seems to be used for the nuns (ibid. 312).

[183] *PL* 162, col. 1081. Neither are they recorded at the English Fontevraudine houses in the 12th or 13th centuries. [184] *PL* 178, cols. 268, 276.

[185] Thompson, *Women Religious*, 146–9, where she makes reference primarily to the Premonstratensians and Arrouaisians. Her analysis is not, however, universally accepted: Milis, for example, certainly considered the Arrouaisian canonesses to be distinct from the *conversae* (Milis, *L'Ordre des chanoines réguliers*, 502–4). According to the *Vita*, Gilbert enjoined constant prayer and meditation upon his lay sisters as well as the nuns (*Book of St Gilbert*, 36). For Cistercian examples of lay sisters, see *Monasticon*, v. 676–7 (Nun Cotham): *EYC* i. 444, no. 564 (Basedale); Graves, 'Organisation of an English Cistercian Nunnery', 335 n. 11 (Stixwould); *Reg. Giffard*, 147–8 (Swine). In every case these women are styled *sorores* not *conversae*. Nichols, 'Internal Organisation', 33 n. 38, lists 11 English Cistercian nunneries with lay sisters, but he does not give references or specify whether they were styled *sorores* or *conversae*.

were styled *sorores* not *moniales*: they performed menial tasks that would certainly come to be associated with the lay sisterhood—including washing and cleaning for the men. At the same time, they also followed a lifestyle very similar to nuns *stricto sensu*.[186] Originally intended by Norbert for service in the world, especially in the care of the sick, in the following generation the women were deliberately restricted by Hugh de Fosse's codification of the Rule to a contemplative role.[187] The position at Obazine in its early days was analogous. Here the women who first joined Stephen's community similarly cooked and cleaned while the men were responsible for the heavier work outside.[188] A more rigid segregation may also have been a consequence of the establishment of independent communities of canonesses or nuns as the asssociation of women with male communities was increasingly regarded as unacceptable. The clearest example of this transition is found at Rolduc. Here the earliest women in the quasi-eremitical community were drawn from the household of Embricho. After years of vicissitudes in which the role and continued existence of the women were frequently questioned, the women were finally established in their own house in 1137. Here (according to the Rolduc annals) they began for the first time to sing the Psalter and the canonical Hours. This indicates that only now did the women acquire 'liturgical independence', and move from *sorores* to *sanctimoniales*. It was probably at this point that those women who did not or could not sing the offices were defined as lay sisters or, in the Premonstratensian houses, as *sorores non cantantes*.[189] Nuns and lay sisters could then be differentiated by a number of criteria; these determinants included whether or not they sang the offices, were literate, or were veiled.[190]

Can this model of development be paralleled amongst the Gilbertines? By contrast with the experiences just discussed, it seems that from their beginning a distinction was drawn between the nuns and sisters of Gilbert's

[186] van Waefelghem, 'Les Premiers Statuts', 53–6; de Fontette, *Les Religieuses*, 14–17, draws attention to the ambivalent position of these women half-way between the two states.

[187] How far his intentions were realized is debatable (C. Neel, 'The Origins of the Beguines' in J. M. Bennett, E. A. Clark, J. F. O'Barr, B. A. Vilen, and S. Westphal-Wihl (eds.), *Sisters and Workers in the Middle Ages* (Chicago, 1989), 252–4).

[188] *Vita Stephani*, 88–90.

[189] By the 13th century these Premonstratensian women now established, like the women of Rolduc, in their own community, were divided between the *sorores cantantes* (or *canonissae*), who wore the distinguishing mark of the veil, and the *sorores non cantantes*, who were now assimilated to the *conversae* (Berlière, 'Les Monastères doubles', 23; de Fontette, *Les Religieuses*, 21–2).

[190] Veiling was an important ritual, and de Fontette (ibid. 22, n. 63) points out that one disciplinary measure in Premonstratensian nunneries was its temporary withdrawal. In 1267/8 the lay sisters of Swine claimed to be equal with the nuns, and demanded that they too wear the veil, as they asserted was the custom elsewhere (*Reg. Giffard*, 147).

establishments; this is certainly the implication of Gilbert's own account of the creation of the first Sempringham community.[191] An early independent source, the letter of William, bishop of Norwich, in support of Gilbert during the lay brothers' revolt, also distinguishes between the *sanctimoniales* and the *sorores*.[192] Moreover, early charters never refer to *sorores* but only to *sanctimoniales* or *moniales* (and just occasionally to *ancillae Christi*), though a distinction is frequently made in charters between the *canonici* and *fratres*. This would suggest both that, whatever might have been the arrangement in other orders, amongst the Gilbertines there was clear demarcation of status, and that the *conversae* had even less recognition than their male counterparts. This different pattern amongst the Gilbertines can best be attributed to the fact that they emerged from a different milieu from those of Prémontré or Rolduc, for example. There the women were initially marginal adjuncts to an essentially male body, and the chief function of all the women was to care for the men's material needs. Gilbert's first community, founded in the following generation, was primarily for women, and from the beginning they needed servants, who, for reasons already noted, were best themselves incorporated under Gilbert's control. In Gilbertine houses, as in the 'Cistercian' English nunneries which so much resembled them, nuns and lay sisters probably existed side by side from the beginning.[193]

The section of the Gilbertine institutes devoted to the lay sisters is considerably the shortest.[194] Perhaps more than any other part of the Rule it is marked by its lack of coherent organization, and it seems clear that the institutes as they are presented represent a collection of sentences promulgated at succeeding general chapters with no later arrangement of the material. The prime obligation of the sisters was to show obedience, devotion, reverence, and honour to the nuns, whom they were to serve in all their necessities without complaint or demur.[195] There was never any

---

[191] *Monasticon*, vi. 2. xix, where reference is made to the care of the *sanctimoniales* and the *laicae* by the canons. The *Vita* distinguishes between the '*inclusio* monialium' and the '*vocatio sororum laicarum*' (*Life of St Gilbert*, 30, 34).   [192] *Book of St Gilbert*, 138.

[193] The Cistercian lay sisters must have performed the same kind of duties as in the Gilbertine double houses (e.g. see C. V. Graves, 'Stixwould in the Market-Place', in J. A. Nichols and L. T. Shank (eds.), *Medieval Religious Women. I. Distant Echoes*, Cistercian Studies, 71 (Kalamazoo, Mich., 1984), 213, and 'The Organization of an English Cistercian Nunnery in Lincolnshire', 344; and Nichols, 'Internal Organisation', 32–3).

[194] *Monasticon*, vi. 2. lii–liii. Additional references to the duties of the lay sisters are found in the institutes relating to the nuns. Other institutes are found in the section (lvi–lvii) headed *capitula institutionum communiter ad moniales et sorores pertinentium* discussed above.

[195] Ibid. lii. That this obligation was restated both in the 1223 and 1268 visitations suggests that the *sorores* were not wholly obedient to the choir nuns. These statutes laid down that if a sister refused to amend her ways on rebuke, on the next occasion she was to

possibility of a lay sister being accepted as a choir nun; like the *conversus*, the *soror* was always a monastic servant.[196] Failure to minister to the nuns brought heavy penalties, after the erring sister had been twice corrected.[197] Similarly, unauthorized entry into the church was followed after due warning by suspension from attendance at the church for thirty days.[198]

No sister was to enter the community until she was 20 years old. The new recruit would be assigned to a mature sister who would teach her her duties, and then after a year she would make her profession to the *magister*. The novices were subject to a *magistra* who was responsible for their instruction in the order after the nuns' Vespers. Four times a year the sisters were reminded of that teaching by a reading of the Rule by the nuns.[199] The novices only attended part of the sisters' chapter, which was held three times a week in the presence of one of the prioresses or the sub-prioress together with the *scrutatrix* for the year and either one of the *scrutatrices* of the cloister or another mature nun. Here all complaints were to be adjudicated except cases that involved a nun as well.[200] The sisters wore the same habit as the nuns' with the exception of the cowl and scapular, which were replaced with sheepskin cloaks and hoods of the same design as the scapular.[201] If infirmity did require that they wore additional fine-woven tunics of wool, these were not to be worn openly but under their other clothes, presumably so that the distinction between the dress of the nuns and sisters might be maintained. All their clothing was to be coarse and old, of black cloth, according to Gilbert's original stipulation that their clothing should be *abjecta*; their bedding was to be as the nuns', except for the latters' coverings and quilts. The essential duties of the sisters were to carry out all manual work within the nuns'

---

remove her black veil and wear a white for as long as the *magister* insisted (Oxford, Bodl. Lib., MS Douce 136, fos. 88ᵛ, 100).

[196] *Monasticon*, vi. 2. li. Here again the Gilbertine arrangements for these 'monastic vassals' were modelled on Cistercian practices. Only one Cistercian lay sister is ever known to have been allowed to cross the divide and take her place in the choir (Donnelly, *The Decline of the Medieval Cistercian Laybrotherhood*, 61).

[197] *Monasticon*, vi. 2. lii. There is no evidence of discord between the lay sisters and nuns at Gilbertine houses (see Nichols, 'Internal Organisation', 33, for dissension at the Cistercian houses of Swine and Sinningthwaite), though see above n. 195.

[198] *Monasticon*, vi. 2. lii. Elkins suggests that this implies that some lay sisters spent long periods in prayer (*Holy Women*, 140): it seems more likely that this regulation is intended to distinguish further between the status of the contemplative nuns and the working sisters, though see above (n. 185) for Gilbert's intention that the sisters as well as the nuns should pray and meditate.   [199] *Monasticon*, vi. 2. lii–liii, lvi.

[200] Ibid. lii.

[201] Ibid. This is in contrast with the Cistercian *sorores*, who wore white veils, while the nuns wore black (Nichols, 'Internal Organisation', 33).

buildings, though if any task was too heavy then the nuns were expected to give assistance. The sisters were responsible for cleaning the church floor, the cloister, and the chapter house for the Easter ceremonies, and additionally performed a wide range of tasks including preparing the thread for the shoemakers as well as brewing and cooking. In the kitchen they carried out menial tasks like chopping vegetables under the command of the nun cook, while they were also responsible for serving at table, and they looked after the female guests in the convent guesthouse.[202] Weaving was also a task of the sisters, though if the weaving was too onerous it was permissible for hired male weavers to be brought in to help under the supervision of a lay brother. No material for weaving was to be received from another house of the order without the *magister*'s permission, nor was any weaving work to be sent from one community to another. Nothing woven (such as towels or veils) by the sisters was to be sold to the laity without licence on pain of excommunication. Like the lay brothers, they followed a simplified liturgical pattern adapted so that as little time as possible was lost from their labouring duties. They communicated eight times a year at the same times as the *conversi*, while their novices communicated only three times during the year.[203]

There is no early indication of the number of *conversae* in the Gilbertine houses. The regulation stipulating the size of individual houses groups nuns and sisters together and there are no more figures until 1376. The latter show that whereas the lay brethren were now an insignificant element in the priories, and in some cases had disappeared altogether, the sisters were still present in some numbers. In general the ratio of nuns to sisters varied between two and four to one; at Sempringham there were 56 nuns and 18 sisters.[204] Early in the thirteenth century bishop Hugh of Wells had fixed the number of nuns at 30 and lay sisters at 10 in the Cistercian nunnery of Nun Cotham.[205] It is likely that the internal arrangements at this Lincolnshire house were similar to those at neighbouring Gilbertine communities. If these numbers do reflect conditions at the latter, then it would seem that the lay sisterhood remained as numerically important until at least the end of the fourteenth century. The reason for

---

[202] *Monasticon*, vi. 2. lii. St John Hope suggested that at Watton the western range of the nuns' cloister doubled as the lay sisters' quarters and at the upper level as the guest-house ('The Gilbertine Priory of Watton, in the East Riding of Yorkshire', *Archaeological Journal*, 58 (1901), 18). [203] *Monasticon*, vi. 2. lii.
[204] Owen, *Church and Society*, 144–5. 6 sisters were also found at St Katherine's, Lincoln, where they were clearly employed in the hospital attached to the canons-only priory. The 'Cistercian' nunneries of Fosse, Gokewell, and Heynings also recorded sisters at this time.
[205] *Monasticon*, v. 677.

their success and survival when compared with their male equivalents may well be that while the lay brethren could readily be replaced by hired secular labourers (who had in any case been employed for many tasks since the earliest days of the order) such an opportunity was not open for the women. Suspicion of secular servants working within the precincts or the community had occasioned the introduction of the lay sisters at the beginning; it was much less easy to replace female menial labourers working within the convent than it was to replace male labourers working without.

The canons

The Gilbertine institutes for the canons are heavily dependent on models found in the Cistercian institutes, *Ecclesiastica Officia*, and *Usus Conversorum*. In this they were typical of the institutes of reformed Augustinian canons such as Prémontré, Arrouaise, and Oigny, all of which borrowed heavily from the white monks.[206] However, in contrast with the well-ordered arrangement of the latter customaries, which in the case of the mid-twelfth-century Premonstratensian statutes are carefully organized in *distinctiones* in imitation of the *Decretum*, the Gilbertine statutes are a hodge-podge collection in thirty-seven chapters, which, though covering most aspects of the daily life and liturgical round of the canons, are difficult to categorize neatly, and are occasionally even repetitive.[207]

Gilbertine canons in double houses had a dual function: they lived a regular life common to all reformed Augustinian communities of the twelfth century, and they served the spiritual needs of the nuns, to whom they were in theory, though increasingly not in practice, subordinate. While the daily life and observances of the Gilbertine canons in men-only communities must have been almost indistinguishable from that of their neighbours in other reformed Augustinian congregations, or amongst the white monks, where the Gilbertines did have to be more innovative was

---

[206] So, for example, the opening chapter of the Gilbertine Rule for canons (ibid. vi. 2. xxvii) copies the prohibition from the Cistercian Institute 78 forbidding boys save novices to be brought up in the priories; ch. ix (ibid. xxviii) opens with regulations governing the creation of a new community, taken from Institute 12, while ch. xii (ibid. xxix–xxx), which is the longest and is primarily concerned with the ecclesiastical office, is almost wholly taken from the *Officia Ecclesiastica*.

[207] For example, ch. xxxiv (ibid. xxxv) is a lengthy collection of rules relating to bloodletting, with the rubric 'de minuendis et quomodo se debent habere in minutione'. Virtually all is taken from the *Ecclesiastica Officia* ch. xc (*Monuments Primitifs*, 198–201). This is followed by a shorter chapter, headed 'de minutione et loco et tempore minutionis' (*Monasticon*, vi. 2. xxxv–xxxvi), whose first sentence is taken verbatim from the Cistercian Institutes (Canivez, *Statutes*, i. 23), which reiterates some of the material in ch. xxxiv, while adding material relating to the blood-letting of the women in Gilbertine double houses.

in devising regulations for their canons in double houses. Each of these required a minimum of seven canons, and a maximum of thirty, unless resources allowed a larger number.[208] Following the lay brothers' revolt, the utmost care was taken that they neither spoke to or heard the nuns except at mass, which was celebrated daily by only two or three canons in the nuns' half of the conventual church, or when absolute necessity demanded.[209] The full community of canons only visited the nuns' church on fourteen of the most solemn feasts of the year. They entered through a door cut in the dividing wall of the presbytery, after which they processed around the nuns' cloister, though always unseen, curtains being hung around the cloister and at the church door to this end. These solemn processions, the liturgical high points of the Gilbertine year, included the whole community, the canons being followed by the nuns, ranked in order of seniority of profession, the lay sisters, religious novices, and the novices of the *conversae*.[210] Only then was a sermon preached in the nuns' church, while only those of the highest authority, such as the papal legate, bishops, and archdeacons, might preach in the nuns' chapter.[211]

Secular business and necessary communication were also carefully monitored. Crucial to security arrangements were the turntable windows in the window-house (*domus fenestrae*) which constituted the frontier post between the two sectors. These were controlled, on the canons' side, by a responsible canon subject to the cellarer, and known as the *frater fenestrae* or *fenestrarius*, while two reliable nuns fulfilled a similar role for the women. The smaller window served for communication between the nuns and canons, and between the nuns and their close relatives, while the larger (*magna fenestra versatilis*) enabled food, all of which was prepared in the women's kitchens, to be passed through to the men's refectories.[212]

---

[208] *Monasticon*, vi. 2. xxvii. These figures should be compared with the later maxima prescribed at the end of the 12th century (see below, Ch. 3).

[209] *Book of St Gilbert*, 138.

[210] *Monasticon*, vi. 2. xlix. The reference to the cloth dividing the men from women suggests that this pre-dates the later arrangements, when the nuns' part of the church was carefully demarcated by the dividing wall (ibid.). The only other occasion on which any canon would enter the nuns' church was on Good Friday, when two canons entered the deserted church to place the Cross on the ground. After it had been venerated by the women the men removed it (ibid. xlix–l). [211] Ibid. xxxi.

[212] The dimensions of these windows were carefully laid down (ibid. xlv–xlvi). Severe penalties were imposed on all responsible, from the prior to the carpenter, for increasing the size of these windows. Graham (*St Gilbert*, 57) wrote that the turntable windows connected the men's refectories with the nuns' quarters. Such an arrangement is not borne out in the excavated record, and it seems more likely that food was conveyed from the nuns' kitchen through the window-house to the canons' frater, a distance of 350 feet at Watton. It is not surprising that in the late Middle Ages the canons had their own kitchen (St John Hope, 'The Gilbertine Priory of Watton', 28).

The rigid segregation institutionalized in the Gilbertine Rule was given physical shape in the topography of the double priories. Excavations at Sempringham and Watton suggest that the ensemble was enclosed by a wall, while the nuns' quarters, grouped around a cloister lying to the north of their church, were themselves separated from other conventual buildings by a wall and ditch.[213] A free-standing building housed the parlour, where some conversation amongst the nuns was allowed, the prioress heard confessions, the Rule was occasionally expounded, and high-ranking female guests entertained.[214] The canons' buildings at Watton, and probably at the other priories, were similarly disposed around a cloister to the north of their own church, and the whole, along with monastic offices and workshops, lying some distance to the east of the nuns' lodgings, and the majority of the buildings sited in the outer court.[215] The two groups of buildings were linked by a passage which held the window-house. Both the layout and the structure emphasized an isolation of all senses except hearing, and even that was strictly regulated.[216] Unfortunately, no Gilbertine double house has been adequately excavated or its architecture discussed. Moreover, most standing remains (such as the prior's lodging at Watton) date from the later medieval period and reflect an expression of the monastic life very different from the first Gilbertine generations. The most impressive remains of a Gilbertine double house are at Chicksands, but the church and part of the cloister were destroyed in the sixteenth century and the post-Dissolution transformation of the remaining wings of the cloister as a house for the Osborn family makes it difficult to reconstruct the original layout with precision.[217] Neither is

---

[213] The institutes laid down that 3 marks per annum was to be used to enclose the nuns' quarters with a ditch and wall or hedge (*Monasticon*, vi. 2. xlv).

[214] Ibid. xlvii, l; Graham, *St Gilbert*, 55–6. The guest-house itself was remote from the nuns' dwellings, and staffed by the lay sisters (*Monasticon*, vi. 2. li).

[215] A miracle story refers to the monastic kitchens and adjacent workshops at Sempringham (*Book of St Gilbert*, 102). Like the Cistercians and other of the 'new' orders which employed lay brethren, the Gilbertines almost certainly housed their *conversi* in the west claustral range of the priories, though later changes to the plan of priories that have either survived or have been excavated do not permit any such quarters to be located at the present time. Early buildings, however, including a chapel, may well have been separate from those of the canons rather than integrated into the church/cloister complex, as was the case at Cistercian Meaux (C. Norton and D. Park (eds.), *Cistercian Art and Architecture in the British Isles* (Cambridge, 1986), 66). In Cistercian abbeys the lay brethren also ate in a separate refectory (ibid. 161, 185). Cf. Colvin, *The White Canons*, 361 and n. 3.

[216] A point well made by Elkins, *Holy Women*, 141–4.

[217] Sempringham was excavated shortly before the Second World War, which prevented completion. Preliminary findings are discussed in R. Graham and H. Braun, 'Excavations on the Site of Sempringham Priory', *Journal of the British Archaeological Association*, NS 5

a detailed comparison of Gilbertine plans with those of other post-Conquest English nunneries of a similar size and status possible, since there has been hardly any investigation of the latter either.[218] The only 'Cistercian' nunnery to have received more than the most cursory architectural and archaeological attention is Marham, founded *c*.1249.[219] Yet it is an inadequate comparator: Marham was a late foundation, very poor (only Catley was as scantily endowed amongst Gilbertine houses), and there is no evidence of internal arrangements parallel to those in Gilbertine houses. Its church was undivided, and like many post-Conquest nunneries consisted of a simple aisleless parallelogram. Though its length (194 feet) was only some 30 feet less than Watton, and its width, at 30 feet, only half Watton's (which had to accommodate two aisles), the Gilbertine church seems to have been a considerably more sophisticated building.

Doubtless the first buildings of Gilbertine foundations consisted of modest, easily erected structures, probably of wood, which would gradually be replaced as resources allowed. How far the first double houses were segregated is unclear, though it seems that from the beginning the women were in some way separated from the lay brothers' enclosures.[220] The earliest descriptions of the layout of the communities are found in the bishop of Norwich's letters written to the pope in favour of the Gilbertines at the time of the lay brethren's revolt. The *conversi* had alleged that the canons and nuns worshipped together in the same church; in his letter of support bishop William *again* stressed the segregation of the nuns, drawing particular attention to the fact that not even the prior was allowed to see or talk with the nuns and that the eucharist was

(1940), 73–101. The most detailed excavation of a double house was that at Watton, carried out by W. H. St John Hope between 1893 and 1898 and described in 'The Gilbertine Priory of Watton', 1–34. The site is also discussed and illustrated in D. Knowles and J. K. S. St Joseph, *Monastic Sites from the Air* (Cambridge, 1952), 246–7. This survey also provides a brief description of Catley (250–1), whose buildings have now entirely disappeared. The fullest description of Chicksands, including a reproduction of a 17th-century plan of the conventual buildings, is found in *VCH Bedfordshire*, ii. 272–5. The only Gilbertine priory to have received a full archaeological study is St Andrew's, York, an atypical house, both as regards its urban site and date of foundation (R. L. Kemp, *The Church and Gilbertine Priory of St Andrew, Fishergate*, Archaeology of York, 11, fasc. 2 (York, 1995)).

[218] For a brief overview, and discussion of the potential for future archaeological research, see R. Gilchrist, 'The Archaeology of Medieval English Nunneries: A Research Design', in R. Gilchrist and H. Mytum (eds.), *The Archaeology of Rural Monasteries*, BAR British Series, 203 (1989), 251–60.

[219] J. A. Nichols, 'The Architectural and Physical Features of an English Cistercian Nunnery', in J. R. Sommerfeldt (ed.), *Cistercian Ideals and Reality*, Cistercian Studies, 60 (Kalamazoo, Mich., 1978), 319–28.　　　[220] *Book of St Gilbert*, 154.

received in such a way that neither giver nor receiver saw the other.[221] His report on the episcopal inquiry states that the canons had their own oratories and enclosures (*claustra*) completely distinct and separate from the nuns'. They only joined the women at a signal, when they crossed to the conventual church where they celebrated mass and then returned to their own quarters. This arrangement was now changed, at the pope's command, so that only two or three canons celebrated while the remainder stayed in their own oratories, a regulation of which the bishop makes clear both he and Gilbert disapproved. At the same time the *conversi* who used to go to the nuns' church for the night office and Matins were now to attend only the canons' church.[222] Similarly, the letters of other bishops emphasize the nuns' claustration. Henry of Blois wrote that the canons only had access to the nuns at times of urgent necessity, and then only when witnessed by both men and women in the community; Roger of Pont l'Évêque reported how the canons, though in the same enclosure, lived and ate apart.[223] The prior of Bridlington explicitly stated that the *magister* had stipulated that the canons' dwelling lay well apart from the nuns' quarters and churches.[224] Yet, again, these arrangements may not reflect conditions in the very early years. Constable has pointed out that it would have been very difficult logistically for the nun of Watton to meet her lover had the Gilbertine layout as described by the bishops been fully in place, while the presence of an anchorite living next to the conventual church at Watton 'suggests a degree of openness'.[225] This hypothesis is supported by archbishop Roger's remark that he had ordered Gilbert to separate the nuns from the canons according to the papal injunction.[226]

By the 1160s, therefore, the design of the Gilbertine house appears to have been established. It was certainly in place when the *Vita* was written. This again emphasized how the canons normally lived and worshipped far apart from the nuns. They only entered the nuns' enclosure to administer sacraments, and then only in the presence of many witnesses. The nuns who had occasion to speak with the men might be heard, but never seen with uncovered faces. Messages were passed between the community and outside world by four senior religious, two men and women, who likewise could only speak with each other and

---

[221] Ibid., 138, 140, letters 1 and 2.   [222] Ibid. 138, letter 1.
[223] Ibid. 146, 150, letters 4, 6.   [224] Ibid. 154, letter 8.
[225] Constable, 'Aelred of Rievaulx', 219, 223–4.
[226] *Book of St Gilbert*, 152, letter 7. This echoes bishop William of Norwich's statement.

could not be seen. The canons worshipped in their own oratory but mass was celebrated in the conventual church, which was divided by a wall, 'so that the men cannot be seen, nor the women heard'.[227]

This dividing screen or wall seems to have reached almost to the roof. One (or perhaps two) openings containing turntables were set in it at the eastern end, so contrived that no one could be seen through the aperture, through which holy water, the stone for the kiss of peace, and the consecrated elements were passed from the canons to the nuns.[228] At Sempringham the shrine of the founder was also inserted into this wall, so that it was approachable from both sides, appropriately symbolizing the Gilbertine double community.[229] The excavated church at Sempringham was that rebuilt in the early fourteenth century, by which time the twelfth-century church was seriously dilapidated, though remains of a thirteenth-century crypt were also found, and the design of its twelfth-century predecessor can only be surmised.[230] Changes may well have been introduced as the *conversi* declined in importance, and Graham plausibly suggested that the north aisle added to the canons' nave was intended for the laity who visited the church on Palm Sunday and Good Friday, and also in order that they might have more convenient access to Gilbert's shrine.[231] The original church was about 250 feet long, though it was significantly lengthened later to some 325 feet, making it

---

[227] Ibid. 46. Unfortunately, none of these churches survives above ground, though two-aisle naves in parish churches are not unknown. Perhaps the best example is at Hannington (Northamptonshire), dating from the late 13th century, a church whose advowson was held for a short while by Sempringham. Though the two naves are open, being separated by an arcade, the plan of this church gives some idea of the Gilbertine design (N. Pevsner, *Northamptonshire* (2nd edn., rev. B. Cherry, Harmondsworth, 1973), 245).

[228] *Monasticon*, vi. 2. liii. This complete segregation was relaxed in 1307, when papal permission was given for grated windows to be made through which the nuns might observe the Mass (*Cal. Papal Letters*, ii. 22). The seeming remains of the turntable were found during the excavations at Watton ('The Gilbertine Priory of Watton', 10). The tiny window where confessions were heard was probably set close by. Confessions were carefully supervised by nuns and canons (*Monasticon*, vi. 2. liii).

[229] *Book of St Gilbert*, 130, 190—where the chest holding Gilbert's relics is said to have been placed on a marble wall, which might suggest that at this point the dividing wall did not reach to the roof (Graham and Braun, 'Excavations', 82). As Foreville has pointed out, pilgrims visiting the shrine were also divided by gender (*Book of St Gilbert*, p. xxvi n. 1). For examples of this practice, see ibid. 294, 296, and 298 where the father of a *miraculée* stated that he was not present at her cure because he was not allowed entry to the nuns' inner chancel.

[230] Graham and Braun, 'Excavations', 81, 84–5, 93. The excavated church at Watton appeared to be the late-12th-century rebuilding of the church destroyed by fire in 1167 ('The Gilbertine Priory of Watton', 13).

[231] Graham and Braun, 'Excavations', 80, 93–4. By analogy with Cistercian abbeys, the *conversi* probably worshipped in the western half of the nave.

comparable to several of the more substantial Augustinian houses, such as Bristol or Christchurch.[232]

There was nothing unusual or novel about such architectural arrangements. The housing of male and female religious who lived in close proximity to each other was naturally a problem that exercised all such communities.[233] Most of the twelfth-century communities for men and women also prescribed segregation; indeed, after the Second Lateran Council's decree forbidding nuns from singing in the same choir as men, they had to.[234] The immediate model may well have been Cluniac Marcigny, where, though the dwellings of the monks and nuns were separate, a church was shared. This had two choirs divided by a wooden screen in an arrangement akin to that of Sempringham. At Obazine the nuns' church was divided into two unequal parts by a wall running laterally north–south. The eastern, smaller section was for the use of the monks, who passed the eucharist through an opening in the wall, which was also pierced by an iron grille. Communication with the outside world was here maintained by way of a corridor leading from the nuns' cloister and with two doors, the keys to that at the cloister end being held by the prioress, while a lay brother held the key to the outer door.[235] Abelard expected Heloise's nuns to be carefully segregated from the monks. The administration of communion and the last rites to sick nuns in the infirmary were to be given in the presence of the whole convent, though they were separated by a screen. The monks would celebrate in their own church, and those few who officiated in the nuns' church were not to be seen by the women, which must imply some sort of partition within the church.[236] At Fontevrault Robert's followers were famously divided by gender and status, living in buildings each appropriately dedicated.[237] The men normally worshipped in their own church (dedicated as at Sempringham to St John the Evangelist). A single priest-monk accompanied by a deacon and clerk would visit the nuns' church of St Mary only to hear confessions and to celebrate mass. The high altar was screened from the body of the church; a connecting door was only opened at communion.[238]

---

[232] Ibid. 90–1.

[233] For some Anglo-Saxon solutions, see above, 'Continuity and native tradition', and Yorke, '"Sisters Under the Skin"?', 97.   [234] *Histoire des Conciles*, v. i. 732–3.

[235] *Vita Stephani*, 98–100. See Golding, 'Hermits, Monks and Women', 132.

[236] *PL* 178, cols. 278, 285. The nuns of Prémontré may well also have communicated via a window, since Jacques de Vitry complained that their 'windows were turned into doors', a criticism echoed in some of the 13th-century Gilbertine statutes (de Fontette, *Les Religieuses*, 17 and n. 31).   [237] Smith, 'Robert of Arbrissel', 180.

[238] *PL* 162, cols. 1063, 1081–2.

Conclusion

The order devised by the early Gilbertines between *c*.1148 and 1223 possessed a well-articulated command and disciplinary structure in which all elements in the community, male and female, clerical and lay, had a clearly defined place subject to the all-powerful authority of the *magister*. They had apparently resolved the two most pressing and divisive tensions so often found in twelfth-century reform groups. The status of the *conversi* had been firmly established and their subservience assured; their decline in following generations would be due to economic rather than disciplinary reasons. The women who had followed Gilbert, seemingly in such large numbers, had been regularized and their function and role in the community defined. Thus they stood sharply contrasted to those women in other orders, whose origins the Gilbertines closely paralleled, who were by the early thirteenth century regarded, at best, as unfortunate anomalies. Such an integration had, however, been costly.

Not only were the disciplinary regulations perhaps among the harshest and most punitive ever devised for female communities, but the women's status was undermined almost from the beginning. The opening chapter of the institutes for the nuns (which seems to date from the order's early years) reads, 'let the more care be taken that everything necessary for the nuns be administered more quickly and faithfully, and let their church and other buildings be prepared and made more finely, constructed with more care and more nobly than [those of] the men'.[239] Moreover, the earliest papal privileges (of 1178) are addressed primarily to the nuns, who were clearly still regarded as the most important element in the double houses. The alienation of any possessions without their general assent is expressly forbidden, while the whole exterior economy of the communities was entrusted to the canons, who would 'faithfully guard the *temporalia* for the maintenance of the nuns'.[240] Within a generation all this had changed. By the time Gilbert's *Vita* was written, the subordinate status of the women was recognized; it was essential that communities of girls (*puellarum*) be ruled by the governance of monks or clerks to both protect and teach the nuns.[241] There are other indications of the relative deterioration of the women's position. Benefactions which in the early

---

[239] *Monasticon*, vi. 2. xliv.   [240] Cheney, 'Papal Privileges', 59.
[241] *Book of St Gilbert*, 46. This is a paraphrase of Gratian's dictum that nuns be ruled by monks (*Decretum* C. 18, q. 2, cc. 21–4). I have examined the decline in the nuns' status more fully in 'The Distortion of a Dream', 60–78.

years had been typically addressed to the *sanctimonialibus* are now increasingly directed to the convent. During the thirteenth century addresses to 'the prior and convent' become standard, and no one examining grants made to Gilbertine houses at this time would realize from the wording of the charters that these communities included women at all.[242] An analysis of the Gilbertine statutes of the thirteenth and early fourteenth centuries reinforces this conclusion. There are clear signs that resources intended for the nuns are being diverted for the benefit of the canons alone, while efforts are made to maintain the strict seclusion of the women from the outside world.[243] By 1371 the nuns of Sempringham were sufficiently desperate at their declining status to appeal to the crown that the canons continue to minister to them, and that property ceded by their benefactors for the express use of the nuns should not be alienated to the men.[244]

How is this state of affairs to be explained? As has already been seen, the introduction of the canons represented a fundamental shift in the Rule's organization, and it is possible to interpret the male element as a parasitic organism mutating Gilbert's original vision for his communities. In one sense, too, the canons' emergence as the dominant partners in the Gilbertine polity can be seen as an inevitable consequence of the communities' inner dynamic. Gilbert had proved both autocratic and weak. He had driven his lay male followers to actual rebellion, and his conduct during the nun of Watton scandal revealed a fundamental lack of control over his female disciples. His communities were hardly model advertisements of the desirability, or even possibility, of double houses. Gilbert responded to, rather than dictated, developments, and legislated on the hoof. There is little evidence in contemporary sources that he ever had a clear coherent plan for an institution where men and women would live in heavenly harmony under the benevolent dictatorship of the *magister*; rather he assembled an eclectic *florilegium* of monastic statutes from a large corpus of material, which the *Vita* admits included not only 'the great and most important regulations, but also some small and trivial ones'.[245]

---

[242] Amongst many examples, see the early grants of Godwin the Rich and Ralph de Badvent to Sempringham (*Sempringham Charters*, xv. 158, 159) and the grants by Gilbert of Benniworth to Nun Ormsby *c*.1200 (*Gilbertine Charters*, 45–6). An exception to this trend is the foundation charter of Shouldham addressed to the 'nuns and their clerical and lay brethren (*Monasticon*, vi. 2. 975).   [243] See below, Ch. 3: 'Disciplining the community'.

[244] *Cal. Pat. R, 1370–1374*, 87, 110.

[245] *Book of St Gilbert*, 48. For an illuminating, and contrary, interpretation, see S. Elkins, 'All Ages, Every Condition and Both Sexes: The Emergence of a Gilbertine Identity', in J. A. Nichols and L. T. Shank (eds.), *Medieval Religious Women. I. Distant Echoes*, Cistercian Studies, 71 (Kalamazoo, Mich., 1984), 172.

Gilbert's shortcomings demonstrated the need for a strong leader. Roger, prior of Malton, was in some sense a natural candidate. But he came from a different milieu, a cloister where nuns were unknown, and it is hardly surprising that the nuns' role was increasingly questioned. With Roger at the helm, the path was set for the canons to achieve total control. Whether or not it was coincidental that Roger was appointed as *magister* just as the position of women in the religious life was everywhere being challenged, this conjunction certainly affected the future orientation of the order. By the beginning of the thirteenth century the age of radical experimentation in forms of religious life for women was not over, as the emergence of the beguines testified, but the attempt to integrate women fully into reformed monastic life had run into the sands.

It is ironic that the Gilbertine order, of all the new communities which catered for women, should be the one in which women ultimately had the least authority. The English 'Cistercian' nunneries allowed their prioresses, elected by the nuns, considerable authority and even permitted their engagement in temporal affairs. Their *magistri* acted as the nuns' representatives, not their rulers, and the men of these communities were clearly regarded as ancillary to the nuns, rather than vice versa.[246] By the end of the twelfth century the Arrouaisian nunnery of Harrold was ruled not by a prior, but by a prioress in conjunction with a *magister* who, as at the Cistercian houses just described, seems to have been subject to the prioress's ultimate authority.[247] Premonstratensian nunneries, too, were ruled by a woman, first styled *priorissa* and later *magistra*; the fact that these were forbidden from receiving the profession of canons attached to their houses suggests that they retained a considerable degree of control over these communities, while *formulae* of the few surviving grants to English Premonstratensian nunneries suggest that the nuns were superior to the brethren in these houses.[248] At Fontevrault the early pre-eminence of the nuns survived throughout the medieval period. The abbess retained the supreme authority she had had during the time of Robert of Arbrissel. It was expected that she would represent the order in secular business outside the abbey walls, and that she would be the community's chief business manager. Moreover, the monks who

---

[246] Graves ('Organisation of a Cistercian Nunnery', 338) points out that the *magister*'s 'role as representative of the house was clearly a matter of convenience, not of prerogative'. See also Nichols, 'Internal Organisation', 27.

[247] *Records of Harrold Priory*, 9–10, 54–9.

[248] Thompson, *Women Religious*, 139, 141 n. 51, 142. The later *provisor* of the nunnery of Orford who looked after its finances (ibid. 257) was seemingly analogous to the *magistri* found in English 'Cistercian' nunneries.

served as administrators in Fontevraudine nunneries were subject to the prioress.[249]

Such divergences in custom are not easy to explain, but various hypotheses can be proposed. In the case of the 'Cistercian' nunneries the very absence of a definitive Rule for nuns may have worked in their favour. A Cistercian prioress might take over all the powers and wield the same authority as a Cistercian abbot precisely because there was no administrative machinery in the Rule for such a phenomenon. Moreover, neither the *custodes* nor the *magistri* were integral to the Rule, and they were often, indeed, appointed only on a temporary basis. There were thus no opportunities within the structure, such as existed in the Gilbertine institutes, for the *magister* to assume authority from the prioress. The Premonstratensian and Arrouaisian nuns seem to have gained autonomy, rather paradoxically, as a consequence of their orders moving away from too close an involvement with female religious. The prioress was thus able to fill a power vacuum left by the departure of the prior and canons. At Fontevrault, it is possible (as Gold suggests) that women were fully integrated into the organizational structure rather than being peripheral accessories to predominantly male groups, while the 'structured inclusion of men' gave a greater cohesion to the community.[250] While such an explanation is appealing, the same could also be said of the Gilbertine organization. A more plausible reason can perhaps be found in Robert of Arbrissel's belief that his submission, and that of his male followers, to female authority had a penitential and humbling function, whereby salvation was achieved by self-mortification. A further explanation may be found in Robert's choice of Petronilla as his successor—it is inconceivable that Gilbert would have followed suit. She, like Roger of Malton, was a forceful and dominant leader; both were well suited to steer their communities through the difficult times following the founders' deaths. But the choice of a woman to rule Fontevrault and a man to rule Sempringham ensured the divergence of the two communities which at first sight had appeared so similar.[251]

There is one final point. Gilbertine nunneries were with very few exceptions considerably wealthier than their 'Cistercian' or even Augustinian counterparts. As will be seen later, their patrons and

---

[249] P. S. Gold, *The Lady and the Virgin: Image, Attitude and Experience in Twelfth-Century France* (Chicago, 1985), 98–108. Abelard's letter of direction for the Paraclete also emphasizes that the abbot should be subject to the abbess's authority (*PL* 178, cols. 276–7 (Epist. VIII)).   [250] Gold, *The Lady and the Virgin*, 111–12.

[251] The contrast is also made by Gold, ibid. 97–8.

benefactors were attracted from similar social strata with similar resources for pious giving. It can be hazarded that the very solidity of the Gilbertine constitution contributed to the relative temporal success of the priories. Benefactors understood when they bestowed grants on a Gilbertine foundation that it was well ordered, that the nuns were subject to firm discipline and had a place subordinate to the canons. When men and women came to purchase insurance for their souls it was well to know that the community with which they did business was secure.

3

The Life Within

Entering the House

There could be no closer tie between benefactor and priory than the placing of one or more members of the grantor's family as a nun or canon, or the reception of the grantor him- or herself as a member of the religious community.[1] Men and women entered the priories for a number of reasons. As the customary of the Augustinian canons of Springiersbach put it: 'some come from monasteries of our own order, nearby or distant, either as deserters of their place and profession or in order to follow the canonical way of life more strictly. Some come from communities of monks; these have neither been oblated by their kin nor as yet professed as monks, but have left during their novitiate. Some are secular clerks. Some are laymen, and these are of two kinds; some of them are young, and because of their age and intelligence are suitable for instruction in letters and promotion to clerical status, while others, older and of duller understanding, emulate the canonical life while retaining their lay status and, being placed under a Rule, are governed by a discipline appropriate for them.'[2] A nunnery was 'a career, a vocation, a prison, a refuge: to its different inmates the medieval nunnery was all of these things'.[3] Gilbertine nunneries were no exception. We can hardly ever explain, however, why recruits chose the Gilbertine alternative. Charters never record specific motives, and it can only be assumed that in the majority of cases the Gilbertines drew their nuns and canons from local families which had already developed ties with the house. One of Gilbert's miracle stories provides one possible explanation for a canon's entry into the community.

---

[1] There is now a substantial literature on monastic recruitment, though less attention has been devoted to nunneries of the 12th and 13th centuries. For a useful introduction to the subject, see J. H. Lynch, 'Monastic Recruitment in the Eleventh and Twelfth Centuries: Some Social and Economic Considerations', *American Benedictine Review*, 26 (1975), 425–47.

[2] *Consuetudines Canonicorum Regularium Springersbachenses-Rodenses*, ed. S. Weinfurter (Corpus Christianorum: Continuatio Mediaevalis, 48 (Turnhout, 1978), 123–4).

[3] Power, *Medieval English Nunneries*, 25.

While travelling between England and Normandy, a ship carrying a group of magnates including John, constable of Chester, the grandson of Eustace fitzJohn, the founder of Malton and Watton priories, and himself a leading patron of the order, ran into a storm. The holding up of Gilbert's scapular, which John had acquired as a relic from *magister* Roger, soon brought relief. One of the company, William, witnessed the miracle. He was perhaps in the household of one of the lords; certainly he was still a layman. He reported later how then he had had little appreciation of the order but that afterwards, when he had definitely decided to take the habit, that miracle was the chief factor in his decision to join the Gilbertines.[4]

Though we know little of why adults joined the community, in the case of mature women recruits it is likely that they entered as widows. Certainly that appears to be the implication behind Alvingham's promise to receive the wife of Lambert de Scoteni as a nun whenever it pleased her.[5] In many cases the right of entry was probably claimed as an insurance measure to guard against the contingencies of old age or hard times. Typically benefactors would reserve the option to enter a priory when they wished, while if they chose to stay in the world confraternal privileges would be granted.[6] Often it was agreed that both husband and wife should enter religion if they desired. One charter, that of Ridel and Alice of Keisby, specifies that either or both might enter Sempringham if they so wished; if they stayed in the world, then they were to receive burial rights.[7] Perhaps most of these anticipants of future entry expected to be received on their deathbed, though it is only occasionally possible to detect with certainty an *ad succurrendum* entrant.[8]

Some, perhaps the majority, were pledged as children: for although the Gilbertine Rule, like that of most of the new orders, frowned upon

---

[4] *Book of St Gilbert*, 290. Another *miraculée*, Felicia, a woman from Anwick, a village adjacent to Haverholme, vowed that if cured she would become a nun at Sempringham 'if permitted by the convent'. She clearly did not leave the world, however, for she reported in her testimony that to commemorate the miracle she visited the shrine every year with an offering. (*Book of St Gilbert*, 270–2.) Was her social status too lowly to admit her reception, was she otherwise unsuitable for life as a religious, or did she change her mind?

[5] Oxford, Bodl. Lib., MS Laud Misc. 642, fo. 60.

[6] e.g. 'Haverholme Priory Charters', 25–6.   [7] *Sempringham Charters*, xvii. 34.

[8] e.g. the grant by Juliana of Otby to Alvingham 'with her body before she received the habit of a nun' (Oxford, Bodl. Lib., MS Laud Misc. 642, fo. 79ᵛ). Another example is Nicholas II de Stuteville, who entered St Andrews, York, at the end of September 1233 and was dead by 19 October (*EYC* ix. 20; *Cal. Cl. R. 1231–4*, 264). *Ad succurrendum* grants are discussed below, p. 141.

oblates, there is clear evidence that even if this prohibition was not ignored in the letter, it was in spirit.[9] Perhaps the clearest example of what could only be defined as oblation is found in an Alvingham charter where Roger de Neville 'commended his daughter' into the hands of master Gilbert of Sempringham in the nuns' chapter at Alvingham 'that she might be made a nun amongst them when adult'.[10] Equally compelling evidence for the practice is found in Aelred's account of the nun of Watton. She had been received into the community at the age of 4 at the request of archbishop Henry Murdac of York. Henry was a supporter of the Gilbertines and was perhaps too powerful a patron to offend; it may also be the case that in the early years the Gilbertines were less strict about oblation than they were later to become.[11] It is also clear that the priories were educating children both male and female, and that though not all of these would stay in the community, these facilities were intended primarily for oblates. The Rule forbade the education of boys unless they were novices or probationary novices, while in 1223 pope Honorius III prohibited the order from admitting any girl to its priories to be brought up or educated unless she intended to become a nun, which clearly implies that there were girls in the priories who would expect to be made nuns on reaching adulthood.[12] It is likely that the majority of entrants to Gilbertine communities were given as children by their parents or other kin. This is certainly implied by most of the charters which refer to the granting of land along with one or more sons or daughters. The practice of oblation was too well established and useful to be resisted; too many potential benefactors would be offended or inconvenienced by its abolition, for all its potentially disruptive consequences in the cloister

---

[9] There is no full English study of oblation, but see J. H. Lynch, *Simoniacal Entry into the Religious Life, 1000–1260* (Columbus, Ohio, 1976), 36–50 and references there given. The frequency of Cistercian statutes against the practice indicates that they too found it extremely difficult to eradicate (ibid. 39–40, 57 n. 62). See also J. H. Lynch, 'The Cistercians and Under-Age Novices', *Cîteaux*, 3–4 (1973), 283–97.

[10] Oxford, Bodl. Lib., MS Laud Misc. 642, fo. 67ᵛ. This charter is dated 1179, by which time Gilbert is generally supposed to have given up the overall control of the order to Roger. This evidence suggests that, as has been argued above, he still retained personal authority over his communities.   [11] Constable, 'Aelred of Rievaulx', 206–7, 219.

[12] *Cal. Papal Registers*, i. 90; *Monasticon*, vi. 2. xxvii. This regulation is copied verbatim from the Cistercians (Canivez, *Statuta*, i. 31). At the end of the 12th century a peasant benefactor gave land to Alvingham with her brother to be held till he came of age. If he then wished to become a canon, or died before reaching adulthood, the canons would continue to hold the land freely; if he continued in the lay state then they would do him service for this land (Oxford, Bodl. Lib., MS Laud Misc. 642, fo. 108). See p. 170 for an illuminating example of a boy received into a priory to be brought up there until he decided whether or not to enter the cloister.

and its implicit denial of free will. A seemingly acceptable compromise was to refuse to profess nuns and canons before they reached adulthood (in this instance, at the age of 15), but to continue to receive children in the expectation that they would sooner or later enter the cloister.[13]

It is impossible to determine how many entered the priories as adults. The charters which refer to promises by a community to receive the donor when he or she was ready to leave the world naturally do not specify whether this option was ever taken up, or at what time. In most cases it is likely that entry was deferred until late in life. Some would delay until their deathbed, when they were received as *ad succurrendum* recruits.[14] These were usually regarded as fully religious as those who had joined the monastic community earlier in life, and indeed some who recovered from what had been imagined to be mortal illness found it very difficult to extricate themselves from these monastic vows. The Gilbertine Rule laid down that those who died thus habited were to be recorded in the martyrology of the house and their names written in the *breves mortuorum*.[15] That deathbed reception could be arranged in advance is implied in a charter of Fulk of Reedness in favour of Alvingham, which stipulated that if he wished to receive the religious habit either during his lifetime or at death he would be received honourably as a free man in the community.[16]

The ideal community

The Gilbertine Rule was unique in its stipulation of the maximum numbers that could be accommodated in each community. This section of the Rule dates (at least in the form in which it has been preserved) from between *c*.1185 and *c*.1195.[17] There were both economic and disciplinary

[13] This procedure of the *futurus monachus* was that sanctioned by Peter the Venerable. This typically Cluniac compromise allowed families to promise children to the abbey, and presumably also permitted their upbringing there, but delayed the actual reception till the age of 20 (Lynch, *Simoniacal Entry*, 39, 56 n. 59).

[14] The fullest general treatment of this topic remains L. Gougaud, 'Deathbed Clothing with the Religious Habit', in *Devotional and Ascetic Practices in the Middle Ages* (London, 1927), 131–45, but see also Lynch, *Simoniacal Entry*, 27–36, and Knowles, *Monastic Order in England*, 635–6, where he draws attention to the flouting of the Cistercian prohibition on *ad succurrendum* entry. [15] *Monasticon*, vi. 2. lv.

[16] 'honorifice sicut liberum hominem in congregacione sua' (*Gilbertine Charters*, 111).

[17] *Monasticon*, vi. 2. lviii. Mattersey, founded *c*.1185, figures in the list, Shouldham, founded in the mid-1190s, and certainly not before 1193, does not. Neither does Marlborough, which may have been founded as early as 1189. It was not, of course, unusual for the numbers of individual houses to be regulated according to their temporal means. See Lynch, *Simoniacal Entry*, 3–4, for early Carolingian and papal attempts at a more general control.

reasons for the imposition of these limits. There is a clear correlation between the scale of a community's complement and its economic base. The largest priory was Watton, followed by Sempringham, Chicksands, and Sixhills. Watton, Sempringham, and Chicksands were the wealthiest of the double houses throughout the Middle Ages and at the Dissolution. Similarly, the smallest house, Catley, was also the poorest.[18] The limitation on numbers can be related to another of the Gilbertine *capitula*, which stipulated that each double house should contain at least seven canons, or more 'si possessio domus permiserit', while fixing a maximum strength of thirty, unless additional endowments were received to cater for the increase 'so that the nuns be not harmed'.[19] The relative under-endowment of nunneries was always a problem. Poverty brought material discomfort and spiritual tensions: nunneries were often under pressure from their patrons to accommodate more religious than they could afford, and the only way these strains could be relieved was to accept endowments on entry. But this practice brought its own problems, for in an age more and more wary of simony in all its forms these grants, especially if fixed or required, could easily be interpreted as the purchase of spiritual reward.[20] There is clear evidence that canon lawyers were increasingly concentrating their attention on nunneries rather than male communities at the end of the twelfth and beginning of the thirteenth centuries, and that nunneries were forced into uncanonical positions by economic stress.[21]

Like all new orders, the Gilbertines vigorously opposed simoniacal entry. The Rule 'following the canons abhorred the heresy of simony'

[18] This correlation is neatly demonstrated in *Medieval Religious Houses*, 194.

[19] *Monasticon*, vi. 2. xxvii. There are occasional indications that endowments were made specifically in order that the size of the community might be increased. These grants were usually made with the expectation that the new canon would be responsible for saying masses for the benefactor and his family.

[20] For a general consideration of monastic simony, see Lynch, *Simoniacal Entry*. He makes the point (432) that these grants were *stricto sensu* dowry grants, i.e. the obligation to make a fixed payment for the reception of a novice 'over and above the statutory number of religious which [could] be supported from the endowment'. Lynch discusses the particular problems of the nunneries (158–9, 193–4). See also S. P. Thompson, 'Why English Nunneries had no History', in J. A. Nichols and L. T. Shank (eds.), *Medieval Religious Women. I. Distant Echoes*, Cistercian Studies, 71 (Kalamazoo, 1971), 138–9; and Burton, *Yorkshire Nunneries*, 21–3.

[21] The often-quoted canon 64 of the Fourth Lateran Council recognized the scale of the problem: 'Since the simoniacal stain has infected so many nuns to such a degree that they receive scarcely any sisters without a price, and they wish by pretext of poverty to palliate a crime of this sort, we prohibit entirely that this be done from now on' (cited Thompson, 'Why English Nunneries had no History', 139).

and forbade any payment to be demanded for the entry of any canon or nun, though anything freely given could be accepted.[22] Indeed, the new recruit was expected to make a gift of his property to the community, excepting only what had already been given to God or religion, or left to a lay person.[23] How far the prohibition of simony was respected or indeed could be enforced is a different matter. Sometimes, it seems clear that reception was dependent on a financial bargain. It would, for example, be hard to deny that the arrangement whereby Robert of Kirkby's daughter was received as a nun at Sempringham at the same time as her father gave property for which an additional payment of 20 shillings was received was suspect in canon law.[24] The problem is to determine how far gifts that so frequently accompanied a recruit were genuinely voluntary.[25]

One way to resolve those difficulties which so tempted nunneries to accept simoniac entrants was as far as possible to balance economic resources against the complement of nuns: this was what was being attempted by the Gilbertines at the end of the twelfth century.[26] But if avoidance of poverty and the sin of simony were factors which lay behind the Gilbertine restrictions, so too may have been the desire for good discipline. The numbers prescribed at the end of the twelfth century relate not to the nuns and canons, but to the nuns (and lay sisters, who are explicitly included in the figures) and brethren (including both canons and *conversi*), who were outnumbered two to one in all of the double houses. Such an arrangement may well have been intended to reduce the possibility of further internal unrest in the community.

It remains to ask how realistic were the prescribed maxima. Unfortunately, there is no record of the actual numbers of inmates of Gilbertine houses at this time, though at the time of the founder's death in 1189 the author of the *Vita* estimated that there were 700 men and 1,500 women

---

[22] *Monasticon*, vi. 2. xxi–xxii. Lynch has shown how the Gilbertine Rule was influenced in its vocabulary by canonists' texts (Lynch, *Simoniacal Entry*, 167–8 and 176–7, nn. 88–90). It is probably unwarranted to assume, as does Lynch (167), that this section of the Rule dates from *c*.1180; it may equally date from early in the 13th century. Another institute, which may be derived from Gilbert's original codification, suggests that what was condemned was not the offer of money but its concealment or retention by the entrant (*Monasticon*, vi. 2. lvi). [23] Ibid. xxvii.

[24] *Sempringham Charters*, xvi. 33. The payment for the land may have been intended to conceal the more serious offence of simoniacal entry.

[25] These are considered in more detail below, pp. 151–2.

[26] A similar attempt was made by bishop Hugh of Lincoln a few years later when his constitutions for the nunnery of Nun Cotham restricted numbers to 30 nuns, 10 *conversae*, 3 chaplains, and 12 *conversi* (*Monasticon*, v. 677).

in the order.[27] These figures are almost certainly an exaggeration.[28] The absence of figures from other houses, especially nunneries, at this time makes any comparison of the relative size of Gilbertine communities nearly impossible.[29] Undoubtedly some houses of the reformed orders were of considerable size. On Robert of Arbrissel's death in 1117 there were said to be between two and three thousand in the communities of Fontevrault.[30] In England, some of the early Cistercian houses were extremely large: in 1168 there were 140 monks and 500 *conversi* and lay servants at Rievaulx and, though this figure was perhaps extraordinary, there were 70 monks and 120 *conversi* at Waverley in 1187.[31] Though these figures may be inflated, there can be no doubt that during the twelfth century many Cistercian houses could stand comparison with the larger Benedictine communities.[32]

It is when the maxima of the Gilbertine houses are compared with such Benedictine abbeys that the contrast becomes most clear, and the implications of the size of the community for the communal and individual well-being of the Gilbertines are apparent. At this time the largest abbeys were probably St Albans, Christ Church, Canterbury, and Bury St Edmunds. In *c*.1210 the maximum number of monks at St Albans was fixed at 100; at Catley, one of the least endowed and significant of the Gilbertine houses, the total figure for monks and nuns was 95.[33] Even allowing for the much more luxurious communal and individual life-style of the Benedictine establishment, it is clear that Catley could never maintain its maximum complement with its meagre endowments.

Evidence for the size of Gilbertine communities in the thirteenth century is sparse, but does suggest that many houses continued to attract large numbers of recruits, which often resulted in financial difficulties.

---

[27] *Book of St Gilbert*, 192; cf. 54–6, 250.

[28] Though in 1176 cardinal-legate Hugh had also written that there were some 1,500 nuns in the order (ibid. 349). Foreville believes that the maxima were 'probably an underestimate' of the actual population (ibid., p. xxxiii).

[29] But see the case of Nun Cotham (above, n. 26).

[30] Knowles, *Monastic Order in England*, 204. The maxima can also be compared with the population of ten Fontevrault priories in 1209. These contained in general rather fewer nuns than the prescribed figures for the nearly contemporary Gilbertine priories, and far fewer men. Thus Le Breuil had 52 nuns and 9 monks, the highest number of monks recorded in these priories, and Boulauc 70 nuns, a prior, two priests, a clerk, and 31 lay brethren (Gold, *The Lady and the Virgin*, 110–11 n. 104).

[31] *The Life of Ailred of Rievaulx by Walter Daniel*, ed. and trans. F. M. Powicke (London, 1950), 38 and n.

[32] Knowles, *Monastic Order in England*, app. xvii. 713–14. Most Cluniac priories had 20 or fewer monks and it has been suggested that the average French Benedictine house at this time comprised some 30 monks.   [33] Ibid. 714.

In 1248 Bullington received papal permission to appropriate the church of Prestwold because there were 100 women in the community who were suffering in health for lack of necessities, and in 1310 the house, when requesting episcopal permission for the appropriation of Ingham, claimed that the excessive size of the community was a prime cause of poverty.[34] In 1247 there were said to be 200 women at Watton, and even though this was one of the wealthiest Gilbertine houses such a number must have been a great burden on its economy.[35] In the same year papal permission was given for the appropriation of Horbling to Sempringham, since there were 200 women living under the Gilbertine Rule who often lacked the necessities of life. Even allowing for probable exaggeration of their plight in a request for appropriation, the mid-thirteenth-century population of the mother house was evidently substantial.[36] Ten years later there were 52 nuns and 10 *conversi* at Chicksands who had to be dispersed to other houses of the order because of dearth, which seems to indicate that here too extreme poverty resulted from over-population.[37] It does seem that in general during the thirteenth century nunneries were larger than monasteries, and that this was recognized as a prime cause of their poverty, so that they were frequently required to reduce their numbers.[38] Finally, in 1319 the Sempringham chronicle records that the archbishop of Canterbury blessed 52 nuns of Sempringham, 25 of Haverholme, and five of Catley, together with one *summa scrutatrix*, and though it is unlikely that these figures reflect the full complement of these communities, they probably represent the relative size of the three houses.[39] By the end of the century the clerical subsidy returns show that the Gilbertine double houses remained the most popular nunneries in their region. The appeal of Sempringham, though reduced, remained strong.[40]

The Rule and the novice

By the time that the first extant codification of the Gilbertine Rule was made, elaborate rituals surrounded the reception of a novice into the order. However, during the order's first years we should perhaps envisage a much less structured arrangement, in which Gilbert played a very

---

[34] *Cal. Papal Letters*, i. 258; London, BL, Harl. Chart., 43 H 35.

[35] *Book of St Gilbert*, pp. xxxiii–xxxiv.   [36] *Cal. Papal Letters*, i. 232–3.

[37] *Annales Monastici*, ed. H. R. Luard, 5 vols., Rolls Series (London, 1864–9), iii. 205.

[38] J. R. H. Moorman, *Church Life in England in the Thirteenth Century* (Cambridge, 1945), 301n.; Power, *Medieval Nunneries*, 212–15.

[39] *Le Livere de Reis de Britannie e le Livere de Reis de Engleterre*, ed. J. Glover, Rolls Series (London, 1865), 336–7.   [40] See Owen, *Church and Society*, app. 2. 144–5.

active role. This is consonant both with the personal authority that Gilbert exercised in the communities and with the later institutional authority of the Master. Gilbert seems generally to have received all new recruits, whether or not they were intended for the priory at Sempringham.[41] Roger Musteil pledged his grant of Legsby to Sixhills in the hands of Gilbert, his uncle, 'when he received my two daughters into the order of his nuns', and Supir de Bayeux gave land in East Wykeham to Sixhills, with his daughter whom 'Gilbert of Sempringham the Master has received to make a nun'.[42] The impression conveyed by these early charters is of a close-knit bond between the holy man, the community, and local gentry families: the ties between local society and community remained a feature of the order till the Dissolution.

As the order expanded, and certainly following Gilbert's death, it was necessary to adopt less personal arrangements for the reception of novices and their profession.[43] Central to the Gilbertine Rule, as to all of the new orders, were an insistence on free choice by the postulant and a realistic recognition that a long training was necessary in order to assess his or her aptitude for the rigours of the monastic life. These fundamentals underlay the reluctance to accept oblates, who by definition had not acted of their own free will, and the prohibition on the forcing of anyone to enter the community without their consent.[44]

A postulant girl had to be 12 years old, and a novice 15. She was first required to spend some days in the lay sisters' guest-house to test her vocation and spiritual and physical suitability. Before presentment at the nuns' chapter she would be interviewed first by the lay sister in charge of the guest-house and then in the parlour by the prioress, who would stress the austerity of their regime. The new novice would be received by the Master, who would celebrate in the nuns' church. Thereafter she was under the care of a novice mistress and was kept totally segregated from the other nuns until her profession.[45] This could not take place until she had learnt the Psalter, hymnal, and canticles, and could recite the antiphoner

[41] His involvement in the reception of the young daughter of Roger de Neville at Alvingham has already been noted.

[42] *Gilbertine Charters*, 17, 29, 30. Juliana, a leprous nun of Sempringham cured at Gilbert's tomb, is said to have been received into the order by Gilbert himself (*Book of St Gilbert*, 282). [43] *Monasticon*, vi. 2. li–lii.

[44] Ibid. lvi. However, there is evidence in the 13th century that nuns were being unwillingly confined in Gilbertine priories (see below, 'Disciplining the community').

[45] Juliana, a Sempringham nun, entered the priory as a girl, contracted leprosy, and stayed in the infirmary for 12 years being cared for by Clarice, the novice mistress (*Book of St Gilbert*, 282–4).

by heart, though recruits over 20 years old could be dispensed from these obligations, unless they had the ability to learn them. During this period, in many respects novices were treated like the lay sisters, with whom they communicated eight times a year. It was recognized that not all novices would have the ability to be received as choir nuns; they could, if they wished, transfer to the lay sisterhood before their profession, while any who it seemed to the prioress or novice mistress had not fully learned the offices were given the option of joining the lay nuns (*laicae monachae*) to undertake manual work until such time as they had reached the required standard. Those who refused were at this point to leave the community. The Rule does not describe how the novices were to be professed nuns, though it is likely to have been a similar ritual to that observed by the canons.

In many respects Gilbert followed the Cistercian norms governing the recruitment and training of canons. No boy was to be educated in the community unless he was a novice or intended to be one, and none was to be received till he was 15 years old.[46] The new recruit was to be assigned to a canon who would teach him the Rule and correct him if disobedient, 'the older ones with words, but the younger with words and beatings'. The novice had few duties within the priory, and priests, if novices, were not allowed to celebrate mass. Like the novice-nun he had to know the Psalter, hymnal and canticles, and learn the antiphoner by heart, though those aged above 30 could be excused. When the novice was adequately prepared with a knowledge of the liturgy, the Augustinian Rule, and the Gilbertine institutes, he could be professed, though the new canon remained under the care of the novice master for a further forty days.[47]

Social and geographic origins

Evidence for the number and origin of recruits is almost exclusively derived, particularly during the late twelfth and thirteenth centuries, from charters. The sample of known entrants thus obtained is naturally very small when compared with the total population of the communities, and it can do little more than provide an indication of the social origins of the recruits, and demonstrate the close relationships that existed between some benefactors and the priories. These local communities provided a

[46] See below, p. 171.
[47] Some would also be elevated to priestly rank by the Master, but excessive celebrations and feasting at this occasion were prohibited ('nec fiat in novarum missarum celebratione onerosum convivium, vel inutilis convocatio secularium', *Monasticon*, vi. 2. xxvii).

convenient, and perhaps relatively cheap, home for daughters (and, less clearly, for sons) destined for the religious life. Heloise, the daughter of Supir, a member of the leading local knightly family of de Bayeux, was an early entrant at Sixhills; the daughter of Walter *dominus* of Dorrington was received as a nun at Catley.[48] Another example is Matilda, daughter of Alexander de Cressy, who entered the same house *c.*1182. She may well be that daughter who was cured of a mortal illness by Gilbert's coverlet which had been spread over him while the saint lay dying.[49]

For, just as the new orders opened opportunities in the lay brotherhood for men who had previously been denied a place in the monastery, so many of the new houses for women were less socially exclusive than the great Benedictine nunneries of western Europe like Shaftesbury or Quedlinburg. Hagiographers of the new founders are concerned to show that their appeal cut across social classes and that, like Robert of Arbrissel, they accepted all sorts and conditions of women. Some of these undoubtedly would have found it difficult to enter older-established, more conservative institutions, either because they were unable to provide a substantial endowment, or because they did not meet the social standards set by the more exclusive nunneries.[50] Yet it remains true that the majority of entrants to the new orders came from knightly, if not noble, families, and, in spite of the wishes of eremitical idealists such as Robert of Arbrissel, their new communities often quickly became almost, if not quite, as noble as their predecessors. So long as nunneries demanded or needed 'dowry gifts', so long as their benefactors were drawn primarily from the knightly classes and noble families, and so long as there was no real option for young women of this class other than to marry or enter the cloister, most nunneries, even of the new orders, would attract the majority of their inmates from the knightly milieu.

[48] *Gilbertine Charters*, 30, 82. The de Bayeux were lords of Thoresway; the head of the family, Hugh, held about 20 fees in 1166. Both Supir and Hugh were generous patrons of Sixhills (I. J. Sanders, *English Baronies: A Study of their Origin and Descent, 1086–1327* (Oxford, 1960), 88).

[49] *Book of St Gilbert*, 316. Alexander, a minor knightly tenant of the Hanselin fee in both Nottinghamshire and Lincolnshire, was in many respects a typical supporter of the Gilbertines and was also a patron of Haverholme (*Red Book of the Exchequer*, i. 341). The holdings of his descendant, perhaps a grandson, Alexander II in 1242 are given in *Book of Fees*, ii. 1024, 1025, 1036, 1038. He was probably related to Hugh de Cressy, a royal official in the time of Henry II (L. C. Loyd, *The Origins of some Anglo-Norman Families*, ed. D. C. Douglas and C. T. Clay, Harleian Society, 103 (1951), 35. See also 'Haverholme Priory Charters', 33. In addition he was a supporter of the Templars (*Records of the Templars*, 87).

[50] Leyser, *Hermits and the New Monasticism*, 49. Hildegard of Bingen was extremely concerned to maintain the social exclusivity of her community.

It has been convincingly suggested that many small English nunneries were founded to provide for the daughters of the patron, while some nunneries founded by widows may well have been intended to provide a refuge for themselves.[51] This does not seem to have been the case in the majority of the Gilbertine houses.[52] Only three of Gilbert's own family are known to have entered Gilbertine communities. His niece, Matilda, was a nun at Haverholme and the founder received his grandnieces, the two daughters of Roger Musteil, as nuns at Sixhills, along with the substantial gift of their father's manors in Legsby and North Willingham.[53] However, there are some indications that patrons expected to find a place for members of their family in the priories that they favoured. One or more daughters of Hugh de Scoteni, William of Friston, and Hamelin the dean, all men closely associated with the foundation of Alvingham, became nuns there, and Hamelin himself retired to the cloister he had endowed.[54] The daughter of Philip I of Kyme, who had been associated with his father, Simon, in the foundation of Bullington, was received as a nun there, and though her reception was not accompanied by any large grant, the impressive list of witnesses to this transaction suggests the solemnity of the occasion.[55] In Lincolnshire there are indications that the wealthier free peasants were also sending sons and daughters to the Gilbertines, though in their case it is impossible to determine whether the entrant was a choir nun or canon, or a lay sister or brother, since the charters describe all recruits indiscriminately and ambiguously as *soror* or *frater*. Most of these recruits were drawn from the immediate vicinity of the priories.[56]

We know much more about the social status and recruitment of Gilbertine nuns than canons. The Gilbertine Rule does, however, suggest that the order was keen to attract lay recruits of standing. Each house was allowed to receive 'inter canonicos' two or more laymen 'magnae auctoritatis', who would normally occupy the lowest stalls in the church. If one of these proved to be 'careful, prudent, and discreet in religious

[51] Burton, *Yorkshire Nunneries*, 19–20. See also Thompson, *Women Religious*, 167–75.

[52] Though Alvingham did agree to receive the wife of the son of one of its founders when it pleased her 'as their lady and advocate' (Oxford, Bodl. Lib., MS Laud Misc. 642, fo. 60).

[53] *Book of St Gilbert*, 284; *Gilbertine Charters*, 17. Clearly the founder did not perceive this arrangement as simoniac.

[54] Oxford, Bodl. Lib., MS Laud Misc. 642, fos. 60, 65ᵛ, 95ᵛ.

[55] The heads of six local communities with which the family had connections head the list: the abbots of Kirkstead, Bardney, Barlings, Revesby, and Tupholme, and the prior of Kyme. Other witnesses included representatives of local gentry families such as the d'Arcis, Chauncis, and Benniworths (London, BL, MS Addit. 6118, p. 725).

[56] Discussed in more detail in Golding, 'Gilbertine Priories', 339–41.

matters' he might serve as deputy for the cellarer and even, if the Master judged it useful, be tonsured and promoted to cellarer.[57] This passage is difficult to interpret, and there are no immediate parallels with the customs of other orders. These entrants might be analogous to the *conversi* of the Benedictines, recruits who came to the monastery relatively late in life, and who, though they were regarded as fully a part of the monastic community, would not normally be expected to proceed to the priesthood.[58] In these Gilbertine recruits we seem to see an opportunity provided for someone akin to a lay steward or bailiff, but one who lived within the community. Such a post might well appeal to the retired local administrators on whom the order depended so heavily for material support.

Charters describing the entrance of a son or male relative of the grantor are very rare.[59] More frequent, though far from common, are charters where the benefactor himself arranged to join the community. However, a charter of Philip I of Kyme confirms the grant of $1\frac{1}{2}$ bovates to the nuns of Bullington by William son of Richard, once the steward of Philip's father, when he entered religion. This also suggests that the Gilbertines could sometimes expect to recruit from the ranks of administrators of baronial households.[60] Though on occasions they certainly did attract recruits of some calibre, such as Nicholas II de Stuteville, who entered the priory of St Andrew's, York, in September or early October 1233, in general it is likely that the majority of the canons came from a similar social background to that of the nuns.[61] Some secular clergy, like Martin, a priest at the parish church of Watton, might decide to become canons, perhaps in retirement at a priory with which their church was connected.[62] Other early recruits were from the ranks of the local gentry. Richard, a younger member of the de Cauz family, gave a third of two bovates in Ruskington to Haverholme, 'et susceperunt . . . Ricardum in consortio suo et sancte conversationis habitum pro voto suo sibi contradiderunt'. The same priory agreed to receive Richard son of Walkelin of Eyndon, who granted 12 bovates as a *frater* 'when he wished and reasonably

---

[57] *Monasticon*, vi. 2. xxvii.

[58] The customary of Springiersbach also refers to laymen whom age and lack of aptitude precludes from a clerical profession, 'who are commonly called *conversi* or *fratres*'. These are not to be confused with the *conversi* of the Cistercians or Gilbertines, for they were in some way associated with the canons, though neither vested nor tonsured (*Consuetudines Canonicorum Regularium Springersbachenses-Rodenses*, 130–1).

[59] Burton, *Yorkshire Nunneries*, 21, also noted that entry grants for women are much more common than for men.   [60] *Danelaw Charters*, 57, no. 89.

[61] *EYC* ix. 20; *Cal. Cl. R. 1231–4*, 264.   [62] *Book of St Gilbert*, 292.

could'.[63] When Ridel of Keisby was received as a canon at Sempringham, his grandson (also confusingly named Ridel) gave three acres in Keisby— not in itself a substantial dowry, but the family had already proved generous benefactors to the priory.[64] It is possible that when men entered the priories they tended to make a cash rather than a land grant.

Entry benefactions

It is hard to ascertain whether there was a 'fixed charge' for entry. On balance this seems unlikely. Such a negotiation would be more suscep- tible to charges of simony and it is more probable that any arrangement for entry was made on an individual basis and was the subject of consid- erable bargaining. Perhaps some were received into the community with- out any payment.[65] A number of criteria might come into play: the size of property offered; its value to the community; the status of the entrant; and the relationship of the family to the community. Thus patronal families might well expect a 'better deal' than other benefactors. More- over, just as a burial grant might well represent one in a series of grants by one individual or family, so too a family might make a number of grants to a community, only one of which would be associated with a recruit. When Supir de Bayeux gave his daughter to the nuns of Sixhills she was accompanied by a toft and bovate in East Wykeham, but in another charter he gave his half of the church of East Wykeham along with additional land there. When the daughter of Walter of Dorrington was received at Catley the nuns were given 12 acres of arable, two acres of meadow and cattle pasture, but the same charter also records the grant of two bovates and a toft and pasture for 200 sheep.[66] Entry grants could be very substantial. Herbert son of Adelard of Orby gave 18 bovates when his daughter was received at Sempringham, while Humphrey son of Walter of Well gave six carucates with his three daughters when they entered the mother house.[67] Other grants of several bovates were not unknown. This

[63] 'Haverholme Priory Charters', 34, 48.

[64] *Sempringham Charters*, xvii. 234–5. Another charter records how R. de Keisby gave 13 acres in Keisby on condition that when either he or his wife Alice (or both) wished to enter the community they might have free entry, and if they wished to remain in the world they should have burial rights. This donor might be identified with the elder Ridel (*Sempringham Charters*, xvii. 34).

[65] A point well made by Lynch, 'Monastic Recruitment', 433–4, who states that only cases where grants *were* made would turn up in charter evidence. For a discussion of the size of entry gifts see ibid. 434–6.   [66] *Gilbertine Charters*, 8, 30, 82.

[67] *Sempringhan Charters*, xv. 226, xvi. 78.

said, it would seem normal to grant one or two bovates with each entrant. Such a gift would be generous but not crippling for the majority of the entrants' families. Typical of these is the gift by Walter de Boynton of four bovates in Burnby when his two daughters were received as nuns at Watton. Walter was a prominent member of the late twelfth-century Yorkshire gentry; in 1200–1 king John appointed him deputy to William de Stuteville as sheriff of Yorkshire and castellan of York. He probably held the whole of the Percy estate in Burnby, assessed at $2\frac{1}{2}$ carucates in 1086. If so, he had alienated perhaps a fifth of his total estate with his two daughters: such an arrangement may well have been cheaper than providing them with secular dowries.[68]

The Gilbertine priories provided a convenient home for the sons and daughters of the local gentry, a refuge for gentle widows, and a place of retirement for knights of moderate standing. For all the Rule's emphasis on austerity within the cloister and its condemnation of simony and oblation, there is no evidence that the life followed by the Gilbertine nuns and canons was substantially different from that of their Benedictine counterparts. The heroic days of the first generation of Gilbertine communities when hundreds had flocked to Gilbert, when a Cistercian abbot had abandoned his own abbey to become an anchorite at Watton, soon passed. After Gilbert's death, to all appearance the nuns and canons followed a quiet life, their daily existence only occasionally disturbed by the arrival of a corrodian or the daughter of a rebel against royal authority sent to a Gilbertine house to spend the remainder of their lives in mediocre comfort.

Involuntary residents

Occasionally Gilbertine convents were seen as suitable places for penance for errant lay women. In 1309 archbishop Greenfield issued a mandate to the official of the archdeacon of Cleveland to order the notorious Lucy de Thweng, wife of William Latimer, who had now been the mistress of Nicholas, lord Meineill, for some five years (after a number of other amorous adventures), to reside in Watton priory where she was to do penance. Greenfield recognized that there could be problems: Lucy might not be found and she might escape, though Watton was recognized to be both a secure and 'honesta' house. While there she was not to suffer an onerous regime, but 'sub habitu laicali divine contemplacionis obsequiis

---

[68] *EYC* xi. 40–1, 296; ix. 113. He frequently appears as a witness to Percy and Stuteville charters in favour of Fountains abbey.

devocius famuletur'.[69] Another entrant, 'a girl, the daughter of Gilbert, canon of Lincoln, called Margaret', was put into Alvingham by Robert son of Walbert in the mid-twelfth century, presumably in an attempt to avoid scandal.[70] But saddest of all the inmates of Gilbertine priories were the daughters of enemies of the realm placed there for safe-keeping. Following the defeat and deaths of Llywelyn ap Gruffudd and David his brother, their daughters were sent to Gilbertine nunneries. Robert Manning, their contemporary, wrote how as a young child Gwenllian, daughter of Llywelyn, was sent to England 'in hir credille' at the king's command to be made a nun at Sempringham. Here she was brought up and lived until her death fifty-four years later, early on 7 June 1337. Her cousin, David's daughter Gwladys, had died the year before at Sixhills.[71] Other daughters of the dead princes were sent to Alvingham, 'having compassion on their sex and age', in November 1283.[72] Though the king claimed that he had chosen Alvingham because of the order's piety, the reason for his choice of the Gilbertines was probably more pragmatic. The order had no houses outside England and there was little likelihood of external interference in these arrangements. Moreover, North Lincolnshire was very remote from Wales. It was, therefore, unlikely that future Welsh resistance would focus on these representatives of the native dynasty. In 1301 licence was given to the priory to acquire land in mortmain for Gwenllian's maintenance, and she later wrote to Edward II asking that he remember her since Edward I had promised her when she entered Sempringham £100 in lands or rents and the treasurer Walter Langton had paid her £20 per annum.[73]

In 1306 Marjorie Bruce, the youngest daughter of Robert Bruce, was sent to Watton priory; Christiana, Bruce's sister and widow of Christopher de Seton, went to Sixhills, and Elizabeth, the widow of Richard Siward, to Chicksands.[74] Daily maintenance of 3d. was provided. Female relatives

[69] *Reg. Greenfield*, ii. 49–50, xlix. For the fullest and most vivid account of Lucy's career, see W. L'Anson, 'Kilton Castle', *Yorkshire Archaeological Journal*, 22 (1913), 85–90. There is no evidence that Lucy did ever take up enforced residence at Watton: if she did her presence can hardly have been anything but disruptive.

[70] Oxford, Bodl. Lib., MS Laud Misc. 642, fo. 149.

[71] *Peter Langtoft's Chronicle*, ed. T. Hearne, 2 vols. (Oxford, 1725), ii. 243. See also *Cal. Pat. R. 1281–92*, 321–2.

[72] Oxford, Bodl. Lib., MS Laud Misc. 642, fo. 42; T. Rymer, *Foedera*, ii (1273–1307), 429.

[73] *Cal. Pat. R. 1301–7*, 6. These lands became the nucleus of the endowment of Stamford priory. *Calendar of Ancient Petitions relating to Wales*, ed. W. Rees (Cardiff, 1975), 458, where the letter is unconvincingly dated to the first months of Edward III's reign in 1327.

[74] *Calendar of Documents relating to Scotland*, ed. J. Bain, 4 vols. (Edinburgh, 1881–8), ii: *1272–1307*, 508, 519. Christiana stayed at Sixhills till 1314 (*Cal. Pat. R. 1313–18*, 104).

of English rebels were also sent for safe-keeping to Gilbertine houses. In 1322 the prior of Sempringham was commanded to receive and keep in safe custody, Margaret, the wife of Hugh Audley the younger, who had joined Lancaster's revolt. She was sent there with two yeomen and a damsel and was still there in 1326–7, when she received 5s. a day maintenance for herself and her household.[75] In 1324 the king ordered Margaret, daughter of Roger Mortimer, to be taken to Shouldham, Joan, the second daughter, to Sempringham, and Isabella, the youngest, to Chicksands. Fifteen pence a day was to be set aside for Margaret's expenses and 12d. for Joan and Isabella and a mark for a new robe each year.[76] In 1327 Margaret, daughter of Hugh Despenser the younger, was sent to Watton to 'be admitted without delay' and to be professed 'as quickly as possible'; her sister Eleanor was sent on the same terms to Sempringham.[77]

Corrodies

The granting of corrodies by religious institutions to members of the laity is a well-known and well-documented feature of the late-medieval church. Indeed, it has frequently been used as an indicator of its spiritual laxity by 'Protestant' historians. The corrody was 'first and foremost a grant of money or victuals, or of other means of livelihood, made by a monastery . . . to dependants upon its bounty'.[78] By the mid-thirteenth century corrodies were established not only in Benedictine abbeys but also in communities of the reformed orders including the Gilbertines, and they continued to be granted till the Dissolution.

They fall into three main categories. Perhaps most frequently they were given to the laity in return for a grant of property or for a cash payment. Such arrangements were tempting to both community and corrodian: the former increased its own resources or was enabled to ease a cash-flow problem, while the latter gained an annuity which could be quite substantial. Such arrangements had their dangers, both financial

---

[75] *Cal. Cl. R. 1318–23*, 403; *Cal. Memoranda Rolls, Michaelmas 1326–Michaelmas 1327*, 218, 336. The Sempringham chronicle tells how parliament ordered her to be kept in guard at the priory (*Le Livere de Reis de Brittanie*, 345).

[76] *Cal. Pat. R. 1321–4*, 405; *Cal. Cl. R. 1323–7*, 88–9. See also *Cal. Memoranda Rolls, Michaelmas 1326–Michaelmas 1327*, 218, 289, 311–12, 363.

[77] *Cal. Cl. R. 1323–7*, 624. Sempringham was allowed quittance of rent arrears for receiving and clothing Eleanor.

[78] The fullest introduction remains A. H. Thompson, 'A Corrody from Leicester Abbey, AD 1393–4, with some Notes on Corrodies', *Leicestershire Archaeological Society Transactions*, 14 (1926), 114–34. For the most trenchant hostile view, see G. G. Coulton, *Five Centuries of Religion*, 4 vols. (Cambridge, 1923–50), iii. 240–7.

and spiritual: many monasteries, both great and small, found themselves in some embarrassment because of over-indulgent distribution of corrodies, while episcopal visitations and injunctions testify to the problems introduced into the cloister by corrodians. It was for this reason that the general chapter of 1347 warned Gilbertine priors not to burden their houses with corrodians.[79] A less reprehensible and dangerous form of corrody was granted to old or retired lay servants of a monastery, or similarly given to active workers on the monastic payroll, such as master masons, or to vicars of nearby appropriated churches. Both the above types of corrody were granted voluntarily by the religious house, though the motives for the grants might vary considerably. The third class of corrodian was imposed from outside. From at least the mid-thirteenth century the crown attempted with varying success to place retired royal servants in religious houses where they were to receive sustenance for the rest of their days.[80] Though initially (and theoretically) such impositions were confined to houses of royal foundation, where this policy can be seen as an extension of the commonly held belief amongst monastic benefactors and founders that 'their' monastery had an obligation to provide for their material needs and those of their family, within a very few years the crown was attempting to extend the scope of this 'obligation' to all religious houses. For reasons not fully understood, the high point of requests for royal corrodies came in the first third of the fourteenth century.

Though examples of all these types of corrodians are encountered in Gilbertine houses, they are not frequent, which may be because corrody arrangements were by nature temporary, usually operative for the lifetime of only one individual, and records may well not have been preserved in the priory's archives, unless the corrody is mentioned in a charter conveying land to the house in perpetuity.

The earliest grants of the investment- or annuity-type corrodies seem to date from the early thirteenth century. In 1215 Alice, the widow of Robert de Portmort, brought a claim of dower against the prior of Alvingham. The land in question had been sold to the priory by her inpecunious husband, who had disposed of all his land in Alvingham and

---

[79] Oxford, Bodl. Lib., MS Douce 136, fo. 96ᵛ.

[80] These are discussed by J. H. Tillotson, 'Pensions, Corrodies, and Religious Houses: An Aspect of the Relations of Crown and Church in Early Fourteenth-Century England', *Journal of Religious History*, 8 (1974), 127–43, and J. R. Wright, *The Church and the English Crown, 1305–1334* (Toronto, 1980), 227–32. See also M. C. Hill, *The King's Messengers, 1199–1377* (London, 1961), 73–81.

the neighbouring village of Cockerington to the priory. There seems little doubt that Alice was in financial difficulties, and that her plea was genuine and arose out of economic desperation. In return for her quitclaim of the land the prior granted five loaves to be given to her every Sunday for the remainder of her life.[81] A Watton charter furnishes another example of a widow quitclaiming her dower rights in return for a corrody, this time to be paid at Christmas, of a measure of corn or of 12*d.* while she remained a laywoman (which may suggest that she also had the option of entering the community at a later date).[82] At about the same time the prior of Sixhills granted an unspecified corrody to Robert of Hudham for his confirmation of a grant of land in Linwood, and a 'liberacio' to William Malet for another confirmation.[83] A clear example of a corrody granted in return for payment is found at Malton when prior William of Ancaster gave Walter Westiby and his wife ten convent loaves and seven measures of convent beer each week for as long as they lived together, with the promise of burial when they should die, in return for half of their chattels.[84] Similar arrangements were made by the prior of Chicksands in 1240. In the settlement of one plea of warranty of charter, Reginald *cocus* and his wife were granted 14 loaves 'for a canon' and 4 gallons of beer a week for their acknowledgement of the priory's right to 85 acres and some meadow in Cople, while Fulk le Moyne and his wife were granted 14 loaves 'for a canon' for their quittance of claims to lands in Stotfold and Taplow.[85] However, the most detailed description of this type of corrody is found in the Alvingham cartulary. In 1260 William of Redbourn sold his capital messuage in Cockerington with all his land there to the priory. In return he was to receive an annual grant of nine quarters of the wheat used to make the community's bread, five quarters of barley, half a quarter of oat flour, four cartloads of mutton (worth 8*d.* a load), a bushel of peas, two stones of cheese, a basket of herrings, a cartload of hay and another of turves, ten shillings to buy a robe at Boston fair, and a house which the priory undertook to keep in good repair. This was a substantial obligation, but the investment was probably worth it: the canons had gained a large estate in a village adjacent to the priory where

[81] *Final Concords*, i. 116.

[82] *Yorkshire Deeds VI*, ed. C. T. Clay, Yorkshire Archaeological Society Record Series, 76 (1930), 102.　　　　　　　　　　　　　　　[83] *Gilbertine Charters*, 18, 31.

[84] London, BL, MS Cotton Claudius D XI, fo. 268.

[85] G. H. Fowler, 'A Calendar of the Feet of Fines for Bedfordshire preserved in the Public Record Office of the Reigns of Richard I, John and Henry III', *Publications of the Bedfordshire Historical Record Society*, 6 (1919), 118, 121–2. For a grant of 1211 where the benefactor received a money payment and a measure of wheat, see ibid. 42.

they had developed a prosperous grange.[86] By 1260 outright gifts of lands were becoming scarce, so this transaction marked a windfall which could not be ignored. Thereafter references to this type of corrody disappear until the last years before the Dissolution, though it would be wrong to assume from this that they were no longer being granted.[87]

Even less well documented are corrodies granted to retired servants and other employees of the houses. Such corrodies appear to date back to the early years of the order, for the Rule provided that seculars who retired to the priories and who relinquished their property should have their food and clothing provided as for a *conversus*. They were not to be subject to the lay brethren but were to be obedient to the prior, cellarer, and sub-cellarer. When they died they were to receive the prayers and ceremonies accorded to a deceased canon.[88] The Malton cartulary contains a brief list of such grants made in the mid-thirteenth century, and may perhaps be taken as representative of the situation obtaining in other Gilbertine priories at this time.[89] A total of seven corrodies are recorded. They varied according to the status of the recipient. Two, Ralph son of Geoffrey of Amunderby and William of Hainton 'our servant', were each granted the corrody of a free servant for as long as they lived and were faithful to the prior.[90] Two others were to receive corrodies when they came to Malton, which may suggest a rather looser relationship between the community and the recipient. Thus William Luvel was to be received in the priory whenever he came, together with a horse and a *garcio*, 'in recognition of his good work'. He was to be fed and given drink as a free servant, his *garcio* was to be treated as one of the priory's stable lads, and the horse stabled and victualled with those of the canons.[91] William also

---

[86] Oxford, Bodl. Lib., MS Laud Misc. 642, fo. 72ᵛ (margin).

[87] The assessment for the clerical subsidy in the diocese of Lincoln in 1525 shows that several houses, including Bullington, Chicksands, and Clattercote, were burdened with corrodies, some of them substantial. (*A Subsidy Collected in the Diocese of Lincoln in 1526*, ed. H. Salter, Oxford Historical Society, 63 (1913), 42, 214, 285). Dissolution documents similarly record a few examples of corrodies, at Malton and Sempringham, for example (*Yorkshire Monasteries: Suppression Papers*, ed. J. W. Clay, Yorkshire Archaeological Society Record Series, 48 (1912), 132; London, PRO, SC 6, Ministers' Accounts, Henry VIII/2130, pr. J. Youings, *The Dissolution of the Monasteries* (London, 1971), 222–3. See also *The State of the Ex-Religious and Former Chantry Priests in the Diocese of Lincoln, 1547–1574*, ed. G. A. J. Hodgett, LRS 53 (1959), 38, 58.

[88] *Monasticon*, vi. 2. xlii. Clearly there are parallels here with *confratres*; perhaps the difference between the two was primarily that this sort of corrodian lived in the priory, while the *confrater* normally remained in the world.

[89] London, BL, MS Cotton Claudius D XI, fo. 268ᴿ⁻ᵛ.

[90] William's corrody was granted with the assent of the Master of the order.

[91] He was also to receive two pairs of felted shoes each year.

agreed to act as a business representative for the priory. Sometimes a corrodian was both a priory servant and a benefactor. Ingelram de Percy granted $1\frac{1}{2}$ bovates and two tofts in Snainton, and agreed to act for the canons in business. In return he received the corrody of a free servant, or of a brother at one of the granges, as well as 10s. per annum for his clothing and two pairs of shoes. The most generous of these corrodies went to the clerk, Robert of Thornton. He received $1\frac{1}{2}$ loaves and $1\frac{1}{2}$ measures of ale every day, a priest's pittance, and a house in the priory court which was to be built and maintained at the canons' expense. He also received a house in Broughton to store his goods for 3s. per annum, with the proviso that on his death half of these goods would pass to the priory.

To provide for the material needs of a retired and faithful servant of a community was one thing, to look after a retired royal official or soldier at the crown's behest quite another. Though monasteries of royal foundation suffered most heavily from the demands of the crown, they were not alone in being faced by 'requests' for the support of retired royal servants, and by the beginning of the fourteenth century complaints (both general and specific) against the practice were frequent. The clerical complaint made to the king in 1309 is typical and sums up ecclesiastical feelings on the matter: the king should abstain from asking for corrodies or pensions in religious houses because they led to poverty and the diminishing of the religious life.[92]

By comparison with some monasteries the Gilbertines were not overburdened with royal corrodians. The names of some twenty-six of these are known, dating from the reign of Edward I to c.1340. The only Gilbertine houses to receive corrodians were Sempringham, Lincoln, Bullington, Malton, and Watton. These were amongst the wealthiest priories, suggesting that the crown may have had some regard to the ability of a community to support such inmates. All but two of the corrodians were men, though in 1314 the king requested St Katherine's, Lincoln, to grant Eleanor Darcy the allowance of a nun of that house for life at the instance of Henry de Beaumont.[93]

Disciplining the Community

The majority of the disciplinary measures and sanctions employed by the Gilbertines are grouped somewhat illogically, but understandably, in the

---

[92] *Councils and Synods*, ii. 1271–2. See also Wright, *Church and the English Crown*, 231–2.
[93] Henry was the patron of the order (*Cal. Cl. R. 1313–18*, 99). In 1320 Elizabeth, the widow of John of Louth, was sent to Sempringham in consideration of the good service her husband rendered to Edward I and II (ibid. *1318–23*, 326).

section of the Rule nominally devoted to the lay brothers.[94] The most severe penalties, including expulsion from the order, were reserved for those found guilty of theft, conspiracy, arson, or homosexual practices. Any male member of the order found to have sexual relations with a nun or lay sister was to be imprisoned or expelled. A woman did not have even this opportunity, but to avoid scandal was to remain enclosed in a cell within the nuns' court where she was to pass the rest of her days in fasting and prayer, living to all intents and purposes as an anchoress. Those who proved unwilling to submit to the order's authority were either to be expelled or, if they were allowed to stay in the house in the hope of repentance and died still stubborn, were not to be treated as a member of the community in any way, but as a guest who had happened to die there. Anyone found guilty of revealing the secrets of the order to the laity, or of defaming an individual or the order, was to be excommunicated and not absolved until the Master had come to the priory, when the case would be heard and due punishment administered.

Unlike virtually all nunneries in medieval England, including the 'Cistercian' foundations, Gilbertine communities were not subject to diocesan visitation.[95] The bishop's influence over the order was limited to a watching brief and confirmatory presence at the election of a new Master. As a result, much less is known of conditions within their cloisters than elsewhere, but it is legitimate to suppose that Gilbertine communities were subject to the same strains and problems of discipline as were faced by other communities of women, for they inhabited a similar environment and suffered from equal disadvantages. There were always likely to be disciplinary problems in nunneries that were comparatively poorly endowed, in which there is very little evidence of vocation or commitment, which were regarded as convenient institutions for the upbringing of children who might well not intend to proceed to the novitiate, or as a quiet place of retirement from the world for either the widows or other female kin of patrons, or for corrodians who had either been wished upon them by the crown or taken in through financial necessity. Echoes of these strains can be detected in the miracle stories associated with Gilbert. A nun of Sempringham was said to have a shameless tongue and a restless, suspicious nature, annoying all the sisters with her cares: she refused to accept correction from Gilbert. A canon would

---

[94] *Monasticon*, vi. 2. xxxi, xliii–xliv.

[95] The clearest account of episcopal visitation in general remains C. R. Cheney, *Episcopal Visitations of Monasteries in the Thirteenth Century* (Manchester, 1931). The fullest study of visitations of nunneries in the later Middle Ages is Power, *Medieval English Nunneries*, 482–98; for the 13th century, see especially Burton, *Yorkshire Nunneries*, 26–36.

not be disciplined and fell into uncontrollable anger so that even threats of corporal punishment or imprisonment were of no effect and he threatened to leave the order. A nun at Catley in charge of the infirmary was seized by anger towards another sister; she cried out the Devil's name and was instantly possessed. A few nights later she had a vision in which three men, SS Clement, Andrew, and Gilbert himself, stood at her bed. Clement interceded for her, asking Gilbert to have pity on her, but Gilbert refused, 'rather indignantly' since she had given herself to the Devil and, 'having scorned me and spurned my rules (*institutis*), *just as many other women do* [my italics], she has deserted the discipline of her order'. St Andrew too failed to sway Gilbert to forgive the woman, so Andrew asked Clement to aid her. He persuaded her to repent and make confession to Gilbert, who finally relented and gave her his blessing. These stories were probably included in the miracle series with a didactic purpose to promote harmony within the cloister. Indeed, in his account of the Catley nun the author points the moral explicitly: 'By this we are warned not to be easily provoked to anger, nor to speak ill of our neighbours . . . we are warned too that we ought to be careful in observing our vows, lest we are damned with the impious.'[96]

Individual cases of ill-discipline or apostasy are almost unknown in Gilbertine records. In the early years of the thirteenth century, pope Innocent III appointed judges-delegate to hear the case of Agnes, who had been shut up in Haverholme priory by her father and grandmother in order to deprive her of her inheritance. In this instance the community asserted that she had taken the habit out of devotion, though they refused to back this statement on oath. The outcome of this case is unknown. Neither do we know if Agnes had fled the priory, nor who was in the right. Certainly the community may have had a vested interest in retaining Agnes, for they stood to lose her entry gift if she left.[97] Was hers an isolated instance of dissatisfaction or does it represent the tip of an iceberg of discontent?[98]

---

[96] *Book of St Gilbert*, 102–4, 310. Foreville points out (312 n.) that St Andrew was the patron saint of the parish church at Sempringham, while the account itself states that the nun showed special devotion to Clement since her own village church was dedicated to him.

[97] *The Letters of Pope Innocent III (1198–1216) concerning England and Wales*, ed. C. R. and M. G. Cheney (Oxford, 1967), 89, 92, nos. 545, 563.

[98] See, for example, the case of Margaret at Chicksands discussed below, p. 321. In 1386–7 Edmund Randulph broke into Chicksands and abducted Beatrix Sheldon, who was then in the prior's custody. There is no indication that she was a nun, and it seems most likely that she had been placed in the prior's care as a ward (*Cal. Pat. R. 1385–9*, 182). It does, however, appear that generally fewer nuns apostasized than male religious during the Middle Ages. According to figures collected by Harper-Bill, only 10 out of a total of 274

Episcopal visitors of nunneries of other orders commented on a wide range of misdemeanours, some petty, others more serious, including immorality and shady financial dealings. Burton has identified three main areas of complaint in Yorkshire nunneries: 'criticisms of the prioress and of individual nuns, of general patterns of behaviour and observance and of financial mismanagement'.[99] These dissatisfactions are paralleled in reports of internal Gilbertine visitations and those of papal legates during the thirteenth century. The earliest of these dates from 1223 when a legatine visitation visited Sixhills.[100] The most serious institutional problems arose from the increasingly autocratic behaviour of the Master and of the priors. These were difficulties encountered by all the orders during the thirteenth century as abbots became ever more independent from their communities, with separate incomes and living quarters assigned, and though there were considerable differences in organization between the Gilbertines and Benedictines, both orders had to resolve deeply divisive questions of financial autonomy and constitutional proprieties.[101] The authority of the Master had always been considerable; now, in the generations following Gilbert's death, he was apparently arrogating powers that constitutionally lay with the general chapter. Early in the thirteenth century the chapter petitioned the pope that he confirm its right to make changes to the Rule and that neither the Master nor priors amend the liberties and constitutions of the order. Priors were accused of travelling with excessive display accompanied by more servants and horses than the Rule stipulated: they were using precious drinking–cups and increasingly given to ostentation.[102] By the time of Ottobuono's visitation of the order in 1268 there had been no improvement: the Master was cautioned to rule by love not fear, and to enforce his authority over priors and sub-priors who were themselves over-harsh in their governance. At the same time the Master was criticized for receiving both male and female novices without the communities' advice. This action may well have been prompted

---

signications to the crown were for the apprehension of female religious (C. Harper-Bill, 'Monastic Apostasy in Late Medieval England', *JEH* 32 (1981), 4–5). Burton (*Yorkshire Nunneries*, 34–5) is more pessimistic, suggesting that there was a 'high degree of apostasy in the Yorkshire nunneries'.

[99] Ibid. 30.

[100] Oxford, Bodl. Lib., MS Douce 136, fo. 100^{r-v}. That the inquiry ended with a requirement that all its decisions be recited in the general chapter and observed by the whole order indicates that these rulings were intended as authoritative legislative pronouncements.

[101] For a discussion of arrangements typical of the Benedictines, see B. F. Harvey, *Westminster Abbey and its Estates in the Middle Ages* (Oxford, 1977), 85–94.

[102] London, BL, MS Cotton Claudius D XI, fo. 11.

by financial difficulties as the Master sought to maximize income by taking in recruits with entry grants.[103] There is a further hint of financial crisis leading to relaxation of constitutional niceties in the legate's warning to the priors not to manumit their unfree peasants or to free customary land without their chapter's consent.[104] These were extreme measures that might provide short-term relief but could produce long-term misery.

Linked with the growing autocratic control of the priors and Master was the declining status within the double houses of the nuns, who found themselves increasingly subordinate to the canons.[105] Resentment of their position was to boil over in the late fourteenth century, but clear signs of discontent are already apparent a hundred years earlier. This was not confined to the Gilbertine nunneries. When archbishop Giffard visited the 'Cistercian' nunnery of Swine (Yorkshire) in 1267/8, the canons and *conversi* were accused of appropriating funds 'which used to be committed to the nuns'. As a result the nuns suffered from a poorer diet than the men, and lived on 'bread and cheese and ale'.[106] In 1238 the revised Gilbertine statutes had insisted that the nuns should receive the same food as the canons, and that they should not have to drink water when beer was bought for the canons.[107] A generation later, in 1268, the control of the communities' finances by the nuns was confirmed, as was the stipulation that even in necessity they should not hand over money to the canons without the consent and knowledge of the prioress and other discreet nuns.[108] Again the Master was ordered to see that the nuns were not fed less adequately than the canons. All of these problems, too, seem to have their roots in financial mismanagement. The Rule had laid down

[103] Oxford, Bodl. Lib., MS Douce 136, fo. 88ᵛ. This rebuke was echoed in other nunneries where it is clear that communities were taking on more recruits than their resources could support for immediate financial benefit, or in order to please a benefactor (Burton, *Yorkshire Nunneries*, 32–3). Certainly, as shown earlier in this chapter, the Gilbertine priories are known to have been over-populated at this time.

[104] It is interesting to compare this ruling with that made by Ottobuono at Westminster abbey in 1268 when the prior and convent were forbidden from negotiating substantial cash or land deals without the abbot's consent (Harvey, *Westminster Abbey*, 90). The contrast between the two communities points up the relative strength of the Master compared with a great Benedictine abbot, but in both institutions the legate was concerned with financial probity.

[105] I have discussed this development in more detail in 'The Distortion of a Dream', 60–78.

[106] *Reg. Giffard*, 148, cited in Burton, *Yorkshire Nunneries*, 31, 53 n. 134. There is a hint of similar problems at Nun Cotham earlier in the century (*Monasticon*, v. 677).

[107] Oxford, Bodl. Lib., MS Douce 136, fo. 100ᴿ⁻ᵛ.

[108] Ibid., fos. 90ᵛ (this insists that care of finances be entrusted to the three 'religious and discreet' nuns rather than the prioress. If one of the three became prioress then she was to give up her key); 93ᴿ⁻ᵛ.

that the nuns had the care of the communities' money; they authorized expenditure and sales, and their assent was necessary for the alienation of possessions.[109] With the growing authority of the Master, priors, and canons following Gilbert's death, the nuns were squeezed out from their positions of control, especially of the economy. Resources that should have been theirs were diverted: in 1268 it was ordained that pittances intended for the nuns should not be used for any other cause, while entry grants were to be used for the benefit of the nuns alone, a clear indication that recruitment was seen as an answer to the order's financial difficulties.[110]

This fundamental shift in the constitutional and economic balance of power, away from the nuns to the canons, and especially to the Master and priors, surely affected morale within the nuns' cloisters, and was probably the single most important cause of the ill-discipline and irregularities to which the visitations draw attention. The 1223 statutes make it clear that luxury and ostentation were invading the priories. Both nuns and canons were warned against wearing more fashionable dress and cloaks of fine furs. More seriously there were signs that the elaborate provisions for security and segregation were breaking down. In 1268 the need for separation between nuns and canons was re-emphasized and it was insisted that nuns continue to wear the veil. Some relaxation of the original Rule was allowed, perhaps in order to prevent more serious and illicit infringements. Thus nuns were allowed to speak (under strict supervision) with their friends and relatives.[111] Moreover, by the third quarter of the thirteenth century the rigour of the Rule was so far relaxed as to allow individual nuns a personal income, though this seems to have required the assent of the Master of the order. Walter, prior of Bullington, granted Helena of Pinchbeck half a mark per annum from the priory lands of Houton to be paid to her during the time of Boston fair, with the proviso that on her death this sum should go to the community, while in 1273 Patrick, Master of the order, notified all priors of the order that a rent of eight shillings per annum given by William Russell of Edlesburgh and which was assigned to Joanna, the sister of his wife, and to his two daughters, Hawise and Sarah, nuns of Bullington, should be paid to them for their lifetime. After their death half the money should be used to maintain lights burning before two of the altars of the priory church, while the rest should be used to provide a pittance on the feast of St John

---

[109] *Monasticon*, vi. 2. xliv–xlv; Cheney, 'Papal Privileges', 57–65.
[110] Oxford, Bodl. Lib., MS Douce 136, fo. 88ᵛ. [111] Ibid., fos. 89, 88ᵛ.

the Evangelist.[112] All the evidence, therefore, suggests that the experience of Gilbertine nuns during the thirteenth century was indistinguishable from the smaller nunneries affiliated to the 'new' orders which were to be found all over England. Their tensions and disabilities were common amongst all such communities and the response to them was individual or corporate discontent.

If the position of the canons relative to the nuns was improving, we might expect to find less evidence of unrest amongst them. Nevertheless, occasionally canons were accused of serious crimes. In 1242 a canon of Newstead was found guilty of murder, a crime of which Adam de Helmsley, canon of Watton, was accused in 1277, while in 1336 a canon of Malton was similarly indicted, but generally evidence for ill-discipline amongst the Gilbertine canons is as scant as for the nuns, and nearly all the recorded cases date from the fourteenth and fifteenth centuries when most monastic orders were experiencing an increasing incidence of apostasy.[113] For the Gilbertines, as for all religious communities since the beginning of Western monasticism, the greatest disciplinary issue was that of the recalcitrant or apostate monk. Such cases are hard to quantify, but there is considerable evidence to suggest that apostasy was a real, though perhaps not a major, problem throughout the Middle Ages.[114] Motives for apostasy varied from the more or less laudable desire to move to a stricter house, through the temptations of the world, whether of the flesh or of a lucrative secular benefice, to flight from monastic justice and, worst of all, the attempt to factionalize the house from outside. Every order and congregation had devised methods to deal with the disruptive or wandering monk to save his soul, punish his body, and preserve unity within the house. The Gilbertine Rule laid down a sliding scale of penalties for fugitives. If an apostate returned within one week he was reduced to the lowest rank for one year, given diminished food allowances, and for as many days as he was a fugitive was subject to discipline within the chapter. Absentees for more than a week and less than forty days suffered the same punishment but were also punished by fifteen

---

[112] London, BL, Harl. Charts. 44 A 44 and 44 I 19. For a clear example of the relaxation of the Rule at Alvingham during the priorate of Ralph in 1282, see Oxford, Bodl. Lib., MS Laud Misc. 642, fo. 57ᵛ.

[113] *Cal. Cl. R. 1242–47*, 82; ibid. *1272–9*, 385; London, BL, MS Cotton Claudius D XI, fo. 288ᵛ.

[114] The fullest and most recent discussion is Harper-Bill, 'Monastic Apostasy', 1–18. Much of the following introductory paragraph is dependent on this work. For further discussion of monastic ill-discipline, see J. Sayers, 'Violence in the Medieval Cloister', *JEH* 41 (1990), 533–42.

disciplines and were deprived of communion for a year.[115] A fugitive for more than forty days was subject to anathema; if he returned penitent he could never be promoted above the lowest rank and after a year's excommunication was received back to communion only once or twice in the second year.

Pressure could also be exerted from outside. The papacy itself could be appealed to for support. This was ironic since Rome was one of the most common destinations of the apostate, who often looked to the Curia for pre-emptive absolution or legal support, or for more lucrative office than could be gained at home. Houses which were subject to episcopal visitation could use the good offices of the diocesan to excommunicate and/ or imprison the reprobate, and even exempt orders like the Gilbertines might invoke the bishop's coercive powers.[116] Probably the most effective remedy, however, was an appeal to the crown for aid. As early as 1269 a royal mandate was issued to arrest vagabond canons and lay brethren of various priories, and to deliver them to the Master or his proctor to be tried according to the order's discipline.[117] More often, however, the crown intervened in individual cases. The usual procedure was for the head of the house or his representative to come to chancery, signify the missing fugitive as excommunicate for forty days or more, and request the crown's aid in bringing him to justice. A writ would then be issued to all sheriffs, or, if the likely whereabouts of the apostate was known, to the local sheriff ordering his arrest and return to his house. A group of twelve significations from the Master of the order or from individual priors to the king survive dating from 1286 to 1415, though the majority were written between *c.*1360 and *c.*1390. They follow a standard form in which the prior asks the crown's help, usually through the offices of the sheriff, to track down the offender, who is normally said to be wandering through

---

[115] *Monasticon*, vi. 2. xliii–xliv. The text is ambiguous here but might imply that for every week a fugitive the penitent had to spend a year in the lowest position.

[116] In 1280 two canons fled from St Andrew's, York. Their colleagues requested archbishop Wickwane to excommunicate them (*Reg. Wickwane*, 29–30). In 1296 the Master of the order requested bishop Oliver Sutton of Lincoln to cause his rural deans to proclaim the excommunication of brother William of Billingborough (*Reg. Oliver Sutton*, v. 133–4). William was one of the canons chosen to elect the master in 1283 (ibid. i. 43). Excommunicated for contumacy, disobedience, and apostasy, it is likely that his only offence was to run away from his priory. For late-14th-century examples, see A. K. McHardy, 'The Crown and the Diocese of Lincoln during the Episcopate of John Buckingham, 1363–98', D.Phil. thesis (Oxford University, 1971), 272–4, 280–2.

[117] *Cal. Pat. R. 1266–72*, 393. There are isolated references to runaway *conversi* in the last quarter of the century (see e.g. *Cal. Pat. R. 1272–81*, 430). Such mandates were to become common a century later (see e.g. ibid. *1381–5*, 211).

the country in secular dress to the danger of his immortal soul and the great scandal of his order.[118] The normal procedure on receipt of such complaints seems to have been for the crown to appoint a small group to arrest the miscreant. They would then deliver him to the Master or his attorney. With one exception the apostates were male members of the order, and, as far as can be judged, only two were *conversi*.[119] The evidence, exiguous as it is, suggests that apostasy was not a major problem in the order, and that it was largely confined to the Yorkshire houses, which were experiencing considerable economic problems at this time which may have contributed to dissatisfaction. Only the Yorkshire priories and Haverholme and Shouldham are known to have had recalcitrant canons or *conversi*, though in two other instances the priory concerned is not specified.[120]

Sometimes both crown and bishop intervened. One of the fullest and most interesting cases is that of Ralph of Richmond, prior of Malton. This episode is a useful reminder that there can be more to complaints of apostasy than meets the eye. In 1286 the Master appealed to the crown for help in apprehending Ralph of Richmond, who had fled since the previous December and who was now going about Yorkshire in secular habit.[121] There are no further references to Ralph in the royal records but the story can be completed from the register of archbishop le Romeyn of York. On 25 January 1287/8 the archbishop ordered the abbot of Fountains not to accept the profession of Ralph, an apostate of the order of Sempringham, since he had heard how the order had lodged complaint against him at the general chapter of the Cistercians, and that he had been excommunicated both by archiepiscopal authority and by that of the order. At the Cistercian chapter it had been decided that the abbot of Clairvaux would adjudicate the case when he next visited Fountains, and until that time the profession of Ralph was to be deferred. On 30 June 1289 a mandate was issued to receive surety from the abbot and community of Fountains that they would hand over Ralph, who had now been released from the archbishop's prison ('nunc carceri mancipatum pro

---

[118] London, PRO C 81/1791/1–12. These are discussed by Wright, *The Church and the English Crown*, 222–3.

[119] John de Bynne and Robert Ancreuson, who left Ellerton shortly before 8 February 1370 (London, PRO C 81/1791/12).

[120] It is hard to believe that Hugh of Kelstern, 'once' canon of Nun Ormsby, who stole a horse and saddle valued at 16s. in 1396, was not also an apostate (*Some Sessions of the Peace in Lincolnshire, 1381–1396*, ed. E. G. Kimball, LRS 56 (1962), 38).

[121] London, PRO C 81/1791/1.

nostro beneplacito'), to the archbishop when required on pain of a fine of
£200. When this was done the archiepiscopal bailiff of Ripon was ordered
to hand Ralph over on a day to be fixed by Hugh of Bubwith, monk of
Fountains. It is only at this point that Ralph is identified as a former prior
of Malton. A little over a month later the chancellor and another official
were ordered to examine Ralph to see whether he wished to enter a
'stricter' order or to remain with the Gilbertines—an indication that at
a time when even the Cistercians were under some criticism for growing
laxity of observance they were still generally regarded as more rigorous
than the other orders.[122]

Transfers from a more lenient to a stricter house had long been a
problem; in the twelfth century it was believed the number of dissatisfied
monks was increasing. This was attributed in part to the increase of the
monastic population in general, and in part to the disruptive tendencies
of the burgeoning of the new orders.[123] The only recorded *transitus* affecting the Gilbertines at this time was that of Adam, first abbot of Meaux,
who after ten years was so dissatisfied with life there (not least because of
the abbey's great poverty) that he moved to Watton intending to live
there as an anchorite.[124] In theory such moves could not be denied, and
so long as formal approval was obtained it seems likely that there was
little practical opposition. The difficulty arose if a discontented, perhaps
over-idealistic, religious found that for some reason he could not enter his
new home, or discovered on arrival that he really wanted to return to his
former house. Such instability was both personally and communally
disruptive and had to be curbed. The danger was the more acute when,
as in the case of Ralph of Richmond, the runaway was himself the head
of his house.[125]

Not all errant canons were necessarily lost to the order for ever. Henry
de Seton, a canon of Ellerton, left the house without licence and went to
Rome. Here he was persuaded or himself decided to return. A papal
penitentiary sent a letter by Henry to Archbishop le Romeyn asking for
the archbishop's good offices with the Master of the order on the bearer's
behalf. In addition the pope wrote to le Romeyn with a similar request,
in which he cited the statute of Gregory IX regarding errant monks.
Accordingly le Romeyn wrote to the Master asking him to receive Henry
as a lost sheep. Nothing further is heard of the matter, and it must be

---

[122] *Reg. John le Romeyn*, ii. 58–9, 62–3.
[123] Lynch, *Simoniacal Entry*, 38 and 56 n. 55, for contemporary references to the problem.
[124] *Chronica Monasterii de Melsa*, i. 107.   [125] Harper-Bill, 'Monastic Apostasy', 10.

presumed that the repentant Henry returned to Ellerton.[126] If he did he may have been an exception.

Any closed community was subject to problems of personal antipathies, acts of individual rebellion and anger. These could be exacerbated by the organizational structure of the order. The early Gilbertines prided themselves on an elaborate system of checks and balances in which each component group within the community had rights and responsibilities under the very considerable authority of the Master.[127] That polity was distorted after the death of Gilbert as the canons increasingly took control and the nuns were relegated to an inferior role within the institution. It was this transfer of authority that provided an atmosphere in which discontent could take root, particularly as the order faced progressive financial hardship.

The view from outside: comments and criticism

Rather surprisingly, in view of the possibilities for scandals and slanders in a double house, the Gilbertine order attracted little adverse criticism from outsiders. Walter Map devoted a paragraph to Gilbert and his foundations and commented on their most striking feature, that men and women were found together in the same community, but was forced to admit (perhaps reluctantly), 'nothing sinister is as yet reported of them. But there is fear of it, for too often the tricks of Venus pierce the walls of Minerva; nor is there meeting of these two without consent.'[128] Perhaps more surprising is the account of the order given by Nigel de Longchamp in the *Speculum Stultorum* (1179–80). Nigel's satire on the religious orders of all kinds is wide-ranging and often bitter, yet the Gilbertines are treated gently. The order is a new one which ought to be commended because it is good. Nigel comments on the wall which divided the canons from the nuns while allowing both to blend their voices in singing the offices. At the same time, when Burnel the ass describes his own order and how he will take elements from all the other rules, he says that he does not know how much to take from such a new order, but he will insist that only in secret will a sister ever stay with a brother—which is perhaps

---

[126] *Reg. Romeyn*, i. 184–6. The statute *ne religiosi* ordered that fugitives should be taken back into their order if it could be done without scandal (Harper-Bill, 'Monastic Apostasy', 5). The court of Rome 'acted as a magnet for monastic fugitives of all types' (ibid. 14–16).

[127] *Book of St Gilbert*, 54.

[128] Walter Map, *De Nugis Curialium*, ed. and trans. M. R. James, rev. C. N. L. Brooke and R. A. B. Mynors (Oxford, 1983), 114–17.

an oblique reference to the scandal of the nun of Watton a generation earlier.[129]

Gerald of Wales tells two stories of Gilbert and his nuns. As is often the case in Gerald's writings, the tone is ambiguous: we are never sure if his intention is to improve or amuse.[130] In the *Gemma Ecclesiastica* he writes how a nun inflamed by desire for the aged Gilbert admitted her lust to him. The next day in chapter, after preaching a sermon on the virtue of continence and resisting fornication, Gilbert suddenly threw off his cape and revealed his emaciated body to the nuns, 'hispidus, macilentus, scaber, et horridus', turning round three times so that he might be seen by all from all sides. The cure was immediate.[131] The other story is contained in the *Speculum Ecclesiae*. After a long introduction in which Gerald describes the arrangements made in Gilbertine houses to separate the nuns from the canons, he recounts how there was a canon and a nun whose voices excelled all others. Hearing each other over the dividing partition in the church, they met secretly and the same night eloped over the convent wall. In Gerald's view such behaviour could only be the direct result of the Devil's temptation. When this was brought to Gilbert's notice he initiated a number of reforms: the nuns were no longer to be allowed to sing the offices; their hair was to be cut very short and they were not to comb or look after it; and their veils were no longer to be white or coloured.[132]

Thereafter the order almost entirely disappears from satirical literature. However, in the first half of the fourteenth century the anonymous author of *L'Ordre de Bel-Eyse* has his community borrow the idea of a double house from Sempringham: 'c'est bon ordre, come me semble.' However, unlike Sempringham, where there were ditches and high walls separating the brothers and sisters, 'que desplest a plusours', in the new order there should be no prevention of the brethren visiting the sisters nor should there be any watchword.[133] More obscure is an apparent reference in the register of bishop Grandisson of Exeter. In 1348 the bishop ordered his officials to put an end to the activity of a group of evil

---

[129] *Nigel de Longchamp's Speculum Stultorum*, ed. J. H. Mozley and R. R. Raymo (Berkeley and Los Angeles, 1960), ll. 2401–12, 2451–9.

[130] Though it should be noted that Gerald criticized the Arrouaisians in Ireland, where canons and nuns lived in dangerous proximity (*Giraldi Cambrensis Opera*, iv. 183).

[131] Ibid. ii. 247–8.

[132] Ibid. iv. 184–6. The manuscript text is defective but the substance of the account is clear.

[133] *The Political Songs of England*, ed. T. Wright, Camden Society, 1 (1839), 138–9.

men in Exeter who had constituted themselves as an 'order' with an elected abbot, put on a scurrilous play in the theatre (*in theatro*) of the city, and had generally conducted themselves in a riotous manner. Their order was said to be *de Brothelyngham*. Coulton plausibly suggested that this name was 'doubtless a parody on the actual monastic order of Sempringham'. If this hypothesis is true then it may be that by this time the order had become a commonplace of satirists and parodists.[134] By this time, the Gilbertines had lost their novelty. They were an established element in the monastic landscape, while at the same time those organizational features which had made them appear so distinctive had largely disappeared.

Education and Learning

Education

Evidence as to whether the Gilbertines educated children who were not novices of the order, or who did not intend to make a profession, is scanty. The Rule makes it very clear that boys were not to be taught within the *monasterium* or *in locis monasterii* unless they were novices or received as probationary novices. It is presumably this group which is meant in the general agreement between the Cistercians and the Gilbertines in 1164, when it was forbidden for a house of either order to accept as novices those boys who had been given by their parents to be educated in a house of the other order without the latter's consent.[135] Such a probationary novice is found in a charter of the second half of the twelfth century in which Walter, son of Hugh of Burgh-le-Marsh, granted his land there to Bullington priory, and it was agreed that his son William should be made a canon on reaching the age of majority if he desired. Meanwhile the convent undertook to provide food, clothing, and education for him. If Walter died while William was still in the canons' care, the boy's guardian was to promise the prior to look after William's interests, to defend his land, and to perform the services due for it. William was thus recognized to all intents and purposes as an oblate who was to be the responsibility of the canons while he remained a minor, though it was clearly acknowledged that at majority he might wish to leave the community to inherit his land.[136]

---

[134] *Records of Early English Drama: Devon*, ed. J. M. Wasson (Toronto, 1986), 9, 439; G. G. Coulton, *Medieval Panorama: The English Scene from Conquest to Reformation* (Cambridge, 1938), 610–11. [135] London, BL, MS Stowe 937, fo. 145ᵛ.

[136] *Danelaw Charters*, 10, no. 13. A century later John le Romeyn, the future archbishop of York, was educated at St Katherine's, Lincoln.

In 1223 pope Honorius III forbade the order to admit any girl to any of its houses to be brought up or educated unless she intended to become a nun.[137] This suggests that within a generation of Gilbert's death the order was accepting girls without a monastic vocation into their convents for education. It is difficult to know what to make of the 'magister scolarum ecclesie Maltone' or 'eiusdem ville', as he is variously described, who acted as principal papal judge-delegate in a case heard in the chapel of St Michael at Malton involving the claims of Alvingham priory to an advowson in 1245.[138] The fact that the *magister* was obviously a member of the Gilbertine community, as the context of the documents makes clear, and is sometimes described as a master of the scholars of the vill, again seems to imply that the priory was fulfilling an educational function outside the monastic community.

This education was probably fairly basic, and for Gilbertines requiring further study the order maintained establishments at Cambridge and Stamford. The earliest surviving reference to the community in Cambridge is a mandate sent by Nicholas IV in 1290 to the archdeacon of Stow, requiring him 'to grant the place held by the friars *de penitencia* [or 'of the Sack'] which they are about to leave, to the Master and brethren of Sempringham, who often sent members of their order to study at the castle of Cambridge'.[139] Obviously the canons did not literally study within the royal castle (which at this time was being rebuilt by Edward I); the text probably refers to a site near the castle originally held by the Carmelites, who had first settled there in 1249. A few years later the majority of this community transferred to a new site at Newnham. It seems likely, however, that some refused to move and this splinter group became known as the Brethren of Blessed Mary or the Pied Friars, remaining in the parish of All Saints by the Castle until they disappear from all records early in the following century.[140] Both the quasi-eremitical life of the early Carmelites and the fact that, following the move to the new, more conventual buildings at Newnham, there was vacant accommodation available may have encouraged the Gilbertines to make this their first headquarters. Obviously, this could only be a temporary solution if the Gilbertines wished to settle permanently in Cambridge.

Once again, it was partly as a result of changes amongst the more ephemeral groups of friars that new accommodation was provided. The friars of the Sack were established in Cambridge by 1258 and had their

[137] *Cal. Papal Letters*, i. 90.
[138] Oxford, Bodl. Lib., MS Laud Misc. 642, fos. 4ᵛ–5.
[139] *Cal. Papal Letters*, i. 514.   [140] *VCH Cambridgeshire*, ii. 282, 286–7.

conventual buildings outside the town boundary on the west side of Trumpington Street where Peterhouse and the Fitzwilliam Museum now stand.[141] Within twenty years, however, the Council of Lyons (1274) decreed that in future this order could recruit no new members, and, as a result, though the friars were not formally disbanded their extinction was assured.[142] It was no doubt as a result of this council that Nicholas IV in 1290 believed that the Cambridge friars were about to disperse. His mandate allowed the Gilbertines to take over the property on payment of a fair price, which was either to be used for the papal Holy Land subsidy or for some other fund as the pope should determine. In this belief, however, Nicholas was too precipitate, for the friars of the Sack remained in Cambridge till 1307, when their property was made over to the new foundation of Peterhouse.[143] Too hasty in this respect, Nicholas was too slow in providing a new property for the Gilbertines, since on 12 June 1290, only a few days after the pope's mandate, Cicely, daughter of William of St Edmund's, received licence to alienate to the Gilbertines two acres in Cambridge together with the advowson of the chapel of St Edmund's.[144] Cicely was the head of a leading Cambridge family, one of whose members had been mayor, and which held considerable urban and rural property in Cambridge and its suburban parishes.[145] The main holding of the family lay on the east side of Trumpington Street, almost opposite the friars of the Sack, where Old Addenbrooke's hospital was later to stand. The chapel was a private one held by the family and served by *custodes* or *rectores* who seem to have been clerics of substance, and it may be that the chapel itself fulfilled a quasi-parochial role.[146]

The fact that both the papal mandate and the royal licence were issued at the same time, though they related to different properties, suggests that by mid-1290 the canons of Sempringham were actively looking for a new permanent property either within the town or just outside it, and that they had no certain idea where precisely they wished to settle. The impetus for this move may have been dissatisfaction with their quarters near the castle; it may also have been encouraged, as Lobel has suggested, by the fact that only a few years before (1284) the bishop of Ely had

[141] Ibid. 290–1.

[142] The friars of the Sack are discussed in R. W. Emery, 'The Friars of the Sack', *Speculum*, 18 (1943), 23–34.

[143] *Cal. Papal Letters*, i. 514; H. P. Stokes, *Outside the Trumpington Gate before Peterhouse was Founded*, Cambridge Antiquarian Society, 44 (1908), 28.

[144] *Cal. Pat. R. 1281–92*, 363.

[145] *VCH Cambridgeshire*, ii. 254; Stokes, *Outside the Trumpington Gate*, 56–9.

[146] Ibid. 59–60.

received royal authority to move his scholars from their lodgings in the hospital of St John to two hostels in the bishop's houses (also outside Trumpington gate).[147] Certainly in both cases scholars of the regular clergy were initially housed in unsuitable accommodation and the pressure to establish an independent home must have been strong.

It is clear that at this time, if not before, active steps were being undertaken to improve the learning of the Gilbertine canons. In September 1290 the pope gave the prior and brethren of St Gilbert licence to have 'within their house [presumably Cambridge] a discreet and learned doctor of theology to teach those of the brethren who desire to study that science'.[148] The following year he granted an indulgence to all those who visited the chapel of St Edmund on the feast-days of SS Edmund and Gilbert, and on the anniversary of the chapel's dedication, though the fact that he granted similar indulgences on the same day to both Chicksands and Watton may suggest that the pope at this time was favouring the order in general, rather than just its Cambridge house.[149] In 1291 the Barnwell chronicler recorded that the canons of Sempringham first established themselves at the chapel of St Edmund and were very assiduous in attending lectures and disputations.[150] The following years saw a substantial increase in the house's temporal possessions in the town. In 1293 the foundress received another licence to alienate a messuage, 60 acres of land and 40s. annual rent to the priory, and six years later Nicholas de Bolingbroke received a similar licence to grant a messuage and 67 acres in the town.[151] Thereafter the canons' acquisitions were small. Though the prior was granted a general licence to acquire lands in mortmain to the value of £10 per annum in 1314, this was not fully taken up, and only in 1318 and 1332 did the canons acquire further lands and rents in Cambridge valued *in toto* at £2 2s. 8d. Though there is some evidence that the priory had also acquired land (whether licensed or not) in other parishes of the town and in the town field, there is no indication that it ever acquired lands outside Cambridge or its suburbs, nor did it acquire the advowson of any churches.[152]

The priory, then, was never a wealthy landholder in the town, and the fortunes of the house can hardly have been aided by an accidental fire in

---

[147] *VCH Cambridgeshire*, ii. 305; M. D. Lobel, *Historic Towns: Cambridge* (London, 1974), 11. [148] *Cal. Papal Letters*, i. 516.

[149] Ibid. 534.

[150] 'lectionibus audiendis et disputacionibus multum insistebant' (*Liber Memorandum Ecclesie de Bernewelle*, ed. J. W. Clark (Cambridge, 1907), 212.

[151] *Cal. Pat. R. 1292–1301*, 25, 421.

[152] Ibid. *1313–17*, 177; *1317–21*, 110; *1330–34*, 321; *VCH Cambridgeshire*, ii. 255.

1348/9 which apparently destroyed all its charters and archives.[153] By this time benefactions to the priory seem to have dried up almost entirely. By the middle of the following century the priory was in desperate straits. The order petitioned the crown for assistance, since the priory that had been founded 'for the education and maintenance of scholars, canons regular of that order studying in sacred theology and other liberal sciences, has nothing in its endowment save the site of the priory and lands to the value of ten marks per annum, and that the said order used to exhibit scholars, elected by the Master and common chapter of the order to study in the said priory, at great costs, and is now so impoverished that it can do so no longer'. The royal response was to grant another general licence to the priory to acquire lands in mortmain to the value of £100 per annum.[154] This was clearly a futile gesture, and there is no evidence that any lands or rents were acquired under its terms.[155]

As far as can be seen, St Edmund's received only Gilbertine canons as students and probably comparatively few of them. Indeed, the order would have been better advised to have sent its canons who wished to attend the schools (or those whom the order wished to do so) to other halls and colleges, as did most other monastic institutions. By the time of the Dissolution the assessed income of St Edmund's was a little under £15. Compared with the income of Barnwell (over £250) the priory's resources were minute, and even the next poorest hall, St Katherine's, had an income of nearly £40, and that institution had only been founded in 1473.[156] The priory of St Edmund, though a laudable attempt to improve the academic standing of Gilbertine canons, could hardly be said to have been a wholly successful venture.

But if the economic base of the priory was weak, can anything be said of the quality of intellectual life within its walls? As noted above, there is no evidence that the house was ever open to students other than Gilbertines. Though Robert Manning tells of how he met Robert Bruce and his brothers Thomas and Alexander while they were all in Cambridge, it does not seem possible that they were at St Edmund's, and it is even

---

[153] *VCH Cambridgeshire*, ii. 255.   [154] *Cal. Pat. R. 1446–52*, 76–7.

[155] Indeed, it seems likely that the greater part of the priory's income, at least in the years preceding the Dissolution, came from payments made by other Gilbertine houses towards its support. These payments seem to have been made on a sliding scale according to the income of the individual priories. They were not large sums, but the priory was probably always a drain on the resources of the order as a whole. The *Valor Ecclesiasticus* records annual payments ranging from 16s. paid by wealthy houses such as Sempringham and St Katherine's, Lincoln, to 4s. paid by Newstead. Only Catley, Ellerton, and Sixhills do not appear to have paid anything.   [156] *VE* iii. 506.

arguable that Manning himself studied in Cambridge before the priory was founded.[157] Very few names of individual canons who studied at St Edmund's are known: all were students in the fifteenth century and it may be significant that all but one of those identified were, or later became, priors of Gilbertine houses. Most were associated with the wealthier priories: Sempringham, Lincoln, Malton, and Watton. It may be that the Cambridge house was not used by the generality of the canons, but operated as a centre which those Gilbertines marked out for high office within the order might attend, or which those who had already attained office might visit in order to further their education.

Though it is likely that in the latter years of its existence St Edmund's attracted few Gilbertine scholars, the evidence of the Barnwell chronicler cited above does suggest initial enthusiasm for the venture. In addition there is evidence that in the early years of the fourteenth century, only a decade after the Cambridge priory was established, the Gilbertines attempted to settle at Stamford. In 1301 Edward I licensed the alienation in mortmain by master Robert Luterel to Sempringham of lands and rents in Ketton, Cottesmore, Casterton, and Stamford, in recognition of the charges borne by the priory in the maintenance of Gwenllian, daughter of Llywelyn ap Gruffudd.[158] There is nothing in this licence to suggest that the grant was other than it seemed, an unexceptional benefaction of assorted lands to a religious house. In 1303, however, the episcopal register of John Dalderby makes it clear that Luterel intended rather more, for in a letter to the prior and convent the bishop wrote that this land had been conveyed 'wishing that scholars, proportionate to the augmented number of your convent, studying the scriptures and philosophy, may live in the manor [sc. that granted by Luterel] together with a secular or regular chaplain to celebrate in the chapel of Our Lady in the same manor . . . though there has been a chantry founded in the said chapel for a long time past'.[159] In return for this grant the priory agreed to maintain three chaplains for Robert's soul and for the souls of his family: one in Irnham parish church to be nominated by Robert and his successors; one in the chapel at Stamford (presumably the chaplain referred to in Dalderby's letter); and one in Sempringham itself. The priory also confirmed that the grant would be used for the maintenance of scholars. If they neglected their obligation they were to pay £20 per annum in alms for the poor to the bishop.[160] Though no other reference to the chapel of

---

[157] See below, p. 182.   [158] *Cal. Pat. R. 1301–7*, 6.

[159] *VCH Lincolnshire*, ii. 469.

[160] Lincolnshire Archives Office, Episcopal Register III (Reg. Dalderby), fo. 8.

Our Lady has been found prior to this date, it seems that Robert was subsuming a pre-existing chantry in a more ambitious foundation. Why he did so is uncertain. Robert came from an important Lincolnshire gentry family based in Irnham and is almost certainly to be identified with master Robert Luterel who was instituted to the living of Irnham in 1262 on the presentation of his father Sir Andrew Luterel, but thereafter the episcopal records are silent concerning him.[161]

The early history of the schools at Stamford remains unclear. The first scholars recorded there are the Gilbertines mentioned in Dalderby's letter, and though it has been argued that the canons would scarcely have gone to Stamford had there not already existed the nucleus of an educational establishment, it is hard to see any evidence to support this contention. Even less plausible is the notion that the Carmelite friars were in the forefront of the Stamford enlightenment.[162] Yet the myth of Stamford dies hard. As recently as 1965 it was alleged that 'there is considerable evidence for these schools. At the end of the thirteenth century the reputation of the Stamford schools was very high. A large number of celebrated scholars are known to have lived and worked in the town.'[163] Whatever the obscurity of the early years of the Stamford schools, their life was short. Inevitable rivalry with Oxford and the resultant pressure of the Oxford masters resulted in the closing of Stamford's schools in the 1330s. Nothing is known of the life of the Gilbertine establishment during these years. Thereafter there was no need for the order to maintain a house in the town, and in 1373 Sempringham paid 40s. to alienate a tenement and 10 acres of land in Stamford to the Augustinian friars in order that the latter might enlarge their dwelling.[164] Nevertheless, the Gilbertines appear to have kept some of the lands granted by master Robert Luterel in their own hands till the Dissolution, for in 1535 they were still receiving £8 3s. 4d. per annum from lands in Ketton and Cottesmore, and, though no lands in Stamford were recorded amongst the *temporalia*, 5s. per annum was being paid to the duke of York for lands there.[165] It seems clear, therefore, that following the collapse of the Stamford

[161] *Rotuli Ricardi Gravesend*, 11. His family had considerable, if ambiguous, ties with Sempringham.

[162] The fullest account remains that of A. F. Leach in *VCH Lincolnshire*, ii. 468–7.

[163] A. Rogers, *The Making of Stamford* (Leicester, 1965), 55–6.

[164] *Cal. Pat. R. 1370–4*, 235. Three years later the friars were accused of having acquired this land without licence and the land temporarily escheated to the crown until the escheator certified that the friars had purchased the land from the prior of Sempringham and that the licence had been duly obtained.   [165] *VE* iv. 102.

schools the canons pulled out of the town but retained most of the lands granted in 1303 to provide a rental income.

Gilbertine libraries, *c.*1150–*c.*1300

Virtually nothing is known of the contents of early Gilbertine libraries and only a handful of twelfth-century manuscripts of Gilbertine provenance survive.[166] Perhaps the most interesting is one which belonged to Sempringham, containing various texts including Maurice of Kirkham's polemic *contra Salomitas*, dedicated to Gilbert of Sempringham, and a letter of *magister* Bernicius of Lincoln to Gilbert.[167] In addition it includes a metrical and prose life of St Brendan, sermons and letters of Bernard of Clairvaux, the commentary of Macrobius on the *Somnium Scipionis*, the *Achilleis* of Statius, and excerpts from the prophecies of Merlin.[168] The manuscript is inscribed 'Liber canonicorum Sancti [*sic*] Marie de Semplingham' and quite possibly was there before the death of Gilbert himself. At some point, however, it came into the hands of the bibliophile and scholar Robert Fleming, dean of Lincoln, who donated it, along with many other volumes of his collection, to Lincoln College, Oxford, his uncle's foundation, in 1465. Two of Chicksands' manuscripts date from the twelfth century, though they do not seem to have come into the priory's hands until at least two centuries later. One is an illuminated commentary of Augustine upon St John's Gospel which contains a fifteenth-century inscription: 'Hic liber attinet ecclesie S. Johannis Baptiste de Hardwyk qui olim Prioratui de Chycksand pertinebat.'[169] It is by no means clear, however, how Chicksands acquired the manuscript or when it passed into the hands of Hardwick church. The other is a twelfth-century copy of Origen's *Homilies on the Old Testament*, a manuscript that remained at the priory to be seen by Leland on his travels. This is a well-written copy, with illuminated initials and a few coloured drawings (for example, a crowned king on fo. 2^r) on the opening folios. Again there is no indication when the manuscript came to Chicksands, and the only reference to the priory is to be found on the last, mutilated folio

---

[166] See D. N. Bell (ed.), *The Libraries of the Cistercians, Gilbertines and Premonstratensians*, Corpus of British Medieval Library Catalogues, 3, British Library (London, 1992), 153–6.

[167] Oxford, Lincoln College, MS Lat. 27.

[168] For the work of Maurice of Kirkham, see above, Ch. 1: 'From Sempringham to Cîteaux'.

[169] Cambridge, St John's College, MS 216. Hardwick was a church appropriated to the priory.

where in a later (thirteenth-century?) hand is written '. . . nialium de Chikesand'.[170]

A few more manuscripts date from the thirteenth century. Two books survive which may well have belonged to St Katherine's, Lincoln: a missal, together with other liturgical material for Gilbertine use, begun in the late twelfth century and finished *c*.1250, and a composite volume (containing *inter alia* the Vulgate texts of the Old Testament from Jeremiah to Wisdom, a group of sermons, including one for the feast of St Gilbert, and treatises on the sacraments and preaching, and Innocent III's *De contemptu mundi*).[171] Clattercote possessed a composite (and now incomplete) volume containing devotional writings of Bernard of Clairvaux and a number of sermons written in the thirteenth and early fourteenth centuries in various hands, the gift of *frater* Thomas de W., presumably a canon of the house.[172]

In the mid-1530s Leland compiled a list of the more interesting volumes in Lincolnshire monastic houses, including Gilbertine priories. These include twelfth- and thirteenth-century works, though it is by no means certain that they were acquired at this date.[173] Bullington owned Robert of Bridlington's commentary on the Pauline epistles, and St Katherine's, Lincoln, the same author's commentary on the Old Testament. St Katherine's also had biblical commentaries by Gilbert the Universal and William de Montibus. Bullington possessed one other work of exegesis, the *Unum ex quattuor* of Clement, the twelfth-century prior of Llanthony Prima. In addition, there was 'a little book of the liberties of England' (which was perhaps analogous to the copies of Magna Carta and related texts found at the beginning of the Alvingham cartulary) together with Giles of Rome's *De regimine principum*.

This sparse evidence for the size and contents of Gilbertine libraries suggests that they were no great repositories of learning. Gilbertine foundations were relatively poor and small communities, and there was probably a correlation between size of house and size of library. Their holdings

---

[170] Oxford, Bodl. Lib., MS Auct. E. inf. 4. See N. R. Ker, *English Manuscripts in the Century after the Norman Conquest* (Oxford, 1960), 47; O. Pächt and J. J. G. Alexander, *Illuminated Manuscripts in the Bodleian Library. 3. British, Irish and Icelandic Schools* (Oxford, 1973), 23.

[171] Lincoln Cathedral, MS 115 (missal); see R. M. Thomson, *Catalogue of the Manuscripts of Lincoln Cathedral Chapter Library* (Woodbridge, 1989); *The Gilbertine Rite*, ed. R. M. Woolley, i, pp. xi–xvi; London, BL, MS Royal 4 B VIII (composite texts).

[172] Oxford, Bodl. Lib., MS Rawl. A. 420.

[173] J. R. Liddell, '"Leland's" Lists of Manuscripts in Lincolnshire Monasteries', *EHR* 54 (1939), 88–95. The 14th-century acquisitions by Sempringham priory included a number of earlier works, including Peter Lombard, as well as Cassian and Augustine.

were similar to those of other nunneries, and, interestingly, to many of the small Augustinian priories of East Anglia and the East Midlands.[174] Their collections may well have been built up through personal gifts and bequests, like the four books given to Sempringham early in the fourteenth century by the canon (and later Master of the order) John de Glynton.[175]

The canons

Like other new orders of the twelfth century that drew their inspiration from the Cistercians, or shared the same ideals, the Gilbertines were not noted for their intellectual or their literary activity, nor were intended to be so. The Gilbertine Rule required service books to be of standard form and all books to be strictly unilluminated. For the Gilbertines, as for the Cistercians, from whose Rule these regulations were derived, books were working tools, not artistic treasures. Gilbertine canons were forbidden to copy anything other than service books without the permission of the Master.[176] Indeed, it may be that the Gilbertines adhered more rigidly to their own Rule in this respect than did the Cistercians, who by the end of the twelfth century were not only active in the writing of spiritual and devotional texts but were also producing chronicles and foundation histories of considerable sophistication.[177] By contrast, after the death of St Gilbert no work known to have been written by a Gilbertine has been identified until Robert Manning's *Handlynge Synne* in the early fourteenth century.

Yet, for all that a premium was not placed on learning amongst the canons and nuns of the order, like all religious they had to possess some literacy skills. They needed to be able to read the services in church, or to act as lector at collation or at chapter, and they all had to read daily in the cloister. In addition accounts had to be kept, cartularies compiled, legal cases prepared: no community could afford to neglect such tasks. The tension between the demands of secular necessity and the ideals

[174] I owe this suggestion to Dr Tessa Webber.

[175] N. R. Ker, *Medieval Libraries of Great Britain: A List of Surviving Books* (2nd edn., London 1964), 304.

[176] *Monasticon*, vi. 2. xxxi. Cf. Canivez, *Statuta*, i. 26. The Cistercian legislation is clearly laid out by C. H. Holdsworth, in Norton and Park (eds.), *Cistercian Art and Architecture in the British Isles*, 319–93, and see also C. H. Talbot, 'The Cistercian Attitude towards Art: The Literary Evidence', ibid. 56–64, and A. Lawrence, 'English Cistercian Manuscripts of the Twelfth Century', ibid. 284–98.

[177] C. J. Holdsworth, 'John of Ford and English Cistercian Writing, 1167–1214', *TRHS*, 5th ser. 11 (1961), 117–36.

of spiritual austerity is perhaps nowhere more apparent than in the Gilbertines' attitude to intellectual pursuits.

At the time of reading all canons were to sit in the cloister, each facing away from his neighbour, and they were to read individually except when it was necessary to read or consult a book together. They were not to discuss their reading except where it was unclear, or if there was a query relating to the readings to be made in the refectory. Caps could be worn, so long as it could be seen whether or not the reader was asleep. If a canon had to leave the cloister he could either return his book to the cupboard or ask another canon to look after it for him during his absence. If he needed to consult a work being read by another canon he was to pass his own book to that canon in exchange. Unlike the nuns, all canons were expected to be able to read and no alternative employment was to be found for them during the reading period.[178]

There was also strict control over the copying of books. No one was to write secretly, nor to write anything without the permission of the Master of the order. Such a prohibition was to be taken very seriously, and if broken the culprit could be in danger of losing office or even of being expelled from the order. The unlicensed volume itself was to be sent, as the Master decided, to another house, and its scribe or commissioner and the house to which he belonged were to lose the work for ever. The only works that lay outside this draconian rule were service books. Those who were allowed to write were to do so simply, 'et omnino caveat vanitatem profundi vel pomposi dictaminis'. No canon was to have any books of his own nor take a volume from the library of another house without the Master's permission. Equally firm were the measures to ensure that books remained secure in the convent's custody: all books, whether liturgical or otherwise, were to be under the care of the precentor and no one was to be allowed to carry a book, seal, or calendar at his belt while in the house.[179]

The precentor was in charge of the canons' reading, arranging, for example, the readings at collation, yet it appears that the library itself was situated in the nuns' quarters. The *scrutatrices* of the nuns' cloister were made responsible for passing books through the window dividing the nuns' and canons' quarters when the canons required them. Books were specifically stated to belong to the nuns ('de iure sanctimonialium sunt') and were not allowed to be sent from one house to another without the assent of the Master or the *circatores* and with the consent of the nuns.[180] Unfortunately, there is little evidence to show how far these requirements

---

[178] *Monasticon*, vi. 2. xxx–xxxi.   [179] Ibid. xxxi.   [180] Ibid. xxi, xxiii.

and prohibitions were maintained. However, the general chapter held by Philip de Burton, Master of the order, in July 1300 gives some slight indications. Under pain of excommunication members of the community who were sick or at the point of death were forbidden to give any of their own possessions, including books, to any of their servants, so it was clearly now accepted that individuals might own books.[181] The same chapter ordered that all *cantores* (or precentors) should show their books to the *procuratores* of the house in order that they might be added to the list of books in the house that they compiled ('ut in matricula cantorum cum ceteris libris scribantur'), and so that fraud and theft might be avoided they were to be placed in common custody, and every year at Lent these books, along with the others, were to be available for reading. The clear implication is that some of the precentors as librarians had been appropriating volumes held by the convent to their own use.[182]

If the canons were required to be literate, the lay brethren, like their counterparts in other orders, were expressly forbidden to be so. Following the Cistercian regulations, they were to have no books and were to learn nothing save the Paternoster, Credo, and Miserere, and any other necessary texts. All these were to be learnt by heart, not from a written text ('non litera sed corde tenus').[183]

In view of the relatively small and unimpressive contents of Gilbertine libraries it is perhaps not surprising that the order is in marked contrast to most other new orders of the twelfth century in that it never attracted scholars or produced substantial literary works.[184] The order's sole chronicle was the Sempringham continuation of *Le Livere de Reis de Britannie e le Livere de Reis de Engleterre*: 'it does not amount to very much.'[185] The manuscript comprises a list of the priors of Sempringham till 1396, English annals from 442 to 1274, and the Chronicle itself, which contains entries between 1280 and 1326. Some of these relate to events affecting the order but it is a slight and unimportant work, and can hardly be compared with the more substantial compilations of many Cistercian houses.

At the same time as the chronicle was being compiled Robert Manning

---

[181] Oxford, Bodl. Lib., MS Douce 136, fo. 104.   [182] Ibid., fo. 104ᵛ.

[183] *Monasticon*, vi. 2. xxxvii.

[184] The Premonstratensians in Britain likewise produced only one author of note, Adam of Dryburgh.

[185] M. D. Legge, *Anglo-Norman Literature and its Background* (Oxford, 1963), 291. The work was edited from the very inaccurate transcript in the PRO made from the Vatican MS Barberini 2689 by J. Glover in *Le Livere de Reis de Britannie*, 322–55. See also *Descriptive Catalogue of Materials Relating to the History of Great Britain and Ireland*, 3 vol., Rolls Series (London, 1862–71), iii. 206.

was a canon of Sempringham. He was probably born, or spent his early life, at Bourne, some six miles from the priory, and most of what is known of his life is derived from his own statements in his works.[186] Manning was educated at Cambridge, where he says he was an associate and fellow-student with Alexander Bruce, a younger brother of king Robert of Scotland. Whether or not he was a student of the newly founded Gilbertine college of St Edmund is unknown: it does, however, seem likely that he entered Sempringham *c.*1302, shortly after leaving Cambridge, and it is at least possible that he was a novice at St Edmund's, where the prior, Philip de Burton, was a future Master of the order.[187] He spent the next fifteen years at Sempringham, as he wrote in the Prologue to *Handlyng Synne*:

> Y dwelled yn the pryorye
> Fyftene yere yn cumpanye
> In the tyme of gode dane Ione
> Of Camelton, that now ys gone:
> In hys tyme was y there ten yeres
> And knewe and herd of hys maneres;
> Sythyn with dane Ione of Clyntone,
> Fyve wyntyr wyth hym gan y wone;
> Dane Felyp was mayster that tyme
> That y began thys englyssh ryme
> The yeres of grace fyl than to be
> A thousynd & thre hundred & thre.[188]

What his status was here is unknown, though it has been plausibly suggested by a number of authorities that he was master of the novices, a position that would have particularly fitted him for, and given him an interest in, the translation of texts from Latin and French to English for the 'lewed'.[189] It was certainly while at Sempringham that he began work on his translation and adaptation of *Manuel des Pechiez*, *Handlyng Synne*. Later, Manning moved to Sixhills, as he wrote in his preface to his

---

[186] The fullest account remains R. Crosby, 'Robert Mannyng of Brunne: A New Biography', *Publications of the Modern Language Association of America*, 57 (1942), 15–28. E. Seaton argued in 'Robert Mannyng of Brunne in Lincoln', *Medium Aevum*, 12 (1943), 77, that Manning was in Lincoln in 1327, and by implication had then left Sempringham priory, but her case is not convincing.   [187] Crosby, 'Robert Mannyng', 24.

[188] *Handlyng Synne*, ed. F. J. Furnivall, EETS, os 119, 123 (1901–3). The priors are John of Camelton and his successor John of Glinton; 'dane Felyp' is the Master, Philip of Burton.

[189] See the prologue to his *Story of Englond*, cited in Crosby, 'Robert Mannyng', 15–16; see also 25–7.

translation of Peter Langtoft's chronicle, which he began to translate perhaps in the late 1320s:

> Of Brunne I am, if any me blame
> Robert Mannyng is my name
> Blissed be he of God of hevene
> That me Robert with gude wille nevene
> In the thrid Edwardes time was I
> When I wrote alle this story
> In the hous of Sixille I was a throwe
> Danz Robert of Malton that ye know
> Did it wryte for felawes sake
> When that wild solace make.[190]

The work was finished in 1338 since Manning found that he had run out of material:

> Now must I nede leue here, of Inglis forto write,
> I had no more matere of kynges lif in scrite.
> If I had haued more, blithly I wild haf writen.[191]

Manning remains a relatively minor figure of Middle English literature; as a writer he is unique in Gilbertine history. No work by any other canon from the beginning of the thirteenth century till the Dissolution in either the vernacular or Latin has survived. All the evidence, therefore, conveys the impression that Gilbertine houses were neither great patrons of manuscript production nor of learning. Both quality and quantity are unexciting.

The nuns

When we turn to the educational attainments of the nuns there is rather less evidence, and some of that is contradictory. From his first days at Sempringham on his return from the French schools, Gilbert had begun to educate not only the boys but also the girls of the district, an educational experiment that was unusual, though perhaps not unique, in twelfth-century England. He clearly, therefore, had no theoretical objection to the education of women, and the Rule makes it clear that his nuns were expected to be literate, though at the same time it also implies that some were not since those 'who could not read nor hold office in the church'

---

[190] *Peter Langtoft's Chronicle*, i, p. ci. Robert of Malton has not been identified, though he was probably prior of Sixhills, and was perhaps earlier a canon at Malton.

[191] Crosby, 'Robert Mannyng', 16.

were to work during the time set aside for reading, 'even though they knew the Psalter'.[192] A novice who was clearly unable to learn was given the option of becoming a lay nun, lay sister, or of leaving the community, but, as we have seen, the essential educational requirements for a nun before she could be professed were fairly basic.[193] At the time set aside for reading, the nuns, like the canons, were to sit back to back in their cloister, and no literate nun was to be allowed to sit in cloister after Prime without a book. If one was observed to be sitting idle rather than reading she was to be given another task by the sub-prioress or *scrutatrix* of the cloister.[194] The general running of the library and the convent's books was in the hands of the *precentrix*. She chose the book to be read at collation, kept the key of the book cupboard (which was to be firmly shut except at reading time), and at the end of the chapter on the first Sunday of Lent was to divide the books for the next year's reading, while at the same time those nuns who had not read their books of the previous year asked pardon. No one, unless they had asked permission of the prioress, sub-prioress, or *precentrix*, was to take a book being read by another. Like the canons the nuns were forbidden to copy any books, prayers, or meditations without the assent of the Master of the order, and the same severe penalties applied to those nuns who broke this rule. Similarly they were not allowed without permission to hire or bring scribes into the nuns' church ('scriptores conducere et retinere in ecclesiis monialium'), which suggests that they were reliant on outside help in the production of manuscripts.[195] From this evidence, therefore, it would appear that the expected norm was that Gilbertine nuns could and should be able to read, though it was accepted that some might not be able to do so, and it is also clearly suggested that they might also be scribes and produce devotional works. Yet the language of speech was presumably to be English since the Rule clearly states that the use of Latin was in normal circumstances forbidden.[196]

How far does what is known of the intellectual life and education of the Gilbertine nuns accord with evidence from English nunneries of the same period, which they so closely resembled in organization, size, and economy? The fortunate survival of episcopal visitation records for the dioceses of

---

[192] *Monasticon*, vi. 2. xlviii.   [193] Ibid. li.   [194] Ibid. xlix.

[195] Ibid. l. The verb *scribere* can be interpreted either as the act of copying or composing. Here, it is likely that copying is meant, though the warning that letter-writing should be free of all pomposity of style indicates that letters might be composed by the nuns. Bella Millett has suggested to me that a similar distinction between letter-writing and other writing is found in the *Ancrene Wisse*. The scribes might have been hired for administrative services as well as to copy books.   [196] *Monasticon*, vi. 2. xlix.

Lincoln and York, of which extensive use was made by Miss Power, makes possible such a comparison with nunneries that lay in the same geographical context as the Gilbertine houses. In general nunnery libraries were unimpressive and primarily consisted of service books.[197] Since Gilbertine communities were double houses it is, of course, impossible to state whether the books known to have been owned by them were the nuns' or the canons'. Certainly, though they do not indicate high intellectual activity, they were somewhat more academic and theological in tone than those books known to have been in other nunneries. It is also interesting that in Gilbertine houses the library was administered by a nun, not a canon. Since no books are known to have been possessed by individual nuns, perhaps because the rule against such possession was still largely being observed, it is impossible to use this as an indicator of individual literacy.[198] It has been suggested that an illustrated copy of *La Lumiere as Lais* (now York, Dean and Chapter Library 16 N 3) by Peter of Peckham, written in the last quarter of the thirteenth century, was owned by Shouldham priory.[199] *La Lumiere* was a popular work, and though explicitly addressed to the clergy enjoyed a wide readership amongst religious in general. Indeed, the fact that it was written in the vernacular may well have appealed to a community where the level of Latinity left something to be desired.[200] There is no further evidence concerning the use of the vernacular by the nuns until the fourteenth century. A

---

[197] Power, *Medieval English Nunneries*, 238–55. The most impressive and lavish manuscript to survive from a Gilbertine priory is the Psalter of Robert de Lisle (now London, BL, MS Arundel 83 II), given before 1339 by Robert to his two daughters, nuns at Chicksands (L. F. Sandler, *The Psalter of Robert de Lisle in the British Library* (London, 1983), 11–13.)

[198] In the prologue to his translation of the 'Life of St Gilbert' (1451) Capgrave stated that the work was undertaken at the request of the Master of the order, who 'desired gretly the lyf of Seynt Gilbert schuld be translat in the same forme', i.e. like that of Capgrave's translation of the life of St Augustine. This was to be for the benefit of the 'solitarye women of your religion whech unneth can vndyrstande Latyn, that thei may at vacaunt tymes red in this book the grete vertues of her maystyr' (*John Capgrave's Lives of St Augustine and St Gilbert of Sempringham*, ed. J. J. Munro, EETS os 140 (1910), 61). Late-medieval episcopal visitations certainly endorse the evidence of Capgrave cited above that nuns in general were ignorant of Latin. English translations of important texts, such as the Benedictine Rule itself, devotional texts, and charters (as happened at Godstow) were produced for many nunneries during this period and many such translations specifically state that the work was undertaken because of the nuns' ignorance of Latin.   [199] *Book of St Gilbert*, p. cix.

[200] M. D. Legge, ' "La Livere as Lais"—a Postscript', *Modern Language Review*, 46 (1951), 191–5. There is no evidence, *pace* Foreville, that Peter ended his life as a Gilbertine at Shouldham (*Book of St Gilbert*, p. cix). See A. B. Emden, *A Biographical Register of the University of Oxford to AD 1500*, 3 vols. (Oxford, 1957–9), iii. 1447, and M. D. Legge, 'Pierre de Peckham and his "Lumiere as lais" ', *Modern Language Review*, 24 (1929), 37–40.

now-lost manuscript once in the library of the Yorkshire bibliophile Henry Savile of Banke is listed in a seventeenth-century catalogue as 'Litera missa a magistro Waltero Hilton ad dominam sacerdotissimam quandam ordinis sancti Gilberti in qua ordo et regula vivendi est descripta quam Ricardus de Hampull rogatu eiusdem dominae a Latino in Anglicum idioma transtulit'.[201] As with most English nunneries, what education the novices received came from the precentress: how far such education was available to those who were not, or who had no intention of becoming, novices is debatable. What seems most likely is that amongst the Gilbertines, as elsewhere, there was a tension between the desire of the community for contemplative solitude and the demands of local benefactors and patrons who regarded the education of their children as a right, and who were, moreover, often prepared to pay for this privilege.

Virtually nothing is known of the spiritual life of the Gilbertine nuns (and nothing of that of the canons and lay brethren); such indications as there are tend to be oblique at best.[202] The nuns left no writings of their own, the contents of their early libraries are unknown, and evidence from the fourteenth and fifteenth centuries scarcely suggests that they were at the forefront of learning or spirituality. The Gilbertine women, like their counterparts in other communities, were expected to devote themselves to contemplation and prayer, and perhaps particularly to meditation upon the Psalter.[203] Their spiritual exercises were structured by the liturgy and the daily *horarium*. Such were by definition silent or spoken activities, leaving no trace in the written record. There is an occasional tantalizing glimpse. An early fourteenth-century manuscript contains a prayer in French verse allegedly sent by St Bartholomew from the Virgin Mary to a 'holy nun' of Sempringham. Such epistolary prayers are not uncommon expressions of both lay and monastic piety.[204]

[201] A. G. Watson, *The Manuscripts of Henry Savile of Banke* (London, 1969), 57. Another 14th-century manuscript (London, BL, MS Harl. 2406) includes an exposition in English of a letter of Walter Hilton written to a 'friend' for the dedicatee, who was most likely a Gilbertine nun. She clearly lived in a community, referring to her sisters and the chapter, and 'seynt Gillebert' is specifically mentioned as one whose aid is to be sought in her difficulties.

[202] For comments on the spirituality of Cistercian lay brothers, which might be applied to the Gilbertines, see Holdsworth, 'The Blessings of Work', 66–8.

[203] Christina of Markyate was said to have her Psalter open on her lap at all hours of the day, and though she was a recluse, not a nun, her meditations probably differed little from those of nuns (*The Life of Christina of Markyate*, 98. cf. 92). During the night she 'devoted herself to prayer and contemplative meditation' (ibid. 34).

[204] New York, Pierpont Morgan Library, M700, fo. 122ᵛ. The prayer carries the rubric: 'Iceste enveya n̄re dame seinte mar' a une seinte nonayne de Sympringham par seint bartholome k'chascun iur le dirra de lui sucur enavera.'

Sometimes the nuns might be preached to, and there is evidence that Gilbert travelled round his nunneries giving sermons; at Chicksands he rebuked the nuns for being less devout than those of nearby, and Benedictine, Elstow, even though the latter were (as the *Vita*'s author avers) 'less strict in their religious observance'.[205] There are some indications, too, that the Gilbertine nuns enjoyed the support of powerful figures in the ecclesiastical hierarchy who functioned as their spiritual advisers and who paralleled the activities of earlier churchmen such as Anselm or Thurstan of York in their patronage of holy women. The fullest account is provided in Aelred's eulogy of the piety of the nuns of Watton, praising their fervour in prayer, spiritual and mystical exercises, and their visions, which apparently reached an unusual intensity. But it should be remembered that this was written in the context of Aelred's account of the nun of Watton, and it may be that he was exaggerating the spirituality of the community in order to contrast the evil behaviour of the scandalous nun the more forcefully. There is some further evidence in Aelred's work, however, that the Gilbertine nuns had a reputation for piety that extended beyond their own cloisters, since in a sermon on visions he refers to a Gilbertine nun's experience of a vision of Christ, while she was engaged in private prayer.[206] We know too that a generation later the learned and influential William de Montibus thought highly of the order and that he wrote sermons for the nuns.[207] The Gilbertines produced no Hildegard nor Heloise, nor even a Christina of Markyate, nor should we expect them to. Their houses catered for the daughters and widows of local knightly society and fulfilled a social as much as a religious need.

---

[205] *Book of St Gilbert*, 108.

[206] Aelred, 'De Sanctimoniali de Wattun', *PL* 195, cols. 791–2; 'Sermones de Oneribus', ibid., cols. 370–2. Discussed in Elkins, *Holy Women*, 100–1.

[207] William de Montibus' writings for Gilbertine nuns are preserved in two manuscripts: Oxford, Bodl. Lib., MS Lyell 8, and London, BL, MS Royal 4 B VIII. The latter's provenance is probably St Katherine's, Lincoln. The sermons in the Oxford manuscript are all in praise of Gilbert and his foundations (see A. de la Mare, *Catalogue of the Collection of Medieval Manuscripts bequeathed to the Bodleian Library Oxford by James P. R. Lyell* (Oxford, 1971), 17–18. These sermons are discussed by J. Goering, *William de Montibus*, Pontifical Institute of Medieval Studies, Toronto, Studies and Texts, 108 (1992), 7–8, 222–6, 518–19. L. C. Bracelond ('Nuns in the Audience of Gilbert of Hoyland', in J. B. Sommerfeldt (ed.), *Simplicity and Ordinariness: Studies in Medieval Cistercian History IV*, Cistercian Studies, 61 (Kalamazoo, Mich., 1980), 139–69) suggests that Gilbert of Hoyland may have addressed some of his sermons to Gilbertine nuns.

PART II

Founders and Foundations

4
Gilbertine Foundations

By the time of his death in 1189 Gilbert had founded nine double houses and four for canons only.[1] The former included all the double communities except Shouldham; the small house of Tunstall had already failed. The four single houses are hard to identify with certainty, but were probably St Katherine's, Lincoln, Malton, Newstead, and Mattersey.[2] By the Dissolution there was a total of twenty-three Gilbertine houses, ten of them double communities.[3] At least six more, three of them in England, one each in Scotland and Normandy, and another at Rome, had a more ephemeral life and survived for no more than a few years.[4]

A general pattern of monastic foundations and endowments during the late eleventh and twelfth centuries has long been established. After the Conquest the first generation of Norman colonists tended to make grants of English lands to abbeys in their homeland. Well before 1100, however, some Anglo-Norman magnates (especially the wealthier ones) began to found independent Benedictine houses, such as that of earl Hugh at Chester. The first half of the twelfth century was the time of most rapid Augustinian growth, soon followed by the most vigorous period of Cistercian expansion. Consequent on the prohibition of further Cistercian establishments, the Premonstratensians enjoyed their greatest popularity.[5] This chronology of growth is clearly found in both Lincolnshire and Yorkshire. In 1066 there were no religious foundations anywhere to the

---

[1] *Book of St Gilbert*, 54–6.

[2] Clattercote was also in existence, but at this stage was a hospital for lepers of the order. The *Vita* also refers to Gilbert's foundation of hospitals. Marlborough may also have been founded by 1189.

[3] *Medieval Religious Houses*, 194–9. Additionally, the small priory of Bridge End founded at the end of the 12th century had become a cell of Sempringham by 1535 (ibid. 197).

[4] These are discussed below, 'Failures'. To these should perhaps be added the small hermitage in Holland Marsh, regarded by Foreville as a modest, but independent, establishment fulfilling an economic function analogous to that of Bridge End, though it is more likely to have been a place of retreat administered by the canons of Sempringham (*Book of St Gilbert*, p. xxxv). It should be noted that no mention of this establishment is made in Henry II's confirmation charter to the order (1154 × 1161) (London, BL, MS Cotton Claudius D XI, fo. 30).

[5] The best regional account, and that most relevant here, is D. M. Owen, *Church and Society in Medieval Lincolnshire* (Lincoln, 1971), 47–8. The chronology of foundations is

north of Lincoln. This region had suffered heavily during the Danish
invasions, and most monasteries in the county had been destroyed. Some,
such as Bardney or Crowland, revived; others, like Barrow-on-Humber,
never recovered. This is the single most important factor in explanation of the monastic desert that existed in much of the county at the
Conquest. Further devastation and disruption in the years immediately
following 1066 prevented speedy recovery. The first post-Conquest
community to be founded was that of the cathedral at Lincoln, transferred there from Dorchester by bishop Remigius in 1072. Thereafter a
few alien priories were established in the last quarter of the eleventh
century, but no indigenous foundations were made until the last years of
the reign of Henry I.[6] A dramatic change occurred in the second quarter
of the twelfth century. During some thirty years from *c.*1130 to *c.*1160
houses belonging both to the old Benedictine and to new orders sprang
up all over north Lincolnshire.[7] Augustinian houses were established at
Wellow (*c.*1132), Nocton, Thornholme (both *t.* Stephen), and Thornton
(1139); the Cistercian abbeys of Louth Park, Kirkstead, Revesby, Bytham
(later Vaudey), and Swineshead were founded in 1137, 1139, 1143, 1147,
and 1148 respectively, while the Premonstratensians had abbeys at
Newsham (1143), Barlings (1154–5), and Tupholme (1155–6).[8] North of
the Humber a few Benedictine abbeys were founded between 1066 and
1100, but during the first half of the twelfth century there was a significant increase in monasteries, mostly Augustinian priories and Cistercian
abbeys. There were about ten new Augustinian houses and rather fewer
Cistercian abbeys.[9] By contrast there were no new independent Benedictine abbeys founded after *c.*1100 and only one Cluniac priory (Monk
Bretton).

studied from the point of view of an individual family by J. Ward, 'Fashions in Monastic
Endowment: The Foundations of the Clare Family, 1066–1314', *JEH*, 32 (1981), 427–51.
For developments before *c.*1100 see B. J. Golding, 'Anglo-Norman Knightly Burials', in C.
Harper-Bill and R. Harvey (eds.), *The Ideals and Practice of Medieval Knighthood* (Woodbridge,
1986), 35–48.

  [6] Additionally, a number of religious houses outside the county held lands in Lincolnshire in 1086 (see Owen, *Church and Society*, 47–52).

  [7] Between *c.*1130 and *c.*1180 about 41 independent religious houses (excluding hospitals)
were founded in Lincolnshire. This figure is derived from the list in Owen, *Church and
Society*, 146–53. It cannot be regarded as absolutely accurate, since the dates of foundation
are in nearly all cases only approximate. It also omits all foundations that were dependencies
of already existing houses, whether, like Deeping, of an English monastery (Thorney) or
alien priories.

  [8] There was only one new Benedictine abbey, Humberstone, founded *c.*1160.

  [9] Including two Savigniac foundations at Byland and Fors (which moved to Jervaulx in
1156).

This chronology is adequate for male communities, but rather more complicated if applied to nunneries and double houses. Constraints of function, space, and time determined the development of the first Gilbertine priories: they were primarily intended for women, and nearly all were located in either Lincolnshire or Yorkshire and were founded between *c*.1130 and *c*.1160. Nowhere was the dramatic increase in the number of religious communities for women more apparent than in eastern England. Recent studies make it unnecessary to examine this phenomenon in detail, but it is worth reminding ourselves of its central features.[10] At the time of the Norman Conquest there were only ten nunneries, nearly all of them in southern England, nearly all founded by aristocratic families for aristocratic families, and nearly all relatively wealthy corporations, at least when compared with later establishments. The immediate post-Conquest period saw hardly any additions to this tally, and the real expansion only occurred *c*.1100. The unparalleled growth of nunneries in England during the second third of the twelfth century came a few years after the surge in male foundations, but proportionately exceeded the latter in scale. Its dynamic came from below. As we have already noted, few radical monastic reformers or hermits went out of their way to encourage female followers, while most actively distanced themselves from women. Female demand for a place in the cloister far outstripped supply, and it was to fill this need that founders and patrons who might earlier have established male communities now turned their attention to the nunneries.

Expansion was particularly marked in Lincolnshire and Yorkshire, where there were the highest concentrations of nunneries in medieval England. It is not easy to account for this. Elkins draws a distinction between developments south and north of the Welland, typifying the former as a region where there was considerable variation in responses to the needs of religious women from the old Benedictine abbeys, from the new orders, from founders of varying status, and from women themselves living in small, more or less self-governing groups, while arguing that northern nunneries were marked by a homogeneity of organization based, however loosely, on Cistercian models, and where the norm was for 'necessary physical and spiritual services . . . provided by religious men who were full members of the monastery'.[11] This distinction is perhaps too rigid; certainly, however, female foundations in the north were frequently modelled on the 'new monasticism'. But the reason is simply that

---

[10] See Burton, *Yorkshire Nunneries*; Elkins, *Holy Women*; and Thompson, *Women Religious*.   [11] Elkins, *Holy Women*, esp. 75–7.

there was little 'old' monasticism (and certainly no 'old' nunneries) here to exert any influence, and a twelfth-century northern lord, of whatever status, who wished to found a religious house would naturally tend to turn to the more fashionable 'new' orders when insuring his soul.[12]

About half of the twelfth-century Lincolnshire foundations were for women. The first was the community set up by Gilbert at Sempringham *c*.1131. The only Benedictine nunnery (Stainfield) was not founded until the mid-1150s, at about the same time as the creation of the only Premonstratensian nunnery in the shire, the tiny house of Orford. The sole house in the county for Augustinian canonesses at Grimsby was not established till the mid-1180s. Most prolific amongst the Lincolnshire foundations for women were the 'Cistercian' nunneries. Between *c*.1135 and *c*.1184 seven such communities were founded.[13] Their status and organization remain obscure and controversial and have already been discussed: certainly they bore very close similarities to the Gilbertine double houses.[14] It is in this context of monastic proliferation that the six Gilbertine houses established in north Lincolnshire before 1160 must be seen.

Though it is difficult to establish a clear chronology for the founding of nunneries in Yorkshire, by the end of Stephen's reign there were probably about ten houses for women, with the pace of foundation quickening in the early 1150s. By the end of the century there were twenty-three nunneries (including double houses) in the county. But Yorkshire saw only one Gilbertine double house: Watton. This contrast with Lincolnshire, where over half of the nunneries founded at this time were Gilbertine, has been remarked on, but not satisfactorily explained.[15] The two shires had close political, tenurial, and cultural ties; many leading baronial and knightly families had interests, and were active patrons of religious houses, in both counties. Certainly some of the Yorkshire nunneries, particularly the 'Cistercian' ones, were influenced by Gilbertine practices, but they were never assimilated into the order, though contemporaries occasionally described them as 'Gilbertine'.

With the exception of Sempringham and Haverholme, founded before Gilbert's journey to Cîteaux in 1147, all of the successful double houses

---

[12] Even so, there was a significant minority of Benedictine nunneries founded during the second half of the 12th century in Yorkshire (Burton, *Yorkshire Nunneries*, 5–11).

[13] Stixwould (*c*.1135), Heynings (after 1135), Gokewell (before 1148), Nun Cotham (1147–53), Legbourne (after 1150), and Greenfield (before 1153).

[14] See above, Ch. 2: 'Continuity and native tradition'.

[15] See Burton, *Yorkshire Nunneries*, esp. 10–11.

established by 1189 are usually said to have been funded between 1148 (when Gilbert returned from France) and 1154, a *terminus ad quem* seemingly chosen to coincide with the death of king Stephen. In fact it is rarely possible to date the foundation charters (where these exist) with great accuracy, and in any case these charters may well have been issued some time after the actual foundation. There are no surviving foundation histories of any Gilbertine priories to give an account, however apocryphal, of their early days, or to indicate the dynamic behind the bare details of a foundation given in the charters. Neither is there evidence amongst the Gilbertines when any of their conventual churches were dedicated, a *rite de passage* in a community's history that was often regarded by contemporaries as well as by modern commentators as indicating the real date of foundation.[16]

While the impetus given to monastic foundations by the 'anarchy' of Stephen's reign may have been exaggerated, contemporaries certainly saw some connection between the unsettled state of temporal affairs and the desire by the laity, especially the knightly class, to establish monasteries. In Walter Daniel's biography of Aelred, the saint is said to have been told by the bishop of Lincoln 'to accept grants of lands from knights in generous free alms', and Aelred obeyed, 'since he had realized that in this unsettled time such gifts profited knights and monks alike, for in those days it was hard for any to lead the good life unless they were monks or members of some religious order'.[17] William of Newburgh, who was primarily interested in monastic foundations in Yorkshire, made an explicit comparison between the castles built by the lords of Stephen's reign and the *castra Dei* that they founded, and wrote that many more monasteries and nunneries were founded during Stephen's reign than in the previous hundred years.[18] But though it cannot be denied that many new monasteries were established during Stephen's reign it is perhaps too simplistic to see a direct causal relationship. The earliest Cistercian abbey was founded in England in 1128, the first Gilbertine community in *c*.1131, the first English Premonstratensian house in 1143. The early years of a new order were usually the most productive in terms of new foundations; the upsurge in the number of communities of the new orders in the two

---

[16] The fullest treatment of the chronology of foundations and foundation charters remains V. H. Galbraith, 'Monastic Foundation Charters of the Eleventh and Twelfth Centuries', *Cambridge Historical Journal*, 4 (1934), 205–22. Ironically, the clearest account of the motivation and process by which a Gilbertine priory was founded relates to a late and ultimately unsuccessful plantation, Dalmilling (Ayrshire). This foundation is discussed below, 'Failures'.

[17] *The Life of Aelred of Rievaulx by Walter Daniel*, 28.

[18] William of Newburgh, *Historia Rerum Anglicanum*, i. 53.

decades from *c*.1130 to *c*.1150 may be as attributable to this factor as to political unrest. It must also be remembered that the disturbances of Stephen's reign were themselves detrimental to the safety of the religious, a fact recognized in the *Vita*'s account of one of Gilbert's visions in which the saint is said to have been troubled by the wars of the reign, both on account of the region's devastation and through fears for the destruction of his new order.[19] But as beneficial to the foundation of Premonstratensian and Gilbertine priories as the political situation may have been the decision of the Cistercian general chapter in 1152 that no new abbeys be founded. This policy decision was shortly followed by the death of Bernard of Clairvaux. The vacuum thus created could be exploited by the new orders of canons.[20]

Often the new foundations lay very close to each other. This is most marked in Lincolnshire, which was a more densely settled and populated region than Yorkshire, though even north of the Humber difficulties might be experienced.[21] The smaller density of settlement and the fact that there was more land, particularly pasture, available for expansion may explain why male communities in Yorkshire were normally substantially wealthier than their Lincolnshire counterparts. Alvingham lay in the next parish to Louth Park, and only two or three miles to the north of Legbourne. Within a distance of some ten miles were the houses of Bullington, Barlings, Stainfield, Bardney, Tupholme, and Stixwould. The monastic garden of Lincolnshire was rapidly becoming overcrowded, and it is no wonder that we find general agreements between the Gilbertines and Cistercians as well as individual understandings between houses, attempting to regulate the acquisition of property and to avoid acrimonious competition for labour and lands.[22] No longer a desert, the region was now too fruitful. As a result of this overcrowding and pressure on available land, few of these communities gained more than modest endowments or wealth. Their sphere of influence was local, almost parochial in extent. Of the houses mentioned above, only Kirkstead, Revesby, Barlings, and Thornton had incomes over £200 in 1535, and only Thornton (£591) had an income over £300. Moreover, most of these houses were founded by lesser local lords. They stood as witnesses to the piety and pretensions of the knightly, not the magnate, class. The amount of land available for

---

[19] *Book of St Gilbert*, 106–8.

[20] Knowles, *Monastic Order in England*, 346; Colvin, *The White Canons*, 29–30.

[21] The uncomfortable proximity of Old Byland and Rievaulx abbeys is well known, while conflict between neighbouring abbeys for lands was common.

[22] See below, pp. 280–2.

the demands of piety was limited, even though it was sometimes possible for houses to be founded on unreclaimed or uncultivated lands, thereby allowing the benefactor to gain a reputation for good works with little effort.[23]

It is in this context that the foundation and early endowments of the Gilbertine houses must be seen. All had to take their chance in the competition for land and other endowments from benefactors of modest means whose resources were frequently limited. It was not an easy world for the first generation of nuns and canons, and the conditions that they faced set the course of obscurity and poverty the priories were to endure until their dissolution. It should, however, be stressed that this poverty was relative to male religious communities. The wealthiest of the Gilbertine nunneries, Watton, Sempringham, and Chicksands, all had net incomes in 1535 over £200. Only ten of the Benedictine nunneries were in this category: Watton was the sixth wealthiest nunnery in the country at the Dissolution. Only one Cistercian nunnery (Tarrant) had an income higher (£214) than £200 in 1535, while two more had incomes in excess of £100. A very crude averaging of incomes reinforces this picture. In 1535 the average income of a Cistercian nunnery was just under £50, of a house of Augustinian canonesses about £86, while that of the Gilbertine double houses was over £160. How should this relative prosperity be explained? What did benefactors find particularly attractive about the order? Motives are extremely difficult to analyse. Donors seldom explained why they were favouring one community, let alone why they were favouring one rather than another, but the following factors may have been influential. Gilbert was a local man and his order was limited to England.[24] The majority of Gilbertine foundations were confined to eastern England where the saint had laboured while alive and where his bones rested after death. It is also significant that all but one of the Gilbertine double houses were founded during Gilbert's own lifetime.[25] His popularity both as a charismatic holy man and as a spiritual leader close to the Angevin court was an undoubted driving force. Moreover, in spite of the early crises, associated above all with the scandal of the nun of Watton, Gilbert's Rule was carefully structured, providing an ordered society for nuns and canons which compared favourably with the much more ambiguous approach to religious women shown by the Cistercians and other new orders,

[23] Owen, *Church and Society*, 49.

[24] Though for attempts to establish priories beyond England, see below, 'Failures'.

[25] The exception is Shouldham, founded by Geoffrey fitzPeter, one of the order's greatest patrons.

while at the same time it was less exclusive and aristocratic in its clientele than the Fontevraudine priories in England.

Sempringham

The mother church of the Gilbertines emerged from the small quasi-eremitical community that Gilbert had established next to the parish church *c*.1131. This church was the nucleus of the foundation's resources, and the initial community of women, lay brethren, and sisters must have been supported by the parish tithes and the produce of the glebe, as well as by income from Gilbert's other church of West Torrington.[26] All accounts of the foundation agree that the community at Sempringham was established in its rudimentary form in 1131. Most would argue that 'about 1139 [the community was] raised to the status of the priory of St Mary on adjoining lands given by Gilbert de Gant'.[27] This hypothesis that Sempringham became a 'priory' under the patronage of Gilbert de Gant is hard to sustain. Indeed, it is doubtful whether it is even legitimate to call Gilbert's community a priory until the order was formally organized in the years immediately following 1147. The *Vita* never describes the settlement at Sempringham as a priory before the journey to Cîteaux; nor does it mention the establishment of the priory on a site somewhat to the west of the parish church shortly afterwards.[28] Neither does it indicate any involvement of Gilbert de Gant in the foundation. The earliest reference to the role of the de Gant family is found in a charter of Gilbert II de Gant dated between 1139 and 1153 in which he granted one knight's fee in Thorpe for the soul of his father 'per quem religio illa sanctimonialium inchoata et fundata est'.[29] Gilbert's father, Walter, had died in 1139, having taken the habit at Bardney, and though he has recently been

---

[26] While in the household of bishop Alexander, Gilbert had used the revenues from Sempringham and West Torrington churches for the relief of the poor. The *Vita* implies that both these churches were similarly used for the maintenance of the nascent community (*Book of St Gilbert*, 20–1, 30–1).

[27] *Book of St Gilbert*, pp. xx–xxi. The source of the belief that Gilbert II de Gant was the founder of the priory would appear to be the jurors' statement in 1274–5 that Sempringham held three carucates 'super quas prioratus fundatus est', by gift of Gilbert de Gant made 160 (*sic*) years or more earlier (*Rotuli Hundredorum*, ed. W. Illingworth and J. Caley, 2 vols., Record Commission (1812–18), ii. 254). This chronology is obviously faulty. See also Graham, *St Gilbert*, 12, and *Medieval Religious Houses*, 195. The role of the Gant family in the foundation of Sempringham is also discussed in M. Abbott, 'The Gant Family in England 1066–1191', Ph.D. thesis (Cambridge University, 1973), 230–5.

[28] Graham and Braun, 'Excavations', 75.

[29] *Sempringham Charters*, xv. 223. Unfortunately, no original charters of Walter de Gant relating to lands in Sempringham survive.

described as the lay founder 'as donor of the land on which Gilbert was to establish his first priory', there is no evidence for this role.[30]

In 1086 there were three manors in Sempringham; the largest was held by Alfred of Lincoln.[31] Over half of this land had been subinfeudated to Jocelin, Gilbert's father, who also held a quarter of the church. Since the *caput* of Alfred's barony lay at Thoresway, some 40 miles to the north, it is likely that Jocelin was the dominant lord in the village.[32] The next largest manor was held (seemingly in demesne) by Gilbert I de Gant, and formed part of the sokeland of Folkingham, the *caput* of Gilbert's Lincolnshire lands. He also had shares in two churches, presumably those at Sempringham and Aslackby. Robert de Todeni, lord of Belvoir, held one carucate in the vill.[33] Like so many eleventh-century villages in Lincolnshire, therefore, Sempringham was a community of divided lordship with a divided church: such an arrangement was to have important implications for the development of Gilbert's priory, for it meant that he would have to rely upon the generosity and goodwill of several local families for survival.[34] By 1131 Gilbert of Sempringham's father was almost certainly dead, as he does not appear amongst the known benefactors to his son's community. The family estates had passed to Gilbert's younger brother Roger, since Gilbert as a cleric could not himself inherit.[35] It was to this group of local lords that he had to look for initial support.

The clearest indication of the lands held by the priory in the twelfth century is provided by Richard I's confirmation charter of 1189. By this date the priory held the whole vill of Sempringham. Yet there is no mention of any grant by Walter or Gilbert II de Gant in Sempringham, though it does confirm the latter's grant of a fee in Thorpe and a mill in Birthorpe.[36] It seems likely that by the 1130s the de Gant manor in

[30] *Book of St Gilbert*, p. xvii; cf. Foreville's view that Gilbert II was the founder (see above, n. 27).

[31] *Lincolnshire Domesday*, 130. It had previously been in the possession of earl Morcar. Shortly after 1066 Ulf, a leading Lincolnshire thegn, bequeathed these lands to Ramsey abbey. As the editor of the Lincolnshire Domesday wrote, 'it would be presumptuous to offer any explanation of this discrepancy', and, whatever the tenurial complications in the years immediately following the Conquest, it is clear that by 1086 Ramsey had not received the manor and that Alfred was in undisputed possession (ibid., pp. xlii–xliv).

[32] Sanders, *English Baronies*, 88. Jocelin also held lands at Alvingham, Cockerington, and West Torrington of Alfred, but the greater part of his estates lay in Sempringham (*Lincolnshire Domesday*, 130, 126). [33] Ibid. 114, 98.

[34] For the tenurial structure in Lincolnshire, see the introduction to the *Lincolnshire Domesday*, and F. M. Stenton, *Types of Manorial Structure in the Northern Danelaw* (Oxford, 1910). Other Gilbertine priories, notably Alvingham, were to face a similar problem.

[35] *EYC*, vi. 252–4.

[36] *Sempringham Charters*, xvi. 227. Birthorpe lay in Sempringham parish. Abbott

Sempringham had, in any case, been subinfeudated. Adam de Amundeville granted 11 bovates to Sempringham 'which Gilbert de Gant once my lord gave to me for my service', while Godwin the Rich of Lincoln granted a carucate there *c*.1177, which he held of the fee of countess Alice de Gant, who had succeeded her father, Gilbert II, in 1156. The total amount of land granted from this fee amounts to two carucates three bovates, approximating to the assessed holding of two carucates six bovates in 1086.[37] All this strongly suggests that the de Gants' role in the foundation of Sempringham (*pace* the jurors of 1274–5 and later authorities) was a passive one, and extended no further than confirming the grants of their tenants. There is further, if negative, evidence for this hypothesis. It is surprising, if either Walter or Gilbert had played an important part in the foundation, that there is no mention of them in the *Vita*. Additionally, there is no evidence that Gilbert II de Gant viewed the Gilbertines with special affection. He founded the Cistercian abbey of Rufford, of which he was a generous patron, and clearly had a close relationship with the Augustinian priory of Bridlington, where he wished to be buried. These were the chief foci of his piety. His father's chief ties had been with Bridlington, which he founded, and Bardney, where he died.[38]

If neither Walter nor Gilbert II de Gant can any longer be regarded as the 'founder' of Sempringham, what of the other lords and their tenants? Early in the priory's history Ralph de Badvent confirmed to 'master Gilbert and the nuns of Sempringham' (a terminology which in its lack of reference to any canons or clerks suggests an early date) his father Richard's grant of one carucate which Agnes *de Bellafago* had given to him for his service.[39] Richard's grant, however, though generous in its terms, cannot be regarded as the foundation grant, for the wording of the charter

suggested ('Gant Family', 232) that by the 13th century it would be natural to ascribe this grant to Gilbert, rather than Walter (who would have been alive 160 years before), since Gilbert was now the usual family Christian name (see above, n. 27).

[37] *Sempringham Charters*, xv. 159–60. Adam also held a fee in Edenham of Simon de St Liz, husband of Alice de Gant, in 1166 (C. T. Clay, 'The Family of Amundeville', *Lincolnshire Architectural and Archaeological Society Reports and Papers*, 3/2 (1948), 131).

[38] GEC vii. 672–3; *EYC* ii, no. 1138, 429–30, 432–6; *Rufford Charters*, ed. C. J. Holdsworth, 4 vols., Thoroton Society Record Series, 29, 30, 32, 34 (1972, 1974, 1980, 1981), i, pp. xx–xxvi.

[39] Sanders, *English Baronies*, 12, where it is stated 'she [i.e. Agnes] does not seem to have retained any Belvoir lands'. Agnes is probably to be identified with Robert de Todeni's sister who married Hubert de Ria, and the carucate is probably that which belonged to the de Todeni fee in 1086. Certainly, Hubert de Ria granted the church and land in Aslackby which had earlier belonged to the de Todeni fee (*Sempringham Charters*, xv. 224–5, xvi. 227).

presupposes the house's existence. This leaves Roger son of Jocelin for consideration. Apart from the *prima facie* argument that Gilbert's own brother and the inheritor of their father's lands would be the most likely first patron, his donation ranks first in the list of benefactions confirmed by royal charter in 1189. This was the largest grant made in the village of Sempringham. Close consideration of the charter of Roger, which can be dated between 1148 and 1155, and which appears as the first charter on the Exchequer roll of 1410, confirms this view. After the conventional greeting Roger states that, having seen the affliction of the handmaidens of Christ and having compassion on the poverty of the community which had been begun at Sempringham, he has given nine bovates of his land in Sempringham and Billingborough, together with a mill in Cockerington, with the consent of his lord, Ralph de Bayeux. Later, 'manu misericordie Dei qui flagellat omnem filium quem recipit', he gave the remainder of his land in Sempringham and Billingborough, which amounted to four carucates three bovates. In addition Roger is known to have given the parish church of St Andrew, Sempringham, with its dependent chapel of Pointon to the community, while Roger and Gilbert's sister, Agnes, gave Gilbert their other demesne church of West Torrington.[40] It will be argued below that it was difficult for a community to flourish unless it possessed the parish church. In 1086 half of the church of Sempringham was held by Gilbert de Gant, a quarter by Alfred of Lincoln, while the other quarter was presumably in the possession of Robert de Todeni. It is likely that the whole church had come into the hands of Jocelin by the time he granted his son the living, and no other interest in the church is recorded when Roger gave it to the priory. This suggests that he was by now the dominant lord in the village; his support for his brother was essential if the community was to flourish.[41]

All the demesne lords had played their part in the foundation of the priory, while their own lords had, at least passively, supported the new foundation with their confirmations. But when we look for an initiator of this corporate effort it is surely to Roger son of Jocelin, rather than to the de Gant family, that we should turn. There is one final question: the date of the establishment of the priory. If it is no longer the case that a 'new' priory was established *c.*1139 there is at least the possibility that the new buildings were not required until after Gilbert's return from Cîteaux and

---

[40] *Sempringham Charters*, xv. 158–9, xvi. 226. *Registrum Antiquissimum*, iii. 26. This suggests that at least part of Gilbert's inheritance had been divided between his brother and sister.

[41] The confirmation of this grant by Hugh de Bayeux (who succeeded his father in 1158) is printed in *Monasticon*, vi. 2. 947.

the introduction of the canons. Of the four charters relating to Sempringham on the Exchequer roll of 1410 none can be dated before 1148. While a charter recording a grant of land can post-date the actual grant (sometimes by many years), there is little compelling evidence for the development of the landed estates of the community at Sempringham until after the return of Gilbert from France, that is, at the same time as the other Gilbertine priories of north Lincolnshire were being endowed.

Haverholme

According to the *Vita*, following the establishment of the community at Sempringham 'many rich and noble Englishmen' began to grant estates to Gilbert and under his 'guidance began to build many houses in many regions'. Gilbert was reluctant to accept these grants, and rejected a number, but ultimately perceiving the expansion to be God's will and unwilling to 'obstruct the devotion of generous donors' he acquiesced in his movement's growth.[42] This is hyperbole. Only one new community was founded before Gilbert's visit to Cîteaux, and there is little evidence that 'earls and barons' were offering 'lands, estates and many possessions'.[43] However, the *Vita* is correct in attributing the commencement of this process to bishop Alexander of Lincoln.[44] In 1137 he proposed to establish a daughter house of Fountains at Haverholme, which lay in the marshes of the river Slea, a few miles north-west of the episcopal manor of Sleaford. This gift was accepted and lay brethren sent to construct the buildings. Two years later monks were dispatched from Fountains to the new foundations of Kirkstead and Haverholme. However, having inspected the site, they were dissatisfied and in exchange received land on another episcopal estate. This became the abbey of Louth Park.[45] The reason for the monks' discontent is unknown, but the new site was certainly more suited for agriculture than marshy, undrained Haverholme. The same year Alexander decided to pass the unwanted land to Gilbert. In his lengthy foundation charter Alexander describes how he has given

[42] *Book of St Gilbert*, 38–40.

[43] Ibid. 38–40. For the involvement of the magnates in Gilbertine foundations, see below, Ch. 5: 'Contexts for growth': 'The feudal matrix'.

[44] *Book of St Gilbert*, 38–9. The role of bishop Alexander as a patron of Gilbert has been cogently argued by Dyson, 'Monastic Patronage', 14–24, and see above, Ch. 1: 'From Sempringham to Cîteaux': 'The first communities'. The completion of the work of foundation is attributed to Henry II, presumably a reference to the recent royal foundation of Newstead (*c*.1171) and, perhaps, Marlborough.

[45] *Monasticon*, v. 414 (from the Louth Park chronicle).

to the nuns land sufficient for their needs, the island of Haverholme, and two mills. Yet for all his expression of concern for the community's well-being it is clear that this grant was no more sufficient for the Gilbertines than it had been for the Cistercians.[46] Two other lords, Ralph Halselin and Robert de Cauz, had an interest in Haverholme, and their support had to be obtained and their potential losses compensated.[47] Indeed, on closer examination it is apparent that Alexander did little more than provide a rather unsalubrious site. The year 1139 was a fraught one for the bishop: he would have had little time to devote himself to the affairs of his foundation. Furthermore, Haverholme island does not appear to have been part of the manor of (Old) Sleaford but to have lain on the bounds of Ruskington and Anwick. In neither of these places did the bishop have an interest, and it may even be questioned by what right Alexander donated the island, unless he had purchased or otherwise acquired rights from the Hauselin or de Cauz families. Certainly the early history of the priory is dominated by these local gentry families and without their support there would have been little future for the nuns. As in the case of Sempringham itself, it looks as if Haverholme was far from flourishing for a decade after its foundation. In 1141 Simon Tuschet gave lands in Ashby de la Laund 'ne illius loci supradicti [sc. Haverholme] virginibus deo dedicatis vite necessaria in aliquo defecerint'.[48] Moreover, and again there are parallels at Sempringham, it was local families who ensured its eventual survival.[49]

The North Lincolnshire Foundations

Until Gilbert returned from France in 1148, only two communities had been established. Both were poorly endowed and with an uncertain future. During the next few years there was considerable growth, especially concentrated in the region from which the founder had sprung. Five double houses were successfully founded in north Lincolnshire. They lay

[46] Though a charter of Ralph d'Aincurt does refer to the nuns at Haverholme 'quas ibi congregavit magister Gilebertus de Sempringham sub protectione . . . Alexandri episcopi' (London, BL, MS Lansdowne 207a).

[47] *Monasticon*, vi. 2. 948–9.

[48] This is the only grant which can be firmly dated before the reign of Henry II. It bears the unusual dating clause 'in anno quo commissum est prelium inter regem Stephanum et comitem Cestrie Ranulphum' ('Haverholme Priory Charters', 37–8).

[49] This is clearly demonstrated in Henry II's confirmation charter of 1175, which, although crediting Alexander with the foundation, shows the role of the neighbouring lords to have been paramount (*Cal. Ch. R.* iv. 403–4).

within a twenty-square-mile area and can be treated as a group.[50] They
share a number of features: in particular, the scale and type of initial
benefactions are similar, and the early benefactors were for the most part
recruited from the same social stratum. All these foundations are usually
ascribed to between 1148 and 1154.[51]

Alvingham

Alvingham lies about four miles to the north-west of the small town of
Louth. In the twelfth century it was close to the sea: active reclamation
from the sea and fen was extending the possibilities for agriculture, particularly sheep farming, though arable farming was also practised on the
higher clay-lands. It was a region of divided lordship and with a high
proportion of free peasants and sokemen, whose generosity towards the
new priory would do much to consolidate the community's local estates.

In the absence of a foundation charter there has been no general agreement as to the founder of Alvingham priory.[52] In fact, it is likely that no
one demesne lord was in a position to make a foundation by himself, for
their estates were too modest to endow even a small house. In 1086 there
were four manors in Alvingham, held by vassals of different tenants-in-
chief.[53] Stenton emphasized how complicated grants of churches to the
Gilbertines could be, ascribing this to a confusion of interests and relating
it to the frequent division of Lincolnshire villages into several lordships,
each holding a fraction of the church.[54] This phenomenon and explanation can be extended beyond parish churches to transactions in land. It is
more realistic to think in terms of a co-operative foundation rather than

---

[50] Alvingham, Bullington, Catley, North Ormsby, and Sixhills. Tunstall was also founded
but failed to survive.

[51] *Medieval Religious Houses*, 194; *Book of St Gilbert*, p. xxxi.

[52] Tanner was unsure: 'by whom founded, it does not certainly yet appear, whether by
Will. de Friston, Hugh de Scoteni, Hameline the dean or some other' (T. Tanner, *Notitia
Monastica: An Account of All Abbeys, etc. in England and Wales*, repr. J. Nasmith (Cambridge, 1787), Lincolnshire I). Dugdale did not venture an opinion. Graham hazarded a
foundation by Hugh de Scoteni or one of his tenants between 1148 and 1154; Stenton stated
categorically that the priory was founded by Roger son of Jocelin, a view followed by
Foreville, who adds that his work was completed by his nephew, Roger Mustel (*VCH
Lincolnshire*, ii. 192; *Gilbertine Charters*, p. xvi; *Book of St Gilbert*, p. xxxi). However, there
is no evidence for Roger Mustel's support of Alvingham, though he was a patron of Sixhills
and Bullington (Golding, 'Gilbertine Priories', 256–62). The foundation is investigated in
more detail, ibid. 7–11.)

[53] *Lincolnshire Domesday*, 23, 44, 126, 161. This fragmentation was to continue into the
13th century.

[54] *Gilbertine Charters*, pp. xxiii–xxiv. See below, Ch. 7: 'The donation of the churches'.

the act of a single benefactor: a venture in which each holder in demesne contributed something towards the initial endowment of the priory.

If no one founder stands out, it may be possible to suggest an initiator. Bishop Robert de Chesney issued the first confirmation charter in favour of Alvingham.[55] It confirms all the priory's possessions in general terms, but emphasizes the grants of three benefactors: Amfridus of Legbourne, William of Friston, and Hugh de Scoteni. Amfridus was not a benefactor in Alvingham; William had granted five tofts and four bovates, and Hugh a toft and bovate in the village. Clearly neither of these was adequate to maintain a foundation, however small. Yet the Scotenis at any rate certainly regarded themselves as having a special patronal relationship with the priory, for Sibyl, wife of Hugh's son, Lambert, later described herself as the community's lady and advocate.[56] No charters of Roger son of Jocelin survive. We have seen that he was a vital figure in the establishment of Sempringham, and it is likely that he was prime mover at Alvingham too. He gave his quarter-share of the parish church, of which Hamelin the dean, who held the other three quarters, was parson. Hamelin's charter clearly implies that Roger's grant preceded his own, but it is hard to see how Roger alone could have been responsible for the foundation since his estate in Alvingham was very small and was not sufficient to maintain a new community.[57] Hamelin's role is more shadowy. His only grant in Alvingham was his share of the church and his part in the foundation may well have been a minor one, the consolidation and corroboration of an existing foundation by a local ecclesiastical dignitary. None of these charters can be dated with any precision. The earliest date for Hugh's grant is 1148; the terminal date for his first charter is 1160.[58] William of Friston made at least one of his grants by 1153.[59] Hamelin's grant must be dated between 1160 and 1167.[60] Neither the founders, nor their initial grants, nor the time of their foundation of

---

[55] Oxford, Bodl. Lib., MS Laud Misc. 642, fo. 12aᵛ. Printed in *English Episcopal Acta. I*, 43–4, where it is suggested that it dates from early in the episcopate. The fact that it was addressed only to the nuns of Alvingham and makes no mention of the canons suggests that it pre-dates the latters' introduction.

[56] Oxford, Bodl. Lib., MS Laud Misc. 642, fo. 60. See below, Ch. 6: 'Patrons and benefactors': 'The founder as patron'.

[57] *Gilbertine Charters*, 103; *Lincolnshire Domesday*, 126.

[58] When one of the witnesses, Humphrey, subdean of Lincoln, apparently died (le Neve, *Fasti Ecclesiae Anglicana 1066–1300, iii. Lincoln*, 21).

[59] One of the witnesses to his charter, Gervase, abbot of Louth Park, was succeeded by Ralph of Norway by 1153 (*Heads of Religious Houses*, 137).

[60] His charter mentions bishop Robert and includes among the witnesses Robert, archdeacon of Lincoln (*Fasti. iii. Lincoln*, 25).

Alvingham are certainly known. It is clear, however, that even with a co-operative effort the early endowments of the priory were sparse, and it was to be several generations before the future of the community was secure.

Bullington

Bullington is situated about ten miles north-west of Lincoln. By contrast with Alvingham the region was heavily wooded and poorly drained, with few opportunities for substantial agricultural expansion. By the mid-twelfth century Bullington was dominated by one lord, Simon, son of William.[61] His origins are unclear, though it has been suggested that the family (which took the toponym 'of Kyme' in the following generation) descended from William, tenant of Walden the engineer in 1086.[62] Though the family possessed only $1\frac{1}{2}$ fees in chief, they held an additional 30 mesne fees and by the second half of the twelfth century possessed 'probably the largest holding of any knightly family in the kingdom . . . far larger than that of many of the barons'.[63] The family estates were held of at least ten different lords, and though the chronology of their acquisition is uncertain it seems most likely that they were accumulated during the first half of the twelfth century.[64] Davis has persuasively argued that Simon son of William was able to extend his hold over the three consti-tuent manors in Bullington and Goltho between 1158 and 1166, when the two manors which he did not hold (those of the earl of Chester and William de Romare) were in royal custody. As a vassal of the earl of Chester and as a servant of the king, Simon would have been well placed for aggrandizement.[65] Additionally, as a tenant of other Lincolnshire lords, including the bishops of Lincoln and Durham, Simon may well have been increasing his standing locally, gradually building up his holdings from a number of lords. If this is so, then the foundation of a priory very

---

[61] The vill was divided in 1086 between the bishop of Durham, the earl of Chester, and Ivo Taillebois. In 1212 only one lord was recorded there, Simon of Kyme, who held of the bishop of Lincoln (*Lincolnshire Domesday*, 31, 76, 85; *Book of Fees*, i. 171).

[62] It is possible that Simon's father, William, is William son of Anschetel, who at the time of the Lindsey Survey (1115–18) held the manor on which the priory was situated. The family is discussed in Golding, 'Gilbertine Priories', 217–37. See also Golding, 'Simon of Kyme: The Making of a Rebel', *Nottingham Medieval Studies*, 27 (1983), 23–5; W. Farrer, *Honors and Knight's Fees*, 3 vols. (London and Manchester, 1923–5), ii. 118–19; R. H. C. Davis, 'Goltho: The Manorial History', in G. Beresford, *Goltho: The Development of an Early Medieval Manor, c.850–1150*, English Heritage Archaeological Report, 4 (1987), 127–30.   [63] Farrer, *Honors and Knight's Fees*, ii. 118.

[64] Davis, 'Goltho', 127.   [65] Ibid. 129–30.

close to his own hall and sited in his park would have signalled his arrival in county society.

Between 1148 and 1155 Simon son of William granted the Gilbertines part of his demesne in Bullington, a portion of his park and wood, and lands to the north and east of the nuns' houses, which presupposes that the community was already established there in some form. Additionally he gave the two churches of Bullington and Langton; a mill; lands in Faldingworth (which were to be the nucleus of the priory's grange there), together with pasture for 600 sheep.[66] The original endowment of Bullington was considerably greater than that of any of the priories of the North Lincolnshire group, yet unlike most other Gilbertine houses the majority of its profits were derived from its other granges rather than from its home demesne, where there was little further development. The very dependence upon one family may be at least partly responsible for the priory's comparative failure. It relied to a very great extent upon the generosity of the Kymes, and they determined where its estates were to be. Bullington was a small village, and there was probably little more available land for the Kymes to give here.[67]

Catley

Catley was by some way the poorest of the double houses. In 1535 it had a net income of only £34, half that of the next poorest, Haverholme. Moreover, if the limitations placed upon the size of the priories in the 1190s indicate their relative prosperity and ability to maintain their communities, then it is apparent that even by this time Catley's poor endowment

---

[66] *Gilbertine Charters*, 91. Henry II's confirmation charter (*Danelaw Charters*, 2–3, no. 1) is almost certainly to be dated to the summer of 1155 ('Gilbertine Priories', 12 n.). A charter of Roger of Benniworth associates Simon's son, Philip I of Kyme, with his father as founder (*Gilbertine Charters*, 95). There is a slight problem as to where the original foundation was made, for though the foundation charter states that the park of Bullington was the original site, Henry II's confirmation charter refers to the grants made to the nuns of *Lindelai*. In the royal confirmation charter to the order issued between 1154 and 1161 there is also a reference to the nuns of 'Liguelega' (London, BL, MS Cotton Claudius D XI, fo. 30). There was a settlement of this name in the parish of Lea in the west of the county, and Canon Foster (*Lincolnshire Domesday*, p. lx) stated that the priory was first established here. However, since the Kymes are not known to have held any land in this area, and since the total possessions of Bullington in Lea amounted to only seven acres of meadow, this early settlement seems unlikely. Lindelai can mean 'limewood': if this is understood here then the name would seem to be the name of that wood in which Simon's park was situated.

[67] Particularly as the Kymes maintained an active interest in their estate here. In 1259–60 they received a greater income from it than from any other of their Lindsey lands (London, PRO Exchequer Accounts, Miscellaneous, E.101/505/11).

was recognized.[68] Yet at first sight the foundation of Catley seems as generous as any. Peter son of Henry of Billinghay gave the island of Catley with all its appurtenances including fisheries and a water mill; the site for a grange; a number of *culturae* of both arable and meadow land; two carucates in Walcot; the site of a vaccary; pasture for 400 sheep; and the church of Billinghay with its dependent chapel of Walcot and a carucate of arable in Billinghay (which may represent the glebe of the church).[69] The initial endowment was comparatively lavish and was certainly as large, and probably larger, than that of any of the Gilbertine houses in the area; the community enjoyed the support of local lords and, more importantly, their tenants, and it was later prepared and able to enter the land market to enlarge its holdings. Why, then, did the priory not flourish?

Three reasons can be proposed. It may not be coincidental that Peter of Billinghay is the most obscure of all the founders of Gilbertine houses. In 1166 he held one fee of the archbishop of York in Billinghay, but no other holding is recorded.[70] He also held a quarter fee of the Mowbray honour, though in Yorkshire rather than in Lincolnshire, and it has been suggested that he was one of Roger de Mowbray's household knights. The fact that he does not appear in Roger's *carta* of 1166 strongly suggests that he had not yet been enfeoffed with land.[71] Even in an age of small-scale benefactions and benefactors it was unusual for so modest a knight to undertake the foundation of a religious house.[72] By 1181 Peter was dead and was succeeded by his son, whose wardship was held by the archbishop, lord of his Lincolnshire fee.[73] There are signs that by this date the manor of Billinghay was in serious difficulties, and indications

---

[68] The maximum number of nuns and sisters was fixed at 60, lower than that at any other house.

[69] *Gilbertine Charters*, 72–3. The date of foundation cannot be precisely determined, though it was certainly established before December 1157 (ibid. 83).

[70] *Red Book of the Exchequer*, ed. H. Hall, 3 vols., Rolls Series (London, 1896), i. 414.

[71] *Charters of the Honour of Mowbray, 1107–1191*, ed. D. E. Greenway, British Academy Records of Social and Economic History, NS 1 (1972), pp. lxi, 224–5, no. 349. He figures fairly frequently as a witness to grants by Roger of Mowbray, e.g. of land in the Isle of Axholme to the Northamptonshire house of Sulby (*Danelaw Charters*, 293, no. 393) and of another grant in the Isle to St Leonard's hospital, York (*Charters of the Honour of Mowbray*, 201, no. 307).

[72] Not surprisingly his known grants to other religious houses seem limited to one of a toft in Billinghay to the Templars (*Records of the Templars in England in the Twelfth Century: The Inquest of 1185*, ed. B. A. Lees, British Academy Records of the Social and Economic History of England and Wales, 9 (1935), 86).

[73] Peter's heir in the Mowbray fee was his brother, Philip, a benefactor of Byland and Newburgh abbeys, as well as of Gilbertine Malton, to which he gave land in Hovingham which he had inherited from his brother (*Charters of the Honour of Mowbray*, 133–4, no. 188. See also ibid., pp. xl n., 225).

that at the time of his death Peter had financial problems.[74] Though the family continued to hold the fee of the archbishop for at least one more generation, its direct interest in the manor was probably almost wholly extinguished at the foundation of Catley. Moreover, the establishment of Catley must have left Peter with little for himself, or his heirs. It is noteworthy that only one additional grant from the family is known. When Peter II came to confirm his father's grants he gave *de dono meo* one acre in Billinghay.[75] This paltry benefaction suggests either that the family had lost interest in the priory, or, more likely, that there was no more to give. Perhaps the founder had been too generous for his own good, and, paradoxically, for the priory's good as well.

In such circumstances it was advisable, perhaps essential, to have the support of the patron's lord. There is no evidence that Peter's lord, the archbishop, supported his tenant's foundation or even confirmed his grants, while the Aincourts, lords of the other fee in the village, were almost equally unforthcoming.[76] While other priories frequently relied on the collective goodwill of local lords, Catley was unable to attract additional substantial local benefactors. The only patrons of baronial status were Ralf I and II Halselin and John de Aincourt. The Halselin family spread their grants widely, being benefactors of the Templars in both Nottinghamshire and Lincolnshire, as well as favouring neighbouring Haverholme.[77] Similarly the Aincourt family were benefactors of Haverholme, the Templars, Rufford, and Kirkstead.[78]

---

[74] In 1191 a Peter of Billinghay owed a total of £8 13s. 4d. to Aaron of Lincoln, for £3 3s. 4d. of which the prior of Catley stood pledge. This was probably Peter I de Billinghay rather than his son, Peter II. In 1191 the latter was only 11 years old, and, though he could have contracted the debts before Aaron's death in 1189, it seems more likely that they were those left unpaid at his father's death (*Pipe Rolls 3 and 4 Richard 1*, PRS, NS 2 (1926), 19–20). On the archbishop's death the wardship was assumed by the crown. Peter's son was then 15 years old. The manor of Billinghay had rendered £6 10s. 8d., but the archbishop had raised the farm to £16 'so that (as the jurors say) the *villata* and men are harmed (*distracti*)'. No land was held in demesne. Most of the tenants seem to have been *nativi*, though there were two free tenants rendering quitrents of a silver-plated spur and a pound of pepper. If the land had been stocked with 2 ploughs, 20 cows, 2 bulls, 100 sheep, 10 pigs, and a boar, the value of the estate was estimated at £11 1s. 6d. (*Rotuli de Dominabus et Pueris et Puellis de xii comitatibus*, ed. J. H. Round, PRS 35 (1913), 3–4). See also *Pipe Rolls, 30 Henry II*, PRS 33 (1912), 40; *31 Henry II*, PRS 34 (1913), 78, 79; *33 Henry II*, PRS 37 (1915), 48, 76, and *2 Richard I*, PRS, NS 1 (1925), 86.   [75] *Monasticon*, vi. 2. 968.

[76] *Gilbertine Charters*, 77–8, 79–80.

[77] *Records of the Templars*, 88, 93, 96, 98. For Haverholme, see 'Haverholme Priory Charters', 9–13, 19.

[78] For benefactions to Haverholme, see 'Haverholme Priory Charters', 38–9. For the family's involvement with Rufford, see *Rufford Charters*, i, pp. xxxvi–xxxvii; with Kirkstead, *Monasticon*, v. 419; with the Templars, *Records of the Templars*, 84, 85.

Moreover, the region around Catley was crowded with competing religious houses. Only a few miles away lay Haverholme, Temple Bruer, the Augustinian priories of Kyme and Nocton Park, and the wealthy Cistercian abbey of Kirkstead. Here the monastic garden was particularly overgrown. Another reason for the lack of prosperity may have been Catley's failure to attract *spiritualia*. It derived the lowest proportion of its total income from churches amongst any of the Gilbertine double houses and held only two rectories, Digby and Billinghay.[79] The failure to acquire churches inhibited the development of granges and cut the community off from such lucrative revenues as tithes.[80] Finally, Catley's position in the Witham fenland area was not conducive to economic success: 'before the improvements of the eighteenth century they [i.e. the fens] formed a swampy area of little value.'[81] Even with a seemingly substantial initial endowment it was impossible for Catley to flourish in this environment. A combination of factors, economic, tenurial, and geographic, worked against the priory. Its lack of success is a useful reminder that the foundation endowment was only the first determinant of a religious house's development.

Nun Ormsby

Nun Ormsby was as close a neighbour to Alvingham as Haverholme was to Catley. However, its setting was quite different, lying on the wolds about 250 feet above sea-level at the head of a small valley which opened into the flat marshland below. While its foundation endowment was smaller, the priory (though never wealthy) was considerably more prosperous than Catley. The foundation charter names Gilbert son of Robert as the *primus fundator*. Gilbert was a sub-tenant of William le Gros, count of Aumale, and the latter's involvement, extending beyond mere consent and confirmation, was explicitly stated in his vassal's charter.[82] Already by the mid-twelfth century lords were becoming concerned at the alienation by their tenants of land in free alms with a resultant loss of services and income. Gilbert's charter provides rare evidence for the arrangements

[79] It also received a pension from Dunsby church.

[80] See below, Ch. 8: 'The grange': 'The grange and the church.'

[81] H. C. Darby, *The Domesday Geography of Eastern England* (3rd edn., Cambridge, 1971), 93.

[82] *Gilbertine Charters*, 39. See also two charters of earl William. These can be dated between 1151 and 1160 (ibid. 41–2). In 1086 (and at the time of the Lindsey survey) there were three manors in Ormsby, of which the largest was the Aumale fee, the others being held by the bishop of Lincoln and Ivo Taillebois (which ultimately passed to the earldom of Chester) (*Lincolnshire Domesday*, 141, 50, 86).

that were made to compensate a lord for such losses.[83] Gilbert held his land in Ormsby of Odo de Fribois, a leading tenant of William le Gros in both Yorkshire and Lincolnshire.[84] In his charter Gilbert announced that the earl had assigned to Odo the service of Stephen de Lund (another Yorkshire tenant of the Aumale fee) for the service of the land which had been granted to the nuns in free alms. It was this kind of support from the great lords, who were not often 'direct' patrons of the Gilbertines and who were often (as here) not even resident in Lincolnshire, which was essential if the new priories were to survive.[85]

Gilbert's grant consisted of half of his two churches of Ormsby and Utterby together with a third of all his land, amounting to 20 bovates in the two villages, besides other closes and parcels of land, including six acres which he had given from his demesne on the occasion of his wife's death. This clearly indicates that the charter post-dated, perhaps by some years, the actual foundation. Moreover, the reference to a dead wife, and the fact that Gilbert was giving a third of his land, suggest that it was his wife's dower that was being used to endow the new priory.[86] It is doubtful if Gilbert's endowment would have been sufficient in itself to establish a new priory. Twenty bovates was not a particularly large estate and, more importantly, the new community really needed control over the whole of the parish church. As Stenton noted, Ormsby 'soon after its foundation received gifts from each fee'.[87] The most significant of these was that of Ralph of Wyham, a tenant of the bishop of Lincoln, who gave his share in the churches of Ormsby and Utterby, thereby completing the nuns' control over them, along with a *cultura* of arable, land to the north of Ormsby which had belonged to the church of St Andrew, Utterby, before it was consecrated, and all his land within the close where the nuns lived.[88] With the church and a sizeable estate in Ormsby achieved, the

---

[83] For the development of free alms tenure and the question of the canons' liability to forinsec and other services, see Golding, 'Gilbertine Priories', 95–109 and the references there cited.

[84] William had granted his lands in Ormsby to Odo of Fribois for 1/7th of a fee, and a survey dated between 1238 and 1241 shows Gilbert of Ormsby holding half the villages of Ormsby and Utterby of Robert of Fribois (*Book of Fees*, i. 156, cf. ii. 1023; ii. 1474). For the Fribois family, see B. English, *The Lords of Holderness, 1086–1260: A Study in Feudal Society* (Oxford, 1979), 146, 171, and *EYC* iii. 72–3.

[85] For a similar case of a lord's encouragement of a vassal's foundation, see Rannulf of Bayeux' support for Peter of Goxhill's foundation of Newhouse (*Red Book of the Exchequer*, i. 387).

[86] For examples of nunneries founded with a wife's dowry, see Thompson, *Women Religious*, 177. [87] *Gilbertine Charters*, p. xii.

[88] 'totam partem mean infra clausum earum ubi habitant' (ibid. 40).

nuns could now proceed to the consolidation and expansion of their local estates.

Sixhills

Sixhills occupied a similar position to North Ormsby at about the same altitude on the edge of the wolds, with easy availability of both arable and pastoral land, but facing westwards, a few miles east of Market Rasen. No foundation charter survives and the priory's early history poses as many problems as those of Alvingham and Sempringham. In 1086 there were three estates in the village. Of these the largest was sokeland belonging to Hainton and held of Roger le Poitevin.[89] The other manors were smaller but less fragmented: one, which contained the church, was held by Ilbert de Lacy of the bishop of Bayeux, the other was held in demesne by Reiner de Brimou.[90] As in the case of Sempringham and Alvingham, therefore, any religious community established in the village would have to attract the support and goodwill of several lords in order to prosper.

Following Dugdale and Tanner, Graham, the editors of *Medieval Religious Houses*, and Foreville have ascribed the foundation of Sixhills to the de Greslei family.[91] This assumption seems to have been based on a statement in a now-lost extent of 1322/3 which reads '. . . de Grelle . . . fundator erat ejusdem abbathiae [sc. Sixhills]'.[92] Albert I de Greslei was a Domesday tenant of Roger le Poitevin in Lancashire and the family continued to hold of Stephen of Blois after Roger lost his lands.[93] But Robert I de Greslei, Albert's son, does not seem to have held lands in Sixhills in 1115–18, though he did hold five bovates in nearby Nettleton of the crown, which was once part of Roger's fee.[94] Though a grant by Albert de Greslei of two bovates and a toft in Hainton along with

---

[89] This was assessed at just over 2½ carucates and was held by 30 sokemen (*Lincolnshire Domesday*, 92). By 1115–18 Roger's lands had escheated to the crown and were held by Stephen of Blois, count of Mortain.

[90] *Lincolnshire Domesday*, 43, 160. The de Brimou manor was the more prosperous, being valued at 30s. By 1115–18 the tenurial pattern had changed: Ilbert's lands had been granted (with the whole of the Lacy barony) to Hugh de la Val on the forfeiture of Ilbert's son, Robert, and Ralph de Criol had acquired Reiner de Brimou's land (ibid. 245, 256, 257; Sanders, *English Baronies*, 130–1, 138).

[91] *Monasticon*, vi. 2. 964; Graham, *St Gilbert*, 35; *Medieval Religious Houses*, 196; *Book of St Gilbert*, p. xxxi.   [92] *Monasticon*, vi. 2. 964.

[93] Sanders, *English Baronies*, 130–1; W. Farrer, *Lancashire Inquests, Extents and Feudal Aids, AD 1205–AD 1307*, Lancashire and Cheshire Record Society, 48 (1903), pp. xv, 52–3.

[94] *Lincolnshire Domesday*, 94, 251. However, by 1185, when Albert III de Greslei's lands were in wardship, the family did have a manor in Sixhills which was then held by Thomas and Gilbert Basset (*Rotuli de Dominabus*, 8).

other grants both there and in Sixhills is mentioned in Henry II's general confirmation charter of 1186–8, they are given no special prominence.[95]

Stenton ascribed the foundation of Sixhills to William son of Hacon. He, with his wife Ediva and son, Thomas, gave the church of Sixhills and one carucate there; a mill on Tealby water; two bovates in North Willingham; five bovates in Nettleton, together with a sixth part of the church 'which belongs to that land'.[96] This almost certainly represents the priory's foundation endowment. William's family is of considerable interest. Stenton long ago argued that it was established in the shire before 1066 and that Ediva was a form of the common Old English name Eadgyfu.[97] Hacon had one plough-team in Hainton in 1086 which he held of Roger le Poitevin. Moreover, Manasser I de Arsic is recorded to have granted his $6\frac{1}{2}$ bovates in South Willingham to Hacon at an annual farm of 20s. If this is so—and certainly the name Hacon suggests an Anglo-Scandinavian origin—then it seems likely that here we have a family of native origin which survived the Conquest more or less intact and remained of local standing until at least the mid-twelfth century.[98] Hacon was probably dead by the time of the Lindsey Survey (1115–18). He was succeeded by William. At some point William also acquired an interest in the Sixhills manor of the Bayeux fee. Certainly the grant to the priory of all his land in Sixhills comprising one carucate appears to represent the bishop's manor, on which the church was founded, in 1086. But the family was also acquiring land from other sources. In 1212 Hugh de Scoteni (who died between 1150 and 1155) was said to have granted Hacon and his heirs a knight's fee comprising six bovates in Hainton, four bovates in Barkwith, and four in Strubby.[99] This must be a garbled entry, for no Hacon of Hainton held there in the mid-twelfth century, and the only person of that name known is the Domesday tenant, but it may well be a confused reference to an earlier enfeoffment by Hugh's predecessor, later confirmed by Hugh to Hacon's heirs. This hypothesis is supported by a reference in the Lindsey Survey. Ralph de Criol (whose lands later passed to the Scotenis) held two bovates in Strubby and a carucate in Barkwith and Hainton, and it is probably these lands that are referred to in 1212. Moreover, in the early twelfth century William son of

---

[95] *Gilbertine Charters*, 36. Moreover, Albert II de Greslei did not succeed his father, Robert I, until 1157–8, i.e. until after the priory's foundation (Sanders, *English Baronies*, 130).

[96] *Gilbertine Charters*, pp. xi, 1. The reference to the divided church is a striking example of the tenurial fragmentation in the area.   [97] Ibid., p. xi.

[98] *Lincolnshire Domesday*, 91, 256; *Book of Fees*, i. 171.   [99] *Book of Fees*, i. 170.

Hacon also held $7\frac{1}{2}$ bovates in Cuxwold, and $1\frac{1}{2}$ carucates in Clee of Hugh de la Val.[100] While the dynamic behind this story of advancement by the son of a pre-Conquest tenant cannot be recovered, what is certain is that by the mid-twelfth century William son of Hacon was established as a not insignificant member of the Lincolnshire knightly class. By the end of Henry I's reign he was a sheriff of Lincolnshire.[101] The native family had come to terms with the new rulers: Hacon and William had retained their family lands and had acquired others. Like their Anglo-Norman contemporaries they now marked their advance by the establishment of a modest priory.[102]

On balance, then, it seems likely that William son of Hacon was the founder of Sixhills. His charter is entered first in the long Exchequer transcript of documents and his grant is the first following the confirmation of the king's own small grant to the community to be listed in Henry II's general confirmation charter. While it is true that William's charter presupposes the existence of the priory and contains no explicit statement of foundation, it is clear that this grant formed the nucleus of the priory's holdings. But it is equally apparent that William's generosity was not in itself enough to support the nuns. As was the case with most of the Gilbertine foundations, if Sixhills was to survive it would need the support of many other local lords.

The Mid-Century Expansion

Watton

At the same time as Gilbertine priories were being established in their north Lincolnshire heartland, the first communities were also appearing

---

[100] *Lincolnshire Domesday*, 256, 247, 248.

[101] J. A. Green, *The Government of England under Henry I* (Cambridge, 1986), 155, 205. William also appears to have held property in Lincoln (*Records of the Templars*, 82) and is also probably to be identified as the holder of land in the far north of the county at Barrow-on-Humber. William of Hainton witnessed a charter in favour of Rufford abbey granting land in Barton-on-Humber (*Danelaw Charters*, nos. 246, 349, pp. 183, 263).

[102] A parallel can be drawn between this family and that of Adam fitzSwein. At exactly the same time Adam, another native survivor, was engaged in the foundation of a Cluniac priory, Monk Bretton, in Yorkshire. See B. J. Golding, 'The Coming of the Cluniacs', *Proceedings of the Battle Conference in Anglo-Norman Studies 3 (1980)*, ed. R. A. Brown (Woodbridge, 1981), 69. By 1166 William was dead, and in that year his son Thomas (who was associated with him in the foundation of Sixhills) is recorded as holding one fee of Lambert of Scoteni, though charter evidence indicates that he was a considerably more important figure than the *carta* return would suggest (*Red Book of the Exchequer*, i. 386). He

further afield. Both Watton and Malton priories were founded by one of the greatest magnates of twelfth-century Yorkshire, Eustace fitzJohn. Eustace, whose origins were modest, first appears at the royal court *c*.1119. Thereafter until his death in 1157 he enjoyed an illustrious, if chequered, political career. He was a loyal servant of Henry I, and frequently served as a royal justice in the north during the last years of the king's reign. Described by the author of the *Gesta Stephani* as the king's 'summus et popularis amicus', he was rewarded with considerable favours and granted substantial estates. By his first marriage to Beatrix, the daughter and heiress of Ivo de Vesci, he succeeded to the lordships of both Alnwick and Malton, and on her death married Agnes, the sister and joint heiress of William, constable of Chester, from whom his family gained the hereditary constableship. On Henry's death Eustace supported Matilda and shortly after his accession king Stephen seized some of Eustace's castles. He promptly went over to the side of king David of Scotland, of whom he already held some fiefs, and fought on the Scots' side at the battle of the Standard. Shortly afterwards, however, he was pardoned by Stephen and recovered his lands and offices.[103] Eustace is an archetypal parvenu, a loyal servant of the crown, of modest background, perhaps not even an eldest son. His services and marriages brought him substantial wealth. With his fellow justice and neighbour in the north, Walter Espec, a man of similar origins and career, he 'did much to promote a revival of the religious life in northern England'. These royal servants were concerned to insure their souls adequately, though not grandiloquently; the majority founded English Augustinian or similar communities. By so doing they marked their own social and political promotion and furthered the monastic cause in their regions of influence.[104]

Around 1150 Eustace founded three religious houses: Malton, Watton, and a Premonstratensian abbey at Alnwick.[105] Watton and Malton were

continued to be a benefactor to the Gilbertines and was also a patron of Newhouse abbey, to which he granted land in Grimsby (this grant had Hugh, the first recorded prior of Sixhills, as its first witness (*Danelaw Charters*, no. 259, pp. 193–4)).

[103] Green (*Government of England*, 153–4, 250–2) places Eustace in his social and political contexts. See also GEC xii (part 2), 272–4; G. Barraclough, 'Some Charters of the Earls of Chester', in P. M. Barnes and C. Slade (eds.), *A Medieval Miscellany for Doris Mary Stenton*, PRS, NS 36 (1960), 24–38. [104] Green, *Government of England*, 153–4.

[105] He was probably also responsible for the foundation of North Ferriby, of the Order of the Temple of the Lord at Jerusalem, but there is no documentary evidence for its existence earlier than 1160. I owe this reference to Janet Burton. See also *Medieval Religious Houses*, 168. He was also a benefactor of other Yorkshire houses, especially Bridlington and Fountains. Eustace's religious foundations (especially Alnwick) are discussed in Colvin, *The*

the first Gilbertine priories in Yorkshire, and, indeed, with the possible
exception of Chicksands, the first foundations outside Lincolnshire. They
thus represent a new stage in the expansion of the order. According to
Rose Graham, Watton was founded on the advice of archbishop Henry
Murdac in expiation of Eustace's part in the Scots' invasion of 1138.[106]
This statement has been repeated by most later commentators but no
evidence for it has ever been presented.[107] Graham referred to the foundation charter printed in the *Monasticon*, but this makes no reference to
Murdac's influence. Neither does Murdac's own confirmation charter,
issued at the request of Eustace fitzJohn and William Fossard.[108] Thus,
although Eustace's foundations should undoubtedly be seen in the context of the upsurge in monastic foundations during and immediately
following Stephen's reign, there is no explicit evidence that Watton was
founded as an act of contrition. Moreover, there is some indication that
the foundation at Watton was inspired by Eustace's second wife, Agnes.
She was certainly associated with her husband in the foundation charter,
and in a charter issued by Agnes alone she makes it clear that the vill of
Watton was part of her *maritagium*. Her charter, unlike the foundation
charter, was witnessed by master Gilbert and two of his canons.[109] Agnes

---

White Canons, 53–4. See also C. A. Newman, *The Anglo-Norman Nobility in the Reign of
Henry I: The Second Generation* (Philadelphia, 1988), 76. For Fountains see R. Gilyard-Beer
and G. Coppack, 'Excavations at Fountains Abbey, North Yorkshire, 1979–80: The Early
Development of the Monastery', *Archaeologia*, 108 (1986), 149. He had already become a
benefactor of the Augustinian priory of Norton (Cheshire), which had been founded (at
Runcorn) by Eustace's predecessor as constable of Chester, William fitzNigel (J. Tait, 'The
Foundation Charter of Runcorn (later Norton) Priory', *Chetham Society Miscellany*, NS 100
(1939), 16; J. P. Greene, *Norton Priory: The Archaeology of a Medieval Religious House*
(Cambridge, 1989), 5).

[106]   Graham, *St Gilbert*, 38.

[107]   See e.g. Colvin, *The White Canons*, 54; *VCH Yorkshire*, iii. 254; *Book of St Gilbert*,
pp. xxxi–xxxii.

[108]   *English Episcopal Acta. V. York, 1070–1154*, ed. J. E. Burton (Oxford, 1988), 100–2,
no. 129. Burton suggests a date of 1151. In 1086 there were two estates at Watton: one,
assessed at 3 carucates, was held of the king by its pre-Conquest tenant, while the other,
which was much larger and consisted of 13 carucates, was held by Robert of Mortain, who
had granted it to Nigel Fossard (*VCH Yorkshire*, ii. 225, 287, 320). This manor had been
held by four tenants T.R.E.; the descendant of one of these later sold a carucate to Stephen,
abbot of St Mary's, York (*c*.1080–1112). On the death of Robert of Mortain, Nigel Fossard
became tenant-in-chief (*EYC* ii. 325–6). The Fossards continued to hold Watton until the
mid-12th century, when William I Fossard was lord, but it is unknown when Eustace
acquired his tenancy here. In 1166 William de Vesci, Eustace's son and heir, held seven
Fossard fees (ibid. ii. 331).

[109]   *EYC* ii. 406–7, no. 1109. Another charter (ibid. 407–8, no. 1111), issued by Agnes's
half-brother, refers to Eustace's grant 'prece et assensu Agnetis'. Her land in Watton had
been held by two tenants, who received other lands in Yorkshire and Northamptonshire in
compensation (ibid. 406–9, nos. 1109, 1111, 1112).

was a cousin of Gilbert de Gant, Gilbert of Sempringham's lord, and her family was to continue close relations with the Gilbertines over several generations.[110] The endowment of Watton included the founder's manor in the village along with the grant of a tenant, Orm, and his three bovates of land which was to become the nucleus of the priory's grange in North Ferriby.[111] It was also necessary to obtain the consent of Eustace and Agnes's lord, William Fossard, to the foundation. This was duly given in the presence of Henry Murdac, and at Eustace's request he released the nuns from his claim to the service of two knights, assigning his grant for the maintenance of 13 canons to support the nuns.[112]

Chicksands

Chicksands is in one respect an anomaly amongst the early Gilbertine double houses, since it was not only the first but was for many years the sole Gilbertine foundation outside Lincolnshire and Yorkshire.[113] Unusually for Gilbertine houses, a very early original charter, probably the foundation charter, survives detailing the initial endowment of Payn de Beauchamp and his wife, the countess Rohaise. It can almost certainly be dated between 1151 and 1153.[114] Though it has recently been suggested that the countess Rohaise was the sole founder, there is no evidence in the foundation charter to support this hypothesis.[115] Nevertheless, she may have been the prime instigator of the foundation. Thompson has shown how many twelfth-century English nunneries were founded by aristocratic women, and that sometimes the wife's role in a joint husband-and-wife foundation is obscured in the foundation document. On occasion it can be proved, for example, that the foundation was made on dower land, or that the joint foundress or her daughters entered the new foundation. Though there is no indication that this happened here, Rohaise was

---

[110] John, constable of Chester, and Agnes's grandson, was said by the author of the *Vita* to greatly revere Gilbert's holiness, and he possessed two relics of the saint, his staff and scapular, by which miracles were effected (*Book of St Gilbert*, 288–90, 304). John was a generous benefactor of monasteries and founded the Cistercian abbey of Stanlaw (Cheshire).

[111] *EYC* ii. 404.

[112] *EYC* ii. 405–6. The charter concludes with a note that William had handed over his quittance and Eustace's petition to the archbishop ('in manu mea tradidit').

[113] It did, however, lie in Lincoln diocese.

[114] London, BL, Harl. Chart. 45 I 7 (pr. *Monasticon*, vi. 2. 950). The first witness is Henry Murdac, archbishop of York. He died in 1153, and though he was elected in 1147, he did not take full possession of his see until 1151 (*Heads of Religious Houses*, 146 and n.). Burton points out (pers. comm.) that Murdac, though he could not enter York till 1151, was active as archbishop from the time of his election. [115] Elkins, *Holy Women*, 56–7.

closely involved with the foundation and herself granted the nuns a substantial grange in Chippenham (Cambridgeshire) from her own lands.[116]

Payn de Beauchamp succeeded his brother Miles as lord of the barony of Bedford and married *c*.1144 Rohaise, widow of Geoffrey I de Mandeville, first earl of Essex.[117] By the time he and his wife founded Chicksands they were already benefactors of the collegiate church of St Paul, Bedford (which later became the Augustinian priory of Newnham). Their choice of a Gilbertine foundation is difficult to explain. The foundation charter makes it clear that the community was already established, probably just as a group of nuns, at the parish church.[118] As at Haverholme there is no mention of lay brethren or canons and the nuns are described in the same terms, serving God 'sub custodia Gileberti de Sempingeham'.[119] The charter also confirms earlier grants made by Adela, wife of Wigan, in Cople and by Adela, wife of Walter de Mareis, in Campton. The association of these female benefactors in the confirmation might suggest a wider interest in the foundation of a nunnery by a group of local women of influence.

The initial grant was a substantial one. All the lands were part of Hugh de Beauchamp's fee in 1086, though it should be emphasized that very little was given from the Beauchamps' demesne land in Chicksands. Instead they gave the holdings of three tenants: Richard *monachus*, Avenel, and Warner of Hawnes.[120] The grant of the church seems here, as elsewhere, to have provided a nucleus of the estate. In addition they gave a grange and 40 acres in the neighbouring village of Hawnes; again this was a holding of two tenants, Norman the priest and Geoffrey Lohareng, who were obliged to assign the land to the nuns in the presence of many witnesses. Payn and Rohaise also granted most of Appley wood, their

---

[116] Thompson, *Women Religious*, 167–77; G. H. Fowler (ed.), 'Early Charters of the Priory of Chicksand', *Publications of the Bedfordshire Historical Record Society*, 1 (1913), 112. The fact that Rohaise was so concerned that the body of Geoffrey de Mandeville II, earl of Essex, her son by her first marriage, be buried at Chicksands rather than at his father's foundation of Walden also suggests considerable loyalty to the Gilbertine foundation (Graham, *St Gilbert*, 37–9).

[117] For the early history of the family, see Chambers and Fowler, 'The Beauchamps, Barons of Bedford', 1–24.

[118] Though Thompson ('English Nunneries: A Study of the Post-Conquest Foundations, *c*.1095–*c*.1250', Ph.D. thesis (London, 1985), 294) suggests that a phrase such as 'women serving God in that place' is a standard formula and does not necessarily imply the prior existence of a community.

[119] *Monasticon*, vi. 2. 950. Canons were certainly present by 1164, when Becket's flight to the Continent was aided by a canon–chaplain of the priory.

[120] These tenants received other lands in compensation. All three occur as small tenants of the Beauchamp fee in 1166 (*Book of Fees*, i. 319–22).

demesne plantation (*virgultum*) near Hawnes church, together with half a virgate and the dwelling held by Lefstan, its warden. Some of this woodland was probably intended to provide timber for the conventual buildings, for the charter goes on to grant the service of Godric the carpenter (with a quarter virgate and *mansura*) *ad reficiendum domos sanctimonialium*. The nuns were also given the reversion of the church of Hawnes on the death of Philip of Broi.[121] In Willington they received a mill together with a half virgate and *mansura*, while tenants in Cople had added to the foundation, their grants being confirmed here. Together these grants amounted to a sizeable foundation in and around Chicksands, and a secure base for the later expansion that was to make Chicksands one of the wealthiest Gilbertine priories.

Communities for Canons Only

The introduction of Augustinian canons into the Gilbertine communities after Gilbert's return from Cîteaux transformed the structure and organization of the early nunneries. It also made possible the creation of Gilbertine priories, which did not contain women but only canons and lay brethren and which were scarcely distinguishable from other contemporary reformed Augustinian foundations. By the end of Gilbert's life four priories (probably St Katherine's, Lincoln, Malton, Newstead, and Mattersey) for 'canons living on their own' had been established.[122] These foundations marked a fundamental shift in the order's orientation. With one exception, after *c.*1155 there would be only one more double house, and the priories of canons would come to predominate in the order, with a resulting decline in the status and influence of the Gilbertine nuns.[123] Why this change should have come about is not easy to explain. Undoubtedly the introduction of 'scholars' and 'clerks' to rule the Gilbertine women gave the canons in the double houses an enhanced status and profile, and the appointment of Roger, who had been prior of Malton, as Gilbert's successor may have contributed to the growing importance of the Gilbertine canons as a whole, but these factors do not explain why benefactors should necessarily wish to found single-sex Gilbertine houses. It has been argued that these replaced double houses as a result of a growing suspicion of communities of both sexes, and this may well be true: certainly after the mid-1150s there was a marked decline in the number of

---

[121] The notorious criminous clerk whose activities contributed to the dispute between Henry II and Becket (Barlow, *Thomas Becket*, 93).   [122] *Book of St Gilbert*, 54.
[123] I have discussed this transition in more detail in 'The Distortion of a Dream', 60–79.

'Cistercian' nunneries, which also included a male element, and attitudes to the segregation of the religious were clearly hardening during the second half of the twelfth century.[124] This does not, however, account for the early Gilbertine foundations for canons only: those of St Katherine's and Malton. One suggestion for the latter is that it functioned as a retreat house for the canons, but there is no evidence for this in the surviving records, nor are there obvious parallels for this in other orders.[125] It may not be coincidental that three of the early single-sex foundations were connected with care for the sick. The eleemosynary role of the order was commented on in the *Vita*: 'he [sc. Gilbert] founded and controlled hospitals for the poor and infirm, for the sick and for lepers, for widows and orphans.' According to Graham, 'instead of the charge of nuns the canons of Malton had three hospital houses', implying that the canons were not associated with nuns because they had eleemosynary duties.[126] From its earliest days St Katherine's was linked with the Hospital of the Holy Sepulchre; Ellerton was founded for the maintenance of thirteen poor men as well as a community of canons; Malton had control of three small hospitals in or near the town, while Clattercote began life as a hospital for the sick of the order.[127]

Malton

Eustace fitzJohn's benefactions to his religious foundations were substantial and, if anything, his grants to Malton were more generous that those to Watton. The foundation comprised his demesne manor; a carucate and woodland in Malton; the demesne manor and two mills in Wintringham with the hamlet (*villula*) of Linton; and the two churches of these manors.[128] In 1086 there were four manors at Malton. Two of them, assessed at 11 carucates, were held by the king, another (of one carucate) was held by the archbishop of York, and a fourth (of $1\frac{1}{2}$ carucates) was held by Robert of Mortain. The royal lands and the Mortain manor (which later escheated to the crown) ultimately passed to Eustace.[129] In 1086 the manor of Wintringham (assessed at 20 carucates) and Linton (assessed at

---

[124] Elkins, *Holy Women*, 122.   [125] Ibid. 90.

[126] *Book of St Gilbert*, 54; Graham, *St Gilbert*, 37. In his letter to the Malton canons, Gilbert states that they can be more rigorous in their spiritual life and in the observance of the Rule since 'you are freer from the concerns that occupy others in the order', and Gilbert writes that it was for this reason particularly that he brought them together (*Book of St Gilbert*, 164).

[127] The foundations of St Katherine, Ellerton, and Clattercote are discussed below: 'Eleemosynary foundations'.   [128] *Monasticon*, vi. 2. 970.

[129] *VCH Yorkshire* ii. 201, 212, 221, 311.

four carucates) was held by Ralph de Mortemer. Clay rightly observed 'the origin of the tenure of the Mortemer fee in Yorkshire by Eustace fitzJohn is extremely obscure', though he plausibly postulated a marriage alliance between the Mortemer and de Vesci families, from whom Eustace's claim to Malton derived.[130] If this is so, then it is apparent that Eustace, for all his generosity to his new foundations, was granting them lands acquired either through royal favour or by marriage, rather than his patrimonial lands, which were concentrated in East Anglia.[131]

However, though Malton necessarily had to look to other local lords, such as the Flamvilles or Lascelles, to consolidate its holdings, the canons were firmly established in the Vale of Pickering, on fertile land with easy access to pasturage and arable, and with good communications to the local markets of York and Scarborough. Eustace had laid the foundations for future prosperity.

Mattersey

Mattersey, a small house in Nottinghamshire, was probably the last Gilbertine priory to be established before Gilbert's death. The foundation is normally ascribed to Roger, son of Rannulf of Mattersey, some time before 1192.[132] Unfortunately, no foundation charter of the house survives and the evidence for Roger's foundation rests on the Hundred Rolls, which record that the priory's site was the gift of Roger of Mattersey, senior. Little is known of Roger's family. It first appears early in the twelfth century and seems to have held the majority of its lands in Lancashire, where Roger's father was given five carucates in the barony of Penwortham in *maritagium* by Warin Bussel, when he married Warin's daughter, Isobel.[133] However, the fact that the family was always known

---

[130] *EYC* iii. 485–8.

[131] Clay (ed.), *Early Yorkshire Families*, 99. Eustace's predecessors' main sphere of influence appears to have been in the Marches (GEC xii (part 2), 269–71). As we have seen, his foundation of Watton was made with the *maritagium* of his wife.

[132] See *Monasticon*, vi. 2. 965, citing Tanner, *Notitia Monastica*, Nottinghamshire, XI; *VCH Nottinghamshire*, ii. 140. If Roger was the founder then the foundation must be earlier than 1186 when Roger died leaving his son, Ranulf, a minor. The confirmation charter issued in the mid-13th century by his descendant, Isabella de Chauncy, and included in an *inspeximus* of Edward III, is of little value for the early history of the house. It merely confirms all Isabella's grants to the house: the demesne lands in Mattersey and Thorpe, with other lands in Gamston, West Retford, Missen, and Bolton (Lancashire) and the advowsons of Mattersey, Gamston, Missen, and Bolton (*Monasticon*, vi. 2. 965–6). It makes no specific mention of Roger.

[133] *Lancashire Inquests, Extents and Feudal Aids*, ed. Farrer, pp. xvi, 29, 71. Farrer suggested that Ranulf's total holding of the Penwortham barony amounted to a fee comprising $8\frac{1}{4}$ carucates.

as 'of Mattersey', or sometimes 'of Gamston' (also in Nottinghamshire), suggests that it was in Nottinghamshire that the family had its origins. In 1086 Roger de Buisli held lands in all the Nottinghamshire villages where the Mattersey family was later to endow the Gilbertine priory, and it is possible that the family was initially a tenant of the Buisli honour. In 1212 the heirs of Ranulf of Mattersey were recorded as holding three fees in chief: two in Nottinghamshire at Gamston of the fee of Lancaster and one each in Fleet and Luton in Holland (Lincolnshire). Additionally, Ranulf son of Roger held four carucates in chief in Lancashire in Bolton and neighbouring settlements. We have here, therefore, a modest knightly family similar in social status to Peter of Billinghay, founder of Catley, and to so many of the other early benefactors of the order. Such families seldom appear in the records of government and their endowments of religious houses were necessarily limited.[134]

It is hardly surprising to find, therefore, that Mattersey was never a wealthy house, and its complement of ten canons stipulated by the order *c*.1195 suggests that from the beginning it was recognized as one of the least well endowed. Virtually all of its property lay in north Nottinghamshire along the valley of the river Idle (the priory site itself lay on an island in that river). The Hundred Rolls show the largest estate held by the priory to be 11 oxgangs in Mattersey granted by the founder, and this probably constituted the home demesne.[135] Though the initial endowment is hard to recover, a dispute with the neighbouring priory of Welbeck that occurred in 1192 shortly after the foundation reveals the Gilbertines to be holding a number of advowsons including Mattersey, Misson, Gamston, and Elkesley (all in Nottinghamshire), and Bolton (Lancashire).[136]

Royal Foundations for Gilbertine Canons

Gilbert was fortunate to enjoy the friendship and patronage of Henry II, who provided emphatic support during the lay brothers' revolt, and who failed to take more than token retributive action over Gilbert's own support for archbishop Becket. The king was also active in protecting the

---

[134] The Mattersey family appear as benefactors of the Nottinghamshire houses of Rufford and Blyth but their donations are far from substantial.

[135] The Hundred Rolls indicate that the greater part of the priory's holdings were of the fee of Lancaster (*Rotuli Hundredorum*, ii. 26, 303–4).

[136] London, BL, MS Harley 3640 (Welbeck Cartulary), fo. 129. These churches probably formed part of the original endowment. See also A. H. Thompson, *The Praemonstratensian Abbey of Welbeck* (London, 1938), 35–6.

order with royal privileges and began the long association of the order with the crown that was to prove so advantageous to the Gilbertines in the coming centuries. In addition Henry founded at least one Gilbertine priory, the small community of Gilbertine canons in north-west Lincoln-shire at Newstead.

Newstead

Newstead-in-Ancolne was the first of two royal Gilbertine foundations. Henry II's foundation charter (which is preserved in an *inspeximus* of Edward II) can probably be dated to July 1171.[137] Hallam has argued that most of Henry's monastic foundations date from after the death of Becket, and that many can be directly related to the archbishop's murder.[138] The reasons for these foundations include penance (which was the explanation offered by several contemporaries, including Gerald of Wales), but they may also include an element of thanksgiving for the defeat of the rebels in 1174, as well as a desire to regain ecclesiastical support for the crown after the disaster of December 1170. It is tempting to explain the foun-dation of Newstead as an act of expiation for Becket's murder only six months earlier. However, Hallam excludes the Gilbertine priory from this 'penitential' programme of foundations, arguing that it was founded some time before 1170. In 1163–4 the canons of Sempringham were first granted £8 10s. from the royal estate of Hibaldstow. Hallam has sug-gested that this represents the foundation of Newstead (which lay in Hibaldstow). She goes on to point out that from 1169–70 'the nominally similar sum of £8 10s. goes to Gilbert of Sempringham from the '"*soka de castra*"'. This sum reverted to Sempringham following Gilbert's death, and Hallam hazards a suggestion that the money was paid directly to Gilbert from 1169 to ensure his personal control over it at the time of the lay brothers' revolt.[139] Certainly the nucleus of Newstead's endowment as given in the 1171 foundation charter was that 'quae solebant reddere michi annuatim octo libras et decem solidos', and these lands lay in or near Hibaldstow in the soke of Caistor. Yet the situation may have been a little more complicated than appears at first sight. The sum of £8 10s. was only paid to the canons of Sempringham from 1163–4 till 1166–7; no payments are recorded thereafter until 1170, when the pipe roll for 1169–70 records lands given to *Gilbert of Sempringham* (my italics) valued at £4

---

[137] When the king was at Bur-le-Roy (Eyton, *Court, Household and Itinerary of King Henry II*, 159).

[138] E. M. Hallam, 'Henry II as a Founder of Monasteries', *JEH* 28 (1977), 131–2.

[139] Ibid. 120.

5*s*. for the half year. It is possible that the payment was withheld from the Gilbertines during the late 1160s as a penalty for Gilbert's earlier support of the exiled archbishop, though it might have been expected that this sanction would have been employed somewhat sooner after the Northampton fiasco. Was the resumption of this payment, this time in land rather than cash, a result of the last temporary restoration of relations between the king and archbishop in 1170? If so, the following scenario can be proposed. Henry II originally made an annual cash payment to the order derived from one of his estates in north Lincolnshire. This payment was interrupted, perhaps because of Gilbertine support for Becket, and then resumed in 1170 with the grant of the lands from which the earlier pension had been obtained. These may have been intended as a grange of Sempringham or another Gilbertine house: there is no evidence that an independent foundation was yet envisaged. Following Becket's death another change of plan occurred, and a new priory was set up with an increased, though hardly lavish, grant. This may well have been intended as expiation for the murder. Gilbert had been a close friend of both the king and archbishop, and Newstead was dedicated, uniquely amongst Gilbertine houses, to the Holy Trinity, whose feast Becket had promoted.[140]

In any case, Henry's endowment was far from generous. With its assessed income of only £38 in 1535, Newstead was amongst the very poorest of the Lincolnshire religious houses.[141] The foundation comprised a little over $2\frac{1}{2}$ carucates in Cadney and Howsham (which lay in the royal soke of Caistor); a bovate and the site of a grange in Hibaldstow; and five bovates of land in Hardwick (in Nettleton parish) which belonged to a certain Ivo, who was compensated with other royal demesne land.[142] A number of scholars have remarked on Henry's shrewd and even parsimonious grants to religious houses; his foundation of Newstead was no exception, and was nothing like as generous as, for example, the king's support of Witham or Amesbury. Indeed, the canons may well have found the privileges they were granted in the foundation charter—the freedom from all royal dues and exactions, the freedom from all temporal services, and the right to have their suits heard *coram rege*—of more value than the lands.[143] For all his personal support of Gilbert, Henry's bene-

---

[140] A. Binns, *Dedication of Monastic Houses in England and Wales, 1066–1216* (Woodbridge, 1989), 171–2. [141] *VE* iv. 71.

[142] The lands in Hardwick may have later passed to Sixhills, for Henry granted that house all the land which Ivo fitzAlden held there, which had escheated to the crown (*Gilbertine Charters*, 35–6).

[143] *Monasticon*, vi. 2. 966. This point is also made by Hallam, 'Henry II', 120.

factions to the order were limited: a fairly generous grant to Haverholme, the modest grant of land in Nettleton to Sixhills which had escheated to the crown, and the foundation of Newstead (and, perhaps, also of Marlborough) do not amount to a great deal.[144] Little more was ever added to the royal endowment of Newstead. Henry II confirmed, and perhaps instigated, an agreement whereby the Cistercian abbey of Long-villers (Picardy) demised to the canons land in Hibaldstow and Gainsthorpe that had been granted by Reginald, count of Boulogne, and his wife Ida, in return for an annual payment of 100*s.* by the priory. Henry's son, John, added land worth 66*s.* in Howsham in January 1201.[145] The absence of other surviving charters makes it very difficult to construct the later endowment history of this priory. However, it is apparent that the priory received very few further benefactions, other than the church and land in Barnetby-le-Wold given by Robert II de Greslei early in the thirteenth century.[146] Newstead was clearly seen as a royal foundation: up until the Dissolution the priory continued to give alms to the poor for the souls of its founders, Henry II and John.[147] It may be for that reason that it failed to attract the support of other, less exalted supporters.

Marlborough

Of all the successful Gilbertine priories, Marlborough was the most distant from Sempringham. It owed its existence and continuing support to the Angevin kings, but was never to flourish, and it remains amongst the least known of Gilbertine houses. The date and circumstances of its foundation are unclear. It was certainly in existence by 1199, when it is listed amongst the priories in John's general confirmation charter to the order.[148] A writ of 1229 refers to the taking of the ale custom as in the time of *H. regis avi nostri*, and for this reason it has been suggested that the house was founded in the time of, and perhaps by, Henry II.[149] However, the priory does not figure in the list of priories in the Rule. Its omission from this list, which can be dated to *c.*1195, and the fact that it

---

[144] For Haverholme, see *Cal. Chart. R*, iv. 404–5; for Sixhills, see *Gilbertine Charters*, 35–6; Marlborough is discussed below.

[145] *Monasticon*, vi. 2. 966. This grant may be associated with contemporary moves for Gilbert's canonization. Less than two months later, John was himself to write to the pope in support of the canonization campaign.

[146] *Lincolnshire Records: Abstracts of Final Concords, Richard I, John, and Henry III (1193–1244)*, ed. W. O. Massingberd (London, 1896), i. 100; *Reg. Hugh de Welles*, i. 149–50.   [147] *VE* iv. 71.

[148] *Cartae Antiquae. Rolls 1–10*, ed. L. Landon, PRS, NS 17 (1939), 32, no. 57.

[149] *Cal. Cl. R. 1227–31*, 190; *VCH Wiltshire* iii. 316.

is the last named priory in John's confirmation charter, which seems to arrange the priories more or less in order of foundation, suggests a date not much before 1199. Certainly of all the Gilbertine priories it enjoyed the closest ties with the crown during the thirteenth century, and in 1399 it was described as 'of royal foundation'.[150] It was situated only a few hundred yards from the royal castle of Marlborough, in Marlborough barton.[151] The castle came to prominence at the beginning of the thirteenth century, and under Henry III was one of the favourite royal residences. Its proximity, and the fact that there were no other local religious houses, must have contributed to the favour the priory found with Henry III. The relationship between castle and priory was formalized by 1265, when the prior had to provide one of his canons to celebrate in the castle chapel of St Nicholas for an annual stipend of 50s.[152] The absence of a foundation charter makes it very difficult to determine the extent of the initial endowment, and it may be that at the beginning the priory gained most of its income from royal grants of cash and goods rather than from landed endowments. Some of these grants that are only recorded during the reign of Henry III may date back to the foundation. In 1232 Henry III allowed that whenever the king came to Marlborough the community should have a tithe of all bread purchased for his household, a tithe of ale, and of meat or fish served as the household's first course (or, if neither meat nor fish was served, then whatever was).[153] The priory already possessed the right to the ale custom ('tolsester') from every brewhouse in the barton. Further grants were made for building works. In 1235 20 trees were ordered to be given to repair the priory's house, and a total of 21 oaks were given in 1244 and 1246 for the provision of buildings and roofing shingles. There was then a pause until 1269 when a further three oaks were given to repair the bell tower, and this was followed in 1271 by six more to repair the dormitory.[154] Neither was the furnishing of the church neglected, for in 1246 a goldsmith was commissioned to make a silver-gilt chalice for the canons' church.[155]

It is only in the 1230s that the first grants of land to the priory are recorded. The benefactors were largely drawn from the royal household:

---

[150] *Cal. Pat. R. 1396–9*, 560. The *Vita* states that four houses for canons only had been founded by Gilbert's death in 1189, the year in which Henry II also died.

[151] This was a small estate belonging to the castle lying just outside the borough of Marlborough.

[152] *Cal. Liberate R.* v. 180, 201. In 1271 the king ordered the constable to pay arrears due for this maintenance (ibid. vi. 201). [153] *Cal. Ch. R.* i. 145.

[154] *Cal. Ch. R.* ii. 156; *Cal. Cl. R. 1234–7*, 127; *Cal. Cl. R. 1242–7*, 272, 486; *Cal. Cl. R. 1268–72*, 161, 444. [155] *Cal. Liberate R.* iii. 36.

men such as Geoffrey Esturmy, the hereditary warden of Savernake forest, who granted 30 acres of his demesne wood in 1235.[156] But the priory never received substantial landed endowments, and as royal support dwindled after the death of Henry III the canons relied increasingly upon grants from the burgesses of Marlborough and knightly families in the surrounding regions. As was the case with Newstead, royal favour was no guarantee of prosperity: like Newstead Marlborough also appears to have been a foundation on the cheap that involved little outlay from the crown.

Eleemosynary Foundations

The Gilbertine Rule laid down careful provision for the sustenance of travellers. However, there were no specific ordinances for the care of the poor at the gate.[157] The guest-house (*maior hospitum*) of the canons was to be served by two members of the community, one a canon, who would normally be the sub-cellarer, the other a lay brother who 'knew how to look after guests'.[158] The *maior hospitum* was clearly intended for the more prestigious guests, not the indigent, who were looked after in the *domus elemosinarie*. This represents a continuation of the old two-tier system of treatment of guests.[159] None of the community was to be allowed to eat with the guests, except such as were of great authority, that is, bishops and archbishops, and only bishops, archdeacons, and the sick were to be given meat in the guest-house. Women guests were received in their own hostel within the nuns' enclosure, but out of sight of the nuns' quarters.

---

[156] *Cal. Ch. R.* i. 194, 219; *Excerpta e Rotulis Finium*, i. 299–300. Geoffrey's support for the canons did not prevent him illegally seizing and imprisoning two of the prior's men who had gone to Savernake forest to take thorn branches for the priory's enclosures, a right granted by the king in 1232 (*Cal. Cl. R. 1234–7*, 276; *Cal. Chart. R.* i. 143).

[157] *Monasticon*, vi. 2. xxvi, li.

[158] The sub-cellarer had a particularly onerous task at the Gilbertine hospital of St Katherine's, Lincoln, and it may be for this reason that his appointment, and that of the *custos infirmarie* there, was reserved to the Master of the order (*Monasticon*, vi. 2. xxi). In some of the new orders a distinction was soon drawn between the service of the church, attended to by the clerks, and that of the hospice, which was the responsibility of lay brethren (Leyser, *Hermits and the New Monasticism*, 61–2). This distinction does not seem to have been so rigidly made in Gilbertine houses, though the lay brethren and sisters undoubtedly carried the main burden of nursing and care.

[159] A similar distinction between the *hospitium* for the wealthy sick and mounted guests, and the *domus elemosinarie* for the indigent and travelling poor, is found at La Trinité, Vendôme (P. D. Johnson, *Prayer, Patronage and Power: The Abbey of La Trinité, Vendôme, 1032–1187* (New York, 1981), 160).

Only the prioress or those delegated by her were to visit the guests. They were to be attended by lay sisters, described as *hospitales sorores*, and by two or three 'discreet and mature' nuns who would be responsible for taking the guests into the nuns' buildings if necessary. Rules were rigorous. Under no circumstances was meat to be given to visitors, noble or ignoble, without the express licence of the Master, and guests were only allowed to stay one night. It is clear from the continuation of this section of the Rule that the order expected most of its lay visitors to be connected with its houses in some way, rather than 'casual' travellers, and in this expectation it rightly expected problems. There was inevitably tension between the demands of lay patrons and relatives of nuns for hospitality and the need of the nuns for seclusion. As far as possible the nuns were to avoid converse with their visitors. Even the prioresses and other office holders in the priories were not to speak with such unless in the presence of the *summae scrutatrices* or *claustri speculatrices*, or those specially noted for their piety. The prioress was allowed to talk with 'honeste mulieres' in the guest-house, but with no others, and other nuns could only talk, and that sparingly, if given leave. Significantly, such leave would only be given to avoid 'offensio, dampnum et odium magnatum foeminarum', while only the lay sister in the guest-house could talk with travelling women ('peregrine mulieres'). Special rules were laid down for cases when the visitor was a relative of a nun. If the relative was male then he was to speak either at the large window or at the guest-house gate, but, if the prioress agreed, nuns were allowed to speak at the little window if the guests were *nobiles* or *advocatae* of the house. Even more stringent were the rules if a boy was taken into the women's guest-house. Then no one should enter, and if they did enter by mistake, they were to leave immediately until the boy was safely gone. It seems clear that these rules for guests and their welcome relate primarily to the 'upper-class' visitors, not the poor. We know nothing of how the inmates lived in the infirmary, or of their numbers, and the only reference to the infirmary, other than in charters, is found in one of the miracle stories of St Gilbert. William of Houghton, described as a *pauper laicus*, reported how he had lain sick in the infirmary of the poor at Watton priory for two months, finally going mad. He was then healed by being placed and tied in a litter once used by Gilbert, and his cure was testified by *frater* Norman (clearly a lay brother) who was then warden (*custos*) of the hospital.[160] Nor is anything known of the drain of eleemosynary work, together with the costs of

---

[160] *Book of St Gilbert*, 292.

entertaining guests and visitors, on the priories' resources, though these were probably considerable.

Charters detailing grants made specifically for the maintenance of services for the sick and the poor can be found for many Gilbertine houses. A very early charter in favour of Haverholme granted half of the church of Ruskington for the maintenance of the nuns, lay brethren, 'et pauperum dei qui ibi suscipientur ad hospitandum'.[161] In the mid-thirteenth century Simon le Porter of Bullington granted two shillings annual rent for the sustenance of the poor at the priory gate.[162] In 1261 William of Redbourne sold land in Cockerington to Alvingham in order that the income might be used for the maintenance of the guest-house, and at about the same time Hugh son of Edric of Grimoldby granted a toft in Cockerington for the same purpose.[163]

The largest collection of grants relating to the canons' charitable work is found in the Malton cartulary, where a group of fifteen charters describes lands given for the support of the poor. The purpose of these grants is described in various terms, such as 'maxime ad vestiendos pauperes in hospitali eiusdam domus', 'ad sustenacionem domus elemosinarie', or 'ad sustenacionem infirmorum secularium' (which makes it clear that the infirm referred to are those 'at the priory gate' or, alternatively, in the lay infirmary, rather than canons in the priory infirmary). The land given does not amount to a great deal, the largest donation being two bovates in Grimston, and three of the eight grants are of tofts only, which would then presumably be leased out for a cash income.[164] Virtually all of these grants are of lands rather than money rents.[165]

---

[161] 'Haverholme Charters', 14, no. 16. Philip of Kyme gave the church of St Alban, Spridlington, for the maintenance of the infirmary of the nuns of Bullington (London, BL, MS Addit. 6118, fo. 383[r–v]).

[162] London, BL, Harl. Chart. 54 I 46. A similar grant was made by Clemencia the Fleming of Covenham to Nun Ormsby (*Gilbertine Charters*, 47). In 1333 Roger Lock of Kilnwick gave a selion 'for the sustenance of the poor at the gate' of Watton (*Yorkshire Deeds*, vi. 106).

[163] Oxford, Bodl. Lib., MS Laud Misc. 642, fos. 83[v]–4. The rubric to these charters reads 'Carte de terris emptis pro subcelararium'. This is the only reference to transactions by an obedientary in the cartulary, and shows that the care of the guest-house at this period remained, as stipulated in the Rule, in the hands of the sub-cellarer.

[164] London, BL, MS Cotton Claudius D XI, fos. 182–184[v]. These grants are listed as *carte elemosinarie*. Their number should be compared with Fountains, where a considerable number of grants were made for the lay infirmary, and over 200 for the relief of 'poor at the gate' (J. Wardrop, *Fountains Abbey and its Benefactors, 1132–1300*, Cistercian Publications, 91 (Kalamazoo, Mich., 1987), 118–20).

[165] This contrasts, for example, with the position at Fountains, where most of the grants in favour of the lay infirmary were of money rents (ibid. 118).

These benefactions were made to Gilbertine priories, all of which had a responsibility to care for the local poor and infirm. In all probability, every Gilbertine priory had a small *domus elemosinarie* for the poor and distributed food for them at the gate. However, a number of Gilbertine houses had more specific charitable functions. These foundations are analogous to those Premonstratensian English houses that have been identified as 'hospital monasteries' with special responsibilities to the poor.[166]

St Katherine's, Lincoln

By far the largest of the Gilbertine charitable foundations (and, indeed, the wealthiest of the Gilbertine communities for canons only) was St Katherine's, Lincoln, situated just to the south of Lincoln across the river Witham.[167] Its foundation was succinctly described in the *Valor Ecclesiasticus* as 'founded for orphans thrown into danger by the negligence of their friends and taken into the hospital of St Sepulchre to be cared for and brought up', as well as for 'the support of poor people and other works of mercy from certain rents granted to St Katherine's by the gift and foundation of Robert Bloet, second bishop of Lincoln after the Conquest and founder of St Katherine's'.[168]

In fact, St Katherine's was founded not by Robert Bloet but by bishop Robert de Chesney (1148–66), probably early in his episcopacy, and perhaps as early as 1148. It was his only religious foundation, and can presumably be ascribed to the close relationship which continued between Gilbert and the bishops of Lincoln even after the former had left episcopal service. Chesney was criticized by Gerald of Wales in the *Vita Sancti Remigii* not only for alienating lands to his nephews but for giving four churches of his manors (which used to be held by the household clerks of the bishop) and one prebend to the order of Sempringham. These can

---

[166] Colvin, *The White Canons*, 309.

[167] The priory is described by R. E. G. Cole, 'The Priory of St Katherine's without Lincoln of the Order of St Gilbert of Sempringham', *Lincolnshire Archaeological and Architectural Society Reports and Papers*, 27 (1904), 264–336. Though the priory was not a double house, the presence of lay sisters as nurses was envisaged from the first. In 1376 there were six sisters, and five are mentioned by name in the *Valor Ecclesiasticus*. They were also mentioned in late-medieval wills, being left, for example, 10s. by Joan, widow of Robert of Appleby, a Lincoln merchant in 1408, and 6s. 8d. in a will of 1526 (*The Register of Bishop Repingdon 1405–19*, ed. M. Archer, LRS, 57, 58, 74 (1963, 1982), i. 143–4; *Lincoln Wills I, AD 1271–1526*, ed. C.W. Foster, LRS, 5 (1914), 174). In 1314 the king sent Eleanor Darcy to the priory with the request that she be granted a corrody, equivalent to the allowance of a canoness of the house. This must either mean that Eleanor was to be received as a sister of the hospital, or, more likely, that she was to be provided for as for a Gilbertine nun in a double house (*Cal. Cl. R. 1313–18*, 99).   [168] *VE* iv. 34.

be identified as the churches of Newark, Norton Disney, Marton, and Newton-on-Trent, while the prebend is that of Canwick, which together formed the nucleus of St Katherine's foundation.[169] The foundation charter only survives in an *inspeximus* of Edward III of a confirmation issued by Henry II. The latter can probably be dated between 1156 and 1166.[170] In addition to the churches the endowment included five bovates at Wigsley; two *mansurae*, other houses and lands in Newark; four bovates in the fields of Newark; 20 acres of heathland; a *mansura* and two bovates held by the church of Newark; the chapel of Sts Philip and James (which had earlier been given to the cathedral) in Newark castle; and a tithe of all Newark borough tolls (except during fairs). Additionally, three bovates with their *mansurae* were given in Balderton and four shillings' worth of land in Newark that was once held by *magister* Malger of Newark, as well as the church of Bracebridge, a bovate, *mansura*, and appurtenances there.[171] The foundation included the grant of the 'care and custody' of Holy Sepulchre hospital, along with the possessions of its poor and the brethren.

The early history of this hospital too is obscure. Modern commentators unanimously assert that it was founded by bishop Robert Bloet, but no certain evidence for this statement has been discovered.[172] What is clear is that the foundation cannot long have remained independent. The form of the royal confirmation charter suggests that the grant of the hospital to the Gilbertines represented a separate transaction from the other grants of land to St Katherine's. Indeed, until the Dissolution

---

[169] For Chesney's career, see *English Episcopal Acta. I*, pp. xxxv–xxxvi; *Giraldi Cambrensis Opera*, vii. 34–5. It may be that the market, shops and prebend, and houses in London, purchased from the Templars by Chesney for the cathedral endowment were intended as compensation for the alienated churches (ibid. 35, 198).

[170] For the text of this charter, see *Registrum Antiquissimum*, i, no. 194. It is probably a consolidation of several grants: a charter granting the castle chapel and other Newark lands is also known (*English Episcopal Acta. IV*, 194–5, no. XII). See also *English Episcopal Acta. I*, 98, no. 164, where it is demonstrated that the grant of Bracebridge probably dates from between 1156 and 1162. Its nature is discussed in *English Episcopal Acta. I*, 97–8, nos. 163–4. The second part of the charter grants the church of Bracebridge to the canons. This church had been confirmed to the chapter of Lincoln some time between 1156 and 1169. The foundation included the grant of the 'care and custody' of Holy Sepulchre hospital, along with the possessions of its poor and the brethren. Chesney's foundation endowment was to form the most substantial element of the priory's income until the Dissolution (*English Episcopal Acta. I*, 97, no. 163; *Registrum Antiquissimum*, i, no. 194).

[171] *English Episcopal Acta. I*, 97, no. 163; *Registrum Antiquissimum*, i, no. 194. Malger was a canon of Lincoln: it is tempting to suggest that the land he was granted by Chesney in Nettleton was in recompense for the land that had been lost to the new foundation (*Fasti*, 131; *English Episcopal Acta. I*, 104, no. 177).

[172] See e.g. *English Episcopal Acta. I*, 201, and Owen, *Church and Society*, 55.

the priory-hospital had two functions, operating both as a community of Gilbertine canons and as a hospital served by lay brethren and sisters. How far the two were constitutionally autonomous is difficult to assess.[173] The rule restricting community numbers seems to divide them, limiting the brethren in Lincoln to 16, and those in the 'Hospital' to 45, while there were to be only 20 sisters.[174] The absence of many charters in favour of St Katherine's makes it difficult to be certain, but some sort of distinction appears to have continued to be made between St Katherine's and Holy Sepulchre.[175] Some further indication is given by final concords of the late twelfth and thirteenth centuries. Fines distinguish between the two communities, though at the same time it is clear that they had a prior in common.[176] Perhaps the most conclusive evidence that the communities held their lands separately is found in the Hundred Rolls, where a careful distinction is drawn between the holdings of the *fratres laici* of the Hospital, and those of the prior and convent of St Katherine's. The lay brethren's holdings were substantial; by contrast, no other Gilbertine house is known to have had its lands divided in such a way at this time.[177] It seems likely, then, that these brethren belonged to Holy Sepulchre hospital, rather than to St Katherine's, and are to be equated with the lay brethren of Holy Sepulchre to whom the dean and chapter of Lincoln granted a mill in 1198, and land in Whisby between 1245 and 1254.[178] For how long this distinction lasted is unclear. Certainly no such distinction is drawn in the accounts of the *Valor Ecclesiasticus*, and late-medieval wills which frequently record bequests to the Hospital and its inmates always refer to it as St Katherine's. Indeed, alone of the Gilbertine houses

---

[173] Certainly some 'hospital-priories', such as St Bartholomew's Smithfield, did maintain separate organizations and finances. See C. N. L. Brooke and G. Keir, *London, 800–1216: The Shaping of a City* (London, 1975), 325–8.   [174] *Monasticon*, vi. 2. lviii.

[175] The grants of Hamelin and Isabella, earl and countess of Warenne, were addressed to the canons and brethren and poor of the Hospital of St Katherine. In the early 13th century Baldwin son of Baldwin Wake granted and confirmed lands to the brethren of Holy Sepulchre hospital 'who are of the order of Sempringham' and the *pauperes* there, and this charter makes no mention of St Katherine's, though the two *canonici* who appear among the witnesses were probably members of the latter house (London, BL, Harl. Chart. 57 D 27 (pr. Cole, 'The Priory of St Katherine's', 325–6)).

[176] William is styled prior of Holy Sepulchre hospital in 1218: two years later William was described as prior of St Katherine's (*Final Concords*, i. 133; *Heads of Religious Houses*, 203). Ralph is described as prior of St Katherine's in 1245, and of Holy Sepulchre in 1252 (*Final Concords*, ii. 82, 98).

[177] However, it should be observed that only St Katherine's figures in the Hundred Rolls' list of religious houses holding property in the city of Lincoln (*Rotuli Hundredorum*, ii. 316).

[178] *Registrum Antiquissimum*, vii. 103, 160, nos. 2068, 2133. Further evidence that the lands were accounted for separately occurs in 1255–6, when a felon, Richard le Gros, was said to have held a toft of the grange (or granger?) of Holy Sepulchre's (*Cal. Inq. p. m.* i. 90).

St Katherine's appears to have maintained its level of receipts of benefactions until the Dissolution, an indication that its charitable function retained its appeal, when that of the religious had largely declined.[179]

Ellerton

Care of the sick was also an integral function of the foundation of Ellerton on Spalding Moor, close to the Humber estuary. The founder was William son of Peter (or 'of Goodmanham'). His foundation charter suggests that he had connections both with Geoffrey fitzPeter, founder of Shouldham, and with Hugh Murdac, founder of St Andrew's, York, since the grant was made for the salvation of their souls.[180] Ellerton priory was established between 1199 and 1203 for canons of the order of Sempringham, and for the feeding of thirteen *pauperes*, and shortly afterwards Gilbert II, Master of the order, and the prior and convent of Ellerton acknowledged their obligation to provide for those 'in hospitale ecclesie de Ellerton', and agreed that in default they could be forced to undertake this duty by

---

[179] This continued support for the hospital was not necessarily typical of late-medieval urban charitable activity. Hospitals were increasingly being founded, operated, and funded by secular authorities or individuals, the role of the religious in the care of the sick was declining, and, indeed, a number of old-established 'religious' hospitals were in serious difficulties (Rubin, *Charity and Community*, 294–6 and references there cited). One reason for the continued support of St Katherine's may have been the fact that medieval Lincoln was comparatively under-provided with hospitals. Only six were founded in the city, and by 1350 two of these had probably disappeared (*Medieval Religious Houses*, 325, 371). By contrast, there were at least ten hospitals in late-medieval Exeter, and nine in the much smaller town of Beverley (ibid. 325, 314). Moreover, none of the Lincoln hospitals was a secular foundation: care of the sick in late-medieval Lincoln remained in the care of the religious, who continued to receive the benefactions of the burgesses. A comparison of the bequests made to St Katherine's in the early 16th century and in the years immediately preceding the Dissolution with those made to other Gilbertine houses in the diocese reveals that the former was receiving many times more such grants than other priories. Indeed, it would seem that virtually every testator in the diocese made a bequest, however small, to the hospital or its inmates, frequently described as the 'fatherless children'. The majority of these grants were indeed small, often amounting to only a few pence, but cumulatively they must have contributed significantly to the priory's economy. A number of these bequests are detailed in Cole, 'The Priory of St Katherine's', 302–3.

[180] He was also a witness to Hugh Murdac's own foundation. William, who was a minor mesne tenant of the Fossard fee in the East Riding of Yorkshire, had already had dealings with the Gilbertines. William Fossard had given (or more likely, sold) 3 carucates in Hawold (in Huggate) to Watton priory. These lands were held by a tenant, Roger son of Roger Hay, who needed to be compensated, as did Roger's own tenant, William son of Peter. The latter claimed that he had lost a service of 3s. per annum by the grant, and in the following generation (*c*.1180–6) William Fossard II granted land in York to Watton for 3s. to be paid to William of Goodmanham in compensation (*EYC* ii. 415–16, 422–3, nos. 1122, 1130).

the authority of the archbishop of York.[181] A number of other charters dating from this initial period and thereafter demonstrate that the care of the *pauperes* continued to be taken seriously. Henry de Puiset confirmed the grant of a meadow at Cliffe which William son of Peter held of him 'ad sustentionem eorum tresdecim pauperum, qui ibi pascentur in perpetuum', and Alan of Wilton granted considerable lands in several local villages for the same purpose.[182] When the Hay family acquired some or all of William's estates they took over the patronage of the priory, and it is clear that as late as the end of the fourteenth century they continued to support the eleemosynary activities of the canons.[183] In 1387 the prior and convent made an agreement with Germanus Hay, *advocatus* of the priory, in which the former acknowledged their obligation to maintain thirteen 'pauperes ex primaria fundatione'. The patrons had apparently had the right to nominate one of the *pauperes* for the community: this privilege was now extended to the nomination of eight of the thirteen. Moreover, the convent agreed that if it was remiss in its treatment of the poor and restitution was not done within a month of the patrons' complaint being upheld, then the latter would assume the right of presenting all thirteen *pauperes*. Finally the convent granted an obit to Germanus and Alesia his wife and agreed that if these obits were not performed, and for every *pauper* presented but not received, it would pay to Germanus and his heirs £10. The elaborate nature of this agreement and the heavy burdens and penalties laid on the community by Germanus suggest that the latter may himself have made substantial grants to the priory at this time.[184] After this date, however, there are no further records of the charitable functions of the house, and, by contrast with St Katherine's, none of the bequests made to Ellerton in the late Middle Ages refer to the poor or infirm.

Fordham

The vicarage of the wealthy church of Fordham was granted to Henry, rural dean of Fordham, by king John in 1204, and some time between

[181] *EYC* ii. 425–6, nos. 1133, 1134, Geoffrey, earl of Essex (created 1199) is mentioned, and in 1203 the prior of Ellerton was vouched to warranty concerning land in 'Howham' (*CRR* iii. 36). It should be noted that the number of *pauperes* was the same as that stipulated for the establishment of a Gilbertine house of canons. However, a number of hospital communities that followed a Rule or quasi-Rule comprised thirteen inmates (see Clay (ed.), *Early Yorkshire Families*, 145, and Rubin, *Charity and Community*, 115).

[182] *Monasticon*, vi. 2, 977–8: *EYC* ii. 125–6, no. 788.

[183] For the Hay family and its connections with William son of Peter, see Clay (ed.), *Early Yorkshire Families*, 40–2 and the references there cited.

[184] *Monasticon*, vi. 2. 977. For a similar right of a benefactor to nominate men for

then and 1227 it passed into the hands of the Gilbertines. A royal charter of 1227 records the grant of the church, 'which is of the king's donation', to the priory and nuns of Sempringham, the income from which was to be used to provide food ('ad procurationem faciendam') for the annual chapter of the order at Sempringham during the three rogation days.[185] The priory, however, was separate from the church (which remained in the hands of Sempringham until the Dissolution) and it is not known whether or not its foundation antedated the grant of the church. Certainly the priory was never wealthy. Nothing is known of its eleemosynary function apart from a reference in the Hundred Rolls to a grant by Walter son of Robert confirming his ancestors' grant of 60 acres of arable and five acres of meadow 'xiii pauperum in perpetuum sustinendorum victum et vestitum in hospit' de Fordham'.[186] Rubin has suggested that the term *hospitale* in this context implied an almonry dispensing 'outdoor relief', performing a similar function to that of many small rural houses of the time: it 'did not mean the creation of a permanent dependent group of poor within the community'.[187] While it is true that there were a number of such foundations at this time, and though the foundation of Fordham can in no way be compared with that of St Katherine's, Lincoln, by analogy with Ellerton, though on a smaller scale, where the foundation for the maintenance of thirteen poor men is described in very similar terms, and where it seems likely that the poor were maintained in the convent, it is not impossible that Fordham too provided permanent quarters for its own poor.

Clattercote

The early history of Clattercote priory, which lies a few miles north of Banbury on the Oxfordshire–Warwickshire border, is obscure and little studied. According to Mason, 'bishop Chesney granted demesne land there [i.e. Clattercote] to the small Gilbertine priory of St Leonard of Clattercote'.[188] This bland statement goes further than the earlier comment of Salter that the Gilbertine house was originally a hospital of lepers, founded by the time of Chesney and possibly by that bishop.[189] The editors of *Medieval Religious Houses* repeated this view, and went on

maintenance in a Premonstratensian house (Hornby), see Colvin, *The White Canons*, 309. See also Clay (ed.), *Early Yorkshire Families*, 130.

[185] *Cal. Ch. R.* i. 65: see Rubin, *Charity and Community*, 137, and *VCH Cambridgeshire*, ii. 256–8. [186] *Rotuli Hundredorum*, ii. 502.
[187] Rubin, *Charity and Community*, 137. [188] *VCH Oxfordshire*, x. 195.
[189] Ibid. ii. 105.

to state that 'it was for members of the order who contracted leprosy, limited to 55 *c*.1185–90'.[190] Unfortunately, the editors erred in identifying the *hospitalis* of the Rule with Clattercote rather than the hospital of Holy Sepulchre, Lincoln, founded by bishop Robert Bloet, the custody of which was granted by bishop Chesney to St Katherine's priory.[191] The identification with Clattercote is the more surprising since the same chapter of the Rule went on to limit the number of *fratres apud sanctum Leonardum* to ten.[192] Clattercote was the only Gilbertine priory dedicated to St Leonard and there can be no doubt that this is the priory referred to, and that it was already in existence by the late 1180s as a Gilbertine priory. Was it, however, founded as a priory? There are some difficulties in accepting this hypothesis.

Though the foundation charter of bishop Chesney does not survive, amongst the transcripts of Oxford charters made by Salter is one entitled 'concessio annui redditus prioratui de Clatercote'.[193] It consists of a notification by Richard Gravesend, bishop of Lincoln, granting an annual rent of 50*s*. to the priory. The witnesses enable it to be dated to between 2 February 1259/60 and 22 September 1260. It preserves the content of the original grant, describing how Chesney gave three hides from his demesne in Clattercote with all appurtenances, together with a further 60 acres in a *cultura* called *Costive* with 10 acres in *Pingworthe*, and common pasture for their animals, for the support of the *infirmi* of Clattercote and their brethren. In addition he granted a tithe of all his rents in Banbury, Cropredy, and Farnborough, a tithe from the town and hundred of Banbury, and a tithe of his corrody whenever the bishop stayed on his manors of Banbury and Cropredy. This would appear to have been the initial grant: a new section goes on to state that these tithes had been commuted to an annual payment of nine marks ten shillings, and a third section tells how the grants of various episcopal tenants had been confirmed.[194]

---

[190] *Medieval Religious Houses*, 187. This reference to the limitation of numbers is based on the chapter in the Institutes limiting the numbers of *conversi*, nuns, and lay sisters in Gilbertine houses, which can be dated on internal evidence to between *c*.1185 and *c*.1189 (see above, Ch. 3: 'Entering the house': 'The ideal community').

[191] *VCH Lincolnshire*, ii. 188–9.   [192] *Monasticon*, vi. 2. lviii.

[193] The transcript, which is largely accurate, is taken from the Memoranda register of bishop Longland (1521–47), fo. 162. This document was not used by Salter in his *Victoria County History* article on the priory (though it is possible that Salter's transcript post-dates the writing of the *VCH* entry).

[194] Only two of these have been identified. William Bassett held the manor of Stutford West in Swalecliffe and was the bishop's sub-tenant in Wardington (in Cropredy). William de Buissei was lord of Prescote in the bishop's fee of Cropredy (*VCH Oxfordshire*, x. 232, 216, 207).

It is impossible to date these grants with precision. After Robert's death in 1166, while the bishopric was in the king's hands, money was paid to the *infirmi* of Clattercote from the Exchequer. In 1166–7 £4 17s. 6d. was paid, and in the following year £10 9s. 8d.[195] The year 1166–7 also saw similar payments to the *infirmi* of Lincoln, Northampton, and Newark (and, in 1167–8, to those of Leicester as well). These are probably to be identified with the inmates of the hospitals of Holy Innocents (founded by bishop Remigius) or Holy Sepulchre (founded by Chesney himself) at Lincoln; St Leonard's, Newark (founded by bishop Alexander); St Leonard's, Northampton (allegedly established by William I); and St Leonard's, Leicester (said to have been founded by William the Leper, son of Robert, earl of Leicester). All of these were leper hospitals, as was Clattercote, as we shall see, and at least two of them had associations with the bishops of Lincoln. All lay within the diocese and all were clearly regarded as the especial interest of the bishop. There is nothing in the pipe roll entries to suggest that Clattercote was anything other than a leper hospital; there is no mention of canons or nuns there. Yet it is clear that the Gilbertines did have custody of the hospital, for Robert is said to have entrusted the house and its possessions to Gilbert of Sempringham and his successors. The document states that it was the bishop's particular intention that 'if any in his [i.e. Gilbert's] communities were suffering from appalling sickness or shameful illness such as leprosy or the like they can be separated from the company of the healthy and be shut up (*reclusas collacare*) in the said place of Clattercote'. There are two striking features in this passage. First, it is not implied that the hospital should be exclusively for the care of Gilbertines, though their care is regarded as paramount. Secondly, it assumes that it is the women of the order who are to be sent to Clattercote. There are two possible explanations for this. It may be that sick canons of the order were sent elsewhere, perhaps to the hospital of St Katherine's, Lincoln, or it may be that this arrangement dates from very early in the order's history, while it was still in all essentials a community for women only. It seems most likely that the hospital at Clattercote, originally intended primarily, though not exclusively, for Gilbertine leprous nuns, was a generation later, and certainly by the 1180s, transformed into an institution catering solely for the Gilbertines. It survived as a hospital for several more decades: on 5 March 1216 Innocent III confirmed the possessions, which are detailed,

---

[195] *Pipe Roll, 13 Henry II*, PRS 11 (1889), 58; *Pipe Roll, 14 Henry II*, PRS 12 (1890), 77.

of the *domus leprosorum sancti Leonardi* to the proctors (*proctoribus*) and
convent of the house 'of the order of Sempringham'.[196] Some time between 1256 and 1261 the prior, canons, and lay brethren 'nursing the sick
of Clattercote' granted their property in Wolverton to Chicksands, but
very shortly afterwards, between 1258 and 1262, the Master of the order
issued a notification that was presumably intended for the attention of the
bishop and chapter of Lincoln. This stated that there had been an increase in the temporalities of the house as a result of the benefactions of
the faithful, so that the resources of the priory were now able to sustain
the needs of the brethren there: moreover, in place of the sick who used
to live in the priory, whose maintenance and care was necessarily more
expensive, healthy people (*validi*) were now substituted.[197] Therefore the
Master quitclaims to the bishop of Lincoln the annual payment of six
marks of the total of nine marks ten shillings which the bishop used to
pay in commutation of certain tithes granted to the house by Robert
Chesney.[198] It would appear, then, that by the mid-thirteenth century at
the latest the order no longer felt the need for a hospital, perhaps because
of a decline in the number of lepers, and that the hospital was gradually
transformed into a 'normal' Gilbertine priory of canons.[199] This change
was institutionalized in the notification of master William. Thereafter,
there are no further references to the sick or lepers of Clattercote in
grants, bequests, or other records.

[196] *Letters of Pope Innocent III*, 274, app. 1057. Though there can be no doubt that by this
date the house belonged to the order, the address to the 'proctors' is unique in a Gilbertine
context. Four years later, however, Honorius III addressed a general confirmation to 'the
prior and brethren' of the leper hospital at Clattercote (Oxford, Bodl. Lib., Oxford Chart.
146).
[197] 'Cum domus de Clatercote adeo dono dei et fidelium subsidiis creverit in temporalibus
ut ad sustenacionem fratrum ordinis nostri ibidem commorancium proprie domus ipsius
suppetant facultates, ac in locum infirmorum qui ibidem degere solebant, in quorum exibicione
et custodia necesse fuit profusiores facere expensas, saniori consilio ad nostram instanciam
et rogatum validi subrogentur' (*Registrum Antiquissimum*, ii. 275–6, no. 936).
[198] Fowler (ed.), 'Early Charters of . . . Chicksand', 116–17; *Registrum Antiquissimum*, iii.
275–6, no. 936. The fact that it was the Master rather than the prior of Clattercote who was
responsible for the notification might suggest that the priory was less autonomous than
other Gilbertine houses but, given that the Master did possess considerable authority over
all Gilbertine communities, the leading role he played here may not have been unusual.
[199] Leprosy was certainly dying out in England in the 14th century and may well have
been in decline during the previous century (P. Richards, *The Medieval Leper and his
Northern Heirs* (Cambridge, Mass., 1977), esp. 3–4). It is interesting that just at the time
that Clattercote was ceasing to be a hospital the leper hospital of Stourbridge in Cambridge
was dissolved, and its chapel became a free chapel under the patronage of the bishop of Ely.
Though there were certainly lepers in Cambridge after this date it may be that here, too,
there was a decline in the disease's incidence in the 13th century (Rubin, *Charity and
Community*, 111–18).

Clattercote thus underwent several transformations during its first century. Beginning as a leper hospital, it was placed at an early date (perhaps at its foundation) under the care of the Gilbertines and became an asylum primarily for leprous nuns of the order. The earliest surviving grant (dated *c*.1150–1170) does not mention canons at Clattercote, but was addressed to St Leonard of Clattercote and the 'sanis et infirmis ibidem deo servientibus'.[200] However, by the end of the century it certainly contained canons, and maintained a dual function as hospital and priory till the middle of the thirteenth century.

A similar assimilation of a hospital to a Gilbertine priory seems to have taken place here as at Lincoln. At Lincoln bishop Robert Bloet had established the hospital of Holy Sepulchre for brethren, the poor, and the sick, but after bishop Chesney founded St Katherine's the 'care and custody' of Holy Sepulchre was put into the hands of St Katherine's.[201] It is worth noting that the same terms, *cura et custodia*, are used to describe the cession of Clattercote to Sempringham as are used in the charter of Henry II confirming the takeover of Holy Sepulchre. Similar developments are also found at Malton. Here the Gilbertine priory had the care of three hospitals. One, established at Broughton by Eustace fitzJohn, Malton's founder, was given by him into the care of the priory, another lay in Malton itself, while the third, that of Norton, was founded as a hospice by *magister* William de Flamville on land granted to him by Newburgh priory. He then granted it to the prior and canons of Malton to administer and provide for the needs of the poor who visited it. It seems that this foundation was intended essentially as an almshouse and perhaps also as a hostel for travellers—certainly there is no suggestion that lepers were cared for. However, the principle seems analogous to that of Clattercote in that a pre-existing foundation was given to the Gilbertines for their administration.[202]

---

[200] Oxford, Christ Church Deeds M. 37.

[201] *Registrum Antiquissimum*, x. 95, no. 2765.

[202] There were, of course, many precedents for, and later examples of, the absorption of small hospitals and leper houses into local religious houses. In Lincolnshire Burton Lazars took over the hospitals of Carlton-le-Moorland (*c*.1275) and the Malandry in Lincoln St Katherine's, Lincoln (1456) (Owen, *Church and Society*, 55–6). A later Gilbertine example is found at Marlborough. A small hospital for lepers was established in the town by 1231. Nothing is known of its early history, though it appears, like St Margaret's itself, to have been a royal foundation. In 1393 the king granted the reversion of the leper hospital of St Thomas by Marlborough to the canons of St Margaret's, after the death of the then warden, John Were. He died in 1402, when an inquisition found that St Thomas's possessions amounted to a little land, meadow and pasture in Manton and Marlborough Barton that was now in the hands of Sir Walter Hungerford, together with annual rents amounting to 53s.

Gilbertine Foundations, 1189–*c*.1300

Following Gilbert's death the pace and scale of new foundations slowed considerably. Moreover, with the exception of Shouldham, these priories were substantially poorer than those founded during Gilbert's lifetime. In part these features can be explained within a general pattern of monastic endowments, but they are also attributable to declining enthusiasm for the new order, which had owed so much of its special character to its founder, and which was now increasingly losing much of its appeal as a joint community for male and female religious. Indeed, after 1189 only one new double house, Shouldham in Norfolk, was established, an indication of the growing suspicion of such communities at the end of the twelfth century.

Shouldham

'Geoffrey fitzPeter was the most important baron in England during John's reign': for all that, he was a parvenu.[203] Active as a royal lawyer (he has even been suggested as the author of 'Glanville'), he had been made justiciar by Richard I in 1198 and had earlier, by royal patronage, acquired the marriage of Beatrix II de Say, the co-heiress to the Mandeville honour.[204] His own origins were in Wiltshire and his family were benefactors of Bradenstoke and Winchester, where his father, Peter of Ludgershall, became a monk shortly before his death. William de Mandeville, earl of Essex, died without legitimate heirs in 1189 and his lands were inherited by his aunt Beatrix I de Say, his father's sister. Her son, Geoffrey de Say, was allowed to succeed in his mother's place, but was unable to pay the huge fine demanded and was disseised. Thereupon Geoffrey fitzPeter obtained the Essex lands through his wife Beatrix II, the granddaughter of Beatrix I de Say. The question of the inheritance was certainly confused, and it is not surprising that suit against Geoffrey's claim was raised by Geoffrey de Say after fitzPeter's death in 1213. Indubitably the latter's claim was debatable, and his acquisition of the lands and profits of the

By this time it is doubtful how many lepers there would be remaining in the town, and it had probably outlived its usefulness (see above, n. 199). In any case, its acquisition by the Gilbertines can hardly have constituted a significant increase in the canons' income and its care was probably more of a hindrance than asset (*Cal. Pat. R. 1391–6*, 320; ibid. *1401–5*, 200; *Cal. Inq. Misc.* vii. 123; *VCH Wiltshire*, iii. 342–3).

[203] S. Painter, *The Reign of King John* (Baltimore, 1949), 293. Geoffrey's career is fully discussed in R. V. Turner, *Men Raised from the Dust: Administrative Service and Upward Mobility in Angevin England* (Philadelphia, 1988), 35–70.

[204] W. L. Warren, *King John* (London, 1961), 122, 144; Sanders, *English Baronies*, 71.

earldom (though he was not formally created earl until 1199) was due entirely to his position as one of the most powerful advisers to the Angevin kings.[205] It was natural for an *arriviste* like fitzPeter to establish his credibility by founding a new religious house. His colleague William Brewer had founded at least two: the Cistercian abbey of Dunkeswell and the Augustinian priory of Mottisfont, while an even more distinguished royal servant, William Marshal, founded Cartmel (besides other houses on his Irish lands).[206]

The chief de Mandeville foundation was Walden, a Benedictine abbey established in 1136 by Geoffrey de Mandeville, first earl of Essex. Support for Walden, however, was never secure. Geoffrey's son and heir, Geoffrey II (d. 1167), was influenced by his mother, Rohaise, to favour Chicksands, though he did confirm his father's grants to Walden and eventually found burial there. Geoffrey's brother and heir, William, was also hostile to the monks of Walden, though, like his brother, he was eventually reconciled, and when he died in Normandy he ordered his heart to be brought to Walden for burial.[207] There can be little doubt that the leading patron of Walden at this time was Beatrix I de Say, the founder's sister. Though her own gifts to Walden were fairly limited, she is lauded in the Walden chronicle as the monks' truest friend and *matronarum nobilissima*. As patron she was approached by the prior of Walden to ensure that her son carried out the bequests of his cousin William when he had obtained the earldom. However, as we have seen, Geoffrey de Say retained his position for only a year. The new regime of Geoffrey fitzPeter is vividly portrayed by the Walden chronicler. Soon after receiving his new possessions Geoffrey embarked on a tour of his estates, including Walden. In spite of a friendly reception Geoffrey treated the community with contempt, and accused the abbot of disinheriting him when 'my priory' was converted into an abbey.[208] The next day he proceeded to disseise the abbot of the estates bequeathed by earl William. According to the Walden chronicler, the instigator of Geoffrey's hostility was his wife Beatrix, *auctrix malorum*. After her death in childbirth her body was taken to Chicksands for burial in the nuns' chapter. It is

---

[205] GEC v. 118–25; Painter, *Reign of King John*, 262–3.

[206] Ibid. 77–8; Turner, *Men Raised from the Dust*, 63–7 (Geoffrey fitzPeter), 87–90 (William Brewer).

[207] *Monasticon*, iv. 144–5. William is said to have criticized the monks for possessing all the churches once held by his father, so that he could not find one to give to any of his clerks.

[208] This episode is fully discussed in S. Wood, *English Monasteries and their Patrons in the Thirteenth Century* (Oxford, 1955), 167–70.

perhaps to her that we should look for her husband's patronage of the Gilbertines.

Certainly Geoffrey was an enthusiastic supporter of the new order. It is no coincidence that his letter in favour of Gilbert's canonization and included amongst those sent to the Roman Curia is the only one from a layman preserved in the dossier, with the exception of that of king John, though others were almost certainly written. Moreover, it was to Geoffrey that the archbishop of York and the papal legate wrote asking for support for Malton priory in the canons' struggle to secure the church of Marton.[209] It might have been expected that Geoffrey would continue the association with Chicksands. This was derived from his wife's great-aunt Rohaise, who had married Payn de Beauchamp after Geoffrey I de Mandeville's death, and who with him had founded the Bedfordshire priory. However, Geoffrey preferred the greater prestige of his own foundation—to the undisguised dismay of the Walden chronicler.[210]

The date of Shouldham's foundation is unclear. From the witness list Geoffrey's foundation charter can be dated to between 1193 and 1200, and the fact that he styles himself earl of Essex might suggest a date after 27 May 1199 when he was formally created earl.[211] However, the Walden chronicler makes it clear that Shouldham was founded in the reign of Richard I and that Geoffrey's wife died before Beatrix I de Say. The latter died in 1197 at the latest. The body of Geoffrey's own wife is said to have been transferred to Shouldham from Chicksands and the foundation charter is made for her soul *cum corpore suo*: it also refers to Geoffrey as a vassal of Richard I. We must assume, therefore, either that Geoffrey's charter post-dates the actual foundation or that Geoffrey chose to style himself earl of Essex prior to 1199.[212]

Geoffrey's foundation comprised the manor of Shouldham, together with lands in eighteen other places in north-east Norfolk and one (Wrangle) just across the Lincolnshire border. Though he retained 120 acres of his demesne, the capital messuage and offices, and the homage and services of his own free tenants, this was a lavish endowment, especially when to it were added five churches: All Saints and St Margaret's, Shouldham; Shouldham Thorpe; Stoke Ferry; and Wereham.[213] This

---

[209] *Book of St Gilbert*, pp. xcxii, 232–4. For Marton, see London, BL, MS Cotton Claudius D XI, fo. 60[r-v], and below, Ch. 7: 'Advowsons: disputes and uncertainties'.

[210] *Monasticon*, iv. 146; Elkins, *Holy Women*, 122.   [211] GEC v. 124.

[212] Certainly from 1190 he was taking the third penny due to the earl, and such a powerful baron may not have been too nice in his use of the title.

[213] *Monasticon*, vi. 2. 974–5. Moreover, there is a suggestion in the Walden chronicle that more was envisaged, for when the dispute between Geoffrey and Walden was finally

endowment pattern is somewhat different from that of the Lincolnshire priories. As we have observed, these were often co-operative foundations, and even where a single founder appears to have been responsible, his efforts were supported by other local families without whose help the community could not have prospered. The contrast with Shouldham is particularly striking if the charters enrolled in 1408 are examined. There are fourteen: two (including the foundation charter) were issued by Geoffrey fitzPeter; another is from William de Mandeville, Geoffrey's son, confirming his father's gifts and adding some of his own; two more are from Christiana, William's widow; another, of Christiana de Valognes, confirms these grants; the seventh charter in the series is a grant of rent by Aveline, countess of Essex. Of the remaining seven, three relate to small grants in Lynn, two more to a parcel of 12 acres in Northwood (*sic*: ?Northwold); one to a messuage in Norwich, and the last to the grant of a tenant's homage and service in Rodney. It is clear that Shouldham priory was essentially the creation of one family. This conclusion is reinforced by the 1291 valuation, which reveals that nearly half of the priory's total income from temporalities was derived from the manor of Shouldham, while all the other major estates, including Stoke Ferry, Westbrigg, and Wolferton, had also been granted either by the founder or his son.[214]

The fifty years following the death of Gilbert also saw the emergence of several communities for Gilbertine canons, as well as a number of foundations which for a number of reasons proved ephemeral. The 'successful' priories were themselves amongst the poorest of the Gilbertine houses with few landed endowments and providing for only a handful of religious.

Holland Bridge

The tiny foundation of St Saviour's, Holland Bridge (also known as Bridge End), was the smallest of all the Gilbertine foundations. It lay in the fens only a few miles to the north of Sempringham, and was probably always in some measure dependent upon the mother house; by the Dissolution it had certainly become a cell of its much larger neighbour. It

resolved through the intervention of Richard I, the king is said to have told his justiciar to give lands intended for Shouldham to Walden (ibid. iv. 147). It is unclear if these were additional lands or whether they comprised those which Geoffrey had earlier taken from the monks.

[214] *Taxatio*, 105.

was never staffed by more than a few canons. Their chief function was to maintain the fen causeway linking Holland with Kesteven, which carried the road from Boston to Grantham.[215] Such small establishments combining spiritual with temporal obligations were not unknown in the Lincolnshire marshes: sometimes they were served by a single hermit, in other places the responsibility for the maintenance of bridges, causeways, or ferries was carried by a larger foundation.[216] No foundation charter of the priory survives, but an inquiry of 1334 into the state of the causeway (which was continually subject to criticism during the fourteenth century) shows it to have been founded by Godwin the Rich of Lincoln, with the intention that any income surplus to the requirements of the brethren there should be used for the causeway's maintenance. Since this causeway included thirty bridges, upkeep was a major undertaking, and it is perhaps little wonder that the canons were unable or unwilling to support the work.[217] The causeway chapel of St Saviour which formed the nucleus of the foundation seems to have already existed by the time the canons were settled there, and it is possible that they took over the responsibilities of its priest(s). The date of the foundation is uncertain. It does not appear in the list of Gilbertine houses compiled *c*.1195, but was certainly in existence when John issued his general confirmation charter to the order in 1199.[218]

The priory of Holland Bridge is unusual amongst Gilbertine houses in having a merchant as its founder. Though most of the priories possessed urban property and numbered burgesses amongst their benefactors, since they were normally rural communities there was perhaps little incentive for merchants to become closely involved with their fortunes. Godwin the Rich was (as his name might suggest) one of the most prominent citizens of late twelfth-century Lincoln.[219] His business and landed interests were extensive, and he held property in Lincoln and its suburb of Wigford as well as in Boston, and perhaps in Torksey also. It is not surprising to find him as one of the leading Lincoln merchants fined for their assault on the Jews in 1191, nor to find him frequently involved in mercantile and financial litigation in the city. He seems to have invested

---

[215] This was the road taken by a mad woman of Lynn on her way to the shrine of St Gilbert (*Book of St Gilbert*, 332–4).

[216] See Owen, *Church and Society*, 51. Haverholme priory was responsible for the maintenance of a ferry for foot passengers in the same region.

[217] *Monasticon*, vi. 2. 969–70.   [218] *Cartae Antiquae*, 32.

[219] His career is summarized in G. W. F. Hill, *Medieval Lincoln* (Cambridge, 1948), 392–3.

in property in the countryside, and this may have been the reason for his support of religious houses in rural Lincolnshire.[220]

York

With the exception of St Katherine's, Lincoln, St Andrew's, York, was the only Gilbertine priory to be founded in a large town.[221] However, unlike the Lincoln house, it remained primarily an urban establishment, and though it possessed rural holdings (and even one or two properties described as granges) it would appear that most of this property provided a rental income. Like St Katherine's it was, and remained, an establishment for canons alone. Its founder was Hugh Murdac, a nephew of archbishop Henry Murdac, who had been a royal clerk and justice. He seems to have been a typical royal lawyer rewarded with clerical office. He was rector of Bamburgh between 1161 and 1173 and it is possible that he was also prebendary of Driffield before 1166.[222] By the early 1190s Hugh was a canon of York minster, in which capacity he regularly witnessed charters, and in 1201 he reached the peak of his career when he was the successful royal and chapter nominee, against the wishes of his archbishop, for the archdeaconry of Cleveland. His tenure, however, was limited, for by Michaelmas of that year he had been replaced by William, the king's treasurer, perhaps as a compromise candidate.[223] That such a man should aspire to found a Gilbertine house was not surprising. His uncle, the archbishop, had been a supporter of the order, and was particularly involved with Watton priory, which foundation he had confirmed.[224] Hugh also had links with Yorkshire nunneries: he witnessed a charter in favour of Watton in 1204 and was a benefactor of the nuns of

---

[220] Already by 1177 he and his wife Alice had been received into the fraternity of Sempringham by Gilbert in return for his grant of a carucate in Sempringham which he held of Alice de Gant (*Sempringham Charters*, xv. 159). He also appears as a donor of other rural property to the Templars and to the small nunnery of Fosse outside Torksey (ibid. 392–3; *Records of the Templars*, pp. cciii–cciv, 102. Land in Boston was given to the monks of Durham (Hill, *Medieval Lincoln*, 393).

[221] The fullest discussion of this house is J. E. Burton, 'Historical Evidence', in R. L. Kemp ed., *The Church and Gilbertine Priory of St Andrew, Fishergate* (The Archaeology of York, vol. 11: Historical Sources for York Archaeology after AD 1100, fasc. 2, York, forthcoming). I am grateful to Mr Kemp for a sight of this work prior to publication.

[222] *York Minster Fasti*, vol. 2, ed. C. T. Clay, Yorkshire Archaeological Society Record Series, 124 (1958), 20–1. Henry II described Hugh as *clericus meus* in a notification to the canons of Nostell (*EYC* ii. 155, no. 1457). In a charter of 1188 he is styled *magister*.

[223] C. T. Clay, 'Notes on the Early Archdeacons in the Church of York', *Yorkshire Archaeological Journal*, 36 (1947), 429–30. [224] *Monasticon*, vi. 2. 955.

Clementhorpe.[225] At least one other royal official, albeit of much higher
status than Hugh, Geoffrey fitzPeter, had founded Shouldham priory a
few years previously. Moreover, the Angevin court was actively fostering
Gilbert's cult, and St Andrew's was indeed founded at just the time that
the canonization was in progress.[226]

The site of the new priory was extra-mural and close to the river Ouse,
and the priory was laid out around the church of St Andrew Fishergate.
This church ('quae est ultra fossam in Fischergata') had been given to
Newburgh priory by the latter's founder, Roger de Mowbray, in the
1140s.[227] There is no indication how this church came into the hands of
Murdac, though it may be surmised that he received it during his period
of royal service in Yorkshire. Certainly there is no evidence of any disputes or negotiations between the Gilbertines and Newburgh. The original foundation comprised the church and its adjoining lands, together
with rentcharges on property in York and the suburbs. Apart from the
foundation grant virtually nothing is known of the early history of
the priory, and indeed St Andrew's is one of the least documented of all
the Gilbertine houses. By the Dissolution the great majority of the priory's income was derived from temporalities (it had no *spiritualia*) in
the villages around York rather than in the city itself, but there is no
evidence, apart from a few fines of the thirteenth century and a few later
licences to receive property in mortmain, to indicate the pattern of land
acquisition after 1200.[228]

Marmont

The small priory of Marmont in the fenlands of the Cambridgeshire–
Norfolk border may have been founded as the result of a miraculous
vision. On the night of Gilbert's death Matilda, the wife of Ralph de

---

[225] *Yorkshire Deeds VI*, 94; R. B. Dobson and S. Donaghey, *The History of Clementhorpe
Nunnery*, The Archaeology of York, vol. 2: Historical Sources for York Archaeology after
AD 1100, fasc. 1 (1984), 19.

[226] Burton, 'Historical Evidence', dates the foundation between 1195 and 1202.

[227] *Monasticon*, vi. 320. See also *Charters of the Honour of Mowbray*, nos. 195, 203,
pp. 138, 143. Later in the 12th century the advowson of the church was granted to St
Mary's, York, but neither do the monks here seem ever to have made good what claims they
possessed in it (Burton, 'Historical Evidence').

[228] The first interest in rural property may date from 1202, when an agreement was made
to transfer the property which Hugh had given to St Andrew's outside the west entrance to
the Minster to the dean and chapter, in order to expand the minster cemetery and to lessen
the risk of fire to it and the archiepiscopal buildings, in return for rent from lands in South
Cave (*Monasticon*, vi. 2. 962).

Hauville, had a vision in which she saw the soul of the saint being taken up into heaven.[229] No direct connection between Ralph and the Gilbertines has been established: the nearest priory to Marmont was Shouldham in north Norfolk, though the fact that the *Vita* calls Ralph a *vir bonus* might suggest that he was already known as a Gilbertine patron. The history of the de Hauville family is obscure during the twelfth century, but Ralph is known to have served as a royal falconer successively to Henry II, Richard I, and John, and he held land by serjeantry tenure of the crown in Norfolk, as well as holding of the bishop of Ely just across the Cambridgeshire border.[230] Like other minor Angevin servants, Ralph was active in the wardship market, and gained a number of royal wards, including his own future wife, Matilda.[231] Matilda held two carucates in Hacconby, a village only a short distance from Sempringham, which had earlier been in the possession of Roger le Gros, from whom it had escheated to the throne. Matilda, who was probably Roger's daughter, became a royal ward,[232] Roger, who died shortly before Michaelmas 1202, had been a benefactor of Sempringham, as well as to Hacconby church, Bourne abbey, and the Templars. At his death very little property was left in his possession, but his successor, Matilda, did ensure that her new family continued the support of the order of which he had been a patron.[233] The priory of Marmont was not founded until *c*.1204, when king John confirmed Ralph's gift of all his land in Upwell together with four churches: Dunton, Doughton, and Kettleston (Norwich diocese) and Hacconby (Lincoln diocese), for the construction of a small house where Ralph and his wife were to be buried. In return the community of three canons was to say a daily mass in the church of Upwell for the soul of queen Eleanor, the king's mother.[234] The terms of the charter make it clear that Ralph wanted to found a small monastic chantry for himself and his wife. It was not an ambitious project, and it was probably neither expected nor intended that other benefactors would join his enterprise.

---

[229] *Book of St Gilbert*, 126–8. The vision is discussed by Foreville, ibid., p. lxxx. Visions were not infrequently associated with monastic foundations. For other examples, see e.g. Elkins, *Holy Women*, 70. [230] *Book of Fees*, i. 10, 129, 169.

[231] *Pipe Roll, 3 John*, PRS, NS 14 (1936), 183; *CRR* i. 390; *Rotuli de Dominabus*, 51–2.

[232] Matilda is styled 'daughter and heir of Richard de Dunwich' in *VCH Cambridgeshire*, ii. 258, but this seems to be a case of mistaken identity, for Matilda, daughter of Richard, was the wife of Ralph II de Hauville, the grandson of Ralph I the falconer (F. B. Blomefield and C. Parker, *An Essay towards a Topographical History of the County of Norfolk*, 11 vols. (London, 1805–10), vii. 84).

[233] For Roger, his holdings, and grants see *Book of Fees*, i. 181, 286; ii. 1336; *Sempringham Charters*, xvi. 33, xvii. 165; *Records of the Templars*, 96; *Lincolnshire Assize Roll of 1202*, 479, 482–3, 486. [234] *Monasticon*, vi. 2. 979.

This foundation, therefore, marks the beginning of that transition in pious giving from the monastic to the chantry foundation, that was to gather momentum in the coming centuries.[235]

Failures

Possession of a foundation charter did not necessarily guarantee the success of a new religious house. Goodwill was not of itself sufficient to ensure the future, and, in any case, as we shall see, the communities themselves might not be eager for success. Moreover, the very fact that houses of the new orders were much easier and cheaper to found than Benedictine communities because they demanded fewer resources and, sometimes, less productive land, meant that a greater proportion of them were doomed to failure.[236] Every order can show examples of failed institutions, either never established or but short-lived, but such cases are not unnaturally much less well documented than the successes. In many cases non-viable foundations were moved and re-founded on new sites.[237] Nunneries were especially vulnerable. An attempted Cistercian foundation at Coddenham (Suffolk) failed, perhaps because it was too far from the proposed mother house of Nun Appleton (Yorkshire).[238] Bretford (Warwickshire) was established as a small Benedictine nunnery in the mid-twelfth century, but disappeared after a few years since the two nuns there did not like the site.[239] However, the Gilbertines have the unenviable record of the highest failure rate, with at least five failures before 1300 compared with a total of twenty-two established priories.[240]

---

[235] See below, Ch. 6: 'Benefits': 'Chantries'. An analogous foundation of the 14th century is the Gilbertine house of Poulton (Wiltshire), founded by Sir Thomas Seymour in 1350 (*Monasticon*, vi. 2. 980–1).

[236] Stamford is not considered here: its foundation, and subsequent abandonment, was due to different circumstances and is discussed above, Ch. 3: 'Education and learning': 'Learning'.

[237] For example, the Lincolnshire Cistercians of Otley, founded in 1137, lasted for only one generation because of their meagre endowment: only the generosity of the bishop of Lincoln enabled their refoundation at Thame (Norton and Park (eds.), *Cistercian Art and Architecture in the British Isles*, 29).   [238] *Medieval Religious Houses*, 277.

[239] The fact that there were only two nuns suggests that the house was hardly feasible (ibid. 256).

[240] To the cases considered below should perhaps be added Wintringham (Yorkshire). This is listed as a separate community in Henry II's general confirmation of 1154 × 1161 but can only have had an autonomous existence for a very short time, if at all, for it early appears as a large grange of Malton, which held the advowson of the church. None of the charters in the Malton cartulary relating to this site suggests that it was independent (London, BL, MS Cotton Claudius D XI, fo. 30).

Tunstall

Some time before 1160 Reginald de Crevequer granted to the nuns 'de Insula quae dicitur Tunstall' the island of Tunstall; his part of the island of *Haye*; *Wulfholm*; his meadow between Tunstall and *Haye*, together with 16 acres 'ad construendam abbatiam loca praenominata'.[241] The total grant amounted to almost 100 acres of arable and considerable pasturage. However, the new foundation on an island of the river Ancolne failed to survive, and by the time of Simon and Alexander, Reginald's sons, Tunstall had become a grange of Bullington.[242] Tunstall lay in Redbourne, which had come into Reginald's hands by his marriage to Maud, the heiress of Gilbert fitzJocelin, lord of Redbourne, for whose salvation his foundation was made. It may be that Tunstall was intended as an assertion of Reginald's arrival among the ranks of Lincolnshire county society. Why did the new foundation fail? One reason may well be that the nuns were unable to gain control of the parish church, which was normally considered a *sine qua non* of a successful foundation. This had been granted to Selby abbey by Gilbert, together with his demesne tithes, and this grant was later confirmed by Reginald himself.[243] Selby's strong presence in the village ensured that the Gilbertines had little scope for expansion.

A further reason for Tunstall's failure may well have been the fact that several lords had interests in Redbourne. In 1086, though Jocelin was the largest landholder, there were eight other lords, and in 1212 there were still six lords, including Bullington and Selby, with estates in the vill.[244] As we have already seen, in instances where there was no one lord with sufficient resources to establish a priory sometimes neighbours would join together to make a foundation. In Tunstall there seems to have been no such co-operation. With the exception of the Crevequers other local lords were but little, if at all, interested in the Gilbertines, and this probably explains not only the failure of Tunstall but also the fact that at the Dissolution Redbourne was among the least valuable of Bullington's granges.[245] Finally the situation was not ideal for a new foundation. The Ancolne valley was largely infertile and parts were liable to flooding. Not surprisingly,

---

[241] *Monasticon*, vi. 2. 954.
[242] Golding, 'Gilbertine Priories', 49–50, 74–5, 247 and references there cited. The foundation charter is London, BL, Harl. Chart. 48 I 49.
[243] *The Coucher Book of Selby*, ed. J. T. Fowler, 2 vols., Yorkshire Archaeological and Topographical Association Record Series, 13 (1892), ii. 228–32, 299.
[244] *Lincolnshire Domesday*, 20–1, 53, 83, 120, 132, 162, 170, 190; *Book of Fees*, i. 189, 190.
[245] *VE* iv. 84. The holding was valued at 17*s*. 4*d*.

population was low relative to the county as a whole. There can have been little economic incentive to establish a new priory here.[246]

Ravenstonedale

The manor and advowson of Ravenstonedale were given in the middle of the twelfth century by Torphin fitzRobert for the creation of a Gilbertine house. Torphin, the grandson of Copsi, the Anglo-Scandinavian lord of Waitby and Warcop (Westmorland), was a leading vassal of the counts of Brittany, with substantial estates in Yorkshire where he was a benefactor of Byland and Easby abbeys. In Ravenstonedale he was a tenant of William de Vesci, son of the founder of Malton and Watton priories, and it was most probably this tenurial link that inspired Torphin to found a Gilbertine priory of his own.[247] The site was a remote one, on the western edge of the Pennines, a few miles south-west of Kirkby Stephen. Like Tunstall its status as an independent priory was short-lived, if, indeed, it was ever established as such.[248] Certainly by 1200 it was a grange of Watton, when king John granted (or confirmed an otherwise unrecorded grant of) extensive lands and pasture in the region to the nuns of Watton.[249] The estate continued in the priory's hands till the Dissolution, when the value of its *temporalia* was £93 14s. and of the rectory £26 13s. 4d. This made it by far the wealthiest of all of Watton's estates: fifteen Gilbertine priories had incomes lower than this.[250] Clearly, and in this case unlike Tunstall, Ravenstonedale was economically viable and we must look elsewhere for the reason for its failure.

---

[246] J. Thirsk, *English Peasant Farming*, (London, 1967), 92–3; Darby, *The Domesday Geography of Eastern England*, 88–9.

[247] An English translation of the foundation charter, which was destroyed in the fire in St Mary's tower, York, is given in J. Nicholson and R. Burn, *The History and Antiquities of the Counties of Westmorland and Cumberland*, 2 vols. (London, 1777), i. 518. The priory remains are discussed in E. P. Frankland, 'Explorations in Ravenstonedale', *Transactions of the Cumberland and Westmorland Antiquarian and Archaeological Society*, NS 29 (1929), 278–92; NS 30 (1930), 144–8, and *An Inventory of the Historical Monuments in Westmorland*, Royal Commission on Historical Monuments, England (London, 1936), 198. For Torphin and his lands, see *EYC* v. 53–66, and Clay (ed.), *Early Yorkshire Families*, 57. For Torphin's patronage of Byland and additional genealogical material, see J. Burton, 'Charters of Byland Abbey relating to the Grange of Bleatarn', *Transactions of the Cumberland and Westmorland Antiquarian and Archaeological Society*, 79 (1979), 29–50. For Eustace's lordship of Ravenstonedale, see Green, *Government of England*, 252.

[248] Though it is listed as an independent community in Henry II's general confirmation charter of 1154 × 1161 (London, BL, MS Cotton Claudius D XI, fo. 30), the foundation charter is addressed to the community at Watton, and makes no reference to a new priory.

[249] *Monasticon*, vi. 2. 956. In the confirmation charter of Celestine or Innocent III it appears as a possession of Watton (Cheney, 'Papal Privileges', 63).

[250] *Monasticon*, vi. 2. 957.

Owton

At first sight there seems little reason why Alan of Wilton's putative foundation of Owton in south-east County Durham should have failed. Though a long way from the mother house it was no further from Sempringham than Marlborough, and was within comparatively easy distance of the order's Yorkshire houses. The endowment, too, was not unsubstantial by Gilbertine standards, and could certainly have formed the nucleus of a viable priory. It comprised the whole vill of Owton; twelve bovates in Hutton Rudby; a carucate in Upleatham; two bovates in West Coatham; and half a carucate in Middleton-in-Cleveland. The founder, too, was not unknown in Gilbertine circles and was a considerable benefactor of Ellerton, of whose founder his wife was a kinswoman.[251]

A closer inspection of the grant, however, suggests that there were deep-seated difficulties which ultimately could not be overcome. Though it is not certain that Alan wished his new foundation to be at Owton, since king John's confirmation charter of 1204 (which provides the only reference to the house) merely confirms the *rationabilem donationem* which Alan made 'in order to make a certain priory of the order', the fact that Owton is the first place mentioned in the text and constituted the largest single grant suggests that this was intended as the site. Owton was a manor of perhaps 220 acres forming part of the Brus fee of Stanton. It did not possess a church of its own since it was part of Stanton parish, and Stanton church itself had been given to Guisborough priory between 1119 and 1129.[252] There was, therefore, no possibility that the Gilbertines would ever gain control of the parish church. Moreover, though as the crow flies Owton was not far away from the other properties given by Alan, they were divided by the fast-flowing Tees, which here formed the shire and diocesan boundary. Finally, there may be some doubt as to whether Alan himself was actually in a position to grant these lands. William de Brus held the manor and there is no evidence that he had subinfeudated it to Alan.

Whatever the reasons, there is no doubt that the priory failed to get off the ground. Within a few years the lands in Hutton Rudby, Upleatham,

---

[251] He was also a patron of St Nicholas's hospital, Yarm, and of Healaugh Park. Farrer distinguished, for no apparent reason, between Alan, founder of Owton, and the Alan, benefactor of Ellerton and Yarm, 'whom I suppose to have been nephew of the donor to the canons of Sempringham' (*EYC* ii. 124). Alan did not die till 1230–1, but his gift to Sempringham probably dates from 1204 or not much before.

[252] *VCH Durham*, iii. 366–7, 375. There was a dependent chapel at Owton by the early 13th century.

and Middleton had been granted by Alan to the hospital of St Nicholas, Yarm (which was administered by Healaugh Park), while the land in West Coatham had gone to Healaugh Park itself.[253] Farrer drew attention to the similarities between the foundation at Yarm and that of Alan of Wilton's kinsman, William son of Peter's establishment of Ellerton.[254] Moreover, both founders remembered each other in their foundation charters and prayers were expected for both founders in both houses. It may be that Alan, realizing the drawbacks of establishing a Gilbertine priory at Owton, decided to endow a hospital with the Yorkshire properties, perhaps in imitation of Ellerton.[255]

Dalmilling

The history of the short-lived Gilbertine foundation of Dalmilling is the best documented of all the failed houses of the order.[256] Some time between 1219 and 1228 Walter fitzAlan, Steward of Scotland, wrote to Robert, Master of the order, announcing his intention to found a priory on his land at Dalmilling near Newton-upon-Ayr.[257] His letter details the proposed grants. They were substantial and included pasture ready stocked with 300 cows and 2,000 sheep; a fishery; five ploughgates; two mills and woodland, besides the churches of Dundonald and Sanquhar, worth 100 and 20 merks respectively. Other charters, including the foundation charter and two other grants recorded in the Paisley register, make it clear that the actual donation was even larger than that proposed in the letter.[258] It remains unclear why the Steward should have decided to found a Gilbertine house at all. Walter's grandfather, Walter I, created Steward by David I, founded the Cluniac priory of Paisley, which was colonized

---

[253] *The Chartulary of the Augustinian Priory of St John the Evangelist of the Park of Healaugh*, ed. J. Purvis, Yorkshire Archaeological Society Record Series, 92 (1936), 123, 129–30.   [254] *EYC* ii. 124–5.

[255] It is perhaps significant in the light of what has been said of the tenurial position in Owton that the estate there was the only one of those initially given to the Gilbertines that did not form part of this new foundation.

[256] The charters and other material are to be found in the Malton cartulary, London, BL, MS Cotton Claudius D XI, fo. 227, and in the register of Paisley abbey, *Registrum Monasterii de Passelet*, Publications of the New Club, Paisley, 1 (1897), 21–32, 42–7. Much of the following paragraphs is owed to J. Edwards, 'The Order of Sempringham, and its Connexion with the West of Scotland', *Transactions of the Glasgow Archaeological Society*, NS 5 (1908), 67–95, and G. W. S. Barrow, 'The Gilbertine House at Dalmilling', *Collection of the Ayrshire Archaeological and Natural History Society*, 2nd ser. 4 (1955–7), 50–67.

[257] Ibid. 58–9. This letter is discussed below, Ch. 6: 'Patrons and benefactors'.

[258] Barrow, 'The Gilbertine House at Dalmilling', 59–61; *Registrum Monasterii de Passelet*, 22–3.

from Much Wenlock, and was also a patron of the Cistercian abbey of Melrose. His son, Alan, was likewise a benefactor of Paisley.[259] The Stewards had no interests in Lincolnshire and little known connection with the order of Sempringham.[260] The first positive connection is found when Walter II granted to the community at Sixhills three merks annual rent from land held by his tenant Adam of Ness. It was clearly through Sixhills that the negotiations for the foundation of Dalmilling were conducted. Prior Nicholas of Sixhills carried the letter from Walter to the order's Master, to whom he was expected to explain the full details of the proposal. Presumably he also inspected the proposed site of the new priory. How Nicholas became the confidant of Walter cannot be known.

By 1238 the site was abandoned. On 29 November 1238 the priors of Malton and St Andrew's, York, appointed the order's proctors in Scotland, met with representatives of Paisley abbey at Dryburgh and ceded all the priory's possessions, together with all charters relating to the house, to Paisley. They recited the text of the Master of the order's resignation of the priory, which would be sent before next Pentecost.[261] At the same time the canons at Dalmilling were ordered to deliver seisin to Paisley, and to hand over all the mares and foals so that if any of these were found to be missing after they had been sold to Paisley the sum could be subtracted from the payment the latter was to make to the Gilbertines. This is the first mention of a cash transaction between the houses. When all these affairs had been wound up the canons were speedily to return to England.[262] In another instrument the monks of Paisley pledged to give 40 merks per annum to Sempringham for the property.[263] It is extremely unlikely that the Gilbertines had ever established a community at Dalmilling. In the letter from the priors of Malton and St Andrew's, York authorizing the transfer of Dalmilling to Paisley the canons there, John and Walter, are said to be 'canonicis apud Dalmunyn

---

[259] J. Cameron Lees, *The Abbey of Paisley from its Foundation till its Dissolution* (Paisley, 1878), chs. iv and vii.

[260] A Walter Steward did witness a charter in favour of Sempringham in the mid-12th century, and he was identified by Edwards with Walter I fitzAlan (Edwards, 'Order of Sempringham', 71).

[261] *Registrum Monasterii de Passelet*, 25–7. Walter ordered the priors to hand over the charters issued by himself, the king, and the bishop of Glasgow (Barrow, 'The Gilbertine House at Dalmilling', 66). Those of Walter and the king are duly found transcribed in the *Registrum*, 21–4, 47–8.   [262] Barrow, 'The Gilbertine House at Dalmilling', 61–2.

[263] This was confirmed by Walter fitzAlan (ibid. 63–4, 65–6). See also the acknowledgement by the bishop of Glasgow that he and his chapter would be responsible for ensuring Paisley made due payment (ibid. 67).

constitutis', an unusual phrase which suggests that they may well have been an advance guard sent to oversee the site before the community was established.

No reason was given for the Gilbertines' cession of Dalmilling. Edwards suggested, not wholly convincingly, that worsening Anglo-Scottish relations may have provoked the decision.[264] Certainly the agreement whereby Paisley undertook to pay the annual rent contained the proviso that no penalties would accrue for non-payment if there was war in the land. The initial foundation was clearly large enough to support a Gilbertine house: indeed, it was one of the largest the order ever received. However, it must have been uncertain how much further support the priory could expect in south-west Scotland from other benefactors, and, more importantly, regardless of the potential or real problems of war, Dalmilling was far from the centres of the order. Malton and York, the two most northerly priories, were still some 200 miles away: it must have seemed more realistic to cede the property to Paisley in return for a fixed annual income.

Unfortunately, even this income was not certain, and from the beginning difficulties were experienced in extracting the 40 merks. In 1246 the Gilbertines complained before papal judges-delegate that the moneys due had not been paid and it was agreed that in this instance half of the sum would be remitted.[265] This agreement may be related to an acknowledgement by Paisley that 60*s*. had been withheld from the annual payment because of a papal tax demand. Paisley had attempted to claim exemption on these grounds from the pope, but had failed and now agreed to pay the full sum due.[266] No further complaints were heard until 1296. Then, in the uncertain times of the Anglo-Scottish war, the abbot acknowledged that Paisley owed the Gilbertines 40 merks arrears of rent and agreed to pay this in two instalments.[267] This was but a temporary respite, and another solution was tried in 1319 when the pope authorized the appropriation of the church of Whissendine valued at 50 marks per annum. The choice of Whissendine is interesting and perhaps significant for there, too, there was a Scottish connection. Earl David of Huntingdon had given this church to the Scottish abbey of Lindores between 1195 and 1199.[268] The church was held by Lindores throughout the thirteenth

---

[264] Edwards, 'Order of Sempringham', 77–8.

[265] *Registrum Monasterii de Passelet*, 24–5.

[266] Barrow, 'The Gilbertine House at Dalmilling', 64–5.

[267] The fact that the prior of Malton recognized payment indicates that he was still responsible for the rent's collection.

[268] K. J. Stringer, *Earl David of Huntingdon, 1152–1219* (Edinburgh, 1985), 242. This

century, but the abbey experienced some difficulty in collecting the pension from the church and by 1275 had arranged that this be collected by Sempringham.[269] Moreover, the sporadic warfare between England and Scotland meant unpredictable confiscations of the English property of Scottish houses, so that in 1301 and again in 1304 a royal clerk was presented to Whissendine. Later that year the lands were back in Lindores' hands and the clerk was re-presented by the abbey.[270] Perhaps as a result of this uncertainty the abbey decided to cut its losses, and in 1309 Lindores was given licence to alienate the advowson of Whissendine to Sempringham and two years later licence to appropriate was granted.[271] Papal approval was not gained till 1319. The justification for this was said to be the large numbers in the community and also the fact that the rent from Paisley had not been paid for the past fourteen years because of the wars.[272] Finally in 1343 came a royal mandate to the Exchequer that demands made of Lindores for an annual pension of ten marks and arrears of the same which were owed to the crown should be dropped, since Lindores had had licence to grant the church to Sempringham and had subsequently released to the latter the glebe land and the annual pension which Lindores had received 'from antiquity'.[273]

This, perhaps, should have been the end of the affair. After all, the Gilbertines were now receiving an assured annual income from the appropriation considerably in excess of what they would hope to receive from Paisley. However, it seems that the canons still expected to receive the rent. In 1329 a new claim for non-payment was put in for arrears, while Paisley claimed that money was only due since the Treaty of Northampton of April 1328.[274] The following year Reginald More, the order's proctor in Scotland, was himself granted the annual rent by the canons, perhaps in recognition of his activities on their behalf, perhaps for an

church had earlier been granted to St Andrew's, Northampton, by earl Simon III de Senliz of Northampton (ibid. 146).

[269] A number of Scottish houses had problems at this time in collecting moneys from English churches in which they held interests (ibid. 135–6). The pension in 1291 was £6 13s. 4d., and the *Taxatio* entry (65) reads: 'Iste pensio et decima ejusdem debet exigi sub nomine prioris de Sempyngham a 24 Octobris anno tercio et deinceps per processum annotatum inter recordas de termino Trinitatis anno 17.'

[270] *Cal. Pat. R. 1292–1301*, 596; ibid. *1301–7*, 221, 342.

[271] Ibid. *1307–13*, 195, 320.

[272] The mandate was repeated in 1327 (*Cal. Papal Letters*, ii. 185). A vicarage was ordained by the diocesan two years later, but the rector, William of Newark, seems to have held the living only till 1328, when he resigned on account of the appropriation of the church to Sempringham (*VCH Rutland*, ii. 164; *Cal. Papal Letters*, ii. 282).

[273] *Cal. Cl. R. 1343–6*, 76.   [274] *Registrum Monasterii de Passelet*, 29–31.

unstated financial consideration, and perhaps for prudential reasons, fearing that in future confrontations with the Scots it might be impossible in any case to obtain payment.[275] Finally in 1368, during a bitter struggle between Paisley and Reginald's son, William, the order formally renounced all claims to the rent in William's favour and the complex and ultimately frustrating Gilbertine interest north of the border came to an end, the victim of high politics and war.[276]

Brachy

Most interesting and puzzling of all the Gilbertine failures is the abortive foundation of Aldulf de Brachy on his estates in the Pays-de-Caux (Normandy). The Gilbertine order has long been recognized as a peculiarly English institution: its two foundations outside the kingdom in Scotland and at Rome have been interpreted as late aberrations, doomed to failure not only because of their distance and the logistical difficulties of controlling them from Lincolnshire, but also because the Gilbertines did not *want* to expand. There is some truth in this analysis. After all, Gilbert was obviously unwilling for his communities to increase, and this had been the chief motivation for his attempted persuasion of the Cistercians to take over in 1147. Moreover, the closest analogies with the Gilbertines as an order can be found in Continental Europe, perhaps particularly in France, where small orders of purely local appeal were not uncommon. Most of these were, like Sempringham, communities that had their origins in the devoted followers of quasi-eremitical holy men.[277]

However, the attempted foundation in Normandy makes it clear that during the lifetime of Gilbert the order was prepared at least to investigate the possibility of trans-Channel houses.[278] The founder is a shadowy figure, though not, it would appear, an insignificant one. Perhaps the family's most tantalizing appearance is in the near-contemporary romance of Fulk fitzWarin, where an Adulf de Braci is presented as the outlaw's cousin. He shares in many of the latter's adventures, both at home and abroad, at one point being rescued from prison in a daring escapade.[279]

---

[275] Ibid. 31–2; Edwards, 'Order of Sempringham', 86–7.

[276] *Registrum Monasterii de Passelet*, 42–7.

[277] The majority of these, like Dalon or Obazine, were later subsumed in larger institutions, particularly the Cistercians.

[278] Though attention was drawn to this venture by J. Nichols, *The History and Antiquities of the County of Leicestershire*, 4 vols. (London, 1795–1811), iii, pt. i. 231, it has not been noted since.

[279] *Gesta Fulconis Filii Warini*, in *Radulphi de Coggeshall Chronicon Anglicanum*, ed. J. Stevenson, Rolls Series (London, 1875), *passim*; the 'real' Fulk is discussed by M. Keen,

He first appears in the documentary record in the mid-twelfth century when he is mentioned amongst the benefactors to the Norman monastery of Longueville in a confirmation charter issued by Henry II in 1155.[280] In England he had succeeded to lands in South Croxton (Leicestershire) which his father had held of the Belvoir fee, and thirteenth-century evidence shows that the family also held lands in Knipton and Redmile close by.[281] However, Aldulf's prospects were considerably enhanced *c*.1170 when Henry II granted him the lands previously held or farmed of the crown by Osbert Martel in Bedfordshire and Buckinghamshire. The foundation charter of Brachy describes Aldulf as *nepos* of Osbert, and it is likely that Aldulf was his heir, perhaps on both sides of the Channel.[282] Osbert had held a group of manors to the east of Dunstable at Edlesborough and Eaton Bray, and a little further away at Mentmore and Stone, as well as one at Ravenstone on the northern edge of Buckinghamshire. All of these, with the exception of Edlesborough, passed to Aldulf.[283]

It was probably shortly after he had succeeded to Osbert's lands that Aldulf began to make his pious benefactions. He granted forty acres of his demesne land in Totternhoe to Dunstable priory, as well as confirming lands granted to the same foundation by Osbert Martel in Eaton Bray. He was also a benefactor to the Premonstratensian priory of Croxton, to which he granted land in South Croxton.[284] But his most substantial endowment was the foundation of Brachy. This can probably be dated

---

The Outlaws of Medieval Legend (2nd edn., London 1987), 40, and Painter, *Reign of King John*, 48–54. It is impossible to be certain whether Aldulf I or II is presented in the romance.

[280] *Calendar of Documents preserved in France*, 77, no. 225. He was perhaps a tenant of the Giffards, patrons of Longueville.

[281] *Circa* 1200 Aldulf restored to Hugh de Chemelles, his tenant, half a fee in South Croxton which Aldulf's father had granted to Hugh's parents (*Manuscripts of his Grace the Duke of Rutland*, Historic Manuscripts Commission 14th Report, HMSO (London, 1905), iv. 8, no. 28; *Book of Fees*, ii. 954). All these lands lay very close to the castle of Belvoir.

[282] Osbert probably belonged to the Martel family, which came from Bacqueville-en-Caux, almost adjacent to Brachy. The main branch of the family held lands in Dorset, Essex, and Bedfordshire (L. C. Loyd, *The Origins of some Anglo-Norman Families*, ed. D. C. Douglas and C. T. Clay, Harleian Society, 103 (1951), 60). He may have died or lost his lands as early as 1165–6.

[283] *Pipe Roll 17 Henry II*, PRS 16 (1893), 57; *VCH Buckinghamshire*, ii. 307; iii. 351, 397–8; iv. 440; *VCH Bedfordshire*, iii. 370. Some of Aldulf's lands passed to William de Cantilupe, who married Aldulf II's daughter and heiress, Masceline, others were held by Gilbert de Brachy, who was also a tenant of the Belvoir barony in 1242–3 (G. H. Fowler, 'Calendar of Inquisitions post Mortem, no. 1', *Publications of the Bedfordshire Historical Record Society*, 5 (1920), 210–15; *Book of Fees*, i. 462, 468, 472; ii. 875). The date of Aldulf I's death is unclear, but he may have died in the late 1170s, when his manor in Eaton Bray was again in the sheriff's hands.

[284] G. H. Fowler, 'A Digest of the Charters preserved in the Cartulary of the Priory of Dunstable', *Publications of the Bedfordshire Historical Record Society*, 10 (1926), 79, 63, nos.

between *c*.1170, when Aldulf succeeded Osbert, and 1184, by which time
the English lands were certainly in the hands of Malton priory. The
choice of the Gilbertines may have owed something to the fact that
Sempringham was less than twenty miles from South Croxton. Moreover, a number of tenants of the Belvoir fee were patrons of Gilbertine
houses and two substantial benefactors to Sempringham, Nigel son of
Alexander and Ridel of Keisby, appear as witnesses to one of Aldulf's
charters.[285]

The foundation charter, made with the assent of Aldulf's sons, Gwerne
and Aldulf, is addressed to the 'canons of the order and chapter of
Sempringham', which implies that this was intended as a canons-only
foundation from the start.[286] He granted all his demesne land in the
cultura between the vill of Rainfreville and *le Maygniyl* in Royville except
for 10 acres he had already bestowed on St Wandrille and a total of 19
acres held by Gilbert and Osbert de Royville. There the canons would
establish their house and priory.[287] The canons were endowed with the
churches of Brachy, those of St Audoen and St Mary at Greville, of
Burnebusc and Manneville, with all the appurtenant tithes and other property of the churches. He also gave all his tithes from all his feudal rents
in Normandy. This comprised the Norman element in the foundation,
but to this was added a half of his fee in South Croxton, saving the bovate
that was already held by the canons of Croxton priory and one-eighth fee
held by a tenant, Ralph Puintel.[288] The charter concludes with a statement that Aldulf has brought the first prior from England to his new
foundation and that he has agreed with Gilbert, 'first Master of the
order', that no prior shall be appointed during Aldulf or his heir's lifetime without the election of the convent and the approval of Aldulf and
heir. Thereafter a prior would be appointed either from within the community or from elsewhere in the order according to the institutes 'et
absque assensu ceterorum advocatorum'. These priors were to attend the
annual chapter at Sempringham every year or second year as the chapter
determined.

242, 179. He also witnessed other grants to the priory, e.g. 60, no. 170. For the Croxton
grant, see *Manuscripts of his Grace the Duke of Rutland*, iv. 179.

[285] Ibid. 8, no. 28.   [286] London, BL, MS Cotton Claudius D XI, fo. 217.

[287] 'mansionem suam et prioratum constituant unius conventus de canonicis sui ordinis
secundum quod terra illa et elemosine que date fuerint illis canonicis sustinere rationabiliter
poterint.'

[288] This half-fee is said to be that once held by Roger of Muston, who may be the
Domesday tenant Roger, who held 5 carucates in South Croxton as a sub-tenant of Robert
de Tosny (*Domesday Book*, i. 223b).

Aldulf's gifts were reasonably generous: many small Norman monasteries had been established in recent generations with similar endowments and held property on both sides of the Channel.[289] But Brachy was
not to survive. By 1184 its English lands were administered by Malton
and its Norman property was no longer in Gilbertine hands. The reason
must surely lie in the distance and water that separated it from the
mother house. This had been implicitly acknowledged in the concession
that the prior might only have to attend the general chapter every second
year; in an order where control was so centralized such an arrangement
was clearly anomalous. Distance had already been a factor in the ration-
alization of Gilbertine estates and was to contribute to the demise of
Dalmilling. Indeed, a few generations later Malton would even lease the
South Croxton property, since 'nimis remota minus proficebat'.[290]

Once it had been decided to abandon the foundation of Brachy, the
choice of Malton to administer the lands made some sense, since, though
much further away than many of the Gilbertine houses, it was a priory
for canons only. Aldulf duly confirmed the estate of $3\frac{1}{2}$ carucates and a
moiety of the church to Malton.[291] The canons retained it for about sixty
years, then, recognizing the difficulties of administering so distant an
estate, demised it for seven marks per annum to the hospital of Burton
Lazars, and later to the nuns of St Michael's, Stamford.[292] So ended
direct Gilbertine involvement in Aldulf's optimistic foundation.

Rome

The ancient basilica of San Sisto had been founded in the fifth century,
not far from the Vatican on the Appian Way. Some time between 1202
and 1207, as part of his programme for the regeneration of the charitable
and religious life of the city, Innocent III determined to establish a nunnery centred on the basilica which he was in the process of rebuilding.[293]
At this time the nuns of Rome were not strictly enclosed and the principal aim of the project was to remedy this situation. The new foundation

---

[289] The fullest study remains D. Matthew, *The Norman Monasteries and their English
Possessions* (Oxford, 1962).

[290] London, BL, MS Cotton Claudius D XI, fo. 219.

[291] The church was shared with the Premonstratensians of Croxton, each appointing to
the living alternately.

[292] Both land and rectory continued to be farmed till the Dissolution.

[293] B. M. Bolton, 'Daughters of Rome: All One in Christ Jesus!', in W. J. Shiels and D.
Wood (eds.), *Women in the Church*, Studies in Church History, 27 (Oxford, 1990), 101–15,
esp. 109–12; V. J. Koudelka, 'Le *Monasterium Templi* et la fondation dominicaine de S.
Sisto', *Archivum Fratrum Praedicatorum*, 31 (1961), 5–81.

was to have sixty nuns who would largely be recruited from the small, ancient, and unreformed nunneries of early thirteenth-century Rome. To carry out this scheme Innocent turned to the Gilbertines. He had already encountered the order, since in 1202 he had approved the canonization of Gilbert. This process had lasted some four years, so in its course he would have learnt much through the *Vita* and other sources of the order's constitution.[294]

Innocent was clearly planning on the grand scale. According to the *Gesta Innocentii III* he gave the foundation 'quingentas uncies auri regis et mc libras proviniensium'. As Koudelka points out, this sum was far larger than any other analogous papal grants to monastic foundations, and there can be little doubt that San Sisto was intended to be the flagship of Innocent's religious establishments. Had the Gilbertines accepted the pope's invitation, the future history of the order might have been radically different.

But Gilbertine canons never came to San Sisto. The reasons for their reluctance are unclear. They may not have been willing to expand beyond England. Moreover, by this time it must have been clear that the Gilbertines could expect to make few, or any, more foundations. A place at Rome, however prestigious, may well not have been considered to be worth the trouble. Furthermore, the building work at Rome itself was slow to complete: the rebuilding of the church seems to have encountered difficulties, and that had to be completed before the conventual buildings could be begun. Innocent died with his work here, as so often elsewhere, unfinished. There is no evidence that any Gilbertines had come to San Sisto even on a temporary basis, and it is probable that during these years a lay proctor looked after their interests. Innocent's successor, Honorius III, was eager to complete the work, however, and on 3 August 1218 he wrote sternly to the prior of Sempringham ordering him to send four canons to serve San Sisto by Christmas; if they failed to turn up he would give the church to another order. In spite of this ultimatum the final handover did not take place until the end of the following year, when on 4 December 1219 two canons formally stated that the order was not able to look after the basilica properly and therefore petitioned that the order be released from its obligation. San Sisto passed to the care of the Dominicans. Koudelka has argued forcefully that the initiative for the transfer came from Dominic himself. He had already founded a house

---

[294] Moreover, while at Rome on Gilbert's canonization cause the canons had gained papal approval for their *instituta*.

for women at Prouille: a similar establishment could be made in Rome itself. Honorius took Prouille under papal protection on 30 March 1218. The reason for the delay in transferring San Sisto from the Gilbertines to the Dominicans may be that Dominic was absent from Rome during the latter part of 1218 and much of 1219.[295] So ended the Gilbertine Roman connection: henceforth when Gilbertines came to the Holy City they would be visitors, not neighbours.

This brief survey of the failed foundations suggests that there is no single explanation for non-viability. Only in the case of Tunstall does the poverty of the initial endowment seem to have been a factor; by contrast the endowments of Ravenstonedale and Dalmilling were relatively lavish, and that of Owton certainly not insignificant. The failure of Owton and Ravenstonedale can perhaps best be attributed to the distance of these sites from Sempringham. Dalmilling presented a rare, if not unique, problem: a Scottish foundation whose mother house lay in England.[296] In the face of wars and political uncertainty such a venture was perhaps doomed. Logistical and administrative difficulties were thus compounded. A similar explanation probably underlay the canons' decision to abandon Brachy, but the case of Rome was different. Here the chief disincentive seems to have been the reluctance of the Gilbertines to commit themselves to a venture which they may well (rightly) have seen to be beyond their capabilities. For an order reluctantly established in the first place and with an essentially regional appeal, it was too much for the pope to expect them to willingly spearhead the reform of the nuns of Rome.

If there is one single feature these foundations (with the exception of Tunstall) have in common, it is their distance from the mother house. This need not have been an insuperable problem, but it was certainly a disincentive. Marlborough was the only Gilbertine house established before 1300 that lay outside northern or eastern England, and Marlborough may be the exception that proves the rule for it was especially favoured by the crown. To have spurned such favour may well have been too great a price for the canons to pay for the advantages of a geographically closely knit group. It seems most likely that the Gilbertines, who did not have

---

[295] Koudelka, 'Le *Monasterium Tempuli*', 49–52.

[296] Similar problems were faced by Scottish houses possessing English property, such as Lindores, discussed above, and conversely by English monasteries with Scottish interests. For a useful summary, see Stringer, *Earl David of Huntingdon*, 205–7, and R. B. Dobson, 'The Last English Monks on Scottish Soil', *Scottish Historical Review*, 46 (1967), 1–25, for the experiences of Durham.

the experience of other orders which crossed state boundaries, were, in the last resort, not interested in expansion. Their failures were failures of will, not of resources.

Conclusion

By 1230 all but three of the Gilbertine priories had been established. St Edmund's, Cambridge, was to be founded in 1291 as a centre for Gilbertine canons studying at the University, and two small communities, more akin to collegiate chantries than older-style priories, were founded at Hitchin (Hertfordshire) and Poulton (Wiltshire) in the mid-fourteenth century.[297] Some foundations had already failed both at home and abroad: another, just begun in Scotland, would shortly be added to the list. Most, however, survived. Some, like Sempringham, Chicksands, Watton, or Lincoln, flourished as large and prosperous communities, others, such as Alvingham or Sixhills, were of middling rank in their localities, while several such as Catley, Newstead, or Marmont lived a precarious existence till the Dissolution. While there is nothing particularly distinctive about Gilbertine foundations and patronage, they do need to be seen in the broader context of widespread Augustinian establishments, and other communities for women, which proliferated during the twelfth century and which appealed to the same class of patron. Their continuing prosperity was built in part, but only in part, on the scale of the initial foundation. As already noted, Catley was given a considerable foundation endowment but never built on its early good fortune. Conversely, Alvingham was a small foundation but continued to expand up till, and indeed a little beyond, the Statute of Mortmain. There were varying criteria for success, but all ultimately depended upon the communities' capacity to attract benefactions over several generations. This in turn was dependent upon such factors as the density of religious houses in the region; the readiness and ability of the heirs of earlier patrons to continue familial generosity; the attitude of patrons' lords to the alienation of property; and the financial resources of the priories to enter the land market and perhaps to take advantage of the financial embarrassment of their lay neighbours.

[297] For St Edmund's, see above, Ch. 3: 'Education and learning': 'Learning'.

5

Patterns of Endowment

Contexts for Growth

The mid-twelfth century was the high-water mark of monastic foundations in England. Thereafter the tide of benefactions receded. In part this
was due to changing fashions of pious giving, in part to the fact that there
was a decreasing amount of land available for distribution to the religious.
The majority of the Gilbertine houses, founded as they were between
1148 and 1160, operated in a world where there was an increasing scramble for endowments, where investment in the land market was essential
for expansion, and sometimes for survival, and where competition between the religious was now regulated by formal agreement.[1]

While the prohibition in 1152 on the foundation of new Cistercian
abbeys opened a window of opportunity for 'new' orders everywhere, and
in England for the Gilbertines and Premonstratensians in particular, it
was short-lived. The period of expansion lasted for only a little more than
a generation. Following Gilbert's death there was only one major new
foundation, Shouldham.[2] In Lincolnshire, the Gilbertine heartland, the
thirteenth century saw only one new monastic foundation.[3]

The same slackening is found north of the Humber. This decline in
the number of new foundations is one indicator of change in spiritual
fashion, and perhaps too of the inability of benefactors to maintain earlier
levels of generosity; the fact that these new houses were almost without
exception small and poorly endowed is another. But how far did this
downturn in fortune and popularity affect priories that were already in
existence? To what extent did the Gilbertines continue to attract grants
in the following century, and is it true of them, as has been claimed for
the Lincolnshire monasteries in general, that 'there is no real sign of a
decline in their popularity . . . or of a loss of interest in them before the
mid-fourteenth century'?[4]

[1] See below, pp. 280–2.
[2] After 1200 there were virtually no new Premonstratensian foundations either, and only
two, the creations of bishop Peter des Roches at Halesowen and Titchfield, were of any size.
[3] The tiny alien priory of West Ravendale established in 1202.
[4] Owen, *Church and Society*, 52.

The pattern of endowment of Gilbertine priories was partly determined by these general trends in pious giving amongst the laity, and by increasing pressure on resources that both made potential patrons more reluctant to part with them and led to rivalry and dispute between the religious themselves. But estate creation was also governed by factors specific to each community. Most important was the attitude and wealth of local lords. In instances where a priory had been established by one regional family, its own development was primarily shaped by these patrons. This is seen at Chicksands, where virtually all of the priory's estates were to be found on lands held either by the founding family, the Beauchamps of Bedford, or by their tenants. An even clearer example is Shouldham. Here the Gilbertines were almost wholly dependent upon the generosity of Geoffrey fitzPeter and his family.[5] Priories whose founders retained little interest in their fate had, on the other hand, to depend on a wider spectrum of support. Haverholme, for example, was reliant not on the bishops of Lincoln but on a number of local lords, of whom the de Cauz and Halselin were the most generous. Where there was no one leading family, as at Alvingham, the community owed much to local knightly families, and even the free peasantry of the surrounding villages, whose small grants, steadily accumulated, enabled the creation of substantial estates. Other factors, too, contributed to the fortunes of the priories. The proximity of other religious houses inhibited growth and sometimes distorted acquisitions. Larger houses inevitably had more financial resources and opportunities for land purchases or leases, and profited in the land market at the expense of smaller rivals. All such criteria require assessment in any analysis of the landed property of the Gilbertine priories.

The geography of settlement

The Gilbertine order was essentially regional in scale, of a type familiar on the Continent (especially in France), but unique in England, where all other religious houses were affiliated to supra-national organizations of one kind or other. The localism of the order is one of the features that defined its special character: there was no successful foundation outside England, and the majority of the priories were concentrated in the eastern counties. A local community tended to appeal to local benefactors; these seldom had the resources associated with the great magnates of the realm,

---

[5] However, the fact that so few charters from this house survive may distort the picture.

and the lack of appeal to these potential patrons contributed to the Gilbertines' relative poverty.

All of the Gilbertine double houses were in the eastern half of the country; all but three lay in Lincolnshire.[6] A similar geographical distribution is found amongst the early houses for canons only. Only two (Clattercote in Oxfordshire and Marlborough in Wiltshire) were west of Watling Street. The choice of site for a religious house was a response to a number of criteria, of which the wishes and resources of the founder and the requirements of the community were the most important. These did not necessarily coincide, but once the choice had been made the site itself became a determinant of the future development and distribution of the priory estates. The position of the priory relative to other religious houses, the nature of local lordship, the availability and productivity of agricultural land were all key factors in estate creation. In general, the holdings of the Gilbertines, like those of other orders, were first concentrated in the vicinity of the priories, but since no Gilbertine house was in a position to refuse land grants, however inconvenient or distant, most priories also came to possess some more far-flung estates.

Ten Gilbertine priories are recorded to have possessed property outside their immediate sphere of influence in 1291, though it was practically unknown for any to have lands more than fifty miles from home. Outside north Norfolk Shouldham, whose estates were the most compact of all the priories, held only property in London. Mattersey's sole outlying holding was the church of Bolton (Lancashire), which formed part of the original endowment. The founder was a Lancashire lord and his grants clearly reflect his landed interests. He was prepared to alienate his more distant lands in Nottinghamshire but only limited property nearer home.[7]

However, though the distribution of the Gilbertine estates was primarily established by the benefactors, after property had been received it could then be sold to another community, either within the order or outside it, or exchanged for the mutual convenience and profit of both parties. At one extreme this could result in the cession of the very site of a religious house to another community, as happened in 1139 when the monks of Fountains refused the site given them at Haverholme by the bishop of Lincoln, who then gave it to Gilbert, while the Cistercians were established at Louth Park. About a century later the unsuitability of

[6] One of these (Chicksands in Bedfordshire) was in the diocese of Lincoln; the other two were Watton and Shouldham.

[7] The foundation charter also refers to grants of land in Bolton, but these are not mentioned either in 1291 or 1535. For the foundation of Mattersey, see *Monasticon*, vi. 2. 965–6.

Ayrshire for a Gilbertine priory was recognized, and the lands there were granted to Paisley. The English lands of the abortive Gilbertine foundation in Normandy were passed into the hands of the Gilbertine canons of Malton. Chicksands priory acquired Wolverton from Clattercote, while the nuns of Bullington soon took responsibility for the church of West Torrington, one of the original churches served by Gilbert of Sempringham, but which lay much closer to Bullington than to the mother house.[8] Similar arrangements were made with non-Gilbertine communities. Haverholme provides two good examples of this process of re-structuring. By *c.*1160 the 'Cistercian' nuns of Greenfield had acquired ten bovates in Marston near Grantham. As Stenton pointed out, this land lay far from the other estates of the nuns, and it made sense to convert this to a rental property held by Haverholme, which did have other lands there and in the vicinity. The abbreviated copy of the Haverholme cartulary and the long royal confirmation charter of 1327 shows how the priory was able to develop a sizeable estate at Marston amounting to about 27 bovates, together with a mill, meadow land, and some fifteen tofts.[9] The king himself might intervene in the process. Between 1174 and 1181 Henry II gave Haverholme 100 solidates of land in Staunton and Thurgarton (Nottingham) in exchange for a similar amount of land in Perlethorpe (Nottingham) which the king then assigned to a royal serjeant.[10] These examples relate to re-configurations of property at the level of the village and above. Within the village there was even greater fluidity. Sometimes a patron would re-allocate property that had been granted by a predecessor or tenant. Normally this was for the benefit of the patron, and often the priory had the worst of the bargain. A clear example of this intervention is found at Chippenham (Cambridgeshire). Here countess Rohaise, the wife of Payn de Beauchamp, and her son Geoffrey gave a substantial estate to Chicksands. Her other son, William, when he came to confirm his mother and brother's grants, took back some of the land and gave in exchange 'newly cleared land' and land in 'Blatherwyc', later known as Blethwick Heath and of much poorer quality.[11] More frequent were exchanges of property initiated by the

---

[8] Fowler, 'Early Charters of . . . Chicksand', 116–17.

[9] *Danelaw Charters*, liii–liv, n. 3, 94–6, nos. 144–7; 'Haverholme Priory Charters', 40–3; *Cal. Ch. R.* iv. 411–12. For another good example, see the exchange whereby Watton gave 4 bovates in Burnby to Warter priory for a carucate in Hawold, where the nuns had a grange (*EYC* xi. 296–7).   [10] *Cal. Chart. R.* iv. 404.

[11] M. Spufford, *A Cambridgeshire Community: Chippenham from Settlement to Enclosure*, Local History Occasional Papers, 20 (Leicester, 1965), 12–13, 42–3. See also below, Ch. 8: 'The grange': 'The formation of the grange'.

Gilbertines themselves in order to consolidate and improve their holdings, particularly in places where they possessed granges. The cartularies of Malton and Alvingham and the surviving charter archives of priories such as Bullington or Sempringham contain numerous examples of these small-scale negotiations whereby the priory estates were improved and rounded-off.[12]

These transactions at all levels remind us that an estate was never eternally fixed. Land might be lost, either through litigation or by sale. Chicksands received 24 acres in Clapton from William of Clapton in the third quarter of the twelfth century, but was unable to prevent six of these acres being taken by abbot Benedict of Peterborough (1177–93), who was vigorously expanding his abbey's interest in the village. The priory then sold the remaining 18 acres to Richard of Hotot for 18 marks, doubtless realizing that there was little opportunity to develop this property in the face of Peterborough's rivalry.[13] Such detailed accounts are rarely recorded in the Gilbertine documents, but similar experiences were certainly not uncommon. Though not liable to the vicissitudes suffered by lay tenants, such as the break-up of estates through too few or too many heirs, marriage, enforced sales, or forfeiture, the estates of the Gilbertines were constantly, though often almost imperceptibly, in flux.

Some rough indication of the concentration of the priory estates can be gained from the returns made in 1291 for the *Taxatio Ecclesiastica*. For all their imperfections and imprecision they do provide assessments of the temporal income of religious houses arranged according to deaneries. They show that in most instances the major Gilbertine holdings lay very close to the priories. Thus Sempringham derived 45 per cent of its total temporal income from the deanery of Avelund in which the priory lay, and the two adjacent deaneries to the north, Loveden and Sleaford, each contributed about 15 per cent, the next highest proportion. Two-thirds of Nun Ormsby's income was found in the deanery of Louthesk and Ludborough; and over 55 per cent of that of Haverholme in Sleaford deanery. Only occasionally did a priory obtain a significant income from a more distant property. Catley's estate of Glentworth, which was purchased from Oliver of Wendover in the third quarter of the twelfth century and which lay over twenty miles to the north of the priory,

---

[12] Discussed below, pp. 285–6.
[13] 'Estate Records of the Hotot family', in *A Northamptonshire Miscellany*, ed. E. King, Northamptonshire Record Society, 32 (1983), 18, 47. For Peterborough's interest in Clapton, see E. King, *Peterborough Abbey, 1086–1310* (Cambridge, 1973), 46–50, 90–1.

contributed about 28 per cent of its temporal revenues, and Bullington gained about 30 per cent of its income from lands not in its 'home' deanery of Wraghow but about 10 miles to the west in Aslacoe, where the priory owned two productive granges at Hackthorn and Ingham. A similar picture is found amongst the Gilbertine priories outside Lincolnshire. Shouldham's lands in Shouldham itself accounted for over 45 per cent of its total income while another 16 per cent came from its lands in the nearby vills of Stoke Ferry, Wretton, and Wereham. The less detailed figures for Watton show that all but £1 4s. 5d. of its total assessed temporal income of just over £242 came from the archdeaconry of the East Riding, and over 80 per cent (£170) of Malton's temporal income came from the archdeaconry of Cleveland, most of the remainder coming from property in Lincolnshire. In the case of Malton this figure can be supplemented by evidence in the cartulary which lists the amount of land held in individual villages in 1254 as part of the inquiry made for the valuation of Norwich.[14] This shows that about 60 per cent of Malton's arable land lay in the corridor of the Derwent valley running from Amotherby in the west through Malton itself to Wintringham in the east, a total distance of perhaps ten miles.

In some other instances it is possible to obtain a more detailed analysis of geographical distribution. The Alvingham cartulary provides details of the 1291 valuation of *temporalia* arranged by village, and, to a more limited extent, according to land use, while the *Taxatio* itself provides similar data for the priories of Shouldham, Chicksands, and Clattercote, and for the much smaller houses of Fordham and Marmont. In the case of Alvingham the five granges of Alvingham, Cockerington, Keddington, Grainthorpe, and Yarborough grouped in close proximity around the priory accounted for about 56 per cent of the total temporal income of £91 14s. 2½d., and the only distant holding of any size was the grange at North Conesby.[15] The importance of the local holdings in Shouldham's economy has already been noted, while at Chicksands, though here the holdings were a little more diffuse, about 35 per cent of the total temporal income was derived from estates in the villages immediately surrounding the priory. All of Clattercote's property, with the exception of a tiny rental income in Bodicote, just to the south of Banbury, lay immediately adjacent to the priory with the greater part of it lying in Clattercote itself.[16]

---

[14] London, BL, MS Cotton Claudius D XI, fo. 279.
[15] Oxford, Bodl. Lib., MS Laud Misc. 642, fo. 39. [16] *Taxatio*, 44, 56, 257.

The tenurial matrix

No religious foundation was made in a tenurial vacuum; even the remotest Cistercian establishment necessitated a reshaping of the landholding structure of its region. A new monastery was a new organism inserted into a pre-existing framework that it inevitably distorted. Its creation did not merely forge a relationship between founder and community: it also involved the founder's lord and vassals, in turn establishing new ties of dependence and responsibility. The scope and scale of a foundation, even its very site, were to a very large extent predetermined by tenurial networks. The estates of any monastery necessarily depended on the willingness and ability of its benefactors to bestow property.[17] Grants were increasingly subject to the control of their lords and their willingness to sanction the alienation of land and its services. So a new balance had to be made in a local society, and the new corporation integrated and accommodated. The fortunes of a religious house were dependent upon the resources of its founder. Contrary to the view of the *Vita*'s author, who credited the *comites* and *barones* with the multiplication of the communities, the considerable success of the early Gilbertine houses was largely owing to local knightly society.[18] While the great families of the region, such as those of Mowbray or Aumale, might view the Gilbertines with favour, this normally extended only to the confirming of their vassals' grants, and even where a Gilbertine priory was founded by a great lord, such as the bishop of Lincoln, the consolidation and growth of its estates was usually the responsibility of lesser men, who were of regional and local, rather than national, importance.[19]

By *c.*1150 most great families had either already established religious houses which they continued to patronize, or they no longer had substantial estates left to endow others. When they did make new foundations these tended to be Cistercian. So, when one of the leading barons of

---

[17] The term 'benefactor' is used here, as elsewhere, to signify not only a 'donor' who granted property or rights freely *in puram et perpetuam elemosinam*, but also all those who issued grants or confirmations, whether or not for a monetary or other temporal obligation, for all were bringing some benefit to the community, for which the nuns and canons reciprocated with prayers and/or cash (see below, Ch. 6: 'Benefits': 'Spiritual benefits', for further discussion of this topic). [18] *Book of St Gilbert*, 38.

[19] Though occasionally a great lord would associate himself with his tenant's foundation, as William of Aumale did in the case of Gilbert son of Robert's establishment of Nun Ormsby (*Gilbertine Charters*, 39, 41–2). A parallel and revealing example of the role of the tenant-in-chief in the creation of a new community is found in Hugh de Bayeux' *carta* of 1166, where his father is said to have released his tenant Peter of Goxhill from his obligations when Newhouse was founded *in qua elemosina . . . volero partiri* (*Red Book of the Exchequer*, i. 387).

Lincolnshire, William le Gros, count of Aumale, wished to found a monastery on his Lincolnshire estate at Bytham, it was to the white monks that he turned.[20] The Gilbertines, by contrast, were not high on a twelfth-century magnate's list of pious priorities. This can be sharply illustrated by the activities of Roger de Mowbray. Roger was a liberal patron who spread his generosity widely. He founded two monasteries, the Cistercian abbey at Byland and the Augustinian priory at Newburgh. Neither of these was of the first rank, but they were substantial communities and well endowed by Roger. Yet to the canons of Malton went only land in Dalby and 40 cartloads of wood per annum from his wood of Hovingham for their kitchen.[21] The contrast in scale between the benefactions points to a lack of will rather than a lack of resources. Though Roger was careful not to involve himself too closely with Malton, he was prepared to confirm the grants of his tenants to the canons.[22] This was indeed the main function of the great lords in the development of the Gilbertines' estates—to provide a favourable climate for their own tenants to make endowments by a readiness to confirm alienations. This role should not be underestimated. As generations passed, lords became increasingly reluctant to act in this way. Fearful of the loss of services that grants in free alms implied, their tenants' freedom of action was circumscribed. In such a climate a lord's goodwill was at a premium. Only rarely do we see beyond the charter recording a confirmation to the negotiations that must always have occurred at any such transaction. One early charter relating to Haverholme deserves attention, not only because it provides that unusual glimpse of the lord–tenant–priory relationship, but also because of its early date (probably third quarter of the twelfth century). Geoffrey de Cauz and his brother Adam had granted two bovates in Coteland to the nuns. Geoffrey was a vassal of his kinsman Robert II de Cauz, whom he asked to confirm the grant. Desirous of the salvation of his soul and those of his father and ancestors, Robert agreed, freeing the land from all secular service. His charter goes on to describe what happened: 'I took

<hr>

[20] He also founded Meaux in Holderness (English, *The Lords of Holderness,* 25–6). Gilbert de Gant founded Rufford in 1147, while Robert de Greslei, lord of Manchester and of lesser baronial status than William le Gros, similarly founded a Cistercian abbey, Swineshead, in Lincolnshire. Like William he was associated with the foundation of a Gilbertine priory (Sixhills), but the initiative came from his tenant (see above, Ch. 4: 'The north Lincolnshire foundations': 'Sixhills').

[21] *Charters of the Honour of Mowbray, 1107–1191,* ed. D. E. Greenway, British Academy Records of Social and Economic History, NS 1 (1972), pp. xli–xlii, 132–3, nos. 185–7.

[22] For examples of such confirmations, see ibid. 131–4, nos. 183–4, 188–9. He also confirmed a grant of Thomas of Wappenbury to Sempringham (*Sempringham Charters,* xvi. 153).

my charter [i.e. that by which he had enfeoffed Geoffrey] and again handed it to him saying, "Receive again those lands *in hereditatem* and my permission (*licenciam*) to give them with the meadow land to the nuns of Haverholme" before these witnesses who were then present and saw this gift, i.e. William and Henry canons, Ralph the priest and Thomas the priest of Riskington.'[23]

The involvement of the knights and lesser barons in the creation of small religious houses during the twelfth century has long been recognized, and commentators have stressed how this sort of benefactor found the Augustinians particularly appealing. In them they saw 'a type of foundation within their means, and a religious ideal within their understanding'. Such men have been characterized as 'of modest means but with the instincts of great landlords. Like their betters they wanted that symbol of territorial stability—a religious house where they would be honoured as founders, and buried with decency in the midst of their family.'[24] According to this interpretation, the great advantage of the Augustinians to the 'small-time investor' was the cheapness of their endowment when compared with the demands of either the Benedictines or the Cistercians, combined with the fact that they were very ready to receive grants of churches whose possession by the laity was increasingly coming into question.[25] Moreover, in Southern's phrase, 'they were ubiquitously useful'. By contrast, the Cistercians appealed primarily to the great lord who had extensive lands available for a substantial endowment, but lands which were either economically or politically marginal. How far is this analysis applicable to Lincolnshire, the seed-bed of Gilbertine growth?

Unlike many English shires, twelfth-century Lincolnshire was dominated by no one great family with a consolidated bloc of estates from which local society was controlled.[26] Certainly, there were powerful tenants-in-chief, such as the bishop of Lincoln or the earl of Chester, but the secular lords tended to hold the majority of their lands outside the county: conversely they held few castles or other power bases there. Neither their political nor their pious interests were focused on the shire. By *c*.1130

---

[23] 'Haverholme Priory Charters', 15.

[24] R. W. Southern, *Western Society and the Church in the Middle Ages* (Harmondsworth, 1970), 245. His comments on the motivation of the founders of both Augustinian and Cistercian houses during the 12th century remain the most accessible general study of this issue.   [25] The possession of churches is discussed below, Ch. 7.

[26] The fullest analysis of knightly society in Lincolnshire is C. J. Wales, 'The Knight in Twelfth-Century Lincolnshire', Ph.D. thesis (Cambridge, 1983), a thesis which deserves to be better known.

most of these families had already developed close ties with religious houses elsewhere. Ranulf, earl of Chester (who retained little demesne land in Lincolnshire), had directed his benefactions primarily to St Werburgh's, Chester, which had been founded by his ancestor and where he himself found burial in 1153.[27] Another leading magnate, Conan IV, duke of Brittany and earl of Richmond, spent much of his time in Brittany, and though he made a number of small grants to religious houses in England and founded a small nunnery at Rowney (Hertfordshire), he directed his attentions mainly to his foundation of Carnoët in Brittany.[28] For the most part such baronial foundations as there were were small and insignificant.[29] Only one of the leading landholders, William le Gros, count of Aumale, founded more than one house in the shire: Thornton and Castle Bytham (later Vaudey).[30] Thornton became the thirteenth wealthiest Augustinian priory in the country, and was by far the richest of the twelfth-century foundations in Lincolnshire. At the other end of the scale, Lucy, countess of Chester, founded the small 'Cistercian' nunnery of Stixwould, while the Premonstratensian nunnery at Orford, which was always desperately poor, was founded by Ralph, a member of the powerful de Aubigny family.[31]

The absence of 'natural leaders' within the county meant that their vassals, the mesne tenants, enjoyed a greater degree of autonomy than was often the case elsewhere: vertical ties of lordship were less important in determining social and political alliances, horizontal ties created by intermarriage and neighbourhood were dominant. This development was the more important since so many village communities in Lincolnshire, particularly in the northern parts of the shire, where the majority of Gilbertine foundations were concentrated, were divided amongst several tenants, whose co-operation was often necessary if a religious house was to flourish. Tenurial fragmentation was to influence the foundation, development, and fortunes of many houses. The knights of Lincolnshire were the 'country gentlemen' forming a 'squirearchy' essentially local in outlook and interests. It was these men and women who founded well over half of all houses in Lincolnshire during the mid-twelfth century.

---

[27] GEC iii. 167; Farrer, *Honors and Knight's Fees*, ii, *passim*.

[28] *EYC* iv, *passim*, esp. 82, 92–3.

[29] Though there were exceptions, such as Gilbert de Gant's foundation at Bardney or William de Romare's at Revesby, the largest Cistercian abbey in the county.

[30] English, *Lords of Holderness*, 25–7. In addition to these houses William also founded Meaux (Yorkshire) and was a benefactor of a number of other communities.

[31] For some reservations as to whether Ralph can be regarded as the founder of Irford, see Colvin, *The White Canons*, 328–30.

Lesser baronial and knightly founders were responsible for all the Premonstratensian houses in the county and all but one of the Templar establishments. But their interest was concentrated most upon the Gilbertine double houses and on the 'Cistercian' nunneries.[32]

At the same time this knightly class was very heterogeneous, and the question of definition difficult.[33] At its head stood families whose economic and political status ranked almost with the magnates, with whom they could be linked by marriage. With their considerable landed interests, and perhaps twenty to thirty knight's fees, they sometimes played a part in national politics, could be active at the royal court, and frequently served as royal officials such as sheriffs. Such families included the Kymes, the leading supporters of Bullington priory. Below them came lesser men, minor tenants-in-chief and holders of small baronies. They might occasionally act as sheriffs, but generally their role was confined to the locality.[34] Some were officials in the households of great lords, or were themselves scions of more important families.[35] Amongst them were families like the de Bayeux, who held the barony of Thoresway.[36] Hugh de Bayeux was a benefactor of both Sixhills and Nun Ormsby priories, as well as of Louth Park, the Templars, and the Premonstratensian abbey of Newhouse, which had been founded on land held by his father's tenant, Peter of Goxhill.[37]

---

[32] Only Haverholme amongst the former and Stixwould amongst the latter cannot be attributed to these founders.

[33] Definitions of the terms 'knight' and 'gentry' are notoriously beset with pitfalls, and at no time was the function and status of the knight changing more rapidly than during the 12th and early 13th centuries. See e.g. E. King, 'Large and Small Landowners in Thirteenth-Century England: The Case of Peterborough Abbey', *Past and Present*, 47 (1970), 26–50; R. H. Hilton, *A Medieval Society: The West Midlands at the End of the Thirteenth Century* (Cambridge, 1983), 48–60; and J. E. Newman, 'Greater and Lesser Landowners and Parochial Patronage: Yorkshire in the Thirteenth Century', *EHR* 92 (1977), 280–308.

[34] At least two late-12th-century sheriffs of Lincolnshire, Alfred of Pointon (1170) and Nigel son of Alexander (1185), were benefactors of Sempringham.

[35] The de Meaux family, who were substantial, if not wholly willing, benefactors of Alvingham, were related to the family of that name who were among the most prominent tenants in Holderness; the family of de Cauz, instrumental in the foundation of Haverholme, were related to the Ferrers, earls of Derby, while Geoffrey de Mandeville, who was a benefactor of Watton in Huggate, belonged to the family of the earls of Essex. For de Meaux' grants to Alvingham, see below, pp. 293–4, and for the family see Clay (ed.), *Early Yorkshire Families*, 59–60; for the de Cauz, see *Registrum Antiquissimum*, vii. 209–22; for de Mandeville's grant, see *EYC* ii. 526. The family is discussed in Clay (ed.), *Early Yorkshire Families*, 56–7.

[36] Sanders, *English Baronies*, 88–9. In 1166 Hugh de Bayeux reported that he held $16\frac{1}{2}$ fees.

[37] *Gilbertine Charters*, 4, 36 (Sixhills); 40–1, 56–7 (Nun Ormsby); *Cal. Ch. R.* iii. 248 (Louth Park); *Records of the Templars*, pp. cc, 87, 105–6; *Danelaw Charters*, pp. 171, 173,

The lowest rank comprised families with often no more than one or two fees, with interests correspondingly confined to a few villages. This subgroup was the most susceptible to economic disaster, the most likely to experience a 'crisis' in the thirteenth century.[38] Nevertheless, not all these small knightly families were in distress, and many made grants to the Gilbertines with no indication that they were acting from any financial motive. Thus Robert son of Robert of Thwing granted the church of Legsby, and later the whole village of Legsby in fee farm for £4 per annum to the nuns of Sixhills. At this time Robert held one fee of William de Percy in Lincolnshire (including Legsby, which amounted to half a fee) as well as probably holding another half fee of de Brus in Yorkshire. Robert had seemingly alienated a third of his landed holdings, yet there is no evidence that he was in financial difficulties, and his family was later to achieve moderate prosperity in Yorkshire.[39] Thomas of Etton, who gave the nuns of Watton 195 acres in Etton, was of similar standing. He held about 20 carucates of land in the East Riding, and seems to have held no more than a couple of fees. He and his family were also generous benefactors of the nearby Cistercian abbey of Meaux, to which they gave lands forming the nucleus of the grange of Skerne. Again there is no record of financial instability at this time, and the family survived in the male line into the fourteenth century.[40]

These families, in spite of their varying status, have certain aspects in common. They were primarily local in outlook; they were frequently linked to each other by ties of blood or lordship; they supported the same type of local religious community. In spite of the vicissitudes that many of their number suffered, they were a self-aware and self-confident group, even those with only one or two fees proudly presenting their knightly

175–6, 179–80, 190–1, nos. 238–9, 244, 255 (Newhouse). Hugh's father, Ralph, who died in 1158, was also a benefactor of the Gilbertines, granting 36 arpents of land in Woodgrange to Sempringham (*Sempringham Charters*, xvi. 225, 227), and Supir de Bayeux, a kinsman, granted property to Sixhills (*Gilbertine Charters*, 5, 30, 36). Hugh's tenant, Gilbert de St Laud, married Hugh's sister and was another benefactor of Sempringham (*Sempringham Charters*, xvi. 227; *Book of Fees*, i. 388).

[38] The literature on the supposed 'crisis of the knightly class' is now considerable, but in addition to the works cited above (n. 33) see P. R. Coss, 'Sir Geoffrey de Langley and the Crisis of the Knightly Class in Thirteenth-Century England', *Past and Present*, 68 (1975), 3–37, and D. Carpenter, 'Was there a Crisis of the Knightly Class in the Thirteenth Century? The Oxfordshire Evidence', *EHR* 95 (1980), 721–52.

[39] *Gilbertine Charters*, 2, 7, 17. For the family, see Clay (ed.), *Early Yorkshire Families*, 92–3; GEC xii(i), 735–44; and *EYC* xi. 203–7.

[40] *EYC* ix. 191–5; Clay (ed.), *Early Yorkshire Families*, 25–6.

image on their seals, and building chapels for themselves and their tenants rather than worshipping in the parish church.[41] These benefactors acted together socially and politically. They fulfilled the same functions and offices, they supported each other by acting as each other's pledges, occasionally they fought together, as many were to do in the struggles early in the thirteenth century. As importantly, they witnessed and warranted each other's charters in favour of local religious houses. In return they gained the prayers and other spiritual benefits of the communities, receiving rights of burial or confraternity or placing one of their number as a nun or canon in a local house.

The cohesion of this group was aided by marriage alliances, which were usually local, and the dynastic links thus formed stimulated pious giving to a substantial network of communities.[42] Kinship was a powerful motor in determining benefactions. Agnes of Orby was the sister of Philip de Kyme; she and her husband's family became generous patrons of Bullington.[43] Alternatively, tenants frequently supported houses favoured by their lords. Many of the benefactors of Sempringham were tenants of the de Gant fee; Bullington frequently looked to the tenants of the Kymes, who were themselves tenants of the Cauz, benefactors of Haverholme, in Anwick and Coteland. The family of Millei held of both the Kymes and Scotenis, following the former in giving to Bullington, and the latter as benefactors of Alvingham. Occasionally the direct role of the lord is acknowledged, as when Ivo de Karkenii gave half of the church of South Ferriby to Bullington priory at the request of his lord, Adelard of Orby.[44] Sometimes ties of kinship and lordship overlapped. The Well family were tenants of the de Gants and William de Well was married to Matilda, sister of Gilbert de Gant. Not surprisingly, they were generous

---

[41] Many of the surviving Sempringham and Bullington charters bear fine equestrian seals. Cf. Richard de Luci's sneering comment: 'it was not the custom in the past for every petty knight to have a seal. They are appropriate for kings and great men only' (*The Chronicle of Battle Abbey*, ed. and trans. E. Searle (Oxford, 1980), 214). For the private chapels created by four Lincolnshire families, including the de Bayeux and Amundevilles, who were both benefactors of Sempringham, see Owen, *Church and Society*, 8.

[42] This is illuminatingly demonstrated in the case of the de Arches family by Elkins, *Holy Women*, 94–7. This family, apart from patronizing a number of Yorkshire nunneries, was also involved with at least three Gilbertine double houses: Sempringham, Bullington, and Nun Ormsby.

[43] In the same way the Benniworth family were plugged into the Bullington network through Roger de Benniworth, a son-in-law of Philip de Kyme, who married a niece of Agnes de Orby.   [44] *Danelaw Charters*, 17–18, no. 24.

supporters of Sempringham.[45] But, above all, benefactors were inspired by the example of their neighbours and friends.

An analysis of surviving Gilbertine charters shows that the priories attracted support from across the whole spectrum of the knightly class, particularly in the second half of the twelfth and early years of the thirteenth century. No more than a brief indication of the scope of their pious giving can be given here and one fairly detailed examination must suffice to reveal the Gilbertines' reliance on these lesser men, the honorial barons of Lincolnshire and Yorkshire.[46] Richard I's 1189 confirmation charter to Sempringham lists the most substantial estates that the community had received, along with their donors. Sempringham priory was the mother church of the order, its wealthiest house, and held the bones of the founder. Here if anywhere we might expect to find evidence of benefactions from great as well as lesser lords. Yet of about forty named benefactors only about ten were of baronial rank, and of these even fewer were from families of more than local importance. Heading the list are Gilbert de Gant and his family, especially Alice de Gant, his daughter and heiress. Alice gave land in Sempringham and Heckington, pasture in Barton, mills in Birthorp and Folkingham, and half a fee in Laughton. This was not ungenerous, but neither was it as considerable as might have been expected from a family of such resources. Alice's grants can be seen in perspective when compared with those of her tenants, which she confirmed to the nuns: a carucate in Sempringham given by Godwin the Rich of Lincoln, 18 bovates given by Herbert son of Adelard in Walcot and Folkingham, two bovates in Walcot of the gift of David of Ewerby, 11 bovates given by Adam de Amundeville in Sempringham, and land from Simon son of Sibald in Walcot.[47]

Hubert II de Ria gave his churches of Hannington and Aslackby in Lincolnshire and Buxton in Norfolk to Sempringham as well as lands, pasture, and woodland in Aslackby.[48] Maurice de Craon and his son Guy, lords of Freiston, were responsible for the priory's grange at

---

[45] Wales, 'The Knight in Twelfth-Century Lincolnshire', 235. Wales also suggested (20 n. 73) that Thomas son of William, son of the founder of Sixhills, was a son-in-law of Philip of Kyme. He was certainly active in the Kyme circle.

[46] I have examined in some detail the role of the knightly class as benefactors to Alvingham and Bullington in Golding, 'Gilbertine Priories', 209–72.

[47] *Sempringham Charters*, xv. 161.

[48] Ibid. xv. 224–5. Hubert held between 30 and 35 fees (Sanders, *English Baronies*, 53). These were concentrated in Norfolk, but he had extensive holdings in Lincolnshire and founded the Templar preceptory of Aslackby. The Templars claimed to have been given the church of Aslackby in 1164, and ownership was disputed, though after 1201 the Templars

Mareham.[49] The family also proved generous supporters of Sixhills: Alice de Craon gave land in West Wykeham amounting to one carucate together with a moiety of the church and two bovates in Ludford.[50] While the de Craons were generous to the Gilbertines, William d'Aubigny's support was almost wholly confined to his confirmation of lands granted by his tenants (at their request), William de Rames and Hugh de Hotot in Aslackby and Kirkby Underwood.[51]

The charter shows that knights ranging from the very wealthy to those who stood only a little above the free peasants were making grants to the priory, and this conclusion is reinforced by a survey of the surviving charters of the grantors. Amongst the knightly benefactors William Tisun was probably the most eminent. William held fifteen fees of the Mowbray fee in 1166 and had property in Yorkshire, Nottinghamshire, Leicestershire, and Lincolnshire. His grant of 14 bovates in Thrussington (Leicestershire) formed the nucleus of the priory's holdings there.[52] This grant was supplemented by another of the Mowbray knights, Thomas of Wappenbury, who held five fees of the honour, and who gave pasture for 1,000 sheep in winter and 800 in summer, as well as six acres for the lay brothers'

established their claim (*Records of the Templars*, pp. clxxxvi–clxxxviii). Such duplications of gifts were not uncommon (see S. Raban, *The Estates of Thorney and Crowland: A Study in Medieval Monastic Land Tenure* (Cambridge, 1977), 41–3).

[49] The family also had its own foundation at Freiston, the *caput* of their honour, which was a cell of Crowland, and Maurice de Craon was a benefactor of Cistercian Kirkstead and of the Templars (ibid. 30; London, BL, Harl. Chart. 49 A 1 (Kirkstead); *Records of the Templars*, 89). Guy de Craon also confirmed his tenant Robert Monk's grants to the nuns of Sempringham in Keisby. Robert, who gave land and pasture in Keisby, held one fee of the bishop of Lincoln and half a fee of Maurice in 1166 (*Sempringham Charters*, xvii. 33–5; *Book of Fees*, i. 375, 385). It is possible that Ridel of Keisby, another Sempringham benefactor, held of his fee, though Gilbert de Gant also had a manor in the vill. Ridel of Keisby, who gave property in Keisby, was probably of more modest background, though still of knightly status (*Sempringham Charters*, xvi. 81–2, xvii. 234–6; *Danelaw Charters*, 324, no. 439). The family were also benefactors of the Templars (*Records of the Templars*, pp. cciii, 96). Ridel of Keisby's mother (or possibly mother-in-law) Clarice was also a benefactor of Sempringham and married to Ascelin de Walterville, who himself gave a third of his fee in Laughton (perhaps representing Clarice's dowry) which he held of de Gant to the priory (*Sempringham Charters*, xvi. 31–2, xvii. 235–6).

[50] *Gilbertine Charters*, 30, 4. In Henry II's confirmation charter Maurice is said to have given half the village of West Wykeham and half a carucate in Ludford (ibid. 30).

[51] *Sempringham Charters*, xvi. 33–4. William d'Aubigny seems to have given the land of one of his tenants in Kirkby to the nuns (ibid. xvi. 164). For William de Rames' charters, see (ibid. xvi. 34, 157, 223–5). He held one fee in Stathern (Leicestershire) of Mowbray in 1166 (*Charters of the Honour of Mowbray*, 264). He was associated with his brother, Ralph, in the grant of three carucates in Stathern to Haverholme (ibid. 123).

[52] *Sempringham Charters*, xvi. 83. For the family, see *EYC* xii, and Clay (ed.), *Early Yorkshire Families*, 93–4.

buildings.[53] Less wealthy, but still influential in local society, were Alexander son of Osbert and Nigel his heir, who were generous benefactors of Sempringham at Fulbeck, where the priory was able to establish a grange. The family held four fees of the honour of Richmond, of which three were in Lincolnshire and one in Yorkshire, as well as a fee in Skinnand and another in Ingoldsby, whence the family took its name. Nigel served as sheriff of Lincolnshire between 1185 and 1189, and was also employed as an itinerant justice.[54] Like many of their fellow-benefactors to the Gilbertines, they were also patrons of the Templars.[55] A number of Sempringham's benefactors were, not surprisingly, tenants of the de Gant fee. Herbert son of Adelard, who gave 18 bovates in Walcot and Folkingham, was typical. He held of a number of lords, being a tenant not only of the de Gants but also of the earl of Chester, the de Haia family, Robert fitzHugh of Tattershall, and William of Ingham.[56] He was also typical in extending his liberality to several local communities. He and his wife Agnes of Orby were not only supporters of Bullington and Sixhills, but founded the small Premonstratensian abbey of Hagnaby.[57] The de Well family were de Gant tenants of more modest knightly rank. William de Well held just over six fees of earl Simon of Northampton in 1166 and another quarter fee of Hamon Peche, in addition to the lands he held of the de Gants.[58] Humphrey, William's younger brother, granted six carucates in Cranwell (amounting to half a fee) to the nuns when three of his daughters were received into the community.[59] John of Bulby, who gave parcels of arable land, woodland, and scrub in Bulby, lies at the lower end of the knightly spectrum. His father Hasti or Asketin had an Anglo-Scandinavian name, and the family may have been native. Certainly their

[53] *Sempringham Charters*, xvi. 153; *Charters of the Honour of Mowbray*, 256, 263.

[54] Clay (ed.), *Early Yorkshire Families*, 46–7; *EYC* v. 255–7. Nigel chose to be buried at Sempringham (*Sempringham Charters*, xvi. 225).

[55] *Records of the Templars*, pp. cciii, 86, 88. Nigel also gave property in Kelsterne to Louth Park (*Cal. Ch. R.* iii. 264).

[56] Gilbert de Gant's charter of enfeoffment to Herbert is printed, *The Topographer and Genealogist*, i. 317. R. de Haia's grant of four bovates is *Danelaw Charters*, 351, no. 480.

[57] He was also a benefactor of Bardney and Welbeck (Colvin, *The White Canons*, 68, 107–8). For his benefactions to Bullington, see *Danelaw Charters*, 18, 56, nos. 25, 87, and to Sixhills, *Gilbertine Charters*, 37. His daughter was a nun at Sempringham (*Sempringham Charters*, xv. 226). Herbert is found as a witness to a Gilbert de Gant charter issued to Sempringham (ibid. xvi. 223).

[58] *Book of Fees*, i. 366, 382–3. William was also a benefactor of Alvingham priory, the Cistercian nunnery of Greenfield, and the Cistercian abbey of Louth Park.

[59] *Sempringham Charters*, xvi. 78–9. William son of Walter de Welle witnessed Gant charters in favour of Sempringham (ibid. xv. 161, 223) and other houses (*EYC* ii. 451, 455; iii. 189). For the early history of the family, see GEC xii(ii), 436–7.

resources were meagre, and Stenton argued that the family was of peasant rank. However, the fact that one of John's original charters in favour of Sempringham bears a fine equestrian seal suggests that John at any rate had moved into the ranks of the knights.[60]

The combination of an absolute decline in the number of benefactions made by great lords during the twelfth century and their continuing support of other, more prestigious orders enforced Gilbertine dependence upon those of lesser status. In itself this probably ensured that none of the Gilbertine priories could compete with the wealthier of their Benedictine, Cistercian, or even Augustinian neighbours, but their difficulties were exacerbated by the increasingly catholic tendencies of potential benefactors, who were now distributing their goods more widely—and thinly. Even had such families continued to flourish this was a severe constraint on large benefactions. The old order in which a great family would patronize one house above all others, which it would expect to dominate, and where it would expect representatives to be members of the community and to be buried, was passing away. In Beatrice Lees's telling words, donors 'scattered their comparatively small gifts among many recipients, much as a modern millionaire subscribes to uncounted charities or takes a few shares in a multitude of investments'.[61] This shift in patterns of giving has been noted before, but an explanation is difficult. In part it was due to the new orders' refusal to be so closely involved with their lay patrons. Moreover, the very expansion in the number of religious institutions in virtually all regions may have induced benefactors to widen their choice. The close proximity of religious houses of all orders, particularly apparent in Lincolnshire but also noticeable north of the Humber, stimulated local families to give to all, with little obvious discrimination. It may also be that it was now felt desirable to purchase prayers from as many religious as possible. A further possibility may be familial ties. The more communities a family inherited interests in by marriage, the greater the pressure to make small grants to each of them. But perhaps above all there was a desire for prestige: to have the family name remembered in life and death amongst as many communities as possible. Grants that were ostensibly motivated by piety were an expression of temporal power.

Without the support of the lesser lords the Gilbertine priories could

---

[60] *Sempringham Charters*, xvi. 81, xvii. 29–32; *Danelaw Charters*, pp. xciii–xciv, nos. 434–6, pp. 320–2; London, BL, Addit. Chart. 20622.

[61] *Records of the Templars*, pp. cxcviii–cxcix. She was referring to the nobles, but the comment is as applicable to the knightly class. See also e.g. Raban, *Estates of Thorney and Crowland*, 44.

not have survived: indeed, many would not have been founded at all.[62]
At the same time, reliance on these families ensured that the period of
growth would be a short one, for the benefactors lacked the capabilities to
maintain sustained support. The Gilbertines' success depended upon the
continuing willingness and ability of the knightly class to assist them.
The failure of many of these families to keep up their status to the end of
the thirteenth century ensured that the priories could expect no more
grants from this source, though they might benefit in the short term from
their financial embarrassment. Their fortunes and those of the priories
were intermeshed.

The Chronology of Endowment

The first generations

The rapid growth of the order during the 1150s brought its own problems. Competition for land and workers between rival communities could
be intense and require arbitration at the highest levels.[63] The most notable of such agreements occurred in 1164 at a meeting between representatives of the Cistercians and Gilbertines held at Sempringham and the
nearby Cistercian abbey of Kirkstead.[64] This covered a wide range of
contentious issues. No canon or monk or novice of one order was to be
received by the other. No house was to build a grange or *bercaria* within
two English leagues of another, though any house was permitted to receive up to one ploughland within these limits provided that no payment
or service was attached, and so long as this land was cultivated or used as
sheep pasture by laymen rather than *conversi* and no grange was ever
established.[65] Any quarrels were to be adjudicated by three Cistercian

---

[62] Though peasant grantors conveyed many small parcels of land in individual villages
(particularly in north Lincolnshire) which enabled the consolidation of estates in isolated
villages, they clearly did not have the means to make substantial endowments. The role of
peasant benefactors in the creation of the estates of Alvingham and Bullington is discussed
in Golding, 'Gilbertine Priories', 273–331.

[63] For some Cistercian examples, see R. A. Donkin, *The Cistercians: Studies in the Geography of Medieval England and Wales* (Toronto, 1978), 55–6, and B. Waites, 'The Monastic
Settlement of North-East Yorkshire', *Yorkshire Archaeological Journal*, 40 (1959–62), 492–
3. For the Lincolnshire context, see Owen, *Church and Society*, 64–5.

[64] Printed in *Cartularium Abbathiae de Rievalle ordinis Cisterciensis*, ed. J. C. Atkinson,
Surtees Society, 83 (1889), 181–3. For an earlier (1142) similar agreement between the
Cistercians and Premonstratensians, see Colvin, *The White Canons*, 12 n. 3. See also J. E.
Burton, 'The Settlement of Disputes between Byland Abbey and Newburgh Priory', *York-
shire Archaeological Journal*, 55 (1983), 67–72.

[65] This option was of course theoretically only open to the Gilbertines as the Cistercian
rule forbade the farming out of property.

abbots and by three *fratres* (which probably here means canons rather than *conversi*) of Sempringham. The Gilbertines were also allowed to possess churches within these bounds (again so long as no grange or *bercaria* was developed), houses for the priests serving them, and a barn (*grangia*) to keep tithes or glebe produce and 'suitable' animals. If a river which was neither bridgeable nor fordable divided the two estates, then granges could be held within the forbidden bounds.

Similar agreements were also made between individual houses. In 1174 an accord was reached between Alvingham and its Cistercian neighbour of Louth Park.[66] Drawn up 'for the preservation of peace and unity, and that untroubled and unbroken peace might remain for ever in times to come', it provided that neither house should purchase or lease for a term of years any land, cultivated or waste, in twenty-one named villages near the two houses without the consent of the other community. Only lands granted in free alms or *ex voto* were exempt. The agreement stipulated that if Louth Park neglected to obtain the consent of Alvingham to any acquisition of land then the latter could take one-third of the land on payment of one-third of the purchase price. If Alvingham broke the contract then Louth Park could take two-thirds of the land for two-thirds of the price. Additionally, for as long as Alvingham kept the agreement, the priory could have the tithes from all cultivated lands in these parishes, except from the *novales*, that is, land newly brought into cultivation, but if the agreement was broken then Louth Park could refrain from the payment of tithes on its lands. Finally the agreement echoed the general composition of 1164: no grange, sheep- or cow-fold was to be built or any other land acquired except in free alms within two leagues of either house, without mutual consent. Elaborate arrangements were made for the observance of the accord on both sides, with the ultimate obligation of enforcement being vested in the Cistercian general chapter and the bishop and chapter of Lincoln.

Agreements such as these indicate the considerable pressures on land that prevailed in north Lincolnshire at this time, and the stress that both Gilbertines and Cistercians laid upon the acquisition of grange estates free from the competition of others. Significantly, however, there is no definite evidence that the provisions of this agreement were ever invoked.[67] Either it was regarded as a dead letter from the beginning, or

---

[66] Oxford, Bodl. Lib., MS Laud Misc. 642, fo. 130. Gilbert of Sempringham was amongst the witnesses.

[67] For a possible reference to it, and to a grant of land as compensation to Louth Park, see ibid., fo. 61ᵛ.

permission was always given for land acquisitions within the exclusion zones. Alvingham and Louth Park possessed a number of granges within a two-league radius, and sometimes (as at Keddington) each community had a grange within the same village.[68] Pressure on land was a cause of these agreements: it was also the main reason why they could never work.

There are enough indicators to suggest that the greater part of the Gilbertines' estates had been acquired by, or shortly after, the death of the order's founder in 1189.[69] Of particular value are the charters presented to the Exchequer by the Gilbertine double houses in the early fifteenth century to support their claims of poverty, and hence to taxation relief. The charters chosen for inclusion in the priories' submission to the Exchequer normally relate to their larger properties. The majority of these date from before 1200: thereafter, though substantial acquisitions, such as the grant by Robert Burnell, bishop of Bath and Wells, of the manor of Toft to Sixhills priory in 1279, were not unknown they were unusual.[70] These can be used to supplement the overviews provided by general confirmation charters issued by the early Angevin kings, and by twelfth-century popes, which list the priories' most significant possessions. These can then be compared with the holdings as recorded in later sources, such as the *Taxatio Ecclesiastica* of 1291 and the *Valor Ecclesiasticus*. The interpretation of both the *Valor* and the *Taxatio* presents difficulties. Both are almost certainly under-assessments and are unreliable in their coverage of estates held by the religious. At the same time they do provide a very rough indication of the relative prosperity of the priories and the location and comparative values of a priory's estates. Moreover, since the majority of these had reached their maximum extent by 1291, the *Taxatio* is generally a useful *terminus ad quem* for the measurement of land acquisitions.

Early papal charters survive, though sometimes only partially, for four Gilbertine houses: Alvingham, Chicksands, Malton, and Watton.[71] Though primarily concerned with the spiritual possessions of the priories, they also list the more important temporal properties. That for Alvingham,

---

[68] A number of other Gilbertine priories possessed granges in villages where other houses had substantial estates. See e.g. the resolution of the dispute between Bullington and Stainfield priories concerning lands and pasture near Bullington (London, BL, Harl. Chart. 44 A 23).

[69] In 'The Knight in Twelfth-Century Lincolnshire' Wales argued that pious giving peaked between 1130 and *c.*1170, then fell off until *c.*1200, when there was a brief revival till *c.*1220. This chronology, though a little rigid, generally accords with the Gilbertine experience.   [70] *Gilbertine Charters*, 15.

[71] See Cheney, 'Papal Privileges', 39–65. The privileges are printed 57–65. Further charters for Alvingham and Malton are found in their cartularies: Oxford, Bodl. Lib., MS Laud Misc. 642, fos. 1–4ᵛ, and London, BL, MS Cotton Claudius D XI, fos. 9–19, 26–29ᵛ.

which dates from 1178, shows that the priory had already obtained granges at Newton, North Conesby, and Little Cawthorpe, a mill and other possessions at Swinhop, and a saltpan at Kermundtorp—as well as six churches and their landed endowments. These estates provided a substantial part of the priory's income; the only large estate which does not figure in this list, and which was predominantly a creation of the following century, is Grainthorpe. The papal charter for Malton (also issued in 1178) indicates that it had received ten churches and chapels, the grange of Wintringham and the demesne there granted by William de Vesci, son of the priory's founder, amounting to three carucates, the granges at Mowthorpe and Kirby, and land at Linton, as well as other property including turbaries, meadows, and mills given by Eustace fitzJohn and William de Vesci. The canons had also acquired the lands in Croxton which had been the endowment of the Gilbertine priory in Normandy.[72] The damaged charter for Chicksands which was issued at or about the same time lists the seven churches possessed by the priory along with its lands in Chicksands, Maulden, Campton, Haynes, Stondon, Molesworth, and Chippenham. Again these were amongst the most valuable possessions the priory was to acquire.[73]

Royal confirmation charters are generally fuller than papal ones, frequently recording both the extent of an individual property and its grantor. One of the most detailed is that issued to Sempringham by Richard I shortly after his accession in September 1189. This describes properties in over thirty villages, mostly in Lincolnshire, but including lands and churches in Leicestershire, Nottinghamshire, Derbyshire, and Norfolk. Thirteen churches and chapels and eight granges are specifically named, while there were also substantial properties which had already been organized as granges at villages near to Sempringham such as Walcot and Laughton. When this compendium is compared with properties recorded in the *Valor Ecclesiasticus* it is apparent that, though some new lands had been acquired, with few exceptions the most prosperous holdings were in the priory's hands by 1189.[74]

---

[72] *Papsturkunden in England*, iii. 425–6, no. 154.

[73] A later charter issued jointly for the priories of Watton and Malton and probably dating to shortly after 1200 shows that by that date Watton had acquired land in over twenty vills, and gives special prominence to the nuns' possession of the vill of Watton itself, the church and lands in North Dalton, and property in Hawold, Kilnwick, and Langdale, as well as in Ravenstonedale (Cheney, 'Papal Privileges', 63–5). It is possible that this was issued by Celestine III, but Cheney argued persuasively (50–1) for Innocent III's pontificate.

[74] The only substantial properties held in 1535 and seemingly not recorded in 1189 were at Bitchfield, Rigbolt, and Brothertoft. The priory held one-twentieth of a fee in Bitchfield in 1303 (*Feudal Aids*, iii. 135). In 1292 the priory was given the right to hold an annual fair

At other Gilbertine priories in north Lincolnshire the picture is the
same. Virtually all the estates recorded in the *Valor* as belonging to
Sixhills in 1535 are listed in the confirmation charter issued at the end of
Henry II's reign.[75] The only estates of any size that seem to have been
obtained after 1189 were at Binbrook and Kirmond, which were certainly
demesne lands by 1252, and the manor at Toft purchased in 1279.[76] But
this picture is not confined to Lincolnshire. A comparison of Henry II's
confirmation charter, which can be dated between 1163 and 1179, for the
nuns of Chicksands with the priory's estates recorded in 1291 makes it
clear that the bulk had already been acquired by the time Henry issued
his charter. After *c.*1180 few major acquisitions occurred.[77]

Thirteenth-century developments

The framework of Gilbertine estates had, then, been largely established
by 1200. Even during the twelfth century it had been rare for the
Gilbertines to obtain the grant of whole villages. True, some were fortunate: the endowment of Watton included the whole vill of Watton with
its appurtenances, the priory at Sempringham possessed the whole of the
village, and Sixhills held the village of Legsby, but the benefactors' limited resources, the fact that most Gilbertine foundations were in well-
populated areas, and that in Lincolnshire the majority of villages were
divided between two or more lords, meant that these opportunities were
rare. In the thirteenth century they were almost non-existent, and opportunities for substantial territorial aggrandizement were few, and usually
dependent upon the chance financial embarrassment of a local family and
consequent sale of property. The largest single acquisition was probably
that made by Sixhills in 1279, immediately (and fortunately) prior to the
Statute of Mortmain, when Robert Burnell, bishop of Bath and Wells,
and close adviser to Edward I, transferred his manor of Toft-by-Rasen,
and all his lands in the neighbouring villages of Aby, Strubby, Saxilby,
and Beelsby.[78] A grant, made at almost exactly the same time, to
Sempringham, was of nearly equal value; this comprised the manor and

---

on the manor of Rigbolt (*Cal. Ch. R.* ii. 429). The lands at Brothertoft may be associated
with the hermitage on Holland Marsh which lay at nearby Wyberton.

[75] *Gilbertine Charters*, 35–8.   [76] *Cal. Ch. R.* i. 392; for Toft, see below.

[77] The only significant property to come into the priory's hands thereafter was at Tadlow
(Cambridgeshire), where Fulk le Moyne confirmed all the dower land held by Sybil his
mother and amounting to nearly 60 acres in the village (Fowler (ed.), 'Early Charters of
. . . Chicksand', 109). The family were already patrons of the priory and were tenants of the
Beauchamp patrons of Chicksands.   [78] *Gilbertine Charters*, 15.

chapel of Rigbolt and appurtenant lands in Gosberton and Surfleet, which was assessed at £6 6s. 8d. in 1535.[79]

Changing conditions demanded new policies, and there are, indeed, indications of a changing strategy towards the Gilbertine estates, and perhaps a more carefully planned programme of acquisition. Consolidation of older properties, rather than extension into new areas, became the norm; exchanges of land were more frequent, as were demises of property judged less valuable or convenient in order to finance purchases or rented lands elsewhere. The priories, therefore, acquired land in only a few more villages during this century, but where they already held lands they continued to expand their holdings. The rate of acquisition decelerated, new properties tended to be smaller, reflecting the less ambitious scale of benefactions, though at the same time enterprising priors, of whom William of Ancaster, prior of Malton, is the best known, continued actively to promote the temporal well-being of their communities.

Decline in large-scale benefactions meant that the nuns and canons had to look elsewhere to maintain their income. Churches of which they held the advowson were appropriated wherever possible;[80] lands were increasingly rented if they could not be obtained by gift or purchased outright; the purchase of land, though far from unknown in the twelfth century, increased; less desirable properties held by the priories were leased, or, as often, exchanged. Exchanges enabled community and lay grantor mutually to consolidate their estates, and were one of the chief means by which the priories could rationalize their estates, making for their more efficient exploitation. All the priories for which detailed records survive can be demonstrated to have actively exchanged lands. These exchanges occurred at all levels. A priory might exchange property with another Gilbertine or non-Gilbertine house, or with a lay tenant, in one village for land in another. Thus the nuns of Bullington gave a toft, *cultura*, and four selions in Beckering, where they had only a slight interest, to Simon of Beckering in return for a toft, four selions 'on the west of their [i.e. the canons'] grange near their land', and another ten selions in two other *culturae* in West Torrington, where Bullington already possessed a substantial estate.[81] Typically, here land was disposed of in a village where little was held in return for land in a grange-village, and it is noteworthy that nearly all recorded exchanges relate to lands in villages where a grange was held. Often the priories were prepared to grant more land

[79] *Sempringham Charters*, xvi. 35; *VE* iv. 102.

[80] The exploitation of *spiritualia* is discussed in more detail below, Ch. 7.

[81] London, BL, Addit. MS 6118, p. 764. For earlier exchanges see above, pp. 265–7.

than they received, if by so doing they could consolidate their holding.[82] At the level of the village, the Gilbertines aimed to bring scattered selions into consolidated *culturae*, and ultimately where possible to develop these into granges. Often only small amounts of land were involved, which itself testifies to the care with which the religious were now managing their resources. Moreover, as the construction of estates came increasingly to resemble the placing of missing pieces in a complex jigsaw puzzle, it was often useful to employ the good offices of a local land agent to acquire property for their use rather than negotiate with a number of donors or vendors. At the end of the twelfth and beginning of the thirteenth century Alvingham priory used Rabod, the vicar of the parish church of the neighbouring village of Keddington, in this way. He spent more than £3 in acquiring two bovates, four acres of arable and meadow, and two tofts for the priory.[83] In Scopwick the nuns of Catley seem to have employed Gilbert son of Gibbe of Keal in similar fashion. He acquired $5\frac{1}{2}$ bovates and three tofts from various 'donors' which he then granted to the priory for a nominal rent.[84]

Another possibility was to lease land. By definition this expedient cost money, and could only be second-best to outright gifts, or perhaps even purchases. It is noteworthy that very little property was rented in the priories' first years; this policy was a response to a harsher climate. Analysis of these rents has attendant difficulties. Their nature varied: they could be merely nominal, quitrents by which the donee recognized the tenure; alternatively, they might be the recognition of a sale, whereby a nominal tenure was created in return for an unstated lump-sum; they might represent the commutation of forinsec service owed to the benefactor's lord; they might be 'economic' rents fixed, at any rate in part, by supply and demand, but perhaps also determined as 'beneficial' rents, or lowered because a large down-payment was made at the time of the grant.[85] Records of short-term leases are less likely to have survived than those

---

[82] I have discussed the exchanges made by Alvingham and Bullington in Golding 'Gilbertine Priories', 53–5. It is, of course, possible that unequal exchanges could have been 'topped up' by a cash payment.

[83] Oxford, Bodl. Lib., MS Laud Misc. 642, fos. 124ᵛ–125ᵛ. One of these purchases was made on the express understanding that he convey the land to a religious house ('ad dandum terram . . . cuicumque domui de religione . . . voluerit'). Waites has suggested that Guisborough abbey was employing an agent for the purchase of parcels of land in the slow business of consolidation ('The Monastic Grange as a Factor in the Settlement of North-East Yorkshire', *Yorkshire Archaeological Journal*, 40 (1959–62), 642).

[84] *Gilbertine Charters*, 76–7. Though there is no mention of a sale, it is hard to credit that these donors all gave their lands to Gilbert without some payment.

[85] All these types of rent are discussed in detail in Golding, 'Gilbertine Priories', 94–128.

of permanent alienations. There is some evidence to suggest that the priories were leasing property in the late twelfth century, but the practice increased as outright grants declined. Indeed, the priories may have leased land in the hope that it would later be conveyed to them in perpetuity.[86]

The surviving cartularies of Malton and Alvingham, as well as the Bullington charters, make it clear that the priories were prepared to spend considerable sums on rented property. It appears that certain types of property were particularly desirable, and for them the Gilbertines were especially willing to pay. These included mills and meadow land. By contrast, in general, arable or pasture was rented only when it constituted a relatively large holding, from which the community might expect to derive worthwhile profit, and rents were seldom paid for lands that could not be associated with a grange. The absence of detailed accounts makes it impossible to determine precisely how much the Gilbertines were expending annually on rent, but the abbreviated Malton accounts show that here the canons spent nearly £200 between 1244 and 1257.[87] Such a sum was not insignificant, and, though the annual amounts fluctuated, it could amount, as in 1249, to nearly 10 per cent of the priory's total expenditure. The practice of leasing continued into the following century. In 1302 Sempringham leased the manors of Folkingham and Edenham for a seven-year term, and in 1318 Bullington leased the manor of West Torrington from Philip of Kyme for twenty years. Significantly, these were manors where the priory already had considerable interests, and the leases probably indicate a desire to maximize profits, if only for a short time, from other sources of income, such as courts and similar manorial perquisites.[88]

The thirteenth century is distinguished from the earlier period, therefore, by a diminution of scale. The Gilbertines now thought in terms of the *cultura* or even the single strip of arable, the selion, rather than the village or manor. Efforts were concentrated on the consolidation and development of what they already possessed by whatever means were available. Inevitably this enforced policy cost money: nowhere was this more evident than in the increase in the purchase of lands.

[86] For an early fee-farm surrendered by Watton priory some time between 1186 and 1191, see *EYC* x. 169–70, no. 113. In 1230 Bullington acquired meadow land in Burgh-le-Marsh for a down payment and annual rent for ten years, after which the priory was to hold in perpetuity (London, BL, Harl. Chart. 54 C 19; Cotton Chart. xxviii, 11).

[87] London, BL, MS Cotton Claudius D XI, fos. 279ᵛ–281. The cartularies and accounts rarely record temporary lease arrangements but these certainly existed and contributed further to the priories' outgoings.

[88] S. Raban, *Mortmain Legislation and the English Church* (Cambridge, 1982), 112.

The Gilbertines and the land market

Even in their first generation Gilbertine priories entered the land market on quite a large scale and purchased lands both to establish new grange estates and to round off others.[89] Such enterprise was essential if the communities were to survive in the highly competitive scramble for land that involved religious houses of all types during the second half of the twelfth century. This activity, as well as the fact that they were in many instances obliged and prepared to accept property at fee farm, must mean that some early patrons were giving substantial sums of cash, to which the charters rarely, if ever, allude, to finance these operations. Purchases were clearly carefully planned and controlled, and formed part of a coherent policy of land acquisition and consolidation. In principle all were subject to the Master of the order. The canons were warned not to accept lands at farm and no lands could be purchased or accepted for rent or taken in pledge without the Master's consent. Any purchases over three marks in value required his license; all sealed documents of land transfers required his seal as well as that of the priory, and only in his absence could this rule be overridden in cases of urgent necessity. All documents were to be drawn up in chirograph, and only the Master, the priors, chief scrutators, the confession-priest, sub-priors, and cellarers were to hold seals.[90] The engagement of the canons in the acquisition of land encumbered with debt was expressly forbidden.[91] Nevertheless, it is likely that these prohibitions were dead letters from the beginning. Certainly there is abundant evidence that the Gilbertine priories were purchasing encumbered estates, sometimes on a large scale, while there is little evidence that the Master's written consent was given for these acquisitions.[92] One of the earliest recorded sales is also one of the most detailed, and is probably typical of the sort of arrangements accompanying land sales. Around 1150 Matthew of Tealby sold land in North Willingham and rent in Osgodby to Sixhills for 20 marks to himself, 20 shillings to his son to buy a palfrey, and three marks to Reginald de Crevequer, Matthew's lord. In addition the priory agreed to pay an annual rent of 12 marks.[93]

[89] The agreement between Alvingham and Louth Park presupposed that purchases by both communities were standard practice. See above, p. 281.

[90] *Monasticon*, vi. 2. xxi.   [91] Ibid. xlii.

[92] For the purchase of property mortgaged to the Jews, see below, pp. 295–8. The agreement made between the Cistercian and Gilbertine orders in 1164 explicitly recognized that both were engaged in land purchase.

[93] *Gilbertine Charters*, 14–15. This agreement was made in the chapter house of Lincoln before bishop Robert Chesney and in the presence of many witnesses, including a number of dignitaries of the cathedral. No mention is made of master Gilbert's presence.

A general analysis of patterns of monastic acquisition in the Middle Ages is still awaited, but Raban has argued that land purchases increased in volume after *c*.1200, as land became less readily available and as opportunities for colonization and more intensive settlement declined. As real income was eroded by inflation, one solution was to purchase more property. The lead in this activity was taken by the great, old-established Benedictine houses with their comparatively substantial resources: individual purchases of more than £1,000 were not unknown. The victims of predatory purchase whether by the religious or the upwardly mobile *curiales* and royal bureaucrats were normally the financially embarrassed local knightly families.[94]

More recently Wardrop has shown that Fountains abbey seems to have made the majority of its purchases, large and small, during the period *c*.1160 to *c*.1200.[95] How far is this pattern reflected amongst the Gilbertine houses? Obviously a great deal depended upon individual circumstances: the availability of a surplus to spend; the presence of a vendor eager to sell; the need to fill out and consolidate a property, most typically a grange. Gilbertine houses did make substantial purchases in the second half of the twelfth century. By 1172 the nuns of Catley had spent at least 57 marks in acquiring a substantial property in Glentworth from Oliver son of Oliver of Wendover; we have already seen that Sixhills spent £100 to gain the manor of Ludford from Jocelin of Louvain.[96] The majority of Alvingham's purchases were made before 1200, though a number of substantial acquisitions were also made well into the following century.[97] These, however, seem to have been the result of the canons exploiting the financial embarrassment of a local family when the opportunity arose: virtually all of these later purchases relate to Jewish debts. It could, indeed, perhaps be argued that in the twelfth century the Gilbertines bought because they had to, while in the following century they took advantage of a buyers' market. The example of Malton shows that there at any rate the canons continued to spend very considerable sums up until the middle of the thirteenth century. Between 1244 and 1257 the canons spent £508 18s. 10d. in the purchase of lands.[98] Yearly purchases fluctuated considerably: the lowest amount spent was £5 19s. 2d. in 1250, a year later it

[94] Raban, *Mortmain Legislation*, 142–52. Another possibility was to recover previously alienated land into the demesne: a number of purchases do seem to indicate this sort of resumption. [95] Wardrop, *Fountains Abbey*, 80–1.

[96] *Gilbertine Charters*, 84–7, 6–7.

[97] These are discussed in Golding, 'Gilbertine Priories', 61–5. Bullington also made most of its purchases before 1200.

[98] London, BL, MS Cotton Claudius D XI, fos. 279ᵛ–281.

peaked at £163 17s. 6½d. How far this activity is typical of contemporary Gilbertine houses is difficult to determine. Certainly Malton benefited during these years from a forceful and acquisitive prior, William of Ancaster, but long ago Graham suggested that a comparison between the 1254 and 1291 valuations of the *temporalia* of Sixhills and Alvingham as well as Malton demonstrates that these houses, by contrast with others in the order, were aggressive acquirers of land.[99] This may be true: certainly it would appear that some Gilbertine priories, most notably the three cited by Graham, were in general more active in the land market than some other Gilbertine houses. Chicksands, for example, made few or any such purchases, and neither Sempringham itself nor Haverholme can be shown to have made more than a few acquisitions, primarily to round off pre-existing estates.[100]

The most striking feature of the distribution of land purchases is the (hardly surprising) fact that virtually all were made in villages where the priories possessed granges. Thus, with the exception of a little urban property, an access road in Grimsby Parva, and valuable meadow land on the rich grazings of the saltmarsh at Somercotes and Conisholme, all known purchases by Alvingham were in grange villages. Most was spent in the acquisition of estates in Alvingham itself. As has already been shown, the foundation at Alvingham was a co-operative one dependent upon the goodwill of a number of benefactors. The difficulties of obtaining a large estate in this divided village may well have prompted the purchases. Certainly by the end of the twelfth century the priory had spent a total of 267½ marks in the purchase of lands here.[101] Considerable sums were also spent on the neighbouring grange of Cockerington; by contrast, little was expended on the more outlying properties such as Reedness or Wold Newton. A similar pattern is found on the Bullington estates, where, with the exception of two *nativi* purchased in Orby and Winthorpe (and perhaps intended as labourers on the nearby grange at Burgh-le-Marsh) and a rent charge in Lincoln, all purchases were in grange villages. However, in contrast to Alvingham, Bullington did not concentrate its purchases in a few villages, and made no purchases at all in Bullington itself, which is perhaps a tribute to the generosity of the foundation grant.

---

[99] R. Graham, 'The Finances of Malton Priory, 1244–1257', in *English Ecclesiastical Studies* (London, 1929), 257.

[100] This contrast may be more apparent than real, as only in the cases of Alvingham and Malton do cartularies survive. However, Bullington, for which the records are almost as complete as Alvingham, was much less active, and surviving charters of Sixhills suggest a much greater activity than its north Lincolnshire neighbours, Nun Ormsby and Catley.

[101] Golding, 'Gilbertine Priories', 14–15, 61.

The clearest indication of Gilbertine grange policy is to be found at Malton. The cartulary contains an index arranged by village of all the properties acquired by the priory during William of Ancaster's priorate. The total amounted to something over 140 bovates, as well as pasture land, meadow, and tofts.[102] That these acquisitions were largely, or wholly, sales is clear, though this cannot be certainly proved since the charters describing the specific transactions listed seldom make explicit mention of a cash payment.[103] During this period land was acquired in a total of twenty-five places, though in some only a very small property was involved.[104] Activity was concentrated in five areas. At Levisham and Dunsdale the canons received a very considerable estate from the lands of Ralph Bolebec senior and junior, comprising 52 acres of arable, pasture for 1,000 sheep and 120 other animals, a mill and meadow land with an additional three *culturae* totalling 20 acres, the services of Adam the reeve, his *sequela* and customary bovate holding, and arable land estimated to total four bovates. This was a new estate for the canons. Taking advantage of the financial needs of the Bolebec family, they were able to develop a small grange at Dunsdale, which seems to have administered the Levisham lands. There was already a grange at Rillington two or three miles to the east of Malton in the Derwent valley. Here the estate was more than doubled by the acquisition of three carucates: most, if not all, of this land was purchased from landholders indebted to the Jews.[105]

A similar pattern is found at the other vills where major acquisitions occurred. A total of sixteen bovates was added to the priory's lands in Ebberston, where the canons already had a grange, and in the neighbouring vills of Snainton and Sawdon. At Edston and Swinnington a relatively small estate was transformed by the purchase of fifteen bovates, again largely from the property of a local lord indebted to the Jews, while at Swinton and Amotherby, adjacent settlements to Malton to the west,

---

[102] London, BL, MS Cotton Claudius D XI, fos. 2ᵛ–3.

[103] For example, the charter of Roger of Burley granting four bovates to the canons in Swinton makes no mention of payment, but a fine dated 1246 shows the prior of Malton giving 30 marks to Roger and his wife in return for this land and 4 shillings rent (*Feet of Fines for the County of York from 1232 to 1246*, ed. J. Parker, Yorkshire Archaeological Society Record Series, 67 (1925), 177–8). Similarly, the two bovates in Wombleton listed in the index can be identified with the two bovates granted by Ralph of Thorpe to the canons. This charter is couched as a straightforward grant: it is only the preservation in the cartulary of the release of all interest in this land by Samson the Jew that makes it apparent that the canons had paid for this property (London, BL, MS Cotton Claudius D XI, fo. 111ᵛ).

[104] At Hutton and Norton the canons received only one bovate, and at Scarborough only the land on which their house was built.

[105] London, BL, MS Cotton Claudius D XI, fos. 169–70.

a series of transactions brought a total of sixteen bovates. In all these places the canons already possessed lands which they were keen to expand and by the end of the century had successfully established granges at these sites. Even small accessions might be carefully planned. Since the canons had a large, indeed their largest, estate at Wintringham, there was probably no opportunity or desire to make further substantial additions to the property, but they did purchase a piece of land for the enlargement of the court towards their sheepfold. Elsewhere other purchases were more opportunistic. There would be little prospect of developing a grange at Wombleton since Rievaulx had one there, but when Ralph of Thorpe was obliged to sell his two bovates in the vill the canons were prepared to purchase them to provide a rent income which they shortly exchanged with the canons of Newburgh for rent previously owned by the latter in Malton itself.[106]

Any analysis of Gilbertine land purchases is hampered by the problem of 'concealed' sales, and it is likely that transactions acknowledged in such phrases as *in mea magna necessitate* represent only the tip of the iceberg of acquisitions.[107] Vendors were reluctant to state explicitly that a sale had been made, and usually sales were recorded using the same formulas as were applied to outright gifts, with any mention of the consideration paid (perhaps using such phrases as *in inicio* or *in recognicione*) at the conclusion of the charter.[108] Conversely, a charter may refer explicitly to a sale but still describe the transaction as a *donatio*.[109] At the same time, the line between a sale and an outright gift was a thin one. As already suggested, sales were often recorded in formulas more suitable to grants *in liberam,*

---

[106] Ibid., fos. 111ᵛ–112. Similarly, the half-carucate granted to the canons in Kennythorpe was soon demised at farm to Hugh of Newport Pagnell (ibid., fo. 69).

[107] This is a problem experienced by all monastic historians of the period. For an able discussion in a Cistercian context (where, of course, purchases were forbidden), see L. J. McCrank, 'The Frontier of the Spanish Reconquest and the Land Acquisitions of the Cistercians of Poblet 1150–1276', *Analecta Cisterciensia*, 29 (1973), 57–78, and also Wardrop, *Fountains Abbey*, 70–1, 79–86.

[108] The Malton cartulary lists land purchases made during the priorate of William of Ancaster. It is noteworthy that few of the charters in the cartulary detailing the individual transactions refer to a financial consideration.

[109] As occurs, for example, in a charter wherein Toka of Keddington stated that he had received 11s. from the canons of Alvingham for land in Keddington but describes this grant as a *donatio* in the warranty clause (Oxford, Bodl. Lib., MS Laud Misc. 642, fo. 126). It has on occasion been suggested that sales seldom contain references to salvation for the vendor, whereas a donor normally made his gift 'pro salute', and that this distinction can be used to identify sales from gifts, but little evidence of such a distinction has been found in the Gilbertine charters (see e.g. *The Early Charters of Waltham Abbey, 1062–1230*, ed. R. Ransford (Woodbridge, 1989), p. xxvi).

puram, et perpetuam elemosinam, and drafters of charters saw no inherent contradiction here, perhaps because both types of grant brought spiritual benefits of one kind or another.[110] There was nothing incongruous about the community of Alvingham agreeing to receive as nuns the sister and niece of John of Meaux (together with three nieces of Reiner of Waxham) when John sold his demesne in Alvingham and Cockerington to the community.[111] There was no reason why those who sold land should not receive spiritual and temporal advantages: vendors, like donors, were making available land that the priories could otherwise not have acquired. It is unrealistic to draw a distinction between gifts and sales, for in both cases the benefactors were rendering a service, and in both cases they received their reward.

The reason for this reluctance to publicize sales can sometimes be ascribed to an order's refusal to countenance these transactions; the Cistercians forbade land purchase between 1180 and 1216, and in the case of the Gilbertines it is possible that some purchases may have been concealed to avoid having to gain the Master's assent for them, as well as to evade the prohibition on the acquisition of encumbered lands. Wardrop has also suggested that in the thirteenth century purchases may have been concealed from the vendor's lord. As lords became increasingly reluctant to countenance the alienation of property by their tenants, they were particularly concerned to prevent the loss of lands by sale rather than by eleemosynary grant, since in agreeing to the latter the lord could at least himself partake of the contingent spiritual benefits.[112] There is one other possible explanation. A charter which assured the benefactor of spiritual benefits in return for a grant, and which at the same time also referred to a cash transaction, might be regarded as simoniacal, and as religious houses grew increasingly wary of such accusations, discretion may have seemed essential.[113]

---

[110] e.g. the charter of William of Redburn to Alvingham making over his lands in return for payment of his Jewish debts (Oxford, Bodl. Lib., MS Laud Misc. 642, fo. 72ᵛ). An acknowledged sale can be described in the same charter as a 'donatio' (ibid., fo. 126).

[111] Ibid., fo. 72ᵛ. For further discussion and examples of sales, see Golding, 'Gilbertine Priories', esp. 67–9.

[112] Wardrop, *Fountains Abbey*, 85–6 and nn. 72–4. She draws attention to Bracton's statement that it was advisable for a vendor to avoid stating the payment of a lump sum in a charter if he wished to avoid enquiry into the transaction. Raban has commented how the Provisions of Westminster probably stipulated that licences from mesne lords for alienations to religious houses be required only for purchases (Raban, *Mortmain Legislation*, 142).

[113] For analogous caution in the drafting of fines relating to land transactions which included a monetary consideration, see H. G. Richardson, *The English Jewry under Angevin Kings* (London, 1960), 87 and n. 1.

'Concealed' sales are, by definition, almost impossible to identify. Sometimes a fine indicates a sale, but these were not entered into on every occasion, and there is some evidence that they, too, did not necessarily record an accompanying payment. If a benefactor who is known to have been in financial difficulties and to have made one sale to a priory also made other apparent gifts, then it is likely that these were likewise made in return for some financial consideration. If the priories were obtaining lands in particularly favourable positions then there is an even greater likelihood that they were purchasing that land.

The Gilbertines confined their purchases almost exclusively to their grange properties, and it is clear that in many cases it was necessary to purchase land in order to consolidate and expand grange estates almost as soon as they were created. Many such purchases were of comparatively large holdings, of *culturae* rather than selions, the latter being normally acquired by exchange rather than purchase. Substantial sums were often involved. Sixhills was prepared to pay Jocelin of Louvain the very considerable sum of £100 *c.*1174 and an additional annual payment of £12 for the manor of Ludford. Over two generations Alvingham spent $227\frac{1}{2}$ marks acquiring land in Alvingham and Cockerington from the de Meaux family. Haverholme spent 50 marks in gaining a fee in Dorrington for which the priory also agreed to pay an annual rent of one mark and to perform the knight's service.[114] But not all purchases were of large holdings or made for large sums. They might be, as importantly, small areas of land bought to round off an estate.

There is often no clear correlation between the purchase price and the size of the property. John of Bulby sold a toft of $2\frac{1}{2}$ acres in Bulby to Sempringham for a cloak worth one mark, and another five acres in the same village for two marks. But these were useful properties: they lay close to or adjoined the priory's grange of Woodgrange and were hence of more value than might at first appear.[115] By contrast, Sempringham seems to have had a bargain when it acquired pasture for 160 sheep in Keisby from Ridel of Keisby for two marks and a palfrey valued at 4 marks, but Ridel was a generous benefactor and in any case some of his other grants may have been concealed sales.[116]

A further problem is that we are not always informed which party initiated the land deal. Smaller, more poorly endowed houses like Catley

---

[114] *Gilbertine Charters*, 6–7. The estate at Ludford amounted to nearly $4\frac{1}{2}$ carucates and Jocelin also gave the church of Ludford and land in North Willingham to the community (see also *EYC* xi. 66–9); Golding, 'Gilbertine Priories', 14–15, 61; 'Haverholme Priory Charters', 69. [115] London, BL, Addit. Charts. 20904, 20914.
[116] Ibid. 20907.

may well have had to purchase land in order to survive; wealthier priories invested to increase their temporal income and often took advantage of their lay neighbours' financial embarrassment. Certainly many of the lesser nobility of Lincolnshire, like their counterparts elsewhere in the country, were experiencing economic problems, and the Gilbertines were not alone in profiting from their discomfiture, but it was not solely a buyers' market. The religious could exploit these difficulties where they existed, but sometimes the priories required land from those who had no apparent necessity to sell, and here the price of property investment could be much higher. It is this factor, as well as the type and position of the property required, that accounts for the large fluctuations in the price the Gilbertines were ready to give. Where land could be acquired freely, or where only a modest outlay was necessary, they took advantage of circumstances, but they were also prepared to pay over the odds for the land of those who were not in difficulties, in order, for example, to round off a grange estate.

Sometimes they might lease land prior to acquiring it outright from an impecunious benefactor. In the mid-twelfth century Robert of Pormort leased a demesne bovate and customary lands in Alvingham to the priory for ten years for a lump sum and the agreement that thereafter the nuns might hold it in fee. Later he is found selling property in Alvingham and Cockerington outright: clearly the earlier arrangement had not solved his problems, and the only solution was this more radical one.[117] In some cases the reason for the sale is made explicit. Usually financial difficulties, signalled by such phrases as *in mea magna necessitate*, are responsible, and often the involvement of Jewish money lenders is admitted.[118] Undoubtedly the most fruitful source of relatively cheap property for the Gilbertines were local lords who found themselves in financial difficulties and who were indebted to the Jews.[119] Most of the acquisitions made in this way appear to date from the second quarter of the thirteenth century, which was perhaps the most critical time for the lesser knights. However, enough evidence survives to show that the priories were active in the Jewish land market in the preceding century.[120] Indeed, Alvingham's most lavish

[117] Oxford, Bodl. Lib., MS Laud Misc. 642, fos. 14, 59.

[118] A typical example is Simon de Crevequer's grant to Sixhills for 100*s*. given 'in magnis et arduis necessitatibus meis' (*Gilbertine Charters*, 34). The family were also generous benefactors of Bullington priory, and were in considerable straits during the 13th century (see Golding, 'Gilbertine Priories', 246–52).

[119] A full study of Jewish involvement in the estate creation of English religious houses is still awaited, but see Richardson, *English Jewry*, esp. ch. v, 'Jews and the Land', 83–108.

[120] Wardrop has suggested that 'the central period of pressure' on the knightly families of Yorkshire which granted lands to Fountains lay between *c*.1180 and *c*.1240, a chronology

expenditure on any holding occurred in the mid-twelfth century when the priory first bought half of the de Meaux family demesne in Alvingham and Cockerington for $87\frac{1}{2}$ marks in settlement of a Jewish debt, and then in the following generation spent 140 marks in acquiring the whole of the remainder of the demesne.[121] In 1171–2 Catley acquired a carucate and seven tofts in Glentworth from Oliver of Wendover junior for 30 marks paid to the Jews of Lincoln, and the substantial additional grants by the same benefactor, which enabled the house to establish a grange at Glentworth, suggest that these were also made in settlement of debts.[122] Involvement with Jews was probably just as much a matter for conceal-ment as the sale of property to religious houses, if not more so, though the increasing control of Jewish financial affairs by the crown made se-crecy correspondingly more difficult. Sometimes the role of Jews in land transfer can be inferred from their specific inclusion in warranty clauses. When, for example, in the 1160s William, count of Aumale, confirmed the grant of his tenant Gilbert of Ormsby of lands in Ormsby and Utterby to the nuns of Ormsby and warranted it 'against the king and against all men and also against the Jews', we may probably assume that Jewish lenders had an interest in the property.[123] There is also some evidence in the recorded debts of Aaron of Lincoln to indicate the Gilbertines' in-volvement in Jewish financial affairs. The debts of the prior of Bullington are noted below: the prior of Sixhills was answerable for £12 per annum in payment of the debts of Agnes de Percy, which amounted to £190.[124] More significant, perhaps, are the names of the lay debtors in Lincoln-shire. They read as a roll-call of the benefactors of Gilbertine houses. Here we find, for example, Peter of Billinghay, the founder of Catley, owing £9 5s. 8d., two marks of which were by pledge of the prior; Ailwin Net and Eudo of Mumby, benefactors of Bullington; Walter de Scoteni,

which is consonant with the evidence from Gilbertine houses in Yorkshire and Lincolnshire (*Fountains Abbey*, 211).

[121] Oxford, Bodl. Lib., MS Laud Misc. 642, fos. 10ᵛ–11.

[122] *Gilbertine Charters*, 84–7.

[123] Ibid. 41–2. For a much later example dated 1276 whereby Roger d'Arci granted a substantial holding in Nettleton to Sixhills priory, see ibid. 16. This was almost certainly a sale occasioned by d'Arci's financial difficulties. When in 1249 Malton priory acquired six bovates in Rillington which certainly formed part of an encumbered estate, the grantor being in debt to several York Jews, all parties in the transaction warranted their confirma-tion of this property against both Christians and Jews (London, BL, MS Cotton Claudius D XI, fo. 170ᴿ⁻ᵛ).

[124] See below, p. 301. For Sixhills see *Pipe Rolls 3 and 4 Richard I*, PRS, NS 2 (1926), 22. It is likely that the £12 represents the annual rent due from Sixhills to Agnes for the manor of Ludford (see above, p. 294).

a patron of Alvingham; Alexander de St Vedast, benefactor of Haverholme; Nigel son of Alexander, benefactor of Sempringham.[125] These examples are chosen at random: many more could be added. We can seldom demonstrate conclusively that these men were selling their property to pay off these debts, but it seems reasonable to infer that this was frequently the case. William de Pontfol owed £10 to Aaron pledged on his lands in Ingham: at about the same time he granted two bovates of demesne, about six acres of meadow and a toft, and pasture for 200 sheep to the nuns of Bullington. A relative, Hugh de Pontfol, perhaps his father, owed £2; shortly afterwards his widow sold all her land and rents in Newton and Toft to Bullington for the same sum.[126]

The fullest evidence for Gilbertine intervention in the Jewish land market during the thirteenth century derives from the Malton cartulary.[127] Most of this priory's dealings with the Jews appear to date from the priorate of William of Ancaster, though, as in other respects, this emphasis on William's activity may be just a result of the greater survival of material from his rule. The starrs entered in the margins of the cartulary shew that the canons were dealing with money lenders in both York and Lincoln. The debtors mostly came from local knightly families, such as those of Redbourne or Bolebec. William of Redbourne was clearly in considerable difficulties. His family held land both near Malton and also in north Lincolnshire, and at the same time as Yorkshire property was passing to the canons of Malton the nuns of Alvingham were acquiring William's estate in Cockerington for an unspecified sum and the provision of a large corrody.[128] In 1242 the canons of Malton acquired six bovates in Little Edstone in settlement of William's debts to Josce, nephew of Aaron the Jew of York, Benedict of Nantes, and Jacob son of Leo, Jews of Lincoln.[129] Josce was also a creditor of William son of Thomas of Richburgh. For seven bovates in Welham the canons paid 37½ marks 'pro allevacione partis debiti quo ei tenebar astrictus'.[130] Both of these were substantial acquisitions at a time when genuine gifts were drying up. Though there was not as yet a grange at either of these places, the land at Edstone could be administered from the newly created grange at

---

[125] Ibid. 17–21, *passim.*   [126] Ibid. 21; *Danelaw Charters*, 41–2, 56, nos. 62–3.

[127] For a brief discussion, see Richardson, *English Jewry*, 95–8.

[128] Oxford, Bodl. Lib., MS Laud Misc. 642, fo. 72ᵛ and margin. Money was also paid to William's daughter *prae manibus* for her renunciation of all rights in the property.

[129] London, BL, MS Cotton Claudius D XI, fo. 114. Printed in Richardson, *English Jewry*, 281–4.

[130] London, BL, MS Cotton Claudius D XI, fos. 64ᵛ–5. Printed in Richardson, *English Jewry*, 283.

Sinnington, while that at Welham lay in close proximity to the grange of Sutton. Thus they probably represent a conscious policy of acquisition. At about the same time Malton was also creating a large estate in Levisham by taking advantage of the problems faced by Ralph Bolebec. Ralph was in debt to both Leo son of Solomon and Aaron son of Josce of Lincoln, and a starr of the former shows how the priory obtained pasture for 500 sheep, 60 cattle, 20 mares, and three stallions, along with the site of a *bercaria* and animal houses and 32 acres of arable with 60 quarters of salt from Ralph's holdings in the Lincolnshire marshland village of Fulstow. This acquisition probably formed part of another, larger sale by Ralph comprising pasture for 1,000 sheep and 120 other animals and 52 acres of arable.[131] Even this did not solve the family's problems, however, for in 1250 Ralph's son, Ralph junior, sold his mill in Levisham and the suit of mill of Levisham and Lockton with other parcels of land in settlement of debts to Aaron son of Josci and Samuel son of Leo.[132]

All the evidence suggests that the Gilbertines were pursuing an active policy of acquiring land from financially embarrassed neighbours and that, as always, these purchases were concentrated in villages where they possessed or hoped to develop a grange. Though some dealings may have been more opportunistic, perhaps with a view to later exchange for more profitable or convenient estates, generally the nuns and canons restricted their activities in the Jewish land market, as they restricted their purchases as a whole, to areas with the greatest value and potential for growth.[133]

---

[131] London, BL, MS Cotton Claudius D XI, fos. 116ᵛ–117. In part at least Ralph needed ready money to finance his crusading expedition. The tenurial history of Fulstow is fully discussed by D. M. Williamson, 'Some Notes on the Medieval Manor of Fulstow', *Lincoln Architectural and Archaeological Society Reports and Papers*, NS 4 (1948–51), 1–56.

[132] London, BL, MS Cotton Claudius D XI, fos. 117ᵛ–118. This grant was made with the body of Ralph for burial in the priory. Full possession was not obtained by the canons till 1252, when Hugh of Lockton, Ralph's servant, was ordered to convey seisin (ibid., fo. 118ᵛ).

[133] Under William of Ancaster the priory obtained 2 bovates in Wombleton which had been granted to Ralph of Thorpe by Robert of Bowforth and then regranted to the priory by Ralph. Only a starr of Samson son of Amyot reveals that indebtedness lay behind this transaction. This refers to the debts of Alice Arundel, the wife of Ralph of Thorpe. Perhaps Alice and Ralph had overreached themselves in their own land acquisitions (ibid., fos. 111–12). Alice and Robert were also benefactors of St Leonard's hospital, York, and Easby abbey. For the families, see *VCH North Riding*, i. 77, 336; *EYC* v. 354, ix. 227–8, xi. 196–202). Two bovates was hardly sufficient for a grange estate, however: the chapel of Wombleton was already in the hands of Newburgh abbey, which had a substantial estate here, and by the late 13th century Malton had leased all its lands in Wombleton to the Augustinian house for 4s. per annum (London, BL, MS Cotton Claudius D XI, fo. 112; *VCH Yorkshire*, ii. 521, iii. 226).

Often we can only infer the financial motives behind land deals. Rarely are their workings revealed, but a Bullington charter indicates that Jews were not alone in advancing money to indigent tenants. Philip of Kyme lent £10 to Helewisa the daughter of Ate in return for a gage of a bovate in West Torrington. Philip later passed this land to Bullington to hold until such time as the debt be repaid.[134] Stenton long ago showed how Philip operated in land transactions which brought his lay tenants and Bullington into a complex tenurial network. He drew attention to a charter in which Philip gave the nuns two bovates in Bullington, which his father had given to Richard Noreis and which Philip had first bought back from Richard's heir, then granted to Walter of Barton before buying it back from him also. It can also be shown that this property was exchanged for land the nuns held in Ingham which Philip had bought from Ailwin Net, who is known to have owed money to Aaron of Lincoln.[135] Other factors that stimulated sales are occasionally mentioned. Jocelin of Louvain's sale of Ludford to Sixhills was to finance his journey to Jerusalem on crusade, while Ralph Bolebec raised money for his crusading venture *c.*1240 by selling property in Fulstow (Lincolnshire) to Malton priory for 40 marks and a horse worth three marks.[136]

The chance survival of charters or cartularies and the fact that not all cash transactions were explicit means that our understanding of Gilbertine purchasing policy is at best impressionistic.[137] We can demonstrate that

[134] *Danelaw Charters*, pp. l–li, nos. 103–4, pp. 67–8. Since the priory held on to the land, it would appear that the loan was never repaid.

[135] This property is probably the 2½ bovates which Philip had earlier granted the nuns and which were held by Ailwin in Ingham (ibid., pp. li–lii, nos. 9, 59, pp. 7–8, 39).

[136] Jocelin's charter refers to money which 'ego ab eis suscepi Jeresolimam profecturus ad sumptus itineris mei'. For Ralph Bolebec's transactions, see London, BL, MS Cotton Claudius D XI, fo. 19ᵛ, cited in Owen, *Church and Society*, 125. Ralph also granted considerable property in Fulstow, including pasture for 900 sheep, to Louth Park (*Cal. Ch. R.* iii. 265). At the same time he was negotiating with lay neighbours in Yorkshire to raise capital before his departure. When he left for the Holy Land he gave his seal into the safe-keeping of the prior of Malton (*Feet of Fines for the County of York from 1232 to 1246*, 139 n. 2). Bolebec was also indebted to the Jews, and much of the family lands in Yorkshire also came to Malton. The financing of crusading expeditions by the sale or mortgaging of property is discussed by S. Lloyd, *English Society and the Crusade, 1216–1307* (Oxford, 1988), esp. 183–93, and C. Tyerman, *England and the Crusades, 1095–1588* (Chicago, 1988), esp. 195–9. Another grant associated with a crusading journey, that made by William Fossard I to the nuns of Watton of three carucates in Hawold 'maxime pro itinere quod facturus eram Ierosolimam', was almost certainly made in return for a sum towards the financing of William's expedition, though no money is said to have changed hands (*EYC* ii. 396).

[137] A general context to these purchases, at least during the 13th century, is provided by Raban, *Mortmain Legislation*, 142–52, and see the same author's 'The Land Market and the Aristocracy', in D. Greenway, C. Holdsworth, and J. Sayers (eds.), *Tradition and Change:*

virtually all of the priories, even small houses like Catley, were active, and
that comparatively large sums of money were on occasions spent, but it is
rare indeed to be able to quantify in detail the land purchases of a
community. That opportunity is offered in the abbreviated accounts of
Malton, which show that, between 1244 and 1257, the priory under its
prior William of Ancaster spent a total of just over £500 'pro terris
perpetuis emptis'.[138] This sum sometimes represented a substantial percentage of the total annual expenditure, and it is clear, as Rose Graham
suggested, that much of any annual surplus was being invested in lands.[139]
However, the annual purchase of lands fluctuated considerably. In 1250
less than £6 was spent, the lowest sum during the nine-year period. The
following year the canons invested nearly £163 in property, the highest
amount of any year, accounting for nearly 30 per cent of the year's total
expenditure. When to this sum is added nearly £200 spent during the
same period in the leasing of lands ('pro terris et pratis conductis') the
full scale of the canons' activity is apparent. Yet we must be careful to
keep this level of expenditure in proportion: between *c*.1220 and *c*.1250
Richard Hotot of Northamptonshire, a knight of very moderate means
and background, spent over £534 on land purchases, and he may not
have been exceptional. To contemporaries, therefore, the activities of
prior William were probably not remarkable.[140] It should also be remembered that the lords, both lay and ecclesiastical, who were most active in
the market for encumbered estates, were rich and powerful and frequently had contacts at court. These were advantages the Gilbertines did
not possess.[141]

It remains to ask where the priories gained the resources for such
activities. There are a number of possibilities. Though there is no statistical evidence for their involvement in the wool trade during the twelfth
century, the fact that from the earliest years the priories were receiving
substantial grants of sheep pasturage indicates the importance of wool in
their economy at this time, and in 1193 the entire annual wool yield of the
order was taken as contribution towards Richard I's ransom.[142] It may be,

Essays in Honour of Marjorie Chibnall (Cambridge, 1985), 239–62, for an important comparison with lay magnates' purchasing policy during the same period.

[138] London, BL, Cotton Claudius D XI, fos. 279ᵛ–281.

[139] Graham, 'Finances of Malton Priory', 140–2.

[140] 'Estate Records of the Hotot Family', 8–10, 32–3.

[141] See Coss, 'Sir Geoffrey de Langley', 1–34, esp. 4–5, 17–24, and Raban, 'The Land
Market and the Aristocracy', 239–62.

[142] *Chronica Rogeri de Hovedene (AD 732–1201)*, ed. W. Stubbs, 4 vols., Rolls Series
(London, 1868–71), iii. 210.

too, that wool was already being mortgaged to raise ready money in the late twelfth century as it was to be, often years in advance with disastrous consequences, a century later.[143] Then there was the not inconsiderable income from rents. Land that could not readily be incorporated into a grange or cultivated from one was frequently alienated, either permanently in fee or for a term of years. Though the majority of these arrangements were made in the thirteenth century, there is some evidence that even in the twelfth century some lands were at rent, and that occasional grants of rent charges were also being made to the priories. It is also likely that the priories were themselves borrowing money in order to invest in land. In 1192 the prior of Bullington was recorded as owing £304 to Aaron of Lincoln, making him one of the largest debtors in the county.[144] At the same time unwanted land was being sold to other religious houses; the money thus gained could be used to pay for more desirable properties.[145] Finally, the communities doubtless also received cash benefactions, donations from recruits, and offerings at Gilbert's shrine (though these were not likely to yield as much cash as at larger Benedictine houses). These are notoriously imponderable, for they were not usually recorded in charters or cartularies, but they were probably not insubstantial, and could be used for the purchase of property if required.

By the last quarter of the thirteenth century land purchases by the Gilbertines had virtually dried up. Purchases (like other forms of benefactions) were affected by the new circumstances created by mortmain legislation, and though it is likely that many of the acquisitions in mortmain also represented purchases, increasing financial pressures on the priories clearly reduced their ability to trade as they had once done. Occasional opportunities still occurred. In 1275 Thomas de Boulton, in want of money and on his deathbed, sold his manor of Swinton to the canons of Malton for the very large sum of 220 marks 10 shillings, perhaps the largest single purchase made by the priory. The canons had been developing their grange at Swinton for several decades: the

---

[143] T. H. Lloyd, *The English Wool Trade in the Middle Ages* (Cambridge, 1977), 289–90.

[144] Golding, 'Gilbertine Priories', 66–7. The prior had already paid £7 10s. and contracted to pay the remainder at £5 per annum (*Pipe Rolls, 3 and 4 Richard I*, 231). Graham suggested that the unexplained debts of Malton priory midway through the following century were also the result of direct borrowings from Jews (Graham, *St Gilbert*, 124).

[145] Stixwould nunnery, for example, paid 30s. to Gilbert of Sempringham and the community at Sempringham for a bovate in Honnington (London, BL, Addit. MS 46701, fo. 8ᵛ). And see *The Coucher Book of the Cistercian Abbey of Kirkstall*, ed. W. T. Lancaster and W. P. Baildon, Publications of the Thoresby Society, 8 (1904), 67–70, for an exchange between Kirkstall and Haverholme.

availability of the manor from a dying and indebted lord was a chance not to be missed.[146]

Though it may be that some major purchases continued to be made on a significant scale a little after grants in free alms had largely ceased, in general the chronology of purchases marches much in step with the pattern of acquisitions as a whole. Purchases were necessary to consolidate grange properties almost as soon as they were created, and, as we have argued, too rigid a distinction between gift and sale should not be made. The nuns and canons may have understandably taken more care over their purchases: certainly in the cases of Alvingham, Bullington, and Malton priories, where detailed study has proved possible, it is apparent that they were almost exclusively concerned to invest capital in their grange estates, and especially on those granges that lay close to the priory.

The impact of the Statute of Mortmain

The Statute of Mortmain of 1279 marks a legal watershed in the history of land acquisitions by the Church in England. In theory it prevented the alienation of any land to the religious by gift, sale, or lease, and its corresponding purchase or sale by the religious, on pain of forfeiture. In practice, notwithstanding this general prohibition, the crown was prepared, at a price and with varying enthusiasm, to sanction such alienations. The first licences were granted in 1280. Their enrolment on the Patent Rolls, the accompanying inquisitions *ad quod dampnum*, and analogous royal documents, along with other monastic records, provide the fullest account of the scale and chronology of accessions of landed property by the religious in the late Middle Ages.[147]

However, this material does not answer all the questions relating to church property and the benefactors of the religious during this period. Land was not the only currency of pious exchange: gifts of cash, vestments, ornaments, and books were also frequent, and probably increased as a result of the restrictions and difficulties now experienced in the transfer of land. Such grants, if *post mortem*, can be traced in the wills of benefactors, but *inter vivos* grants of this nature are but rarely recorded. To use records of land grants during this period as a measure of the

---

[146] Thomas's son had claimed that his father was not of sound mind when he made the grant, but this charge was rejected by the jurors (*Yorkshire Inquisitions of the Reigns of Henry III and Edward I*, vol. 1, ed. W. Brown, Yorkshire Archaeological and Topographical Association Record Series, 12 (1891), 152–3).

[147] The fullest account of the legislation and its impact on the Church is Raban, *Mortmain Legislation*.

popularity of an individual community or of the relationship between benefactor and house is misleading. Perhaps more seriously, the mortmain documents usually only record successful alienations, that is, grants that were ultimately made in spite of restrictions and the exaction of sometimes heavy fines. Raban convincingly demonstrated that though there was a marked decline in grants to church corporations before 1279 and that as far as gifts, though not sales, were concerned, 'the crown had chosen to lock the stable door long after the horse had bolted', nevertheless the Statute did curb and distort patterns of acquisition, particularly in the first two decades of the new controls. Purchases of property were first halted altogether and thereafter were never to assume their former importance.[148] After 1300 the crown did license, though sometimes with marked reluctance, the alienation of lands in mortmain, usually in return for a fee. The agrarian crises and then the economic stagnation experienced by many communities after the Black Death (and especially during the fifteenth century) prevented further expansion. In other words, mortmain legislation imposed a premature brake on acquisitions that would soon in any case have been restricted by economic factors. Hicks has recently suggested that even this interpretation of the depressing impact of legislation did not go far enough, for he argues that the cost of licences could be a major disincentive to potential benefactors, though it might not necessarily deter the religious as purchasers. Moreover, during the fifteenth century political reasons may account for the relative small number of licences granted. Those that were given perhaps indicate shifting levels of royal patronage rather than royal leniency or complacency.[149] Finally, evasion as well as manipulation of the Statute was possible, and successful evasion is hard to identify.

It remains to determine to what extent these general conclusions are true of Gilbertine houses and their landed acquisitions. Of all the priories founded before 1279 only two, Catley and Holland Bridge (which may by this time have been regarded as merely a cell of Sempringham), failed to make any recorded acquisitions under the Statute. Within the order there was a considerable disparity between a minority of wealthy priories headed by St Katherine's, Lincoln, and the remainder, none of whom received more than seven licences.[150] There is usually no corroborating evidence to

---

[148] Ibid., esp. 142, 188–92.

[149] M. Hicks, 'Chantries, Obits and Almshouses: The Hungerford Foundations, 1325–1478', in C. M. Barron and C. Harper-Bill (eds.), *The Church in Pre-Reformation Society* (Woodbridge, 1985), 138–41.

[150] St Katherine's received 22 specific licences, Sempringham, and Malton 13 each, Chicksands had 11, and Watton 10. In the case of three priories only one was received.

prove that all licences were followed by actual acquisitions, but in the absence of evidence to show that such acquisitions did not take place, it has been assumed that any licence did represent an increase in property.[151] It is surely significant that, with the exception of Chicksands, those priories making the most post-1279 acquisitions were by 1254 the wealthiest Gilbertine houses, and that they all, including Chicksands, comprised the wealthiest group of priories at the Dissolution.[152] It does not, of course, follow that the number of licences necessarily correlates with the size of the grants made. In 1318 St Katherine's received a licence to acquire a mere $1\frac{1}{2}$ acres in Barton-on-Humber: conversely Mattersey, which received only three specific licences, obtained under one licence in 1344, a messuage, $2\frac{1}{2}$ cottages, a mill, six bovates of arable, 20 acres of meadow, and annual rent of 13*s*. $1\frac{1}{2}d$.[153] Nevertheless, it remains true that the wealthier houses not only received, and paid for, more licences; they also acquired more land under them.

In general, the chronology of licence acquisitions by the priories follows that established by Raban. Sempringham and Chicksands procured a licence each in 1290 (somewhat earlier than the much larger houses of Spalding and Crowland); St Katherine's (1291), Newstead (1294), and Malton (1295) followed. Rather surprisingly, the wealthy priory of Watton did not receive a licence till 1300. The last priories to gain licences were Haverholme, which was allowed to appropriate the church of Thorp-by-Newark in 1348, and Nun Ormsby, which was similarly allowed the appropriation of Ludborough four years later. While overall demand for licences grew steadily after 1300 and peaked in the 1330s, by contrast the Gilbertine priories made the greater number of their acquisitions a little earlier, in the first decade of the century, when eighteen licences were granted, and in the second, when they received seventeen. Only fifteen were gained from 1320 to 1349, and a further fourteen during the following decade. It is difficult to explain this pattern in the light of national trends, but it may be that Gilbertine acquisitions after 1320 were depressed as a result of the economic crisis that many of their houses experienced at this time.

There was a further flurry of acquisitions at the end of the century, but only two of these seem to be a result of the tightening of the Statute in 1391, which, amongst other stipulations, closed the loophole whereby grantors could bypass the Statute by an enfeoffment to use.[154] It is always

[151] On this question see, in general, Raban, *Mortmain Legislation*, 153–4.
[152] W. E. Lunt, *The Valuation of Norwich* (Oxford, 1926), 518–19.
[153] *Cal. Pat. R. 1313–17*, 317, and *1343–5*, 308.
[154] Raban, *Mortmain Legislation*, 157.

difficult to positively identify such enfeoffments, but it seems that no more than seven were made for the benefit of Gilbertine houses, the first being licensed in 1336. In 1392 Thomas, vicar of St Martin's, Fincham, was allowed to grant 28 acres of marsh in Wolferton to Shouldham for the soul of Thomas, chaplain of Wolverton, whose feoffee he probably was, and in the same year four feoffees (or executors) of Walter de Kelby, . a leading merchant of Lincoln and formerly mayor and MP for the city, paid 20 marks to alienate messuages and shops in city parishes to St Katherine's to celebrate divine service in the priory church for Walter's soul.[155] The clearest example of a licensed enfeoffment, however, is the last known. This dates from 1407, when William Thirnyng, knight, and eight others paid £20 for licence to enfeoff Thomas la Warre, clerk, of 50 acres of meadow and 300 acres of pasture in Tirrington by Sixhills, and for him to grant the land to Sixhills to celebrate divine service for Thomas, and the souls of his parents and other benefactors.[156] By 1407, however, acquisitions by Gilbertine houses were to all extents and purposes at an end. Indeed, this was the last, but for an isolated grant by Sir Thomas Burgh of messuages and land in Weston and Mattersey to Mattersey priory in 1480.[157]

It did not become standard practice for the crown to charge fines for licences until 1299; thereafter fines were normally exacted for the grant of specific licences, and these could represent a substantial additional cost for a religious house.[158] No fines were charged for any of the seven licences granted to Gilbertine houses before 1299; the first recorded were charged in June (to St Katherine's) and July (to Sempringham) in that year. It is impossible to correlate the fine demanded with the property acquired, but one thing is clear: appropriations were expensive. The largest fine paid by any priory was of £40 given by St Katherine's in 1314 for the appropriation of Stapleford; the following year Shouldham paid £26 13s. 4d. for the appropriation of Stanford. Returns, however, could be commensurably high. In 1291 Stapleford had been valued at £14 13s. 4d., Stanford at £13 6s. 8d. Malton paid £13 13s. 4d. in 1352 for the appropriation of Brompton: the Dissolution value of the rectory was £53 6s. 8d.[159]

---

[155] *Cal. Pat. R. 1391–6*, 113, 105; Hill, *Medieval Lincoln*, 249.

[156] *Cal. Pat. R. 1405–8*, 334. Thomas la Warre, a canon of Lincoln, was an 'honest broker' involved in land transfers to several Lincolnshire houses (Raban, *Mortmain Legislation* 122). In 1430 the earl of Northumberland and twelve others, together with the prior and convent, were pardoned (on payment of 40s.) for their acquisition of this land on a life lease from the priory (*Cal. Pat. R. 1429–36*, 65).

[157] *Cal. Pat. R. 1476–85*, 209.   [158] Raban, *Mortmain Legislation*, 23–5, 55–71.

[159] It should be pointed out, however, that the following year Marlborough paid the same sum for the appropriation of East Kennett, which was valued at only £4 in 1535.

On the other hand, licences appear to have been granted for some appropriations without fine. In 1310 Bullington was freely allowed to appropriate Ingham on condition that prayers were said for the salvation of the king and his ancestors and successors.[160] It may well be that the crown was prepared to forgo a fine if spiritual payment was proffered instead. In 1344 Shouldham was licensed to appropriate Fincham on condition that chantries were established for the good estate of Edward III, queen Philippa, and their children, and in 1399 Marlborough was pardoned its acquisition of various lands by grant of Sir John Lovell without licence on condition that prayers were offered for the king and queen.[161] Sempringham seems to have been particularly favoured or fortunate. In 1309 licence was freely given for the appropriation of the churches of Thurstanton and Norton Disney, and two years later similar licence was obtained for the appropriation of Whissendine.[162] The priory did have the advantage of powerful supporters. Henry de Beaumont, the priory's patron, was instrumental in obtaining the licence for Whissendine. It may also be that the crown felt under some obligation to the order, which was at this time caring for a number of children of the king's enemies. Certainly the crown allowed Sempringham a major acquisition of five messuages, three carucates of arable, and 22 acres of meadow in 1301 because the king had charged the priory with looking after Gwenllian, the daughter of Llywelyn ap Gruffudd.[163]

The difficulties and expense of gaining licences could be considerably reduced by the use of sponsors at court.[164] The help afforded Sempringham in 1309 by Henry de Beaumont has already been noted; in 1311 he acted on Sempringham's behalf again, and also aided St Andrew's, York, to acquire one of the largest estates the priory ever gained. Other great barons also lent their support. Henry de Lacy was instrumental in obtaining a licence for Alvingham to recover land of his own grant in 1303. Edmund de Mauley and Aylmer de Valence came to the aid of Bullington and Chicksands respectively in 1310 and 1317. Lesser lords could also help. Nicholas de Grey and William de Latimer helped Malton in 1316 and 1352, and a noted benefactor of Marlborough, the king's knight Sir John Lovell, did the same in 1383. Royal clerks could be as useful. Philip de Barton acted on Malton's behalf in 1346, and two years later *magister* Simon de Islip helped Haverholme gain the appropriation of Thorp.

---

[160] *Cal. Pat. R. 1307–13*, 294.

[161] *Cal. Pat. R. 1343–5*, 270; *1396–9*, 560. Alvingham appropriated Grainthorpe in 1352 without fine (ibid. *1350–4*, 360). [162] *Cal. Pat. R. 1307–13*, 157, 320.

[163] *Cal. Pat. R. 1301–7*, 6. [164] See Raban, *Mortmain Legislation*, 39, 61.

Simon, at this time a canon of Lincoln (he became archbishop of Canterbury a year later), was clearly of considerable influence at court and was active in support of several Lincolnshire houses including the cathedral and Thorney abbey.[165]

Licences to alienate were either specific or general. The latter allowed a community to acquire property to a stated annual value, though they did not prevent any acquisition under their terms being subject to the normal processes of inquiry, notably the *inquisitio ad quod dampnum*.[166] The majority of these licences were for the acquisition of relatively small sums, and this is certainly the case where these licences were received by Gilbertine houses. The most generous were granted to Bullington (1310) and St Katherine's (1316), allowing property valued at up to 40 marks per annum, but the great majority of the twelve recorded were for sums of £10 or less. With the exception of Marlborough, which paid £10 for a £10 general licence in 1409, all were granted between 1310 and 1346 and were freely given. Their most interesting feature is that they were seldom completely taken up: and when they were a considerable length of time had usually elapsed since they were first granted. Malton, granted a £10 licence in 1346, does not seem to have employed it until 1381; it was used up in 1387. Watton received two licences. The first (granted in 1331) was only fully used in 1402; the second (of 1335) was exhausted in 1347. The most extreme cases of non-use are Ellerton and Mattersey. The former was granted a general licence in 1331, which does not seem to have been used at all. Mattersey received a £10 licence in 1344. Some land was acquired under this licence the same year, but it was not used again till 1480, when an additional £5 was paid for the accession. This would suggest that though the will to acquire property was still strong, it was no longer possible for these small communities to attract benefactions.

There is little evidence that Gilbertine houses endeavoured to evade mortmain legislation. Where confiscations and pardons are recorded, they seem to have been the results of misunderstandings and technical breaches of the law. Alvingham ran into difficulties, which took a generation to resolve, over property acquired in Alvingham, Yarborough, and Grainthorpe just at the time the Statute was promulgated. There was general uncertainty whether the grants had preceded or followed the Statute. The priory was finally pardoned in 1327 in return for a twenty-shilling fine. That year also saw the pardon of St Katherine's, Lincoln, and Sixhills

---

[165] Ibid. 122.   [166] Ibid. 41–55, 63–71.

for entering upon property before the inquisition *ad quod damnum* had been returned to chancery and before licences had been issued.[167]

It is now generally agreed that mortmain legislation was 'more than a bureaucratic inconvenience' for even the wealthier abbeys.[168] Costs of acquisition were prohibitive in most circumstances. The possession of general licences to alienate may have lessened the Statute's impact, but, as has been shown, few of these licences granted to the Gilbertines were ever fully used up, suggesting that in their case the legislation was largely irrelevant. By the end of the thirteenth century the Gilbertine estates had reached what was to all intents and purposes their maximum extent.

All the evidence indicates that the Gilbertine priories were, like their Augustinian cousins, local houses for local men and women. They had put down deep roots in their immediate neighbourhoods, where they controlled much landed property as well as many parish churches, but, with few exceptions, they had no wider influence.[169]

---

[167] Ibid. 76–7 (Alvingham), 50 (Lincoln and Sixhills). Both the latter houses had already received general licences. For the problems encountered by Shouldham when it tried to appropriate Caister church irregularly, see ibid. 51–2.   [168] Ibid. 186.

[169] The distribution of Augustinian estates is discussed by D. M. Robinson, *The Geography of Augustinian Settlement*, 2 vols., British Archaeological Association Reports, 80 (1980), i. 308–33, where it is demonstrated that over 50% of all manors, nearly 70% of all recorded granges, and almost 75% of other lands valued at £5 or over lay within 10 miles of any individual Augustinian house.

6

Benefits and Benefactors

Patrons and Benefactors

No religious order, however world-forsaking, could afford to cut itself off
entirely from secular society and influence. Every house needed a protector and defender of its interests. Just as a vassal expected support, as well
as a fee, from his lord in return for military service, so the eleemosynary
tenant would expect protection from the benefactor. But when discussing
the nature of this reciprocal relationship a problem of definition is immediately encountered. Strictly speaking, the term 'patron' should be applied only to the founder and his/her family and successors, and perhaps
in some cases to the founder's own lord, whose consent was necessary to
the alienation of his tenant's estates.[1] However, the term can also be used
in a non-technical sense to indicate those particular benefactors who
enjoyed a special relationship with a community, as evidenced, for example, by the grant of confraternity, burial rights, or corrodies. So, W.,
prior of Malton, appointed a perpetual chaplain in the priory to celebrate
for the soul of John Mansel, once provost of Beverley, 'our special patron
and helper', in recognition of all the good work done by John for the
community.[2] Such supporters were normally, and hardly surprisingly,
among the more generous benefactors to the priory.[3] In order to avoid
ambiguity in the discussion that follows, the use of the term 'patron' will
be confined to the founder and his kin.

Occasionally there are references to 'advocates' of Gilbertine houses.

---

[1] S. Wood, *English Monasteries and their Patrons in the Thirteenth Century* (Oxford, 1955),
passim. The identity of patron and founder is sometimes made explicit, for example, in the
late-15th-century visitations of the Premonstratensian abbeys where the 'fundator sive
patronus' of each community is listed (*Collectanea Anglo-Premonstratensia*, ed. F. A. Gasquet,
Camden Society, 3rd ser. 10 (1906), ii. 3).

[2] 'speciali patrono et adiutori nostro.' London, BL, MS Cotton Claudius D XI, fo. 267ᵛ.
On his death he was to receive the same rites as for a prior of the house. W. is either
William, prior in the late 1220s and early 1230s, or the mid-13th-century William of
Ancaster.

[3] Alexander fitzOsbert and Nigel his son were styled *fundatores* of the grange of Fulbeck,
which belonged to Sempringham, and received benefits commensurate with that status
(*Sempringham Charters*, xv. 222).

The meaning of this term varied according to the time and place of its usage, but in post-Conquest England it was normally synonymous with 'patron'. Though the original meaning of a lay protector inside and outside courts of law still persisted, and a distinction between 'patron' (i.e. the founder) and 'advocate' (i.e. the defender) was still drawn by canon lawyers in the thirteenth century, and though in some few instances the appellation 'advocate' was primarily applied to a person who could be vouched to warranty by the community, it was normally understood that the specific legal functions of the advocate would be subsumed in the general obligations of the patron.[4] In the late twelfth century we find Lambert de Scoteni giving land to Alvingham 'with my wife Sibyl whom the nuns agreed to receive as a nun in their community when it pleased them as their lady and advocate'. The de Scoteni family had been primarily responsible for the foundation of Alvingham; it was natural that Sibyl be regarded as 'advocate'.[5] About a century later the earl of Richmond was described as 'patron and special advocate' of Alvingham. Though the earls of Richmond were not themselves notable benefactors of Alvingham, they were lords of Gayton soke, in which the priory lay. As chief lords their goodwill was a useful asset for the priory.[6]

Patronal rights and responsibilities were not absolute but relative: there is a sliding scale of patronal authority that was determined by a number of criteria, such as the power (and piety) of the founder, the size and prestige of the community, the nature of the order, and so on. The degree of control exercised by lay founders and benefactors over the Gilbertines was extremely limited when compared with the interference some Benedictine abbeys, in particular, had to endure from their patrons. There is, for example, no evidence that any Gilbertine patron ever attempted to establish any claim to the custody of a priory during a vacancy or actively participated in the election of a prior.[7] The freedom of the order from all kinds of outside control was exceptional. Since it was itself responsible for its internal discipline, bishops, as well as lay patrons, were excluded

---

[4] For the interchangeability of the terms see Wood, *English Monasteries*, 8, 16–21. See also Wardrop, *Fountains Abbey*, 139.

[5] 'sicut dominam et advocatam.' Oxford, Bodl. Lib., MS Laud Misc. 642, fo. 60. Lambert's father had been instrumental in the priory's foundation.

[6] Ibid., fo. 42. The grant of confraternity rights to John is described below, p. 328. In 1251 Agnes de Percy was styled advocate of Malton (London, BL, MS Cotton Claudius, D XI, fo. 267ᵛ).

[7] Though Aldulf de Brachy clearly intended to have a say in the appointment of the prior of his Gilbertine foundation in Normandy when he stipulated that his approval was necessary, and that no other 'advocatus' should be involved (London, BL, MS Cotton Claudius D XI, fo. 217).

from interfering in the priories' affairs and the Master was, to all intents and purposes, omnipotent in the administration of his order.[8] However, it is misleading to argue that the Gilbertines 'did not recognize any patrons at all'.[9] There are enough indications to suggest that in most cases the larger Gilbertine houses acknowledged a patron. The clearest evidence comes from Sempringham itself. Sempringham lay in the honour of Folkingham. When in 1307 Edward II granted the manors of Folkingham and Edenham to his second cousin, Henry de Beaumont, the latter assumed the role of patron previously held by the de Gants.[10] On his death in 1339/40 Henry de Beaumont was said to have held the advowson of the priory, and that he took his responsibilities seriously is demonstrated by the fact that shortly after acquiring the lordship of Folkingham he used his influence at court to obtain licence for the priory's acquisition of lands in mortmain.[11] But the clearest evidence that lay patronage of Sempringham was vested in the Beaumont family comes in 1397. At that time John, lord Beaumont, had just died and his son and heir, Henry, was a royal ward. In consequence, and more especially because of dissension within the order, the priory 'being of the patronage of Henry' was taken into the king's custody and committed to the care of a consortium headed by John of Gaunt.[12]

Sempringham was not alone in having a patron. In 1299 seisin of the advowson of the hospital [*sic*] of Shouldham, founded by Geoffrey fitzPeter, was granted to Maud de Beauchamp, countess of Warwick, who had inherited the possessions of Geoffrey. Over a hundred years later Margery, the widow of Thomas Beauchamp, earl of Warwick, was similarly allowed to have livery of the advowson.[13] The earls of Warwick maintained very

---

[8] The diocesan bishop was, however, involved in the election of the Master, and for an example of an 'unofficial' episcopal interference see below, p. 316.

[9] Wood, *English Monasteries*, 4.

[10] *Cal. Cl. R. 1307–13*, 2. On Gilbert V de Ghent's death in 1298 the barony had been divided between three heiresses, but the aforesaid manors were granted by Edward I to John de St John. On the latter's death in 1303 the king assigned them to Sempringham priory for seven years at an annual rent of £150 (Sanders, *English Baronies*, 46; *Cal. Pat. R. 1301–7*, 105).

[11] *Cal. Inq. P. m.* viii, 195; *Cal. Pat. R. 1307–13*, 195, 320. See also ibid. *1343–5*, 45–6, for royal confirmations in favour of the priory granted at the request of Henry and Eleanor de Beaumont. In a deed of Lindores abbey Henry is specifically described as patron of Sempringham (ibid. 45).

[12] Less than a month later, however, the crisis was over, and the commission was revoked on 28 January 1397 (*Cal. Pat. R. 1396–9*, 50–1, 59). Later Beaumonts made generous bequests to the priory, and between 1441 and 1460 a special office was even presented for John, viscount Beaumont (*The Gilbertine Rite*, i. 64, where the recipient is wrongly identified as John, viscount Beaumont, d. 1396 (i, p. xxiv)).

[13] *Cal. Cl. R. 1296–1302*, 287; ibid. *1402–5*, 75. See also ibid. *1405–9*, 184. At least twice

close ties with the priory during the fourteenth century, making bequests
to Shouldham, where several female members of the family were nuns; it
is hard to believe that references to possession of the advowson are the
result of jurors' mistaken assumptions. Whatever the theory of the
Gilbertine Rule, and though possession of the advowson brought no
material advantage, the earls of Warwick clearly believed that they had
rights in the priory, and were prepared to exercise them.[14]

Royal patronage

Perhaps more than any other, the Gilbertine order was under the direct
protection of the crown. The king alone amongst the laity was permitted
by the Rule to be met in procession, an honour which canon law granted
to the *patronus*.[15] In this sense, therefore, the king could be regarded as
the order's paramount patron. Such support could be vitally important,
as it was, for example, during the Interdict, when in 1208 king John
allowed the Master of the order to hold all lands and possessions which
had been taken into the king's hands.[16] Gilbert was an Angevin saint *par
excellence* who had enjoyed the favour and the friendship of Henry II.
Though only two houses, Newstead and Marlborough, were royal foundations, successive kings from Henry II onwards regarded the order as
under their special protection. In a famous passage in the *Vita*, Henry is
said to have exclaimed on hearing of Gilbert's death: 'Truly I realize now
that he has departed this life, for these misfortunes [i.e. his sons' rebel-
lion] have befallen me just because he no longer lives.'[17] Even when the
Gilbertines supported Becket and enabled his escape to France after the
Council of Northampton, Henry had personally intervened to protect
Gilbert from harassment by the royal justices.[18] Later the king was to play
a crucial role in the resolution of the lay brothers' revolt, twice writing to
the pope on Gilbert's behalf. In the second, stronger letter he had threatened to withdraw the grants made to the order by himself and his barons

in the 14th century the earl of Warwick was given licence to enfeoff tenants with property
including the advowson of the priory (*Cal. Pat. R. 1340–3*, 516, and ibid. *1361–4*, 48). In
1358 Thomas de Seymour was said to have the advowson of Poulton, but this was a very
small foundation that should perhaps be considered primarily as a chantry foundation (*Cal.
Inq. p. m.* x, no. 437, 346).

[14] See below, n. 41; Wood, *English Monasteries*, 5 and n. 8.   [15] Ibid. 4.
[16] Ibid. 98 n. 2; *Rotuli Litterarum Clausarum*, ed. T. D. Hardy, 2 vols., Record Commission (London, 1833), i. 112. This privilege followed a few days after the king had given the
custody of Shouldham priory to its founder, Geoffrey fitzPeter.
[17] *Book of St Gilbert*, 92. See above, pp. 53–4. During his lifetime Gilbert had been a
visitor at Henry's court, and according to the *Vita* had acted as spiritual adviser both to the
king and to queen Eleanor (*Book of St Gilbert*, p. 92).   [18] Ibid. 71–3.

unless the pope supported Gilbert against the villeins and lay brethren who were disrupting the established order. A patron, particularly one as powerful as Henry, could take as well as give.[19]

The fullest collection of royal privileges is contained in the Malton cartulary.[20] Six of these were issued by Henry II. The first, which is probably the earliest general confirmation charter for the order to survive, dates from between 1155 and 1162. One of the most important privileges obtained was the right of free election of the Master by the communities, while the care of the order's property during the vacancy was given to the prior of Sempringham. This was a privilege not unique to the Gilbertines (Henry had made a similar concession to the Premonstratensian house of Newstead, for example) but it did constitute a valuable freedom.[21] Henry also gave the even more important privilege that the canons were only to sue or to be sued in the royal courts. Other charters followed, some repeating the privileges, others granting specific protections, as of the orders' animals, or freedoms, such as quittance of all tolls in all towns in England and Normandy.[22] Some related only to an individual priory, as when Henry intervened in a dispute between Malton and Rievaulx concerning pasture rights near Pickering in 1175.[23]

Just as the Angevin establishment had rallied round in solidarity at the time of the rebellion, so it now came to support the campaign for Gilbert's canonization. King John himself visited Sempringham with his court in January 1201, and two months later wrote (admittedly in a cursory manner) to the pope adding his support for the canonization.[24] Both Richard and John confirmed the privileges granted by their father to the order.[25] Henry III also issued charters in the order's favour, and in 1228 the Master of the order is found addressing a letter to the king as *speciali advocato sub Deo.*[26]

A royal patron, like any other, sometimes required reward for support. The king might, for example, demand a corrody for a retired servant, or he might use a Gilbertine priory as a suitable depository for the daughter

---

[19] Ibid. 142–4, 161–3.   [20] London, BL. MS Cotton Claudius D XI, fos. 30–3.
[21] See Colvin, *The White Canons*, 292–3.
[22] London, BL, MS Cotton Claudius D XI, fo. 30. See also Oxford, Bodl. Lib., MS Laud Misc. 642, fo. 168.   [23] London, BL, MS Cotton Claudius D XI, fo. 31.
[24] *The Book of St Gilbert*, 170, 214.
[25] John also confirmed the lands of Malton held in the royal forest of Pickering (London, BL, MS Cotton Claudius D XI, fos. 30ᵛ–32ᵛ; *Cartae Antiquae, Rolls 1–10*, ed. L. Landon, PRS, NS 17 (1939), 31–3).
[26] *Cal. Cl. R. 1227–31*, 117. Henry was a particular supporter of Marlborough priory, a royal foundation.

or widow of an enemy. The crown might also expect to obtain a place for a nominee in the priory. A rare surviving draft letter from Edward I to the sheriff of Bedford, which can probably be dated to 1274, refers to the 'ancient and approved custom' whereby each queen of England on her accession had the right to nominate a nun to every nunnery in the realm. Estagra de Chanceus had been presented to Chicksands, but though letters had twice been written the priory had refused to accept her. As a result the sheriff was urged to attempt persuasion once more, and then to compel the priory to receive her by distraint.[27] Clearly such demands excited opposition, just as did the reception of royal corrodians. We do not know the outcome of this incident, and it is the only indication that the Gilbertines were burdened with this type of request. Though it was not unknown for the king to use his influence to nominate a nun—for example, Edward I wrote to Romsey nunnery in 1294—such requests were usually directed at the older, wealthier nunneries of royal foundation on the occasion of the king's coronation. I have found no record of the general right claimed in 1274, and it would seem that the king, or perhaps more likely the queen, who was notorious amongst contemporaries both for her piety and her high-handedness, was claiming a privilege for which she had no justification.

The bishop as patron

Three of the early Gilbertine priories were founded by bishops of Lincoln: Haverholme by Alexander, and St Katherine's, Lincoln and Clattercote by Robert de Chesney. Only one of these priories, however, was a double house.[28] In general, comparatively few post-Conquest nunneries were episcopal foundations. None of the non-Gilbertine nunneries in Lincolnshire were, while in Yorkshire there was only one: Clementhorpe, founded by archbishop Thurstan between 1125 and 1133.[29] Yet the role of the bishop in the support of these institutions remained important. First, episcopal patronage, however limited, encouraged others to follow

---

[27] PRO SC 1/30/49.

[28] Though Clattercote originally functioned as a hospital for both male and female Gilbertines. Additionally, Robert de Chesney demised the bishop's mill at Sleaford to the nuns of Sempringham for 40s. per annum (*English Episcopal Acta. I*, 153–40). Other churchmen also founded Gilbertine houses: St Andrew's, York was a foundation of Hugh Murdac, archdeacon of Cleveland, and the small community of Fordham was established by Henry the dean.

[29] For Yorkshire, see Burton, *Yorkshire Nunneries*, 18. For a general interpretation of the episcopal role in the foundation and support of English nunneries, see Thompson, *Women Religious*, 191–210.

the bishops' example, while the wide-ranging interests of a Thurstan or an Alexander ensured a considerable audience for their activities. Secondly, surviving charters make it very clear that diocesan bishops took their responsibilities to protect nunneries as well as monasteries very seriously. Their active involvement in issuing confirmation charters, which were often witnessed by leading lay figures of the region, may well have served to stimulate further benefactions.

It was, of course, normal practice for the bishop to oversee and confirm donations of churches to religious houses, but such confirmations were not restricted to grants of *spiritualia*. Sometimes grantors addressed their charters directly to the bishop, as did Ralf of Wyham when he gave property in Ormsby to the nuns there.[30] In this way it was surely hoped to add ecclesiastical to lay or royal authority against those who might make future claim to the land. Frequently grants were made and confirmed in the presence of the diocesan. Maurice de Craon gave lands to the nuns of Sixhills in the hands of bishop Robert de Chesney at his castle of Sleaford and in the presence of a number of other clerics, including the abbot of Vaudey and the cellarer of Kirkstead, as well as Gilbert of Sempringham himself.[31] These were undoubtedly solemn occasions, similar to that when Gilbert's own sister Agnes and her sons Roger and Hugh Musteil conveyed land in Sempringham and Billingborough to the community in the presence of bishop Robert.[32] Bishop Robert was also present on the occasion when Philip of Kyme granted the church of Ingham to Bullington priory, when the body of Philip's mother was translated to lie next to that of her husband in the nuns' chapter house.[33] It was at ceremonies such as these that the active participation of the bishop in the affairs of the community shows clearest.

Bishops did not only confirm grants at the request of the grantor: they also acted for the grantee, providing protection and support for the community. This is often spelt out in commonplace formulas similar to the analogous charters of privileges issued by the papacy. Sometimes the promise of spiritual rewards and the threat of ecclesiastical sanctions are made explicit. These are proclaimed most exhaustively in Alexander's foundation charter of Haverholme. All the faithful making benefactions

---

[30] *Gilbertine Charters*, 40.

[31] Ibid. 3–4. The presence of Gilbert might suggest that he was still a regular attender at the episcopal court. A complicated transaction whereby Matthew of Tealby granted land in Willingham to Sixhills was made in the chapter house at Lincoln in the presence of bishop Robert and many of his chapter (ibid. 14).   [32] *Sempringham Charters*, xv. 227.

[33] *Danelaw Charters*, no. 58, pp. 38–9.

to the new community or protecting it from evil-doers are received into the fraternity of the cathedral; all those who harm it are cursed with Judas, Simon Magus, and Dathan and Abiram.[34]

While Gilbertine priories were exempt from episcopal visitation, and hence were not subject to such direct control and care as was the case with most English nunneries, it was still the diocesan's responsibility to preserve their well-being, and it is likely that the canonical injunctions that bishops ensure that the number of nuns in a community did not exceed its resources were applicable to the Gilbertines, even though the order had its own regulations.[35] The Alvingham and Malton cartularies contain many charters indicating the involvement of these priories' diocesan bishops as protectors.[36] They included general confirmations of all property as well as charters confirming individual grants. Bishops also adjudicated in disputes between rival religious houses, as did bishop Robert de Chesney when he confirmed an agreement between Alvingham and the neighbouring 'Cistercian' nunnery of Legbourne concerning a disputed mill in Cockerington.[37] Finally, it was the bishop's responsibility to confirm a newly elected Master, though his actual control over the election was severely restricted and his consent amounted to little more than courtesy.[38] Occasionally a bishop might try to intervene more directly in the affairs of the order. In 1298 the archbishop of York, Henry of Newark, wrote to the priors of the order, describing himself as *nutritus* and *alumpnus* of the order and strongly recommending that they elect the prior of St Katherine's as their new Master.[39]

The founder as patron

If the king was the patron of the order, what of individual priories? Though the king could and did issue confirmation charters and privileges to specific communities (as Henry II did, for example, to Sixhills and St Katherine's, Lincoln), in the local context of each house there was a need for other, perhaps more accessible, supporters.[40] The nuns and canons

[34] *English Episcopal Acta. I*, 25.   [35] See e.g. *Councils and Synods II*, i. 123–4.

[36] Most of these are protections of the priories' *spiritualia*. See London, BL, MS Cotton Claudius D XI, fo. 209. The charters of Robert de Chesney in favour of Alvingham are conveniently printed in *English Episcopal Acta. I*, 43–7.   [37] Ibid. 45–6.

[38] *Reg. Gravesend*, 8–9; *Reg. Sutton*, i. 40–3, 230–4. Such consent was seemingly linked to confirmation of the order's *spiritualia*.

[39] Hamilton Thompson suggested that the archbishop had been educated at St Katherine's, and perhaps sent by the canons from there to the Gilbertine house at Cambridge (*Reg. Romeyn*, ii. 295–6, xxxvii and n., xlii).

[40] *Gilbertine Charters*, 35–8 (Sixhills); *Registrum Antiquissimum*, i. 121 (Lincoln). In both cases prayers were to be said for the king and his family.

required powerful neighbours to confirm their charters, and whom they could vouch to warranty; they needed advocates to plead their case in courts and to press for royal privileges and licences (such as those to alienate in mortmain). Sometimes they also needed physical protection from their local enemies and detractors. Such support was normally provided by the descendants of the founding family.[41] So John de Lacy, constable of Chester and descendant of the founder of Malton, wrote to W. de Rideford, his seneschal, and all his bailiffs in Lindsey ordering them to do all in their power to protect and defend the canons of Malton, 'scientes nos habere illos de cetero specialiter commendatos'.[42]

Foundation charters of the early Gilbertine priories make it clear that these communities were established above all to provide prayers for the souls of the founder and his kin. Eustace fitzJohn founded Malton 'wishing to provide for the salvation of my soul, and those of my wife, children and parents' and Watton 'for the souls of our fathers and mothers, sons and daughters, brothers and sisters and our friends'.[43] Catley was founded by Peter of Billinghay 'for the souls of my ancestors and heirs'; Bullington for 'the salvation of the soul of Simon son of William, of Agnes my wife and of all my ancestors', while Nun Ormsby was founded by Gilbert of Ormsby 'for the salvation of my soul and of all my kin living and dead'.[44] Payn de Beauchamp founded Chicksands and expected prayers for his family, and made specific mention for the soul of Simon de Beauchamp, his uncle.[45] Some foundations were made for the benefit of a wider clientele. Alexander, bishop of Lincoln, stated that he had founded Haverholme 'for the comfort and profit of our mother church, and for ourselves and our friends and for the souls of king Henry [I] and my uncle Roger who was the bishop of Salisbury, and for the souls of my father and mother and my departed friends'.[46] Such a range of recipients of prayers is perhaps unusual at this date, and may be explained by the fact that Haverholme was an episcopal foundation. It seems to have taken longer for this expansion in the numbers for whom prayers were expected to spread to foundations by the laity. The wider scope of Gilbertine foundation charters is fully seen for the first time in the charter of Henry II establishing Newstead early in the 1170s. This was made for 'the salvation of my soul and queen Eleanor and my heirs, and all faithful

---

[41] As late as 1401 the earls of Warwick were described as having the *advocatia* of Shouldham priory (*Cal. Inq. p. m.* xviii, no. 500, 141).

[42] London, BL, MS Cotton Claudius D XI, fo. 209.   [43] *Monasticon*, vi. 2. 955, 970.

[44] *Gilbertine Charters*, 72 (Catley), 91 (Bullington), 39 (Nun Ormsby).

[45] *Monasticon*, vi. 2. 950.   [46] Ibid. 948–9.

kings who are to come after me and for the good estate of my kingdom and for the souls of king Henry my grandfather and Geoffrey my father and all my ancestors'.[47]

The two Gilbertine houses founded at the end of the twelfth and the beginning of the thirteenth century were also expected to pray for the soul of the king, which is perhaps a recognition that after the deaths of Gilbert and Henry II there could no longer be so close a personal bond between the crown and the order, and that it was now necessary to purchase royal support more overtly. Shouldham was founded for 'the soul of my lord Henry king of England, and for the soul of Beatrix de Say my wife with her body, and for the souls of my father and mother, and for my own soul with my body if I die in the kingdom of England, and for the souls of all my ancestors and successors, and for the salvation of my lord king Richard, and of my own and of my heirs': the order of priority should be noted.[48] A similar order is found in the foundation charter of Ellerton issued by William son of Peter 'for the salvation of our lord John, most illustrious king of England, and that of our reverend father Geoffrey by the grace of God archbishop of York and that of Sir Robert of Turnham [king's steward and William's lord], of Geoffrey [fitzPeter] earl of Essex and of Alan of Wilton [Robert of Turnham's steward] and Mary his wife [a kinswoman of the founder], and for the salvation of my soul and Alice my wife and my lords, friends and men and of all those who will maintain this my gift, and for the souls of my lords Henry and Richard, kings of England, and of Peter my father and Christiana my mother and Hugh Murdac [the founder of St Andrew's, York] and of all my predecessors and ancestors'.[49] Ellerton was the last Gilbertine house of any size to be founded before the mid-fourteenth century: in the roll-call of those for whose spiritual benefit the community was founded we see the natural and political 'extended family' of the founder displayed. To make the foundation on behalf of the souls of so many was an act both charitable and prudential, for it helped to establish ties between the priory and men of influence whose support was so necessary for its well-being.

It is rare for a charter to spell out the motivation, other than the desire for spiritual benefits, and process by which a benefaction was conveyed.

---

[47] Ibid. 966. This phraseology is similar to that of the king's confirmation charter in favour of St Katherine's, Lincoln, made 'for the souls of king Henry my grandfather, Matilda the empress my mother, for my salvation and that of queen Eleanor and my heirs and for the good estate of my kingdom' (ibid. 969).   [48] Ibid. 974.
[49] Ibid. 976.

Ironically, the clearest account relating to a Gilbertine foundation concerns the unsuccessful plantation at Dalmilling (Ayrshire). In a letter dated between 1219 and 1228 and addressed to Robert, Master of the order, Walter fitzAlan states that he proposes to found a Gilbertine house at his own cost for the safety of his soul and that of his ancestors and successors, and for the increase of religion and the salvation of souls, 'realizing that there is no zeal to be compared with that for souls'. Walter then goes on to describe in some detail what he proposes to give. This letter was sent to the Master by the hand of Nicholas, prior of Sixhills, with whom Walter had discussed his plan, and it closed with a request for an early reply to his proposal. Here, then, we have a rare glimpse of the negotiations which preceded a foundation, fleshing out the bare bones of a foundation charter.[50]

The foundation of a religious community operated on two levels. On the one hand it represented an individual, and reciprocal, relationship between the founder and his/her foundation; on the other, the ties so established were expected to last, binding the community and the founder's descendants through the generations in a never-ending symbiotic alliance. There was inevitably tension between these two aspects since each succeeding generation wished in turn to insure its soul: tastes changed, there were new fashions in religious giving, and the loyalty of a family to a foundation of an increasingly distant ancestor could not be assured.[51]

This does not, of course, mean that on occasion these links could not last for many generations. In some cases their echoes continued to be heard in the sixteenth century. Newstead was still making an annual payment of £1 14s. 8d. in alms for the poor for the souls of its founders Henry II and John in 1535, and on 1 April 1542 John Aske of Aughton exchanged lands in Sussex with the crown for Ellerton priory and its

---

[50] The letter is printed in Barrow, 'The Gilbertine House at Dalmilling', 58–9. There is, however, some evidence from contemporary charters relating to non-Gilbertine foundations to suggest that discussions were not unknown: indeed, it is reasonable to suppose that they were standard procedure. Roger de Mowbray gave churches to Kenilworth priory 'by the counsel and care' ('consilio et industria') of prior Bernard (*Charters of the Honour of Mowbray*, 127).

[51] There is now a copious literature on changing patterns of religious endowments, but three recent and illuminating studies approaching this question from differing perspectives are J. Ward, 'Fashions in Monastic Endowment: The Foundations of the Clare Family, 1066–1314', *JEH* 32 (1981), 429–51; M. G. A. Vale, *Piety, Charity and Literacy among the Yorkshire Gentry, 1370–1480*, Borthwick Papers, 50 (York, 1976); and N. Saul, 'The Religious Sympathies of the Gentry in Gloucestershire, 1200–1500', *Transactions of the Bristol and Gloucester Archaeological Society*, 98 (1980), 99–112. For an example of the bitterness that a shift in monastic patronage could occasion, see below, pp. 368–70.

estates, along with other properties belonging to Yorkshire houses.[52] John's family lands of Aughton adjoined those of Ellerton, but as strong a motive for the acquisition of the priory was the fact that his family and predecessors had been for generations benefactors and supporters of the house. Like many other gentry and magnate families, the Askes were concerned that the Dissolution had destroyed a religious community with which they had for so long been associated, and where their ancestors had found burial.[53] The priory of Ellerton had been founded at the beginning of the thirteenth century by William son of Peter of Goodmanham.[54] He seems to have died without issue. Some of his lands passed to his nephew, some to his sister Alice, the wife of Adam de Linton, and some to the Hay family, who inherited the function of patron of Ellerton from William. The Hays of Aughton in turn died out and their property passed (probably early in the fifteenth century) to a cadet branch of the Aske family.[55] All of these families played an active role in the priory's affairs, and the office of patron was passed from family to family with their estates. Such evidence for the survival of a patronal relationship for so long is rare. Nevertheless, this does not mean that it did not exist: records relating to the Gilbertine priories in the late Middle Ages are so exiguous as to make this sort of evidence unusual.

However, the relationship between patron and house could be soured. Patrons of Gilbertine houses might expect rights of hospitality, and they might literally outstay their welcome. In April 1272 the king wrote to the sheriff of York after the order had complained that, contrary to its statutes that secular women were not to remain in a Gilbertine house for longer than three nights without special licence of the Master, Agnes de Vesci had imposed herself on the community at Watton with 'a great crowd of women with dogs and other animals' to the impeding of the religious life there. In his own capacity as protector and defender of the order, the king ordered the sheriff to go in person to Agnes to warn her

---

[52] *VE* iv. 71. Aske's lands also included the site of the nunnery of Thicket (*Calendar of Letters and Papers, Foreign and Domestic, of the Reign of Henry VIII*, ed. J. S. Brewer *et al.*, 23 vols. in 38, HMSO (London, 1862–1932), xvii, no. 283.8).

[53] Margaret Aske was buried in Ellerton in 1465 and her son, Sir John Aske, in 1497. His sister was a nun at Watton (*Testamenta Eboracensia*, ed. J. Raine, Surtees Society, 53 (1869) iv. 89, 123). Cf. Richard Zouch's request to Cromwell for the priory of Stavordale, 'a foundation of my ancestors', or the plea of lord de la Warre for the priory of Boxgrove 'whereof I am founder, and there lieth many of my ancestors', and asking that this house where he had 'made a poor chapel to be buried in' be not suppressed (T. Wright, *Letters relating to the Suppression of Monasteries*, Camden Society, 26 (1843), 51, 119–20). Many similar cases could be cited. [54] *EYC* ii, no. 1133.

[55] Clay (ed.), *Early Yorkshire Families*, 42.

to leave lest further action be taken against her.[56] In times of political unrest a patron might attempt to interfere in the internal affairs of the religious. This seems to have happened at Chicksands in 1223. In that year Fawkes de Breauté came to the royal court demanding that the prior of Chicksands should return to him his ward Margaret, the daughter of Ralph son of William, whom he claimed he had committed to the nuns' care. The prior responded that she had been in the nunnery, but that William de Beauchamp (*advocatus suus*) had come and taken the girl away uninvited and without the prior's knowledge. William was ordered to attend court and explain himself. In his testimony he stated that Ralph had been his tenant and had died before the civil war broke out. William had then received Margaret and her sister and given their wardship to one of his knights, who looked after them till the outbreak of war. Then William had been disseised of his lands and Fawkes, his supplanter, had taken the girls, placing Margaret in Chicksands. When the war was over and William recovered seisin he came to the priory, where Margaret revealed herself as his tenant's heir, claiming that Fawkes had wished to make her a nun against her wishes. According to William, she left the priory of her own free will and came to his house, where she was married to one of his free men in the presence of the prior. Here we see the two rivals for political power in Bedfordshire during the civil war jockeying for power in a local cloister.[57]

The relationship between Gilbertine priory and patron was primarily spiritual. Its nature is summed up in a statement of 1297/8, when the advowson of Shouldham was said to be 'worth nothing save in the prayers and alms that are done in that house'.[58] Just occasionally there are hints of other, more mundane services. A community might witness charters issued by its patron in favour of another house, and at Malton the canons looked after the family papers of the de Vescis.[59] Generally, however, patrons looked for their rewards in the next world, not this, though normally rights of burial, confraternity, and perhaps the obligation of the priory to receive a member of the patron's family into the community

---

[56] Oxford, Bodl. Lib., MS Laud Misc. 642, fo. 36ᴿ⁻ᵛ. The king also wrote in similar vein to Agnes herself. Agnes had never been a friend of the Gilbertines, either at Watton or Malton.   [57] *CRR* xi, nos. 231, 1022, 1626.

[58] Cited in Wood, *English Monasteries*, 14 n. 2.

[59] Towards the end of the 12th century, Thomas, prior of Nun Ormsby, together with two canons of Malton, was amongst the witnesses to a grant in favour of the nuns of Yeddingham by Ralph de Clere, who had earlier granted the church of Ludborough to Ormsby (*EYC* i. 468, 481). For Malton and the Vescis, see *Calendar of Patent Rolls, 1317–21*, 445.

would be assumed.[60] They expected certain privileges from their priories, the provision of specific spiritual benefits, such as the commemoration of their anniversaries or the grant of rights of confraternity, that were not always vouchsafed to other benefactors. Nevertheless, many benefactors, who were not 'patrons' in the particular sense of the word, did obtain similar benefits, and in this way were brought more closely into the community. As *confratres* of the priories they too entered the Gilbertine brotherhood.

Benefits

Spiritual benefits

Any grant, including sales and grants of land for rent, presupposed a reciprocal relationship between the benefactor and the religious community. In return for the grant the benefactor would expect to receive spiritual benefits. This was the essence of eleemosynary tenure. Originally the term *elemosina* was used primarily to describe the charitable or pious nature of a grant rather than a type of tenure, and though from the mid-twelfth century it also bore judicial implications, the original meaning was never lost.[61] This definition was succinctly accepted by Robert Ses of Louth when, in the second quarter of the thirteenth century, he quitclaimed to Alvingham all his rights in a toft, pledging that no services 'nisi tamen orationes' would in future be exacted.[62] There does, indeed, seem to have been a feeling that a grant made absolutely free of temporal service brought commensurately greater spiritual rewards.[63] Prayers for

[60] The Rule also laid down the obligation to visit in their infirmity those who were bound to the order in ties of familiarity ('vinculo familiaritatis') (*Monasticon*, vi. 2. xlii).

[61] The most recent study is B. Thompson. 'From "Alms" to "Spiritual Services": The Function and Status of Monastic Property in Medieval England', in *Monastic Studies 2: The Continuity of Tradition*, ed. J. Loades (Bangor, 1990), 227–62. See also F. Pollock and F. W. Maitland, *The History of English Law*, 2 vols. (2nd edn., Cambridge, 1968), i. 240–51; E. Kimball, in 'Tenure in Frank Almoign and Secular Services', *EHR* 43 (1928), 314–53, and 'The Judicial Aspects of Frank Almoign Tenure', *EHR* 47 (1932), 1–11; A. Nichol, 'Changes in the Assize Utrum between the Constitutions of Clarendon and Bracton', in R. F. Hunnisett and J. B. Post (eds.), *Medieval Legal Records edited in Memory of C. A. F. Meekings*, HMSO (London, 1978), 18–25. Bracton's own views can be found most clearly in *Bracton's Notebook*, ed. F. W. Maitland (Cambridge, 1887), ii. 20–1. I have discussed this matter in a Gilbertine context in Golding, 'Gilbertine Priories', 94–109.

[62] Oxford, Bodl. Lib., MS Laud Misc. 642, fo. 127.

[63] Property was granted to Sixhills 'retaining no earthly profit . . . that it may more abundantly profit our souls in the future' (*Gilbertine Charters*, 13).

the founder and benefactors and their families were, as we have already seen, services incumbent upon all religious houses, however much they were exempt from secular control. In 1285 non-performance of such services was recognized as a valid reason for the resumption of the land into the demesne of the founder or his descendants. The second Statute of Westminster clearly stated that both the king and other lords could recover land given to a religious house if alienated by that house, since such an alienation was contrary to the form of the grant in free alms. Similarly, if land was given for a charity, almsgiving, lights, etc., and these services were not performed for two years, the land might be taken back.[64] This Statute translated into legal terms the essence of the relationship between patron and community. Prayers for the benefactor underpinned that relationship: if they were withdrawn the ties would be broken. Prayers were the cement binding together the lay and spiritual worlds: without them the structure would collapse.

Social, religious, and legal pressures to maintain this relationship were great, and not surprisingly there is no evidence that the Gilbertines were negligent in their responsibilities to their patrons.[65] Grants were made to procure the salvation of the benefactor and his family, and usually expressed this hope explicitly in standard formulas. One of the fullest of such expressions is contained in the charter of Ralph le Noreis, a minor benefactor of Sixhills, whose gift was made 'principally for the love of God and his holy mother Mary ever virgin, for the salvation of the souls of my father and my mother, of my own soul and my wife's, of my children and all my kin, and especially for the souls of Pagan my grandfather

[64] *Statutes of the Realm*, i. 91–2 [Stat. Westm. sec. c. 41]. See Thompson, 'From "Alms" to "Spiritual Services" ', 251–2.

[65] In 1403 the king's escheator was ordered to restore lands in North Dalton to Watton priory which had been taken into the king's hands because it was alleged that queen Matilda had given them in order that the priory find a chaplain to celebrate for her soul and those of her ancestors in North Dalton church. It was claimed that the terms of this grant, confirmed by Henry III and Richard I, were observed until 1386–7, when the service was withdrawn. In addition the queen had given sheep pasture in the village on condition that the community should toll a bell for 360 strokes every night at Vespers in the church or its belfry. This service, too, had been withdrawn for twenty years. Land had also been given to find a lamp to burn continually in the church: this service too had lapsed. The case is a strange one: if the grants were indeed confirmed by Henry III and Richard I (and no such confirmation charters have survived), then the donor-queen must be either Matilda, wife of king Stephen (d. 1152), or the Empress (d. 1167). No grant by either survives, nor is there any evidence that lands in North Dalton were ever held by them. It was perhaps for this reason that it seemed to the justices that the seizure of the property should be of none effect. Whatever the reasons for bringing the case, it is of interest chiefly in demonstrating that the payment of spiritual services was taken seriously and that non-performance could lead to distraint (*Cal. Cl. R. 1402–5*, 77).

and Emma his wife, and lastly for the souls of all their ancestors and my family'. He then expressed the wish that he, all his relatives, and kin would be made partakers of the good works performed by the community.[66] The on-going nature of the bargain was made explicit in another charter of Sixhills priory where the donor pledged that he and his heirs would warrant the grant forever 'that it may always avail for the salvation of our souls'.[67] Sometimes the donor named more distant relatives in his charter. In the third quarter of the twelfth century Philip of Kyme and his wife made a grant for the salvation of themselves, their children and friends, for the souls of their parents and ancestors, and for the soul of the countess Rohaise (mother of the wife of Philip's son and heir, and the widow of earl Gilbert de Gant).[68] This grant also desired salvation for the donor's friends. Such inclusion of friends is not unusual, while grants made for the salvation of all the faithful are frequent. Occasionally hope was also expressed for the salvation of the grantor's lord, an inclusion that probably indicates his confirmation of the grant.[69] Very occasionally the relationship between benefactions and forgiveness is spelt out. In the late twelfth century William of West Torrington gave land to Bullington in order to gain forgiveness 'for all the sins of himself and of Sigerthe his wife'.[70] An early charter in favour of Sixhills was made for the soul of the donor's brother 'that he might have pardon of all his sins in the life eternal', while another was made that the donor 'might earn a good reward from Christ his Lord in eternal life'.[71] Occasionally, too, the grants hint at earlier disputes over the property conveyed and a wish by the grantor to gain forgiveness for high-handed action. In the third quarter of the twelfth century Roger de Clere gave a quarter of the church of Fotherby of his fee to Nun Ormsby, indicating that he had acquired the fee by duel 'in the king's court at London' from Hugh de Twit and 'so I judged it necessary to give some part of the fee to the service of God' and for the salvation of himself and his family.[72] At about the same time, and probably between 1154 and 1172, Oliver, son of Oliver of Wendover, confirmed property that his father had granted in Glentworth 'for the soul of William son of Warin' to Catley. The charter ends: 'and through this gift and confirmation we are reconciled with all the kin of William son of Warin.' Another, and perhaps earlier, charter of Oliver also

---

[66] *Gilbertine Charters*, 33.   [67] Ibid. 1.
[68] London, BL, Addit. MS 6118, p. 72.   [69] See Golding, 'Gilbertine Priories', 333.
[70] 'pro omnibus excessibus meis et uxoris mee Sigerthe' (London, BL, Addit. MS 6118, p. 760).   [71] *Gilbertine Charters*, 3.
[72] Ibid. 43.

confirmed property in Glentworth granted by his father, and this confirmation, as well as the original grant, was made especially for the soul of William son of Warin. As Stenton commented, 'a story which has not been told lies behind a commonplace grant in alms'.[73] It is possible that the dispute had something to do with dowry rights, since one of Oliver's charters specifically states that the property was his wife's dower, and pledges to warrant it 'lest there should be any doubt' that it be so, and he goes on to promise that neither he, nor any one through him, would for gain or any other reason oppose the community, but would rather help and maintain them according to his power. In both these episodes we may detect another, more cynical motive for the grant than a need for expiation. These lands had been subject to dispute: if land was to be given to the religious, then the task of establishing rights to it could be left to the new holders.

Grants were, however, often made for more specific spiritual benefits than those normally expressed in standard formulas. These reveal closer links with the priories and a more personal association of the lay benefactor with the religious. Such benefits could take several forms: the reception of the donor or a member of his family into the priory as a nun or canon; the burial of a member of the family, or the promise of burial on the donor's death; the grant of confraternity rights, or the provision of sundry other benefits, rather more temporal than spiritual, such as corrodies or obits. Though for clarity confraternity, burial, anniversary, and obit rights will be discussed in separate sections, it must be remembered that such rights often overlapped with each other, and that too strict a division between the various types of benefits is potentially misleading concerning the nature of the relationships between benefactor and community. A charter of Brian of Pointon, an early benefactor of Sempringham, illustrates the point. In this one document Brian confirmed a number of earlier grants: unspecified property granted when the chapel of St Andrew was built at Sempringham; the half bovate given when Brian's brother Hugh joined the community; the *cultura* given with one of his daughters; the half acre of meadow and 12 acres of arable given with his other two daughters, and finally the half acre of land and pasture for 200 sheep granted when Brian and his wife were received into confraternity.[74]

Before turning to these rights in detail it is worth looking at the highly interesting charter of Alexander son of Osbert and Nigel his heir in favour of Sempringham, since it provides an insight rarely found in Gilbertine

[73] Ibid. 84–5, 86–7, pp. xxvii–xxviii.   [74] *Sempringham Charters*, xvi. 31.

sources not only into what was expected by a benefactor by way of spiritual benefits, but also into the process of the grant itself. Some time between 1150 and 1160 Alexander and Nigel gave 180 acres of arable and 20 acres of meadow in Fulbeck of their inheritance to the nuns of Sempringham in free alms. For this the nuns 'received father and son as brethren and participants in all their prayers and provided a place of burial in their *atrium* [?porch or cemetery] and a full [burial] service just as for one of the nuns as the founders of that grange in the fields of Fulbeck'. This grant was first made in the chapter of Haverholme priory in the presence of Gilbert, abbot of Swineshead (d. 1172). It was then repeated in the chapter of Lincoln cathedral in the presence of several cathedral dignitaries, Gilbert of Sempringham, Simon, *magister* of Stixwould, William, prior of Warter, and Hugh, prior of Sempringham. Next the grant was made in the chapter of Sempringham before another large group of witnesses, mostly drawn from the local knightly families. Then the party moved on to Cistercian Vaudey, whose monks were given Alexander's section of the chirograph recording the grant to look after. Finally (*deinde*) Alexander went to the grange of Fulbeck, where in the presence of many he assigned (and presumably delivered) seisin.[75]

Confraternity

Though all grants made in free alms gave the grantor a share in the prayers of the community, a grant of confraternity forged a closer link between the benefactor and the priory. It provided a no less real, though less dramatic, tie than did entry into the house. The names of monastic *confratres* were usually recited during mass in their lifetime, and prayers and masses were offered for them as for a member of the community at their death. Post-mortem provision might also include burial, the saying of anniversary masses, and the entry of the *confrater*'s name on the community's mortuary roll.[76] The Gilbertine Rule, though it prescribed detailed instructions for the relationship to be maintained between the cloister and the world, did not specifically mention *confratres*. It did state, however, that departed parents, brothers, sisters, and other close relatives

[75] Ibid. xv. 222.

[76] For confraternity in general, see Knowles, *Monastic Order*, 475–9; Colvin, *The White Canons*, 258–64; W. G. Clark-Maxwell, 'Some Letters of Confraternity', *Archaeologia*, 2nd ser. 25 (1926), 19–60, and 'Some Further Letters of Confraternity', *Archaeologia*, 2nd ser. 29 (1929), 179–216. Rights could be held in several monasteries. Alice de Gant, who chose to be buried at Sempringham, and who had, therefore, probably been granted confraternity, was also remembered at Fountains and York Minster (*Sempringham Charters*, xv. 33; *Charters of the Honour of Mowbray*, 101, 209).

of the brethren were to be remembered by name at the order's annual chapter and in each house of the order. They were also to be made partakers in all the benefits that the general chapter decided to perform for departed brethren, and a special office was to be performed for them upon the eve of St Edmund.[77] The Gilbertine Ordinal shows that upon that day prayers were specially said for parents, relatives, the order's friends, and all those particularly received by the community into their prayers.[78]

The precise nature of the benefits conveyed by a grant of confraternity in a Gilbertine house is never spelt out, and is hence difficult to ascertain. One of the earliest dated grants of confraternity was made by Robert, Master of the order, who in 1251, 'mindful of the devotion of our advocate (*advocate nostre*) Agnes de Percy, and at the fervent request of W., prior of Malton' (i.e. William of Ancaster), gave rights of confraternity and the privilege of burial to Agnes if she chose, promising that she would be treated with all honour as was done for a prior or prioress of the order, while her name was to be written in all the martyrologies of the order.[79] Two features of this agreement should be noted. First, the grant was made by the Master of the order rather than by the prior of Malton, whose patron Agnes was. This is the only case recorded amongst the Gilbertines where this occurred.[80] Secondly, the terms of the grant suggest that Agnes was to be honoured throughout the order; indeed, it may be for that reason that the Master's intervention was necessary. Reference to the universality of the confraternity is unusual, though it is also found in the case of the earl of Richmond discussed below, and such privileges may well have been confined to especial and noble benefactors of the order.[81] One reason why such general grants of confraternity seem to have

[77] This practice was closely modelled on the Cistercian custom (*Monasticon*, vi. 2. lv). It is not made clear whether the day of commemoration is Edmund the archbishop (16 November) or the martyr (20 November). See Clark-Maxwell, 'Some Letters of Confraternity', 29–30, for examples of various orders' commemoration of their *confratres*.

[78] *The Gilbertine Rite*, i. 87.

[79] London, BL, MS Cotton Claudius D XI, fo. 267ᵛ. It should be noted that a woman was not debarred from receiving confraternity in a house for canons only. Malton also received Maud de Rouelle 'in specialem sororem domus sue', and the canons promised to do for her 'sicut pro sorore sua sive viva sive defuncta' (*EYC* vi, no. 91, 192. For further grants by Maud to Malton, see ibid., no. 94 and 193 n.). For a similar grant of confraternity to a woman by the Cistercian monks of Fountains, see Wardrop, *Fountains Abbey*, 259.

[80] Though in 1379 the confraternity granted to Sir William Marmion by Sempringham priory was approved by the Master (London, BL, Addit. Chart. 20620).

[81] It is also worth noting that Agnes, as advocate or patron, might have expected to receive the benefits of confraternity without question. Agnes was hardly a model patron: was this grant at the prior's 'fervent request' an attempt to placate her? An even earlier grant

been comparatively rare may be that it was impossible for every house to commemorate every notable benefactor of every community: certainly this was a problem faced by the Premonstratensians, whose own obituaries became increasingly localized in scope.[82]

Another detailed confraternity grant was made at the end of the thirteenth century by R. of Richmond (probably Ralph, active in the last quarter of the thirteenth century), prior of Alvingham, to J., earl of Richmond (probably John of Brittany, earl from 1269 to 1305). The arrangements can perhaps be taken as typical of those for a *confrater*, at least for one of high status. In return for John's support of the house as 'a patron and special advocate', he was received into full confraternity and given the promise that when they heard of his death the canons would circulate his obit together with the schedule of benefits throughout the order. If he chose to be buried at Alvingham he would lie before the high altar, and would be ever remembered because his name would be written in all the canons' martyrologies. The earl was lord of Gayton soke in which the priory lay: it was thus important for the canons to favour him as the most important magnate in the area. In this case a grant of confraternity represented a reward for secular protection.[83]

It seems likely that a *confrater* would normally expect to receive right of burial within the community. A grant of confraternity, typical of several others, in which Ralph, son of Tamar of Cawthorpe, was received with his wife into the fraternity of Alvingham in order that the canons should perform for them at death 'exactly as was done for brethren of the house', suggests that this right was a normal feature, though the case of the earl of Richmond suggests that it was up to the *confrater* whether he chose to take up the option.[84] Confraternity might also precede a benefactor

of confraternity with the whole order was made to Godwin the Rich of Lincoln, founder of the small priory of Holland Bridge *c*.1199, who, with his wife Alice, was received into confraternity by Gilbert of Sempringham himself ('Gilbertus et conventus susceperunt nos in plenam fraternitatem ordinis sui per omnia tam vivos quam mortuos' (*Sempringham Charters*, xv. 159). Confraternity with the Premonstratensian order, as distinct from that with an individual house, was also confined to great lords and ladies (Colvin, *The White Canons*, 258–60).

[82] Ibid. 260–1.

[83] Oxford, Bodl. Lib., MS Laud Misc. 642, fo. 42. In fact John was buried in the Carmelite priory at Plöermel, Brittany (GEC x. 814).

[84] Oxford, Bodl. Lib., MS Laud Misc. 642, fos. 136ᵛ–7. Burial within the monastic precincts was not apparently 'a normal part of confraternity' in 13th-century Westminster (Harvey, *Westminster Abbey*, 39), but this does not address the question whether the individual *confrater* wished for burial in the abbey. It was, of course, common practice for an individual to be a *confrater* of several houses, and a choice of burial place would then need to be made.

entering the priory as a canon; in this way it functioned as a half-way state between life in the world and in the cloister. Thus William Aguillun I, the founder of Malton's grange at Mowthorpe, was received as a 'special brother in all houses of the order' and the canons agreed to admit him as a canon when he so wished.[85] It has recently been argued (following Cheney) that confraternity only lasted during the lifetime of the recipient, and that a distinction should be drawn between the benefits of confraternity and the privileges of being treated as a member of the community after death.[86] However, the lack of precise definitions in most charters makes it impossible to determine with certainty what was expected by the recipient of confraternity. What are we to make, for instance, of the privileges given to Ralf Abbot and his wife when he confirmed land conveyed to Sixhills by his brother when their mother was received into the community? He and his wife were to receive burial with the nuns 'and would be partakers of all the good works done in their house and it would be done for them in all things for ever as for a brother and a sister (*pro fratre et sorore*)'. This phrasing surely implies a grant of confraternity to the couple. Burial and spiritual benefits are here elements in a 'package-deal'.[87] Another telling example is that of Humphrey of Alvingham, *nepos* (probably nephew) of William of Friston, one of the founders of Alvingham. In return for a small grant of two selions and a headland in the fields of Alvingham (the only grant Humphrey is known to have made to the priory), he and his wife Avice were 'received into spiritual fraternity, and when our last day has closed, [the priory] will receive us into its burial ground (*in sepultura sua*) in charity, and perform for us the full service as for a brother or for a sister of the house'.[88] It was possible for a benefactor to receive rights of confraternity at one house and burial at another. In the mid-twelfth century, for example, Oliver of Wendover, Petronilla his wife, and his two sons received rights of confraternity from Bullington, but the family was also a benefactor of Catley, and it was there, rather than at Bullington, where Petronilla was buried.[89]

How far the grant of 'spiritual benefits' can be distinguished from 'confraternity' is questionable. It has been suggested that there was a gradual tightening of the definition of 'spiritual benefits', which in the early Middle Ages need mean no more than the grant of a regular share

[85] *EYC* ii. 387–8. There is no evidence that William ever took up this option.

[86] Wardrop, *Fountains Abbey*, 246. Cf. C. R. Cheney, 'A Monastic Letter of Fraternity to Eleanor of Aquitaine', *EHR* 51 (1936), 489.   [87] *Gilbertine Charters*, 25–6.

[88] Oxford, Bodl. Lib., MS Laud Misc. 642, fo. 20ᵛ.

[89] London, BL, Addit. MS 6118, p. 798; *Gilbertine Charters*, 85.

in the intercessions of the monks, so that by the end of the fifteenth century '"spiritual benefits" and "confraternity" are interchangeable terms'.[90] This hypothesis is probably correct, though I would suggest that, in Gilbertine circles at least, interchangeability of terms was possible at a much earlier date. It is perhaps misleading to look for too close a definition of confraternity: what was expected from the Gilbertines may well have varied according to the status of the benefactor, the closeness of the relationship, and the amount of property conveyed. Most likely, then, there was a sliding scale of privileges, from the grant of unspecified benefits to the performance of funeral and remembrance services as for a member of the community, or even, as in some of the cases cited above, as for a prior or prioress.[91]

If we know little of the precise implications of confraternity, we know even less of the ceremonial that undoubtedly accompanied the reception of the new *confrater* into the community. The example of Godwin the Rich noted above suggests that a grant of confraternity with the order may have normally been made in person by the Master (in Godwin's case, Gilbert of Sempringham), while a late twelfth-century charter of Robert Putrel in favour of Bullington ends, 'this charter was made in the chapter of the nuns when . . . Robert . . . was received into fraternity'.[92] The charter of Alexander son of Osbert seems to imply that the grant of confraternity was made in the chapter of Haverholme priory. In another charter Alexander's son Nigel states, 'in order that this deed be not ignored or infringed by anyone, I have made this confirmation to them in the common chapter of the whole order before master Gilbert when he received me as a brother and participant in all good things of the order'.[93] Sometimes, however, the grant of confraternity seems to have been made at a separate ceremony. William Tison granted 14 bovates in Thrussington (Leicestershire) to Sempringham for 10 shillings per annum. There were at least two stages in the ritual of giving. William swore to warrant the grant on the altar of St Mary in the priory church, and in the hands of Humphrey the sub-dean of Lincoln in the cathedral chapter in the presence of the canons. The charter continues: 'this first grant (*concessio primo*) was made in the presence of master Gilbert at Lincoln.' The

---

[90] Harvey, *Westminster Abbey*, 371–2.

[91] For a distinction between confraternity and other benefits, see Wardrop, *Fountains Abbey*, 250. Cheney ('A Monastic Letter', 489) hints at varying interpretations of confraternity prior to the 13th century.   [92] *Gilbertine Charters*, 93.

[93] The witnesses to this transaction included the priors of three Gilbertine houses: Walter of Chicksands, Henry of Haverholme, and Hugh of St Katherine's, Lincoln (*Sempringham Charters*, xv. 222–3). See above, pp. 325–6.

witnesses are then given and the document goes on: 'but afterwards the gift and confirmation of this alms was made in the nuns' chapter at Sempringham, in which chapter the fraternity (*fraternitas et societas*) of all the common benefits of the house was granted to me and the soul of my father was received into their common prayers.'[94] The personal tone of the charter of Simon Tuschet addressed to the nuns of Haverholme perhaps suggests something of the real relationship that could exist between benefactor and house. Describing himself as 'your brother in Christ', he spoke of how, seeing the good life of the nuns, he was compassionate towards them, and especially to the church of Haverholme, and so, lest the community fall into want and in order that he might be a partaker of the prayers of the community, he gave them land in Ashby-de-la-Laund.[95]

Grants of confraternity were made for many reasons: as a *quid pro quo* for protection; in return for generous benefactions; and, it would appear especially, as spiritual rewards for temporal concessions. In particular, there does seem to be a close connection between such grants and litigation settled by final concord.[96] Indeed, in every case in which the prior of Alvingham made an agreement with a lay plaintiff, the latter was made a participant in all prayers and benefits of the house. A similar correlation can be seen in many other cases involving Gilbertine priories. As is well known, final concords do not always indicate the conclusion of real and contested litigation: as often as not they are the result of 'fictitious' litigation, a device to ensure the enrolment of a grant or agreement between consenting parties in the royal records.[97] Confraternity was a cheap way to buy off the claims, actual or potential, of descendants and to prevent further disputes by binding the benefactor's family and the priory more closely together. Similarly, confraternity might be used to placate the claims of tenants, whose lords had granted their property to a religious house. Thus, Bullington priory granted confraternity to William of Kyme, William of Ingham, Jordan de Insula, and Hugh de Neville. The advowson of Ingham church had been granted to Bullington by

---

[94] *EYC* xii. 130–1, no. 106. It may be that the elements of the transaction were divided to avoid any accusation of simony where confraternity was being given in return for a grant (perhaps itself a 'hidden sale') for which an annual rent was required.

[95] This charter has a curious dating clause: 'in anno quo commissum est prelium inter regem Stephanum et comitem Cestrie Ranulphum' ('Haverholme Priory Charters', 37–8).

[96] This correlation is discussed in Golding, 'Gilbertine Priories', 348–50. For similar grants made by Westminster Abbey, see Harvey, *Westminster Abbey*, 400.

[97] *Abstracts of Feet of Fines relating to Wiltshire for the Reigns of Edward I and Edward II*, ed. R. B. Pugh, Wiltshire Archaeological and Natural History Society, Records Branch, 1 (1939), pp. ix–x. In several cases confraternity was granted to a plaintiff whose ancestor had given the advowson of a church.

Philip I of Kyme, but in 1214 William of Ingham and Jordan, tenants of the Kymes, claimed it in a plea of darrein presentment brought against the prior. The settlement of the case was not achieved till 1219 when the plaintiffs acknowledged the prior's right.[98] Equally, lords might feel aggrieved at the loss of rights brought about by grants of tenants to the priories: their consent to such alienation was often achieved by the grant of confraternity.[99] Confraternity could also be granted in return for confirmation of grants by the benefactors' lords or heirs.[100]

Even in cases where no litigation was involved, confraternity might often be exchanged for the remission of the obligation to perform temporal services. Spiritual favours could be 'bought' in exchange for temporal services. This is explicitly stated in a late thirteenth-century charter of John le Breton. John quitclaimed an annual rent owed by Alvingham for a grant by his ancestor, Geoffrey, and received in return a grant of confraternity for himself, his wife, and heirs.[101] The fact that confraternity was given not only to the grantor, but very often to his wife and often to his children as well, may also indicate a desire on the part of the community to ensure that the latter too raised no claims.[102]

Though in most cases confraternity accompanied quite large grants, this was by no means always the case. Thorald son of Warin was given confraternity in return for half an acre given to Bullington priory.[103] It is probable, however, that a small benefaction in return for confraternity does not represent the sum total of land granted.[104] It was not even necessary for confraternity to be given in return for a grant in free alms. Walter of Buslingthorpe sold land to Bullington for two marks, a cow for his wife, and 16*d.* for his son to buy boots; an annual rent of 6*s.* was also to be paid. A grant of confraternity seems almost superfluous in this case, and it suggests that the canons may have been using the confraternity as

---

[98] London, BL, Harl. Charts., 52 B 20, 52 B 32. The fine is printed in *Final Concords*, i. 125.   [99] For examples, see Golding, 'Gilbertine Priories', 349.

[100] For examples, see Golding, 'Gilbertine Priories', 350–1, and *Sempringham Charters* xv. 225, where the grantor 'prayed all prelates of holy church to confirm and maintain the grant'.

[101] 'prior et conventus in compensacione temporalium spiritualiter concesserunt . . . quod simus participes omnnium bonorum que fient in domo sua.' Oxford, Bodl. Lib., MS Laud Misc. 642, fo. 32ᵛ. Cf. an early charter of Walter of Buslingthorpe to Bullington where he and his family received confraternity 'pro amore Dei et huius negotii causa' (London, BL, Addit. MS 6118, p. 735).

[102] One Haverholme charter names all the recipients in the family: Henry le Wildebof (the donor), Albreda his wife, Thomas, Geoffrey, William, and Richard his sons, and Sibyl his daughter ('Haverholme Priory Charters', 46).

[103] *Danelaw Charters*, no. 6, pp. 5–6.   [104] Golding, 'Gilbertine Priories', 351.

an additional inducement to persuade Walter to part with property they particularly wanted.[105] This raises the question whether such grants were simoniacal. Certainly, according to a strict definition of simony the provision of spiritual benefits conveyed by confraternity in exchange for property was uncanonical, and it has recently been suggested that charters of Fountains abbey may have been so constructed and phrased as to separate elements of sale or lease from the grant of confraternity, and it is concluded that 'usually no direct relationship between a grant of land and a grant of spiritual benefits was indicated'.[106] Such scruples cannot readily be found in Gilbertine charters, and it may be that the Cistercians were particularly sensitive to charges of simony which other orders were prepared to ignore. So we find, for example, William, son of Richard of Lincoln, quitclaiming rights in a wood to Sixhills 'that (*ut*) we may be partakers of their prayers and fraternity for ever'.[107] An even clearer example was a confirmation of Henry of Stonegrave of a tenant's grant to Sempringham 'that we may participate in all benefits of St Mary's church, Sempringham. For this the brethren gave me two silver marks.'[108]

No single account can summarize confraternity grants to Gilbertine priories. They were common from the time of the houses' foundation till at least the end of the thirteenth century, and their apparent decline thereafter may be merely due to a lack of evidence, as the number of charters after this date is considerably reduced. In the late Middle Ages the chief sources of information regarding confraternity grants to the laity become obit lists and individual letters of fraternity. Nevertheless, we should probably not assume from the scarcity of the evidence that the Gilbertines were either not granting many confraternity privileges to the laity at this time or that the order had lost in popularity relative to other communities, since the survival of confraternity letters appears to be random. The apparent concentration of confraternity grants at the end of the twelfth and beginning of the thirteenth century may reflect the larger number of benefactions made at this time. As we have noted, the great majority of grants were made to members of the local gentry families. It was these families whose goodwill was most necessary for the well-being of the priories, and though confraternity does not seem to have been linked to the size of the benefaction, the fact that it was often associated with litigation or quitclaims by heirs or lords demonstrates its use as a bond uniting religious and lay community.

---

[105] London, BL, Addit. MS 6118, p. 735. For another, similar example see Golding, 'Gilbertine Priories', 351.   [106] Wardrop, *Fountains Abbey*, 246–8.
[107] *Gilbertine Charters*, 19.   [108] *Sempringham Charters*, xvi. 79–80.

Burial

Death did not divide community from benefactor: if anything, ties were strengthened. The choice of a particular monastery for burial implied a specific and mutual commitment between the deceased and the religious community. Just as burial in the proximity of a saint was believed to afford protection and patronage on the day of judgement, so the religious were advocates through their prayers of the lay people who chose burial amongst them. The Gilbertine Rule's *de officio mortuorum* makes it clear that the order placed no restrictions on lay burials within its houses, and right of burial was open to both rich and poor, should they so choose, and saving the rights of mother churches.[109] Provision is made for the laity to be buried within Gilbertine churches, and there is considerable documentary, and a little archaeological, evidence that lay people took advantage of this facility throughout the order's existence. Women were to be buried 'remotis viris' in the nuns' choir, while *redditores seculi* were interred *ad altare secundum*, presumably a side or nave altar.[110] After the annual general chapter, a memorial service for the dead was to be held in each house for all those of the order whose names were recited and remembered in chapter, and for all those for whom the Master or priors of individual houses, with the advice of their convents, promised prayers at the request of influential supporters (*prece nobilium*). Those who were joined to the order *familiaritate* (?in confraternity) were to be especially remembered in a memorial feast on the eve of the feast of St Edmund.[111] Special prayers were also to be said on the anniversary of the 'principal founder and foundress' in the house which they had founded, while the order made arrangements for the commemoration of the deaths of parents and kin of the community in the general chapter, the Rule implying that these were automatically received into confraternity.[112]

In death, therefore, many of the lay *familia* of the Gilbertines were in close association with the canons and nuns. Like the latter, in many cases the deaths of benefactors were reported to the whole congregation by the obit-bearer, and it is probable that, *mutatis mutandis*, the same procedures of announcing the death were followed. In its treatment of the deaths of

---

[109] See Innocent III's charter in favour of Alvingham (*Monasticon*, vi. 2. 961).

[110] Ibid. liv–lv: 'Corpora . . . omnium foeminarum ponantur in choro earum [sc. sanctimonialium] . . . redditorum secularium [ponantur] ad altare secundum.' The term *redditor* should probably be translated 'benefactor'. There is archaeological evidence from Watton priory that by the mid-14th century laymen of note could be buried in the presbytery of the nuns' quire (St John Hope, 'The Gilbertine Priory of Watton', 10–11 and pl. vii).

[111] *The Gilbertine Rite*, i. 87.   [112] *Monasticon*, vi. 2. lv.

ad succurrendum entrants the Rule states that their obit should be carried *sicut pro familiari*, which certainly implied that lay supporters of the order were thus remembered, and also that their names were recorded in the houses' martyrologies.[113] The Rule laid down that within three days of death the *scripta* of the dead should be carried to each of the Gilbertine houses and that the *portitor* should be given 'panis regularis' and drink in all the houses.[114] The fullest description of the *portitor*'s duties is contained in a later addition to the Rule, dating perhaps from the fourteenth century. This restated the earlier regulations, and added that the bearers of the obit on their return to the house from which they came had to swear to the *procuratores* that, after leaving Marlborough (mentioned presumably because it was the most remote of the Gilbertine priories and hence the last to be visited), they had returned without delay. They were not to stay more than one night in any house unless delayed by storm or serious illness, and indeed the date of their arrival at every house had to be written on the obit. Nor were the schedules of the obits to be given to any other obit-bearer to carry, nor were the packs of others to be carried unless the *portitor* was returning home. The penalty for disobedience in these matters was harsh: the *portitor* was to be permanently expelled from the community.[115]

Burial within the convent, whether within the cemetery, chapter house, or (most exalted of all) in the priory church, was a mark of close emotional ties. To be buried amongst a large community was an expression of sentiment and brought mutual prestige; 'to be buried in one place was a concrete expression of family solidarity.'[116] In a sense it represented a deeper link than that of confraternity, since whereas benefactors could have rights of confraternity in several houses, they would normally be buried in one place only. In rare circumstances, of course, the heart and/ or other parts of the body could be buried separately. The chief reason for such a division of the body was probably to ensure that more than one

---

[113] Ibid. lv.   [114] Ibid. liv–lv.

[115] Oxford, Bodl. Lib., MS Douce 136, fo. 105ᵛ. That this arrangement for the bearing of the obit continued until the Dissolution is clear from two bequests made to Watton. In the first, William Rowkshaw, rector of Lowthorpe, left 6s. 8d. to William *abitor* of Watton 'ad annunciandum meam mortem per totum ordinem de Sempryngham', and a few years later Robert Arkesay of Hutton Cranswick left 26s. 8d. to the prior of Watton in order that he might have absolution and be given confraternity, and 'if it please my lord to make me a brother, then I wil that the obiter have 6s. 8d. for the cariage of it through the religion' (*Testamenta Eboracensia*, iv. 233, v. 136). For the office of obit-bearer in general, see N. R. Ker, 'Mortuary Briefs', in *Miscellany I*, Worcestershire Historical Society (1960), 53–9, and R. B. Dobson, *Durham Priory, 1400–1450* (Cambridge, 1973), 249.

[116] Wood, *English Monasteries*, 131.

community with which the dead person had links received a token of that tie. Sometimes it was claimed that the burial place of the heart indicated the true affection of the deceased. So, for example, on the death of William de Mandeville, earl of Essex, in 1226–7, his body was buried at Shouldham but his heart at Walden 'in sign of the great love that he bore to us', as the Walden chronicler put it.[117] It seems more likely, however, that this was done to reconcile the conflicting claims of Walden, founded by the de Mandeville earls of Essex, and Shouldham, founded by their successor as earl, Geoffrey fitzPeter, to the family's patronage. A similar conflict of interest was seen in the burial of William's widow, whose body was also buried at Shouldham, while her heart lay at Binham, a foundation of her family, the de Valognes.[118]

The place of burial is rarely specified. No detailed list of burial places survives for a Gilbertine house, and virtually all the available information derives from charters.[119] Sometimes the charters refer to burial 'in capitulo', which might mean burial in the chapter house, but may merely indicate burial within the community.[120] Important benefactors, notably patrons, were almost certainly buried in the chapter house. Simon son of William, founder of Bullington, and his wife, together with the countess Rohaise, the widow of Gilbert de Gant, were buried in the chapter house of Bullington, and Simon's son, Philip, granted land, the rent from which was to be used to provide lights in the priory church and around the tombs.[121] Occasionally there are references to burial in the nuns' cemetery, and Alexander son of Osbert and his son Nigel wished to be buried in the *atrium* of Sempringham priory.[122]

Burials were, of course, more than matters of emotion. They meant endowments, especially of land, and for the small Gilbertine houses the grants that accompanied burials were probably more important than the

---

[117] *Monasticon*, iv. 140. See also Turner, *Men Raised from the Dust*, 63–7. Isabella de Beauchamp's body was buried at Beaulieu, her entrails at Missenden, and her heart at Tewkesbury, 'because the heart was sent there true love was revealed' (*Annales Monastici*, ed. H. R. Luard, 5 vols., Rolls Series (London, 1864–9), i. 165). Heart burials require a full study: I have considered some aspects of this subject in more detail in 'Burials and Benefactions: An Aspect of Monastic Patronage in Thirteenth-Century England', in W. M. Ormrod (ed.), *England in the Thirteenth Century: Proceedings of the 1984 Harlaxton Symposium* (Harlaxton, 1985), 64–75. [118] GEC v. 133.

[119] An entry in the now-lost Haverholme cartulary recorded that Ralph de Normanville and A. his wife were buried before the altar of St John the Baptist in the priory church ('Haverholme Priory Charters', 22). [120] e.g. *Gilbertine Charters*, 4, 74.

[121] Ibid. 98.

[122] The mother of Oliver of Wendover was said, for example, to lie in their cemetery at Catley (ibid. 85).

prestige that the burial of a notable could bring to his or her resting place. Just as was the case in dowry and confraternity grants, personal and economic considerations went hand in hand. The translation of the body of Philip I of Kyme's mother to lie beside her husband Simon in the chapter house of Bullington was no doubt a moment of great solemnity that revealed an emotional solidarity between Bullington and the Kymes. But not only did the family see a representative buried in the priory it had founded—the priory received the church of Ingham, one of the most valuable of its livings.[123]

Burial grants fall into two main types: those made with the body of a member of the donor's family at the time of burial, or, and perhaps more frequently, grants made by the donor with a promise of burial when he or she should die. Very occasionally these grants are associated with the provision of an obit, the celebration of an annual mass upon the anniversary of the death of the donor or the donor's kin. It was natural for the founders of houses or their descendants to find their final resting place amongst the communities which they had founded. The Rule's provision that the founders should have an annual obit in their houses implies that they were normally buried in their foundations. Four generations of Kymes were buried at Bullington over a period of more than a century. The founder, Simon son of William, and his wife were buried in the chapter house, though there is no record of a grant made on the occasion of their burial. Simon's younger son, Simon, directed that he was to be buried in the priory, when he granted a large holding in Maplethorpe and Hardwick.[124] Some time after the death in 1220 of Simon I of Kyme (Simon son of William's grandson) his heart was given to the priory, with arable land in Brethage, by his son Philip II, and later in the century Philip's own son William gave meadow in Lee next Trent together with his heart to be buried in the conventual church.[125] In the case of the Kymes there was no competition between foundations in the first generations after the priory was established. The only other community of which the family was patron was the Augustinian priory of North Kyme, founded by Philip I, which was always a small house. It was on Bullington that the family lavished most attention. For other Gilbertine patrons it was different.

Some families were, of course, patrons of more than one house: they had a choice of burial place which often precluded loyalty to one

---

[123] *Danelaw Charters*, no. 58, pp. 38–9.

[124] Another charter refers to grants in Hardwick to be made to the priory if Simon should die whilst on crusade (London, BL, Addit. MS 6118, p. 719).   [125] Ibid. 717, 723.

community alone. The de Vescis were patrons of Alnwick and Norton, as well as of Malton and Watton. We do not know the burial place of Eustace fitzJohn, the founder, but his son, William, who died in 1183, having taken the habit *ad succurrendum* at Alnwick, was buried there. His grandson William (who died in Gascony in 1253) was taken to Watton for burial, but his first wife was buried at Alnwick, while his second wife, who survived him, found burial at the Greyfriars, Scarborough. The burial place of John's son, William, who died in 1297 is unknown, though the fact that he died at Malton and that his son (who predeceased him, being killed at Conwy in 1295) was buried at Malton priory might suggest he too was buried there.[126] A similar choice faced the de Gant family, the early patrons of Sempringham. Representatives of the family found burial in several of the houses they founded, but only one of the family, Alice, daughter of Gilbert III de Gant, was buried at Sempringham, to which she gave a lavish endowment.[127] A significant change occurred in the fourteenth century. As we have seen, the patronage of the priory passed to the *arriviste* de Beaumont family. They had no links with any English religious house, and it seems most likely that the Beaumonts cultivated their close association with Sempringham to stress their new status. Certainly at least three successive heads of the family from Henry II (d. 1369) to Henry III (d. 1413) chose burial at the priory and in so doing emphasized their new position as local lords and patrons.[128]

Inevitably, it is impossible to determine the burial places of all the lay founders of Gilbertine houses. There is no indication, for example, where Payn and Rohaise de Beauchamp, founders of Chicksands, or their descendants were buried, though Joan Daubeny, who married into the Beauchamp family and who was dead by 1240/1, left rents for the care of the sick and for a light to burn in the priory church with her body 'in her last will'.[129] The burial place of the founders of Sixhills is unknown, as is that of the founders of Nun Ormsby, though the earls of Aumale, the founders' lords, who were closely involved in the foundation, were buried at their own establishment at Thornton.[130] In some cases the founders

---

[126] GEC xii, pt. II. 275–80; *Monasticon*, vi. 2. 957. Some of the Eures, who succeeded the Vescis as lords of Malton and who inherited the patronage of the priory, were buried there in the 14th century.

[127] *Monasticon*, v. 491; *Sempringham Charters*, xv. 161. See below, pp. 341–2. Interestingly, only one member of Gilbert of Sempringham's own family seems to have been buried in a Gilbertine priory: the mother of William Musteil, Gilbert's sister-in-law, who was buried at Bullington (London, BL, Addit. MS 6118, p. 756). [128] GEC ii. 61–3.

[129] Fowler, 'Early Charters of . . . Chicksand', 107.

[130] For the Aumales, see GEC i. 353.

and early patrons were too obscure for details to have survived: this is true, for example, for Catley and Alvingham. One of the putative founders of Alvingham, Hamelin the dean, later became a canon of the priory and his daughter-in-law certainly found burial there, as did the *nepos* and his wife of another founder, William of Friston.[131] Thomas de Scoteni, the descendant of another of Alvingham's founders, Hugh de Scoteni, stated that he wished to be buried with the community ('inter suos') and that he wished all his friends to know that he had chosen to be buried there. This charter, one of the last to be made in favour of the priory by the Scoteni family, demonstrates that the family were still concerned to maintain their ties with the community and to show these links publicly. Though the family fortunes had collapsed and the priory could, therefore, expect few more material advantages from it, sentiment between family and community still ran high.[132]

If it was natural for founders to seek burial with the community, it was equally important for the priories to obtain the bodies of other, local knightly families. Here they seem to have been less successful. The surviving records of individual priories make a detailed statistical analysis impossible, but the records of Alvingham and Bullington, which have been examined in depth elsewhere, do suggest that comparatively few local families of note chose burial with the Gilbertines and that this failure very probably contributed to the latters' slackening hold on the loyalty of potential benefactors. Though in some cases the benefactions that accompanied such burials were considerable, they were essentially 'one-off' grants.[133] The majority of burials in Alvingham priory were of donors and their families who held land in Alvingham itself and in the adjoining settlements. Most belonged to the local free peasantry, and usually only a very small amount of land accompanied the burial. But, as in the case of the gentry considered above, there are few signs that there were family traditions of burials in the priory amongst the peasant benefactors.

Finally, it is necessary to consider the scale of the grants that accompanied burial or the promise of burial. Here no generalizations are

---

[131] Oxford, Bodl. Lib., MS Laud Misc. 642, fos. 20ᵛ, 24ᵛ. These burials are discussed in Golding, 'Gilbertine Priories', 355–6.

[132] Thomas gave very little to the priory and this grant comprised only 20*d.* annual rent. He further stipulated that he wished his aunt, who was a nun at Alvingham, to receive the rent granted, for the remainder of her life. After her death it might be given to any of his daughters whom he might place in the priory (Oxford, Bodl. Lib., MS Laud Misc. 642, fo. 61ʳ). For the Scotenis' misfortunes, see Golding, 'Gilbertine Priories', 240–5.

[133] These grants are discussed in ibid. 358–9. A similar pattern can be seen at Sempringham and Haverholme.

possible, and there were considerable variations in both the extent and value of these grants. It does seem clear that they were rarely larger, and often smaller, than other grants made by the same family without the promise of specific spiritual benefits. In most cases, it is true, the donor or his family had already made grants to the priory, and in these instances burial grants should be seen as an indicator of close relations between family and community over one or more generations rather than as specific grants conferred for individual spiritual benefit. Moreover, it is impossible to tell whether or not these grants represent a final gift made to complete a series of donations. Certainly, in most cases where a small burial grant is the only recorded donation of a benefactor the family had made earlier grants in favour of the house, and ties with the community already existed. It was perhaps the cumulative impact of these benefactions that persuaded the nuns and canons to grant rights of burial.[134] It cannot be denied that some of these grants were very small. William son of Walter of Fillingham gave a headland to Haverholme with his body, while Henry Selvein of Cranwell gave an acre of meadow to the same house with the body of his wife on the day of her burial. In this case, however, it is very clear that Henry was a more generous benefactor than might be thought from this transaction, for in the same charter he gave the priory the two churches of Quarrington and New Sleaford, and Henry's other grants included a further three bovates.[135] It must also always be remembered that other grants, not of land and unrecorded, may have accompanied those mentioned in the charters and cartularies. Moreover, in some cases at least there was probably more to these grants than is immediately apparent. Small grants might well allow the consolidation of the priory's estates and be commensurately more valuable than their mere acreage might suggest.

At the other end of the scale, however, grants could be substantial, even lavish. Those of countess Alice de Gant, and Nigel of Ingoldsby, both benefactors of Sempringham, have already been mentioned, but similar generosity could be found in most other priories. Hugh de Bayeux gave Sixhills the church of Cadeby on the day his wife was buried with the community, and Thomas, son of William of Saleby gave four bovates with their tofts to the same house with his own body to be buried, while some time after 1233 Geoffrey de Turribus, whose grandfather had provided the nucleus of Alvingham's grange at Cabourn, confirmed to the

---

[134] Holdsworth suggested that several burial gifts made to the Cistercian abbey of Rufford represented the last in a series of grants (*Rufford Charters*, i, p. xl).

[135] 'Haverholme Priory Charters', 41, 20.

priory all the grants in that village, and granted an unspecified amount of land that he had purchased there from a tenant in return for the promise of burial for himself and his wife.[136] Though grants of land with the promise of burial were the most common, they could include the grants of money rent, as when Walter of Fauconberg gave one mark rent per annum from the farm of land in Maplethorpe with the body of his wife to be buried in Bullington, or burial might even be granted in return for confirmation or quitclaim of an earlier grant by the family, as when Stephen of Orford quitclaimed an annual rent of 20s. to the canons of Alvingham for land his father had granted them in Cockerington.[137]

It is, of course, impossible to calculate the total number of lay people who found burial in Gilbertine houses. However, the cartulary and charters of Alvingham and Bullington, both of which were of average size and status in the order, provide some little indication. The names of twenty-seven lay burials (five belonging to the founders' families) at Alvingham and thirteen (of which five were Kymes) at Bullington are known. These figures can be contrasted with the more than ninety burials requested at Fountains abbey.[138] Fountains had an income perhaps some eight times that of the Gilbertine priories: if choice of burial place was in part a recognition of the house's prestige and in part a contribution towards it, the few recorded burials at Alvingham and Bullington are no fewer than might be expected.

The fact that burials were comparatively rare, and frequently confined to only one representative of a family of benefactors, is both an indication of and reason for the failure of Gilbertine houses to attract substantial and long-lived support. Just as families and founders were benefactors of several houses, so too they found burial in a number of different communities. One of the prime functions of a house monastery was as a family resting place, preserving the community of the living and the dead, the lay and the religious; now that the concept of the house monastery was largely defunct so, too, few families were united in death beneath the roof of one abbey church. One of the best examples of the new distribution of burials is provided by the de Gant family. The first Gilbert de Gant was buried in the Benedictine house of Bardney, which

---

[136] *Gilbertine Charters*, 4, 25 (Sixhills); Oxford, Bodl. Lib., MS Laud Misc. 642, fo. 158ᵛ (Alvingham). For a similar example of a benefactor purchasing land which was then given to the community in return for burial, see Wardrop, *Fountains Abbey*, 175.

[137] London, BL, Harl. Chart. 49 I 17 (Bullington); Oxford, Bodl. Lib., MS Laud Misc. 642, fo. 76ᵛ (Alvingham). See also the case of Joan Daubeny, cited above, p. 338.

[138] Wardrop, *Fountains Abbey*, 264.

he had been instrumental in refounding. His son Walter was also buried there. His grandson directed that he was to be buried in the Augustinian priory of Bridlington, which his father had founded and where he had been brought up. He preferred burial there to the Cistercian abbey of Rufford, which he had founded. His brother Robert was buried at the Cistercian abbey of Vaudey, that had been founded on the de Gant estates by a vassal. His daughter was buried at Sempringham, her daughter, Rohaise, at Bullington.[139] All of these houses had been founded within fifty years and all were looking for grants from the same family. It is little wonder, therefore, that communities that relied on benefactors such as these failed to attract burials from one family for more than one or two generations.

If during the late twelfth and early thirteenth centuries the number of burials, particularly of gentry benefactors, was restricted by the claims of other communities, thereafter another factor assumed importance. As the laity increasingly favoured the friars at the expense of the older monastic orders and founded chantries rather than communities, they found new places for burial. Thus, at the end of the thirteenth century William of Kyme was buried at Bullington but Lucy his wife was buried amongst the Franciscans at York.[140] In 1343 Gilbert de Umbraville, who had inherited the lordship of Kyme in 1338, founded a chantry at Dogdike for the souls of himself, his wife, his ancestors, heirs, and all the faithful departed. The family burial place at Bullington had now been forgotten, and the lords of Kyme were subscribing to new forms of spirituality.[141]

Burials fulfilled a valuable cohesive role between the priories and their lay benefactors; perhaps among their more important functions was to enable a lay society to enter a closed community that they supported but rarely saw. When this function was no longer felt to be necessary, the days of the monopoly of monasteries of the spiritual affections of the laity were numbered.

Anniversaries and pittances

Burial amongst a religious community brought its benefits: remembrance at the funeral service and, thereafter, the close physical proximity to the unceasing prayers of the place. The endowment of special ceremonies to mark the anniversary of the death of the benefactor or his family was a

---

[139] These details are given in a genealogy (now lost) printed in *Monasticon*, v. 491. For the grant to Sempringham, see *Sempringham Charters*, xv. 161, and for Rohaise's burial see London, BL, Addit. MS 6118, p. 728.   [140] GEC vii. 352.

[141] Owen, *Church and Society*, 93.

further means of ensuring his memory when dead. The provision of anniversary commemorations for both the religious themselves and for the laity is found from at least the ninth century. These included the performance of a memorial mass and often the provision of a pittance for the community, with perhaps a dole for the poor.[142] By the twelfth century anniversaries were a regular feature of monastic life, and the details of their observance were often carefully recorded. The majority, however, appear to have been appointed to commemorate heads of houses, rather than lay benefactors.[143] Undoubtedly the growing dissemination and elaboration of the doctrine of purgatory provided an impetus to benefactors to establish an annual commemoration of their death and those of their families. The essentials of this ceremony, often styled an obit, consisted of a re-enactment of the funeral and accompanying rites, such as bell-ringing and almsgiving.[144]

At the same time, some of the 'reformed' orders expressed disquiet. There were two main reasons for this. First, the provision of special spiritual benefits for lay benefactors in itself weakened the barrier between the cloister and the world. Secondly (and this was a cause of concern not confined to the monastic reformers), specific endowments for specific spiritual services smacked of simony. Early Cistercian statutes do not expressly condemn these grants, perhaps because they were not yet seen as a significant trend, but by the end of the twelfth century criticism of the practice was growing. The problem was that it was hard to deny to the great and powerful the privileges which they had come to expect as rightfully theirs, and in the late twelfth century it is noteworthy that those who received these privileges were always of high rank, and had also contributed substantially to the material well-being of the monks. By 1201 the Cistercians recognized the growing prevalence of these grants, and forbade them without the consent of the general chapter. Later in the thirteenth century the order took active steps to discourage patrons from applying for the privilege.[145]

---

[142] See K. L. Wood-Legh, *Perpetual Chantries in Britain* (Cambridge, 1965), 2–4; E. Bishop, 'Some Ancient Benedictine Confraternity Books', in *Liturgica Historica* (Oxford, 1918, repr. 1962), 349–56. For the later development of the anniversary, see C. R. Burgess, 'A Service for the Dead: The Form and Function of the Anniversary in Late-Medieval Bristol', *Transactions of the Bristol and Gloucestershire Archaeological Society* 105 (1987), 183–211.

[143] Harvey, *Westminster Abbey*, 39–40. For an elaborate pittance appointed by abbot Walter of Battle, see *The Chronicle of Battle Abbey*, ed. and trans. E. Searle (Oxford, 1980), 253. [144] Burgess, 'Service for the Dead', 183–90.

[145] Wardrop, *Fountains Abbey*, 240–1; Wood, *English Monasteries*, 134–5. For concern voiced by the secular Church, see e.g. the statutes of archbishop Stephen Langton (1213 ×

It may be as a result of the criticism of endowed anniversaries that such endowments are uncommon in the records of the Gilbertine priories.[146] Another reason may well be that the very public, often even civic, nature of later medieval anniversaries, which could be most effectively displayed in a parochial ambience, was hardly suitable for, or suited to, performance within a monastery. Details of Gilbertine obits are rarely spelt out. What is perhaps the earliest dates from the late twelfth century when Geoffrey of Benniworth granted a bovate with its appurtenances and unfree tenant to Nun Ormsby for a pittance to be given on the anniversary of the death of his mother.[147] Only one obit is known to have been endowed at Alvingham. At the end of the thirteenth century a toft in Cockerington was granted in return for an obit to be celebrated annually upon the anniversary of the donor's death. At about the same time an obit was granted to the duke of Brittany, patron of Alvingham, to be observed in all the Gilbertine houses on the anniversary of his death.[148] Likewise only one anniversary is recorded at Bullington, for Sir Robert of *Boleviore* (?Belvoir), who in the mid-thirteenth century left money for pittances on his anniversary and on the feast of St John the Baptist. However, three other pittances given to the priory may well have been associated with the commemoration of an anniversary. The earliest is that of Gilbert son of William of Burgh, who gave three acres in Winthorpe at the end of the

1214) (*Councils and Synods II*, pt. I. 30). It is significant, however, that in the 13th century an obedientiary was appointed at Cistercian Meaux with special responsibilities for supervising the pittances that often accompanied anniversary endowments (cited in Moorman, *Church Life in England during the Thirteenth Century*, 338).

[146] It must be remembered, however, that confraternity rights included the celebration of an obit.

[147] *Gilbertine Charters*, 53–4. At about the same time, William of Wyham, who, with others of his family, was a generous benefactor of Nun Ormsby, gave a bovate in Cadeby from which a pittance might be given on the anniversary of his wife, Agnes (Oxford, Bodl. Lib., MS Dodsworth 135, fo. 156ᵛ). It should be noted that these grants do not refer specifically to a ceremony accompanying the pittance, which should be seen as the monastic equivalent of the almsgiving frequently found at parochial anniversaries.

[148] Oxford, Bodl. Lib., MS Laud Misc. 642, fo. 79 (margin), 42. Obits and pittances were often endowed in many different houses, as did Geoffrey Luttrell (d. 1343), who left 20s. to the nuns of Sempringham (where his daughter was a nun) 'ad essendum in oracionibus earundem ad unam pittanciam'. The same bequest was made to many other Lincolnshire houses (Lincoln, Lincolnshire Archives Office, Episcopal Register VII (Bek), fo. 212ᵛ). See also the bequest made by William Cawood of Boston (d. 1478), merchant of the Staple, who left various sums to all the double houses of the order in Lincolnshire to sing masses for his soul (C. W. Foster, 'Lincolnshire Wills proved in the Prerogative Court of Canterbury, 1471–90', *AASRP* 41 (1932), 180). By contrast with the anniversaries granted in Cistercian houses, the recipient of the Alvingham anniversary was of relatively lowly status, a free peasant.

twelfth century. A little later William, a former burgess of Louth, left 30 shillings in a legacy for this purpose, and Sir William Russell of Edlesburgh gave eight shillings per annum, half for a pittance on the feast of St John the Evangelist and half for lights to burn before two altars in the priory church.[149] The fullest description is found in the account of the last such recorded obit in a Gilbertine house, that of Germanus Hay, advocate of Ellerton priory, and Alesia his wife in 1388. In return for their augmentation of the endowments for relief of the poor at Ellerton, the prior and convent granted an annual obit for Germanus, Alesia, and their kin. This was to be celebrated in the convent church by the prior himself, if he was able to be present on the anniversary of their death, with *Placebo*, *Dirige*, and a mass for the dead. If the community failed to perform this anniversary then it would be fined £10 for each non-celebrated obit.[150] With very few exceptions, like the obit established for Guy de Beauchamp and his wife at Shouldham priory in 1386, such few obits and anniversaries as have been found all date from before 1300 and there is no evidence that benefactors in the later Middle Ages were attracted to establish such institutions in Gilbertine priories.[151]

Chantries

An anniversary provided for the commemoration of the dead once a year and was often funded for only a term of years; a natural development was the perpetual chantry where prayers for the dead would be said daily.[152] Perpetual chantries never comprised more than a small minority of the total number of chantries founded.[153] Not all chantries were intended as permanent foundations, and the perpetual chantry itself may well have developed from endowments for individual, but temporary, spiritual benefits. An interesting example of this type of endowment is found in a charter dating from the turn of the twelfth and thirteenth centuries in which Hamelin, earl of Warenne, granted pasture to St Katherine's, Lincoln, in return for the endowment of two beds in the infirmary and 300 masses to be said for himself and relatives in the first year after the gift, together with 1,000 Psalters.[154] These temporary foundations are by

---

[149] London, BL, Harl. Charts. 47 E 20, 44 I 20, 44 I 19.   [150] *Monasticon*, vi. 2. 977.

[151] Guy de Beauchamp's obit (for himself, his wife, and daughter, Katherine) was established by a group (probably feoffees) in and around Shouldham. Katherine was a nun at the priory (*Cal. Pat. R. 1385–9*, 223).

[152] The fullest treatment of the chantry in England remains Wood-Legh, *Perpetual Chantries*.   [153] See e.g. Vale, *Piety, Charity and Literacy*, 22–3.

[154] *EYC* viii. 117–18.

their nature more elusive and it is likely that many more were founded than appear in contemporary records.

The chantry is often regarded as a successful rival to the monastery for the affections of the laity, 'eventually taking its place as a vehicle of religious benefaction'.[155] While this is broadly true, it must not be forgotten that many chantries were founded in monasteries, or were administered by the religious, and these, therefore, while representing the growing privatization of prayers, also indicate a continuing loyalty to the religious house. Initially, indeed, chantries may well have been founded in monasteries by benefactors too poor to set up a monastery on their own but desirous of obtaining a share in the spiritual benefits of the house by funding a monk or canon to say masses specifically for them. While monastic chantries, though they may not have been styled as such, have been traced back to the twelfth century at least, they seem to have become popular only in the following century, reaching a peak a century later still. The earliest chantries established in Gilbertine houses date from the second quarter of the thirteenth century, but 'proto-chantries' can be found earlier, as when in the late twelfth century Iveta de Arches gave her dower church of Norton to the canons of Malton for the maintenance of two canons in the priory for herself and her husband, Roger de Flamville.[156] A more detailed example of this practice is seen in 1258–9 when Gilbert de Preston granted a carucate in Dunsthorpe to Sempringham in return for confraternity and the concession that a canon-priest or secular chaplain would be found to celebrate in perpetuity at the altar of St John the Evangelist in the priory church for the souls of the donor and his family.[157] The great majority of Gilbertine chantries were, however, established after 1300.[158]

Chantries in which the canons had an interest fall into three main types: those founded within the priory church; those established in parish churches appropriated to the priories; and those in churches in which the Gilbertines would appear to have had little or no other interest. These will be examined in turn. Typically a benefactor would arrange for his presentation of a clerk, and after his death by his heirs, to be made a

[155] Owen, *Church and Society*, 92.

[156] *Monasticon*, vi. 2. 971. For an early example of a Premonstratensian chantry, see Colvin, *The White Canons*, 174.

[157] *Final Concords*, ii. 171–2. The prior also conceded that the family would have the command of this chaplain throughout the octave of St Michael.

[158] During the 13th and 14th centuries chantries were endowed in at least nine Gilbertine houses. The last recorded is in 1392. This accords well with the general pattern of chantry foundations in medieval England.

canon who would celebrate for his soul and those of his family. If the chantry was to function in the priory church then it was usual for the celebrant to be a canon, though secular priests were not unknown. Unfortunately, descriptions of Gilbertine chantries are seldom sufficiently detailed to enable us to determine whether the endowment provided for the recruitment of an additional canon to serve the chantry, or whether it was expected to be served by an existing member of the community as an extra duty. The latter arrangement could cause problems at a small house. Between 1317 and 1390 at least six chantry priests (all canons) served in Marlborough priory. This house was small and poorly endowed: if no extra canons were recruited for these posts the burden on the community must have been excessive.

One of the earliest Gilbertine chantry foundations was that of Hugh de Neville in the second quarter of the thirteenth century at Bullington for the maintenance of two chaplains to celebrate masses for the souls of his family, alive and dead.[159] Often the provision of canons is specified. In 1249 Geoffrey de Lasceles gave two bovates in Malton in return for burial for himself and his wife *more canonicali*, trentals and other benefits, and the provision of two canons to serve in the priory for ever.[160] A little later, in 1260, Alan and Margaret FitzJohn granted a messuage and carucate in West Grafton to St Margaret's, Marlborough, in return for daily prayers and the provision of a suitable canon in the priory to be nominated by the grantors.[161]

Chantries were also appointed in parish churches appropriated to the priory. In 1291 licence was given for *magister* Henry of Newark, dean (and later, archbishop) of York, to establish a chantry of two chaplains to celebrate in the chapel of SS Katherine and Martha built by him in the churchyard of St Mary Magdalene, Newark, which was appropriated to St Katherine's, Lincoln.[162] Henry had close ties with the priory and may

---

[159] London, BL, Addit. MS 6118, p. 768. This charter does not specify whether these chaplains were themselves canons. Early in the 13th century Alan of Wilton gave lands in Habeton and elsewhere to Ellerton to find a lamp to burn before the altar of St Lawrence in the priory church, and to maintain one chaplain at the altar in perpetuity. It is likely, though not absolutely certain, that this was an endowment of a chantry for the benefactor (*Monasticon*, vi. 2. 978).

[160] Their names were also to be remembered before every mass ('cum expressione nominorum nostrorum ante cuiuslibet misse celebracionem') (London, BL, MS Cotton Claudius D XI, fo. 43). The charter is a little unclear, but it may also refer to another chaplain to celebrate at Norton.

[161] The grantors were also to receive £10 per annum during their lifetime (PRO CP 25(1) 251/20/7. See *VCH Wiltshire*, iii. 317).

[162] *Cal. Pat. R. 1292–1301*, 43; London, BL, Harl. Chart. 43 D 3. This chantry failed

have been educated at St Katherine's. Chantries of this kind might be served by secular priests; alternatively, they could be the responsibility of canons. The latter arrangement did have its advantages at places where canons also served the parish church (as they did in the later medieval period at Newark). These were required by canon law for disciplinary reasons to have a fellow canon-companion: if this canon served the chantry there were obvious financial and organizational advantages.[163]

However, the priories largely depended on secular chaplains to serve their chantries. The reason was probably the inability of most Gilbertine houses to spare members of their community to go into parish churches.[164] At the same time, it was customary to pay chantry priests less than the annual income expected from the endowment, and, at a time when the flow of advowsons to religious houses was reduced to a trickle, the nomination of chantry priests increased the possibilities for clerical patronage. It must have been primarily these considerations that led Gilbertine houses to undertake the supervision or trusteeship of chantries in churches in which they otherwise had no interest. In such cases it is not easy to determine why the benefactor should make such arrangements. It may be that he wished to benefit both the church in which the chantry was situated and also the religious house responsible for its maintenance; it may be, too, that by dividing responsibilities he hoped to more readily control the foundation; but in some cases, particularly where the church involved was itself a large and wealthy institution, financial considerations were certainly paramount.

within a few years of its endowment, which consisted of the advowson of Northorpe together with two acres of land there. It was probably expected that the priory would proceed to the appropriation of Northorpe, but as the grant stood it was clearly too small to support two chantry priests, and in 1312–13 Henry's successor as archbishop of York allowed the chapel to be demolished. The chantry had not been sufficiently endowed for its maintenance and was already derelict. Moreover, more land was urgently needed for burials, and so the parishioners were allowed to remove the chapel's materials, its 'stones, timber, lead, glass and iron', which could be used for the construction of a new aisle of the church, on condition that a new chantry be established for Henry and his predecessors as archbishop in the aisle, and that archbishop Greenfield and all other archbishops of York be remembered in the canon of the Mass. Though this chapel did not survive, there were by the end of the Middle Ages fifteen chantries in the church, of which only one was actually controlled by St Katherine's. Other religious houses with an interest in this church's chantries were Newbo, Rufford, Wellow, Shelford, and Thurgarton, described in A. H. Thompson, 'The Chantry Certificate Rolls for the County of Nottingham', *Transactions of the Thoroton Society*, 17 (1913), 68–88; 18 (1914), 138–49. See also ibid. 134 and n., 138.

[163] K. L. Wood-Legh, *Studies in Church Life in England under Edward III* (Cambridge, 1934), 96.

[164] A problem also faced by the Premonstratensians: see Colvin, *The White Canons*, 268.

A very early example of such an arrangement is found at Southwell minster, where Sixhills priory was responsible for the annual payment of six marks towards the maintenance of the chantry of Henry of Nottingham, founded in 1241–2 by the royal justice, Robert of Lexington (a canon of Southwell who had founded three additional chantries there). In 1332 Southwell chapter wrote to the prior and convent of Sixhills asking that they pay the arrears due for this chantry: 'we wonder not a little and not without reasonable cause are disturbed that you, religious men, who so often celebrate divine service, do not regard the peril of your souls in neglecting . . . to pay our rent.'[165]

The involvement of relatively impoverished Gilbertine houses in the maintenance of chantries and chantry priests must always have presented problems. If a new canon was appointed for the purpose he might be nominated by the benefactor and even retain an individual salary, both developments inimical to the communal life. If the community relied on secular priests to fulfil the chantry's functions there was equally the possibility of dissension, such men occupying a position within the house analogous to the lay corrodians. If the priory undertook responsibility for a chantry outside its own walls this was either a drain on the community's own manpower, or necessitated the payment of a secular. The disadvantages for the spiritual well-being of the community were obvious, the financial consequences a gamble.[166] That Gilbertine priories, along with most other religious houses, undertook such responsibilities testifies both to the continuing appeal of these communities to benefactors, and also to the financial needs which made these arrangements possible routes to financial survival.

If a man or woman of moderate means wished to endow a religious foundation for his or her soul, and the family was not already associated with an earlier, perhaps monastic, establishment, then a chantry was the ideal answer, bringing the promise of eternal salvation and an indication of temporal status. In spite of all the potential hazards of monastic chantry foundations, the Gilbertines showed themselves as ready as any to accept both chantries within the priory churches and their administration in parish churches that the canons controlled. Certainly the financial benefits could be substantial: very few Gilbertine chantry priests received

---

[165] *Visitations and Memorials of Southwell Minster*, ed. A. F. Leach, Camden Society, NS 48 (1891), 182, cited Wood-Legh, *Perpetual Chantries*, 143–4.

[166] The latter were recognized at the general chapter of 1347, which warned all priors that they were not to encumber their houses with 'debts, corrodies, chantries or burdens of a similar kind' (Oxford, Bodl. Lib., MS Douce 136, fo. 96ᵛ).

more than the minimum legal stipend of five marks, while the value of the churches themselves was often considerable. Such inducements could not be ignored, and it was these that played a large part in persuading the canons to undertake responsibility for chantries. Why, though, did the laity found chantries under the care of the canons? The increasing individualization of religious practice in the late Middle Ages certainly posed a threat to the popularity of the older religious communities. At the same time, however, the theoretical incompatibility between the monk and the chantry priest can be exaggerated. The former, though dedicated to prayer for the whole Christian commonwealth, had a particular responsibility to pray for the souls of his monastery's benefactors; the latter, though his concern was primarily for the salvation of the founder and his family, was normally enjoined to pray for all the faithful. The involvement of monasteries with chantries brought about at least a partial resolution of the tension between the two. In this way the canons, by adapting their organization to accommodate the chantry, were able to ensure the continuance of benefactions.[167]

[167] *Reg. Greenfield*, iv. 131–2; cf. ibid. v, p. xxii.

PART III

Resources and their Exploitation

7

The Gilbertines and their Churches

When Gilbert returned from his studies in France his father presented him to his two demesne churches of Sempringham and West Torrington. In spite of his reluctance, Gilbert agreed to receive them 'in order that his father's rights in them might be preserved'. A few years later Gilbert used the income from these churches to support his first community of anchoresses, and it is likely that these revenues continued to provide the greater part of their income until *c*.1150.[1] Since the mid-eleventh century the church-owning laity of western Europe had been disposing of their spiritual possessions to more acceptable proprietors, chiefly monks, and by 1150 a 'flood of donations' of parish churches to religious orders was already well under way. The reasons for this transfer of rights, unparalleled in England (or western Europe) until the sixteenth century, have been much discussed and there is no necessity to examine this issue in detail here.[2] The motives for lay donation of churches were mixed, owing something to the growing disapproval of the laity's ownership of tithes and their *ius proprietatis* in churches, a right which was now being reduced to one of *patronatus*, and something to the fact that a lay proprietor probably received relatively little financial benefit from ownership of a church when compared with that enjoyed by a religious owner. Since the laity could no longer be granted any spiritual possessions nor enjoy the temporal benefits of tithes, it made more sense to give or, perhaps as likely, sell their churches, and gain spiritual rewards for their benefactions. Pressures on the laity to 'disinvest' in churches were considerable: the chief beneficiaries were the religious.

[1] *Book of St Gilbert*, 16.
[2] For a general introduction to the 'restitution' movement, see C. Morris, *The Papal Monarchy: The Western Church from 1050 to 1250* (Oxford, 1990), 60–2, and G. Constable, 'Monastic Possession of Churches and "Spiritualia" in the Age of Reform', in *Il Monachismo e la Riforma Ecclesiastica (1049–1122)*, Miscellanea del Centro di Studi Medioevali, 6 (Milan, 1971), 304–31. For a discussion of contemporary developments in France, see G. Mollat, 'La Restitution des églises privés au patrimonie ecclésiastique en France du IXe au XIe siècle', *Revue Historique de Droit Français et Étranger*, 4th ser. 27 (1949), 399–423. The situation in England is briefly discussed in M. Brett, *The English Church under Henry I* (Oxford, 1975), 230–1; see also B. R. Kemp, 'Monastic Possession of Parish Churches in England in the Twelfth Century', *JEH* 31 (1980), 133–60.

However, the process of restitution was long-drawn-out, and advanced at various speeds in different regions. In England and Normandy, ever conservative in matters ecclesiastical, change was slow to gain momentum and restitution was never as complete as in other parts of western Europe. Much also depended on individual bargains made between lay owner, local bishop, and monastery, and the interplay of all their interests. Gilbert's presentation *c*.1120 as rector of his father's churches came at a time of transition and uncertainty in England. By this time attitudes on all sides had subtly changed from the previous generation. Popers and bishops increasingly looked to regulate the transfer of *spiritualia* from the laity to the monks. The classic statement of intent over the operation of restitution had been provided by Paschal II, who in 1102 wrote, in answer to an enquiry of Archbishop Anselm, that all churches should be under episcopal control, and that bishops alone (and not abbots) should be allowed to receive a grant of a church directly from the lay owner.[3] At the same time, however, countervailing arguments against the very possession of churches by the religious were beginning to be advanced.[4]

It is necessary at this point to determine what contemporaries meant by monastic possession of churches. A distinction must be drawn between enjoyment of ecclesiastical revenues, such as tithes, and the profits of the glebe; the lesser right to present priests for institution; and actual service by a regular at a parochial altar—a practice which remained uncanonical throughout the Middle Ages (though, as will be shown, this prohibition was frequently overridden).[5] Ecclesiastical revenues were, as Constable demonstrated, hard to define with precision; they included revenues of the church endowment, tithes (which might or might not have become separated from the parish church), and a wide range of oblations. Their possession by the religious was generally welcomed by the papacy, though successive popes did attempt to ensure that the bishop remained the arbiter and broker in such transactions.[6]

A number of reformers, however, went further. They argued that churches should be served by, and their revenues maintain, priests alone. At one end of the spectrum of reform, not surprisingly, some of the most vociferous criticism of the monks came from the regular canons, who

---

[3] This view was incorporated in the Council of Westminster the same year (Brett, *English Church*, 141–2).

[4] For a discussion of this question, see Constable, 'Monastic Possession', 304–31.

[5] This last point is discussed in a Gilbertine context below, pp. 388–90, but see here M. Chibnall, 'Monks and Pastoral Work: A Problem in Anglo-Norman History', *JEH*, 18 (1967), 165–72.   [6] Constable, 'Monastic Possession', 318–22, and see above, n. 2.

themselves stood to gain most from the possession of churches, and who may well have wished both to stress their distinction from the monks, and to maintain as far as possible a monopoly of ecclesiastical revenues. They argued that these should be reserved for those who served the altars. The monastic *ordo* was not intended so to do (though individual monks might), therefore monks should not receive income from this source. But opposition to monastic possession of these revenues came not only from without, it was voiced at least as strongly from within monasticism's own ranks. Radicals like the Cistercians set their face against ownership of all types of *spiritualia*. The root of their objection lay in concern for monastic poverty as central to the religious life, combined with concern that possession of churches inevitably involved monks in secular affairs and soul-destroying lawsuits. In this they were not far wrong: quarrels over advowsons were the single most frequent cause of litigation involving the Gilbertines and their patrons. The most famous prohibitions are contained in the early legislation of the Cistercians; but the Carthusians, Grandmontines, and the order of Fontevrault all likewise forbade the possession of churches or tithes.[7]

The reformed regular canons had, as might be expected, a more ambiguous attitude, and the practice of different groups and congregations varied quite considerably. There was an even wider range of religious observance amongst the regular canons than in the monastic *ordo*, and (as the author of the *Libellus de diversis ordinibus* recognized) the strictest canons, like the new monks, did not exact tithes or rents, and laboured with their hands.[8] The Premonstratensian canons were the most akin to the reformed monastic orders, and it was the white canons whom the Gilbertines perhaps most resembled. Their first statutes were as uncompromising as those of the Cistercians, clearly forbidding the possession of churches, unless they could be made into abbeys and then presumably adopted for use as the canons' church. But, as Colvin remarked, 'by the middle of the twelfth century this rule seems to have been a dead letter'; tithes and churches were being received by the Premonstratensians during the lifetime of Norbert himself, and with his approval.[9] The reformed

---

[7] *Les Plus Ancien Textes de Cîteaux*, 124; Guigues 1ᵉʳ, *Coutumes de Chartreuse*, Sources Chrétiennes, 313 (1984), 244; *Scriptores Ordinis Grandimontensis*, ed. J. Becquet, Corpus Christianorum, Continuatio Mediaevalis, 8 (Turnhout, 1968), 73–4; *PL* 162, col. 1085.

[8] *Libellus de Diversis Ordinibus et Professionibus qui sunt in Aecclesia*, ed. G. Constable and B. Smith (Oxford, 1972), 62. Occasionally monks are found on the offensive, insisting that regular canons should not hold or serve in churches (e.g. see G. Constable, *Monastic Tithes from their Origin to the Twelfth Century* (Cambridge, 1964), 158).

[9] Colvin, *The White Canons*, 272; Constable, *Monastic Tithes*, 189.

monks' opposition, too, lasted for little more than a generation after their initial and radical enthusiasm. By 1150 all the orders which had stood out against possession of *spiritualia* had weakened. When the order of Savigny joined the Cistercians in 1147 it was allowed to keep all its *spiritualia*, and though some diehards bemoaned the growing laxity, the tide was flowing fast against them.[10] It is significant that when the Gilbertine Rule was codified in the 1150s there is no prohibition of the possession of churches or other *spiritualia*: rather the order is concerned that churches should not be farmed out to others without licence. Thus, in a sense, the wheel had come full circle.[11]

The Parish Church as Property: Revenues and Income

The question of monastic possession of churches was inextricably bound up with the broader issue of simony. Though the concept of *spiritualia* seems not to have been codified until the generation after Gratian, the notion of *res ecclesiastice* was already developed and its immunity from lay control established.[12] In grouping churches and tithes indiscriminately with manors, villeins, rents, ovens, and mills under the rubric, 'Quod redditus non habemus', the early Cistercian legislators had expressed in a stark fashion the value of churches as economic assets.[13] While the precise implications of the grant of a church in the twelfth century are unclear, and while they were certainly changing during the century from 1150, there can be no doubt that these represented a most valuable source of income for exploitation by their owners: churches meant cash.[14] The transference of this element of a lord's seigneurial income to the religious implied a considerable shift of temporal resources. On the one hand, the income provided by tithes and other appropriated 'spiritual' sources could be considerable, and, on the other, the gift of even the advowson of a church was usually accompanied by the glebe land of the parish. This was often extensive and tended to lie close to the church in a compact holding. As such it was frequently used as the nucleus of a grange.[15] It is the high economic value of the churches that underlies the Gilbertines'

---

[10] Savignac Byland had refused the grant of three churches in the mid-1140s.

[11] *Monasticon*, vi. 2. lvi.   [12] Morris, *Papal Monarchy*, 394.

[13] *Les Plus Anciens Textes de Cîteaux*, 124.

[14] Grants of churches to the Gilbertines are discussed below: 'The donation of the churches'. The income could be used for the general support of the community or for specific needs. So Philip of Kyme granted the church of St Alban's, Spridlington to Bullington for the maintenance of the nuns' infirmary (London, BL, Addit. MS 6118, p. 729).   [15] See below, Ch. 8: 'The grange': 'The grange and the church'.

concern to acquire them, and which explains the frequent litigation to which both canons and laity resorted in order to maintain their rights to them.

The earliest indication of the value of *spiritualia* to the Gilbertines is found in the 1254 Valuation of Norwich. By this time the priories had acquired almost all their churches and in many cases their appropriation had been secured. Many priories were now receiving a very considerable proportion of their total income from *spiritualia*. Unfortunately, the Malton cartulary is the only source for the 1254 valuation of the Gilbertine houses, and this gives two sets of figures, both purporting to be assessments for the taxation. These figures differ markedly, one set being consistently and considerably lower than the other.[16] According to the lower valuation, eight of the thirteen houses which derived income from both temporal and spiritual sources drew at least half of the total from their churches.[17] The proportion of total income provided by *spiritualia* in the higher valuation is much less, but even according to these figures Alvingham, Bullington, and Malton received more than half of their income from ecclesiastical sources, while only Clattercote, Marlborough, York, and *Pons* (presumably Bridge End) drew solely temporal income.

Though neither the incomes recorded in the *Taxatio Ecclesiastica* of pope Nicholas IV in 1291 nor the *Valor Ecclesiasticus* of 1535 show the priories obtaining as much from *spiritualia* as in 1254, it is clear that such income was still important. In 1291 Bullington derived over £140 (56 per cent of its total assessed income) and Alvingham over £40 (or nearly 30 per cent of its income) from churches, and in 1535 Bullington (58 per

---

[16] London, BL, MS Cotton Claudius D XI, fo. 278. The higher set of figures was used by Lunt in his study of the Taxation (*The Valuation of Norwich*, 518), while the lower assessments were used by Rose Graham in 'Finances of Malton Priory'. Neither seems to have recognized the existence of the other figures entered on the same folio of the cartulary. One possible explanation for the discrepancy is that the lower figures represent the order's own assessment of income (it is called an *estimacio* in the cartulary), while the higher figures are the assessments made by the official valuers.

[17] Sixhills may well have gained the highest proportion (85%) from *spiritualia*, but though at this time this priory did possess more rectories than any other Gilbertine house, it is likely that there is a scribal error here. In 1291 Sixhills derived a little under 25% of its total income from churches. In addition, the small house of Fordham apparently derived all of its income from *spiritualia*, but this was a peculiar case. Fordham may not have been an independent priory at this time but rather a cell of Sempringham. The church of Fordham had been granted to the mother house in 1227 (see above, Ch. 4, 'Fordham'). By contrast, only Mattersey, Clattercote, and St Andrew's, York, are not listed as holding *beneficia ecclesiastica*. According to the other valuation, Mattersey had an income of £10 from *spiritualia* (20% of its total income). Clattercote did not receive its single church of Ratley till 1342, while St Andrew's is not known to have held any churches at this time.

cent), St Katherine's, Lincoln (51 per cent), Sempringham (41 per cent), Alvingham (29 per cent), and Nun Ormsby (25 per cent) still received at least a quarter of their total income from churches and tithes. While all these figures are subject to the many criticisms that can be made of medieval tax assessments, they do provide some indication of the relative importance of the possession of churches in the economy of many Gilbertine priories.[18] The income from a single church could be very substantial: in 1291 the churches of Prestwold and Burgh-le-Marsh, which were held by Bullington, were assessed at £43 6s. 8d. and £20 respectively, and Watton's church at Hothum was valued at £40, as was Ellerton's church at Aughton.[19] Success in obtaining the appropriation of their churches was therefore vital for the economic well-being of the Gilbertine priories.

The Donation of the Churches

By the mid-twelfth century the actual process of transferral of rights in a church was well established. Only occasionally do we get any idea of the motives that inspired the donors to alienate their churches, other than the standard expectation of salvation found when any benefaction was made. However, the donor of the church of Grainthorpe to Alvingham priory does articulate contemporary ideas, giving the church 'since it is better for the care of churches to be in the hands of regular clergy than in those of the laity'.[20] The lay donor passed the church into the hands of the diocesan bishop, either in person or by charter, and the bishop would then cede the church to the religious house.[21] The consent of the bishop had become a *sine qua non* of such transactions for it enabled the diocesan both to monitor the grant and also to control the presentation of future incumbents. The bishop might also be required to adjudicate between the rival claims of the new holders of the advowson and the sitting incumbent.[22] Soon his oversight would allow him also to ensure that the incumbent received a decent livelihood.[23] Yet it is only at the

[18] The veracity of the *Taxatio Ecclesiastica* was considered by Graham, who concluded that there was significant under-assessment in 1291 compared with the true value of the *spiritualia* ('The Taxation of Pope Nicholas IV', *EHR* 23 (1908), 434–54). For the 1535 figures, see A. Savine, *English Monasteries on the Eve of the Dissolution* (Oxford, 1909), 276–7.

[19] *Taxatio*, 63b, 59, 303. Aughton alone was assessed at nearly two-thirds of all Ellerton's *temporalia*. Similarly, the church of Billinghay appropriated to Catley and valued at £11 6s. 8d. was worth nearly a third of all that priory's temporal holdings (ibid. 70).

[20] Oxford, Bodl. Lib., MS Laud Misc. 642, fo. 96.

[21] Of several Gilbertine examples, see e.g. *Danelaw Charters*, 8–9, no. 11.

[22] e.g. *Danelaw Charters*, 21–2, no. 31.   [23] See Brett, *English Church*, 141–8.

very end of the century that it becomes commonplace for donors to stress that they had obtained the consent of their bishop for the grant of churches. Geoffrey fitzPeter's foundation charter of Shouldham (which dates from the 1190s) carefully distinguishes between the temporal property and the churches of Shouldham All Saints and St Margaret's, Thorpe, Wereham and Stoke All Saints, which he gave 'with the consent and agreement of John, bishop of Norwich, our spiritual father'.[24]

Throughout this period virtually all the donors of churches treated them as seigneurial assets. They were inherited like other types of property: Philip I of Kyme described the church of Prestwold which he gave to Bullington as coming from his inheritance from his father Simon.[25] Sometimes, even though the lay donor had granted a church to the religious, he still expected residual patronal rights. The church of Brompton was given 'quantum fas est laicae personae' to the canons of Malton by Eustace fitzJohn shortly after the priory's foundation, but *c.*1200 Roger, Master of the order, and prior Cyprian agreed with Eustace de Vesci (the donor's grandson) that during the latter's lifetime and during that of his eldest son (if any) he should present a suitable clerk to the living in return for an annual pension of 20*s.* to the canons.[26] Brompton was a wealthy living and continued to be controlled by the Vescis for many years. Between 1215 and 1219 prior Adam recognized the collation by Eustace de Vesci's brother, Richard de Vesci, canon of Beverley and rector of Brompton, appointing a vicar to the church and chapel of Falden appurtenant to Brompton. In 1245, on Richard's death, William II de Vesci, Eustace's son, presented his chaplain, Hugh of Grimston, to the prior 'ut fidelitatem et benevolenciam nostram merito debeamus commendare'. The prior then wrote to the archbishop asking him to duly institute Hugh. After inquiry the archbishop obliged, reserving the 20*s.* pension.[27] Such arrangements were acceptable so long as there was goodwill. But on William's death without an adult heir there were problems. Peter of Savoy gained the heir's wardship and he and William's widow, Agnes (no friend of the Gilbertines), brought a plea against Malton's right to the advowson. The prior was successful and thereafter we hear no more of Vesci presentations.[28]

Moreover, like all transfers of seigneurial property, the gift of a church

[24] *Monasticon*, vi. 2. 974–5.

[25] 'ex cuius hereditate haec donatio procedit' (*Danelaw Charters*, 57, no. 89).

[26] London, BL, MS Cotton Claudius D XI, fo. 39. Brompton was the last Gilbertine church to be appropriated, in 1518.   [27] Ibid., fos. 43ᵛ–44.

[28] Ibid., fo. 43ᵛ (margin). In 1284 Agnes was also unsuccessful in her claim to the advowson of Langton (ibid., fo. 45ᵛ).

required the assent of the donor's lord, and for all the 'pious phrases' which Roger de Mowbray employed in his charter confirming his tenant's grant of the church of Norton to Malton, he was continuing to exercise traditional rights without which the canons could not have maintained their claim to their new benefice.[29] The lord's assent was essential if future disputes were not to arise, and many of these confirmation charters have survived. To be sure of avoiding litigation it might be wise to obtain a whole series of confirmations. John, constable of Chester, gave the canons of Malton the church of Winterton 'especially because the priory was founded on land acquired by my grandfather Eustace'. This grant was confirmed by his son, Roger de Lacy, and his grandson, John de Lacy (who also released the canons from their obligation to provide hospitality for the family), while the Bardulf family, who also had rights in the church, issued their own series of confirmations.[30] Lords might also encourage their tenants to grant churches to favoured priories.[31] Such transactions might be complicated. Herbert son of Adelard was tenant of Ivo de Karkenii at South Ferriby. Ivo had apparently granted the moiety of the church to Bullington at the request of Adelard, but the nuns do not seem to have gained control until Agnes, the wife of Herbert and daughter of Simon I de Kyme, Bullington's founder, took action. Purchasing for 15 marks the moiety of the church which Herbert had apparently given her in dower 'that I, sc. Agnes, may do as I like with it', she then granted it 'to the church which Simon my father founded on his fee'.[32]

Tenurial complexities were exacerbated by the frequently divided ownership of churches, particularly in the Danelaw, where so many of the Gilbertine houses were located. Here the manor was prior and superior to the parish, and the church was normally shared amongst the lords and their tenants.[33] In a number of instances the priories were only able to secure possession of a portion (usually a moiety) of a church. This inevitably limited the potential for its exploitation.[34] Sometimes two lords would grant their share of the church to different priories. This

[29] *Charters of the Honour of Mowbray*, 131, no. 183.

[30] London, BL, MS Cotton Claudius D XI, fo. 205[r-v].

[31] e.g. Bullington's two churches of Hackthorn and Burgh-le-Marsh were given by tenants of the Kyme fee (*Danelaw Charters*, 8–9, 21, nos. 11, 30. See Golding, 'Gilbertine Priories', 148–9). [32] Ibid. 147–8; *Danelaw Charters*, 17–20, nos. 24–7.

[33] See D. Roffe, 'Pre-Conquest Estates and Parish Boundaries: A Discussion with Examples from Lincolnshire', in M. L. Faull (ed.), *Studies in Late Anglo-Saxon Settlement* (Oxford, 1984), 115–22.

[34] This was the case, for example, at Stainton-le-Vale, where Lambert de Scoteni gave his two-thirds of the church to Alvingham but the nuns never obtained the whole (Oxford, Bodl. Lib., MS Laud Misc. 642, fo. 60; *Gilbertine Charters*, 107).

happened at Hackthorn, where the church was held jointly by Bullington and St Katherine's, Lincoln. Sometimes another religious house shared the church, as in the case of Wiggenhall St Peter, which Shouldham shared with Crabhouse nunnery, or Kirkby Underwood, shared by Sempringham with Lincoln cathedral, while sometimes a moiety continued to be held by a lay patron until the Dissolution, as was the case with the living of Grimoldby, of which a moiety was held by Nun Ormsby. In such cases the patrons either appointed alternately or, more occasionally, appointed a priest to each half of the living. The parish church of Alvingham was in the hands of two lords; so too was its neighbouring church of Cockerington St Mary, where the nuns were again fortunate to obtain benefactions from both William of Friston, who held two-thirds, and Hugh de Scoteni, who held the other portion.[35] Perhaps the most extreme example of fragmentation was found at Fotherby. Here the nuns of Nun Ormsby had to negotiate with three parties with interests in the church. While it is impossible to determine the full story, it seems most likely that in the mid-twelfth century the church was held by Mark de Twit. He certainly gave half of the church to his daughter when she married Hugh de Wildeker. Hugh later gave it to the nuns with the consent of his wife and father-in-law. The remaining moiety was held as part of his fee in Ormsby by Hugh de Twit, perhaps Mark's son. But Roger de Clere and William son of Amfrid of Haugh each claimed a quarter of the fee in the king's court in London. The matter was settled by duel and the successful claimants then each gave their share in the church to the priory.[36]

The early Gilbertine foundations had all acquired the majority of their churches by the end of the twelfth century. In virtually every instance the foundation charter was accompanied by the gift of one or more parish churches, often including the church of the parish in which the new community had settled, or proposed to settle. Indeed, it has been argued above that failure to obtain a grant of the parish church could be a factor (and sometimes the deciding factor) in the eventual failure of the priory itself.[37] Of successful early foundations only Clattercote, Marlborough,

---

[35] For Alvingham, see below, pp. 362, 389. William of Friston's grant of his share in Cockerington St Mary was confirmed by bishop Robert de Chesney (1148–66), while Hugh de Scoteni granted his share of a third of the church 'constituta in illo loco ubi idem conventus manet', together with all its appurtenances and the land that his tenants had given to the church (Oxford, Bodl. Lib., MS Laud Misc. 642, fo. 60). Hugh probably died *c*.1155. He also gave the church of St Leonard's, South Cockerington, to the priory.

[36] *Gilbertine Charters*, 42–3. The charters make it very clear that the portions of the church belonged to the divided fee. [37] See above, Ch. 4: 'Failures'.

and Newstead did not possess their local parish church. In the case of Clattercote there was probably never a church in the village, and local inhabitants would presumably have attended either the chapel of Claydon or the latter's mother church of Cropredy.[38] Marlborough lay in the parish of Preshute. This church was already appropriated to Salisbury cathedral: there was, therefore, little possibility that it would ever come into the Gilbertines' hands. Moreover, the priory had close relations with Marlborough castle, and by the mid-thirteenth century was providing a canon to celebrate in the castle chapel. Ties were undoubtedly closer with the castle than with the local church.[39] Newstead was in the parish of Cadney, which was held by (and probably already appropriated to) Thornholme by the time Henry II established the priory.[40]

Frequently founders gave the local parish church to their new foundation. Simon son of William gave the churches of Bullington and Langton to Bullington priory 'for its maintenance' ('ad sustentationem suam') and Eustace fitzJohn gave the churches of Malton (described as a 'locum religioni aptum') and Wintringham to Malton priory.[41] Where the founder did not possess the entire church, as at Nun Ormsby, he gave his portion and hoped (with reason) that other lords with an interest would contribute their share.[42] At Alvingham, Roger son of Jocelin held a quarter of St Adelwold's church; the remaining portion was in the hands of Hamelin the dean, who was himself the rector. Both ceded their rights to the priory, probably at its foundation. Hamelin resigned his office into the hands of the bishop of Lincoln, who thereupon invested the nuns with the church in the chapter of Sempringham.[43]

Having obtained the local church, the new community had to decide what to do with it. There were two options: either to incorporate it into the priory complex, where it could be divided into two, one part for the laity, one part for the religious, or to maintain it as the parish church and obtain its appropriation. In both cases the Gilbertines had the option of serving it themselves. There were, of course, many precedents amongst

---

[38] Clattercote, too, was an unusual case, founded initially as a hospital for the order (see above, Ch. 4, 'Clattercote'; *VCH Oxfordshire*, x. 194–5, 191).

[39] *VCH Wiltshire*, xii. 180–1; *Cal. Liberate R.* v. 180, 206.

[40] See e.g. *Reg. Hugh de Welles*, iii. 167. A slightly later foundation, Mirmont, did not obtain the church of Upwell (Cambridgeshire), but the priory here was never to flourish. Haverholme now lies in the parish of Ewerby, but changes in the course of the river Slea which forms the parish boundary strongly suggest that in the 12th century the priory lay in Anwick, the church of which was early granted to the nuns.

[41] *Gilbertine Charters*, 91; *Monasticon*, vi. 2. 970.   [42] *Gilbertine Charters*, 39, 40.

[43] Oxford, Bodl. Lib., MS Laud Misc. 642, fo. 12a^v; *Gilbertine Charters*, 103. See also Golding, 'Gilbertine Priories', 134.

contemporary foundations for adopting the first possibility. Augustinian canons in particular very frequently took over communities of secular clergy or a parish church. However, they often found this arrangement had its disadvantages, and moves from a noisy, cramped site to more peaceful surroundings were commonplace.[44] There is very little evidence that many Gilbertine priories took over a pre-existing church for their own conventual use. The disadvantages of continuing to use a parish church as both a priory church and a church for the local population were far more obvious when the priory included nuns, and there is no clear indication that any Gilbertine double house ever adopted this practice. The original foundation at Sempringham was physically part of the parish church of which Gilbert was rector, the first nuns being enclosed as anchoresses on its north side, but once the order was formally established after 1147 the *Vita* makes it clear that the canons and nuns had their own priory church which was only seldom open to the laity and for pilgrims to St Gilbert's shrine.[45]

At Chicksands there is some uncertainty. The church here formed part of the original endowment of the priory, but it was either extra-parochial, or a chapel of Campton in which parish the priory lay. It was certainly poorly endowed and there is a little evidence that it was used as the priory church, since it was dissolved with the priory in 1539.[46] In the case of the priories founded for canons, only at St Andrew's, York, and Malton may there have been dual use of the church, at least for a time. The canons serving God *apud sanctam Andream* were given the church there with its adjoining lands, though for how long this church remained parochial is far from clear.[47] At Malton the church continued to serve the parish as well as the priory and, though appropriated, was looked after by a canon of the priory, not a vicar.

But the acquisition of the local church was but the first stage in the creation of a network of local parishes under Gilbertine control. The pattern of alienation was largely determined by the status of the priory's

[44] J. C. Dickinson, *The Origins of the Austin Canons and their Introduction into England* (London, 1950), 148–53.

[45] *Book of St Gilbert*, 32, 46. See also Graham and Braun, 'Excavations', 73–101. The laity did attend the priory church on Palm Sunday and Good Friday (ibid. 80).

[46] *VCH Bedfordshire*, ii. 271, 276; *Cal. Letters and Papers, Henry VIII*, xv. g.282 (124), 117, where its steeple and churchyard are mentioned. However, it must be admitted that regular institutions were made to the vicarage of Chicksands in the 13th century and there is no suggestion that the vicar at this time was a canon of the house. (See e.g. *Rotuli Ricardi Gravesend*, ed. F. N. Davis, C. W. Foster, and A. H. Thompson, Lincoln Records Society, 20 (1925) 200.)   [47] *Monasticon*, vi. 2. 962.

founder(s). In a number of instances, where a Gilbertine house had been established by a wealthy patron, the founding family was often responsible for granting all, or a high proportion of, churches to the priory. All of Chicksands' churches were given either by Payn or Simon de Beauchamp; Bullington received nearly all of its churches from the Kyme family; the Vesci family gave most of Malton's churches; Shouldham was equally indebted to Geoffrey fitzPeter for its *spiritualia*.[48] St Katherine's, Lincoln, was founded by bishop Robert de Chesney and obviously could not expect to receive all of the churches in his patronage, though it did get the prebend of Canwick and the churches of Newark, Norton Disney, Marton, and Newton-on-Trent, alienations that were themselves criticized as excessive by Gerald of Wales. As a result, it relied on additional grants from local lords to build up its substantial holdings of advowsons.[49] Other priories had to acquire their churches from a number of local lords of comparatively lowly status and means.[50] By *c*.1200 the process of acquisition was almost complete. Though most priories gained one or two more churches thereafter, consolidation was now more important than procurement: the defence of advowsons already in possession and the appropriation of churches whose revenues were not yet under the priories' control.[51]

What did the nuns and canons expect to receive when a church was passed into their hands? Until the codification of canon law relating to patronal rights during the twelfth and beginning of the thirteenth centuries, there was a certain ambiguity as to what was being ceded. Uncertainty was inevitable in this period of transition when a church ceased to be regarded as a piece of seigneurial property and started to emerge as the spiritual centre of a parish: a unit of an archdeaconry and diocese rather than of a manor and honour. An essential component of the grant was

[48] For Chicksands, see *Monasticon*, vi. 2. 950–1. The Bullington advowsons are discussed in Golding, 'Gibertine Priories', 142–51; for Malton, see the cartulary (London, BL, Cotton Claudius D XI), for Shouldham, see the foundation charter (*Monasticon*, vi. 2. 975). This pattern of endowment from baronial families is a common one: for example, the Mowbrays gave all their churches in Yorkshire to Newburgh (for this and other cases, see Newman, 'Greater and Lesser Landowners', 281 n.).

[49] *Cal. Ch. R.* iv. 52; *Giraldi Cambrensis Opera*, vii. 34.

[50] Haverholme, for example, received five-sixths of the church of Anwick from Ralf son of Fulk of Anwick and the remaining sixth from Geoffrey son of Roger of Anwick; its moiety of Dorrington came from Walter of Dorrington; William of Ashby gave the church of Ashby de la Laund; and Walter the knight of Thorp the church of Thorp-by-Newark ('Haverholme Priory Charters', 31, 71–2, 89–90, 45).

[51] This slackening has been noticed elsewhere, e.g. Newman showed that the barons of Yorkshire made only seven grants of advowsons during the 13th century, and the record of the knights (who gave twenty-five), though better, does not stand comparison with the previous century (Newman, 'Greater and Lesser Landowners', 284–91).

naturally the right of advowson, but almost certainly a grant of a church also included its glebe land. The distinction drawn by the drafter of the charter whereby in the early 1180s Agnes, the heiress of William de Percy, granted to Sixhills both the advowson (*ius patronatus*) of St Helen's, Ludford and the church itself with all its appurtenances shows unusual and precocious sophistication.[52] Charters of donation frequently refer to the church and its appurtenances. Sometimes the endowment is specified. Robert de Chesney's grant of the church of Newark to his foundation of St Katherine's, Lincoln, included 20 acres of heathland, a *mansura* and two bovates in the fields of Newark, and William Foliot's grant of Saxby church to the same priory was accompanied by two bovates belonging to the church.[53] Glebe lands were granted to the parish church either by the local lord or by the parish community, sometimes both. Only rarely do we see how these endowments were built up, but light is shed on the process in a charter of Geoffrey of Keddington, who granted St Margaret's church there to the nuns of Alvingham, along with the lands that had been given to it both from his own lands and from those of his men, 'that is, one acre from every bovate, half from one side of the village, half from the other'.[54] As revealing is the list of grants of very small pieces of land (sometimes as little as a rood) given to the churches of Newton-on-Trent and Marton which were held by St Katherine's, Lincoln 'de dono rusticorum episcopi et non de dono episcopi'.[55]

Advowsons: Disputes and Uncertainties

Rights to churches and advowsons were as hotly contested as those pertaining to any other components of seigneurial property. Sometimes the religious could profit by these disputes. The grant of a church disputed

[52] *Gilbertine Charters*, 2. Other charters of Agnes conveying churches to Sallay and Whitby abbeys at about the same time do not make this distinction (*EYC* xi. 74). For changing formulas in charters giving churches, see Kemp, 'Monastic Possession', 137.

[53] *Cal. Ch. R.* iv. 52; *Reg. Sutton*, v. 86.

[54] Oxford, Bodl. Lib., MS Laud Misc. 642, fo. 122. This charter is discussed by F. M. Stenton in *Danelaw Charters*, pp. lxx–lxxi. Keddington is one of the villages of its region where a church is recorded in 1086, but Geoffrey's charter suggests that its endowment did not occur until the following century. That this allocation of land may have been more widespread is suggested by a mid-12th-century charter relating to the chapel of Hothorpe (Suffolk), whose endowment comprised one acre from each side of the village from every virgate (R. M. Thomson, 'Twelfth-Century Documents from Bury St Edmund's Abbey', *EHR*, 92 (1977), 809).

[55] *Registrum Antiquissimum*, ii. 330–1. The churches themselves had been given to the priory by bishop Robert de Chesney. The church of St Andrew, Utterby seems to have been granted lands on the occasion of or just prior to its consecration: this glebe passed with the church to Nun Ormsby.

between two or more tenants to a priory could be an acceptable compromise to end conflict. We have already observed how Nun Ormsby obtained the church of Fotherby after its ownership had been contested in the royal courts and by duel; Sixhills similarly gained the church of North Willingham. This was divided between two lords, William son of Goer and Matthew of Tealby. William's motives for his grant of rights in the church are unusually explicit. 'Since I am set in old age I see my end approaching', his charter reads: so, wishing to provide for his soul's salvation, he gave his right in the church to the nuns. Moreover, the dispute concerning the moiety of the church which was going on between him and Matthew had been settled, 'since I wish to keep nothing unjustly for me or mine which belongs to his fee. Truly also it is good to me that the nuns should have that part of the church which Matthew claimed and gave to them, without claim of me or mine.' This was done for the salvation of the souls of himself and his kin, 'that I might earn a good reward from Christ the Lord in the life eternal'. Here, then, is the act of an old man making his peace with his God and his neighbour in a solemn ceremony at Lincoln cathedral, pledging his faith in the hand of the archdeacon and in the presence of the chapter, who are asked to witness the grant. At about the same time William's daughter and her husband Walter de Scoteni confirmed William's grant and also gave up their claim to the moiety, ceding it to Matthew of Tealby, who then ceded it to the nuns. Thus all parties were satisfied and Sixhills gained a valuable living.[56]

More often, however, the Gilbertines had to fight to preserve their own rights, and the grant of an advowson to a priory was by no means a guarantee that it would be successful in maintaining its hold upon the church. Every Gilbertine house was involved at some time or other in such litigation, even though as far as possible this was avoided by obtaining confirmations from interested parties. It was common practice for heirs to issue confirmations of their predecessors' grants: alternatively, advowson rights are frequently the subject of final concords which may or may not represent real litigation. Frequently the priory would grant confraternity rights in return for quitclaims of advowsons. This was probably a cheap way to buy off actual or potential claims of descendants, while at the same time reaffirming ties between the priory and the families that supported it.[57] Some churches granted to the priories were never

---

[56] *Gilbertine Charters*, 3, 13. The church was valued at £10 in 1291 (*Taxatio*, 57).
[57] Golding, 'Gilbertine Priories', 348–9. For examples, see e.g. *Final Concords*, i. 99, ii. 208. Between the 1220s and 1260s Sempringham priory made fine concerning the advowsons

secured, or were lost to other claimants after only a short period; others were only obtained after long struggle. Many parties had an interest in a parish church: the incumbent, the donor's family, and the donor's lord, and opposition could be expected from all these quarters, while in cases where the advowson was divided the possibilities for rancour were extended to other tenants, both lay and ecclesiastical. These disputes might take long to surface. They were most often initiated by the descendants of the original donor, sometimes several generations later. Attempts to recover advowsons alienated in the twelfth century were particularly common in the following century as either the heirs of the donor or their lords tried to regain control of 'their' churches. The trade in advowsons was not all one-way, and the enthusiasm of the previous century for granting churches to the monks was giving way to a more cautious, pragmatic approach as the value of advowsons to provide relatives or clerks with a living was increasingly appreciated.[58]

Struggles for advowsons could therefore be lengthy and extraordinarily complex. The Gilbertines might well 'inherit' an advowson dispute: indeed, benefactors were particularly anxious to offload their most troublesome benefices on to the religious. Alvingham was given the advowson of Yarborough in 1275. This had been disputed between two local families since 1190; after the priory gained possession the struggle continued for over five decades and the community was only secure in 1333.[59] Ormsby priory was given the advowson of Covenham St Bartholomew in the third quarter of the twelfth century by Robert de Hallei, and this grant was confirmed by his son, Ralph.[60] However, in 1245–6 Ralph II de Hallei, the nephew of Ralph I, claimed the advowson from the prior, who quitclaimed his rights in the church to Ralph in return for two bovates. Two years later bishop Grosseteste placed Gervase, Ralph's nominee, in charge of the church till he had been ordained, and thenceforth the advowson remained in the hands of the family.[61] It is not clear why Ralph determined to recover the advowson. Certainly he was not himself a patron of Ormsby and may well have directed most of his pious benefactions

of at least five of its churches (Horbling: *Reg. Hugh de Welles*, iii. 134; Birthorpe: *Final Concords*, i. 192; Norton Disney, ibid. ii. 3; Kirkby Laythorpe: ibid. 218, and Cranwell: ibid. 223).

[58] See Newman, 'Greater and Lesser Landowners', 281, 290–3.

[59] This case is discussed in Golding, 'Gilbertine Priories', 137–41.

[60] Oxford, Bodl. Lib., MS Dodsworth 135, fo. 157ᵛ. For the Hallei family, see *EYC* xi. 207–12. Robert was also a benefactor of Sixhills.

[61] *Final Concords*, ii. 34; *Rotuli Roberti Grosseteste, Episcopi Lincolniensis 1235–53*, ed. F. N. Davis, LRS 11 (1914), 98.

to Rufford abbey. There is a hint in the Rufford transactions that Ralph
was in financial difficulties—certainly he was in debt to the Jews in 1254.
Covenham was a wealthy benefice, and, though Ralph could not himself
use its revenues, churches still retained some value for the laity.[62]

Malton priory had difficulties in securing at least two of its churches.
Some time between 1154 and 1166 Walter de Neville gave his share of the
advowson of the church of King's Walden (Hertfordshire) with the assent
of his lord, Geoffrey de Valognes. The other moiety was held by Albanus
Heyrun of the de la Mare fee. He likewise gave his share in the church to
the canons in return for confraternity. The incumbent was Adam of
Stewkley, son of the archdeacon, and his rights had next to be safe-
guarded in the confirmation charter of bishop Robert Chesney.[63] Adam
does not seem to have been satisfied with these assurances, and his position was only settled after litigation in the church courts between 1164
and 1166 which determined that he would pay annual pensions of one
mark to the canons and three marks to Walter de Neville, son of the
donor: an agreement which clearly illustrates the degree of control still
exercised by the lay lord who had nominally ceded all his rights to the
church. On the deaths of Adam and Walter the priory was to have full
possession of the church.[64] Malton's troubles were but beginning, however. Adam's successor was dilatory in paying his pension to the canons
and in 1206 the three papal judges-delegate appointed 'to protect the
order of Sempringham from its wrongdoers in England' ordered the
rector to pay what was owed or incur a further penalty. Two generations
later the canons' very right to the advowson was questioned. In 1259
Walter de Neville claimed that his ancestors had always presented to
King's Walden; prior John denied this claim and produced the charter of
donation. For his part Walter denied that the priory had ever received
seisin and claimed that another charter, that of John de Neville, the
donor's son, confirming the grant, was a forgery and that its seal was not
John's. The prior then put himself on the grand assize, but before the
case was heard a fine was made between the claimants and Walter conceded his rights.[65]

Problems were also experienced at Marton. The advowson had been

---

[62] *EYC* iii. 210; *Rufford Charters*, iii. 519–20.

[63] London, BL, MS Cotton Claudius D XI, fo. 226. Chesney's confirmation charter is
printed in *English Episcopal Acta. I*, 100.

[64] London, BL, MS Cotton Claudius D XI, fo. 226ᵛ; *English Episcopal Acta. I*, 100–1.
Since King's Walden was so far from Malton it was agreed that the pension be paid to the
Gilbertines at Chicksands for transmission to the Yorkshire house.

[65] London, BL, MS Cotton Claudius D XI, fo. 232.

granted in the 1160s to the hospital of Norton (which was under the control of the almoner of Malton) by Roger de Flamville. This grant was confirmed by Roger's son, Hugh, and by their lords, Roger and Nigel de Mowbray.[66] Later it was confirmed to the almoner of Malton *ad perpetuos usus proprios* by Roger, Master of the order, as well as by William de Chemillé, archdeacon of Richmond, and William, bishop-elect of Angers.[67] However, opposition to the canons soon emerged. Matilda de Flamville, Hugh's wife, and others, including master Honorius, the new archdeacon of Richmond, attempted to prevent the canons taking possession of the church. Papal intervention was necessary, and Innocent III ordered the church to be restored to the canons and the losses made good, while judges-delegate ensured that the canons were instituted to the church. The details of the dispute are lost, but what is significant are the forces that were mobilized on the canons' behalf, for it was not only the pope who came to their rescue but also archbishop Geoffrey of York and one of the Gilbertines' most notable and powerful patrons, Geoffrey fitzPeter, earl of Essex. He was asked by the archbishop and by the papal legate, John of Salerno, to safeguard the canons' rights and to aid them in the recovery of the church. The archdeacon appears to have incited the parishioners of Marton to withdraw from the church and to refuse to pay tithes and other offerings. This was forbidden and all priests were warned by the archbishop not to give the sacraments to the parishioners to the prejudice of their church and the priory. The dispute was finally settled *c.*1201 by the papal legate and judges-delegate. Matilda de Flamville confirmed the church to Malton and in 1203 the rural dean inducted the canons to Marton and a vicarage was ordained.

It is only in the last charters relating to the dispute that some light is shed on its cause. Master Roger and the canons swore never to quarrel again with Matilda 'our advocate' regarding any of her pasture land in the manor of Marton (perhaps a reference to an otherwise unrecorded but related dispute over tithes) and to remit all lands to Hugh de Flamville which his father had granted save all lands belonging to the churches of Malton and Norton. At the petition of Matilda the canons also agreed to render an annual rent of three marks to the nuns of Nun Monkton, who swore that they would never revive a claim to the church of Marton.[68] This is the first indication that another religious house was involved. It

[66] Ibid., fo. 60. Three of these charters are printed in *Monasticon*, vi. 2. 972. The Mowbray charters are printed in *Charters of the Honour of Mowbray*, 132, 134, nos. 184, 189.
[67] London, BL, MS Cotton Claudius D XI, fo. 60. These charters can be dated to *c.*1196.   [68] London, BL, MS Cotton Claudius D XI, fos. 61ᵛ–62.

would seem that the canons had become caught up in an inheritance dispute. Roger de Flamville had married Juetta de Arches, heiress to the Arches fee which Roger held in her right in 1166. Juetta's parents were founders of Nun Monkton, and her sister was prioress there. Roger was dead by Easter 1169 and was succeeded by Hugh, who married Matilda. Hugh should not have inherited any of his mother's lands, which certainly later passed to her descendants from her first marriage to Alan de Brus, but in 1212 Matilda claimed that she had been given a third of Hugh de Flamville's inheritance on marriage, which she certainly argued (though unsuccessfully) belonged to the Arches inheritance.[69] It is at least possible that Matilda was defending what she perceived to be her dower interests in Marton, and that she was prepared to support the nuns of Monkton, founded on the Arches fee, against the canons of Malton, who were favoured by her husband's family. The complexities of advowson litigation must have taken up a great deal of the communities' time and money. That they were prepared to engage in this activity testifies in itself to the value placed upon the possession of churches.

Litigation with rival religious communities was often as bitter and protracted as with the laity. Watton's troubles over the chapel of Skerne (East Riding, Yorkshire) lasted for more than a century, as the Gilbertine priory contested right with the neighbouring Cistercian abbey of Meaux. The root of the problem here was that Skerne, where Meaux was developing a large grange, lay in the parish of Hutton Cranswick, the church of which was held by Watton. To this potential cause of disputes over the rights of the mother church and the liability of the Cistercians to pay tithes on these lands was added further tension, since some lands given to the Cistercians in Skerne by Thomas I of Etton had earlier been granted to Watton by the same donor.[70] At the end of the twelfth century the rector of Hutton, Thomas of Etton (who is described as a clerk and friend of archbishop Geoffrey of York and who was presumably a kinsman of the donor), attempted to extort tithes on this land from Meaux. Prolonged litigation followed, and after more than two years and in spite of excommunication by the papal legates, Thomas (who was, as the Meaux chronicler bitterly regrets, skilled in the law) won his case at Rome and arbitration, weighted in his favour, decided that tithes should be paid on some of the lands while not on others.

---

[69] See Clay (ed.), *Early Yorkshire Families*, 1–2, 29–31. Clay argued that Hugh could not have had an interest in Marton: certainly he should not.

[70] *EYC* vii. 191–5; *Chronica Monasterii de Melsa, a fundatione usque ad annum 1396, auctore Thoma de Burton, abbate*, ed. E. A. Bond, 3 vols., Rolls Series (London, 1866–8), i. 316–18.

In the following generation Thomas II of Etton, who was heavily in debt to the Jews, first temporarily and then permanently granted all his land in Skerne and some in Hutton Cranswick, together with the advowsons of Hutton Cranswick and its dependent chapel of Skerne, to Meaux.[71] Unfortunately, he had no right to grant these advowsons, since in 1219 the prior of Watton had vouched him to warrant his father's grant of them to Watton, producing Thomas I's charter of donation and his son's own confirmation charter as evidence. Thomas II had acknowledged that the charters were genuine, and admitted that since he believed the presentation would remain to him he had unjustly impeded the prior's right.[72] By the 1220s Watton, though possessing little or no land in Skerne, did have an important interest in Hutton Cranswick. The interests of Meaux and Watton were beginning to impinge on each other with disturbing implications. Abbot Michael (1235–49) of Meaux shortly afterwards established a grange at Cranswick and it may well have been this act that precipitated the major dispute.

In January 1251/2 the abbot of Meaux impleaded the prior of Watton before the justices in eyre at York.[73] He alleged that the canons of Watton had been presenting to the livings of Hutton and Skerne, notwithstanding that the monks of Meaux held the advowson. At length, however, a compromise was hammered out by archbishop de Gray and the justices whereby the advowson of Hutton was confirmed to Watton, while that of Skerne, now raised to the status of a parish, went to Meaux. Immediately the monks set about obtaining the appropriation, and in 1253 were successful, through the good offices of a monk of Kirkstall, in obtaining papal letters to this end. The papal indult stated that the patronage had been granted to Meaux by Thomas de Etton. Obviously Innocent IV was not aware of Watton's claim, or, if he was, chose to ignore it.[74] While master John le Romeyn held the rectory of Hutton there was no trouble, but when his successor as treasurer of York and rector of Hutton, the even more notorious pluralist John Mansel, was presented to the living by Watton he soon 'violently ejected' the Cistercians from Skerne and held both livings.[75] Mansel next revived the issue of tithes that had been

---

[71] These grants can probably be dated between 1221 and 1227 (ibid. 374–7).

[72] *Rolls of the Justices in Eyre for Yorkshire*, ed. D. M. Stenton, Selden Society, 56 (1937), 55–6.

[73] *Feet of Fines for the County of York from 1246 to 1272*, ed. J. Parker, Yorkshire Archaeological Society Record Series, 82 (1932), 64. The fullest account of the dispute is contained in the partisan chronicle of Meaux compiled at the end of the 14th century (*Chronica Monasterii de Melsa*, ii. 111–14). [74] *Cal. Papal Letters*, i. 292.

[75] *York Minster Fasti*, ed. C. T. Clay, Yorkshire Archaeological Society Record Series, 123 (1957), 24–5.

settled some fifty years earlier. By this time the terms of the arbitration had been forgotten and a new jury met to consider the case. This established which lands had been held free of tithe. However, tithes from these lands had also been forcefully taken by the seneschal of John le Romeyn, the previous incumbent of Hutton, who later caused them to be restored to Meaux. This would suggest continuing uncertainty as to the respective rights of abbey and priory in the first half of the thirteenth century.

Though the dispute over tithes was finally resolved, shortly afterwards the question of rights to Skerne surfaced again. John Mansel died in 1264/5 and Meaux appointed to Skerne before Watton's candidate, Matthew, could be instituted to Hutton. Matthew brought a case in defence of his rights in the *sede vacante* capitular court at York, which decided to sequestrate the goods of Skerne but implicitly recognized the rights of Meaux by warning that if the monks did not present a suitable candidate the chapter would. Shortly afterwards another attempt was made to secure the appropriation. A Lucchese merchant, with whom the house probably had business dealings, was promised 40 marks to put the abbey's case at Rome. Here the monks were successful, but unfortunately the chapter of York was less amenable and the abbey was never able to secure the appropriation. It was for his reason that in 1280 abbot Robert finally decided to cut his losses and to give up the church to Watton. The prior received the abbot into fraternity, and a toft and other lands in Huggate were granted to the monks to compensate them for the payment of tithes from some of their lands.[76] Thus a dispute which had begun nearly a century earlier was resolved. It had involved not only the two communities, but at various stages the donor of the advowson and his family, the archbishop and chapter of York, the papal Curia, and royal justices.

Watton's troubles in the parish, however, were far from over. Almost immediately on gaining the advowson the prior presented *magister* Martin of Grimston to the church.[77] It was not to prove a happy choice. The first

[76] *Chronica Monasterii de Melsa*, ii. 155–6; *Feet of Fines for the County of York from 1272 to 1300*, ed. F. H. Slingsby, Yorkshire Archaeological Society Record Series, 121 (1955), 39–40.

[77] On 16 June 1280 (*The Register of William Wickwane, Lord Archbishop of York, 1279–1285*, ed. W. Brown, Surtees Society, 114 (1907), 98). Martin was probably related to *magister* Thomas of Grimston, a prebendary of York and archdeacon of Cleveland, whose executor he was. Martin was himself an archiepiscopal official and pluralist, receiving the vicarage of Kildwick in 1302, Feliskirk in 1305, and Cowlam in 1310. He had given up Kildwick by 1305–6 (*The Register of Thomas of Corbridge, Lord Archbishop of York, 1300–1304*, ed. W. Brown and A. H. Thompson, 2 parts, Surtees Society, 138, 141 (1925, 1928), i. 72, ii. 173; *The Register of William Greenfield, Lord Archbishop of York, 1306–1315*, ed. A. H. Thompson, 5 parts, Surtees Society, 145, 149, 151–3 (1925–40), i. 1, 130).

hint that anything was wrong came in July 1307, when the official of York was told to act in the case between the prior of Watton and master Martin 'claiming to be the rector of Skerne'.[78] A year later he was charged with immorality with six named women, including his serving girl. He admitted some of the charges, denied others, and was threatened with the loss of his benefice if he sinned again.[79] In February 1308–9 the York official was again mandated to hear the case pending between Martin and the prior. The court finally met in July 1309. Once again the issues were the interrelated ones of tithes and the status of Skerne. The canons claimed that tithes had always been paid by the people of Skerne to the church of Hutton Cranswick. Martin had refused to pay tithes in defiance of the Council of Tours (which in 1282 had laid down stern penalties against non-payers of tithes). The canons requested that it be reaffirmed that Skerne lay in Hutton parish and that tithes be paid to Hutton. The archbishop's judgement went wholly in the canons' favour and Martin himself was ordered to be removed from office.[80] Was the long struggle worth it? In 1291 the chapel of Skerne was valued at £10, the rectory of Hutton Cranswick at £40. In the same year the priory's *temporalia* in the archdeaconry of the East Riding alone were assessed at over £240.[81] In purely economic terms, therefore, possession of Skerne did not make a significant contribution to the priory's revenues. Its importance was, rather, symbolic. Collectively rights in churches were valuable: to protect these claims was essential.

Success was not, of course, inevitable. Many grants could not be secured and never came to fruition. In the interplay of conflicting interests the Gilbertines sometimes lost out to other houses or to a lay lord. Alvingham failed to secure the advowson of Wold Newton given in the mid-twelfth century by Walter Bec. Here the dominant landholder was the bishop of Durham. The church was already situated on his manor in 1086; the Becs were prominent tenants of the bishop and frequently served as his officials. Alvingham's failure here is hardly surprising.[82] In 1164 Hubert de Ria gave the church of Aslackby with a dependent chapel to the Templars, who founded a preceptory in the village. However, in

---

[78] *Reg. Greenfield*, iii. 127.　　　[79] Ibid. 133.

[80] Ibid. iii. 159–62. Hamilton Thompson plausibly suggested that Watton's claim 'was welcomed by the archbishop as a means of getting rid of an incumbent of doubtful reputation' (ibid. iii, p. xlviii).　　　[81] *Taxatio*, 303, 305.

[82] Discussed in Golding, 'Gilbertine Priories', 136–7. Bullington never made good its claim to the church of Tetford, which, though included in the list of churches confirmed to the priory by Philip of Kyme, continued in lay hands throughout the 13th century, and it was unable to maintain its hold on Bilborough and its chapel of Strelley (Nottinghamshire) for more than a generation (ibid. 150–1).

Richard I's 1189 confirmation charter in favour of Sempringham Hubert is said to have given the church to the Gilbertines, and it is also listed as belonging to Sempringham in Innocent IV's charter.[83] Hubert had certainly granted land in Aslackby to Sempringham, and the Templars were experiencing problems there with lay tenants in the 1190s. There was clearly tenurial confusion in the village and the Gilbertines may well have taken advantage of the complicated position to press their claims. For how long they were successful is unclear, but by the fourteenth century Aslackby was firmly back in the hands of the Templars' successors, the Hospitallers.[84]

Appropriations

By the beginning of the thirteenth century the distinction between possession of the right of advowson (the *ius patronatus*) and possession of the church *ad proprios usus* (the *ius proprietatis*) was clearly established.[85] In the former case the possessor had only the right to present a candidate to the living to the bishop for ordination, and had no claim to the income of the church. Such possession was not without value for it enabled the exercise of patronage in favour of a kinsman, friend, or servant; it did not have direct financial benefits, though in some circumstances the possessor of the advowson could impose the payment of an annual pension upon the rector. This represents a situation midway between ownership of the advowson and full appropriation. In the latter case the appropriator had a right to all the income from the church, including the glebe land, the greater and lesser tithes, and all offerings made to the church.

During the twelfth century, however, there was considerable ambigu-

---

[83] *Records of the Templars*, 80, 96. In 1185 the church was said to render nothing to the Templars. In Innocent IV's confirmation of the privileges of the order, the churches of Hale and Heckington are listed as being in the possession of Sempringham, yet there is little evidence that these were ever owned, or even claimed, by the priory (*Monasticon*, vi. 2. 960). In 1195 the brethren of St Lazar's unsuccessfully claimed the advowsons against the holders, Bardney abbey, which continued as rector until the Dissolution: the alleged interest of Sempringham is not mentioned (*Rotuli Curia Regis*, i. 9, 10).

[84] *Records of the Templars*, pp. clxxxvi–clxxxviii and references there cited. Interestingly, the church of Billingborough was recorded as being held of the Templars by Roger Burnel in 1185 but to render nothing, while in 1189 Roger is recorded as the grantor of the church to Sempringham. In this instance Sempringham retained the church (ibid., p. clxxxviii n.).

[85] On the theory and practice of appropriations, see G. W. O. Addleshaw, *Rectors, Vicars and Patrons in Twelfth- and Early-Thirteenth Century Canon Law*, St Anthony's Hall Publications, 9 (York, 1956), and C. Cheney, *From Becket to Langton* (Manchester, 1956), 122–36. For a general discussion of this topic in preceding generations, see Constable, 'Monastic Possession', 304–31.

ity between these forms of possession. As already shown, when a twelfth-century donor gave a 'church' it was far from clear how much of it the donee would end by possessing. The monastery might manage to gain control over the tithes and offerings, that is, achieve full appropriation, but it might only be possible to hold the glebe land or gain the right to presentment and a pension. At the same time, the substantial increase in the number of donations to the religious from lay patrons gave rise to fears that the priests serving these churches were subject to exploitation by their new masters. As a result full appropriation became increasingly difficult, and liable to diocesan and papal control. As early as 1102 Anselm had forbidden monks from taking so much of the revenue from their churches that there was not enough left for the maintenance of the priests, and there are a number of individual instances through the twelfth century in which bishops stipulated that the priest should be adequately provided for; but it was only at the end of the century that reforming bishops made any systematic attempt to regulate the possession of churches by the religious in their dioceses. They enjoined that the appropriator or rector should ordain a suitable payment in cash or kind, the vicarage, for the maintenance of the vicar, a perpetual appointee, appointed by the rector to serve the church and holding the vicarage till death, resignation, or deprivation. Such ordination of vicarages had to be formally sanctioned by the diocesan bishop.[86]

During this period of transition in the second half of the twelfth century, when bishops were gradually extending control over parish churches and the nature of rights to churches was being defined, it is often uncertain whether religious houses did enjoy all rights to many of the churches they were given. A confirmation charter of Geoffrey, bishop-elect of Lincoln (1175–81), in favour of Bullington lists twelve churches that the prior had been granted 'ad proprios usus eorum possidendos', which might imply that appropriation of the churches had already taken place. Of these churches, however, Hameringham was never formally appropriated, Ingham was not appropriated until 1310, and the canons' claim to the church of Tetford was never made good.[87] Another explanation is possible. It may be that the priory was obtaining episcopal consent for appropriation prior to actually proceeding to taking the rectories, just

---

[86] 12th-century developments are considered in Brett, *English Church*, 230–3; Cheney, *From Becket to Langton*, 121–5, 133–6; and Kemp, 'Monastic Possession', 147–58. The fullest discussion of this topic remains R. A. R. Hartridge, *A History of Vicarages in the Middle Ages* (Cambridge, 1930).

[87] *Registrum Antiquissimum*, ii. 29; *Danelaw Charters*, 4–5, no. 4.

as in a later period priories might obtain licences to acquire property in mortmain so that when an opportunity arose they might act immediately.[88]

Appropriation was the ideal: it could not always be achieved. In some cases it is likely that the priories were prevented in their ambitions by ongoing disputes with the family of the original donor. This certainly appears to have happened at Dunsby-by-Brauncewell. Here the nuns of Catley were granted the church by Alexander de Cressi. But a dispute with the donor's heirs occurred in the late 1230s. By this time it was becoming increasingly difficult for religious houses to gain episcopal permission for appropriation, and Catley never proceeded to full ownership of the church but had to be content with a small pension until the Dissolution.[89] There were particular problems in the case of divided churches, and in many cases appropriation proved impossible or difficult. Sixhills obtained a sixth of Nettleton church from the priory's founder, William son of Hacon, in the mid-twelfth century, and then a further third when Ivo son of Alden's land escheated to the crown a few years later; but the remaining half remained in lay hands.[90] In 1210 an assize of darrein presentment adjudicated a case between the prior and William Blanchard concerning a moiety of the advowson (presumably the half in lay possession), when the prior conceded his claim to William because he was ill and could not continue the case. Ten years later, Richard, William's son, and the prior agreed that the church should be shared between them, making presentations alternately.[91] In 1242 Richard acknowledged the prior's right to the advowson and in 1271 Matilda, his daughter and heiress, confirmed the existing arrangements in return for rights of confraternity for herself and her husband.[92] Once again litigation had precluded the priory gaining effective control over the church and its revenues.

Often, however, appropriation seems to have followed the grant of the church very speedily or even immediately. The nuns of Catley were given the church of Billinghay by Peter son of Henry of Billinghay in his foundation charter 'to be held for their own use'.[93] Sixhills had acquired

---

[88] Certainly, in the 13th century it was not unknown for monasteries to gain papal approval for appropriations which were only carried out at a later date, if at all. See *The Cartulary of Cirencester Abbey, Gloucestershire*, ed. C. D. Ross and M. Devine, 3 vols. (Oxford, 1964–72), i, p. xxviii.

[89] *Gilbertine Charters*, 90; *Rotuli Roberti Grosseteste*, 49–50; *VE* iv. 122.

[90] *Gilbertine Charters*, 1, 35.   [91] *CRR* vi. 55; *Final Concords*, i. 153–4.

[92] *CRR* xvi. 390; *Final Concords*, ii. 270.

[93] *Gilbertine Charters*, 72. At about the same time bishop Robert de Chesney confirmed Peter's grant and appropriation (*Registrum Antiquissimum*, ii. 29; see also *English Episcopal*

all its *spiritualia* within a very short time of its foundation. All its churches with the exception of Legsby were confirmed to the priory by bishop Hugh I *c.*1189–91, and though there is no explicit mention of appropriation, the omission of Legsby (which was not appropriated till 1270) from the list would suggest that appropriation had indeed taken place by the time Hugh issued his confirmation.[94] Certainly all these churches were appropriated by the time of Hugh of Wells, and one church (Cadeby) is specifically said to have been ordained 'long since'.[95] Similarly, all of Nun Ormsby's six appropriations had been achieved by *c.*1189–91.[96]

In this early period while all interested parties were feeling their way towards clearer definitions and, in the case of the bishops, tighter control, appropriations were easily obtained, and in normal circumstances the Gilbertines might have expected to proceed to the appropriation of every church they were given without delay or difficulty. During the thirteenth century, however, there was a sharp decline in the number of appropriations. In part this was because many of the churches held by the Gilbertines had already been appropriated, though few approached the completeness achieved by Chicksands, all but one of whose churches still in the priory's hands in 1535 had been appropriated by the end of the twelfth century.[97] Moreover, after about 1200 it became progressively more difficult of religious houses to appropriate their parish churches. The tide was rapidly turning against appropriations. To reforming bishops such as Grosseteste, in whose diocese so many Gilbertine priories and their churches lay, appropriation represented the unacceptable face of monasticism. Virtually no new licences for appropriation were granted during Grosseteste's episcopate, and none were in favour of a Gilbertine

---

Acta. I, 65, no. 97). On the other hand, Digby church, which had been given to Catley by 1184, was probably not appropriated till after 1200. It does not appear amongst the appropriated churches confirmed to Gilbertine priories by the dean and chapter of Lincoln, though it was certainly appropriated by the time of bishop Hugh of Wells (*Gilbertine Charters*, 73; *Registrum Antiquissimum*, ii. 25–32; *Rotuli Hugonis de Welles*, iii. 79).

[94] *Registrum Antiquissimum*, ii. 29–30; *Reg. Gravesend*, 44. The income from two churches, East Rasen and Saleby, was set aside by Roger, Master of the order, to buy fish (*Gilbertine Charters*, 22). [95] *Rotuli Hugonis de Welles*, iii. 80–2.

[96] *Registrum Antiquissimum*, ii. 30.

[97] The exception is revealing. Astwick was a dependent chapel of Stotfold when the latter was appropriated in the 1190s. Though still described as a *capella* in 1243, shortly thereafter it became a parish church, and, though a pension was paid to the priory, the now independent church was never fully appropriated (*VCH Bedfordshire*, ii. 206: *Registrum Antiquissimum*, ii. 31–2; *Rotuli Grosseteste*, 321). Similarly, Sixhills failed to appropriate only one church of which it held the undivided advowson. The advowson of the church of Toft-by-Rasen was given to the priory by Robert Burnell, bishop of Bath and Wells, in 1279, but the priory gained nothing more of this church's assets (*Gilbertine Charters*, 15).

house.[98] At the same time papal authorization was increasingly necessary and, following the Statute of Mortmain in 1279, the consent of the crown was also required. Appropriations to all of the Gilbertine priories either ceased altogether or were drastically curtailed. Such few Gilbertine appropriations as were licensed during Grosseteste's episcopate were papal not episcopal. In 1247 Innocent IV allowed Sempringham priory to appropriate Horbling, 'there being 200 women living under their Rule who often lack the necessities of life'. The following year he similarly licensed the appropriation of Prestwold (Leicestershire) to Bullington priory, in consideration of the priory's obligation to maintain one hundred women 'who for lack of necessities were suffering in health', as well as licensing Sempringham to appropriate Walcot.[99] In none of these cases is the appropriation described in the episcopal registers; recourse was clearly being had to the papal Curia in order to bypass episcopal control, and probable prohibition. Alvingham appropriated only one of its churches—Grainthorpe in 1448—after the early thirteenth century. Bullington only succeeded in appropriating two churches after *c.*1200.[100] At the end of the thirteenth century and during the fourteenth century appropriations increased a little. The reasons are not difficult to find. As benefactions to religious houses declined, partly because of changing fashions and partly as a result of mortmain legislation, and as the financial position of many houses worsened, appropriation was one of the few ways open for them to capitalize assets. However, the business of appropriation was now time-consuming and costly. Licences to amortise could be expensive; to proceed without due licence could be dangerous and doubly expensive. Episcopal permission continued to be necessary, and papal authorization

---

[98] For Grosseteste's attacks on appropriation, see his sermon at the Council of Lyon, cited in Hartridge, *History of Vicarages*, 76; *Rotuli Grosseteste*, p. v. Grosseteste also attempted to recover benefices from the religious where charters confirming the appropriations from the chapter of Lincoln could not be produced. Though the Gilbertines seem to have been exempt from this measure, it was probably prudent for them to obtain these confirmations, such as those of Roger the dean and chapter of Lincoln issued at the end of the 12th century (*Roberti Grosseteste episcopi quondam Lincolnensis epistolae*, ed. H. R. Luard, Rolls Series (London, 1861), p. lxxi, cited in Graham, *St Gilbert*, 107. For Roger's confirmations, see *Registrum Antiquissimum*, ii. 24–32).

[99] *Cal. Papal Letters*, i. 232–3, 258–9; Golding, 'Gilbertine Priories', 162. It is far from certain that there were actually 100 women in Bullington at this time; the figure clearly relates to the upper limit imposed on the female community by the Rule. By this time only a plea of poverty was accepted as a valid reason for appropriation. For another, slightly later, example, see bishop Gravesend's licensing of the appropriation of Old Sleaford and Ruskington churches to Haverholme (*Liber Antiquus de Ordinationibus Vicariarium tempore Hugonis Wells, Lincolniensis Episcopi, 1209–1235*, ed. A. Gibbons (Lincoln, 1888), 105).

[100] Golding, 'Gilbertine Priories', 163.

became (at least in theory) obligatory after 1366.[101] That rather more appropriations were carried out at this time when compared with the most restrictive years of the thirteenth century testifies to the priories' economic difficulties. In a number of cases financial advantages were only short-term. As rectors, the priories were now responsible for the upkeep of the chancels: often they had to choose between meeting the financial needs of their own community and repair of their churches, and the choice was often in the former's favour.[102]

Poverty was by now the only excuse for the validation of appropriation. A typical claim is that of Bullington as it proceeded to appropriate Ingham in 1310. Bishop Dalderby recognized the prior's claim of poverty in his approval, which referred to the heavy burden of taxation endured by the priory and its probable further increase, and to the priory's proximity to the public street so that 'on that pretext frequent crowds of noble and poor people come to it', with the result that the convent could not support the heavy expense of hospitality. At the same time the number of nuns and lay sisters in the priory allegedly placed an unbearable strain upon its resources.[103] Though we may doubt the sincerity of all the claims of poverty made by religious houses in support of requests for appropriations, there can be no doubt of the problems faced by Mattersey in 1280. The archbishop of York's instrument licensing the appropriation of Mattersey church is one of the fullest of such documents.[104] It describes how the canons had been reduced to near-total penury by the disastrous fire which destroyed much of the buildings and all the priory's muniments. The canons were allowed to retain all garb tithes from lands then in cultivation (with the exception of eight bovates), and the tithe of all hay. The dwelling of the rector, the glebe lands, and all church offerings were to be the vicar's. No tithes were to be paid on the canons' own lands and buildings, including their tannery and mills in the parish. The canons were to be responsible for the payment of procurations and synodals and were to make an annual payment of 20s. to the vicar and a further four

---

[101] See in general K. L. Wood-Legh, *Studies in Church Life under Edward III* (Cambridge, 1934), 126–53.

[102] Thompson, *The English Clergy and their Organization in the Later Middle Ages* (Oxford, 1947), 128–31.

[103] Golding, 'Gilbertine Priories', 162–3. Many commentators have noted the more or less standard forms of pleas of poverty in the 13th and 14th centuries. See e.g. Hartridge, *History of Vicarages*, 104–11; J. R. H. Moorman, *Church Life in England in the Thirteenth Century* (Cambridge, 1945), 39–41; Thompson, *English Clergy*, 110. For complaints of poverty as legitimate justification for appropriation, see Wood, *English Monasteries*, 138–9.

[104] *Reg. Wickwane*, i. 70–3.

shillings for the repair and upkeep of books and ornaments and four pence as wax-scot. As was customary, the canons were to pay for all necessary work in the chancel, while all other extraordinary expenses were to be shared equitably. This represents a rather more generous allowance than that given to most vicars in churches appropriated to the Gilbertines in earlier generations, and indicates a growing concern for the well-being of vicars, which frequently found expression in the augmentation of existing vicarages as the century progressed.[105]

Vicarages

The appropriation of a parish church led inevitably to two options for the religious house. It could either provide a priest from within the community to serve the parish (an option that is discussed in more detail below), or it could appoint a vicar or stipendiary priest to act in the community's stead.[106] Early appropriations to the Gilbertines (such as those approved by the dean and chapter of Lincoln in the 1190s) make no mention of the provision of vicarages. What, then, did the vicar receive? He may have taken all the spiritual income in return for the payment of a pension. Such arrangements were known but were not advantageous to the religious. The vicar was then in fact, though not in theory, no different from a rector, and there was a tendency for those vicars to assume rectorial status, to the loss of the appropriator. Moreover, the religious would obviously receive only a fraction of the church's potential income. At the same time, an increase in pension without diocesan permission had been forbidden by Alexander III. Finally, at a time of rising agricultural prices the vicar stood to gain more from the exploitation of the glebe than the payment of a money rent the real value of which was declining.[107] It is more likely that the early Gilbertines relied on stipendiary priests who lacked security and were poorly remunerated. In many cases arrangements were probably made on an *ad hoc* basis, and were dependent on a

---

[105] For this appropriation Wickwane appears to have exacted a *quid pro quo*, for the collation to the vicarage was reserved to the archbishops of York for ever. This right was exercised two days later when William de Langtoft was collated to the vacant vicarage.

[106] The growing concern for the temporal welfare of the vicar during the 12th and early 13th centuries and the corresponding formalization of the vicarage have been much discussed. See, in particular, Kemp, 'Monastic Possession', 133–60; Hartridge, *History of Vicarages*; Addleshaw, *Rectors, Vicars and Patrons*; and Cheney, *From Becket to Langton*, 122–36. For the situation in Lincolnshire, see Owen, *Church and Society*, 26–7, 73–4.

[107] Kemp, 'Monastic Possession', 150–2.

number of criteria, including the status of the incumbent, the value of the church, and the attitude of the diocesan.

As the century progressed, diocesan bishops increasingly insisted that adequate provision be made for priests in appropriated churches, and that perpetual vicarages be assigned to them. The nature of these varied: sometimes the vicar received a pension, sometimes a portion or the whole of the tithes, or even glebe land; normally he was provided with a house. Sometimes he would receive the church offerings, and (more rarely) was given a food corrody.[108] The chronology of vicarage creation is far from certain. Bishop Hugh of Wells compiled (probably during 1228 and 1229) the so-called *Liber Antiquus de Ordinationibus Vicariarum*, a useful and important, though potentially misleading, description of vicarages established in his diocese to date.[109] It has been thought that this detailed vicarages created by Hugh alone, but while it is clear that Hugh was a reformer responsible for the creation of numerous vicarages, in many cases the *Liber Antiquus* merely describes or confirms arrangements made in the time of Hugh's predecessors, notably Hugh I.[110] The existence of the *Liber Antiquus* and additional material contained in Hugh's episcopal registers provides a picture of vicarages ordained by Gilbertine houses within the diocese of Lincoln; for the houses in the dioceses of York and for the churches appropriated to Shouldham (Norwich diocese) the information is generally much later and less full.[111]

However, even in Lincoln diocese it is rarely possible to determine with accuracy when the vicarages were established. It is possible, though perhaps unlikely, that they were created when the bishops confirmed the appropriations. As has been seen, these confirmations were for the most part made by the mid-1190s. A rare example of such a confirmation

---

[108] For early examples, see Brett, *English Church*, 232; Cheney, *From Becket to Langton*, 133–5; Kemp, 'Monastic Possession', 154–7.

[109] *Liber Antiquus de Ordinationibus Vicariarum tempore Hugonis Wells. Lincolniensis Episcopi 1209–1235*, ed. A. Gibbons (Lincoln, 1888); D. Smith, 'The Rolls of Hugh of Wells, Bishop of Lincoln, 1209–35', *BIHR* 45 (1972), 175.

[110] For the earlier view, see Hartridge, *History of Vicarages*, 36–9; for reappraisal, see especially Cheney, *From Becket to Langton*, 131–3 and 'Appendix II: early vicarages in the diocese of Lincoln', 182–8, and Owen, *Church and Society*, 26–7.

[111] However, one contemporary example from the diocese of York shows similar arrangements there. After establishing their rights to the church of Marton, the canons of Malton were inducted by the archdeacon of Richmond in 1203 on condition that a perpetual vicarage was assigned. This was to consist of all the alterage except the offerings of the dead, the tithes of wool and sheep, and all land of the church except a messuage for the vicar. The new vicar next acknowledged that all garb tithes and tithes of vegetables 'both from the gardens and the fields' belonged to the priory, along with the tithes from the land and court of the canons in Grafton and all the tithes of hay in the parish. The vicar was to be responsible for synodals and procurations (London, BL, MS Cotton Claudius D XI, fo. 61^{r–v}).

specifically associated with the creation of a vicarage is found in two
charters of Hugh I of Lincoln confirming Lambert de Scoteni's grant of
two-thirds of the church of Stainton-le-Vale to Alvingham. In one the
canons were instituted to the church *ad usus proprios*, saving the rights of
the sitting incumbent during his lifetime, and in the other the church was
confirmed to the canons on condition that a satisfactory perpetual vicarage was created.[112] A few other ordinations can be securely dated. The
vicarages of Stotfold and Cople (Chicksands) were said to be ordained
auctoritate concilii (i.e. the Lateran Council of 1215), and four: Billingborough (Sempringham), Anwick (Haverholme), Cadeby (Sixhills), and
Auford (St Katherine's, Lincoln), were ordained by master Reginald of
Chester, whom the Anwick ordination refers to as the bishop's official,
while the bishop himself was in foreign parts.[113] Hugh was out of the
country from 1209 to July 1213 and again in 1215, when he was present
at the Lateran Council, so these ordinations must have occurred during
one of these periods, yet they are described in the *Liber* as recent, a
phrase which Cheney argued implied an early appropriation.[114] This group
of ordinations is of particular interest. Some time between 1215 and 1219
archbishop Stephen Langton adjudicated a dispute between Hugh of
Wells and the Gilbertine order concerning these four churches (and a
moiety of Cranwell, held by Sempringham priory).[115] Unfortunately, the
details of the case are unknown, but it appears to have centred on the
order's right to appropriate these churches. The Gilbertines claimed that
by virtue of their privileges they could appropriate churches of which
they held the advowson; and the implication seems to be that they were
denying the right of the diocesan bishop to interfere because their papal
privileges freed them from episcopal control. Langton allowed the appropriations to proceed subject to the provision of suitable vicarages, but
ruled that the Gilbertines should not use these privileges during Hugh's
episcopate. The ordinations recorded in the *Liber Antiquus* must be the
response to this settlement, and cannot be early.

In some cases the vicar continued to pay a pension to the religious, and
Professor Cheney suggested that all such vicarages were early, being

---

[112] Oxford, Bodl. Lib., MS Laud Misc. 642, fo. 4ᵛ. These charters can be dated between
1186 and 1200.

[113] 'dum essemus in partibus transmarinis' (*Liber Antiquus*, 22, 23, 55, 66, 86–7). Reginald
first appears as bishop's clerk in 1213 and disappears in 1219. He was subdean from 1217
to 1219 (*Fasti: Lincoln*, 23, 115).

[114] Cheney, *From Becket to Langton*, 182. The bishop's confirmation of the ordination of
Billingborough vicarage is dated 1218 (*Liber Antiquus*, 87).

[115] *Registrum Antiquissimum*, ii. 44–6.

established before there was a shift to a situation where the vicarage consisted of 'a portion of miscellaneous revenues'.[116] The vicars of a number of churches appropriated to the Gilbertines did pay pensions, but in every case but one they only received the *alteragium* or lesser tithes.[117] It seems likely that in many cases where churches were early appropriated pension arrangements of this sort were later adjusted so that the greater tithes which may once have belonged to the vicar were now in the priories' hands. These amendments are recorded in the *Liber Antiquus*. Some support for this hypothesis is furnished from the case of the churches of Stotfold and Cople. Both were appropriated to Chicksands by bishop Hugh I before 1200. Some arrangements had to be made for the support of their priests, but no vicarages were ordained here till after 1215, when the vicars received a toft and the lesser tithes (except those of linen) and paid an annual pension.[118] What we see in the *Liber Antiquus* is the situation after the stabilization of the vicar's revenues and responsibilities; though it may indicate earlier arrangements and individual bargains in which the payment of pensions figured.[119] All that can be concluded is that the Gilbertines started to establish vicarages in the last quarter of the twelfth century, and that the process was substantially complete (at least in the diocese of Lincoln) by the time of Hugh of Wells's death in 1235.

Even after the codifications of the reforming bishops there was still a wide variety in the types of vicarages ordained and in their value. Though in 1215 the Fourth Lateran Council had expanded the decision of the Council of Westminster, prohibiting monks from so exploiting their churches that those who served them were in need, it was only in 1222 that the Council of Oxford laid down rules which protected the rights of the vicar, and, especially, established five marks as his minimum annual stipend in English dioceses, thereby setting a benchmark for the valuation of future ordinations.[120] The most common feature of the vicarages was the grant of the *alteragium*, either in whole or excluding elements such as (most commonly) flax, or, as in the case of Friskney, salt (an indication of

---

[116] Cheney, *From Becket to Langton*, 133.

[117] The exception is Cawthorpe, where the vicar received all the church revenues (except the tithes from Alvingham's demesne in the parish) and the glebe land, and paid an annual pension to Alvingham. As Kemp has pointed out, in parishes where the religious had a large estate from which tithes were not due, the incumbent might not be as well off as appears at first sight (*Liber Antiquus*, 60; Kemp, 'Monastic Possession', 151 n.).

[118] *Registrum Antiquissimum*, ii. 31–2; *Liber Antiquus*, 22–4.

[119] Kemp ('Monastic Possession', 159 and n.) gives examples of cases from Reading abbey in which vicars received assigned revenues but also paid pensions.

[120] Brett, *English Church*, 128; Hartridge, *History of Vicarages*, 20–1, 40–1.

that commodity's importance in the marshes of Candleshoe wapentake). From these exclusions it is clear that the term *alteragium* normally included the lesser tithes, as well as the customary altar offerings.[121] Very occasionally no mention was made of the alterage, but in these cases the altar dues were specifically detailed. Thus at Sempringham the vicar was to receive 1*d*. at All Saints' Day, 3*d*. at Christmas, 2*d*. at Easter, and 1*d*. on the church's patronal festival. He would also get the 'second legacy' or 'mortuary' payment and 1*d*. at every funeral and wedding.[122] In these cases, too, it was customary for the vicar to receive a payment in food. At Sempringham this consisted of 11 quarters of marketable (*paccabilis*) wheat and two servant's loaves (probably from the priory kitchen) every day for his servant.[123] At other vicarages the vicar received similar payments of wheat, and sometimes hay.[124] However, food payments were not confined to vicars who received the *alteragium*, though in these instances (Cockerington, Grimsby Parva, and Grimoldby) such allowances were significantly much less generous.[125]

Nearly as universal a feature of the vicarage was the provision of a toft for the vicar's residence.[126] The implication of this provision must be that, even in churches that were close to the appropriating priory, the canons expected to appoint a secular priest rather than serve the churches themselves.[127] Sometimes the toft was described in a little more detail: that of Bracebridge lay to the east of the church; in Canwick there were two tofts, one next the church, the other south of the church to make a house for the vicar ('ad curtilegium vicarii faciendum').[128] The importance of the appropriated church as a source of revenue to the religious is well illustrated at Auford, where half of the vicar's dwelling was reserved

---

[121] See ibid. 37. *Alteragium* was defined in the ordination of the vicarage of Auford (St Katherine's, Lincoln) in 1219–20 as all the offerings, proceeds, and obventions, excluding garb tithes (*Liber Antiquus*, 93).

[122] Ibid. 54. The meaning of the *secundum legatum* is discussed by Hartridge, *History of Vicarages*, 227–9. Similar provisions were made for Burgh-le-Marsh and Winthorpe (Bullington), Ormsby, Utterby, and Fotherby (Ormsby), and Alvingham, where the oblation fees were double what they were in the other parishes, presumably because there were two churches here under the vicar's care (*Liber Antiquus*, 59, 60).

[123] Ibid. 54. For similar maintenance grants in cases where the vicarage was close to the monastery, see Kemp, 'Monastic Possession', 157–8.

[124] The vicars of Burgh and Winthorpe also had the altar bread.

[125] For rather more lavish allowances in Lincolnshire established by other houses, see Owen, *Church and Society*, 73.

[126] Only in the cases of Billingborough (Sempringham) and Anwick (Haverholme) is this not specified. However, in the former instance reference is made to the 'houses and other appurtenances' of the church (*Liber Antiquus*, 55).

[127] The care of churches is discussed below, pp. 388–91.   [128] *Liber Antiquus*, 56.

to the canons of St Katherine's to make a tithe barn.[129] There are one or two examples where the vicar also had a landed endowment. The vicar of West Torrington (which belonged to Bullington) had all the *alteragium*, tithes of all the crofts, and corn tithes of four bovates 'assigned to the vicar', which should have provided him with a very substantial income.[130] It was normally taken as read that the rector would maintain the chancel of the church, though in the case of Anwick (Haverholme) this obligation was spelt out: the prior and convent would bear the cost of repairing the books, vestments, and chancel of the church.[131] Another cost normally carried by the priories was the responsibility for the payment of all burdens, including procurations and sinodals, though at Billingborough, Anwick, and Cadeby the vicar himself bore the charge of the latter.[132] The receipt of an annual money payment was not unusual, the sum varying between 6s. 8d. (at Birthorpe, Grimsby Parva, and South Elkington) and £1 10s. (at West Wykeham).[133] There is no indication why some vicars received such a payment, others not: in some cases the recipient did not receive food or other payments as well, though this is by no means a general rule, and the fortunate cleric of Burgh-le-Marsh had a food allowance, all altar offerings, and £1 6s. 8d. per annum.[134] An additional burden that was usually borne by the priory was the provision of a chaplain to aid the vicar.[135]

In cases where the church was divided between two or more rectors the arrangements for the vicar were inevitably somewhat more complicated.[136] Dorrington was appropriated jointly to Haverholme and Shelford. Haverholme provided the vicar with a bovate of arable land, the prior of Shelford gave a toft and croft 'of equal value'. The priors split the

---

[129] 'ad faciendum . . . horrea sua ad reponendum decimas garbarum ad prefatam ecclesiam et capellam pertinentes, que conceduntur eis integre in proprios usus convertende' (ibid. 66). For a similar arrangement made by Elsham priory at Kingerby, see Owen, *Church and Society*, 72.   [130] *Liber Antiquus*, 58.

[131] Ibid. 55, 87.

[132] Ibid. 55, 66. The only exception was at Auford, where the vicar had to bear all burdens but on account of this received an annual payment (*auxilium*) of 10s. (ibid. 66). It was normal for the value of a vicarage to be higher in instances where the vicar was responsible for the payment of spiritual dues (see Hartridge, *History of Vicarages*, 43–5; Kemp, 'Monastic Possession', 158 n.).

[133] *Liber Antiquus*, 54, 57–8, 60–1. The vicar of Winthorpe received one mark *per annum* from Bullington for his clothing (ibid. 59).   [134] Ibid. 59.

[135] Chaplains or deacons were provided at Winthorpe, Burgh-le-Marsh, Utterby, Fotherby, Grimsby Parva, and Chicksands. Only at Auford was the vicar himself made responsible for a chaplain at the dependent chapel of Rigsby (ibid. 60).

[136] The Church recognized the problems caused by divided rectories and made efforts to eradicate them, without much success (see Cheney, *From Becket to Langton*, 129–30).

expenses of procurations equally.[137] At West Wykeham, which was divided between Sixhills and Markby, the rectors were equally responsible
for the vicarage, but Markby additionally granted to the vicar, whom they
had presented, all the oblations and obventions of their men in the vill,
the tithes from two bovates, and an additional stipend of 5s.[138] Watton
priory and Guisborough shared the rectory of Hessle (East Riding, Yorkshire). In 1247 the two houses came to an arrangement whereby the Augustinians demised their share of the church to Watton for 26 marks per
annum though they retained the right of presentation to the vicarage. Such
an agreement was probably the most sensible in cases of divided rectories,
particularly as here where Watton was much closer to the church in question than Guisborough.[139] Potentially more confusing were cases where
the advowson of part of the appropriated church continued to rest in lay
hands. At Anwick, where Haverholme had acquired all but a sixth of the
church, the vicar was to receive five-sixths of the alterage and the garb
tithes from all of the demesne land in the village, and the tithe of another
bovate, while he also received all of the glebe belonging to his portion
with the turbaries and other appurtenances. In this parish certainly the
vicar did not do badly in spite of the problems of the divided rectory.[140]

Finally, how generous were the canons in their provision of vicarages?
The Fourth Lateran Council had laid down that vicars should receive a
reasonable portion, and later English councils repeated this stipulation.[141]
The *Liber Antiquus* and rolls of bishop Hugh of Wells give the valuation
of forty-two vicarages in churches held by Gilbertines. Of these twenty-
eight (66 per cent) were valued at less than five marks, and a further six
at five marks only. This figure should be compared with the total number
of vicarages recorded in the *Liber Antiquus*, where fifty out of 134 vicarages (37 per cent) were assessed at less than five marks.[142] It is true that
these assessments were probably lower than the vicarages' actual values,
but the comparison remains valid.[143] There are two possible explanations

---

[137] *Liber Antiquus*, 56.   [138] Ibid. 57–8.   [139] London, BL, Addit. Chart. 1050.
[140] *Liber Antiquus*, 55.
[141] For the Lateran council decree, see C. J. Hefele, *Histoire des Conciles*, ed. and trans.
H. Leclercq, 8 vols. in 16 (Paris, 1902–21), v, pt. 2. 1359–60. For the Oxford Council, see
Councils and Synods, with other Documents relating to the English Church. II. AD 1205–1313,
ed. F. M. Powicke and C. R. Cheney, 2 vols. (Ocford, 1964), i. 112. For examples of other
legislation of the 13th century dealing with this problem, see ibid. 314 (Statutes of Worcester III, 1240), 165 (Statutes of Chichester I, 1245 × 1252); ii. 171 (Legatine Council of
London, 1268), 1025–6 (Statutes of Exeter II, 1287). Reforming bishops such as Grosseteste
made frequent attempts to augment vicarages wherever possible.
[142] Hartridge, *History of Vicarages*, 41.
[143] Ibid. 41–2; Graham, 'The Taxation of Pope Nicholas IV', 434–54.

for the relatively low values of the Gilbertine vicarages. They may have
been established before the reforming days of the Lateran Council, the
Council of Oxford, and bishop Hugh of Wells. Alternatively, and perhaps
more likely, the relative poverty of these churches meant that the value
of the vicarage could not be higher. Hartridge (following Coulton) suggested that frequently a vicarage was valued at a third of the total value
of the church, and that this reflected the Gelasian quadripartite division
of tithes between bishop, clergy, fabric, and the poor, only the last two
elements being due to the monastery.[144] However, this correlation is not
often found in the case of the Gilbertine vicarages, and though it may be
significant that the two vicarages known to have been ordained after the
Lateran Council were indeed valued at one-third of the churches' total
value, the sample is too small to suggest that this was a result of the
Council's legislation. Of the thirty-nine churches where the value of the
vicarage and the total value is given, a third had vicarages assessed at less
than a third of the total assessment. Yet, though so many of the vicarages
were poorly endowed, there are only two clear examples (and these very
late) of a vicarage being augmented, even though from the thirteenth
century reforming bishops were active in increasing vicarial incomes,
while poor vicars themselves petitioned for the increase of their living.

However, the growing reluctance to authorize appropriations is certainly reflected in the much more detailed descriptions of vicarages and
of the rights and responsibilities of the vicars, as shown above in the case
of Mattersey. In 1203 William son of Peter of Aslaby granted a moiety of
the church of Sancton (East Riding, Yorkshire) to Watton priory, by
which date Alexander of Sancton had already given his share. In 1249
archbishop Walter de Gray approved a pension from the church for a
pittance of five marks to the nuns of Watton, and the following year, on
the death of one of the rectors, the living was consolidated.[145] However,
the nuns of Watton had to wait sixty years for the appropriation. This
was approved in 1309, when pope Clement V allowed it in order to
provide clothing for the nuns. The vicarage was ordained the following
year. It was assessed at 10 marks. If this sum was not paid then the living
was to be sequestrated and, having been warned, the prior, sub-prior,
cellarer, and sacrist were to be excommunicated. While the *mansio* of the
rectory was to remain to the convent, an acre plot was to be assigned for
a house and garden for the vicar, who was to have a kitchen and stable as

[144] Hartridge, *History of Vicarages*, 42–3; Constable, *Monastic Tithes*, 43.
[145] *The Register. or Rolls, of Walter Gray, Lord Archbishop of York, with Appendices of Illustrative Documents*, ed. J. Raine, jun., Surtees Society, 56 (1872), 108, 109.

well as a hall, two chambers, and a larder. The priory was (as customary) to maintain the chancel, provide books and ornaments, and pay 10s. in procurations to the archdeacon. All other ordinary expenses were to be borne by the vicar while extraordinary costs were to be shared equally.[146] Vicars were now, therefore, generally much better provided for, and it was perhaps as well for the Gilbertines that they had managed to procure the appropriation of the majority of their churches before new episcopal stringency took effect.

The Care of Churches

In the early years of the order it was only in very unusual circumstances that the canons themselves cared for their churches. Formal papal approval for the Gilbertines to present one of their canons to a church of which they held the advowson was first given in response to the order's petition by Alexander III in the 1170s. Four (or at least three) canons could be chosen, one of whom would then be presented to the bishop for institution.[147] Canons regular had been allowed to carry out parochial responsibilities since the Council of Poitiers (1100), and it is significant that the papal privileges obtained by the Gilbertines were also granted (and in almost identical phraseology) to the Premonstratensian houses of Welbeck (by Alexander III) and Easby (by Urban III), and again to the whole order by Clement III in 1188.[148] But, as in the case of the Premonstratensians, there is little evidence that churches held by the Gilbertines were normally served by canons until the end of the thirteenth century at the earliest.[149]

Normally the incumbent at the time when the advowson or appropriation was passed to the religious might expect to continue in office for his lifetime. Indeed, his assent to the transaction was frequently regarded as

---

[146] *Cal. Papal Letters*, ii. 64; *Reg, Greenfield*, iii. 174–6. The priory had neglected to obtain royal approval for their act, and were only pardoned for this offence, and for similar unlicensed appropriations of Hutton and Skerne, in 1317 (*Cal. Pat. R. 1313–17*, 669).

[147] London, BL, MS Cotton Claudius D XI, fo. 10ʳ⁻ᵛ, transcribed in *Papsturkunden in England*, i, no. 171. This privilege was confirmed by later popes including Honorius III and Innocent IV (ibid., fos. 11ᵛ, 14ᵛ).

[148] Colvin, *The White Canons*, 277; *Papsturkunden in England*, i, nos. 198, 240.

[149] Cf. Colvin, *The White Canons*, 277–9. One of the earliest recorded cases is the appointment of canon Walter de Codington of St Katherine's, Lincoln, to that priory's valuable living of Newark in 1301 (*Reg. Corbridge*, i. 223).

necessary or advisable.[150] Rectors might also swear to give up their rights, as did Reginald de Mareis, rector of Ingham, who swore in the chapter at Lincoln to renounce all claims to the church to Bullington, though frequently in other cases the diocesan bishop acted to preserve the incumbent's rights, only licensing an appropriation if these rights were maintained.[151]

Even where the parish church lay very close to the priory and was held by the priory it was customary for it to be served by a rector, or more usually by a vicar. An exception to this practice is, however, found at Alvingham. The situation here was doubly unusual. There were two churches (of Alvingham and Cockerington St Mary) standing immediately outside the priory gates and lying in the same churchyard ('in uno et eodem cimiterio'). It was customary for them to be served jointly by a vicar, who had the care of souls in both parishes, and by one of the canons.[152] However, the Gilbertines did not appoint vicars to their rectories in every case, but sometimes relied instead on stipendiary chaplains. This appears to have happened particularly in the northern province. Thirteenth-century archbishops of York were concerned at the non-appointment of vicarages and seem to have tried to force the Gilbertines to act, since twice the papacy came to the canons' protection. In 1259 Alexander IV allowed them to continue to serve churches in which vicars had not been appointed, with chaplains, and ordered that vicarages should not be ordained against the order's will, notwithstanding any indult granted to the archbishop of York or any others.[153] Malton priory would appear to have been especially reliant upon chaplains. In 1271 archbishop Walter Giffard confirmed the appropriation of Malton, Wintringham, Norton, and Marton churches to be served either by the canons themselves or by secular priests, and four years later the bishop of Lincoln conceded that the priory might appoint chaplains to King's Walden, 'no vicarage having yet been instituted'.[154] Certainly the Gilbertines seem to have looked to their canons to serve churches more frequently in the later Middle

---

[150] See e.g. Hamelin Croc's assent to his nephew's alienation of the church of Grainthorpe to Alvingham, saving his rights as parson (Oxford, Bodl. Lib., MS Laud Misc. 642, fo. 96).

[151] London, BL, Cotton Chart. xii. 3. See e.g. bishop Hugh I of Lincoln's approval of the appropriation of Stainton-le-Vale to Alvingham (Oxford, Bodl. Lib., MS Laud Misc. 642, fo. 4') [152] *Liber Antiquus*, 59.

[153] *Cal. Papal Letters*, i. 366. This concession should be seen as one of a series of papal privileges granted to the order in the 1240s and 1250s limiting episcopal authority. Most of these are concerned with the taxation of vicarages (e.g. ibid. 230, 284, 297, 301, 332).

[154] London, BL, MS Cotton Claudius D XI, fo. 42.

Ages. In 1289 the prior of Malton was cited to appear before the archbishop of York to answer for the appropriated church of Marton, where
no vicars had been instituted, and in 1308 he was similarly cited for the
churches of Old Malton, Wintringham, and Norton.[155] The implication
here that these churches, all of which lay close to the priory, were served
by the canons or, perhaps more likely, by stipendiary priests, was made
explicit a century later when in 1402 archbishop Scrope confirmed the
appropriation of Old Malton and Wintringham (with their attendant
chapels), Norton and Marton, and approved the arrangement whereby
the churches (excluding Marton) were served by canons or temporary
secular priests rather than by perpetual vicars.[156]

Sometimes the rector of a Gilbertine church would himself appoint a
vicar: in these instances the rector would probably be non-residentiary.
Such a practice was not uncommon at the end of the twelfth and the
beginning of the thirteenth century, though it was generally deplored
since it did of course negate the very thrust of episcopal legislation to
ensure that the priest in charge received a satisfactory income.[157] By
c.1200 there was a vicar at King's Walden who paid 12 marks per annum
to the canons of Malton, and an *aureus* to the rector.[158] A generation later
Richard de Vesci, rector of Brompton, appointed a vicar to serve the
church and its dependent chapel of Falden. The vicar was to have all the

---

[155] *The Register of John le Romeyn, Lord Archbishop of York, 1284–1296 and of Henry of
Newark, Lord Archbishop of York, 1296–1299*, ed. W. Brown, 2 parts, Surtees Society, 123,
128 (1913, 1917), i. 340; *Reg. Greenfield*, iii. 32–3. Wintringham was a wealthy rectory which
was valued at £23 6s. 8d. in 1291 (*Taxatio*, 303b). See also *Fasti Parochiales V*, ed. N. A. H.
Lawrance, Yorkshire Archaeological Society Record Series, 143 (1983), 72. Norton was
given to Malton in the mid-12th century by Roger de Flamville and Juetta his wife. It lay
very close to the priory and was almost certainly staffed by one or more canons of the house
(ibid. 30). There was still a rector of Norton in 1173 when an agreement was made relating
to Norton and its dependent chapel of Welham (London, BL, MS Cotton Claudius D XI,
fo. 55[r–v]. Cf. *EYC* iii. 495–7).

[156] *Calendar of the Register of Richard Scrope, Archbishop of York 1398–1405, part 1*, ed.
R. N. Swanson, Borthwick Texts and Calendars: Records of the Northern Province, 8
(1981), i. 51. There were two dependent chapels at Malton, dedicated to St Leonard and St
Michael. These were served by chaplains, at least one of whom was hereditary in the late
12th century, who were provided with housing (including an early 'barn-conversion', the
horreum of Norman *mercator*) (London, BL, MS Cotton Claudius D XI, fo. 48[r–v]). In 1308/
9 the priors of Watton and Ellerton were cited in the same way to answer for the churches
of Watton, North Dalton, Kilnwick, and Birdsall (Watton) and Ellerton (Ellerton), and it is
likely that in these cases also the churches were served by stipendiary chaplains or by the
canons (*Reg. Greenfield*, v. 232, 230. Cf. ibid. iii. 157–8). Archbishop Scrope similarly
confirmed the serving of Ellerton by a stipendiary chaplain (*Cal. Richard Scrope*, i. 66).

[157] Kemp, 'Monastic Possession', 149. For examples of vicars themselves 'subinfeudating'
their revenues, see Cheney, *From Becket to Langton*, 131.

[158] London, BL, MS Cotton Claudius D XI, fo. 226[v].

offerings with the exception of the tithes of corn, which remained to the rector.[159] These arrangements seem to have been most frequent when the living was a large and/or wealthy one or when the rector was himself of high status. In 1294 Bullington made an agreement with the newly appointed rector of Ingham, master William of Lowther, whereby all the profits of the church were granted for eighteen months to the priory in return for a sum of £40 to be paid to William or his proctors, either at Bullington, Paris, Bologna, or the papal Curia, depending on where William was when payment fell due. Judging from the places he intended to visit, William was probably a canon lawyer. Such an agreement brought profit to the incumbent while at least in theory ensuring that the church continued to be served in his absence.[160] Incumbents like William were, however, the exception. The majority were of relatively lowly status, often recruited from the priories' locality. Very few were *magistri*, and typically those that were held the wealthier vicarages and rectories. Few played a more extensive part in diocesan affairs, and it is only on the rare occasions that the bishop appointed to a Gilbertine living that episcopal clerks are sometimes presented. The priories' livings were seldom sufficiently lucrative to tempt careerists, pluralists, or bishops eager to reward their officials or clerks.[161]

[159] Ibid., fo. 43.
[160] London, BL, Harl. Chart. 44 A 54. See Golding, 'Gilbertine Priories', 178–9.
[161] The status of appointees to churches of Alvingham and Bullington is discussed ibid. 166–80.

8

The Gilbertine Economy

Like all religious communities in medieval England, the economy and material prosperity of the Gilbertine priories was determined by the quantity and quality of their landed possessions, both arable and pastoral. They relied for their income on a portfolio of assets which included profits from the sale of agricultural produce (wool in particular) from their demesne land, ideally organized in granges; proceeds from *spiritualia*, which usually comprised revenues from glebe land and, where appropriation had proved possible, the greater tithes of the parish, as well as offerings at the altar; manorial perquisites such as fines and customary payments; rents from property that had been either permanently alienated or temporarily demised, and which might include payments from urban property; and incidental sources of income, of which the possession of mills and fisheries was probably the most significant. The relative importance of these commodities fluctuated according to prevailing economic conditions in the country at large, but were also determined by a number of other criteria, amongst which the scale of endowments (which was itself governed, as we have seen, by various factors) was the most influential.

This chapter will examine these sources of *temporalia* income, paying particular attention to the grange, which was as central and distinctive a feature of the Gilbertine economy as it was of the Cistercians. Any such survey is severely hampered by the absence of detailed accounts for the priories. The only exception is the summary of income and expenditure of the priory of Malton during the years of William of Ancaster's priorate (1244–57).[1] This provides a valuable insight into the organization of the priory's temporal properties in the mid-thirteenth century, but it is hard to be sure how far Malton's position was typical of Gilbertine houses as a whole. Malton was in Gilbertine terms a large and prosperous community: its assessed income in 1535 was approximately £197; only four other priories (Lincoln, Chicksands, Sempringham, and Watton) were wealthier. Moreover, Malton was a priory for canons only. Its fortunes cannot

---

[1] London, BL, MS Cotton Claudius D XI, fos. 279ᵛ–281.

therefore be used to determine how far the Gilbertine double houses suffered from the financial pressures and difficulties faced by many contemporary female communities.

There is convincing evidence that nunneries in the thirteenth century were experiencing greater economic hardships than their religious brethren. This was partly the result of generally poorer endowments from poorer patrons, but was also linked to over-recruitment relative to their economic base. The difficulties encountered in balancing resources against numbers were exacerbated by increasingly draconian canonical restrictions on simoniacal entry during the thirteenth century, which were now specifically directed against female communities.[2] There are some indications to suggest that the Gilbertine double houses were suffering similarly in the thirteenth century. Appropriation of churches to Sempringham and Bullington in the 1240s was licensed by the papacy in view of the large number of women in the priories, and their consequent poverty, and ten years later, in 1257, the community at Chicksands, numbering fifty nuns and ten *conversi*, had to be temporarily dispersed because of lack of resources.[3]

In spite of the lack of accounts it is possible to gain a little idea of the relative importance of the varying sources of income in the mid-thirteenth century. The Malton cartulary contains the assessments made of all Gilbertine priories for the Valuation of Norwich of 1254.[4] This gives not only the total assessed income from *temporalia* but also the

---

[2] Gilbertine recruitment and the question of dowry gifts are discussed above, Ch. 3: 'Entering the house'. For the general context, see J. H. Lynch, *Simoniacal Entry into the Religious Life, 1000 to 1260* (Columbus, Ohio, 1976), esp. 193–4 and 202 n. 59; S. P. Thompson, 'Why English Nunneries had no History: A Study of the Problems of the English Nunneries Founded after the Conquest', in J. A. Nichols and L. T. Shank (eds.), *Medieval Religious Women. I. Distant Echoes*, Cistercian Publications, 71 (Kalamazoo, Mich., 1984), 137–9. The relationship between resources, numbers, and simony was made explicit in bishop Hugh of Wells's visitation of the Cistercian nunnery of Nun Cotham (Lincolnshire) early in the 13th century when he both forbade simoniacal entry and limited numbers in the community, since 'the number of nuns was greater than the resources of the house can sustain'. Similar restrictions on numbers were imposed on Gilbertine priories but, as argued above (Ch. 3: 'Entering the house': 'The ideal community'), this was as much for disciplinary as for economic reasons. The Nun Cotham restrictions are discussed by Lynch, *Simoniacal Entry*, 158–9 and 173 nn. 40–1 (where the bishop is mistakenly identified as Hugh I of Witham), and C. V. Graves, 'Stixwould in the Market Place', in Nichols and Shank (eds.), *Distant Echose*, 215–16. For the poverty of Yorkshire nunneries, see Burton, *Yorkshire Nunneries*, 24–6.

[3] For the appropriations, see above, Ch. 7; for Chicksands, see *Annales Monastici*, ed. H. R. Luard, 5 vols., Rolls Series (London, 1864–9), iii. 205.

[4] The fullest account of this valuation remains W. E. Lunt, *The Valuation of Norwich* (Oxford, 1926).

sum assessed as *immobilia*, that is, the estimated value of granges and other property currently held in demesne if they were to be granted at farm.[5] The difference between these two figures therefore represents the assessed income from rents and manorial profits. These figures show that the priories only derived between a third and a half of their total income from their demesne. Unfortunately, it is impossible to ascertain how much of the remainder was obtained from rental revenues and how much from other sources, nor does the assessment include income from the sale of wool, which was probably the single most important element in the priories' revenues at this time.

These figures can be somewhat supplemented by the Malton accounts. The summary of receipts between 1244 and 1257 records income from a number of sources: the six churches then appropriated to the priory (presumably including all proceeds such as tithes, glebe produce, and offerings); mills; land at farm; wool sales; tithes of wool and lambs; and fines and amercements.[6] Of these, by far the most important item was wool sales, which normally accounted for between 60 and 70 per cent of total income, and in one year (1250) contributed more than 80 per cent of the total.[7] Annual rents increased steadily, gradually rising from £47 17s. in 1244 to £60 13s. 4d. by 1254, a figure which represented just under 10 per cent of the total income. Fines naturally fluctuated from year to year but were always insignificant, as was the income from tithes of wool. Revenue from mills was also modest, and none at all was recorded in 1252, 1256, or 1257.

The Grange

For the Gilbertines, as for the Cistercians and all communities influenced by the white monks, the grange was both a spiritual and an economic imperative. Its rationale was derived from an early institute of the Cistercians, forbidding the construction of any habitation outside the walls of the monastery for fear of spiritual danger. This prohibition was repeated verbatim in the Gilbertine Rule, and to it was added the sanction that any such building should be totally destroyed.[8] The grange was therefore fundamental to the Gilbertine economy and its existence

---

[5] London, BL, MS Cotton Claudius D XI, fo. 282[v].

[6] From 1255 income from the newly appropriated church of King's Walden and 'from the sub-cellarer's pigs' is included.   [7] Only in 1255 was there a slump to 37%.

[8] Canivez, *Statuta*, i. 17–18. *Monasticon*, vi. 2. xl.

was central to the Gilbertine Rule.[9] Essentially the grange was a self-contained monastic farm intended to be managed by lay brethren under the supervision of the cellarer. It lay at the centre of a more or less consolidated estate of arable or pastoral land, which was in some instances demarcated from the property of neighbours by ditches, banks, or other means.[10] Often, too, as the grange estate was extended the new lands would themselves be enclosed to more effectively incorporate them into the holding.[11] It thus symbolized the monks' withdrawal from the temporal world, and emphasized their rejection of manorial values.

It was the ambition of every priory to incorporate as far as possible all its holdings into consolidated, self-contained estates. The creation of the grange was slow and laborious and might take several generations to achieve: sometimes it was never accomplished. It involved the steady accumulation of large and small pieces of property by gift, exchange, lease, or purchase. Problems were exacerbated by intense competition for benefactions between local communities, often only a few miles from each other, all looking for grants from a finite pool of potential benefactors, who found themselves with fewer alienable resources as the thirteenth century progressed. The successful creation of the grange owed much to the fact that the corporate body of the priory could afford to be more patient than an individual in the slow assemblage of lands. To uncover the Gilbertines' activity may sometimes seem as toilsome as the acquisitions were themselves. In the case of some priory estates, hundreds of charters record the gradual business, in others, where no cartulary or substantial charter archive survives, the process remains elusive, and even where charters are present they rarely reveal the full story behind each individual transaction, the motives of the benefactor and the community.

---

[9] There is now a large literature on the general development of the grange in the monastic economy, but the fullest study remains C. Platt's survey, *The Monastic Grange in Medieval England: A Reassessment* (London, 1969), while the pioneering work of T. A. M. Bishop in 'Monastic Granges in Yorkshire', *EHR* 51 (1936), 193–214, is still of value. This can be supplemented in the Cistercian world by a number of studies of individual abbeys or groups of abbeys such as J. Wardrop, *Fountains Abbey and its Benefactors, 1132–1300*, Cistercian Publications, 91 (Kalamazoo, Mich., 1987), ch. ii, or D. H. Williams, *The Welsh Cistercians*, 2 vols. (Tenby, 1983), esp. ii. 227–42. There are few full studies of Gilbertine granges, but for Malton see B. Waites, 'The Monastic Grange as a Factor in the Settlement of North-East Yorkshire', *Yorkshire Archaeological Journal*, 40 (1959–62), 627–56. For the granges of Alvingham and Bullington, see Golding, 'Gilbertine Priories', 20–93.

[10] Bishop suggested ('Monastic Granges', 193 and n. 2) that the grange was predominantly an arable estate, but there were certainly granges devoted primarily to sheep or dairy farming.

[11] See William son of Robert's grant to Nun Ormsby of three headlands adjoining the priory's 'court' in North Kelsey which he allowed the community to surround with a hedge or ditch (*Gilbertine Charters*, 60).

Many Gilbertine granges were found in or near well-populated settlements. In most areas where the Gilbertines had interests, there were few areas on the frontiers of settlement available for exploitation. This was particularly the case in north Lincolnshire. As a result, their demesne often marched with the land of others and it was rare for any of their granges to be totally consolidated or enclosed. Moreover, in areas where great lords held few estates in demesne, the Gilbertines depended on the grants of lesser men to provide the nucleus of their estates around which they could gradually assemble other holdings.

Though the Gilbertine Rule (unlike that of the Cistercians) did not forbid the creation of granges more than a day's journey from a priory, it was certainly envisaged that granges should be not too far away, both in order that the lay brethren serving there might easily return to the priory church for great festivals and, more importantly, that the canons might have a measure of practical control over them, especially since the discipline of the *conversi* could never be assured.[12] In many cases, indeed, the largest and most valuable grange lay immediately adjacent to the priory, like the home farm of Alvingham priory described in a mid-twelfth-century papal confirmation as the grange 'quae extra abbaciam vocatur'.[13] Normally accommodation was of the simplest with a rudimentary oratory and farm outbuildings, especially the barn.[14] Indeed, the very word 'grange' originally meant barn or storehouse. These were sometimes used for the storage of parish tithes, and Bishop went so far as to suggest that the ownership of tithes and glebe land was 'the chief factor in deciding where they [the canons] should acquire temporal property'. Possession of the tithes certainly meant that a storehouse and a centre for their sale were required. These *grangiae* could become the nucleus of a later grange, as seems to be the case, for example, at East Rasen, where Sixhills priory was given the site of a grange to store their tithe.[15]

[12] The Cistercians, too, experienced disciplinary problems in their granges, lay brothers being accused of excessive beer drinking, and worse.

[13] Oxford, Bodl. Lib., MS Laud Misc. 642, fo. 39. Bishop argued ('Monastic Granges', 195) that granges 'must be clearly distinguished from the home farms'. Such a distinction cannot be maintained either in terms of their economy or organization.

[14] Platt convincingly modified earlier interpretations of grange buildings, which saw them as abbeys in miniature (*Monastic Grange*, 17–48).

[15] This lay in the *curia* of the donor, who gave the priory the right of free entry and exit for the access of its wagons and carts and access to its houses lying next to the *curia* (*Gilbertine Charters*, 21). See also Bishop, 'Monastic Granges', 204–6; Waites, 'The Monastic Grange', 638–41. The correlation between grange and parish church is discussed below. The 1164 agreement between the Cistercians and Gilbertines allowed the establishment of *grangiae* in order to store tithes and the produce of the glebe.

The barns are seldom described, and no Gilbertine granges survive in anything like their original state above ground. Sites that have been identified suggest that they frequently consisted of a number of enclosures which contained the domestic buildings and constituted the grange court.[16] Some were defended by ditches, as was Catley's grange at 'Sleygtes' in Digby, where the nuns were licensed for the *conversi* to dig a ditch at least 24 feet in width and to enclose it on all sides as best they might against losses and dangers.[17] Little is known of the scale of Gilbertine grange buildings but there are some indications in the charters, as when six acres was given at Thrussington 'to construct the buildings of their [i.e. the nuns of Sempringham's] lay brothers'.[18]

The formation of the grange

Bishop contended that one of the features of the monastic grange, at least in Yorkshire, was the speed of its creation. This, he argued, was not an evolutionary process but an event completed in one generation and in this way, as in others, to be distinguished from the manorial estate, which was of slower, more organic growth. The grange was in this sense a revolutionary creation cutting across old tenurial and parochial boundaries and establishing a new structural organization which owed nothing to past history. This provided the dynamic for the monks and canons to follow a deliberate and planned programme of land acquisition including purchases as well as outright benefactions, and often involved considerable expenditure in buying out the claims of others.[19] Now, it is true that the Gilbertines, like the Cistercians and Augustinians, concentrated their land and bought primarily in areas where they had or wished to develop a grange. It is also true that they followed a much more rigorous policy of land exchanges and consolidation in these places. As will be shown in more detail below, they also attempted to operate a grange in a parish where they held the church. All these factors certainly indicate a degree of forward planning.

Undoubtedly, too, the canons did on occasions, by the generosity or financial need of a benefactor, acquire a large estate at one instant. Sixhills

---

[16] e.g. at Malton's granges of Linton, Rillington, and Wintringham, described in Platt, *Monastic Grange*, 215–16, 227–8, and 245.

[17] *Gilbertine Charters*, 74.

[18] *Sempringham Charters*, xvi. 153. Malton's grange at Mowthorpe was built around a croft of four acres (*EYC* ii. 387–8). Like many granges, it lay on the edge of settlement, on the boundary between Mowthorpe and Thoralby (see Platt, *Monastic Grange*, ch. 3, 'The Grange Estate', 49–75). [19] Bishop, 'Monastic Granges', 200–1.

purchased the manor of Ludford from Jocelin of Louvain and agreed to pay him £12 per annum; at about the same time (in the third quarter of the twelfth century) the same house acquired, probably as another purchase, the village of Legsby. One hundred years later Robert Burnell, bishop of Bath and Wells, granted Sixhills his manor of Toft by Newton.[20] Strictly speaking, such properties were manors rather than granges, but the opportunity for the community to develop them as granges was of course available. In his foundation charter to Bullington, Simon son of William gave all 'Aldefeld', which was later described as a grange in Faldingworth.[21] The foundation of Chicksands' grange at Hawnes also seems to have been completed at one time, in this instance as a result of the generosity of Payn de Beauchamp's tenants.[22] Such rapid foundations are, however, unusual. Much more often the creation of the grange was 'a long and painful process' occupying many years, as the priories gradually accumulated lands by gift, rent, purchase, or exchange.[23] If the ultimate ambition of the communities was to incorporate all holdings in a settlement into a grange, this was seldom realized. Waites has shown that at only three out of thirteen Malton granges that he identifies in the Ministers' Accounts was this ideal reached.[24] In this sense then, the creation of a grange was an ongoing process rarely completed and extending over many generations.

However, it is often difficult to establish with any certainty when a grange was established. The clearest evidence for the existence of a grange is provided by the *Valor Ecclesiasticus* and the Ministers' Accounts. Yet even here the record is unsatisfactory and a number of granges known in the sixteenth century, and long before, do not appear in these sources, and sometimes it is only in a charter that a reference to a grange is found. For example, neither the mid-thirteenth-century Malton accounts nor the Ministers' Accounts list Winterton (Lincolnshire) as a grange, yet a charter refers to land between the *grangia* and the *bercaria*, and it is apparent from the Dissolution income that this was one of the most productive of the priory's estates.[25] Early lists of granges are found only occasionally and these may be incomplete. The first papal confirmation to Malton issued in 1169 refers to two granges, at Wintringham and Kirby Misperton. Eleven years later Mowthorpe had been added to the list.[26]

[20] *Gilbertine Charters*, 6–7, 15. [21] Ibid. 91–2.

[22] Fowler (ed.), 'Early Charters of . . . Chicksand', 103.

[23] Platt, *Monastic Grange*, 214, referring to the creation of Fountains abbey's grange at Kirby Wiske. This creation is examined in illuminating detail by Wardrop, *Fountains Abbey*, 74–9. [24] Waites, 'The Monastic Grange', 656.

[25] Bishop, 'Monastic Granges', 196–7; London, BL, MS Cotton Claudius D XI, fo. 209.

[26] *Papsturkunden in England*, ii. 426–7.

Honorius III's confirmation charter of 1220 lists four more, two more had been added by the time Gregory IX issued a confirmation in 1234, and a further three are recorded in 1244. Thereafter the rate of expansion declines, but even so by the beginning of the fourteenth century there were perhaps another six, giving a total of about eighteen.[27] Henry II's confirmation charter to Chicksands mentions five granges: at Hawnes, Chippenham, Keysoe, Meppershall, and Hargrave.[28] Alexander IV's confirmation charter (1254–61) in favour of Alvingham lists nine granges. Only one grange recorded at the Dissolution (Yarborough) is absent from here.[29] It is clear that most granges were operative by the mid-thirteenth century: in other words, their chronological development parallels that of the Gilbertines' endowments in general.

Successful grange formation depended on a number of factors. Of particular importance was the nature of lordship in the parish. In places of divided lordship, such as was especially the case in north Lincolnshire and Yorkshire, the goodwill of a number of potential benefactors was clearly necessary. The Gilbertines were seldom at liberty to dictate where they should be granted lands. Of course, they could take advantage of the financial embarrassment of local landholders to expand their holdings, but it is doubtful if they could often tell their benefactors precisely what land to sell. Mostly they had to accept land wherever it was granted, and make of it the best they could. Though grants were often made by local landholders in villages round the priory, so that the wishes of the priory to have granges close at hand were satisfied, this was not inevitably the case.[30]

Success also owed much to local geography and agricultural practice, factors which not only determined the nature of the agricultural economy but also the speed and ease of estate consolidation. It was much easier, for example, to create a grange on the marshes of Swinefleet on the banks of the Humber, where several Gilbertine as well as other houses had interests, than in the much more densely populated and settled areas of Bedfordshire or north Lincolnshire. The ideal grange lay in a fertile region on the fringes of cultivation, whether between settlement and the moors or the marshes, as was often the case with Gilbertine (or Cistercian) granges in Yorkshire, or between the fields of two settlements, sometimes crossing

---

[27] Ibid. ii. 426–7. The granges are conveniently listed in B. Waites, 'The Monasteries and the Development of North-East Yorkshire', MA thesis (London University, 1958), 423–4.   [28] Fowler (ed.), 'Early Charters of . . . Chicksand', 119–25.

[29] *Monasticon*, vi. 2. 960.

[30] Thus Bullington's distant grange of Prestwold (Leicestershire) was the result of a grant by the Kyme family, and its geographical position precluded any great value to the nuns (Golding, 'Gilbertine Priories', 75–8).

parish boundaries, as was often the case with granges sited in more populated areas.[31] The initial nucleus of the grange was ideally a comparatively large holding, in a situation where there were abundant possibilities for future expansion and consolidation. The grange should also lie within easy reach of the priory and be of ready access by road or water. Waites has demonstrated how the granges of Malton satisfied many of these criteria. The majority lay upon the gravels of the Vale of Pickering, at the foot of the hills that bordered the valley to north and south. Many were centres of arable production with as many as 11 ploughs on the estate, while at the same time they had easy access to sheep pasturage and rich meadow land. All lay on, or close to, the main road through the Vale leading to Malton town, and water and land routes gave a convenient approach to markets such as York, Hull, and Pickering.[32] These desiderata were seldom achieved, particularly by the Lincolnshire and more southerly houses. Such areas were already well colonized by the middle of the twelfth century. There were few places, as there were in Yorkshire, formerly fertile, but laid waste and deserted in the previous century, for the Gilbertines to spur into renewed agricultural activity; equally, there were comparatively few opportunities for further reclamation of waste or wooded lands. Significantly, the Gilbertine charters contain very few references to assarted land. In an established landscape the canons could not so readily impose their own agricultural system upon it. Instead they had to compromise and adapt their ideal of a completely consolidated and integrated estate set apart from the lands of their neighbours.

Though the 'ideal' grange is most frequently found among those of the Yorkshire and Lincolnshire Gilbertines, an excellent and well-documented example is Chippenham (Cambridgeshire), a grange of Chicksands.[33] Its nucleus was a gift of Rohaise, the wife of Payn de Beauchamp, and

[31] Waites, 'Monastic Settlement', 478–95; 'The Monastic Grange', 637–8. In his study of the monastic grange Platt utilized Tithe Commissioners' apportionments, schedules, and maps to great effect to demonstrate the consolidated estates of the Cistercian granges. The Cistercians were exempt from the payment of tithes on estates acquired before 1215 and lands newly brought into cultivation after that date. These exemptions remained with the lands after the Dissolution and survive in some cases as a trace element of the medieval estate in the 19th-century archive. While this material has many limitations, in cases where these sources can be utilized it provides valuable evidence of the structure of grange estates (Platt, *Monastic Grange*, ch. 3, pp. 48–75, esp. 57–8). Though the Gilbertines also enjoyed the privilege of non-payment of tithes on their lands, it has only seldom proved possible to identify Gilbertine grange estates through this means.

[32] Waites, 'The Monastic Grange', 637.

[33] Chippenham has been the subject of an important study by M. Spufford, *A Cambridgeshire Community: Chippenham from Settlement to Enclosure*, Local History Occasional Papers, 20 (Leicester, 1965).

co-founder of the priory, consisting of the grange site and adjacent land, common pasture and turbary rights, and some meadow land. Before 1166 her son Geoffrey had confirmed this grant and added to it 120 acres of arable in the field east of the grange, seven acres in Stonehill and his demesne land in Sound field, and pasture for 500 sheep and lambs.[34] This is the only charter relating to the grange in the Chicksands archive, but the picture can be elaborated from the Hospitallers' cartulary. The Hospitallers held a large estate, the gift in 1184 of William de Mandeville (Geoffrey's brother), which included the whole village, with the exception of the church (which belonged to Walden abbey) and the land of Chicksands. William confirmed some of his brother's grants to Chicksands but withdrew the lands in Stonehill and Sound, giving in exchange 116 acres of newly cleared land and 10 acres in 'Blatherwyc' and adding to this additional lands in the latter field amounting to 40 acres and 10 acres of sheep pasture. Dr Spufford has pointed out that this exchange was very much to de Mandeville's advantage. He regained valuable meadow land, while the priory received relatively unfertile land of limited productivity.[35] This is a useful reminder of how dependent the communities were upon their benefactors: what was given could as easily be taken away. It was the grantor who largely determined the shape of the Gilbertine grange.

A post-Dissolution survey of 1544, together with an estate map of 1712, allows all these lands to be identified. Together they show that the grange consisted of a consolidated estate amounting to some 300 acres on the southern edge of the village.[36] In this respect the priory had achieved its ideal, even though the church was not acquired. The land was probably used for both arable and sheep pasturage. Undoubtedly the southern fields were relatively poor and may only have been used intermittently. Indeed, some of the lands may have gone out of cultivation altogether even before the mid-sixteenth century, when there is clear evidence of this.[37] The most productive land must have been the sheep pasturage, and as the arable retreated the number of sheep on the Chicksands grange increased. This was not, however, to the priory's immediate advantage since ultimately it proved impossible for the Gilbertine house to compete with the interests of Walden abbey and the Hospitallers, and by the end

---

[34] Fowler (ed.), 'Early Charters of . . . Chicksand', 112–14.

[35] Spufford, *A Cambridgeshire Community*, 14.

[36] The buildings themselves were described as lying in a 'grounde compassed with a ditch containing by estimate iiii acres'. The acreage was very similar to that of other Gilbertine grange enclosures.   [37] Spufford, *A Cambridgeshire Community*, 42–3.

of the thirteenth century the Chicksands grange was leased to the latter.[38] It was almost certainly never brought back under the canons' direct control, and at the Dissolution was farmed along with the manor of Chippenham to a lay lessee.[39]

Chicksands' grange at Hawnes was one of the first granges to be established and, like Chippenham, was well consolidated.[40] Virtually all of its land lay closely grouped on the southern edge of the parish adjacent to the boundaries with Clophill and Chicksands, and centred on Grange Farm and Dove Close, where lay the grange buildings, which comprised just over $9\frac{1}{2}$ acres. The estate amounted to over 380 acres of arable, and about 140 acres of woodland. This grange, the second most productive of Chicksands' estates in 1291, combined with possession of the parish church, represented the ideal that was so seldom attained by Gilbertine priories.

The acreage of Gilbertine granges could vary considerably. There were some 300 acres of arable at Chippenham, and 380 acres at Hawnes. Malton's granges at Amotherby and Ebberston were estimated at about 200 acres in the thirteenth century and at the Dissolution the granges of Malton varied between 60 acres at Aymunderby and 225 acres at Swinton, though the *total* acreage of property in a grange village could be as high as 495 acres.[41] Gilbertine granges were normally smaller than their Cistercian counterparts, perhaps because they were generally more poorly endowed by less wealthy benefactors.[42] The absence of medieval surveys makes it difficult to determine the extent of Gilbertine granges other than by reference to the Ministers' Accounts, which do not always record acreages. However, in 1535 Southgarth, the home grange of St Katherine's, Lincoln, contained about 250 acres: the demesne of the priory enclosure together with 'Goldyngdales' amounted to 17 acres, there were nine acres of marsh and ten of enclosed moorland, and 230 acres of arable in the fields outside the priory. A short distance away the grange of Canwick comprised 30 acres of meadow (of which 24 were marshland), 24 acres of a close (of which 20 acres was brushwood) and 360 acres of arable, a third of this land being brushwood.[43] This evidence is consonant with the

---

[38] Ibid. 29.   [39] Ibid. 38–9.   [40] PRO IR 29/1/23.
[41] As it was at Rillington. London, BL, MS Cotton Claudius D XI, fo. 283. Waites, 'The Monastic Grange', 656, app. 3. Such variation is consistent with Cistercian experience. At Meaux in 1396 the largest grange was 1,417 acres, the smallest was 85 acres in extent, while the granges of the Welsh Cistercians were considerably larger (Platt, *Monastic Grange*, 77 and n., 78 n.).   [42] Bishop, 'Monastic Granges', 203, 209.
[43] *VE* iv. 30. The canons' grange at Boultham was much smaller, consisting only of 30 acres of arable, another 28 acres (of arable?), of which 24 acres were in the fens, 11 acres of enclosed pasture, and 100 acres enclosed at Landesike, which was probably rough pasture.

much earlier assessment for a clerical subsidy in Lincolnshire made *c*.1199–1200 which suggests acreages at grange villages varying between one (120 acres) and five carucates (600 acres).[44]

Of more importance than the actual acreage of the grange was its productivity and agricultural potential, which were determined by many other factors: soil geology, geographic and climatic conditions, the resources of exploitation, and, perhaps most importantly, the opportunity to acquire other revenues in the neighbourhood, especially those of the parish church.

The grange and the church

Possession of the local parish church was one of the ideals of the successful grange. The importance of possession of the tithes and glebe land has long been recognized, and Bishop went so far as to suggest that such possession was 'the chief factor in deciding where they [i.e. the canons] should acquire temporal property'.[45] Conversely, failure to acquire the church might lead to the disposal of a grange to another monastery.[46] Glebe land, which was more likely to consist of a consolidated holding than of isolated selions in the open fields, often formed the nucleus of the grange. From this central core, suitable for the site of a few farm buildings and a small oratory (a 'locum ad habitandum ut ibi faciant domos et grangias et ceteras suas', as Simon son of William's grant to Bullington in Faldingworth was described), the canons could move outwards, slowly expanding and consolidating their estates.[47] Possession of the church had another, less tangible advantage. It established a sphere of influence within the parish for the priory. Other religious houses would tend to be excluded from the territory, or would at least find it difficult to maintain a large holding there. The parish church itself could have tenants, who would then become the tenants of the priory when it acquired the church.[48] Parishioners' grants to the church would now, in effect, be made in favour of the priory, while the latter's hold upon the spiritual affections

[44] PRO E. 179/242/113. This assessment records the total land held in a given village, which may (as already seen) exceed the land consolidated in a grange. However, since all such property would at least be administered from the grange centre, the distinction between the two may be more apparent than real.

[45] Bishop, 'Monastic Granges', 204–6. See also Waites, 'The Monastic Grange', 638–41.

[46] For some Cistercian examples, see Waites, 'Monastic Settlement', 493.

[47] *Gilbertine Charters*, 91. Here *grangia* probably has the meaning 'storehouse'.

[48] Two charters relating to the church of Kilnwick held by Watton refer to tenants of the church; in another charter two sisters gave land to the priory on condition that 6*s*. per annum was paid to the church, which already belonged to the priory (*Yorkshire Deeds VI*, ed. C. T. Clay, Yorkshire Archaeological Society, Record Series, 76 (1930), 98, 100–1, 104).

of the parish could be strengthened. A clear indication of the importance
of the glebe endowment in the creation of the grange is seen in a charter
whereby Geoffrey of Keddington confirmed to Alvingham all the grants
that had been made to the parish church from his own demesne and from
the land of his tenants, 'scilicet, de singulis bovatis una acra, dimidia ex
una parte ville et dimidia acra ex alia'.[49] The grant of the church lands
here, amounting it would seem to at least a fifteenth of the total arable in
the vill, must have provided a substantial nucleus for the grange. The
connection between the church and grange is also suggested in the grant
by Amfridus of Legbourne of St Helen's, Cawthorpe, to Alvingham,
along with a considerable grant of land 'to increase the brethren's grange'
that lay to the west and north of the church.[50]

While the glebe provided a consolidated nucleus for growth, possession of tithes was a catalyst for the creation of a grange.[51] Tithes required
a storehouse and a centre for the sale of their surplus. We have already
seen how the word *grangia* could be translated 'storehouse' or 'barn', and
that this was perhaps its primary meaning. It was a natural progression
from the storehouse to the more developed monastic grange associated
with the twelfth-century orders. Waites has stressed that if the creation of
the grange preceded possession of the church, then tithe ownership was
not important in the grange's establishment.[52] This is true, but, as has
been suggested above, possession of the glebe land may, initially at any
rate, have been as important in the economy of the priories as possession
of the tithes. The evidence, though slight, suggests that the priories often
held the glebe land of the church, even where it was not appropriated.[53]
Nevertheless, possession of the church did not guarantee a grange's survival. Bullington was developing its grange at Prestwold (Leicestershire)
during the first half of the thirteenth century, following the acquisition of
the church towards the end of the previous century. Prestwold was the
centre of a small group of estates in north Leicestershire including Hoton,
Cotes, and Burton-on-the-Wolds. These seem to have been too far away
from Bullington to be developed effectively. The only connection between the village and the priory was the coincidence that the Kymes,

---

[49] Oxford, Bodl. Lib., MS Laud Misc. 642, fo. 122. Though a church is recorded here
in 1086, it would seem that its chief endowment occurred in the mid-12th century. See also
Danelaw Charters, p. lxxi.

[50] However, this would hint that here the grange was created before the priory obtained
an interest in the church. The grant also confirmed lands given by Amfridus' *rustici* to the
church (Oxford, Bodl. Lib., MS Laud Misc. 642, fo. 136).

[51] A point well made by Waites, 'The Monastic Grange', 639–40.

[52] Ibid. 639.   [53] *Gilbertine Charters*, p. xxiii.

founders and chief benefactors of the priory, had interests in both places. This is a salutary reminder that the siting of a grange owed as much to the choice of the grantor as it did to the priory. For all that the priory had the church, other, more local religious houses had extensive holdings in the area. By 1535, though the canons retained the rectory, all *temporalia* here seem to have been disposed of, an indication of the priory's failure to maintain Prestwold as a viable holding.[54]

How far were the priories able to achieve their aim of a correlation between the church and grange? It would be otiose to examine every Gilbertine house in detail, and here two Yorkshire (Watton and Malton), two Lincolnshire (Alvingham and Bullington), and Chicksands priories will be examined. As has been noted above, there are difficulties in establishing precisely whether or not an estate was organized as a grange. The chief sources are the Dissolution accounts, reinforced by other specific, earlier references to granges or manors.[55] At the Dissolution Watton held at least eleven granges, of which four lay in the parish of Watton itself.[56] In seven of the eight 'grange parishes' the priory also had the appropriation of the church.[57] At Birdsall Watton held the rectory, but no other lands here are recorded.[58] Watton was, then, largely successful in obtaining the appropriation of the parish church in the villages in which it had a grange. Only in Hawold was this not possible, and it is probably significant that this grange was (with the exception of one of the granges in Watton itself, Burn Butts) the least profitable at the Dissolution.[59]

As has already been observed, it is not easy to establish the number of

[54] Golding, 'Gilbertine Priories', 75–8, 146–7.

[55] In the remarks that follow, the 'home farm', often referred to as the 'site and demesne' of the priory, has been considered as a grange.

[56] It is likely that lands in Watton Carr assessed at the very considerable sum of £54 5s. were also organized as a grange, or administered from one of the other granges in Watton.

[57] Watton, Sancton, Hutton Cranswick, Kilnwick, Hessle, North Dalton, and Ravenstonedale. The exception was Hawold, which lay in Huggate, where the parish church was already in the hands of St Mary's, York. The rectory of Kilnwick is not listed amongst the holdings of Watton in the Ministers' Accounts, but its tithes are recorded as belonging to the priory and the rectory is amongst those Watton properties granted to Holgate at the Dissolution (*Cal. Letters and Papers, Henry VIII*, 16 (1540–1), 715). Only a moiety of the church was held at Hessle.

[58] *Pace Fasti Parochiales V*, ed. Lawrance, 2–3, where Birdsall is assumed (on no authority) to be appropriated to Kirkham. There appears to be confusion here with Bilsdale near Helmsley, which was a Kirkham church. The church of Birdsall had earlier been granted to St Mary's, York. It was certainly in Watton's hands by 1291 (*Taxatio*, 303). At the Dissolution another rectory, Beswick, is recorded, but it is not clear if this was a separate living or formed part of Kilnwick (*Letters and Papers, Henry VIII*, 16 (1540–1), 715).

[59] However, additional property in the parish of Huggate was assessed at the not inconsiderable sum of over £26 (*VE* vi. 957).

the Malton granges. At the Dissolution only five properties are described as granges. To this number can be added those additional seven granges listed in 1244, and perhaps also the lands at Snainton and Norton where the canons had a court.[60] By contrast with many Gilbertine houses, Malton held comparatively few churches and these were, again unusually, some distance from the priory. Indeed, of the ten churches of which the priory held either the rectory or a share of the tithes, half were in another diocese and shire.[61] It is hardly surprising that no grange was established in connection with any of these churches, and only from two of these parishes, Winterton and South Croxton, did the canons derive any temporal income at the Dissolution. The only places where the canons held the church and a grange were Malton itself, Wintringham, and Norton. The chief reason for this failure to acquire churches is the fact that by the time of Malton's foundation most of the local churches had already been ceded to other religious houses. So, for example, the church of Appleton-le-Street in which Malton's granges of Swinton and Broughton lay had been granted to St Albans in the mid-twelfth century. At about the same time Ralph de Clere had given the church of Sinnington, where the canons had another grange, to his foundation of Yeddingham nunnery. Kirby Misperton passed into the hands of St Mary's, York, in the late eleventh century and Ebberston went to the archbishops of York a generation later. Mowthorpe lay in the parish of Kirby Grindalythe, whose church had been part of the foundation of Kirkham priory, and a moiety of Rillington had been granted to Byland abbey in the late twelfth century, again before Malton had developed an interest here. So, from the beginning Malton's expansion was circumscribed, and it is no coincidence that the Dissolution income from Wintringham church and the landed property in the parish, that included two granges, amounted to over £57, considerably in excess of any other priory estate, including its holdings in Old and New Malton.

In 1535 the *Valor Ecclesiasticus* listed eight holdings of Chicksands as granges or manors. To these should be added Houghton Conquest, described as a grange in the Ministers' Accounts and, probably, Cople and Tadlow, large single holdings valued at £10 and £5 respectively in the

[60] The Ministers' Accounts describe Welham (in Norton) as a grange, and the court at Norton may have been connected with it, while the grange at Sutton (also in Norton) listed in 1244 may represent the same property as Welham, or at least the two may have been administered together. Another 1244 grange, Ryton, in Kirby Misperton, may be listed with the latter holding in the Ministers' Account.

[61] Winterton, Helpringham, and Ancaster were in Lincolnshire; South Croxton was in Leicestershire; and Kings Walden, the most distant, in Bedfordshire.

Accounts.[62] In five instances the priory had the appropriation of the parish church.[63] In four places the advowson of the church had already been alienated by the time Chicksands acquired an interest in the village: Chippenham (Cambs.) was in the hands of Bradwell by the early twelfth century; Tadlow had been given to Bradwell by Meinfelin, the founder, in the twelfth century; Wolverton had been granted to Walden abbey by its founder, Geoffrey de Mandeville; the advowson of Meppershall had passed to Lenton by the time of Henry II.[64] This leaves Hargrave and Houghton Conquest, both of which advowsons remained in lay hands. Here there was no rivalry with another religious house. The reason why the priory was unable to acquire the advowson in these places may be connected with the fact that its benefactor was a sub-tenant in the manor and did not himself hold the advowson.[65] Only at Linslade did the priory have the appropriation of the church but virtually no *temporalia*. At Chicksands, as at Watton and Malton, it is noteworthy that the least prosperous granges tended to be those where the parish church was not appropriated.[66]

Alvingham possessed ten granges in 1535. By the end of the twelfth century the priory had appropriated the churches in five of these parishes.[67] In addition the priory had been granted the church of Wold Newton but had failed to make good its claim here against Durham cathedral. It also held the advowson (though not the appropriation, which was not achieved until 1448) of Grainthorpe. Yarborough grange probably preceded the acquisition of the church in 1275, though the grange is not noted in Innocent IV's confirmation charter. In four places (Wold Newton, Cabourn, North Conesby, and Swinefleet) Alvingham had no

---

[62] *Court of Augmentation Accounts for Bedfordshire*, ed. Y. Nicholls, Publications of the Bedfordshire Historical Record Society, 63 (1984), 44, 50, 51. In *c.*1230 the prior of Chicksands was said to hold a hide and virgate in Tadlow of the Beauchamp of Bedford barony (G. Fowler, 'Domesday Notes', *Publications of the Bedfordshire Historical Record Society*, 1 (1913), 68).

[63] Chicksands, Caysoe, Stotfold, Hawnes, and Cople. The status and even the existence of Chicksands church by the 16th century is unclear.

[64] However, Chicksands' grange at Meppershall was centred on the chapel of St Thomas, which may itself have possessed landed property. The chapel was still in existence and in the priory's hands in 1319, when it appears in a confirmation charter of Walter Reynolds, archbishop of Canterbury (Fowler (ed.), 'Early Charters of . . . Chicksand', 128).

[65] Moreover, Henry II's confirmation charter makes it clear that the priory did originally hold the moiety of Houghton church (ibid. 121).

[66] The smallest granges were Tadlow, Hardgrave, Wolverton, and Chippenham: the exception to this correlation is Houghton Conquest, where the grange brought in £13, making it one of the most profitable of all the priory's estates (*Court of Augmentation Accounts for Bedfordshire*, 44).

[67] Alvingham, Cockerington St Mary's and St Leonards, Keddington and Little Cawthorpe.

interest in the church, and once again it is no coincidence to find that these granges were the least productive in 1535. Indeed, Conesby does not figure at all, which may indicate that the priory had already disposed of its holdings by the sixteenth century. The church at Cabourn was held by Grimsby priory, while North Conesby lay in Flixborough parish, where the advowson was in lay hands.[68]

By the Dissolution Bullington had rather more granges than Alvingham. Of the fourteen of whose existence there can be no doubt, only five lay in parishes of which the priory possessed the appropriation. As in the case of the other priories considered above, in some instances, such as Redbourne, where the church belonged to Selby abbey, or Southrey in Bardney parish, the Gilbertines arrived too late on the scene to acquire the church. However, six of the granges were in parishes where the church was retained in lay hands, at least initially. We cannot tell why Simon son of William, the founder of two granges in Faldingworth (where he was sole lord), did not grant the church as well; the advowson remained in lay hands throughout the period. At Oxcombe, too, a grange had been established through the generosity of William son of Humfrey and his lord Philip of Kyme but the church did not accompany the gift. It is significant that the canons made strenuous but unsuccessful efforts to claim the church in 1218 and 1286.[69] Perhaps more surprising are the examples of East Barkwith and Toft and Newton. Bullington early established a grange at East Barkwith, but the church remained in lay hands for some hundred years, when the advowson, but not the appropriation, came to Sixhills. Similarly, the priory soon had an interest in Toft and Newton, but the advowson of the former was only granted in 1279 to Sixhills, while Newton remained under a lay patron. When we turn to the relative values of these granges at the Dissolution it is again apparent that the most valuable were in parishes where the canons owned the church. But there is one revealing exception. The most valuable of all Bullington's granges was at Huttoft, which provided an income three times that of the home farm itself. Here, however, the parish church had long been held by Markby priory. Huttoft grange was devoted almost entirely to pastoral and dairy farming. It lay in excellent pasturage country; pasture was granted to the priory for at least 700 sheep; its importance to a community that relied heavily upon its wool production goes without saying.

---

[68] Swinefleet is a different case since this grange was remote in the Humber marshes, far from any settlement.

[69] *Final Concords*, i. 144; *The Rolls and Registers of Bishop Oliver Sutton 1280–1299*, ed. R. M. T. Hill, 8 vols., LRS 39, 43, 49, 52, 60, 64, 69, 76 (1948–86), i. 206.

Huttoft reminds us that possession of the parish church was not a *sine qua non* of a successful grange, just as possession of the church was not a guarantee of prosperity. Nevertheless, it remains true that the dual control of grange and church was the ideal towards which the Gilbertine canons aimed and worked.

Organization

The Gilbertine Rule laid down elaborate provisions for the organization of the grange both as an economic and spiritual unit. Each priory had a *grangiarius* who supervised its economic affairs, and who was the senior *conversus*. He was a member of the small committee of the four *procuratores*, which also included the prior, cellarer, and *procurator* (another *conversus*), which was responsible for the day-to-day running of the community and its granges.[70] It was their duty to inspect the granges to check whether they were duly provided for, or were keeping goods unjustly from the nuns. Any fruit or honey produced on the grange was to be sent to the nuns, after a portion had been retained for the *conversi*. They had, moreover, to present monthly accounts to the *scrutator*. Written accounts would then be sent to the nuns, and kept for consideration at the annual chapter, and for showing to the *summi scrutatores* on their visitations, which took place twice or three times a year. These occasions would also be attended by the keepers of the priory's churches (that is, those who accounted for the income from appropriated parishes), the collectors of farms, those in charge of the shepherds and the cobblers, and the brethren who looked after the priory's mill. The four proctors also had control of the priory's flocks and herds, and, though they were to count them, they had no authority to purchase animals without the prior's permission.

The priory granger had overall supervision of the priory's agricultural economy and of its work-force.[71] His freedom of action was at the same time severely limited. He could only talk with the *conversi* about their work and while standing; he might also only speak with two or three at a time. Here (as so often) we detect the almost obsessive concern for discipline within the order. The granger was allowed an assistant who could talk with the household and guests concerning their needs, and who was expected to be totally obedient in his turn.[72] He does not seem to have a Cistercian parallel. Each Cistercian grange was under the control of its

---

[70] *Monasticon*, vi. 2. xxiv. The cellarer was responsible for a Cistercian abbey's granges (Caninez, *Statuta*, i. 29). [71] *Monasticon*, vi. 2. xxxix.
[72] These rules are derived from Cistercian models (*Usus Conversorum*, vi; *Monuments Primitifs*, 282).

own granger, and the Gilbertines seem similarly to have employed a *conversus* official, also misleadingly styled a granger, to supervise individual estates and workers.[73] He could authorize repair or improvement works at the grange, so long as he took the advice of the *conversi* or hired labourers and communicated what he had done to the prior and cellarer.[74] These grangers were clearly senior lay brothers, and their responsibility was recognized when communities started to lease out granges to them as tenants, a practice already current among the Cistercians by 1262.[75]

Below the priory grangers in authority were other *conversi* with various duties: the brother responsible for threshing the corn; the brother in charge of cheese and butter production; the *hospitalis frater*, who looked after the geese and hens, bees, honey, and sheep, and all things necessary for the nuns and canons in the priory, and who also held the keys of the grange. He, along with the granger and a senior oxherd, was collectively in control of the grange, and all the *conversi* were to be obedient to them.[76] They were to keep tallies of all their transactions, one part to be kept by the *hospitalis frater* and the other by the granger.[77] Significantly, if there were not sufficient *conversi* for these tasks hired workers might be employed. These were to be rewarded with higher pay. The Rule is emphatic that these workers should not be held in disrespect by the *fratres*. They were to be informed of all transactions within the grange, and especially were to be notified several times a year of the number of sheep to avoid false accusation. Those who despised them, or refused to employ them as witnesses, were to be severely punished 'ad terrorem aliorum'.

---

[73] For the Cistercian *grangiarius*, see Platt, *Monastic Grange*, 82, and J. S. Donnelly, 'Changes in the Grange Economy of English and Welsh Cistercian Abbeys: 1300–1540', *Traditio*, 10 (1954), 413–14. It is sometimes difficult to distinguish between the 'priory granger' and the *grangiarius grangiae* (as he is sometimes styled) in the Rule.

[74] *Monasticon*, vi. 2. xxvi. Only once is a *grangiarius* mentioned in a charter. This relates to the extensive property of Nun Ormsby in the marshes near the Humber at Spaldington and Spaldingholme (Yorkshire). Here the community possessed considerable pasturage for sheep, cattle, and other animals, and a 12th-century grant of Robert the Constable gave the nuns rights to pasture horses, cattle, and pigs in this territory. If they did not have sufficient animals of their own they were allowed to make up the number with those of others, and Robert conceded that neither he nor his successors should interfere with the animals in any way without the assent and in the presence of the granger of Spaldingholme 'qui pro tempore fuerit' (*Gilbertine Charters*, 66).

[75] Malton farmed its grange at Amotherby to a granger by the end of the 13th century, and there is also a reference to the granger of the hospital of St Katherine's, Lincoln, holding land in Boby (Bishop, 'Monastic Granges in Yorkshire', 196–8; *Cal. Inq. p. m* ii, no. 689, 424).   [76] A shepherd could be added to this trio if need be.

[77] The keeping of tallies at the granges was employed in virtually all matters: to record crop harvests, the amount spent on provender for horses and oxen, how much was spent on seed corn and vegetable seeds.

Here there is more than an echo of rivalries between the *conversi* and secular workers, which may have their origins in the troubles of the order's early years.

The Gilbertines were as wary of women in their granges as in their convents.[78] No woman was allowed in the grange court without the prior's permission, nor should anyone speak alone with a woman. Women were to milk the sheep in the fields and not in the grange buildings, and where possible young and pretty women were to be avoided as milkmaids. They were to be supervised not by the *conversi* but by secular workers. When they were set to reap they were not allowed within the grange enclosure but stayed outside in the guest-house. Food was to be taken to them by a hired worker rather than by the *frater* who had charge of their food. Similarly, those working in the fields were to be accompanied by a mature *laicus* and subject to his authority and the *fratres* were not on any account to work with them, though if they saw work being badly done they could call the lay supervisor's attention to it. Those women who were employed in the reaping were to be accommodated outside the walls: careful rules were laid down for their supervision from the priory through a small window.[79]

The grange, therefore, provided in its organization a secure milieu for the Gilbertine workers, whether *conversi* or hired. Its structure was sufficiently flexible and articulated careful monitoring of the agricultural production at each grange, while allowing overall control and accounting from the centre. It was in many respects a microcosm of the priory; it reflected the same concerns with rigid organization and stern discipline. Above all, it was about segregation, a farm set apart from its secular neighbours and demarcated as far as possible from temporal society. And yet from the beginning the grange proved the impossibility of this ideal. It could not always be totally enclosed from the common fields; it had always to rely on the labour of the hireling as well as the *conversus*. The grange, then, revealed the contradictions in the ideals of twelfth-century monasticism. For all its distrust and prohibitions of other more secular forms of revenue, the grange could only be one element in the monastic economy: the new orders like the old had to come to terms with changing economic as well as spiritual conditions. When, within a century and a half of their foundation, the granges began to be leased, it was a

---

[78] *Monasticon*, vi. 2. xli–xlii. This prohibition is a much expanded form of that in the Cistercian *Usus Conversorum*, VII (*Monuments Primitifs*, 282).

[79] *Monasticon*, vi. 2. xxvi, xli–xlii.

recognition of change as profound as any experienced by the Gilbertines between their creation and Dissolution.

The *conversi* and hired labourers

Though the grange system of agriculture was by definition intended to be dependent upon the labour of the *conversi*, the very fact that the granges were in general comparatively large farms meant that only in very exceptional circumstances was it possible to staff them by their labour alone. From the beginning the Gilbertines accepted this economic reality, in contrast to the early Cistercians' reluctance.[80] In both Gilbertine and Cistercian houses the lay brethren seem to have had a supervisory role in the operation of the grange, functioning as grangers and overseeing the work of others.[81] However, on occasions laymen also seem to have taken an oversight of the grange.[82] Within the priory itself the *conversi* again seem primarily to have exercised supervisory or skilled functions.[83] Gilbert himself tells how Ogger and his brothers were trained, two to be blacksmiths, the other two to be carpenters.[84] Some further evidence is provided in the miracle stories. *Frater* Robert, a weaver of the order, was paralysed in his hand and arm while weaving after vespers; a witness to his cure, *frater* Gilbert, was serving in the lay brethren's refectory.[85] These stories also contain references to lay servants of the priory, such as Alexander, a priory servant who witnessed his wife's cure, or Walter, a 'lay servant and man of the house of Sempringham', who witnessed the cure of Maximilla of Thorpe.[86]

If the *conversi* were not sufficient to provide more than the core of the labour force at Gilbertine priories and granges, how were the domestic offices staffed and the agricultural economy run? There can be little doubt that considerable use was made of peasant labour. From the early years the use of hired labour was presupposed. The first lay brothers themselves were recruited from the *famuli* attached to the Sempringham

[80] The Gilbertine use of hired labour was explicitly recognized in the agreement made between the order and the Cistercians in 1164.

[81] For this aspect of the grange economy, see Platt, *Monastic Grange*, ch. 4, and Donnelly, 'Changes in the Grange Economy', esp. ch. 4.

[82] Geoffrey was the reeve at Watton's grange at Kilnwick and held two bovates in the village of the prior, which was granted on his death 'to our beloved and faithful Geoffrey Dote' for the not inconsiderable rent of 30s. per annum (*Yorkshire Deeds VI*, 102).

[83] However, it has been argued that at mid-13th-century Cistercian Beaulieu most of the domestic departments, such as the brewery and the bakehouse, were headed by monks who were responsible for rendering their accounts (*The Account Book of Beaulieu Abbey*, ed. S. F. Hockey, Camden Society, 4th ser. 16 (1975), 17–19).   [84] *Book of St Gilbert*, 78.

[85] Ibid. 276–8.   [86] Ibid. 274, 294.

community, and Gilbert's own account of the early foundations refers to the *mercenarii*.[87] The agreement drawn up between the Cistercians and Gilbertines in 1164 ordered that no *mercenarius* be poached by one order from the other, and that if this was done the *frater* responsible would receive the discipline first in his own chapter and then in the chapter of the other house while the worker himself was to return to his original employment.[88] The Rule, too, accepts the existence of the hired labourers and legislates for them. The cellarer was responsible for their hire, and within a month of their joining the service it was his obligation to enrol their names and wages, which he paid them. None of these workers were to be employed in priories where any of their relatives were members, except in case of necessity.

Most of the Gilbertine granges lay in, or near, villages where there was a ready pool of labourers, available either for hire, or granted with their services by the priories' benefactors. The cartularies and charters of Gilbertine houses make frequent references to the grants of *nativi* (with or without their land) to the canons.[89] Very occasionally their function is spelt out. The foundation charter of Chicksands priory included Payn de Beauchamp's demesne wood, together with half a virgate and the dwelling which Lefsten, *custos* of the wood, held. The implication is clear that Lefsten (or his successor) would continue to do the same job for his new lord. This grant goes on to give Godric the carpenter (along with his dwelling and quarter-virgate holding) to the nuns 'ad reficiendum domos sanctimonialium'.[90] Such precision is exceptional: more commonly the *nativus* or groups of *nativi* are given to the priories with no explicit mention of the duties that they were expected to perform. It seems clear, however, that these were intended to provide a supply of labour, permanent or seasonal, on the granges, and it is noteworthy that the great majority of such exchanges of labour occur on holdings on or near those on which the Gilbertines had developed granges, rather than on those from which they received a rental income only.[91] One of the most revealing of charters relating to *nativi* is that of William de Vesci to Watton, the priory founded by his father. Early in 1178 he gave to the priory all the men of Watton whom he had not removed thence before the octave of

---

[87] Ibid. 36–8; *Monasticon*, vi. 2. xix. [88] London, BL, MS Stowe 937, fo. 145ᵛ.

[89] See e.g. *Gilbertine Charters*, 8, 9–10, 15, 27, 34 for some Sixhills examples.

[90] *Monasticon*, vi. 2. 950.

[91] There can be little doubt that Orm of Ferriby, given with his three-bovate holding to Watton priory by William de Vesci, was expected to oversee the running of the priory's estate in North Ferriby (*EYC* iii. 500).

the nativity of St John the Baptist to hold with their children and chattels, either to keep them or remove them as lawful men of the vill. The intention of the patron is clearly that his *nativi* should provide the core of the work-force on the priory's home estate.[92]

Further evidence of the importance of wage labourers in the Gilbertine grange economy is provided by grants of tofts by the priories to peasant proprietors. The tofts themselves were normally obtained as part of the standard one- or two-bovate holding that is the most frequent unit found amongst grants to Gilbertine houses in both Yorkshire and Lincolnshire. The arable holdings would then be subsumed into the grange estate of the priory, while the tofts continued to be available at rent for the former proprietor, who was now employed by the priory.[93] It has also been argued that, since more labourers were required than could be conveniently housed in the grange, the priories developed small 'villages' outside the grange perimeter to accommodate them. Though there is hardly any direct documentary evidence for this in England, a number of grange sites are associated with earthworks of peasant settlements, and an example of this type has been identified at the grange of Sutton belonging to Malton priory.[94] However, since most Gilbertine granges lay near pre-existing settlements, it seems likely that in the majority of cases the canons relied upon the provision of accommodation in tofts in those settlements.

Bishop long ago showed that in villages where the Yorkshire priories had granges they also possessed unfree tenants, most of whom were toftholders, with little or no land of their own. He also pointed out that many of these toftholders who occur in the Yorkshire lay subsidy of 1301 carry occupational names suggesting their role in the priories' economy.[95] Investigation of alienations of tofts by the Lincolnshire priories of Alvingham and Bullington has revealed that here, too, they were concentrated on the grange estates, and that virtually all alienations of property were of tofts. A clear example of a worker (perhaps a manumitted villein) being granted a toft on an Alvingham estate is that of Edric of Grimolby, a *nativus* of Walter of Saltfleetby, who granted him to the priory, which then rented him a toft in Alvingham which had itself been given by a peasant benefactor.[96] Tofts, too, might be acquired and then developed,

---

[92] *EYC* ii. 410.

[93] See Bishop, 'Monastic Granges', 207. Alternatively tofts might be acquired separately (e.g. *Gilbertine Charters*, 50).   [94] Platt, *Monastic Grange*, 86–91, 236.

[95] Bishop, 'Monastic Granges', 204.

[96] Oxford, Bodl. Lib., MS Laud Misc. 642, fo. 84. These grants are discussed in detail in Golding, 'Gilbertine Priories', 189–92.

either by the priory or its tenant. Thus, Robert Storri was granted the site of two tofts in Reedness by Alvingham on condition that he built tofts at his own cost within two years. If he failed to do this he rendered himself liable to a fine of half a mark.[97] Similarly, the canons of Malton are found erecting new tofts for their landless tenants on their granges of Hutton and Rillington.[98]

But the clearest indication of the use of both *nativi* and hired labour is found in the Malton cartulary. This contains a list of some 35 unfree tenants (including in some cases their families) who are variously described as *nativus*, *consuetudinarius*, or *homo*.[99] Graham argued from this that 'there were very few villeins on the estates of Malton'.[100] Certainly, not many names are recorded, but these do not comprise all the peasants granted to the house—it is in any case unusual for a cartulary to list grants of *nativi* separately. Moreover, it is likely that the majority of peasants were granted with their holdings; what is unusual about these grants is that they seem to have been granted without any accompanying land. In two instances their occupations are given: one was a carpenter and the other a shepherd. As far as can be judged, all these grants date from the first half of the thirteenth century, and it is possible that they were all acquired during the rule of prior William of Ancaster who was responsible for the cartulary's compilation. In four instances it is apparent that the men were manumitted, for there are notifications by prior William that 'ex collacione et manumissione' of the donor the peasant has been freed on annual payment of a fine to the convent.[101] One of these pledges that the community 'prefatum Thomam et sequelam suam ecclesie nostre concessos tanquam liberam elemosinam nostram curabimus ut decebit'. Another makes it clear that the freed peasant was provided with a dwelling. Reginald of Snainton, given by Ingelram de Percy, was manumitted and provided with a toft to hold for life for 3*s.* per annum on the understanding that when he died or changed his life the toft and its appurtenances would revert to the priory.

The *nativi* were employed as workers on the priories' estates. It is sometimes difficult to distinguish them from the stipendiary employees,

---

[97] Oxford, Bodl. Lib., MS Laud Misc. 642, fo. 166ʳ⁻ᵛ. Many abbeys, including Nun Ormsby, had property on the rich pastures of Reedness by the Humber estuary.

[98] London, BL, MS Cotton Claudius D XI, fos. 272–3.   [99] Ibid., fos. 239ᵛ–241ᵛ.

[100] Graham, 'Finances of Malton Priory', 146.

[101] That manumission was employed by the Gilbertine priories in the mid-13th century is demonstrated by the 1268 prohibition on the manumission of *nativi* and their lands by priors without the consent of their communities and the Master (Oxford, Bodl. Lib., MS Douce 136, fo. 89).

but the latter can usually be differentiated as workers within the priory itself. The Malton accounts detail the expenses *pro mercedibus serviencium* from 1244 to 1252. The annual bill varied between £9 7s. 8d. in 1248 and £13 10s. in 1251 and 1252.[102] This was a relatively small item of expenditure, suggesting that in this priory at least the *conversi* may still have comprised the major part of the work-force. The cartulary also contains a list of wages paid to workers at Martinmas and Pentecost. Though undated this clearly derives from the priorate of William of Ancaster.[103] It includes payments to workers in the kitchen, bakehouse, and brewery, a cheesemaker and fisherman, those working in the cobblers' shop, the carpenter and his boy, the marshal, carters, and grooms in the stable, servants of the sacristy and the clerk of the church, the forester of 'Blakedale', and (the only woman worker recorded) a washerwoman. Payments were also made to named individuals, whose occupations were not specified, including William of Hainton, who is listed elsewhere in the cartulary as a recipient of a corrody. Wages varied between 5s. for the carpenter and 1s. for the bearer of the obit (who only appears in receipt of payment at Pentecost), while the highest-paid servant of all was the *garcio prioris*, who received 6s. 8d. at Martinmas (though he does not appear to have been paid at Pentecost as well). These workers were almost exclusively household servants, they were not workers at the granges, and the only specifically agricultural workers whose payments were recorded were the 'stackers at harvest', who each received 2s. 6d.[104]

These wages can usefully be compared with the much more detailed, but nearly contemporary, accounts of Beaulieu abbey which date from the year 1269/70. Beaulieu had a somewhat greater income (*c.* £252) than Malton (*c.* £202) in 1291, but both were male communities organized on the same principles. Accounts at Beaulieu were rendered at Easter and Michaelmas rather than at Pentecost and Martinmas. Though the Beaulieu wages are only listed for the year as a whole, it is clear from several of the departmental accounts that more servants were employed in the abbey

---

[102] London, BL, MS Cotton Claudius D XI, fos. 279ᵛ–281. Unfortunately, the expenses for 1253 to 1257, entered on the following folio, do not list these wages. The bill for 1244 is given as xl li. vij s. iijd., but xl is almost certainly a mistake for xj. To this figure should be added the annual payments for the servants' liveries ('pro panno garcionum').

[103] Ibid., fo. 275ᵛ. The list of payments at Pentecost (but not at Martinmas) also includes sums for the purchase of various miscellaneous items, such as soap, oil for the carts, and payments for the carriage of wool, as well as alms for the poor.

[104] The Martinmas wages bill considerably exceeded that at Pentecost, the kitchen wages being, for example, 6s. at Pentecost but only 3s. at Martinmas. Since the workers were not agricultural, it is hard to explain this discrepancy in terms of the agricultural year.

offices in the autumn than the spring, just as seems to have been the case at Malton. The Cistercian house employed five *famuli* and two *garciones* in the bakehouse, and four *famuli* in the brewery, by comparison with the four and two respectively employed at Martinmas in Malton.[105] There was a cheesemaker at the Beaulieu grange at Otterwood who received four shillings per annum: the Malton account suggests that there the cheesemaker only received two shillings at Martinmas.[106] It is most likely that workers at Malton, like their Beaulieu counterparts, received a food payment as well as cash, but the less detailed accounts of the Gilbertine priory do not record these.

One striking difference between the two houses is the status of the forester. At Malton he received 2*s.* at Martinmas and 1*s.* at Pentecost: at Beaulieu the forester received 60*s.* per annum and was responsible for his own department. This reflects the much greater importance of the woodland to the economy of the New Forest abbey.[107] Similarly, the forge at Beaulieu seems to have been a much larger undertaking than at Malton, where the smith received 7*s.* per annum. Though the number of *famuli* at Beaulieu is not specified, their annual stipend came to 40*s.*[108] As at Malton there were, perhaps not surprisingly, no women workers on the Beaulieu estates apart from milkmaids and a *lotrix* at the granges of Coxwell and Soberton, where they received 6*d.* per annum, by contrast with the quite substantial payment of 3*s.* received by their Malton counterpart.[109] No women are recorded at Beaulieu itself.

In general, the hired work-force at Beaulieu was larger than at Malton. This may suggest that at the latter *conversi* continued in the mid-thirteenth century to undertake a greater proportion of the priory's manual work. Unfortunately, there is no hint of the numbers of canons and *conversi* at the Gilbertine house: at Beaulieu it has been calculated that the *famuli* considerably outnumbered the combined population of monks and lay brethren.[110] The *famuli* at Beaulieu seem in general to have been somewhat better paid than their Gilbertine counterparts; this may reflect differentials in wage levels between Hampshire and the North Riding. It

---

[105] *Account Book of Beaulieu Abbey*, 234, 298. It is not possible to compare wage rates since the wages at Malton varied between Martinmas and Pentecost, suggesting either that fewer were employed in the Pentecost term or that they were paid less at this time.

[106] There may also have been another cheesemaker at Beaulieu abbey; one certainly received a bread ration from the bakehouse (ibid. 159, 302–3).

[107] The forester's department contributed £30, some 20% of the abbey's annual income (ibid. 198–201; see also 35). However, it should be noted that in the table of wages of the hired servants a forester is listed as receiving only 4*s.* 10*d.* per annum (ibid. 318–19).

[108] Ibid. 266.   [109] Ibid. 22, 91, 115.   [110] Ibid. 16–23.

seems likely, too, that the Cistercian house was more highly organized, with over thirty departments and offices. As far as can be seen, there were fewer obedientiaries in the Gilbertine houses than amongst their Cistercian (or Benedictine) contemporaries. Those that do occur, such as the cellarer and sub-cellarer, may well have been more powerful, but much greater control was retained by a Gilbertine prior in his house than by a Cistercian abbot or Augustinian prior, a fact reflected in the 1268 revision of the statutes which attempted to prevent the priors from acting without consultation with the priories' proctors and without the consent of the chapters.[111]

The labourers discussed above worked in the priory and its offices. Many more were employed on the granges. The Malton accounts list fourteen granges (rising to fifteen in 1250) and the number of *mercenarii* employed on all but one of these estates at Pentecost (and sometimes also at Martinmas).[112] Most (29) were to be found at Swinton, a grange newly created and perhaps for that reason requiring a large work-force. Swinton was also mainly an arable grange using seven ploughs. There were also substantial numbers at the granges of Mowthorpe (19), Rillington (17), and the home farm (16).[113] A further indication of the role of the hired labourers on Malton's grange estates is provided by their wages bills, which are given for each of the granges from 1244 till 1257. These can be expressed as a proportion of the total expenses of the grange. In a good year they amounted to more than half the total costs.[114] In 1244 the wages as a percentage of overall costs varied between 35 per cent at Rillington, and 70 per cent at Kirby (the smallest grange).[115]

The *conversi* probably remained an integral element of the Gilbertine community and economy until the beginning of the fourteenth century. It was at this time that the priories' granges first began to be leased, and the need for labour correspondingly to decline.[116] The only overview of

---

[111] Oxford, Bodl. Lib., MS Douce 136, fo. 89. See also Graham, 'Finances of Malton Priory', 135–9.

[112] The exception is the grange of Wintringham, the largest and most prosperous of Malton's granges.

[113] London, BL, MS Cotton Claudius D XI, fos. 277ᵛ–278ᵛ. The statistics are conveniently summarized in Waites, 'The Monastic Grange', 654.

[114] Annual expenses were probably lowest, as Graham believed, when 'there was no murrain among stock and no serious loss or damage to property' ('Finances of Malton Priory', 145).   [115] Waites, 'The Monastic Grange', 654.

[116] There is very little direct evidence for a decline in the importance of the Gilbertine lay brotherhood, as there is, for example, in the case of the Cistercians, but the experiences of both orders were parallel, and the first evidence of the leasing of Gilbertine granges is found at Chicksands in the 1320s.

the numbers of *conversi* during the medieval period is found in 1376, when a national clerical subsidy assessment listed the numbers of lay brothers as well as religious. *Conversi* were reported at only four priories.[117] The decline of the Gilbertine *conversi*, like that of the Cistercian brethren, was both an indicator and result of a changing economic climate. As all monastic houses looked increasingly to rents for their income, the lay brethren were now an anachronism.

Wool

Production

From the first years of the order it was recognized that wool sales would be an important element in the Gilbertine economy. The Rule also laid down detailed regulations for the Gilbertine involvement in the wool trade.[118] The foundation charter of Ormsby included the grant of pasture for 200 sheep in Walcot, and for 200 sheep in Billinghay, while in his foundation of Bullington Simon son of William gave pasture for 600 sheep in *Aldefeld* in Faldingworth.[119] Initially at least, the nuns had their own flocks, and the proceeds from the sale of their wool were intended solely for the maintenance of the women. There is a unique reference to this practice in a charter of Christina de Mandeville, countess of Essex, in favour of Shouldham. She gave pasture in Wolferton 'ut inde quantum potest extendi pascantur oves monialium qui eis secundum constitucionem ordinis specialiter assignantur ad faciendum edificia et clausuram circa eis'.[120] In 1193 the wool from all the Gilbertine houses, like that from the Cistercians, was seized to help provide Richard I's ransom.[121] Some hundred years later, Pegolotti's list of monastic wool producers shows that all but the smallest Gilbertine houses, Holland Bridge and Marmont, were selling wool to Italian merchants (see Table).[122]

---

[117] St Katherine's, Lincoln (3); Bullington (2); Catley (1); and Shouldham (1). The entry for Sempringham itself is incomplete (Owen, *Church and Society*, 144–5; J. C. Russell, 'The Clerical Population of Medieval England', *Traditio*, 2 (1944), 205). The decline was similar amongst the Cistercians. There were 5 *conversi* at Louth Park, 4 at Revesby, and 3 at Swineshead, but there were also more choir monks in these communities than canons in the Gilbertine houses (Owen, *Church and Society*, 144–5).

[118] See ibid. 66–9 for an overview of the involvement of Lincolnshire monasteries in wool production. See below, pp. 424, 426.   [119] *Gilbertine Charters*, 73, 91.

[120] *Monasticon*, vi. 2. xliv; G. W. Watson, 'Charters to Shouldham Priory', *Genealogist*, NS 36 (1920), 75–6.

[121] 'et de domibus ordinis de Semplingham totam lanam suam in hoc anno' (*Chronica Rogeri de Hovedene*, iii. 210–11).   [122] See below, pp. 420, 425–6.

Wool production of Gilbertine priories

	Price per sack (marks)			
	Good quality wool	Medium quality wool	'Locks' (i.e. short, poor quality wool)	Annual production (sacks)
Malton	17	11	6	45
Watton	$16\frac{1}{2}$	10	$8\frac{1}{2}$	40
St Katherine's, Lincoln	$22\frac{1}{2}$	$12\frac{1}{2}$	—	35
Sempringham	20	$10\frac{1}{2}$	9	25
Bullington	22	13	$9\frac{1}{2}$	18
Nun Ormsby	19	11	10	18
Sixhills	18	$10\frac{1}{2}$	9	18
Shouldham	$12\frac{1}{2}$	'no medium quality wool, nor "locks", but "britches" (i.e. lowest quality wool), three stones per sack'		
Haverholme	18	10	$8\frac{1}{2}$	16
Chicksands	16	9	—	15
Alvingham	18	10	9	12
Ellerton	15	$9\frac{1}{2}$	—	10
Newstead	15	'no medium quality wool, but "britches" as well as "locks"'		10
Mattersey	19	11	10	10
Catley	19	$11\frac{1}{2}$	$8\frac{1}{2}$	8
Clattercote	17	11	—	7
St Andrew's, York	15	$9\frac{1}{2}$	—	3
Holland Bridge	'almost no wool'			3
Marmont	'no wool'			

Source: Based on the list of Pegolotti in his *La Practica della Mercatura*, transcribed in W. Cunningham, *The Growth of English Industry and Commerce during the Early Middle Ages*, 5th edn. (Cambridge, 1915), 635–7.

The clearest indication of the importance of wool in the Gilbertines' economy is derived from grants of pasture for specific numbers of sheep in the common pasture of villages or manors. It must be remembered, however, that grants were also made, particularly to the northern Gilbertine houses, of moorland pasture where no maxima were fixed, so the total estimates of flocks are minimum figures. Though it is impossible to determine whether the actual number of sheep pastured always corresponded to the numbers allowed in a grant, there is strong evidence from Yorkshire monasteries that such lands were fully used, and were sometimes over-exploited.[123] The Malton cartulary records pasture grants for some 6,000 sheep, and in its region of Yorkshire the priory was third only to Rievaulx and Bridlington in the scale of its pastoral economy. Most of its pastures lay on the edges of the Vale of Pickering in strip parishes that ran northwards from the flood-plain of the river Derwent on to the North York moors, but there were also substantial pastures on the Wolds. Though for the most part the Vale of Pickering itself was avoided by sheep farmers since it was poorly drained and marshy, the fact that Malton possessed a flock at Kirby Misperton in the centre of the Vale suggests that even here the canons expected wool production to be worthwhile.[124]

Smaller priories could also possess substantial pastures. By 1337 Haverholme had been granted pasture for at least 3,680 sheep (and pasture for a further 1,000 sheep at *Wardeberg* (Notts.) is referred to in a suit of 1226).[125] Alvingham was granted pasture for 1,200 sheep in North Conesby at the end of the twelfth century, there was pasturage for 900 sheep on the priory's grange at Cabourn, and for at least 600 sheep in Swinhop.[126] Bullington had pasture for 1,100 sheep at Faldingworth, 660 sheep at Hackthorn, at least 600 in Huttoft, and 500 in Redbourne.[127] Substantial pasturage was not confined to the Gilbertine priories of Lincolnshire and Yorkshire. Chicksands was given pasture for 500 sheep with their yearling lambs in Chippenham, and also possessed considerable sheep runs at Molesworth.[128]

---

[123] B. Waites, *Moorland and Vale-Land Farming in North-East Yorkshire: The Monastic Contribution in the Thirteenth and Fourteenth Centuries*, Borthwick Papers, 32 (York, 1967), 30. [124] Ibid. 28.

[125] *Cal. Ch. R.* iv. 403–19; *CRR* xii (1225–6), no. 2396. In one grant alone, John, constable of Chester, gave pasture for 1,000 sheep at Plumtree.

[126] Oxford, Bodl. Lib., MS Laud Misc. 642, fos. 161ᵛ (North Conesby), 157ᴿ⁻ᵛ (Cabourn), 145bᵛ–146ᵛ (Swinhop).

[127] *Gilbertine Charters*, 91; London, BL, Addit. MS 6118, pp. 795 (Faldingworth), 741, 808, 811 (Hackthorn), 724 (Huttoft), 738–9 (Redbourne).

[128] Fowler (ed.), 'Early Charters of . . . Chicksand', 113–14.

Occasional references to sheepfolds are also found. These were often, though not always, attached to granges, and of course contributed to the fertilizing of the priories' arable. Alvingham possessed one at North Conesby, where there was good pasturage in the water-meadows of the Trent. There was also a sheepfold at Swinhop, where Simon de Chaunci gave land for 600 sheep 'with the house built there'.[129] Sixhills had one at Hainton and the canons were granted additional lands in the mid-thirteenth century to expand it.[130] Even the small house of Catley was allowed to make a sheepfold by Alexander de Cressi on the *brueria* of Dunsby.[131] A number of Gilbertine houses, including Alvingham and Ormsby, also had sheep pasture and folds at Spaldingholme and Swinefleet, on the Yorkshire side of the Humber.[132]

Though the marshland areas of Lincolnshire in particular provided good pasturage, there is little evidence for specialist pastoral farming on the estates of Gilbertine houses. The details of the *temporalia* of Alvingham in 1291 show that, though the house had flocks on its granges at Wold Newton, Cockerington, Alvingham, Keddington, Yarborough, and Conesby, only at the latter two estates did income from fruits and flocks exceed that from arable lands and rents.[133] Alvingham may have concentrated on wool production at North Conesby, where the soil was very barren and ill suited to arable farming. At the end of the twelfth century Thomas d'Arci granted the canons pasture for 1,200 sheep 'on both sides of the vill, but especially on the heath': his son, Norman, released the canons from their obligation to give him one sheep from their flocks, in return for permission to cross his meadows when the sheep were taken down to the river for washing.[134] Specialization also occurred at Swinefleet, even though pasturage is not mentioned specifically in any of the charters. This area was newly reclaimed from the sea and would initially have been of little use for arable production.

There is similarly little evidence of specialization on the estates of Bullington. The only grange that does appear to have been devoted

---

[129] Oxford, Bodl. Lib., MS Laud Misc. 642, fos. 180, 145b^v.

[130] 'ad claudendas et edificandas bercarias ad opus earundem' (*Gilbertine Charters*, 24–5).

[131] Ibid. 82.

[132] Ibid. 61, 63, 66. An Ormsby charter specifically refers to the granger of Spaldingholme who was in charge of the priory's flocks.

[133] Oxford, Bodl. Lib., MS Laud Misc. 642, fo. 39. No flocks are recorded at Grainthorpe grange while flocks are noted at the non-grange lands of Fulstow and Cawthorpe.

[134] Ibid., fos. 161^v, 162^v. A series of agreements and disputes with the d'Arci family during the 13th century testify to the importance of pasturage rights here. See Golding, 'Gilbertine Priories', 33–6. The sheep pastures of Alvingham and Bullington are described in detail, 31–9, and the material is only summarized here.

predominantly to pastoral (and dairy) farming was Huttoft. Here land was given by the Kymes and their tenants at the end of the twelfth and beginning of the thirteenth centuries, especially by Philip II of Kyme. He granted pasture for 600 sheep, 23 acres of meadow, all his land and pasture outside *le Hauedik* and common pasture rights within the dike, a sheepfold and the site of another, and an annual payment of 5s. made to him by Markby priory for the pasturage of 50 sheep. He also released the canons from their annual obligation to provide food for one of Philip's own shepherds.[135]

There is little precise information as to the size of Gilbertine flocks. In 1283 there were 941 ewes, 1,005 wethers, and 503 lambs on the estates of Alvingham. This total of 1,946 sheep should be compared with the flocks of Thornton abbey in the same county, which numbered 7,934 in 1313 with a total clip of over 86 sacks producing an income of nearly £700.[136] In 1293 Haverholme sold over 16 sacks to Italian merchants. This suggests a total flock of *c*.3,200.[137] A generation later, in 1308, Malton was reported to have 160 ewes and 200 sheep at Ryton, approaching 500 at Brompton, 200 at Kirby Misperton, and 600 at Middleton.[138] Much less is known of the pastoral activities of the Gilbertine houses outside Yorkshire and Lincolnshire, though Pegolotti's list shows that Chicksands' and Shouldham's wool productions stand comparison with most of the Lincolnshire communities (see Table). For the most part evidence relating to these houses is circumstantial. The lay taxation of 1297 shows that at Hawnes Chicksands possessed 28 sheep valued at 28s. The greater part of the priory's income here, however, came from its production of wheat, rye, and especially oats, together with income from bullocks and cows. At Sandy, on the other hand, there were 160 ewes valued at £8 and they provided the largest element of the priory's income of £11 13s. 2d. Comparison with evidence from other Bedfordshire communities in this locality suggests that sheep farming was the most important element in their economy.[139] In 1291 Shouldham was reported to have 'animals' (there are no specific references to sheep) on its estates of Thorp, Shouldham, Stoke, Wiggenhall, Wolferton, and Carlton St Peter. At Clench Wardon

---

[135] London, BL, Addit. MS 6118, pp. 724, 725. See also Golding, 'Gilbertine Priories', 37–8.

[136] Oxford, Bodl. Lib. MS Laud Misc. 642, fragment attached to fo. 35ᵛ; Owen, *Church and Society*, 68. In 1316 there were 500 sheep on the grange of St Katherine's, Lincoln, at Scopwick (*Cal. Pat. R. 1313–17*, 601). [137] Pegolotti noted a production of 16 sacks.

[138] *Reg. Greenfield*, v. 224–5.

[139] *The Taxation of 1297*, ed. A. T. Gaydon, Publications of the Bedfordshire Historical Record Society, 39 (1959), pp. xxvii–xxviii, 29, 68.

only animals are recorded: there is no mention of arable land. With the exception of Carlton St Peter these were the most valuable estates held by the priory, which suggests, though it does not prove, that at Shouldham too the canons relied chiefly on wool sales for their income.[140]

Some indication of flock size can also be gained from details of sacks sold by the priories. It is usually estimated that 200 fleeces made up one wool sack. A royal inquiry into Italian wool merchants' dealings in 1294 and the figures given in Pegolotti's list of wool producers make some crude calculations possible.[141] These suggest that the two Yorkshire houses of Malton and Watton had the largest flocks at the end of the thirteenth century, but that Shouldham, Sempringham, and Lincoln were also substantial producers. There are some problems in interpreting the 1294 figures, however. On the one hand, they only list wool traded with Italian merchants during the previous year and do not take account of transactions with other merchants, such as those of Flanders.[142] On the other hand, the wool may include not only that produced by the Gilbertines themselves, but also *collecta*. The figures do, however, give some indication of the comparative scale of the priories' involvement in the trade, which is reinforced by Pegolotti's figures. These suggest that in most, though not all, cases production had risen: they show a similar range of production and suggest that, though the Gilbertines could not compete with the really large producers such as Fountains (76 sacks), Rievaulx (60 sacks), or Jervaulx (50 sacks), the largest Gilbertine houses such as Malton (45 sacks) or Watton (40 sacks) were substantial traders, while in Lincolnshire St Katherine's, Lincoln, and Sempringham were exceeded only by large Cistercian abbeys such as Kirkstead or Revesby, or long-established Benedictine communities such as Spalding or Crowland.[143]

Marketing

The marketing of wool by the priories was carefully controlled. No one was allowed to sell without the authority of the four *procuratores* of the house.[144] While something of the scale of wool production amongst the Gilbertine houses can be gleaned from an investigation of pasture grants, these tell nothing of the processes by which the wool was sold to merchants, whether native or foreign. Such evidence can be obtained only

---

[140] *Taxatio*, 105.

[141] The 1294 inquiry (PRO E.101/126/7/12) is described below, pp. 425–6.

[142] However, the list normally refers to all the wool of the house, which seems to suggest that the Italians were taking the whole clip.   [143] Owen, *Church and Society*, 66.

[144] *Monasticon*, vi. 2. xxv.

from the royal records, particularly of the thirteenth century. These are often exiguous. For the most part they date from the last decades of the century, though we do know that St Katherine's, Lincoln, was trading with merchants of Ghent at Boston fair in 1219, and we must assume that Boston was the chief outlet for other Lincolnshire houses at this time: certainly Alvingham continued to trade there in 1293.[145] In 1294 sheriffs were ordered to organize the seizure of all wool, wool fells and hides in the country.[146] Records of this operation are scanty and survive in detail only for Bedfordshire and Buckinghamshire. Four sacks of the prior of Chicksands were seized, along with 20 ox- and 40 calf-hides. If these figures are compared with those for the neighbouring Cistercian abbeys of Warden and Woburn, it is clear that Chicksands was not especially active in wool production: this might in part explain the financial difficulties the house was shortly to experience.[147] More detailed information for other Gilbertine houses comes from returns made in 1294 by Italian firms (who were not exempt from the projected prise) of all wool that they had already contracted to buy or which they expected to buy that year from the religious.[148] Reports were submitted by all the Italian companies which were active in the English wool market and they show that the Gilbertines traded almost exclusively with Florentine firms.[149] The Pulci traded with St Katherine's, Lincoln, Haverholme, and Catley; the Frescobaldi with Newstead, Malton, Sixhills, and Sempringham; the Mozzi with Bullington and Shouldham; the Cerchi Bianchi with Ellerton, Ormsby, Holy Sepulchre, Lincoln (which, though affiliated to St Katherine's, clearly conducted some of its own financial affairs), Mattersey, and Clattercote; and the Cerchi Neri with Watton. For the most part the wool clips were delivered to the firm's representative at the priory itself, but Malton seems to have sent its clip to Watton for collection, Shouldham marketed at Lynn, Mattersey at Lincoln, Watton at Hull, and Alvingham

---

[145] PRO E. 372/63. For Gilbertine property in Boston see below, 'Urban property'.

[146] The use of wool as an economic weapon in Edward I's disputes with France and Flanders has been much discussed. See in general T. H. Lloyd, *The English Wool Trade*, ch. 3, esp. 75–83.

[147] PRO E. 101/126/7. The comparable figures for Warden and Woburn are 32 sacks, 88 ox-hides, 100 calf-hides and 29 sacks, 13 ox-hides and 50 calf-hides respectively.

[148] Lloyd, *The English Wool Trade*, 82. Bischoff suggests that the inquiry was probably intended for the king's advisers so that they could more accurately predict the income from the royal custom on wool (J. P. Bischoff, 'Economic Change in 13th Century Lincoln: Decline of an Urban Cloth Industry', Ph.D. thesis (Yale University, 1975), 219).

[149] Alvingham was an exception, dealing with the Riccardi firm of Lucca. However, in 1338 Alvingham was dealing with the Bardi, to whom the prior is said to have sold 4 sacks, which were conveyed to Boston for export (*Cal. Inq. Misc.* i. 399).

(at its own cost) at Boston.[150] All of the Gilbertine houses, like many other Lincolnshire communities, traded with one Italian firm only, who purchased the whole of their clip.[151] The date of delivery was fixed at between two weeks and one month after the feast of St John (24 June). As Bischoff suggests, this delivery date allowed ample time after shearing for the wool clip to be collected from the granges and graded and packed for the merchants.[152]

The accounts of Malton priory from 1244 to 1257 provide the only detailed information of income from wool sales of a Gilbertine priory. They demonstrate a considerable fluctuation ranging from £243 19s. 8d. in 1255 to £460 16s. 8d. in 1251. However, income during the first three years from 1244 to 1246 was almost static, which may indicate that the canons had made a bargain with a wool merchant to supply wool for this term. During this period the expenses of sheep farming were very low, the costs of washing and shearing the sheep varying from between 10s. and 18s. and those of wool preparation between £1 5s. and £1 17s. Graham suggested that 'it was utterly impossible for the canons to have obtained the whole of the wool from their own flocks' and that the only explanation was that they acted as wool collectors for other producers in the region.[153] The Rule forbade this practice and prohibited the mixing of the canons' wool with that of any other or the selling of other wool as the canons' own. However, the fact that this prohibition was repeated in the 1268 visitation of the order suggests that the practice was widespread.[154] Indeed, in 1274–5 the jurors of Lincoln complained that the canons of Sempringham together with monks of a number of local Cistercian houses had for the past thirteen years bought wool in the county, and carried it

---

[150] That Malton 'devient delivrer tote lor leyne a Watton j moys apres la seint Jon' is strange, since Malton town was a major wool-collecting centre for the region, two of the four main routes to the coast passing through it (B. Waites, 'The Monasteries of North-East Yorkshire and the Medieval Wool Trade', *Yorkshire Archaeological Journal*, 52 (1980), 111–21, esp. 118–19).

[151] References to native merchants dealing with the Gilbertines are nearly unknown, though in 1338 Ralph *Wlpysone* of Louth is recorded as purchasing 2 sacks from the prior of Ormsby (*Cal. Inq. Misc.* i. 399).

[152] Bischoff, 'Economic Change', 223. He mistakenly writes that the delivery date for all Lincolnshire houses was two weeks after 24 June. He also points out that the Boston fair began in late June, so this would have been a convenient time for the wool to be collected.

[153] Graham, 'Finances of Malton Priory', 150.

[154] *Monasticon*, vii. 2. xl; Oxford, Bodl. Lib., MS Douce 136, fo. 89. The practice was also condemned, and the prohibition disregarded, by the Cistercians (C. V. Graves, 'The Economic Activities of the Cistercians in Medieval England', *Analecta S. O. Cisterciensis*, 13 (1957), 25–8, and 'Stixwould in the Market Place', in Nichols and Shank (eds.), *Distant Echoes*, 225–6). Gilbertines were also forbidden to store the grain of others with their own produce without licence (*Monasticon*, vi. 2. xli).

to Boston market, where it was sold to Flemish merchants, to the loss of 100 marks per annum to the Lincoln merchants.[155] But the suggestion that the Malton canons were buying wool is, as Waites points out, not easy to substantiate. Though the cartulary records grants of pasture for a total of some 6,000 sheep only, this represents a minimum figure, since Malton also held moorland pasture where unlimited grazing seems to have been allowed.[156] According to Pegolotti's list, Malton produced a total of 45 sacks per annum. If this was derived entirely from its own estates, and allowing 200 fleeces per sack, then the priory possessed over 9,000 sheep.[157] These figures can be compared with those for Alvingham in 1283. In that year the priory made £166 from the sale of wool. Alvingham then had nearly 2,000 ewes and wethers. These produced $12\frac{1}{2}$ sacks of better-quality wool valued at $17\frac{1}{2}$ marks a sack, and 2 sacks 21 stones of poorer-quality wool valued at 11 marks a sack. If all the ewes and wethers were shorn then the priory was producing either rather more sacks than is normally estimated at 200 fleeces to a sack, or the excess was indeed made up from *collecta*.[158]

Rental and other Non-Demesne Revenues

As already suggested, by at least the mid-thirteenth century the Gilbertines obtained a substantial part of their income from rents, and the valuations of 1254 and 1291, and the more detailed figures that are available for Malton, show the importance of rental income in the Gilbertine economy. Though permanent alienations were sometimes disadvantageous, parti- cularly at a time of rising prices, and it often proved difficult either for the grantor to recover them, or, until the mid-thirteeenth century, for their further alienation to be prevented, rental income could be used to provide capital for investment in other property or for the relief of financial dif- ficulties. It is also clear that the priories were renting out dwellings for the use of hired labourers on their grange estates.[159] However, the scale of this activity is hard to quantify. It has already been noted that records of leases

---

[155] *Rotuli Hundredorum*, i. 317. A similar complaint was made by the citizens in 1302 (*Rot. Parl.* i. 156–7). [156] Waites, *Moorland and Vale-Land Farming*, 32.

[157] Graham, 'Finances of Malton Priory', 150; Waites, 'The Monasteries of North-East Yorkshire', 113, and *Moorland and Vale-Land Farming*, 32.

[158] Oxford, Bodl. Lib., MS Laud Misc. 642, fo 35ᵛ (attached to folio). In the same year the priory began to sell their wool through the Lucchese merchant Hugolinus (probably James Hugolinus, the agent of the Riccardi who collected small amounts of wool (Bischoff, 'Economic Change', 225)) and his partners.

[159] For a detailed account of rental policy in two Gilbertine priories, see Golding, 'Gilbertine Priories', 181–208.

for a term of years are less likely to have survived than accounts of permanent alienations, and even the latter are probably under-represented in the charter and cartulary records.[160]

The Gilbertine Rule frowned upon the permanent alienation of monastic property. No *spiritualia* were to be given at farm, and other lands, woods, ecclesiastical rents, mills, and all other property were not to be alienated without the majority assent of the chapter.[161] All income from farms and rents was received by a canon. He accounted to the prior and in the presence of the prior and proctors, passed the moneys to be kept by the nuns in their treasury.[162] In spite of the Rule's discouragement, there is considerable evidence that from at least the beginning of the thirteenth century property was being alienated, either in perpetuity, or for a term of years. Though land was rented out in virtually all places in which the Gilbertines had land, even in villages where there were substantial granges, it is clear that the majority of rental income was derived from those places where they were unable, or unwilling, to develop granges.

Rents could be derived from the leasing of arable, or other more valuable property, such as meadow, or from mills or fisheries, or from urban possessions. Unlike many religious houses, the Gilbertines do not seem to have had any industrial revenues, such as iron-works, apart from salt-works on the Lincolnshire coast. Probably all of the Gilbertine priories possessed mills.[163] Mills were a *sine qua non* of the medieval agrarian economy and a valuable source of income. They either brought the Gilbertines multure payments, that is, fees paid by manorial tenants or by those who owed suit of mill, or provided a rental income, which seems to have been the most common form of exploitation.[164] They were easy to administer and needed little attention apart from the upkeep of their buildings, while

---

[160] Only about a tenth of the charters in the Alvingham cartulary relate to the priory's alienations. This is clearly an understatement. The cartulary, for example, makes no mention of lands in Raithby or Beesby, yet both were producing rents in 1291. Similarly, though the Malton rental records income derived from some 150 tofts, only a few are recorded in the charters. In both the Alvingham and Malton cartularies such grants are frequently given as an afterthought, in the margins or at the end of topographical sections, sometimes in different, later hands. Their record was clearly not central to the compiler's brief.

[161] *Monasticon*, vi. 2. lvi-lvii.   [162] Ibid. xliv.

[163] These included even small houses like Clattercote and Fordham (*Taxatio*, 130, 257b). For the mills of Alvingham and Bullington, see Golding, 'Gilbertine Priories', 113–15. The most recent general survey of mills in medieval England is R. Holt, *The Mills of Medieval England* (Oxford, 1988), and for useful brief accounts of monastic mills see S. Moorhouse, 'Monastic Estates: Their Composition and Development', and C. J. Bond, 'Water Management in the Rural Monastery', in R. Gilchrist and H. Mytum (eds.), *The Archaeology of Rural Monasteries*, BAR, British Series, 203 (1989), 52–5, 102–4.

[164] Most of the Templars' mills were similarly farmed (*Records of the Templars*, p. clxii).

at the same time they provided a steady income. Since they were staffed by a hired and skilled servant, the miller, they did not need to be in close proximity to a grange, and could be held in distant vills where the priory held no other property, even if they were not farmed out for rent. However, they were frequently associated with grange estates and then probably served both to grind the community's corn for sale or its own consumption, and that of neighbours. Sometimes, as at Harmston, where Bullington and St Katherine's, Lincoln, shared a mill, the mill would be divided between two priories, in other instances it would be shared with lay proprietors.[165]

Charters and other documentary sources rarely distinguish between water and wind mills, nor between the uses to which a mill might be put, such as the grinding of corn, fulling, or tanning.[166] Virtually nothing is known of corn production and marketing on Gilbertine estates, though the Malton accounts show that very considerable sums were being spent on the purchase of corn, which peaked at £138 in 1248 and 1254, and also that large quantities of wheat, barley, rye, and malt were being bought in.[167] Most priories possessed several mills. The long confirmation charter of Haverholme refers to at least ten.[168] Some were granted along with the obligation of the grantors' tenants to grind there, and it was this right that was probably most valuable to the·Gilbertines, for, even where they did not hold the manor, they had now acquired a valuable manorial perquisite.[169] A charter of the son of the founder of Sixhills shows in detail what the priory could expect. He gave the site of a mill in East Rasen and land

Their function as a manorial perquisite explains why their possession was refused by the Cistercians.

[165] London, BL, Harl. Chart. 52 G 44. Mills, like other forms of feudal property, were frequently divided in ownership. Sixhills had half a mill in Cadeby, two-thirds of one on Tealby water from Hugh de Bayeux' gift and the remaining third from Alan and Hugh Malet (*Gilbertine Charters*, 36).

[166] Most of the references to Gilbertine mills, however, imply that they were water mills. For rare specific references to mills *ad ventum* see *Gilbertine Charters*, 9, 45, and for a *molendinum aquaticum* with its pool, banks, and watercourse see the foundation charter of Catley (ibid. 72). No windmills are recorded amongst the Templars' mills in Lincolnshire (*Records of the Templars*, p. clxiv n. 6).

[167] London, BL, MS Cotton Claudius D XI, fo. 286. These figures are discussed by Graham, 'Finances of Malton Priory', 143–4. She suggests that enough corn was produced on the granges for the needs of the employees there, and implies that the canons relied on wool as their cash crop, while purchasing corn from outside their own resources.

[168] Many of these were water mills. There were mills on the Sleaford river; in Merston, with its dam and meadow; in Hagham; in Cranwell; in Roxham; in Evedon, and at least four in Leasingham (*Cal. Ch. R.* iv. 405, 411, 412, 414, 417).

[169] A local monopoly had been transferred, as Lees put it. Her introduction to the role of the mill in the Lincolnshire Templars' economy is valuable (*Records of the Templars*,

next to it for a dwelling or a vaccary, which might have utilized the meadow land adjacent to the mill. The priory was given land to repair the mill dam when necessary and given licence to move the mill if it so pleased. The grantor pledged that he would do nothing to hinder the flow of water either above or below the mill (a frequent cause of dispute), allowed all who wished uninterrupted passage to grind at the mill, and promised that multure would be paid for his own milling there. But it was not intended that the mill should remain in the priory's demesne: rather, the income from its rental was to be used to purchase fish for the convent's kitchen.[170]

The monetary contribution of the mills to the Gilbertines' economy is hard to establish. We have seen that Malton received only small sums from its mills in the mid-thirteenth century. But it is not certain whether these relate to the annual farms of the mills or payments paid by tenants to mills kept in hand. Values clearly varied considerably. In 1535 Haverholme's mill on Sleaford water was assessed at £8 3s. 4d., or something approaching 12 per cent of all temporal income.[171] In 1291 Clattercote's mill at Fenny Compton was only assessed at 5s. per annum.[172] Perhaps the clearest indication of their economic importance is the fact that the priories were prepared to pay so much for them. The nuns of Catley, for example, paid Oliver of Wendover 27 marks for land and a mill with its conduits, pool, and causeway. This became the nucleus of their grange at Glentworth.[173] Rents, too, might be substantial: Alvingham paid 20 shillings per annum for a mill, mill-house, and associated lands in Swinhop.[174]

As important as the mills in the monastic economy, and often physically associated with them, were fisheries and fish-ponds, which provided fish both for home consumption and for sale in the local market.[175] There

pp. clxi–clxiv). The importance of this right is clearly demonstrated by a charter of Roger of Benniworth confirming his mother's gift of a mill on the river Bain at Donington to the nuns of Bullington with the proviso that his men should *not* grind there without his permission (*Gilbertine Charters*, 95).

[170] Ibid. 22. For a similar detailed grant of a mill and its appurtenances see ibid. 29–30.

[171] *VE* iv. 118. Mattersey's mill on its home farm was assessed at £2 10s. and the farms of Bullington's mills at Donnington-on-Bain and Hemingby at £4 13s. 4d. (ibid. v. 178, iv. 84). It has been estimated that the Cistercian nunnery of Stixwould gained at least 10% and perhaps 20% of its *temporalia* in 1291 from its mills (Graves, 'Stixwould in the Market Place', 227).   [172] *Taxatio*, 257b.

[173] *Gilbertine Charters*, 84–5.

[174] Oxford, Bodl. Lib., MS Laud Misc. 642, fo. 145b'.

[175] On these see M. Aston (ed.), *Medieval Fishponds and Fisheries in England*, BAR, British Series, 182 (1988), esp. C. J. Bond, 'Monastic Fisheries', 69–112, and his 'Water Management in the Rural Monastery', along with C. K. Currie, 'The Role of Fishponds in the Monastic Economy', in Gilchrist and Mytum (eds.), *The Archaeology of Rural Monasteries*, 83–112, 147–72.

is little documentary evidence for fish-ponds in the immediate vicinity of the priories, but most communities possessed at least one or two river fisheries.[176] Sometimes they were given with a mill, the water course or mill-pond fulfilling two functions.[177] Normally, however, the priories were given fishing rights along a specified stretch of water. William of Kyme's grant of a fishery in his water of Dogdyke consisted of four men with two boats and two nets for the two days every year when the nuns of Bullington journeyed to Sempringham for the general chapter.[178] Another fishery held by the nuns of Bullington in the river Ancolne was given for the use of the infirmary.[179] These were clearly primarily intended for the use of the community; it is much more difficult to ascertain the extent to which the Gilbertines produced for the market. There is no evidence of sales in the Malton accounts, and a Sixhills charter refers to a rent being used for the purchase of fish, which might indicate that the nuns did not even possess enough fish for themselves.[180] Fish-ponds, in particular, often involved considerable constructional sophistication and capital; it may be that the Gilbertine priories generally lacked the resources for such investment.

Several of the north Lincolnshire priories had interests in the local salt industry, and it is likely that not all the salt produced at their *salinae* was intended solely for their consumption.[181] Sometimes these were situated some distance from the priory: Sixhills (and Alvingham) had a salt-works at Grainthorpe, and Ormsby had considerable interests at Friskney, where Gilbert of Benniworth gave the salt-workings of four of his tenants, which certainly suggests that the priory was to produce salt

---

[176] Ormsby had fisheries at Grainthorpe, where they seem to have extended into the North Sea ('usque in profundum maris'), and Spaldington on the Humber marshes (*Gilbertine Charters*, 49, 63). [177] See e.g. *Gilbertine Charters*, 77–8.

[178] Ibid. 92. [179] *Danelaw Charters*, 65, no. 99.

[180] *Gilbertine Charters*, 22. There is considerable controversy on this question. Currie (e.g. 'Role of Fishponds', 151–2) has forcefully argued that there is no convincing evidence that monasteries were producing for the market till at least the later Middle Ages and that all the catch was used by the community, while Bond ('Monastic Fisheries') and others argue that commercial activity is the only explanation for the large-scale developments of fish-ponds by some abbeys.

[181] Owen, *Church and Society*, 68–9, suggests that Kirkstead and Revesby were both producing for the market. Coastal salt-production in Lincolnshire is discussed in E. H. Rudkin and D. M. Owen, 'The Medieval Salt Industry in the Lindsey Marshland', *Lincolnshire Architectural and Archaeological Society Reports and Papers*, NS 8 (1960), 76–84; A. E. B. Owen, 'Salt, Sea Banks and Medieval Settlement on the Lindsey Coast', in N. Field and A. White (eds.), *A Prospect of Lincolnshire* (Lincoln, 1984), 46–9; R. H. Healey, 'Medieval Salt-Making', *South Lincolnshire Archaeology*, 1 (1977), 4; and H. E. Hallam, 'Salt-Making in the Lincolnshire Fenland during the Middle Ages', *Lincolnshire Architectural and Archaeological Reports and Papers* NS 8 (1960), 85–112.

commercially.[182] Even one Yorkshire house, Malton, had property in the coastal Lincolnshire village of Fulstow, from which it derived a substantial annual salt render.[183]

Urban Property

The Gilbertines, unlike the Cistercians, never placed any prohibition on the establishment of urban communities or the maintenance of urban property. Indeed, there is a clear understanding in the Rule that Gilbertine representatives travelling to markets would normally be expected to stay at a hostel of the order, for it stipulated that no *conversus* should accept food for himself or his horses from any religious house not of the order, and that no brother should eat in towns or fairs except where the prior of his house or the cellarer provided and when necessity compelled.[184] Though no Gilbertine priory established or controlled a borough, and only three (Sempringham, Shouldham, and Sixhills) are known to have been granted the right to hold a fair, urban holdings played a useful role in the economy of individual houses and it is not surprising that all but the smallest priories possessed at least some lands within a town.[185] Such property could fulfil at least three functions: as a lodging place free from secular temptations for visiting canons and *conversi* of the order; as a profitable source of rent income; and as a base for commercial and administrative activity, a sort of urban grange (sometimes even with its own oratory). The types of such property varied reflecting the different functions of such holdings, and included hostels, shops, and warehouses. The priories were also prepared to lease out urban property on condition that the lessees maintained it in good order for the convent's use for secular and ecclesiastical business when necessary. In addition to the urban holdings of rural priories, six Gilbertine priories, ranging in size from St

---

[182] *Gilbertine Charters*, 17 (Sixhills), 45 (Ormsby), 106 (Alvingham). Catley, though not seemingly possessing its own salt-works, received an annual payment of salt from Gosberton (ibid. 87).

[183] London, BL, MS Cotton Claudius D XI, fo. 122.

[184] *Monasticon*, vi. 2. lxv. For the early Cistercian prohibition of urban property, see Canivez, *Statuta*, i. 13, 30. Like so many of the early Cistercian prohibitions this was soon a dead letter, and most Cistercian abbeys later possessed urban property, and some abbeys were even founded in towns. For a brief account of the urban holdings of the Cistercian nunnery of Stixwould, see Graves, 'Stixwould in the Market Place', 227–8.

[185] For the grants of a fair at Stoke Ferry to Shouldham (1248), a weekly market and annual fair at Ludford to Sixhills (1252), and a fair at Stow to Sempringham (1268) and a market to the same house at Rigbolt (1293), see *Cal. Ch. R. 1226–57*, 392, and *1257–1300*, 101, 330.

Katherine's, Lincoln, to Hitchin, were actually established in towns or their suburbs.[186]

London

Only four Gilbertine houses held property in the capital.[187] Though Sempringham's London house is not mentioned in Richard I's general confirmation charter of 1189, it is likely that it was acquired early in the priory's history and it may be that *hospitium* in which Gilbert of Sempringham was staying in London when he miraculously extinguished a fire.[188] In 1212–13 the order acquired two tenements in Cow Lane (near Smithfield) from St Bartholomew's Hospital, for which it paid 4s. per annum, and shortly afterwards the canons received more property from the Hospital in the same street for 3s. per annum.[189] This was to be the nucleus of the order's London base till the Dissolution.[190] In 1291 Sempringham's holding in St Sepulchre's parish was valued at £1 14s. 8d., but shortly afterwards the priory considerably expanded its property. On 6 November 1294 the prior and convent were given licence to stop up Chick Lane adjoining their houses on the west and to enclose it in order to enlarge the Master's house. On the same day licence was given to John de London to alienate a messuage lying to the south-west of the property.[191] It is not hard to account for this expansion. On 21 September 1294 the Master of the order was summoned to the council of clergy at Westminster: thereafter he was to be summoned regularly to Parliament till 1341, when he gained exemption from appearance. It was essential, if for no other purpose, for the mother house to have a London base to provide the Master with suitable accommodation, just as did many of the larger religious houses of England.[192] Though the holding does not figure

[186] St Katherine's, Lincoln; Malton; Marlborough; St Andrew's, York; Cambridge; and Hitchin.   [187] Sempringham, Chicksands, Mattersey, and Shouldham.

[188] *Book of St Gilbert*, 112 and n.

[189] *Cartulary of St Bartholomew's Hospital*, a calendar prepared by N. J. M. Kerling (London, 1973), 25–7, 157.

[190] Stow referred to Cow Lane where 'the Prior of Semperingham had his Inne, or London lodging', and when the site was granted to Robert Holgate, last Master of the order, at the Dissolution, it was called the 'Master of Sempyngham's "hedhous" in London'. A number of other religious houses, notably Sherborne, Leicester, and Ely, had properties in the near vicinity (M. B. Honeybourne, 'The Extent and Value of the Property in London and Southwark occupied by the Religious Houses (including the Prebends of St Paul's and St Martin's le Grand), the Inns of the Bishops and Abbots, and the Churches and Churchyards before the Dissolution of the Monasteries', MA Thesis (London University, 1929), 442–3).   [191] *Cal. Pat. R. 1292–1301*, 127.

[192] Honeybourne, 'Extent and Value of Property', 304–449. After 1341 it is, as she noted

in the *Valor*, an indication of its size is provided in the grant to Holgate. It comprised a messuage, toft, and *hospitium*, eight messuages in Cow Lane, together with all buildings lying between Cow Lane and Chick Lane.[193]

The order's 'hedhous' was clearly large and fulfilled a useful function as a London *pied-à-terre*; it was not maintained for its economic value. A comparison of the valuation of this property with holdings of Chicksands and Shouldham in 1291 and again in 1392 demonstrates that these two houses were receiving a not inconsiderable income from their London tenements. In 1291 Chicksands had property valued at £9 6s. 8d. in three London parishes (St Mary Colechurch, St Mildred Walbrook, and St Stephen Jewry) and Shouldham's tenements in St Mary Colechurch and St Mildred Walbrook were assessed at £7 10s. 8d.[194] From the first it seems that the property of Chicksands and Shouldham was intended to provide a rent income. After all, in so centralized an order there was no need for priories other than the mother house to maintain a base in the capital and there were nearer trading centres to both priories than London. From the beginning, too, there was a close connection between the London holdings of the two priories. In 1212 or 1213 Geoffrey fitzPeter, earl of Essex and founder of Shouldham, granted Chicksands all his land in the parish of St Mary Colechurch, lying between the land and the *magna scola* of the Jews, and twelve shops with tofts that he had given to Shouldham, in order that the income from this land be used to buy smocks for the nuns.[195] Shouldham's property was also intended to provide an income for the community, Geoffrey giving the shops in order to pay for lights in the priory church and sacramental room. The absence of other charters for either house makes it impossible to determine when, how, and for what purpose their other London lands were acquired, but there is one further piece of evidence to indicate how these properties were used. In 1321, at a time when Chicksands was in dire financial straits, the prior granted to *magister* Roger de la Beere an annual rent of £16 from tenements held for life by Simon le Foundour in the three

---

(ibid. 446), interesting that the order continued to maintain this property, commodious enough to suit a post-Dissolution archbishop. The canons do not appear to have let it at all.

[193] In addition, there were other, smaller holdings leased to a lay tenant towards Holborn Cross in the same parish (ibid. 445–6).

[194] By 1392 Sempringham's income from its London property had risen to £14 6s. 8d., no doubt as a result of the acquisitions of 1294, while Chicksands' had risen to £24 0s. 4d. and Shouldham's to £25 13s. 4d. (A. K. McHardy, *The Church in London 1375–1392*, London Record Society, 13 (1977), 43, 74–5).

[195] Fowler (ed.), 'Early Charters of . . . Chicksand', 109–110.

parishes of St Mary Colechurch, St Stephen Colemanstreet, and St Mildred Poultry, and a few months later Roger acknowledged that this grant and other bonds should be void on the payment to him by the priory of its debt of £180. The priory was clearly leasing out all its London property to one tenant and the episode points up another use of urban property: its income could be demised permanently or temporarily for ready cash.[196]

Lincoln

By the end of the thirteenth century all of the Gilbertine houses in Lincolnshire, including even the smallest, Bridgend, had acquired at least some property in the city. These tenements probably functioned more as centres in which members of the communities could stay when on ecclesiastical or other business than as trading bases; in any case, since in most cases the priories themselves were only a few miles from Lincoln, for the most part these holdings may well have been retained chiefly as a source of rent income.[197] More is known of Alvingham's holdings in the city than those of any other priory and their development can stand as an example. They were concentrated in the suburban parish of St Augustine to the south of the river Witham. This low-lying area was already developed as a commercial area by the beginning of the thirteenth century and leading Lincoln merchants, as well as Bardney abbey, also held property here.[198] Around 1200 *magister* Peter, son of Walter of Newark, granted a plot between the *via regis* and the river. This was later extended by the grant of Peter's neighbour, William le Mercer, who gave land adjacent to the corner of the priory's solar to extend their court. He also granted free access to the priory by the lane running from the *via regis* and the river, between his land and the priory's, on condition that the latter would maintain the gate to the road, while he would take responsibility for the water gate.[199] Finally, between 1267 and 1274 the priory purchased the whole of the tenement once held by William le Mercer from Thomas, son of Robert, citizen of Lincoln, for 12 marks, together with rights of entry for all necessary carrying, except for the priory's carts.[200] At about the

---

[196] It is presumably the temporary demise of Chicksands' London holdings that accounts for the fall in income from this source recorded in 1392, but by the Dissolution the priory seems to have regained control of this income and all tenements were leased out in individual parcels from which the house received a total income of £15 10s.

[197] *Rotuli Hundredorum*, i. 316.

[198] Oxford, Bodl. Lib., MS Laud Misc. 642, fos. 140ᵛ–141ᵛ.

[199] Ibid., fos. 140ᵛ–141.   [200] Ibid., fo. 141ᵛ.

same time, in 1270 Nicholas Tyrthe confirmed to the priory the northern and southern gateway abutting on his own house and the priory's oratory.[201] This reference to an *oratorium* certainly suggests that Alvingham had established what could be regarded as an urban grange: a centre for canons and others visiting the city and which perhaps also provided warehousing facilities, lying as it did between Thorngate, the *via regis* running along the south bank of the Witham, and the Sincil Dyke, which flowed into the Witham. Thus, though the details of the acquisitions and the precise dimensions of the property remain unclear, the general pattern of development is apparent. Over some fifty or more years Alvingham gradually accumulated and consolidated its Lincoln base. The priory's other property in the city was maintained solely for a rent income.[202]

As was the case with Alvingham, other Gilbertine holdings in Lincoln tended to be in the suburbs. Nun Ormsby's small holding acquired *c.*1220 lay in the north-eastern suburban parish of St Peter's Eastgate.[203] Haverholme's property lay wholly in the large and populous southern suburb of Wigford. These holdings are known only from abbreviated entries in the confirmation charter of 1337: very few of the grants can be dated even approximately and those that can suggest that they were made at the end of the twelfth and the beginning of the thirteenth centuries.[204] Bullington's earliest holdings seem to have been in the parish of St Bavon in the Bulwerk, quite close to Alvingham's land in St Augustine's; next to the Bargate at the far southern end of Wigford; and also in the parish of Holy Trinity, Wigford.[205] Here the priory was prepared to invest in property, for in 1264 Abraham, son of James, a Jew of Lincoln, remitted all his claim in lands once of Alan 'the weaver', a debtor both of Abraham and his father, to the priory.[206] By the early thirteenth century Bullington had also acquired property in St Stephen's, Newland, a developing suburb to the west of the city, and in Holy Trinity, Butwerk. There is no evidence, however, that any of these lands were retained for the priory's own use. Most were demised to citizens of Lincoln, some (in Holy Trinity, Butwerk) were granted to the Dominicans.[207] The length of these

---

[201] Ibid.

[202] In the late 12th century Walter son of Walter gave 2*s.* rent p.a. to be taken from his land in Eastgate near St Peter's church before he left for Jerusalem, but he retained the option of resuming the rent for himself if he returned. Ibid., fo. 140ᵛ.

[203] *Gilbertine Charters*, 43–4.   [204] *Cal. Ch. R.* iv. 414–16.

[205] London, BL, Harl. Charts. 45 I 52, 48 C 14, 48 C 15, 47 H 40.

[206] Ibid. 43 A 67b.

[207] Ibid. 47 H 38, 39 (St Stephen's); 48 G 7 (Holy Trinity). For the demises, see ibid. 44 A 25, 26, 27, 44 A 41, 46, 44 B 7, 8, 11. For the Dominicans' acquisition, see 48 G 7.

leases is rarely specified: it was probably seldom longer than the life of the original lessee and there are some indications that the usual term was for 20 years.[208]

During the fourteenth century, however, the fortunes of the city began to decline, and with them the rent rolls of priories holding property there. Between 1291 and 1535 the total assessed value of Gilbertine houses (excluding St Katherine's) in the city fell by some 75 per cent and by the Dissolution only St Katherine's maintained a considerable presence there.[209] In 1535 its property was assessed at £17 4s. 10d. in fifteen urban parishes. The great majority of this was concentrated in Wigford, particularly in the most southerly parish, St Botulph's, which lay only a few hundred yards from the priory itself. In 1275 the income of St Katherine's from rents in the city was said to be £32, far higher than any of the other fifty-five religious corporations and individuals deriving rent income from the city, and nearly twice as high as the city income of the bishop, precentor, and vicars of the cathedral.[210] It is unknown when its property was received, but it is clear that, unlike the other Gilbertine priories, St Katherine's continued to acquire property in Lincoln after the Statute of Mortmain.[211] Religious houses did not go to the trouble and expense of acquiring land in mortmain after 1279 without good reason. In part the continuing acquisition of urban property is a reflection of the continuing popularity of the priory with the Lincoln citizens; in part, however, it seems to indicate the canons' concern to expand their urban property, and it may be that suburban St Katherine's found it easier to maintain and collect rents from such property than did other Gilbertine houses.

York

Just as Lincoln was the chief urban centre for the Lincolnshire Gilbertine houses so York fulfilled that function for the more northern priories of the order. The Lay Subsidy of 1301 reveals that Ellerton, Malton, and

---

[208] In 1321 the priory leased lands in St Margaret's, Pottergate to John Scallarius of Lincoln and his heirs for 20 years for eight shillings per annum and a down payment of nine shillings. John undertook to maintain the property in as good order as when he received it, while the priory would provide all lacking necessities (ibid. 44 B 8).

[209] Bullington's income from Lincoln properties declined from £1 10s. 0d. to 4s. (*Taxatio*, 70; *VE* iv. 84).   [210] *Rotuli Hundredorum* i. 316.

[211] In 1320 the priory had licence to acquire five messuages in the suburb of Lincoln (presumably Wigford) valued at 26s. 8d. per annum. Ten shillings' rent was granted in 1321 by the vicar of All Saints' Hundegate, and a messuage valued at three shillings per annum and 24s. rent in the suburb were acquired in 1335 (*Cal. Pat. R. 1317–21*, 510; *1321–24*, 13; *1334–38*, 94).

Watton all received a small rent income from property in York.[212] The relative paucity of the records for these houses makes it more difficult to determine the overall pattern of landholding and use than in Lincoln. The clearest indication of a Gilbertine house's interest here is derived from the Malton cartulary. Some time before the end of the twelfth century, *magister* William de Flamville granted the canons of Malton and the proctors of the hospital of Norton (whose site he had given to the priory) all his land he had purchased in Huggelford 'ut habeantur predicti canonici in eadem villa proprio recipiantur hospicio'.[213] This suburban property was obviously intended to provide the canons with a base in York, but the remainder of their property in the city was from the first meant to furnish a rent income. By the mid-thirteenth century the canons were receiving 14*s*. per annum from their York holdings.[214] Malton's property appears to have been quite widely scattered in the city. Osbert of Thorp granted the canons all the land Geoffrey Dux held of him in Skeldergate. Geoffrey was to continue to hold this land of the canons for the same rent. Substantial lands were held in Goodramgate, and on the other side of the city the canons had houses next to Micklegate Bar and further down Micklegate. However, the greater part of their property seems to have lain in Huggelford, where the canons were actively purchasing or leasing tenements throughout the thirteenth century.[215]

Boston

Lincoln, and to some extent York also, were important centres for the Gilbertine priories as diocesan headquarters and regional capitals. Property there could also be used to provide a useful, though diminishing, rent income. Neither place seems, however, to have been much used by the Gilbertines for trade: the main trading outlet for Lincolnshire houses was Boston, that for Yorkshire priories, Scarborough. At least four Lincolnshire priories maintained some property in Boston, which was of growing importance in the regional and national economy from the mid-twelfth century onwards.[216] Most Gilbertine properties in Boston lay on

---

[212] Though Ellerton seems to have disposed of all its holdings there by 1535 (*Yorkshire Lay Subsidy (1301)*, ed. W. Brown (Yorkshire Archaeological Society Record Series, 21 (1896), 120, 121).   [213] London, BL MS Cotton Claudius, D XI, fo. 201ᵛ.

[214] Ibid., fo. 274.

[215] Roger son of Tyri, and Alice his wife, granted land to the canons next to a tenement already held by the latter for 16*d*. per annum to light the shrine of St William of York. William Wydefax sold a toft on the Huggelford road to the priory for 20*s*. *prae manibus* and William's mother released her dower rights in this property for 10*s*. (ibid., fos. 202ᵛ–203).

[216] Alvingham, Bullington, Haverholme, and Ormsby. However, neither Ormsby nor Bullington (which received property in Boston from Thomas de Moulton at the beginning

the eastern side of the Witham, either within the Barditch, which functioned both as a boundary and sewer for the town, or, as in the case of
Alvingham, just outside. Nearly all of the charters mention a water front-
age, which suggests that trade was a prime consideration in the acquisition of Boston tenements.

In the third quarter of the twelfth century Reiner of Waxham granted
lands and the buildings thereon in the market-place (*in foro*) of Boston to
Alvingham on condition that each year the canons paid William le Volant
(from whom Reiner held) 10*d*. at St Botulph's fair, the greatest social and
commercial event in the town's year, and which, it is clearly implied, the
priory's representative would attend.[217] This attendance is made explicit
in another charter in which Alexander Gernun granted a plot of land in
his *curia* outside the town bar 'to build a *hospicium* there in which they
[sc. the canons] can stay when they come'; Alexander and his heirs would
have custody of the land and its buildings *extra feriam*.[218] It may be at this
time that the priory appears to have moved from its earlier site in the
market-place, which was demised to Robert the chaplain in fee farm for
24*s*. per annum, perhaps because the canons felt themselves to be too
constricted in the built-up centre of the town. Certainly it seems that the
new property was considerably larger than the old.[219] Early in the thirteenth century Nun Ormsby was granted part of a toft next to the house
in which the community used to stay at fairtime, together with that house
and free entry for their carts and wagons, which suggests fairly bulky
traffic, presumably of wool, carried by the priory to the port.[220] But if
Boston was a major export centre for the order it was there too that the
priory's own purchases were made, as another Ormsby charter makes
clear. John son of Alan of Stickford granted property so that the nuns
might buy veils and cloaks at Boston.[221]

Of the Gilbertine houses outside Lincolnshire, only Malton is known
to have held land in Boston. This was acquired by purchase from Walter
Bars *c*.1245. Walter held lands in 'Wrinegate' and had access to the
'shore' (presumably of the Witham), but was in debt to Pictavin, Jew of
Lincoln, and sold all his land in Boston to Malton on condition that one
chaplain be maintained to sing the divine office in the priory church

---

of the 13th century) appear to have retained land in Boston at the Dissolution. For an
introduction to the role of medieval Boston, see D. M. Owen, 'The Beginnings of the Port
of Boston', in Field and White (eds.), *A Prospect of Lincolnshire*, 42–5; *Gilbertine Charters*,
57 (Ormsby), 99 (Bullington); *Cal. Ch. R.* iv. 416 (Haverholme).

[217] Oxford, Bodl. Lib., MS Laud Misc. 642, fo. 167.   [218] Ibid., fo. 167ᵛ.
[219] Ibid.   [220] *Gilbertine Charters*, 57.
[221] 'ad vela et pepla emenda apud Sanctum Botulphum' (ibid. 45).

before the altar of St Augustine or St Nicholas and that 8*s.* 1*d.* be paid to
the lord of the fee at St Botulph's fair. Moreover, William of Ancaster,
prior of Malton, agreed that after the death of Walter and his wife their
names would be entered on the martyrology together with the charter
itself, 'lest with lapse of time their benefactions fall into oblivion'. On his
wife's death Walter could stay permanently with the canons either as a
corrodian or as a canon ('vel in habitu canonicali vel seculari'). The actual
charter whereby Walter granted the land is very revealing. The grant was
made both to the priors and proctors of Malton and Watton, which
suggests that the two Yorkshire houses were sharing facilities at the port.
The grant itself comprised a *grangia* (presumably a warehouse) together
with an adjacent courtyard and stable. The whole was to be surrounded
with a ditch and wall, which was to be held by the priory, along with the
foundation ditch ('cum fundo sue constructionis'). Free entry was granted
up to the water and it was to be held free of all impediment from the
beginning to the end of St Botulph's fair for 16*s.* to be paid at the fair.
The prior and proctors were allowed to construct other buildings in the
courtyard at their own cost, while Walter and his heirs were allowed their
use outside fairtime so long as they looked after the priories' goods left
there, and maintained the buildings new and old. If these buildings were
destroyed by fire then the priors would be responsible for the rebuilding
and would make good any loss to Walter as determined by the judgement
of responsible laity and religious. If, on the other hand, buildings were
destroyed by the carelessness of Walter or his servants, then the farm of
16*s.* would be remitted for the next three years in order that the buildings
might be replaced.[222] Few grants of urban property to Gilbertine houses
are as fully documented as this and it has, therefore, been dwelt on in
some detail as an illustration of the importance attached to urban property
by the canons. This far outweighed the mere financial potential of the
tenement. So long as the priories relied heavily on wool production for
their income and for as long as wool was exported, outlets such as Boston
were necessary. When the export of wool lessened in the later Middle
Ages there was less need for warehousing and other facilities in ports and
this may be the most significant reason for the declining importance of
such property to the houses.

Scarborough

Scarborough fulfilled a similar function for the Yorkshire houses as
Boston did for those in Lincolnshire. By the second half of the twelfth

---

[222] London, BL, MS Cotton Claudius D XI, fo. 216ᴿ⁻ᵛ.

century the town was a flourishing trade centre and port. A royal borough from the 1160s, Scarborough became an important local market for its agricultural hinterland, and above all functioned as an export centre for wool, and an importing one for fish, notably herring.[223] Both its own burgesses and Flemish merchants played a leading role in the export of wool, and it was probably the trade in these two commodities that accounts for the presence from the late twelfth century of town properties held by many Yorkshire religious houses, amongst them Malton (which derived almost three times as much income from its Scarborough possessions as from those in York) and Watton. Malton was acquiring property here from the 1170s onwards. Prominent among the benefactors were the family of Haldane the reeve, a leading burgess family: the grants consisted of houses, including a 'great stone house', which suggests a warehouse, and rents both inside and outside the borough, including one of 500 herring per annum granted by Haldane's son early in the thirteenth century.[224] Rather less is known of Watton's holdings, but a charter of Malton refers to an adjacent property held by Watton, and in 1319 the prior gave up a messuage to the Dominicans at the request of the king in order that the friars might extend their property, and in return received other property in the town held by the crown.[225]

Other urban properties

While the majority of the Gilbertines' urban holdings were concentrated in London, diocesan centres, and ports, several houses had property in local towns from which they derived a small rent income. Such lands do not appear to have been acquired as a result of a consistent policy by the priories but were haphazard benefactions of their grantors. Thus, for example, Clattercote held $8\frac{1}{2}$ tenements in Banbury of the gift of the bishop of Lincoln which 'may well have belonged to the priory since the

---

[223] J. H. Rushton, 'Scarborough, 1166–1266', in M. Edwards (ed.), *Scarborough 966–1966*, Scarborough and District Archaeological Society (1966), 25–32.

[224] London, BL, MS Cotton Claudius DXI, fos. 147ᵛ–150. Prior's lane ran south from the king's highway and probably led to the herring house that was still used in the 14th century (ibid., fo. 147ᵛ).

[225] Little is known of the later history of these properties, but at the Dissolution Malton's income from its Scarborough lands was £1 3s. 4d. (compared with 6s. 8d. from Boston lands) and Watton's was 14s. However, Watton was at this time receiving £4 8s. from lands in Hull and £8 2s. from Beverley properties, indicating that by the late Middle Ages, at least, these towns (much nearer to Watton than was Scarborough) had replaced that town in importance. In 1536 Malton only received 7s. from its nine recorded holdings in the town (ibid., fo. 147).

borough's foundation'.[226] Bishop Robert was also responsible for the grant
to St Katherine's, Lincoln, of substantial property in Newark, where, in
addition to the grant of the church, he gave two *mansurae* and houses on
the north and east sides of the parish church, along with the tithe of all
the tolls of the borough.[227]

With one or two exceptions, the *Taxatio Ecclesiastica* and *Valor
Ecclesiasticus* suggest that the financial contribution of urban holdings to
the total income of the priories in the later Middle Ages was negligible.
Moreover, it is apparent that in the majority of cases the value of urban
relative to rural property fell, in many cases substantially, between 1291
and 1535. Since the valuations of total income in 1535 are generally much
higher that they were in 1291, and given that the *Taxatio* considerably
under-assessed monastic revenues, it is clear that the proportional contribution of urban holdings to the total income of Gilbertine houses declined very considerably during the later medieval period.[228] Most
Gilbertine houses seem to have acquired their urban property quite early
in their history. Shouldham was granted its lands and shops in London
by its founder Geoffrey fitzPeter, and Sempringham had probably received the greater part of its Lincoln holdings by 1190.[229] Conversely,
with one or two exceptions, there is little evidence that the priories were
continuing to acquire urban holdings after the Statute of Mortmain.

Why, then, was urban property retained at all? Certainly such holdings

---

[226] *VCH Oxfordshire*, x. 49. Bishop Robert de Cheney's foundation charter granted to the
priory tithes of all his rents from Banbury borough and Innocent III's 1216 confirmation
charter refers to nine messuages in the town (Oxford, Bodl. Lib., Oxford Charter, 146).
Clattercote was one of the smallest Gilbertine priories, but in 1535 £3 8s. out of a total
income from *temporalia* of £26 5s. 2d. came from interests in Banbury (£2 10s. from the
bishop of Lincoln, perhaps as commutation of the tithes granted in the 12th century, 18s.
from rents) (*VE* ii. 197).

[227] In 1291 the priory received permission to acquire land in Newark to construct an
access road to its property and in 1316 gained lands in Northgate-by-Newark, though these
may well have been agricultural lands in the suburbs. In 1291 Chicksands and Fordham
benefited from property in Cambridge, but seem to have disposed of it by the Dissolution,
when only Shouldham held land there. Chicksands also derived some income from property
in Northampton, Norwich, and Bedford, but only in Bedford did the canons hold more
than one tenement. This land was concentrated in the High Street, and at the Dissolution
nearly £4 per annum was received from this source (*Court of Augmentation Accounts for
Bedfordshire I*, ed. Y. Nicholls, Publications of the Bedfordshire Historical Record Society,
63 (1984), 47, 50, 53). See also W. N. Henman, 'Newnham Priory: A Bedford Rental, 1506–
7', *Publications of the Bedfordshire Historical Record Society*, 25 (1943), 31, 33, 35, 41.
Sempringham held a toft in Northampton, adjacent to another owned by Rufford (*Rufford
Charters*, i. 18, no. 26).

[228] A similar reduction of urban income has been demonstrated for Augustinian houses
(D. M. Robinson, *The Geography of Augustinian Settlement*, 2 vols., BAR, British Series, 80
(1980), i. 333–4).   [229] Fowler (ed.), 'Early Charters of . . . Chicksand', 110.

may well have been regarded as more easily disposable and ephemeral than rural income, capital assets to be realized when necessary. As early as the first quarter of the thirteenth century Haverholme sold rents worth 8s. per annum derived from the grants of four different pieces of land in the Lincoln suburb of Newland to bishop Hugh of Wells for four marks of silver.[230] But such land was not acquired merely because it could be easily disposed of if necessary: its main purpose was probably to provide a centre for commercial activity. This activity was naturally the most vigorous in the regional centres of Lincoln and York, or at the ports of Boston or Scarborough. But the Gilbertines' urban property is not easy to categorize. In the early years it could offer accommodation for members of the order when visiting other houses or when on secular business; it certainly provided warehousing for the priories' commodities, especially wool, and increasingly it was exploited as a source of valuable rental income. For by the beginning of the fourteenth century the inexorable trend towards a *rentier* economy was already apparent. The Gilbertines, like their Cistercian cousins, could not swim against the economic tide— indeed, it is doubtful if they ever had, even at a time in the twelfth century when their agricultural practices appeared so innovative. They made the necessary adjustments, aided by the diversity of their operations, and survived.

[230] *Registrum Antiquissimum*, ix. 51.

Conclusion

Writing shortly after Gilbert's death, the northern chronicler and Augustinian canon William of Newburgh was full of praise. Gilbert, he asserted, was 'of singular grace in the care of women' and 'in my opinion holds the palm amongst all those we know to have devoted their religious labours in organizing and ruling women'.[1] A little later the chronicler of the Cistercian abbey of Walden presented a different view. When describing the activities of Geoffrey fitzPeter, earl of Essex, he tells how, rather than support Walden, the abbey established by his Mandeville predecessors, Geoffrey (the founder of Shouldham priory), 'like others following vain and novel things, was an admirer of the recently founded Gilbertine order which in an unheard-of way mingled canons and nuns, lay brethren and sisters together'.[2] His ill-concealed pique not only indicates the deep hostility to a new foundation perceived to be attracting benefactions which might otherwise have gone to the older-established abbey, but is certainly also a reflection of the growing distrust of double communities. Even though the Gilbertines were the best-articulated and ordered of all the groups of religious women which became so apparent during the twelfth century and caused such concern to the Church, they were not immune from criticism.

That there was a demand amongst many women for a formalized place in the monastic commonwealth is evidenced by the extraordinary growth of female religious communities during this period; that the Gilbertines had a particularly strong appeal for potential recruits and benefactors is indicated by their wealth, when compared with most other English nunneries. This appeal is in itself attributable to the strength of the order's institutional structure. But compromises had been necessary; by 1200 there were already clear signs of the subordination of the nuns to the canons, which was to become increasingly apparent in following centuries. The Walden chronicler need not have worried. Shouldham was the last Gilbertine nunnery. Thereafter new Gilbertine foundations were for canons alone, and they differed hardly at all from other Augustinian priories of strict observance.

[1] *Historia Rerum Anglicarum*, in *Chronicles of the Reigns of Stephen, Henry II, and Richard I*, ed. R. Howlett, 4 vols., Rolls Series (London, 1884–9), i. 54–5.
[2] *Monasticon*, iv. 146.

Nevertheless, during the thirteenth century Gilbertine nunneries continued to attract grants from local society, and their economic base was relatively secure. Of course, they, like other religious houses, were subject to constraints that are largely attributable to a changing economic climate and a related hostility of the king and great lords to the alienation of property by their tenants, as well as to shifts in patterns of pious giving. As a result, the scale of acquisitions did fall off in spite of the efforts by some of the wealthier communities to increase their holdings by purchase, as well as gift.

Most recent commentators have argued that from the end of the thirteenth century female communities went into a decline from which they never recovered. Following Power, it is claimed that their numbers fell, their economy (which had never been strong) faltered, and ill-discipline increased. This depressing scenario should, however, be seen in the context of a wider 'crisis of cenobitism' that affected all male and female houses, though perhaps not to the same degree. Nunneries were certainly more unstable and vulnerable to stresses, both external and internal; several were closed, or absorbed by larger, more successful houses.[3] Though none of the Gilbertine nunneries failed after 1200, and only one of the English houses for canons only, Stamford, proved unviable (and that for reasons outside the order's control), the Gilbertines could not avoid these developments. In 1330, for example, Chicksands successfully appealed for remission of the clerical tenth because it was so in debt that all its possessions, both *temporalia* and *spiritualia*, were now in the hands of creditors, and many of the canons and nuns had been dispersed to other houses by the prior. Even allowing for some exaggeration the community would appear to have been in a parlous state.[4]

The northern Gilbertines suffered heavily, like so many other religious houses, from the Scottish wars. The property of the Yorkshire Gilbertines was ravaged, and all the priories, though they might themselves have remained free from attack, were subject to crippling financial demands from the king, in spite of the liberties and protection granted to the order by a succession of kings from the time of Henry II. By the time of Edward I these exactions were increasing in intensity. In 1278 payment of £200 to the wardrobe was acknowledged and in 1294 royal protection was granted to the Master and priors of the order for their grant of a moiety of their goods for the crusading tenth.[5] But the fourteenth-century demands were of greater magnitude. In 1310 foodstuffs were required from

[3] Thompson, *Women Religious*, 215–16.   [4] *Cal. Cl. R. 1330–7*, 54, 272.
[5] *Cal. Pat. R. 1272–81*, 253; ibid. *1292–1301*, 90.

the houses of Catley, Chicksands, and Sixhills, and in 1319 Edward II requested a loan to finance measures against the Scottish rebels, and the Master of the order was told to induce his priors to come to the king's aid.[6]

Individual priories began to receive some taxation relief from the beginning of the century. In 1304 Catley was freed from a tallage because all of its lands were held in free alms, and in 1361 taxation of Catley and Haverholme was withheld since the bishop of Lincoln had certified that their goods were insufficient to maintain the community and to provide a tenth.[7] Impoverished Chicksands was pardoned taxation in 1335, 1337, and 1345, and again (with Sempringham and Malton) in 1356.[8] But full relief from royal taxation was not to come till the following century. Between 1407 and 1411 the priories of Alvingham, Bullington, Catley, Haverholme, Nun Ormsby, Sempringham, Shouldham, and Sixhills successfully claimed at the Exchequer that although they had been certified as poor nunneries by the bishop of Lincoln, and were hence exempt from the ecclesiastical tenths granted in 1406, 1407, and 1410, they had still been taxed. Their case was allowed after charters had been presented to the Exchequer for inspection.[9] It does not appear that these exemptions were permanent, however, and it was only in 1445 that the principle of permanent exemption was finally conceded to all the Gilbertine nunneries except Watton, the wealthiest of the houses.[10]

Further causes of economic instability were the failure of the wool crop and consequent heavy debts to Italian merchants. Chicksands seems to have been particularly vulnerable. In 1320 the prior acknowledged his debt of £120 to some Florentine merchants; four years later he owed 400 marks.[11] By 1325 he owed 3,300 gold florins to John Pisaquila, a Genoese merchant operating in London, and to Bartholomew Richi. Harsh measures were called for, and he demised his manor called 'the chapel of St Thomas' in Meppershall together with the grange of Hawnes for the lives of his creditors and an additional 20 years, as well as the profits arising from Hawnes church for the next seven years.[12] At about the same time

---

[6] *Cal. Cl. R. 1307–13*, 261, 262; ibid. *1313–28*, 203. Subsequent demands were frequent and heavy (see e.g. *Cal. Cl. R. 1346–9*, 382).

[7] *Cal. Cl. R. 1302–7*, 201; ibid. *1360–4*, 230.

[8] *Cal. Pat. R. 1334–8*. 112, 536; ibid. *1343–5*, 435; ibid. *1354–8*, 474.

[9] The details of their submission are described in *Gilbertine Charters*, pp. ix–xi.

[10] *Cal. Pat. R. 1441–6*, 332. The nunneries had been free from all clerical taxation since the time of archbishop Chichele (ibid. 315).

[11] *Cal. Cl. R. 1318–23*, 233; ibid. *1323–7*, 164, 326.

[12] *Cal. Cl. R. 1323–7*, 293. He also sold two woods in Chicksands to them. However, an

he also made a life lease of his manor of Wolverton to John Pisaquila and his wife, pledging himself to maintain the manor and to provide wood from the priory estates for the lessors to repair ruinous buildings. Compared with these debts, an additional sum of £35 owed to Matilda le Straunge in 1327 is insignificant. How far these difficulties were typical of the order as a whole is unclear, but there can be little doubt that by then the order was on a downward path of increasing poverty and decline.

In one sense the Gilbertines had been the victims of their own success. Already by Gilbert's death there were allegedly 1,500 women and 700 men in the order, and there are many indications that the Gilbertines had no difficulty in attracting recruits until at least the opening years of the fourteenth century, though thereafter demographic attrition and the decreasing appeal of the religious life for both men and women undoubtedly affected numbers. Till then, however, there was a growing disequilibrium between numbers and resources, as the tide of recruits still flowed while that of grants was ebbing.

Central to the recent interpretations of both Elkins and Thompson is the thesis that by the beginning of the thirteenth century the strategies that had been developed in the previous generation both for the regulation of communities for women, and for their control and oversight by men, were under threat from an ecclesiastical establishment which was ever more suspicious of close ties between male and female religious.[13] As a result, men were now distancing themselves from an active supervisory role. Though the Gilbertines had been more successful than most in deflecting criticism by their creation of a coherent organizational structure, they too suffered in this harsher world. Under a two-pronged assault from a more repressive ideology and a worsening economic climate the Gilbertine dynamic ran down, but for nearly a century the order had created an environment in which men and women could share, however imperfectly, the religious life.

agreement was made whereby if the prior paid £1,200 (of which he had already paid £400) by a stated time then the demise would not proceed.

[13] Thompson, *Women Religious*, 211–16; Elkins, *Holy Women*, 161–4. P. D. Johnson, *Equal in Monastic Profession* (Chicago, 1991), 248–66, comes to a rather more optimistic conclusion.

APPENDIX I

GILBERTINE FOUNDATIONS

HOUSES FOR NUNS AND CANONS

Alvingham (Lincs.): 1148 × 1153: ?Roger, son of Jocelin

Bullington (Lincs.): 1148 × 1155: Simon, son of William

Catley (Lincs.): 1148 × 1154: Peter of Billinghay

Chicksands (Beds.): 1151 × 1153: Payn and Rohaise de Beauchamp

Haverholme (Lincs.): 1139: Alexander, bishop of Lincoln

Nun Ormsby (Lincs.): 1148 × 1154: Gilbert, son of Robert of Ormsby

Sempringham (Lincs.): (i) 1131: Gilbert of Sempringham (ii) c.1148: ?Roger, son
   of Jocelin

Shouldham (Norfolk): ?1193 × 1197: Geoffrey fitzPeter, earl of Essex

Sixhills (Lincs.): 1148 × 1154: William, son of Hacon

Watton: (Yorks.): ?1151: Eustace fitzJohn

HOUSES FOR CANONS ONLY

Cambridge, St Edmund's (Cambs.): 1290: Cicely, daughter of William of St
   Edmund's

Clattercote (Oxon.): ?1150 × 1166: Robert de Chesney, bishop of Lincoln

Ellerton (Yorks.): 1199 × 1203: William, son of Peter

Fordham (Cambs.): 1204 × 1227: ?Henry, rural dean of Fordham

Hitchin (Herts.): 1361–2: Sir Edward de Kendale

Holland Bridge (Lincs.): 1195 × 1199: Godwin the Rich of Lincoln

Lincoln, St Katherine's (Lincs.): ?1148: Robert de Chesney, bishop of Lincoln

Malton (Yorks.): ?1150 × 1151: Eustace fitzJohn

Marlborough (Wilts.): 1195 × 1199: ?King Richard I or King John

Marmont (Cambs.): c.1204: Ralph and Matilda de Hauville

Mattersey (Notts.): c.1190: ?Roger, son of Rannulf of Matttersey

Newstead (Lincs.): ?1171: King Henry II

Poulton (Wilts.): 1350: Sir Thomas Seymour

York, St Andrew's (Yorks.): c.1200: Hugh Murdac

FAILURES

Brachy (Normandy): 1170 × 1184: Aldulf de Brachy (English lands transferred to
   Malton priory by 1184)

Dalmilling (Ayrshire): 1219 × 1228: Walter fitzAlan (endowment leased to Paisley abbey in 1238)

Owton (Durham): *c*.1204: Alan of Wilton (endowment transferred to St Nicholas' hospital, Yarm and Healuagh Park priory, early 13th century)

Ravenstonedale (Westmorland): mid-12th century: Torphin fitzRobert (a grange of Watton priory by 1200)

Rome, San Sisto: 1202 × 1207: pope Innocent III (transferred to Dominicans, 1219)

Stamford (Lincs.): *c*.1301: master Robert Luterel (endowment granted to Augustinian friars, 1373)

Tunstall (Lincs.): ?1155 × 1160: Reginald de Crevequer (joined to Bullington priory by 1189)

APPENDIX II
THE DOCUMENTARY SOURCES

Between *c*.1132 and 1300 there was a total of twenty-nine Gilbertine foundations, of which twenty-three survived and six had a more or less ephemeral existence.[1] Their history, like that of all communities, is dependent upon the scope and scale of surviving archival resources, and these vary widely from house to house. This fact inevitably affects the balance of the present study and explains, for example, why much more is found here concerning the priory of Alvingham than Shouldham, or Malton rather than St Katherine's, Lincoln. Some priories have left virtually no records. While it is hardly surprising that evidence for the small houses of Bridge End, Marmont, or Newstead is negligible, one of the priories from which least has survived is St Katherine's, Lincoln, the wealthiest of the houses for Gilbertine canons, and an early, episcopal foundation.

Yet, by contrast with the majority of post-Conquest English nunneries, a rich Gilbertine archive does survive. Thompson has recently considered the absence of documentary sources (to which might also be added the paucity of archaeological evidence) available to the historian of English nunneries.[2] She attributes this scarcity to a number of factors. These include 'natural causes', such as fire and flood, to which the poorer nunneries may have been more susceptible, though male communities were not immune from these disasters. Certainly in some instances the lack of Gilbertine archives can be attributed to chance destruction, either in the medieval period or later. In 1279 there was a disastrous fire at Mattersey priory, and all its documents were lost.[3] The cartulary of Sempringham itself was destroyed in a fire at Staple's Inn in the eighteenth century.[4] Other cartularies have disappeared: that of Bullington was extant in 1642, when Gervase Holles made an abbreviated transcript, but its whereabouts is now unknown. The same is true of Haverholme (also transcribed by Holles) and Nun Ormsby. Nuns were generally ignorant of Latin, and charters in Latin might have been unintelligible to the nuns in the later Middle Ages and hence not preserved. The Gilbertine nuns, though they were expected to learn Latin for liturgical use, were strongly discouraged from using it in everyday conversation, and certainly by the

---

[1] Additionally there were two small 14th-century foundations, Poulton and Hitchin.

[2] Thompson, *Women Religious*, 1–15. For a recent overview of the archaeological record see R. Gilchrist. *Gender and Material Culture: The Archaeology of Religious Women* (London, 1994).

[3] *The Register of William Wickwane, Lord Archbishop of York, 1279–85*, ed. W. Brown, Surtees Society, 114 (1907), 70–3. As a result of the losses sustained, the canons were allowed to appropriate the parish church of Mattersey in 1280. A register of Mattersey was recorded in a seventeenth-century list of monastic leiger-books (G. R. C. Davis, *Medieval Cartularies of Great Britain: A Short Catalogue* (London, 1958), 73). [4] Ibid. 100.

mid-fifteenth century were not competent in the language.[5] The rather unstructured life of many female communities and their often ambiguous relationship with the new orders may have hindered the preservation of records relating to their early history. But above all it was their poverty which limited record-taking. In general, the smaller a community the smaller its history, and the volume of surviving sources for monastic communities normally increases exponentially with size and income. This is as true for monks and canons as it is for nuns, but nunneries, with one or two notable exceptions, were much smaller than the majority of monasteries.[6]

How far can these conclusions be applied to the Gilbertines? The fact that the Gilbertines were generally better organized than many nunneries may account for the greater survival rates of their records. However, within the order the chance survival of charters and cartularies means that we know far more of relatively small priories, such as Alvingham, Bullington, or Haverholme, than we do of the wealthy communities of Watton or Chicksands, or even the mother house. Moreover, with the sole exception of Malton, whose cartulary survives, we know rather less about the Gilbertine houses for canons than we do about the double houses, and the charters for St Katherine's, Lincoln, are scant indeed.

Of more importance than poverty in limiting the history of the Gilbertines is the non-survival of account rolls, except those preserved in abbreviated form in the Malton cartulary. Finally, since the Gilbertines conducted their own visitations, there are no episcopal visitation records, so valuable a source for the internal life and organization of otherwise obscure nunneries. The historian of the order is largely dependent upon the hagiographic life of the founder, the Gilbertine Rule and later statutes of the order, and charters of individual priories. These can be supplemented to some extent by the archives of central and local government and by episcopal records. Inevitably, therefore, the sources distort our perception of the Gilbertines.

THE *LIBER SANCTI GILBERTI*

The text of the *Vita* survives (at least in part) in three manuscripts: BL MS Cotton Cleopatra B I, dating from early in the thirteenth century; BL MS Harleian 468, a generation or so later, and the fifteenth-century Bodleian Library MS Digby 36. The Cotton manuscript is a miscellany assembled in the seventeenth century: its Gilbertine material comprises the Life; episcopal letters relating to the lay brothers' revolt; a description of the canonization process; visions and revelations experienced at the time of the canonization; other material relating to the

---

[5] See above, pp. 183–4, and below, pp. 453–4. For the Rule's discouragement of Latin, see *Monasticon*, vi. 2. xlix.

[6] Thompson also makes the intriguing suggestion deserving fuller investigation that, since the property of nunneries seems to have changed hands more frequently after the Dissolution than that of the monasteries, records had a greater chance of being lost or destroyed ('Why English Nunneries had no History', 140).

canonization including an account of the translation, indulgences, and letters; and it concludes with the miracle collections. In other words, as Foreville emphasizes, it accords fairly closely with the pattern laid down in the author's prologue. These texts are followed by transcriptions of twelfth- and early thirteenth-century papal bulls in the Gilbertines' favour. This manuscript would seem to be of Gilbertine provenance. So too is the Harleian manuscript, which is very similar to the Cottonian and may well be a copy of it, though it is not quite finished.

Foreville has argued that the Oxford manuscript, by contrast, is not only different in structure but in function. Knowles thought that this text (which he was inclined to accept as the best) 'clearly represents a different tradition', founding his argument on the fact that, besides some minor variants, it contains a different selection and ordering of the letters relating to the lay brothers' revolt.[7] More recently Fredeman, basing her conclusions on an analysis of Capgrave's fifteenth-century English translation of the *Vita*, has suggested another now-lost contemporary, or almost contemporary, life of the founder.[8] But while Knowles ascribed the marked differences between the texts to different manuscript traditions, Foreville sees the reason for their divergence in their function. She argues that while the earlier manuscript was a version prepared for use in a Gilbertine community, the latter did not have a specific conventual association but was rather a work for private devotion, and may have belonged to a lay person. This argument should be examined in more detail.

What are the differences in the organization of the material in the two manuscripts? The Oxford manuscript generally follows the same pattern as the London manuscript in the opening sections down to the collection of documents supporting the canonization, though one or two of the miracles performed by Gilbert in his lifetime are omitted, and some are arranged in a slightly different order. Thereafter the miracle stories of the canonization process precede rather than follow the canonization letters, and the material relating to the lay brothers' revolt only appears after this, rather than being entered between the *Vita* and the canonization dossier. The Oxford text concludes with the *servicium* of St Gilbert, which is absent from the earlier versions.[9] But not only are there differences in the material's organization, there are also significant textual variants. The later manuscript has a slightly different selection of letters relating to the rebellion, and includes far fewer of the canonization letters and miracles. Such miracles as are included are not presented in so detailed or formal a fashion. Foreville has convincingly suggested that the compiler of the Oxford manuscript has made an eclectic selection that aims to avoid duplication of either similar miracle stories or letters. So, for example, only one miracle of healing of blindness will be recorded, and only a letter from a single abbot in the canonization material. There is one other major difference between the earlier and later manuscripts. The thirteenth-

[7] *Book of St Gilbert*, pp. lxvii–lxxi; M. D. Knowles, 'The Revolt of the Lay Brothers of Sempringham', *EHR* 50 (1935), 474. These letters are discussed below, pp. 458–60.
[8] J. C. Fredeman, 'John Capgrave's Life of St Gilbert of Sempringham', *Bulletin of the John Rylands Library*, 55 (1972–3), 112–45. [9] See below, pp. 453, 458–9.

century texts are unilluminated: the fifteenth-century manuscript is quite heavily
decorated with illuminated initials that are particularly elaborate where they mark
'significant points in the structure of the book's contents'.[10] From all this Foreville
deduces that the manuscript was not made for conventual use, though she con-
cedes that it may have been given or bequeathed to a Gilbertine priory: 'it was
assuredly compiled from the Gilbertine material, doubtless for a rich patron with
a special devotion to St Gilbert.'[11] This interesting and stimulating argument is
not wholly convincing. It is perplexing that the later 'private' manuscript actually
contains more documents relating to the lay brothers' revolt than does the earlier
'official' version.[12] It is true that there are differences in the way the 'dossier'
relating to the rebellion is treated in the two versions. In the London manuscripts
this follows immediately upon the *Vita*, while in the later version it is found
towards the end of the manuscript, almost as an appendix. Thus the organization
of material in MS Digby 36 is not quite as it is described in the prologue to the
Vita. However, it does contain (while the London manuscripts do not) the 'lessons extracted and summarized from this account [i.e. the *Vita*] which are to be
read upon his feast-day', which according to the prologue conclude (as they do
here) the work. These appear under the rubric: 'Servicium in sollennitatibus
Sancti Gilleberti Confessoris. primi patris et institutoris ordinis de S' ad usus
predictorum fratrum'.[13] Finally, Foreville makes much of the decoration of the
Oxford volume and argues 'that so sumptuous a volume was hardly made for a
conventual library: it can scarcely have belonged to any of the Gilbertine houses,
unless one supposes that it was given or bequeathed to one'.[14] But the work is not
particularly lavishly illustrated. Certainly it contains many illuminated borders
and initials, but there are no illustrations, and the artistry, though good, is far
from extraordinary. It is, in fact, just the sort of volume that might be expected
in a small religious community in late-medieval England: a fine but unostenta-
tious volume for use by a Gilbertine convent, certainly somewhat different in
format from the thirteenth-century exemplars, with (as Foreville notes) a greater
concern to edify rather than to give the precise details of the canonization process,
but none the less a Gilbertine work, not the possession of a lay person.

JOHN CAPGRAVE'S *THE LIFE OF ST GILBERT*

In the mid-fifteenth century Nicholas Reysby (who is known to have been Master
of the order in 1445) approached the Augustinian friar, Capgrave, after reading

---

[10] *Book of St Gilbert*, p. lxviii.   [11] Ibid., pp. lxix–lxx.

[12] It uniquely includes the formal mandate from Henry II to Gilbert, and the letter of the
papal legate, Hugo Pierleoni, to the pope (ibid. 348–9).

[13] Oxford, Bodl. Lib., MS Digby 36, fos. 110^v–116^v (printed in *The Gilbertine Rite*, i.
115–26). Foreville argues that by the 15th century these texts were included in the order's
service books and so were redundant in a copy of the *Vita* intended for conventual use.
However, they are not found in the surviving Gilbertine missal or ordinal.

[14] *Book of St Gilbert*, p. lxix.

his translation of the life of Augustine, and asked him to prepare a translation of the *Vita* of Gilbert for the edification of the Gilbertine nuns who did not understand Latin.[15] In his prologue to the work (which was finished in 1451) Capgrave states that he has translated the work from the Latin, but has also incorporated some additions from the oral testimony of members of the order along with other relevant material.[16] The translation is divided into two parts. The first, and shorter, consists of thirteen chapters. Though it derives some material from the surviving *Vita*, most has little that can be directly related to the Latin texts of the London or Oxford manuscripts. It omits all mention of the lay brothers' revolt and Gilbert's involvement in the Becket dispute, refers to only one specific miracle, and is primarily concerned to present the holiness of Gilbert's life.[17] It seems possible that these chapters were based upon the *lectiones* in the *servicium*. A less likely hypothesis is that there was another, now lost, manuscript source for Capgrave's version of the Life.[18] The second Life is a much longer version of the *Vita* and is by contrast largely based on the surviving Latin texts. At the same time Capgrave made considerable alterations to his source(s): he shortened many passages, particularly (as Fredeman contends) 'rhetorical, supernatural' and 'lyrical' elements, he also glossed and expanded other episodes, included exegetical passages, and included one or two long digressions, such as a comparison of Athanasius with Gilbert. His treatment of the miracles is different, he omits the formal listing of the witnesses to the 'official' miracles presented for scrutiny to the Roman Curia, and on occasions adds to the miracles' circumstantial details. Though Fredeman's hypothesis of another source for the translation is an interesting one, it remains most likely that (as Foreville argues) the differences should be attributed to Capgrave's own alterations, that were at least in part based upon oral testimonies relating to the founder, and which were intended not as justification for a canonization but as edification of the nuns.

'DE CONSTRUCTIONE MONASTERIORUM'

The *Vita* twice refers to an autobiographical account written by Gilbert and described either as 'De Constructione Monasteriorum' or 'De Fundatione Monasteriorum'. Unfortunately, this is now almost wholly lost.[19] Its only surviving fragments are contained in chapter 25 of the *Vita* describing the lay brothers'

---

[15] *John Capgrave's Lives of St Augustine and St Gilbert of Sempringham*, ed. J. J. Munro, EETS os 140 (1910), 61–142. The only modern study of this work is J. C. Fredeman's controversial article, 'John Capgrave's Life of St Gilbert of Sempringham'.

[16] *John Capgrave's Lives of St Augustine and St Gilbert of Sempringham*, 62. Capgrave consulted John, lord Beaumont, patron of the order, for information about Gilbert's parents (ibid. 62–3).

[17] The miracle (ibid. 75) is similar to, but not identical with, one in the *Vita* (*Book of St Gilbert*, 116).

[18] The arguments against Fredeman's thesis have been cogently stated by Foreville in *Book of St Gilbert*, 358–63.   [19] Ibid. 30, 78.

revolt, and also in the opening, autobiographical section of the Gilbertine Rule.[20] This incorporation of autobiographical material in a saint's Life, though rare, is not unknown: the Life of Geoffrey de Chalard similarly contains fragments of the saint's own writings.[21] Elkins has recently argued that the two works, the autobiographical and the *Vita*, have a different intention. While the former is succinct, simple, and straightforward with no hint of a coherent master-plan, the latter is a carefully crafted ideological justification of the order's foundation written in the light of the early scandals which had threatened its existence. However, though the *Vita* is more elaborate and does sometimes present different emphases, it does not seem to present any significantly different interpretations from the earlier work on which it is clearly based. While it is difficult to date the autobiographical fragment, it is likely, as Elkins points out, that it post-dates 1167: in other words, both *Vita* and autobiography were written after the period of crisis and both had a partisan intent.[22]

THE GILBERTINE RULE

The rule survives in a unique manuscript, Bodleian Library, MS Douce 136.[23] It is a composite work, partly comprising Gilbert's own provisions for his communities, the Rule as prepared following Gilbert's return from Cîteaux in 1148, and other additions made between that time and 1238, when the statutes underwent some revision. The manuscript includes these revisions, but also contains records of a number of Gilbertine general chapters, presumably those at which substantial amendments to the Rule were made. These continued to be added to the manuscript until the last years of the order, and are the most important single source for its development.

SOURCES FOR THE HISTORY OF INDIVIDUAL GILBERTINE HOUSES

Only two Gilbertine cartularies are known to have survived, those of Alvingham and Malton. The former (now Bodleian Library, MS Laud Misc. 642) was originally compiled between 1260 and 1270, though it was still being added to and used in the fifteenth century. It comprises 160 folios, which, besides containing the transcripts of some 1,000 charters, also include papal bulls in favour of the priory and the order, records of litigation involving the priory, genealogical material relating to families of benefactors, agreements with other religious houses, a copy of the 1217 reissue of Magna Carta, and other miscellaneous material.[24]

---

[20] Ibid. 78–80. *Monasticon*, vi. 2. xxix–xxx.

[21] See Milis, 'Ermites et chanoines reguliers', 42.   [22] Elkins, 'All Ages'.

[23] This is the manuscript transcribed, generally with commendable accuracy, in *Monasticon*, vi. 2. xxix–xcvii.

[24] A few of the Alvingham charters were published in F. M. Stenton, *The Free Peasantry of the Northern Danelaw* (Oxford, 1969).

Malton cartulary (now British Library, MS Cotton Claudius D XI) was also compiled in the mid-thirteenth century, during the priorate of William of Ancaster. Like that of Alvingham, it is arranged topographically, with papal, royal, and charters of the founding family (the Vescis) occupying the opening folios.[25] In addition it contains abbreviated accounts for William of Ancaster's priorate.

Two Gilbertine cartularies extant in the seventeenth century, but which have now disappeared, were transcribed by the antiquarian Gervase Holles. In 1639 he transcribed the cartulary of Haverholme, which was then in the possession of the rector of Healing (Lincs.). Unfortunately, he made considerable abbreviations, often omitting the names of witnesses to charters (though it is of course possible that these were not included in the cartulary either—certainly they are not found in either the Alvingham or Malton cartularies) and sometimes merely noting a document's contents.[26] Three years later he also transcribed the cartulary of Bullington. Though this, too, normally omits witnesses and is heavily abbreviated, it is clear from instances where the entries can be compared with the surviving originals that Holles' transcriptions were on the whole accurate.[27] Substantial parts of another cartulary, that of Nun Ormsby, were transcribed by Holles's contemporary, Roger Dodsworth.[28]

However, some other transcriptions and original charters do survive. In the first decade of the fifteenth century a series of clerical tenths were granted to Henry IV, with exemptions for the Hospitallers and poor nunneries.[29] Though from the earliest years the Gilbertines had been granted immunity from royal taxation, this privilege was in fact rarely allowed. The first Gilbertine priory to have complained that they were wrongfully being taxed seems to have been Chicksands in 1403. In order to support their claim the nuns presented a series of original charters demonstrating that the priory's endowments had been made specifically to them, rather than to the canons or prior of the community. The nuns were successful in their petition, and the evidence they adduced was transcribed on the King's Remembrancer's Memoranda Roll.[30] In 1407 the nuns of

---

[25] This cartulary is also substantial, comprising 297 folios. It was once in the possession of Christopher, baron Hatton (Davis, *Medieval Cartularies*, 73).

[26] This transcript is now London, BL, MS Lansdowne 207A. It was edited in *Lincolnshire Notes and Queries*, 17 (1922), 7–48, 65–74, 89–98. This also includes a further six charters transcribed by Francis Peck in 1730–1 and included in London, BL, MS Addit. 4937, fos. 110–16. Holles's collection, which includes more than 200 charters, is a useful addition to the long *inspeximus* and confirmation charter issued in 1336–7, which contains more than 300 grants and confirmations. It is fully calendared in *Cal. Ch. R.* iv. 403–19.

[27] This transcript is now London, BL, MS Addit. 6118, pp. 703–end.

[28] He made extracts from the first 275 folios. They are now Oxford, Bodl. Lib., MS Dodsworth 135, fos. 139–61 (Davis, *Medieval Cartularies*, 83).

[29] The circumstances of this grant are described in *Gilbertine Charters*, pp. ix–xi. However, Stenton does not seem to have been aware of the precedent set by Chicksands and states that Catley was the first Gilbertine house to claim exemption. For the general exemption of the Gilbertines from royal taxation, see above, p. 446.

[30] These charters are translated by Fowler, 'Early Charters of . . . Chicksand', 101–28.

Catley, Haverholme, and Shouldham made similarly successful complaints, and were followed in 1408 by the priories of Ormsby, Alvingham, and Sixhills; three years later Sempringham and Bullington pursued the same tactic. Watton alone of the Gilbertine double houses seems not to have submitted a claim, or perhaps the evidence has not survived.[31] For most of the priories these transcriptions constitute our only charter evidence. However, in one or two instances a significant charter archive has survived. There are some 600 original charters relating to Bullington in the British Library, mostly contained within the Harleian collection, though there are also some in the Cottonian.[32] The British Library also contains about 100 charters of Sempringham priory.[33] For some priories we depend upon the monumental effort of Roger Dodsworth, who made transcripts of a large number of charters relating to the Gilbertine priories in Yorkshire. These, like those of many Yorkshire monasteries, were held in St Mary's Tower, York, until its destruction during the siege of York in 1644. His records provide virtually the only charter material for the priories of Watton and Ellerton.[34]

Archival material for a study of the economy of the Gilbertine houses is almost non-existent.[35] Though the Rule laid down clear instructions for the keeping of records of this kind, only for Malton do they survive at all, and then only because the accounts of the years 1244 to 1257 were copied in abbreviated form into the cartulary.[36] Elsewhere, though it is of course possible to establish something of the economic life and organization of the priories from the charter evidence, and while something too can be gleaned from the *Valor Ecclesiasticus* and the *Taxatio Ecclesiastica*, there is nothing of value.

[31] Watton, unlike the other priories, was in the archdiocese of York, and different procedures may have been followed.

[32] More than 100 of these were published in *Documents Illustrative of the Social and Economic History of the Danelaw from Various Collections*, ed. F. M. Stenton, British Academy, Records of the Social and Economic History of England and Wales, 5 (1920). This collection constitutes the largest printed archive of any Gilbertine house.

[33] Many of these were published, along with those charters transcribed on the King's Remembrancer Roll of 1410, by Major E. M. Poynton in *The Genealogist*, NS xv (1898–9), 158–61, 221–7; xvi (1899–1900), 30–5, 76–83, 153–8, 223–8; xvii (1900–1), 29–35, 164–8, 232–9.

[34] For Dodsworth's work, see N. Denholm-Young and H. H. E. Craster, 'Roger Dodsworth (1585–1654) and his Circle', *Yorkshire Archaeological Journal*, 32 (1936), 5–32. Material relating to Gilbertine houses can be found in the following Dodsworth manuscripts in the Bodleian Library: Watton, MSS 7–8, 94, 95, 121; Ellerton, MSS 76, 94, 95; Malton, MSS 7–8; Bullington, MSS 30, 95, 76; Haverholme, MS 144; Sempringham, MS 76.

[35] The absence of similar material for nunneries in general is well known. See above, pp. 450–1 and references there cited. See also J. H. Tillotson, *Marrick Priory: A Nunnery in Late-Medieval Yorkshire*, Borthwick Papers, 75 (York, 1989), 1–2.

[36] London, BL, MS Cotton Claudius D XI, fos. 279^v–81. See Graham, 'Finances of Malton Priory'. The provisions for the keeping of accounts are described ibid. 250–1.

DOCUMENTARY PROBLEMS AND THE CHRONOLOGY
OF THE LAY BROTHERS' REVOLT

I have argued that the inquiries into the Gilbertine order instigated by the rebellious lay brothers were settled by the pope in 1169, though the personal grievances of the lay brothers themselves continued to be a source of discord within the community until Gilbert's death.[1] However, this chronology differs substantially from that put forward by Foreville, who argues that the legal struggle was far from over in 1169. She suggests that some time between 1169 and 1176 there was another hearing at the Curia, new mandates sent to new judges–delegate, new petitions from English prelates to the pope, including those from the bishop of Norwich and prior of Bridlington included in the dossier preserved in the *Vita*. The king again came to Gilbert's support and sent two royal clerks, Jordan, archdeacon of Lewes, and master O., to the pope to press Gilbert's case. Early in 1176 the papal legate, cardinal Hugo Pierleone, visited Sempringham, and added his voice to those pleading Gilbert's cause at Rome, and the issue was only finally resolved with the confirmation of the order's privileges in 1178. Foreville's case largely rests on her reading of the king's two letters to the pope, and her interpretation and comparison of the papal privileges of 1169 and 1178.[2]

There is nothing in the texts of either the letter of the bishop or the prior to suggest that they were not writing at the same time as the other episcopal supporters of Gilbert's cause in 1166–7. In particular it is hard to see why the bishop of Norwich should have written in the 1170s, 'About the canons, whose purity *I hear* [my italics] has been slandered before your clemency', after he had heard the case and reported on it in 1166.[3] Moreover, the prior's reference to the personal letter sent by Alexander to Gilbert seems to refer to the papal mandates (now lost) sent to Gilbert in 1165 or 1166.[4] Royal support for Gilbert was uninhibited and was doubtless a major factor in ensuring Gilbert's success against the lay brethren. Two letters from Henry to the pope are among the surviving dossier of letters in the *Book of St Gilbert*.[5] The *Vita* describes how a letter was sent by royal messengers with the other letters from the English prelates. It concluded with the king's threat to take back all the lands granted to the order if the Rule was altered, while promising that if the pope lent his support then the king would use his secular powers to maintain the order.[6] However, the texts of the surviving letters differ significantly in the London and Oxford manuscripts (London, BL, MS Cotton Cleopatra B I and Oxford, Bodl. Lib. MS Digby 36). Knowles used the

---

[1] See above, 49–50.   [2] *Book* of *St Gilbert*, pp. lv–lxii.   [3] Ibid. 140.
[4] Ibid. 154.   [5] Ibid. 142–4 (no. 3); 160–2 (no. 12).   [6] Ibid. 82.

version in the latter source, arguing that its readings were generally preferable, while Foreville has favoured the London manuscript.[7] Foreville dates one of these letters (letter 3 in her edition) to 1166–7. This seems to be correct. Henry asks the pope to accept the letters that have been written in Gilbert's support by bishops and other religious men, and that Alexander should aid Gilbert in compelling the *conversi* to obedience to their profession. He then goes on to talk of the threat to the very survival of the order posed by the rebellion. Here in the Cottonian manuscript the letter ends abruptly, without any farewell clause: 'in order that this [i.e. the downfall of the order] might not happen, we pray your holiness to strive with all energy against the wicked'. Henry's second letter (letter 12 in Foreville's edition) is dated by her between 1169 and 1176. It certainly post-dates the issuing of a papal privilege in the Gilbertines' favour for which Henry thanks Alexander III in the first part of the letter. In the second half of the letter, we find the royal threat to regain all Gilbertine property if the Rule was altered, balanced by a promise of royal support if the pope supported the order. This is a marked change of tone in the letter and does not seem a logical progression from the king's earlier thanks to the pope for issuing the privilege to the Gilbertines. It is this latter section which accords closely with the royal letter described in the *Vita*.[8]

We should turn now to the versions in the Oxford manuscript and used by Knowles. In this text letter 3 does not finish as in the Cottonian manuscript, but continues with what is the second section from letter 12 in the Cottonian manuscript: 'Proinde obnixe rogamus quatinus ordinem prefatum faciatis inviolabiliter observari', etc. This linking sentence was rejected by Foreville: 'its final sentence . . . does not seem to anticipate any further points linked to it by "Proinde", "in consequence".'[9] I do not see any such difficulty here, and the complete text as given in the Oxford version of the *Vita* has the all-important merit of a very close accord with the description of the royal letter in chapter 25 of the *Vita*.

This leaves the second letter for consideration. In the Oxford manuscript the text is the same until the sentence praising Gilbert's zeal in ruling his order even at his advanced age. Instead of being followed, as in the Cottonian manuscript, by the demand that Alexander support Gilbert and the threat to confiscate the order's property, the Oxford manuscript continues with two sentences of further praise of Gilbert as monastic founder.[10] Foreville argues that these sentences were added to the manuscript in a different hand: in fact there is no evidence in the manuscript that a different scribe was responsible for this part of the transcription.[11] Moreover, these sentences are allegedly 'unsatisfactory both in syntax and

---

[7] Knowles, 'Revolt of the Lay Brothers', 474–5; *Book of St Gilbert*, pp. lxiii–lxxi.

[8] Foreville connects the description in the *Vita* with letter 3, but the *Vita*'s description of Henry's threat to take back his estates if the order was altered by former serfs, and the statement that the letter was sent with royal messengers, accords exactly with the second part of letter 12. There is no reason why the royal clerks should not have delivered a royal letter in 1167, rather than at a later date: Jordan was certainly archdeacon by 1164.

[9] *Book of St Gilbert*, p. lxxxvi.   [10] Printed by Foreville, ibid. 162 n. b.

[11] I am grateful to Dr Tessa Webber for her palaeographical assistance.

sense for their context'.[12] I would argue, rather, that though the construction of the first sentence is a little clumsy the sense is clear and is a far more logical conclusion to the letter than that in the other manuscript.[13]

If the versions of the royal letters as given in the Oxford manuscript are accepted, then the first letter can be seen as a strong request for papal action against the rebels combined with a threat of a unilateral royal response if nothing was done. This accompanied the supporting letters of several English bishops and religious heads, including several who were supporters of the crown against archbishop Becket, who was rightly perceived as a defender of the *conversi*.[14] The success of this campaign in the late 1160s was followed by the issuing of papal privileges in favour of the order in 1169, which were in turn followed shortly thereafter by a royal letter of thanks combined with a further eulogy of *magister* Gilbert.

In her interpretation and comparison of the papal privileges of 1169 and 1178 Foreville was supported by Cheney. They have suggested that the 1169 privileges were not a definitive settlement, and indeed that they imply that a final process would be held in the future.[15] If the privilege of 30 July 1169 addressed to Gilbert as 'prior' of Malton and that of 20 September addressed to Gilbert, Master of the order, are examined, they appear as rather more final and definitive documents than Foreville and Cheney would allow. The latter argued that though Gilbert was given protection to exercise his disciplinary authority and though the order was confirmed as exempt from episcopal control, which had exceptionally been exercised in the recent crisis, the Curia did not settle the main points as to whether Gilbert had exceeded his authority and whether there had been serious moral lapses in Gilbertine houses. But how far do the papal privileges granted in 1178 exceed in scope those of 1169, and answer these points? The relevant privileges for Malton can readily be compared. Both are said to be in response to the prayers of the community. That of 1169 proceeds to confirm as inviolable the 'ordo canonicus' instituted at Sempringham, before going on to confirm in general and specific terms the temporal possessions of the house. The 1178 document refers (as that of 1169 does not) to earlier privileges granted by popes Innocent II, Eugenius III, and Adrian IV. It also for the first time orders that the institutions made in the time of Theobald, archbishop of Canterbury, and Henry and Roger, archbishops of York, as well as the confirmations of Gilbertine liberties granted by Henry II and the young Henry be maintained. A number of exemptions from

---

[12] Ibid., p. lxxxvi.

[13] I am grateful to the late Dr David Whitton for his assistance in the elucidation of textual difficulties.

[14] The letters of bishop William of Norwich and the prior of Bridlington, which Foreville suggests belong to a second campaign, make no reference to a second hearing and are written in very similar terms to those of the bishops sent in 1166–7.

[15] *Book of St Gilbert*, pp. lviii, 344; Cheney, 'Papal Privileges', 44–5. The royal letter dated by Foreville to 1166–7 refers to the grant of a papal privilege to the order by Alexander III. The text of this has not survived.

episcopal authority and general privileges are recited in both documents. Where they differ is in disciplinary matters. The privilege of 1169 allowed the order to receive any clerical or lay persons fleeing from the world without constraint. This privilege is omitted in 1178, perhaps because it was seen as encouraging social disorder. In 1169 the lay brethren were prohibited from leaving the cloister and no one was to support them without episcopal (?) licence ('absque prelati sui licentia'). In 1178 this practical prohibition was replaced by a theoretical statement of the subservience of the lay brethren, who were to be subordinate and obedient to the prior and canons in all things, nor should they presume to usurp power or money unless under the strict injunction of the prior. Now, though there is perhaps a slight tightening of disciplinary rules in the second privilege, it does not seem that there is any substantive difference between the two. The finality of the judgement of 1169 is further suggested in the other letters of Alexander written in the same year to the diocesan bishops and to Henry II. In the first the bishops and archdeacons are urged to give every support and protection to the Gilbertines in their dioceses, in the second the king is asked to extend royal protection to the order and to bring the recalcitrant lay brothers who were refusing to bow to ecclesiastical penalties to justice.

There is, then, little evidence that the real crisis extended beyond 1169, and there is more evidence to suggest that it marked the conclusion of business as far as the pope was concerned. It is likely that any new mandates or reports would have been transcribed into the dossier. It is also noteworthy that the 'provisional' papal privileges of 1169 are included while those of 1178 are not. Moreover, if we return to the account of the troubles in the *Vita*, it is clear that the author regarded the granting of papal privileges as closing the affair.[16] He accurately paraphrases their content. No one in future was to attempt to alter the Rule without the consent of the greater and wiser part of the community, nor was anything to be added which seemed to threaten their institutions. If problems did arise, then the Master (with the advice of his priors) could make amendments to the statutes. If the dispute was still *sub judice* it is hard to understand the pope giving Gilbert such extensive powers as these. As I have argued above, the explanation for the new papal privileges of 1178 lies in their addressee: Roger, the new prior of the order. The most anxious moment for the Gilbertines was the prospect of the loss of their founder, and, as Gilbert appointed his successor, the Gilbertines also sought confirmation of their order in the name of their new prior.

There is one further document which requires consideration. The Oxford manuscript of the *Vita* contains the text of a letter written by cardinal Hugo Pierleone to the pope on behalf of Gilbert.[17] Hugo was certainly in England early in 1176, when he attended the Council of Northampton, and it was presumably at this time while crossing the diocese of Lincoln ('cum per Lincolniensem

---

[16] *Book of St Gilbert*, 84.

[17] Ibid. 348–9. It should be emphasized, as Cheney pointed out, that 'both the pope's address and the cardinal's title are unusual' (Cheney, 'Papal Privileges', 44 n. 2)

episcopatum transirem') that he stopped at Sempringham, though he may have made other, unrecorded visits earlier. His letter describes the exemplary life of the nuns and their rapid growth in a short space of time to a community of some 1,500. He then goes on to describe how Ogger incited some of the brethren to follow him in attempting to break the statutes of the order as confirmed by pope Eugenius and Alexander himself. At last Gilbert had excommunicated Ogger. The letter ends with an appeal to the pope to listen to the petitions of Gilbert and his followers. How does this letter relate to the rebellion? It certainly posed problems for the chronology presented by Knowles, and is evidence to Foreville that the affair at Sempringham was still active in the 1170s. However, the tone of the letter suggests that the events it describes happened some time earlier. Moreover, only Ogger is singled out for condemnation and he is presented as following an almost personal vendetta against Gilbert. This accords with the statements in the *Vita* where Ogger alone is said to have been recalcitrant and persistent in his wickedness, so that almost to the day of his own death and that of Gilbert himself 'he lost no opportunity to attack the saint'.[18] It looks as if the letter of Hugo should best be interpreted as an attempt to give support to Gilbert in his on-going personal struggle with Ogger, rather than indicating the continuing real threat of general *conversi* unrest. It should be emphasized, too, that the community's 'petitions' are never detailed. Presumably they were pleas for the excommunication of Ogger to be given more bite.

[18] *Book of St Gilbert*, 80.

Bibliography

1. MANUSCRIPT SOURCES

London, British Library

Additional Charters
1050; 20620; 20622; 20907; 20904; 20914

Addit. MSS
6118: copy of Bullington cartulary
46701: Stixwould cartulary

Arundel MSS
83 II: Psalter of Robert de Lisle

Cotton Charters
xii, 3; xxviii, 11

Cotton MSS
Claudius D XI: Malton cartulary
Cleopatra B I: early-13th-century *Vita* of Gilbert
Vespasian E XX: Bardney cartulary

Harleian Charters
43 D 3; 43 H 35; 44 A 23; 44 A 44; 44 A 54; 44 I 19; 44 I 20; 45 I 7 (Chicksands priory foundation charter); 47 E 20; 48 I 49 (Tunstall priory foundation charter); 49 A 1; 49 I 17; 50 F 32; 52 B 20; 52 B 32; 52 G 44; 54 C 19; 54 I 46; 57 D 27

Harleian MSS
468: mid-13th-century *Vita* of Gilbert
2406: devotional miscellany
3640: Welbeck cartulary

Lansdowne MSS
207a: Collections of Gervase Holles

Royal
4 B VIII: sermons of William de Montibus

Stowe MSS
937: agreement between Gilbertines and Cistercians

London, Public Record Office

C81/1791/1–12: significations of fugitive canons
CP 25 (1) 251/20/7: feet of fines
E.101/126/7: 1294 wool inquiry
E.101/505/11: accounts of Kyme manors
E.179/242/113: clerical subsidy assessment, Lincolnshire
E.372/63: pipe roll
IR 29/1/23: tithe map, Hawnes
PRO 31/9/16: *successio magistrorum ordinis*
SC 1/30/49: letter of Edward I to sheriff of Bedford

Cambridge University Library

Additional MS 3041: relic-list of Waltham abbey

Cambridge, St John's College

MS 216: Commentary of Augustine

Lincoln, Cathedral Library

MS 115: Gilbertine missal

Lincoln, Lincolnshire Archives Office

Episcopal Register II (Dalderby)
Episcopal Register V (Burghersh)
Episcopal Register VI (Bek)

Oxford, Bodleian Library

MS Auct. E. inf. 4: Origen's *Homilies*
MS Digby 36: 15th-century *Vita* of Gilbert
MS Dodsworth 135: Nun Ormsby charter transcripts
MS Douce 136: Gilbertine statutes
MS Hatton 92: tract of Maurice of Kirkham
MS Laud 642: Alvingham cartulary
MS Lyell 8: sermons of William de Montibus
MS Rawlinson A. 420: composite manuscript belonging to Clattercote

Oxford, Christ Church

Deeds, M.37: Clattercote charter

Oxford, Lincoln College

MS Lat. 27: tract of Maurice of Kirkham

2. PRINTED SOURCES

ABELARD, *Epistolae*, PL 178.

Abstracts of Feet of Fines relating to Wiltshire for the Reigns of Edward I and Edward II, ed. R. B. Pugh, Wiltshire Archaeological and Natural History Society, Records Branch, 1 (1939).

Abstracts of Final Concords temp. Richard I, John and Henry III, ed. W. O. Massingberd, Lincolnshire Records, 1 (1896).

The Account Book of Beaulieu Abbey, ed. S. F. Hockey, Camden Society, 4th ser. 16 (1975).

AELRED, *De Sanctimoniali de Wattun*, PL 195, cols. 789–96.

——*De Institutis Inclusarum*, ed. C. H. Talbot, in *Aelredi Rievallensis Opera Omnia I*, ed. A. Hoste and C. H. Talbot, Corpus Christianorum; Continuatio Medievalis 1 (Turnhout, 1971), 633–82.

——*Sermones de Oneribus*, PL 195, cols. 360–560.

Ancrene Wisse, edited from MS Corpus Christi College Cambridge 402, ed. J. R. R. Tolkien, EETS 249 (1962).

Annales Monastici, ed. H. R. Luard, 5 vols., Rolls Series (London, 1864–9).

AUGUSTINE, *La Règle de saint Augustin*, ed. L. Verheijen, 2 vols. (Paris, 1967).

BARRACLOUGH, G., ed., 'Some Charters of the Earls of Chester', in P. M. Barnes and C. Slade (eds.), *A Medieval Miscellany for Doris Mary Stenton*, Pipe Roll Society, NS 36 (1960), 24–38.

The Book of Fees, 3 vols., HMSO (London, 1920–31).

The Book of St Gilbert, ed. and trans. R. Foreville and G. Keir (Oxford, 1987).

Bracton's Notebook, ed. F. W. Maitland (Cambridge, 1887).

Calendar of Ancient Petitions relating to Wales, ed. W. Rees (Cardiff, 1975).

Calendar of Charter Rolls preserved in the Public Record Office, 6 vols., HMSO (London, 1903–27).

Calendar of Close Rolls preserved in the Public Record Office, HMSO (London, 1892–).

Calendar of Documents preserved in France illustrative of the History of Great Britain and Ireland. i. AD 918–1206, ed. J. H. Round, HMSO (London, 1899).

Calendar of Documents relating to Scotland, ed. J. Bain, 4 vols. (Edinburgh, 1881–8).

Calendar of Entries in the Papal Registers relating to Great Britain and Ireland, ed. W. H. Bliss, C. Johnson, and J. A. Twemlow, HMSO (London, 1893–).

Calendar of Inquisitions Miscellaneous preserved in the Public Record Office (Chancery), HMSO (London, 1916–).

Calendar of Inquisitions post Mortem and other analogous documents in the Public Record Office, HMSO (London, 1904–).

Calendar of Letters and Papers, Foreign and Domestic, of the Reign of Henry VIII preserved in the Public Record Office, the British Museum and elsewhere in England, ed. J. S. Brewer *et al.*, 23 vols. in 38, HMSO (London, 1862–1932).

Calendar of Liberate Rolls preserved in the Public Record Office, HMSO (London, 1916–).

Calendar of Memoranda Rolls preserved in the Public Record Office, Michaelmas 1326–Michaelmas 1327, HMSO (London, 1968).

Calendar of Patent Rolls preserved in the Public Record Office, HMSO (London, 1891–).

Calendar of the Register of Richard Scrope, Archbishop of York 1398–1405, part 1, ed. R. N. Swanson, Borthwick Texts and Calendars: Records of the Northern Province, 8 (York, 1981).

CANIVEZ, J. M., ed., *Statuta Capitulorum Generalium Ordinis Cisterciensis ab anno 1116 ad annum 1786*, 8 vols. (Louvain, 1933–41).

CAPGRAVE, J., *Life of St Gilbert*, ed. J. J. Munro, in *John Capgrave's Lives of St Augustine and St Gilbert of Sempringham*, EETS os 140 (London, 1910).

Cartae Antiquae, Rolls 1–10, ed. L. Landon, Pipe Roll Society, NS 17 (1939).

Cartularium Abbathiae de Rievalle ordinis Cisterciensis, ed. J. C. Atkinson, Surtees Society, 83 (1889).

The Cartulary of Cirencester Abbey, Gloucestershire, ed. C. D. Ross and M. Devine, 3 vols. (Oxford, 1964–72).

Cartulary of St Bartholomew's Hospital, a calendar prepared by N. J. M. Kerling (London, 1973).

Charters of the Honour of Mowbray, 1107–1191, ed. D. E. Greenway, British Academy Records of Social and Economic History, NS 1 (1972).

The Chartulary of the Augustinian Priory of St John the Evangelist of the Park of Healaugh, ed. J. Purvis, Yorkshire Archaeological Society Record Series, 92 (1936).

Chronica Monasterii de Melsa, a fundatione usque ad annum 1396, auctore Thoma de Burton, abbate, ed. E. A. Bond, 3 vols., Rolls Series (London, 1866–8).

Chronica Rogeri de Hovedene (AD 732–1201), ed. W. Stubbs, 4 vols., Rolls Series (London, 1868–71).

The Chronicle of Battle Abbey, ed. and trans. E. Searle (Oxford, 1980).

Collectanea Anglo-Premonstratensia, ed. F. A. Gasquet, 3 vols., Camden Society, 3rd ser. 6, 10, 12 (1904–6).

Consuetudines Canonicorum Regularium Springirsbacenses-Rodenses, ed. S. Weinfurter, Corpus Christianorum: Continuatio Mediaevalis, 48 (Turnhout, 1978).

The Coucher Book of the Cistercian Abbey of Kirkstall, ed. W. T. Lancaster and W. P. Baildon, Publications of the Thoresby Society, 8 (1904).

The Coucher Book of Selby, ed. J. T. Fowler, 2 vols., Yorkshire Archaeological and Topographical Association Record Series, 13 (1892).

Councils and Synods. I. 871–1066, ed. D. Whitelock, M. Brett, and C. N. L. Brooke (Oxford, 1981).

Councils and Synods, with other Documents relating to the English Church. II. AD 1205–1313, ed. F. M. Powicke and C. R. Cheney, 2 vols. (Oxford, 1964).

Court of Augmentation Accounts for Bedfordshire, ed. Y. Nicholls, Publications of the Bedfordshire Historical Record Society, 63 (1984).

Le Coutumier de l'abbaye d'Oigny en Bourgogne au XIIᵉ siècle, ed. Pl. F. Lefevre and

A. H. Thomas, Spicilegium Sacrum Lovaniense, Études et Documents, fasc. 39 (Louvain, 1976).

Curia Regis Rolls, HMSO (London, 1922–).

Descriptive Catalogue of Materials Relating to the History of Great Britain and Ireland, 3 vols., Rolls Series (London, 1862–71).

Documents illustrative of the Social and Economic History of the Danelaw from various Collections, ed. F. M. Stenton, British Academy Records of the Social and Economic History of England and Wales, 5 (1920).

DUGDALE, W., *Monasticon Anglicanum*, ed. J. Caley, H. Ellis, and B. Bandinel, 6 vols. (London, 1846).

The Earliest Lincolnshire Assize Rolls, AD 1202 and 1209, ed. D. M. Stenton, Lincoln Record Society, 22 (1926).

The Early Charters of Waltham Abbey, 1062–1230, ed. R. Ransford (Woodbridge, 1989).

Early Lincoln Wills: an abstract of all the wills recorded in the Episcopal Registers of the old diocese of Lincoln, 1280–1547, ed. A. Gibbons (Lincoln, 1888).

Early Yorkshire Charters, ed. C. T. Clay, 12 vols., Yorkshire Archaeological Society Record Series, Extra Series, 1–12 (1914–65).

English Episcopal Acta. I. Lincoln 1067–1185, ed. D. M. Smith (Oxford, 1980).

English Episcopal Acta. V. York 1070–1154, ed. J. E. Burton (Oxford, 1988).

'Estate Records of the Hotot Family', in *A Northamptonshire Miscellany*, ed. E. King, Northamptonshire Record Society, 32 (1982).

Excerpta e Rotulis Finium in turri Londinensi asservatis, Henrico Tertio Rege, AD 1216–1272, ed. C. Roberts, 2 vols., Record Commission (London, 1835–6).

FARRER, W., ed., *Lancashire Inquests, Extents and Feudal Aids, AD 1205–AD 1307*, Lancashire and Cheshire Record Society, 48 (1903).

Fasti Parochiales V, ed. N. A. Lawrance, Yorkshire Archaeological Society Record Series, 143 (1982).

Feet of Fines for the County of York from 1232 to 1246, ed. J. Parker, Yorkshire Archaeological Society Record Series, 67 (1925).

Feet of Fines for the County of York from 1246 to 1272, ed. J. Parker, Yorkshire Archaeological Society Record Series, 82 (1932).

Feet of Fines for the County of York from 1272 to 1300, ed. F. H. Slingsby, Yorkshire Archaeological Society Record Series, 121 (1955).

Feudal Aids, HMSO (London, 1899–1920).

Final Concords of the County of Lincoln from the Feet of Fines preserved in the Public Record Office AD 1244–1272 with Additions from Various Sources AD 1176–1250, ed. C. W. Foster, Lincoln Record Society, 17 (1920).

FOWLER, G. H., ed., 'Early Charters of the Priory of Chicksand', *Publications of the Bedfordshire Historical Record Society*, 1 (1913), 101–28.

——'A Calendar of the Feet of Fines for Bedfordshire preserved in the Public Record Office of the Reigns of Richard I, John and Henry III', *Publications of the Bedfordshire Historical Record Society*, 6 (1919).

—— 'Calendar of Inquisitions post Mortem, no. 1', *Publications of the Bedford-shire Historical Record Society*, 5 (1920).

—— 'A Digest of the Charters preserved in the Cartulary of the Priory of Dunstable', *Publications of the Bedfordshire Historical Record Society*, 10 (1926).

GERVASE OF CANTERBURY, *The Historical Works of Gervase of Canterbury*, ed. W. Stubbs, 2 vols., Rolls Series (London, 1879–80).

Gesta Fulconis Filii Warini, in *Radulphi de Coggeshall Chronicon Anglicanum*, ed. J. Stevenson, Rolls Series (London, 1875).

The Gilbertine Rite, ed. R. M. Woolley, 2 vols., Henry Bradshaw Society, 59, 60 (1921–2).

Giraldi Cambrensis Opera, ed. J. S. Brewer, J. F. Dimock, and G. F. Warner, 8 vols., Rolls Series (London, 1861–91).

GUIGUES Ier, *Coutumes de Chartreuse*, Sources Chrétiennes, 313 (1984).

GUIGNARD, P., ed., *Les Monuments primitifs de la règle cistercienne* (Dijon, 1878).

'Haverholme Priory Charters', in *Lincolnshire Notes and Queries*, 17 (1922), 7–48, 65–74, 89–98.

HEFELE, C. J., *Histoire des Conciles*, ed. and trans. H. Leclercq, 8 vols. in 16 (Paris, 1902–21).

The Historia Occidentalis of Jacques de Vitry, ed. J. F. Hinnebusch (Fribourg, 1972).

HUNNISETT, R. F., ed., 'Bedfordshire Coroners' Rolls', *Publications of the Bedford-shire Historical Record Society*, 41 (1961).

The Letters of Pope Innocent III (1198–1216) concerning England and Wales. A Calendar with an Appendix of Texts, ed. C. R. and M. G. Cheney (Oxford, 1967).

Libellus de Diversis Ordinibus et Professionibus qui sunt in Aecclesia, ed. G. Constable and B. Smith (Oxford, 1972).

Liber Antiquus de Ordinationibus Vicariarum tempore Hugonis Wells, Lincolniensis Episcopi, 1209–1235, ed. A. Gibbons (Lincoln, 1888).

Liber Memorandum Ecclesie de Bernewelle, ed. J. W. Clark (Cambridge, 1907).

The Life of Aelred of Rievaulx by Walter Daniel, ed. and trans. F. M. Powicke (London, 1950).

The Life of Christina of Markyate, a Twelfth-Century Recluse, ed. and trans. C. H. Talbot (corr. repr., Oxford, 1987).

The Lincolnshire Domesday and the Lindsey Survey, ed. C. W. Foster and T. Longley, with an introduction by F. M. Stenton, Lincoln Record Society, 19 (1924, repr. 1976).

'Lincolnshire Wills proved in the Prerogative Court of Canterbury, 1384–1468', *AASRP* 89 (1932), 61–114, 179–218.

Le Livere de Reis de Britannie e le Livere de Reis de Engleterre, ed. J. Glover, Rolls Series (London, 1865).

MCHARDY, A. K., *The Church in London, 1375–1392*, London Record Society, 13 (1977).

MANNYNG, ROBERT, *Handlyng Synne*, ed. F. J. Furnivall, EETS OS 119, 123 (1901–3).

Manuscripts of his Grace the Duke of Rutland, Historic Manuscripts Commission, 14th Report, HMSO (London, 1905), vol. 4.

MAP, WALTER, *De Nugis Curialium*, ed. and trans. M. R. James, rev. C. N. L. Brooke and R. A. B. Mynors (Oxford, 1983).

Materials for the History of Thomas Becket, Archbishop of Canterbury, ed. J. C. Robertson and J. B. Sheppard, 7 vols., Rolls Series (London, 1875–85).

LE NEVE, J., *Fasti Ecclesiae Anglicanae, 1066–1300. iii. Lincoln*, compiled by D. E. Greenway (London, 1977).

Nigel de Longchamp's Speculum Stultorum, ed. J. H. Mozley and R. R. Raymo (Berkeley and Los Angeles, 1960).

Papsturkunden in England, ed. W. Holtzmann, 3 vols., Abhandlungen der Gesellschaft der Wissenschaften zu Göttingen, Phil.-Hist. Klasse. neue Folge, xxv. 1–2; Dritte Folge, 24–5; 33 (Berlin and Göttingen, 1930–52).

Peter Langtoft's Chronicle, ed. T. Hearne, 2 vols. (Oxford, 1725).

Pipe Rolls: *The Great Rolls of the Pipe, 5 Henry II to 14 Henry III*, 60 vols., Pipe Roll Society (1884–1976).

Les Plus Anciens Textes de Cîteaux, ed. J. Bouton and J.-B. van Damme, Cîteaux: Commentarii Cistercienses: Studia et Documenta, ii (1974).

The Political Songs of England, ed. T. Wright, Camden Society, 1 (1939).

POYNTON, E. M., ed., 'Charters relating to the Priory of Sempringham', *The Genealogist*, NS 15 (1899), 158–61, 221–7; 16 (1900), 30–5, 76–83, 153–8, 223–8; 17 (1901), 29–35, 164–8, 232–9.

'Records of Harrold Priory', ed. G. H. Fowler, *Publications of the Bedfordshire Historical Record Society*, 17 (1935).

Records of the Templars in England in the Twelfth Century: The Inquest of 1185, ed. B. A. Lees, British Academy Records of the Social and Economic History of England and Wales, 9 (1935).

Red Book of the Exchequer, ed. H. Hall, 3 vols., Rolls Series (London, 1896).

The Register of Bishop Repingdon 1405–19, ed. M. Archer, Lincoln Record Society, 57, 58, 74 (1963, 1982).

The Register of John le Romeyn, Lord Archbishop of York, 1284–1296 and of Henry of Newark, Lord Archbishop of York, 1296–1299, ed. W. Brown, 2 parts, Surtees Society, 123, 128 (1913, 1917).

The Register of Thomas of Corbridge, Lord Archbishop of York, 1300–1304, ed. W. Brown and A. H. Thompson, 2 parts, Surtees Society, 138, 141 (1925, 1928).

The Register of Walter Giffard, Lord Archbishop of York, 1266–79, ed. W. Brown, Surtees Society, 109 (1904).

The Register, or Rolls, of Walter Gray, Lord Archbishop of York, with Appendices of Illustrative Documents, ed. J. Raine, jun., Surtees Society, 56 (1872).

The Register of William Greenfield, Lord Archbishop of York, 1306–1315, ed. A. H. Thompson, 5 parts, Surtees Society, 145, 149, 151–3 (1925–40).

The Register of William Wickwane, Lord Archbishop of York, 1279–1285, ed. W. Brown, Surtees Society, 114 (1907).

The Registrum Antiquissimum of the Cathedral Church of Lincoln, ed. C. W. Foster and K. Major, 10 vols., Lincoln Record Society, 27–9, 32, 34, 41, 46, 51, 62, 67 (1931–73).

Registrum Monasterii de Passelet, Publications of the New Club, Paisley, 1 (1897).

Regularis Concordia Anglicae Nationis Monachorum Sanctimonialiumque, ed. and trans. T. Symons (London, 1953).

Roberti Grosseteste episcopi quondam Lincolnensis epistolae, ed. H. R. Luard, Rolls Series (London, 1861).

Rolls of the Justices in Eyre for Yorkshire, ed. D. M. Stenton, Selden Society, 56 (1937).

The Rolls and Register of Bishop Oliver Sutton, 1280–1299, ed. R. M. T. Hill, 8 vols., Lincoln Record Society 39, 43, 49, 52, 60, 64, 69, 76 (1948–86).

Rotuli Curiae Regis. Rolls and Records of the Court held before the King's Justiciars or Justices. 6 Richard I–I John, ed. F. Palgrave, Record Commission (London, 1835).

Rotuli de Dominabus et Pueris et Puellis de xii Comitatibus, ed. J. H. Round, Pipe Roll Society, 35 (1913).

Rotuli Hugonis de Welles Episcopi Lincolniensis (1209–35), ed. W. P. W. Phillimore and F. N. Davis, 3 vols., Lincoln Record Society, 3, 6, 9 (1912–14).

Rotuli Hundredorum, ed. W. Illingworth and J. Caley, 2 vols., Record Commission (London, 1812–18).

Rotuli Litterarum Clausarum, ed. T. D. Hardy, 2 vols., Record Commission (London, 1833).

Rotuli Ricardi Gravesend Diocesis Lincolniensis 1258–79, ed. F. N. Davis, C. W. Foster, and A. H. Thompson, Lincoln Record Society, 20 (1925).

Rotuli Roberti Grosseteste, Episcopi Lincolniensis 1235–53, ed. F. N. Davis, Lincoln Record Society, 11 (1914).

Rufford Charters, ed. C. J. Holdsworth, 4 vols., Thoroton Society Record Series, 29 (1972), 30 (1974), 32 (1980), 34 (1981).

RYMER, T., *Foedera, conventiones, literae et cujuscunque generis acta publica inter reges Angliae et alios quovis imperatores, reges, pontifices, principes, vel communitates*, 20 vols. (London, 1704–35).

Sancti Anselmi Opera Omnia, ed. F. S. Schmitt, 6 vols. (Edinburgh, 1946–61).

Scriptores Ordinis Grandimontensis, ed. J. Becquet, Corpus Christianorum: Continuatio Mediaevalis, 8 (Turnhout, 1968).

Some Sessions of the Peace in Lincolnshire, 1381–1396, ed. E. G. Kimball, Lincoln Record Society, 56 (1962).

The State of the Ex-Religious and Former Chantry Priests in the Diocese of Lincoln, 1547–1574, ed. G. A. J. Hodgett, Lincoln Record Society, 53 (1959).

Statutes of the Realm (1101–1713), ed. A. Luders *et al.*, 11 vols., Record Commission (London, 1810–28).

A Subsidy collected in the Diocese of Lincoln in 1526, ed. H. Salter, Oxford Historical Society, 63 (1913).

Taxatio Ecclesiastica Angliae et Walliae auctoritate P. Nicholai IV, circa AD 1291,
ed. T. Astle, S. Ayscough, and J. Caley, Record Commission (London, 1802).

The Taxation of 1297, ed. A. T. Gaydon, Publications of the Bedfordshire Historical Record Society, 39 (1959).

Testamenta Eboracensia, ed. J. Raine *et al.*, 6 vols., Surtees Society, 4 (1836), 30
(1855), 45 (1865), 53 (1869), 79 (1864), 106 (1902).

THOMPSON, A. H., 'The Chantry Certificate Rolls for the County of Nottingham',
Transactions of the Thoroton Society, 17 (1913), 18 (1914).

*Transcripts of Charters relating to the Gilbertine Houses of Sixle, Ormsby, Catley,
Bullington and Alvingham*, ed. and trans. F. M. Stenton, Lincoln Record
Society, 18 (1922).

Valor Ecclesiasticus temp. Henrici VIII, auctoritate Regis institutus, ed. J. Caley and
J. Hunter, 6 vols., Record Commission (London, 1810–34).

VERHEIJEN, L., *La Règle de Saint Augustin*, 2 vols. (Paris, 1967).

Visitations and Memorials of Southwell Minster, ed. A. F. Leach, Camden Society,
NS 48 (1891).

Vita Stephani Obazinensis, ed. M. Aubrun, Institut d'études du massif central,
fasc. VI (Clermont-Ferrand, 1970).

The Vita Wulfstani of William of Malmesbury, ed. R. R. Darlington, Camden
Society, 3rd ser. 40 (1928).

WAEFELGHEM, R. VAN, 'Les Premiers Statuts de l'ordre de Prémontré', *Analectes
de l'ordre de Prémontré*, 9 (1913), 1–74.

WATSON, G. W., 'Charters to Shouldham Priory', *The Genealogist*, NS 36 (1919–
20), 74–7.

WILLIAM OF NEWBURGH, *Historia Rerum Anglicarum*, in *Chronicles of the Reigns of
Stephen, Henry II and Richard I*, ed. R. Howlett, 4 vols., Rolls Series (London,
1884–9).

WRIGHT, T., *Letters relating to the Suppression of Monasteries*, Camden Society, 26
(1843).

*York Minster Fasti, being Notes on the Dignitaries, Archdeacons and Prebendaries in
the Church of York prior to the Year 1307*, ed. C. T. Clay, 2 vols., Yorkshire
Archaeological Society Record Series, 123, 124 (1957–8).

Yorkshire Inquisitions of the Reigns of Henry III and Edward I, vol. 1, ed. W.
Brown, Yorkshire Archaeological and Topographical Association Record Series, 12 (1891).

Yorkshire Deeds VI, ed. C. T. Clay, Yorkshire Archaeological Society Record
Series, 76 (1930).

Yorkshire Lay Subsidy (1301), ed. W. Brown, Yorkshire Archaeological Society
Record Series, 21 (1896).

Yorkshire Monasteries: Suppression Papers, ed. J. W. Clay, Yorkshire Archaeological Society Record Series, 48 (1912).

3. SECONDARY WORKS

ABBOTT, M., 'The Gant Family in England 1066–1191', Ph.D. thesis (Cambridge, 1973).

ADDLESHAW, G. W. O., *Rectors, Vicars and Patrons in Twelfth- and Early-Thirteenth-Century Canon Law*, St Anthony's Hall Publications, 9 (York, 1956).

AIGRAIN, R., *L'Hagiographie: ses sources, ses methodes, son histoire* (Paris, 1953).

ASTON, M., ed., *Medieval Fish, Fisheries and Fishponds in England*, 2 vols., British Archaeological Reports, British Series, 182 (1988).

BAKER, D., ed., *Medieval Women*, Studies in Church History, Subsidia 1 (Oxford, 1978).

BARLOW, F., *The English Church, 1066–1154* (London, 1979).

——*Thomas Becket* (London, 1986).

BARRIÈRE, B., *L'Abbaye cistercienne d'Obazine en Bas-Limouisin: les origines—le patrimoine* (Tulle, 1977).

BARROW, G. W. S., 'The Gilbertine House at Dalmilling', *Collection of the Ayrshire Archaeological and Natural History Society*, 2nd ser. 4 (1955–7), 50–67.

BATESON, M., 'Origin and Early History of Double Monasteries', *Transactions of the Royal Historical Society*, NS 13 (1899), 137–98.

BECQUET, J., 'La Première Crise de l'ordre de Grandmont', *Bulletin de la Société Archéologique et Historique du Limousin*, 87 (1960), 283–324.

BELL, D. N., ed., *The Libraries of the Cistercians, Gilbertines and Premonstratensians*, Corpus of British Medieval Library Catalogues, 3, British Library (London, 1992).

BERLIÈRE, U., 'Les Monastères doubles au 12ᵉ et 13ᵉ siècles', *Mémoires de l'Académie Royale des Sciences etc. de Belgique*, 2nd ser. 18 (Brussels, 1923), 1–32.

BERMAN, C. H., 'Men's Houses, Women's Houses: The Relationship between the Sexes in Twelfth-Century Monasticism', in A. Macleish (ed.), *Medieval Studies at Minnesota 2: The Medieval Monastery* (St Cloud, Minn., 1988), 43–52.

BINNS, A., *Dedication of Monastic Houses in England and Wales, 1066–1216* (Woodbridge, 1989).

BISCHOFF, J. P., 'Economic Change in 13th Century Lincoln: Decline of an Urban Cloth Industry', Ph.D. thesis (Yale University, 1975).

BISHOP, E., 'Some Ancient Benedictine Confraternity Books', in *Liturgica Historica: Papers on the Liturgy and Religious Life of the Western Church* (Oxford, 1918, repr. 1961), 349–61.

BISHOP, T. A. M., 'Monastic Granges in Yorkshire', *English Historical Review*, 51 (1936), 193–214.

BLOMEFIELD, F. B., and PARKIN, C., *An Essay towards a Topographical History of the County of Norfolk*, 11 vols. (London, 1805–10).

BOLTON, B., *The Medieval Reformation* (London, 1983).

——'Daughters of Rome: All One in Christ Jesus?', in W. J. Shiels and D. Wood (eds.), *Women in the Church*, Studies in Church History, 27 (Oxford, 1990), 101–15.

—— 'For the See of Simon Peter: The Cistercians at Innocent III's Nearest Frontier', in J. Loades (ed.), *Monastic Studies: The Continuity of Tradition* (Bangor, 1990), 146–57.

BOND, C. J., 'Monastic Fisheries', in M. Aston (ed.), *Medieval Fish, Fisheries and Fishponds in England*, 2 vols., British Archaeological Reports, British Series, 182 (1988), i. 69–112.

—— 'Water Management in the Rural Monastery', in R. Gilchrist and H. Mytum (eds.), *The Archaeology of Rural Monasteries*, British Archaeological Reports, British Series, 203 (1989), 83–111.

BRACELOND, L. C., 'Nuns in the Audience of Gilbert of Hoyland', in J. B. Sommerfeldt (ed.), *Simplicity and Ordinariness: Studies in Medieval Cistercian History IV*, Cistercian Studies, 61 (Kalamazoo, Mich., 1980), 139–69.

BRETT, M., *The English Church under Henry I* (Oxford, 1975).

BROOKE, C. N. L., 'Monk and Canon: Some Patterns in the Religious Life of the Twelfth Century', in W. J. Shiels (ed.), *Monks, Hermits and the Ascetic Tradition*, Studies in Church History, 22 (Oxford, 1985), 109–29.

—— 'The Archdeacon and the Norman Conquest', in D. Greenway, C. Holdsworth, and J. Sayers (eds.), *Tradition and Change: Essays in Honour of Marjorie Chibnall* (Cambridge, 1985), 1–20.

—— and KEIR, G., *London, 800–1216: The Shaping of a City* (London, 1975).

BUHOT, J, 'L'Abbaye normande de Savigny, chef de l'ordre et fille de Cîteaux', *Le Moyen Age*, 46 (1936), 1–19, 104–21, 178–90, 249–72.

BURGESS, C. R., 'A Service for the Dead: The Form and Function of the Anniversary in Late-Medieval Bristol', *Transactions of the Bristol and Gloucestershire Archaeological Society*, 105 (1987), 183–211.

BURTON, J. E., *The Yorkshire Nunneries in the Twelfth and Thirteenth Centuries*, Borthwick Papers, 56 (York, 1979).

—— 'Charters of Byland Abbey relating to the Grange of Bleatarn, Westmorland', *Transactions of the Cumberland and Westmorland Antiquarian and Archaeological Society*, 79 (1979), 29–50.

—— 'The Settlement of Disputes between Byland Abbey and Newburgh Priory', *Yorkshire Archaeological Journal*, 55 (1983), 67–72.

—— 'Monasteries and Parish Churches in Eleventh- and Twelfth-Century Yorkshire', *Northern History*, 23 (1987), 39–50.

BYNUM, C. W., *Docere Verbo et Exemplo: An Aspect of Twelfth-Century Spirituality*, Harvard Theological Studies, 31 (1979).

—— 'The Spirituality of Regular Canons in the Twelfth Century', in *Jesus as Mother: Studies in the Spirituality of the High Middle Ages* (Berkeley and Los Angeles, 1982), 22–58.

CARPENTER, D., 'Was there a Crisis of the Knightly Class in the Thirteenth Century? The Oxfordshire Evidence', *EHR* 95 (1980), 721–52.

CHAMBERS, C. G., and FOWLER, G. H., 'The Beauchamps, Barons of Bedford', *Publications of the Bedfordshire Historical Record Society*, 1 (1913), 3–25.

CHENEY, C. R., *Episcopal Visitations of Monasteries in the Thirteenth Century* (2nd edn., Manchester, 1983).

——'A Monastic Letter of Fraternity to Eleanor of Aquitaine', *English Historical Review*, 51 (1936), 488–93.

——'Master Philip the Notary and the Fortieth of 1199', *English Historical Review*, 63 (1948), 342–50.

——*From Becket to Langton: English Church Government 1170–1213* (Manchester, 1956).

——'Papal Privileges for Gilbertine Houses', in *Medieval Texts and Studies* (Oxford, 1973), 39–65.

CHIBNALL, M., 'Monks and Pastoral Work: A Problem in Anglo-Norman History', *Journal of Ecclesiastical History*, 18 (1967), 165–72.

CLANCHY, M., *From Memory to Written Record: England 1066–1307* (2nd edn., Oxford, 1993)

CLARK, C., 'Women's Names in Post-Conquest England: Observations and Speculations', *Speculum*, 53 (1978), 223–51.

CLARK-MAXWELL, W. G., 'Some Letters of Confraternity', *Archaeologia*, 2nd ser. 25 (1926), 19–60.

——'Some Further Letters of Confraternity', *Archaeologia*, 2nd ser. 29 (1929), 179–216.

CLAY, C. T., 'Notes on the Early Archdeacons in the Church of York', *Yorkshire Archaeological Journal*, 36 (1947), 269–87, 409–34.

——'The Family of Amundeville', *Lincolnshire Architectural and Archaeological Society Reports and Papers*, 3/2 (1948), 109–36.

——*York Minster Fasti: II*, Yorkshire Archaeological Society Record Series, 124 (1958).

——ed., *Early Yorkshire Families*, Yorkshire Archaeological Society Record Series, 135 (1973).

COKAYNE, G. E., *The Complete Peerage*, ed. V. Gibbs, H. A. Doubleday, *et al.*, 12 vols. (London, 1910–59).

COLE, R. E. G., 'The Priory of St Katherine without Lincoln of the Order of St Gilbert of Sempringham', *Lincolnshire Archaeological and Architectural Society Reports and Papers*, 27 (1904), 264–336.

COLVIN, H. M., *The White Canons in England* (Oxford, 1951).

CONSTABLE, G., 'Resistance to Tithes in the Middle Ages', *Journal of Ecclesiastical History*, 13 (1962), 172–85.

——*Monastic Tithes from their Origin to the Twelfth Century* (Cambridge, 1964).

——'Eremitical Forms of Monastic Life', in *Istituzioni monastiche e istituzioni canonicali in occidente (1123–1215)*, Miscellanea del Centro di Studi Medioevali, 9 (Milan, 1980), 239–64.

——'Monastic Possession of Churches and "Spiritualia" in the Age of Reform', in *Il Monachismo e la Riforma Ecclesiastica (1049–1122)*, Miscellanea del Centro di Studi Medioevali, 6 (Milan, 1971), 304–31.

——'Aelred of Rievaulx and the Nun of Watton: An Episode in the Early History of the Gilbertine Order' in D. Baker (ed.), *Medieval Women*, 205–26.

Coss, P. R., 'Sir Geoffrey de Langley and the Crisis of the Knightly Class in Thirteenth-Century England', *Past and Present*, 68 (1975), 3–37.

Coulton, G. G., *Five Centuries of Religion*, 4 vols. (Cambridge, 1923–50).

——*Medieval Panorama: The English Scene from Conquest to Reformation* (Cambridge, Mass., 1938).

Crosby, R., 'Robert Mannyng of Brunne: A New Biography', *Publications of the Modern Language Association of America*, 57 (1942), 15–28.

Currie, C. K., 'The Role of Fishponds in the Monastic Economy', in R. Gilchrist and H. Mytum (eds)., *The Archaeology of Rural Monasteries*, British Archaeological Reports, British Series, 203 (1989), 147–72.

Darby, H. C., *The Domesday Geography of Eastern England* (3rd edn., Cambridge, 1971).

Davis, G. R. C., *Medieval Cartularies of Great Britain: A Short Catalogue* (London, 1958).

Davis, R. H. C., 'Goltho: The Manorial History', in G. Beresford, *Goltho: The Development of an Early Medieval Manor, c.850–1150*, English Heritage Archaeological Report, 4 (1987), 127–30.

DE FONTETTE, M., *Les Religieuses à l'âge classique de droit canon: recherches sur les structures juridiques des branches féminines des ordres*, Bibliothèque de la Société d'Histoire Ecclésiastique de la France, 28 (Paris, 1967).

DE LA MARE, A., *Catalogue of the Collection of Medieval Manuscripts bequeathed to the Bodleian Library Oxford by James P. R. Lyell* (Oxford, 1971).

Delooz, P., 'Towards a Sociological Study of Canonised Sainthood in the Catholic Church', in S. Wilson (ed.), *Saints and their Cults: Studies in Religious Sociology. Folklore and History* (Cambridge, 1983), 189–216.

Denholm-Young, N., and Craster, H. H. E., 'Roger Dodsworth (1585–1654) and his Circle', *Yorkshire Archaeological Journal*, 32 (1936), 5–32.

Dereine, C., 'Les Origines de Prémontré', *Revue d'Histoire Ecclésiastique*, 42 (1947), 352–78.

Dickinson, J. C., *The Origins of the Austin Canons and their Introduction into England* (London, 1950).

Dobson, R. B., 'The Last English Monks on Scottish Soil', *Scottish Historical Review*, 46 (1967), 1–25.

——*Durham Priory, 1400–1450* (Cambridge, 1973).

——and Donaghey, S., *The History of Clementhorpe Nunnery*, The Archaeology of York, vol. 2: Historical Sources for York Archaeology after AD 1100, fasc. 1 (York, 1984).

Donkin, R. A., *The Cistercians: Studies in the Geography of Medieval England and Wales* (Toronto, 1978).

Donnelly, J. S., *The Decline of the Medieval Cistercian Laybrotherhood*, Fordham University Studies, History Series, 3 (New York, 1949).

——'Changes in the Grange Economy of English and Welsh Cistercian Abbeys, 1300–1540', *Traditio*, 10 (1954), 399–458.

DUBOIS, J., 'L'Institution monastique des convers', in *I laici nella 'societas christiana' dei secoli XI e XII*, Miscellanea del Centro di Studi Medioevali, 5 (Milan, 1968), 183–261.

DYSON, A. G., 'The Career, Family and Influence of Alexander le Poer, Bishop of Lincoln', B.Litt. thesis (Oxford University, 1971).

——'The Monastic Patronage of Bishop Alexander of Lincoln', *Journal of Ecclesiastical History*, 26 (1975), 1–24.

EDWARDS, J., 'The Order of Sempringham, and its Connexion with the West of Scotland', *Transactions of the Glasgow Archaeological Society*, NS 5 (1908), 67–95.

ELKINS, S., 'All Ages, Every Condition, and Both Sexes: The Emergence of a Gilbertine Identity', in J. A. Nichols and L. T. Shank (eds.), *Medieval Religious Women. I. Distant Echoes*, 169–82.

——*Holy Women of Twelfth-Century England* (Chapel Hill, NC, 1988).

EMDEN, A. B., *A Biographical Register of the University of Oxford to AD 1500*, 3 vols. (Oxford, 1957–9).

EMERY, R. W., 'The Friars of the Sack', *Speculum*, 18 (1943), 23–34.

ENGLISH, B., *The Lords of Holderness, 1086–1260: A Study in Feudal Society* (Oxford, 1979).

ERENS, A., 'Les Sœurs dans l'ordre de Prémontré', *Analecta Praemonstratensia*, 5 (1929). 5–26.

EYTON, R. W., *Court, Household and Itinerary of Henry II* (London, 1878).

FARRER, W., *Honors and Knights' Fees*, 3 vols. (London and Manchester, 1923–5).

FEISS, H., '*Circatores*: From Benedict of Nursia to Humbert of Romans', *American Benedictine Review*, 40 (1989), 346–79.

FOREVILLE, R., *Un procès de canonisation à l'aube du XIIIᵉ siècle (1201–1202). Le Livre de saint Gilbert de Sempringham* (Paris, 1943).

——'La Crise de l'ordre de Sempringham au XIIᵉ siècle: nouvelle approche du dossier des frères lais', *Anglo-Norman Studies 6 (1983)*, ed. R. A. Brown (Woodbridge, 1984), 39–57.

——'Canterbury et la canonisation des saints', in D. Greenway, C. Holdsworth, and J. Sayers (eds.), *Tradition and Change: Essays in Honour of Marjorie Chibnall* (Cambridge, 1985), 63–76.

FOWLER, G. H., 'Domesday Notes', *Publications of the Bedfordshire Historical Record Society*, 1 (1913).

FRANKLAND, E. P., 'Explorations in Ravenstonedale', *Transactions of the Cumberland and Westmorland Antiquarian and Archaeological Society*, NS 29 (1929), 278–92; NS 30 (1930), 144–8.

FREDEMAN, J. C., 'John Capgrave's Life of St Gilbert of Sempringham', *Bulletin of the John Rylands Library*, 55 (1972–3), 112–45.

GALBRAITH, V. H., 'Monastic Foundation Charters of the Eleventh and Twelfth Centuries', *Cambridge Historical Journal*, 4 (1934), 205–22, 296–8.

GILCHRIST, R., 'The Archaeology of Medieval English Nunneries: A Research

Design', in R. Gilchrist and H. Mytum (eds.), *The Archaeology of Rural Monasteries*, British Archaeological Reports, British Series, 203 (1989), 251–60.

——*Gender and Material Culture: The Archaeology of Religious Women* (London, 1994).

GILYARD-BEER, R., and COPPACK, G., 'Excavations at Fountains Abbey, North Yorkshire, 1979–80: The Early Development of the Monastery', *Archaeologia*, 108 (1986), 147–88.

GODFREY, J., 'The Double Monastery in Early English History', *Ampleforth Journal*, 79 (1974), 19–32.

GOERING, J., *William de Montibus (c.1140–1213): The Schools and the Literature of Pastoral Care*, Pontifical Institute of Mediaeval Studies, Toronto, Studies and Texts, 108 (1992).

GOLD, P. S., *The Lady and the Virgin: Image, Attitude and Experience in Twelfth-Century France* (Chicago, 1985).

GOLDING, B. J., 'St Bernard and St Gilbert', in B. Ward (ed.), *The Influence of St Bernard* (Oxford, 1976), 42–54.

——'The Gilbertine Priories of Alvingham and Bullington: Their Endowments and Benefactors', D.Phil., thesis (Oxford University, 1979).

——'The Coming of the Cluniacs', *Proceedings of the Battle Conference on Anglo-Norman Studies 3 (1980)*, ed. R. A. Brown (Woodbridge, 1981), 65–77.

——'Simon of Kyme: The Making of a Rebel', *Nottingham Medieval Studies*, 27 (1983), 23–36.

——'Burials and Benefactions: An Aspect of Monastic Patronage in Thirteenth-Century England', in W. M. Ormrod (ed.), *England in the Thirteenth Century: Proceedings of the 1984 Harlaxton Symposium* (Harlaxton, 1985), 64–75.

——'Anglo-Norman Knightly Burials', in C. Harper-Bill and R. Harvey (eds.), *The Ideals and Practice of Medieval Knighthood* (Woodbridge, 1986), 35–48.

——'The Distortion of a Dream: Transformations and Mutations of the Rule of St Gilbert', *Word and Spirit*, 11 (1989), 60–79.

——'Hermits, Monks and Women in Twelfth-Century France and England: The Experience of Obazine and Sempringham', in J. Loades (ed.), *Monastic Studies: The Continuity of Tradition* (Bangor, 1990), 127–45.

GOUGAUD, L., 'Deathbed Clothing with the Religious Habit', in *Devotional and Ascetic Practices in the Middle Ages* (London, 1927), 131–45.

GRAHAM, R., *St Gilbert of Sempringham and the Gilbertines* (London, 1901).

——'The Taxation of Pope Nicholas IV', *English Historical Review*, 23 (1908), 434–54.

——'The Finances of Malton Priory, 1244–1257', in *English Ecclesiastical Studies* (London, 1929), 247–70.

——and BRAUN, H., 'Excavations on the Site of Sempringham Priory', *Journal of the British Archaeological Association*, NS 5 (1940), 73–101.

GRAVES, C. V., 'The Economic Activities of the Cistercians in Medieval England (1128–1307)', *Analecta Sacri Ordinis Cisterciensis*, 13 (1957), 3–60.

478   *Bibliography*

——'English Cistercian Nuns in Lincolnshire', *Speculum*, 54 (1979), 492–9.
——'The Organization of an English Cistercian Nunnery in Lincolnshire', *Cîteaux*, 33 (1982), 331–50.
——'Stixwould in the Market Place', in J. A. Nichols and L. T. Shank (eds.), *Medieval Religious Women. I. Distant Echoes*, 213–36.
GREEN, J. A., *The Government of England under Henry I* (Cambridge, 1986).
GREENE, J. P., *Norton Priory: The Archaeology of a Medieval Religious House* (Cambridge, 1989).
D'HAENENS, A., 'Quotidienneté et contexte: pour un modèle d'interpretation de la realité monastique mediévale (xɪᵉ–xɪɪᵉ siècles)', in *Istituzioni monastiche e istituzioni canonicali in occidente (1123–1215)*, Miscellanea del Centro di Studi Medioevali, 9 (Milan, 1980), 567–97.
HALLAM, E. M., 'Henry II as a Founder of Monasteries', *Journal of Ecclesiastical History*, 28 (1977), 113–32.
HALLAM, H. E., 'Salt-Making in the Lincolnshire Fenland during the Middle Ages', *Lincolnshire Architectural and Archaeological Reports and Papers*, NS 8 (1960), 85–112.
HALLINGER, K., 'Woher kommen die Laienbrüder?', *Analecta Sacri Ordinis Cisterciensis*, 12 (1956), 1–104.
HARPER-BILL, C., 'Monastic Apostasy in Late Medieval England', *Journal of Ecclesiastical History*, 32 (1981), 1–18.
——'Bishop William Turbe and the Diocese of Norwich, 1146–1174', in *Anglo-Norman Studies 7 (1984)*, ed. R. A. Brown (Woodbridge, 1985), 147–9.
HARTRIDGE, R. A. R., *A History of Vicarages in the Middle Ages* (Cambridge, 1930).
HARVEY, B. F., *Westminster Abbey and its Estates in the Middle Ages* (Oxford, 1977).
HEAD, T., *Hagiography and the Cult of Saints: The Diocese of Orleans, 800–1200* (Cambridge, 1990).
——'The Marriages of Christina of Markyate', *Viator*, 21 (1990), 75–101.
HEALEY, R. H., 'Medieval Salt-Making', South Lincolnshire Archaeology, 1 (1977), 4–5.
HENMAN, W. N., 'Newnham Priory: A Bedford Rental, 1506–7', *Publications of the Bedfordshire Historical Record Society*, 25 (1943), 15–81.
HERBERT, J., 'The Transformation of Hermitages into Augustinian Priories in Twelfth-Century England', in W. J. Sheils, (ed.), *Monks, Hermits and the Ascetic Tradition*, Studies in Church History, 22 (Oxford, 1985), 131–45.
HICKS, M., 'Chantries, Obits and Almshouses: The Hungerford Foundations, 1325–1478', in C. M. Barron and C. Harper-Bill (eds.), *The Church in Pre-Reformation Society* (Woodbridge, 1985), 123–42.
HILL, B. D., *English Cistercian Monasteries and their Patrons in the Twelfth Century* (Chicago and London, 1968).
HILL, G. W. F., *Medieval Lincoln* (Cambridge, 1948).
HILL, M. C., *The King's Messengers, 1199–1377* (London, 1961).

HILTON, R. H., *A Medieval Society: The West Midlands at the End of the Thirteenth Century* (Cambridge, 1983).

HOLDSWORTH, C. J., 'John of Ford and English Cistercian Writing, 1167–1214', *Transactions of the Royal Historical Society*, 5th ser. 11 (1961), 117–36.

—— 'The Blessings of Work: The Cistercian View', in D. Baker (ed.), *Sanctity and Secularity: The Church and the World*, Studies in Church History, 10 (Oxford, 1973), 59–76.

—— 'Christina of Markyate', in D. Baker (ed.), *Medieval Women*, 185–204.

HOLT, R., *The Mills of Medieval England* (Oxford, 1988).

HONEYBOURNE, M. B., 'The Extent and Value of the Property in London and Southwark occupied by the Religious Houses (including the Prebends of St Paul's and St Martin's le Grand), the Inns of the Bishops and Abbots, and the Churches and Churchyards before the Dissolution of the Monasteries', MA thesis (London University, 1929).

An Inventory of the Historical Monuments in Westmorland, Royal Commission on Historical Monuments, England (London, 1936).

IOGNA-PRAT, D., 'La Femme dans la perspective pénitentielle des ermites du Bas-Maine (fin XIᵉ–début XIIᵉ siècle)', *Revue d'histoire de la spiritualité*, 53 (1977), 47–64.

JAMES, M. R., 'The Salomites', *Journal of Theological Studies*, 35 (1934), 287–97.

JOHNSON, P. D., *Prayer, Patronage and Power: The Abbey of La Trinité, Vendôme, 1032–1187* (New York, 1981).

—— *Equal in Monastic Profession* (Chicago, 1991).

KEEN, M., *The Outlaws of Medieval Legend* (2nd edn., London, 1987).

KEMP, B. R., 'Monastic Possession of Parish Churches in England in the Twelfth Century', *Journal of Ecclesiastical History*, 31 (1980), 133–60.

KEMP, E. W., *Canonization and Authority in the Western Church* (Oxford, 1948).

KEMP, R. L., *The Church and Gilbertine Priory of St Andrew, Fishergate*, The Archaeology of York, vol. II: Historical Sources for York Archaeology after AD 1100, fasc. 2 (York, forthcoming).

KER, N. R., *English Manuscripts in the Century after the Norman Conquest* (Oxford, 1960).

—— 'Mortuary Briefs', in *Miscellany I*, Worcestershire Historical Society (1960), 53–9.

—— *Medieval Libraries of Great Britain: A List of Surviving Books* (2nd edn., London, 1964).

KIMBALL, E., 'Tenure in Frank Almoign and Secular Services', *English Historical Review*, 43 (1928), 314–53.

—— 'The Judicial Aspects of Frank Almoign Tenure', *English Historical Review*, 47 (1932), 1–11.

KING, E., *Peterborough Abbey, 1086–1310* (Cambridge, 1973).

KNOWLES, M. D., 'The Revolt of the Lay Brothers of Sempringham', *English Historical Review*, 50 (1935), 465–87.

——*The Monastic Order in England* (2nd edn., Cambridge, 1963).

——*From Pachomius to Ignatius* (Oxford, 1966).

——and ST JOSEPH, J. K. S., *Monastic Sites from the Air* (Cambridge, 1952).

——and NEVILLE HADCOCK, R., *Medieval Religious Houses: England and Wales* (2nd edn., London, 1971).

——BROOKE, C. N. L., and LONDON, V. C. M., eds., *The Heads of Religious Houses: England and Wales, 940–1216* (Cambridge, 1972).

KOUDELKA, V. J., 'Le *Monasterium* Tempuli et la fondation dominicaine de S. Sisto', *Archivum Fratrum Praedicatorum*, 31 (1961), 5–81.

L' ANSON, W., 'Kilton Castle', *Yorkshire Archaeological Journal*, 22 (1913), 55–125.

LAWLESS, G., *Augustine of Hippo and his Monastic Rule* (Oxford, 1987).

LAWRENCE, C. H., *Medieval Monasticism* (London, 1984).

LECLERCQ, J., 'Comment vivaient les frères convers', in *I laici nella 'societas christiana' dei secoli XI e XII*, Miscellanea del Centro di Studi Medioevali, 5 (Milan, 1968), 152–81.

LEES, J. Cameron, *The Abbey of Paisley from its Foundation till its Dissolution* (Paisley, 1878).

LEFÈVRE, J., 'Les Traditions manuscrites des "Usus Conversorum" de Cîteaux', *Collectanea Ordinis Cisterciensium Reformatorum*, 17 (1955), 11–39.

——'L'Évolution des "Usus Conversorum" de Cîteaux', ibid. 65–97.

LEGGE, M. D., 'Pierre de Peckham and his "Lumiere as lais" ', *Modern Language Review*, 24 (1929), 37–40.

——' "La Livere as Lais"—a Postscript', *Modern Language Review*, 46 (1951), 191–5.

——*Anglo-Norman Literature and its Background* (Oxford, 1963).

LEYSER, H., *Hermits and the New Monasticism: A Study of Religious Communities in Western Europe, 1000–1150* (London, 1984).

LEYSER, K., 'The Angevin Kings and the Holy Man', in H. Mayr-Harting (ed.), *St Hugh of Lincoln* (Oxford, 1987), 49–73.

LIDDELL, J. R., ' "Leland's" Lists of Manuscripts in Lincolnshire Monasteries', *English Historical Review*, 54 (1939), 88–95.

LITTLE, L. K., *Religious Poverty and the Profit Economy in Medieval Europe* (London, 1978).

LLOYD, S., *English Society and the Crusade, 1216–1307* (Oxford, 1988).

LLOYD, T. H., *The English Wool Trade in the Middle Ages* (Cambridge, 1977).

LOBEL, M. D., *Historic Towns: Cambridge* (London, 1974).

LOYD, L. C., *The Origins of some Anglo-Norman Families*, ed. D. C. Douglas and C. T. Clay, Harleian Society, 103 (1951).

LUNT, W. E., *The Valuation of Norwich* (Oxford, 1926).

LYNCH, J. H., 'The Cistercians and Under-Age Novices', *Cîteaux* 24 (1973), 283–97.

——'Monastic Recruitment in the Eleventh and Twelfth Centuries: Some Social and Economic Considerations', *American Benedictine Review*, 26 (1975), 425–47.

——*Simoniacal Entry into Religious Life, 1000–1260: A Social, Economic and Legal Study* (Columbus, Ohio, 1976).

McCRANK, L. J., 'The Frontier of the Spanish Reconquest and the Land Acquisitions of the Cistercians of Poblet 1150–1276', *Analecta Cisterciensia*, 29 (1973), 57–78.

McHARDY, A. K., 'The Crown and the Diocese of Lincoln during the Episcopate of John Buckingham, 1363–98', D.Phil. thesis (Oxford University, 1971).

MASON, E., *St Wulfstan of Worcester, c.1008–1095* (Oxford, 1990).

MATTHEW, D., *The Norman Monasteries and their English Possessions* (Oxford, 1962).

MAYR-HARTING, H., 'Functions of a Twelfth-Century Recluse', *History* 60 (1975), 337–52.

MILIS, L. M., *L'Ordre des chanoines réguliers d'Arrouaise. Son histoire et son organisation de la fondation de l'abbaye-mère (vers 1090) à la fin des chapîtres annuels (1471)*, 2 vols. (Bruges, 1969).

——'Ermites et chanoines réguliers au XII\u1D49 siècle', *Cahiers de Civilisation Médiévale*, 22 (1979), 39–80.

——'L'Évolution de l'érémitisme au canonicat régulier dans la première moitié du douzième siècle: transition ou trahison', in *Istituzioni monastiche e istituzioni canonicali in occidente (1123–1215)*, Miscellanea del Centro di Studi Medioevali, 9 (Milan, 1980), 223–8.

MILLETT, E. N., 'Women in No Man's Land: English Recluses and the Development of Vernacular Literature in the Twelfth and Thirteenth Centuries', in C. M. Meale (ed.), *Women and Literature in Britain, c.1150–1500* (Cambridge, 1993), 86–103.

MOLLAT, G., 'La Restitution des églises privés au patrimoine ecclésiastique en France du IX\u1D49 au XI\u1D49 siècle', *Revue Historique de Droit Français et Étranger*, 4th ser. 27 (1949), 399–423.

MOORHOUSE, S., 'Monastic Estates: Their Composition and Development', in R. Gilchrist and H. Mytum (eds.), *The Archaeology of Rural Monasteries*, British Archaeological Association Reports, British Series, 203 (1989), 29–82.

MOORMAN, J. R. H., *Church Life in England in the Thirteenth Century* (Cambridge, 1945).

MORRIS, C., *The Papal Monarchy: The Western Church from 1050 to 1250* (Oxford, 1990).

MURRAY, A., *Reason and Society in the Middle Ages* (Oxford, 1978).

NEEL, C., 'The Origins of the Beguines', in J. M. Bennett, E. A. Clark, J. F. O'Barr, B. A. Vilen, and S. Westphal-Wihl (eds.), *Sisters and Workers in the Midde Ages* (Chicago, 1989), 240–60.

NEWMAN, C. A., *The Anglo-Norman Nobility in the Reign of Henry I: The Second Generation* (Philadelphia, 1988).

NEWMAN, J. E., 'Greater and Lesser Landowners and Parochial Patronage: Yorkshire in the Thirteenth Century', *English Historical Review*, 92 (1977), 280–308.

NICHOL, A., 'Changes in the Assize Utrum between the Constitutions of Clarendon and Bracton', in R. F. Hunnisett and J. B. Post (eds.), *Medieval Legal Records edited in Memory of C. A. F. Meekings*, HMSO (London, 1978), 18–25.

NICHOLS, J., *The History and Antiquities of the County of Leicestershire*, 4 vols. (London. 1795–1811).

NICHOLS, J. A., 'The Architectural and Physical Features of an English Cistercian Nunnery', in J. R. Sommerfeldt (ed.), *Cistercian Ideals and Reality*, Cistercian Studies, 60 (Kalamazoo, Mich., 1978), 319–28.

——'The Internal Organisation of English Cistercian Nunneries', *Cîteaux*, 30 (1979), 23–40.

——and SHANK, L. T. (eds.), *Medieval Religious Women. I. Distant Echoes*, Cistercian Studies, 71 (Kalamazoo, Mich., 1984).

NICHOLSON, J., and BURN, R., *The History and Antiquities of the Counties of Westmorland and Cumberland*, 2 vols. (London, 1777).

NORTON, C., and PARK, D. (eds.), *Cistercian Art and Architecture in the British Isles* (Cambridge 1986).

ORME, N., *English Schools in the Middle Ages* (London, 1973).

OWEN, A. E. B., 'Salt, Sea Banks and Medieval Settlement on the Lindsey Coast', in N. Field and A. White (eds.), *A Prospect of Lincolnshire* (Lincoln, 1984), 46–9.

OWEN, D. M., *Church and Society in Medieval Lincolnshire*, History of Lincolnshire, 5 (Lincoln, 1971).

——'The Beginnings of the Port of Boston', in N. Field, and A. White (eds.), *A Prospect of Lincolnshire* (Lincoln, 1984), 42–5.

PÄCHT, O., and ALEXANDER, J. J. G., *Illuminated Manuscripts in the Bodleian Library. 3. British, Irish and Icelandic Schools* (Oxford, 1973).

PAINTER, S., *The Reign of King John* (Baltimore, 1949).

PARISSE, M., *Les Nonnes au Moyen Âge* (Le Puy, 1983).

PEVSNER, N., *Northamptonshire* (2nd end., rev. B. Cherry, Harmondsworth, 1973).

PLATT, C., *The Monastic Grange in Medieval England: A Reassessment* (London, 1969).

PLATTS, G., *Land and People in Medieval Lincolnshire*, History of Lincolnshire, 4 (Lincoln, 1985).

POLLOCK, F., and MAITLAND, F. W., *The History of English Law*, 2 vols. (2nd edn., Cambridge, 1968).

POWER, E., *Medieval English Nunneries c.1275–1535* (Cambridge, 1922).

RABAN, S., *The Estates of Thorney and Crowland: A Study in Medieval Monastic Land Tenure* (Cambridge, 1977).

——*Mortmain Legislation and the English Church* (Cambridge, 1982).

——'The Land Market and the Aristocracy', in D. Greenway, C. Holdsworth, and J. Sayers, (eds.), *Tradition and Change: Essays in Honour of Marjorie Chibnall* (Cambridge, 1985), 239–62.

RICHARDS, P., *The Medieval Leper and his Northern Heirs* (Cambridge, Mass., 1977).

RICHARDSON, H. G., *The English Jewry under Angevin Kings* (London, 1960).

ROBINSON, D. M., *The Geography of Augustinian Settlement*, 2 vols., British Archaeological Reports, British Series, 80 (1980).

ROFFE, D., 'Pre-Conquest Estates and Parish Boundaries: A Discussion with Examples from Lincolnshire', in M. L. Faull (ed.), *Studies in Late Anglo-Saxon Settlement* (Oxford, 1984), 115–22.

ROGERS, A., *The Making of Stanford* (Leicester, 1965).

ROISIN, S., 'L'Efflorescence Cistercienne et le courant féminin de piété au treizième siècle', *Revue d'Histoire Ecclésiastique*, 39 (1943), 342–78.

RUBIN, M., *Charity and Community in Medieval Cambridge* (Cambridge, 1987).

RUDKIN, E. H., and OWEN, D. M., 'The Medieval Salt Industry in the Lindsey Marshland', *Lincolnshire Architectural and Archaeological Society Reports and Papers*, NS 8 (1960), 76–84.

RUSSELL, J. C., 'The Clerical Population of Medieval England', *Traditio*, 2 (1944), 177–212.

RUSHTON, J. H., 'Scarborough, 1166–1266', in M. Edwards (ed.), *Scarborough, 966–1966*, Scarborough and District Archaeological Society (1966), 25–32.

ST JOHN HOPE, W. H., 'The Gilbertine Priory of Watton, in the East Riding of Yorkshire', *Archaeological Journal*, 58 (1901), 1–34.

SANDERS, I. J., *Feudal Military Service in England: A Study of the Constitutional and Military Powers of the 'Barones' in Medieval England* (Oxford, 1956).

——*English Baronies: A Study of their Origin and Descent, 1086–1327* (Oxford, 1960).

SANDLER, L. F., *The Psalter of Robert de Lisle in the British Library* (London, 1983).

SAUL, N., 'The Religious Sympathies of the Gentry in Gloucestershire, 1200–1500', *Transactions of the Bristol and Gloucester Archaeological Society*, 98 (1980), 99–112.

SAVINE, A., *English Monasteries on the Eve of the Dissolution* (Oxford, 1909).

SAYERS, J., 'Violence in the Medieval Cloister', *Journal of Ecclesiastical History*, 41 (1990), 533–42.

SCHMITT, J. C., 'La Fabrique des saints', *Annales: Economies, Sociétés, Civilisations*, 39 (1984), 286–300.

SCHMITZ, P., *Histoire de l'Ordre de Saint-Benoit*, 7 vols. (Gembloux, 1942–56).

SEATON, E., 'Robert Mannyng of Brunne in Lincoln', *Medium Aevum*, 12 (1943), 77.

SMITH, D., 'The Rolls of Hugh of Wells, Bishop of Lincoln, 1209–35', *Bulletin of the Institute of Historical Research*, 45 (1972), 155–95.

SMITH, J., 'Robert of Arbrissel: *Procurator Mulierum*', in D. Baker (ed.), *Medieval Women*, 175–84.

SOUTHERN, R. W., *Western Society and the Church in the Middle Ages* (Harmondsworth, 1970).

——*Robert Grosseteste: The Growth of an English Mind in Medieval Europe* (Oxford, 1986).

SPUFFORD, M., *A Cambridgeshire Community: Chippenham from Settlement to Enclosure*, Local History Occasional Papers, 20 (Leicester, 1965).

STENTON, F. M., *Types of Manorial Structure in the Northern Danelaw* (Oxford, 1910).

——*The Free Peasantry of the Northern Danelaw* (Oxford, 1969).

STOKES, H. P., *Outside the Trumpington Gate before Peterhouse was Founded*, Cambridge Antiquarian Society, 44 (1908).

STRINGER, K. J., *Earl David of Huntingdon, 1152–1219* (Edinburgh, 1985).

TAIT, J., 'The Foundation Charter of Runcorn (later Norton) Priory', *Chetham Society Miscellany*, NS 100 (1939), 1–26.

TANNER, T., *Notitia Monastica: An Account of All Abbeys, etc. in England and Wales*, repr. J. Nasmith, (Cambridge, 1787).

THIRSK, J., *English Peasant Farming* (London, 1967).

THOMSON, R. M., 'Twelfth-Century Documents from Bury St Edmund's Abbey', *English Historical Review*, 92 (1977), 806–19.

——*Catalogue of the Manuscripts of Lincoln Cathedral Chapter Library* (Woodbridge, 1989).

THOMPSON, A. H., 'Double Monasteries and the Male Element in Nunneries', in *The Ministry of Women: A Report by a Committee Appointed by his Grace the Lord Archbishop of Canterbury* (London, 1919), app. viii. 145–64.

——'A Corrody from Leicester Abbey, AD 1393–4, with some Notes on Corrodies', *Leicestershire Archaeological Society Transactions*, 14 (1926), 114–34.

——*The Praemonstratensian Abbey of Welbeck* (London, 1938).

THOMPSON, S. P., 'Why English Nunneries had no History: A Study of the Problems of English Nunneries founded after the Conquest', in J. A. Nichols and L. T. Shank (eds.), *Medieval Religious Women. I. Distant Echoes*, 131–49.

——'The Problem of the Cistercian Nuns in the Twelfth and Early Thirteenth Centuries', in D. Baker (ed.), *Medieval Women*, 227–52.

——'English Nunneries: A study of the Post-Conquest Foundations, *c*.1095–*c*.1250', Ph.D. thesis (London, 1985).

——*Women Religious: The Founding of English Nunneries after the Norman Conquest* (Oxford, 1991).

TILLOTSON, J. H., 'Pensions, Corrodies, and Religious Houses: An Aspect of the Relations of Crown and Church in Early Fourteenth-Century England', *Journal of Religious History*, 8 (1974), 127–43.

——*Marrick Priory: A Nunnery in Late-Medieval Yorkshire*, Borthwick Papers, 75 (York, 1989).

TURNER, R. V., *Men Raised from the Dust: Administrative Service and Upward Mobility in Angevin England* (Philadelphia, 1988).

TYERMAN, C., *England and the Crusades, 1095–1588* (Chicago, 1988).

VALE, M. G. A., *Piety, Charity and Literacy among the Yorkshire Gentry, 1370–1480*, Borthwick Papers, 50 (York, 1976).

VAN DAMME, J.-B., 'La "Summa Cartae Caritatis": source de constitutions canoniales', *Cîteaux*, 23 (1972), 6–9.

VAN ENGEN, J., 'The "Crisis of Cenobitism" Reconsidered: Benedictine Monasticism in the Years 1050–1150', *Speculum*, 61 (1986), 269–304.

VAN WAEFELGHEM, R., 'Les Premiers Statuts de l'ordre de Prémontré', *Analectes de l'Ordre de Prémontré*, 9 (1913), 1–74.

Victoria History of the County of Bedfordshire, vol. ii, ed. W. Page (London, 1908).

Victoria History of the County of Buckinghamshire, vols. ii–iv, ed. W. Page (London, 1908–27).

Victoria History of the County of Cambridgeshire, vols. ii, iii, ed. H. C. Darby *et al.* (London, 1948, 1959).

Victoria History of the County of Durham, vol. iii, ed. W. Page (London, 1928).

Victoria History of the County of Lincolnshire, vol. ii, ed. W. Page (London, 1906).

Victoria History of the County of Nottinghamshire, vol. ii, ed. W. Page (London, 1910).

Victoria History of the County of Oxfordshire, vol. x, ed. A. Crossley (London, 1972).

Victoria History of the County of Rutland, vol. ii, ed. W. Page (London, 1935).

Victoria History of the County of Wiltshire, vol. iii, ed. R. B. Pugh and E. Crittall (London, 1956).

Victoria History of the County of Wiltshire, vol xii, ed. D. A. Crowley (London, 1983).

Victoria History of the County of York, vol. ii, ed. W. Farrer (London, 1912).

Victoria History of the County of York, vol iii, ed. W. Page (London, 1913).

Victoria History of the County of York: North Riding, vol, i, ed. W. Page (1914).

WAITES, B., 'The Monasteries and the Development of North-East Yorkshire', MA thesis (London University, 1958).

——'The Monastic Settlement of North-East Yorkshire', *Yorkshire Archaeological Journal*, 40 (1959–62), 478–95.

——'The Monastic Grange as a Factor in the Settlement of North-East Yorkshire', *Yorkshire Archaeological Journal*, 40 (1959–62), 627–56.

——*Moorland and Vale-Land Farming in North-East Yorkshire: The Monastic Contribution in the Thirteenth and Fourteenth Centuries*, Borthwick Papers, 32 (York, 1967).

——'The Monasteries of North-East Yorkshire and the Medieval Wool Trade', *Yorkshire Archaeological Journal*, 52 (1980), 111–21.

WALES, C. J., 'The Knight in Twelfth-Century Lincolnshire', Ph.D. thesis (Cambridge, 1983).

WARD, B., *Miracles and the Medieval Mind* (London, 1982).

WARD, J., 'Fashions in Monastic Endowment: The Foundations of the Clare Family, 1066–1314', *Journal of Ecclesiastical History*, 32 (1981), 427–51.

WARDROP, J., *Fountains Abbey and its Benefactors, 1132–1300*, Cistercian Publications, 91 (Kalamazoo, Mich., 1987).

WARREN, A. K., *Anchorites and their Patrons in Medieval England* (Berkeley and Los Angeles, 1985).

——'The Nun as Anchoress: England 1100–1500', in J. A. Nichols and L. T. Shank (eds.), *Medieval Religious Women. I. Distant Echoes*, 197–212.

WARREN, W. L., *King John* (London, 1961).

WATSON, A. G., *The Manuscripts of Henry Savile of Banke* (London, 1969).

WATT, J. A., *The Church and the Two Nations in Medieval Ireland* (Cambridge, 1970).

WILLIAMS, D. H., *The Welsh Cistercians*, 2 vols. (Tenby, 1983).

WILLIAMSON, D. M., 'Some Notes on the Medieval Manor of Fulstow', *Lincolnshire Architectural and Archaeological Society Reports and Papers*, NS 4 (1948–51), 1–56.

WILSON, D. M., ed., *The Archaeology of Anglo-Saxon England* (London, 1976).

WOOD, S., *English Monasteries and their Patrons in the Thirteenth Century* (Oxford, 1955).

WOOD-LEGH, K. L., *Studies in Church Life under Edward III* (Cambridge, 1934).

——*Perpetual Chantries in Britain* (Cambridge, 1965).

WRIGHT, J. R., *The Church and the English Crown, 1305–1334* (Toronto, 1980).

YORKE, B., ' "Sisters Under the Skin"? Anglo-Saxon Nuns and Nunneries in Southern England', *Reading Medieval Studies*, 15 (1989), 95–118.

YOUINGS, J., *The Dissolution of the Monasteries* (London, 1971).

Index